To all the wondrously defiant, ball-ignoring women I love, especially Laura, Evie, Suzie and Jane. Without you, life would be two parts *Breaking Bad* to three parts *Mad Men* to far too many parts *Fawlty Towers*.

To the late Frank Keating, without whom I would never have had the audacity to even contemplate this labour of love and angst. May your adjectival nouns never rust.

Rob Steen is a sportswriter and co-leader of the BA (Hons) Sport Journalism course at the University of Brighton. He has written for the *Guardian*, the *Independent*, the *Financial Times*, the *Melbourne Age*, the *Hindustan Times*, the *Sunday Telegraph* and *Sunday Times*, where he was deputy sports editor. Winner of the 1995 Cricket Society Literary award and the UK section of the 2005 EU Journalism Award 'for diversity, against discrimination', runner-up for the 1991 William Hill Sports Book of the Year and a finalist in 2014, he has published over a dozen books and written for a multitude of magazines and journals, including *Observer Sports Monthly*, *The Cricketer*, *Sport in Society*, *India Today* and *Marxism Today*, and is also a longstanding columnist for Cricinfo. A pro-semitic North Londoner transplanted to deepest Sussex, only 33% of his remaining dreams are fanciful: peace in the Middle East, untold happiness for his children, Laura, Josef and Evie, and to see his partner, Suzie, finally reach the shores of rude health.

Sp   *for all.*

...sues, tracing their origins, evolution and impact, inside the lines and ... this book offers a thematic history of ...

... from the gladiators of Rome to ...ers ... via the innovator-missionaries of Rugby School; from multi-faceted British exports to the Americanisation of professionalism and the Indianisation of cricket. Rob Steen traces the development of these sports, which captivate the turnstile millions and the mouse-clicking masses, addressing their key themes and commonalities, from creation myths to match-fixing via race, politics, sexuality and internationalism.

Insightful and revelatory, this is an entertaining exploration of spectator sports' intrinsic place in culture and how sport imitates life – and life imitates sport.

"Masterful … Every page is an education, every chapter thought-provoking." *Daily Mail*

"This is social history of the very highest standard." **Mark Perryman**, *Morning Star* and *Huffington Post*

"One of the best and most illuminating narratives on sport that I have ever read" **Sarah Juggins**, *Sports Journalists' Association*

"Steen's opus to fans and fandom is so vast in its scope — nearly every sport imaginable gets a mention at some point — and his style is so humorous and engaging, there are times when I hoped it went on for 500 more pages." **Steve O'Rourke,** *The Score*

"… a compelling narrative that is destined to make this work a classic." **Jon Culley, The Sports Bookshelf**

"Steen provides especially great insight into the close relationship among sport, gambling, and fixed contests that has existed since what feels like the beginning of time. A thoroughly researched history of a most captivating topic. Highly recommended for the sports fan or cultural anthropologist." **Brian Renvill,** *Library Journal* (US)

FLOODLIGHTS AND TOUCHLINES

A HISTORY OF SPECTATOR SPORT

ROB STEEN

BLOOMSBURY

LONDON • NEW DELHI • NEW YORK • SYDNEY

Bloomsbury Sport
An imprint of Bloomsbury Publishing Plc

50 Bedford Square   1385 Broadway
London   New York
WC1B 3DP   NY 10018
UK   USA

www.bloomsbury.com

First published 2014

British Library Cataloguing-in-Publication Data
A catalogue record for this book is available from the British Library.

Library of Congress Cataloguing-in-Publication data has been applied for.

ISBN: HB: 978-1-4081-5215-7
PB: 978-1-4729-2221-2
ePDF: 978-1-4081-8136-2
ePub: 978-1-4081-8137-9

2 4 6 8 10 9 7 5 3 1

Typeset in Palatino Linotype by seagulls.net
Printed and bound in Great Britain by CPI Group (UK) Ltd, Croydon CR0 4YY

Contents

Acknowledgements ix

Introduction: It's Only Bats and Balls (but We Like It) 1

1. The Sound (and Fury) of the Crowd: Sport and Spectators . 35

2. Class Wars: How Spectator Sport Began 103

3. Odds and Sods: Sport and Gambling 166

4. Ringmasters Inc: Sport and Governance 194

5. The First Taboo: Sport and Professionalism

    I. From "Gentlemen" to Shamateurs 253

    II. Pride and Prejudice 307

6. Well-Paid Slaves: Sport and Players' Rights 355

7. The Us Syndrome: Sport and Internationalism 411

8. Reluctant Partners: Sport and Politics 497

9. No Normal Sport in an Abnormal Society: Sport and Race

    I. Disunited States 575

    II. For the Common Wealth 621

10. The Grass Ceiling: Sport and Sexuality 661

Endnotes 726

Index 779

Acknowledgements

One windswept morning many moons ago, I attended an MCC committee meeting at Lord's for the first and almost certainly only time. Not because I'd finally conquered a slightly irrational aversion to egg-and-bacon-with-a-hint-of-tomato ties, but because I was hoping to persuade the club to support a DVD history of cricket, a project wherein, in my wildest and most fanciful dreams, I envisaged myself doing for the game what the American documentarist Ken Burns did for my second favourite sport, baseball. Optimism drained away as soon as Robin Marlar, the reigning MCC president, volunteered his ha'apworth.

Though a valued former colleague at the *Sunday Times*, and an extremely generous and kind reviewer of my books, Robin didn't think I was the man for the job – not one jot. "If you want a *Guardian* history of cricket, Rob's your man," he proposed with a discreet titter (though not so discreet that it wouldn't have been perceptible to Frankie Howerd at 100 paces and Vincent van Gogh post-love sacrifice). Robin, I should add, is about as likely to buy the old leftie rag as he is to renounce fine wine.

Even so, while this book may indeed be perceived as a *Guardian*-esque history of sport, the traitorous truth – as the litter of references between these covers will affirm – is that I'm a *Times* reader these days, albeit not for political reasons (though it is far more illuminating, as one of the robustly unconverted, being preached to by the loyal opposition). Once a *Guardian* man, always a *Guardian* man, they say, but what do they know who only newspapers know? So thank-you, Robin, for the motivation.

Expertise is a curious thing. In 2012, Paul Ehrlich was elected to the Royal Society, raising grave questions about that ancient but worthy club's selection policy: in 1968, after all, Ehrlich had predicted in his book *The Population Bomb* not only that 65 million Americans would die of starvation by 1985, but that it was "even money", come the end of the century, that famine would have wiped out the entire British population. In an undertaking of this possibly hubristic ilk, therefore, it seemed sensible to consult a wide range of voices and laptoppers. It pays to requisition (or even steal) the views of others, whether to toast them as founts of commonsense – and hence reinforce one's own perceptions – or to make a point by contradicting them. It also pays to quote them in order to supply relief from your own ramblings and, above all, to help cover what you weren't old enough, clever enough or there enough to have seen or heard or deduced yourself.

A hefty chunk of my gratitude falls, therefore, on four owners of broad-minded shoulders, fellow scribblers all: Simon Barnes, chief sportswriter of *The Times* until his profoundly regrettable release in August 2014, author, Proust-lover, bird-fancier and sportswriting's resident philosopher-in-chief; Huw Richards, ballgame historian par excellence and sportswriting's most unsung commentator, not to mention the only person ever to serve simultaneously as chief rugby correspondent of the *Financial Times* and chief cricket correspondent of the *Herald Tribune*; Dave Zirin, Washington DC-based columnist, author, activist and sportswriting's conscience-in-chief; and Jed Novick, the finest, sweetest wordsmith ever to support Tottenham, and the funniest if laziest sportswriter I know. As I recently confessed to Simon, when seeking permission to publish one or two lengthier extracts, few days go by when I don't curse him for an insight or idea I wish I'd thought of first. As I told Dave while we were putting mankind to rights at my kitchen table in 2012, there isn't a week that goes by when his edgeofsports.com column doesn't enlighten me about the wrongs perpetrated in the name of the competitive arts in the United States. And as I remind Jed and Huw at least once a month, nobody else was allowed to see my final drafts.

I must also thank all the other industrious and perceptive hacks and historians whose work I have scavenged and pillaged while striving to squeeze a jumbo-sized quart into this half-pint pot (for those I did not manage to contact for permission, I hope you can tolerate admiration from afar). I would also like to thank the following, for their thoughts and steers and helpful reminders of yet another slant on an illuminating tale I may have unaccountably overlooked or underplayed: Alan Little, honorary librarian at the All England Club; Adam Chadwick, the MCC curator; Neil Robinson from the Lord's library; Peter Wynne-Thomas, Nottinghamshire County Cricket Club's doughty historian; Andrew Currie at Bonhams, the auctioneers; my colleagues at the University of Brighton (past and present) – Daniel Burdsey, Thomas Carter, Jo Doust, Ian McDonald, Gary Stidder, John Sugden and Alan Tomlinson – plus a veritable Who's Who of contemporary sportswriting and scholarship: Lincoln Allison, Sir Hilary Beckles, Rahul Bhattacharya, Harsha Bhogle, Matthew Engel, Gulu Ezekiel, Stephen Fay, Nigel Gibson, Gideon Haigh, Andrew Jennings, Boria Majumdar, Mike Marqusee, Toby Miller, Kevin Mitchell, Richard Moore, Kadambari Murali, Nick Pitt, John Price, Mark Ray, Jeffrey Sammons, Colin Shindler, Ric Sissons, Sharda Ugra, Stephen Wagg, John Williams, Jonathan Wilson, Neil Wilson and John Young. That some not only granted permission to reproduce their work but took up my offer to chip in the occasional *bon mot* left me feeling as if I now have a small sense of what Ringo Starr felt like when he roped in Levon Helm, Rick Danko, Todd Rundgren, Jack Bruce, Nils Lofgren, Clarence Clemons and Dr John to join his All-Star Band.

I also owe a deeply humble debt to some of those whose journalistic dreams I have tried to encourage, for reversing roles and teaching me a thing or two – take a bow, Jordan Blackwell, Haydn Cobb, Jonathan Dyson, Duncan Hewitt, Maria Hudd, Gemma Nash, Andrew Nove, Michael Nussbaum and Jimmy Pugh. And a rather more substantial one to the exceedingly honourable Tim Berners-Lee, whose clever little invention made my research both astonishingly quicker (it only took three years) and, I hope, immeasurably better informed. Not that I have given up cardboard and ink, hence my guilty thanks to Amazon and their ruthlessly efficient bookstore-slaying ilk, although I can't say it didn't disturb me to find so many ex-library books suddenly in my possession.

Heartfelt mercis, too, to the Charlottes, Atyeo and Croft, Kirsty Schaper and Sarah Cole, who presided over this venture with enthusiasm, encouragement, patience and just the right amount of what my sister calls "noodging", not to mention such compassionate indulgence on the word-count. I also owe a vast debt to my incredibly diligent copy editor, Julian Flanders. And to Tony Collins, sporting archaeologist of wide and deserved repute, for passing the gauntlet backwards (as a good rugby man should). I'd also like to thank Marshall McLuhan, the Canadian communication theorist who insisted that the medium was the message, and turned up as himself in Woody Allen's *Annie Hall* as the punchline in a hilarious example of a comic skewering academic pretension. Fortunately, his prediction half a century ago, that the electronic age would drive the printed word out of business, has proved premature thus far.

To the spiritual and nutritional supporting cast. Mercis unconfined to the minstrels who accompanied me on those fraught and frankly mindbending final laps – Todd Rundgren, Aimee Mann, Paddy McAloon, Weather Report, Lloyd Cole and The Commotions, Chic, Steely Dan and Tommy James and The Shondells, the last of whose finest four minutes, "Crystal Blue Persuasion", is now imprinted forever on my gently fried, no longer gentrified brain; to Brigitte, Sophie and all the lovely girls at Flint Owl Bakery, purveyors of pitying smiles and the most delicious caffeine fixes in Christendom (or even Jewdom); and to Steveski, for nourishing me with your juicy peaches (those nice people at Universal better not cut that condom scene!).

Thanks a zillion, too, to Suzie: my refuge from all things sporty; Laura, Joe and Evie – my greatest pride and joy; Jane – a sister above sisters; Anne – the best ex-wife a man could wish for;

Andy – a brother from another mother; Jed (again) – a brother from another planet altogether; and Shirley – without whom... let's be conservative and call her a mother to leave all Jewish mothers trailing as distant runners-up, whimpering gibberishly. And, more sombrely, to Jill, a mother-in-law to confound Les Dawson, whose death on the night before I completed the first *War-and-Peace*-ish draft of this book robbed a great many people of the kindest person we have ever known.

Above all, I want to express my gratitude to those who made this book worth writing – primarily the runners and kickers and hitters and keepers who lit my boyhood imagination. While I have dedicated it in part to the memory of that most soulful of sportswriters, Frank Keating, I also want to thank John Carlos. In May 2012, the noblest athlete ever to achieve fame with an Olympic bronze medal spent 36 hours of his still active political life in Lewes, 44 years after the Black Power salute that enshrined him in social as well as sporting history. One unforgettable evening in Eastbourne, he reminded myself, my colleagues and all the students who drew inspiration from him, that spectator sport is about a great deal more than professionalism, profits and latterday prophets.

Rob Steen
Lewes, April 2014

Introduction
It's Only Bats and Balls (but We Like It)
Why Spectator Sport Matters More Than It Did
(And Maybe More Than It Should)

Let's kick off with a confession – albeit not, I suspect, a terribly unusual one. I have what might politely be called a "thing" about balls. Round balls, naturally, but also big balls, medium-sized balls, small balls, dimpled balls and even oval balls. I used to love playing with them, but now I prefer to watch others play with them. To boil all my motivations and urges down to a single, definitive root cause, that's why I felt compelled to write this book.

Helpfully, I also have a "thing" about bats. Long ones, thick ones, stringed ones, flat ones, even tubular ones. I love watching experts flex those bats and hit those balls because I love watching sport. I started to love watching sport nearly half a century ago partly because it stirred my passions and imagination, but mostly because, the more I learned about its history and the more it taught me about geography, the more it told me about people and hence helped me apply a sense of structure and order to, and make sense of, a terrifyingly complex world. For all the times it falls short, for all the times it disappoints and dismays, offends and outrages, I love it because of what it *can* be: it can be beautiful, it can be dramatic, it can defeat prejudice and disadvantage, and it can bring together disparate, even warring peoples. And also because, in a world where the only certainty is uncertainty, it consistently gives us, in the shape of the final score, something absolutely, utterly, gloriously unarguable. You may well feel the same.

As a contemporary joybringer, such is its accessibility via newspapers, television, radio, internet and even what we old timers used to call "telephones", sport has no equal because it is always there and (almost) always real. Yet perhaps what I love most about this elusive, often wicked, flagrantly disloyal and consistently unreliable creature is this: whether in the form of prejudice or general moral dubiousness, it points us in the direction of rights and wrongs – big wrongs, little wrongs, even right wrongs; equal rights, individual rights, even the wrong rights. It also does so more speedily and effectively than any governmental decree or court case. In his latest book, *The News: A User's Manual*, the philosopher Alain de Botton makes a heartfelt plea to the news industry (aka journalism) to ease up on "the darkness" and "allow for moments of pride and collective sympathy". He should read the sports pages more often. For that, to a considerable degree, is their function. End of mission statement (part 1).

David Rakoff, on the other hand, hated sport. Or, rather, he hated baseball. Invited to contribute an essay to *Damn Yankees: Twenty-Four Major League Writers on the World's Most Loved (and Hated) Team*, published shortly before his death in 2012, the Canadian social anthropologist and award-winning satirical writer declined via email:

> *I hate baseball because of the lachrymose false moral component of it all, because it wraps itself in the flag in precisely the way the Republicans do and takes credit for the opposite of what it really is... fancying itself some sublime iteration of American values, exceptionalism, and purity when, in fact, it's just a deeply corporate sham of over-funded competition...*[1]

Then there's Steven Berkoff, one of Britain's more imaginative and trenchant playwrights. In a letter published by *The Times* in March 2012, he conveyed his intense displeasure (and admitted his rather considerable envy) at sport's ubiquity:

> *Sir, As an avid reader of* The Times *for several decades I cannot help but notice how much space it gives to sport, and by contrast how little it gives to the arts. I have no doubt that sport is vital, but the overwhelming attention it receives suggests very much*

> *that the arts are really a minority interest. It is through the arts*
> *that we generate ideas and they are the bedrock of any society*
> *that calls itself civilised. In Monday's paper there were four*
> *pages on the arts and 38 pages on sport. Rather depressing.*[2]

Quite what Berkoff would have made of his favourite news-paper's sports coverage five months later, one shudders to think. One assumes he did his level best to ignore the London Olympics, but doing so would have required him to don blinkers, wear earplugs and perhaps even a clothes peg over his nose, so pungent was the aroma of sport-as-panacea. Page after page of a purportedly serious newspaper – front, back and oodles in between, never mind the expansive daily pullout – was devoted slavishly, and all-too often repetitively, to running and jumping and volleyballing, swamping all else. Berkoff might have been reminded, not merely of the surreality of some of his own productions – in particular a 1969 interpretation of Franz Kafka's supremely alienating *Metamorphosis* – but the words of the drama critic Aleks Sierz, who characterised his modus operandi as "in-yer-face-theatre".

The Times was far from alone. Here was "in-yer-face-sport": all-enveloping, relentless, unavoidable. As an estimated million people flooded the streets of London for the celebratory post-Games parade, Mayor Boris Johnson sought to burnish his credentials as a future prime minister with a typically jolly speech that easily upstaged the efforts of the incumbent. He thanked the Armed Forces, police and even a private security firm for ensuring our safety, then thanked the scores of runners, jumpers, throwers, rowers, wrestlers and pedallers known collectively as Team GB, for bringing sport "back home to a city and a country where by and large it was invented and codified". Above all, he went on, "you brought home the truth about us and this country – that when we put our minds to it, there is no limit to what Britain can achieve".[3]

"We needed a pretext to suspend normal life,"[4] reflected *The Times*. At the annual Trades Union Congress conference in

Brighton, the TUC leader, Brendan Barber, implored the beleaguered Coalition government to "learn from the Olympics". Yet for Berkoff and others, for all the general feelgoodness, a palpable air of fascism swirled about the 2012 Games, as it does for all host nations. Some felt bullied: not just into following something about which they could not ordinarily care less, but bullied into cheering for something they objected to on a fundamental ground – here, at a time of widespread (if relative) economic hardship, was a venture requiring £11bn, maybe more, from the public purse, and with no apparent material legacy.

Then, banishing 99.99% of reservations, came a leggy Jamaican. If no footballer was ever blessed with as prescient a surname as George Best, no runner was ever granted a more propitious start in life than to be christened Usain Bolt. "The sense of being there was palpable at the Stadium last Sunday when Bolt trampled the already shabby remnants of doubts and rumours beneath his flowing stride to repeat the 100-metre dominance that had in the Beijing Games four years ago exhilarated a global audience," marvelled Hugh McIlvanney, the veteran sportswriter who had spent more than five decades observing and capturing the feats of Muhammad Ali, Pelé, Garry Sobers and Carl Lewis for readers of *The Observer* and *Sunday Times*. His enthusiasm remained utterly undimmed.

> *To be present again on Thursday, for the 200m victory that made him the first man ever to complete a double double of sprint gold medals at successive Games, was to be reminded with a shudder of renewed wonder of just how deeply the physical capacities of certain human beings can thrill the rest of us. We are, of course, captivated by more than the sheer athletic magnificence of Bolt. Where that evokes awe, his warm and playful personality spreads pleasure. When he is not making us gasp, he is making us smile, and the two effects merge into a power of attractiveness that leaves us proud and grateful we're of the same species.[5]*

The following June brought a bitter shower of cold water masquerading as news: Veronica Campbell-Brown, the two-time Olympic and reigning 200-metre world champion, had failed a dope test; the 12th Jamaican to do so in five years – nothing, mind, on the Russians, 44 of whose athletes were suspended for performance-enhancing at the time. In Paris a month later, ahead of the weekend's IAAF Diamond League fixture, the question was asked; Bolt was ready. "I am clean, I'm sure about that," he insisted. "I welcome people to test me every day if necessary to prove it to the world. I have no problem."[6] A few weeks later, he returned to London's Olympic Stadium for the Anniversary Games and said much the same thing. To many, the fact that the question had to be asked at all, of such a monument to human possibility, is the saddest of all commentaries on 21st-century sport.

Nearly a year after hailing Bolt's magnificence, a regretful McIlvanney nailed the scale of the dilemma: "Great athletes trying to convince the world they are drug-free may sometimes feel their efforts are like spraying tested urine into the wind. The exercise is often pervaded by the pungent smell of the cynicism about doping that has come to prevail in modern sport. And innocents in touch with reality know that complaints of injustice must in fairness be directed not towards public attitudes but at the huge throng of fellow competitors whose determined seeking of strength and fleetness from the pharmacy has made following the careers of even the most captivating champions a nervous pilgrimage of faith."

Joining the 60,000 who pilgrimaged to the Olympic Stadium that July night, every one of whom had come to see Bolt burn up the track again at the scene of his crimes against sloth, merely accentuated McIlvanney's unease. "Watching him in action, enraptured by the ability to transmute his gangling frame into a ground-devouring machine, it was once again easy to believe that his speed is a phenomenon of unadulterated naturalness. The unpersuadable doubters will, of course, contend that such a thought was as much a prayer as a conclusion, and the faithful must concede they have a point."[7]

Simon Barnes's take was snappier but no less carefully hewn: "It's almost as if we were trying to turn a hero into a villain. It makes uncomfortable thinking. Lord knows it must make for uncomfortable living."[8]

* * *

To the Bloomsbury Institute, set amid the enduringly opulent Georgian magnificence of London's Bedford Square. A few weeks before the 2012 Olympics, the publisher that brought us Harry Potter and muggles and Quidditch is staging a literary evening with Richard Moore, author of *The Dirtiest Race In History – Ben Johnson, Carl Lewis and the 1988 Olympic 100m Final*. Cited ad nauseam as the tipping-point in sport's traumatic relationship with drugs, the author's enduring uncertainty and equivocation over his subject could be found on the opening page, where Moore justifies the title, which refers to the fact that six of the eight runners had, at one time or another, failed a dope test.

"The dirtiest race in history? I mean this in the broadest sense, referring not only to drugs, but also to varying degrees of skulduggery and corruption, and the enduring legacy of the [race]. There are those who take a more ambiguous, even ambivalent view. It was the greatest race of all time, they say. And perhaps it was."[9] The book's final sentences, moreover, find Johnson, cast by society as villain-in-chief and "wilfully ignoring that his name has been wiped from the record books", more upbeat about his legacy than might be supposed:

> *Abruptly, he sits forward and, with the faux aggression of a boxer at a pre-fight weigh-in, asks, "Hey, you tell me: who was the first guy to beat 9.9?"*
>
> *"It was you, Ben."*
>
> *"And who was the first guy to beat 9.8?"*
>
> *"You."*
>
> *"OK," he laughs, settling back into the large leather chair in Farnum's office. The chair is so big and so dark that it seems to consume him. He disappears into it. He looks tiny.*

> *And then he springs forward, repeating his boast for the umpteenth time, "Fifty years! I was fifty years ahead of my time. Make sure you print that."*[10]

A Q&A session finds tempers being kept but views veering wildly, from incredulity that anyone could possibly mount a defence of performance-enhancing drugs to profound disbelief that any sane person could possibly criticise a professional athlete for doing something – trying to improve their chances of success and hence happiness through artificial means – that the rest of us do without blinking, much less thinking. Here, it feels, is the most monochrome of worlds.

At length, Moore feels compelled to make a point, one to which, until then – he later admits – he had not given much thought. The gist is this: the men who competed in that grubby contest are not like you and I. They were not Saturday morning footballers or Sunday afternoon cricketers or Tuesday evening greyhound punters. They were professional sportsfolk; sportsfolk with a very different motivation. Same weapons, different battle – and an immeasurably more strenuous one. So why do we seek purity in them? More to the point, given that our knowledge of the despicable antics of priests and mullahs should have taught us once and for all that the quest for purity is as forlorn as the pursuit of perfection, what earthly right do we have to demand it of them?

* * *

> *Sport has the power to change the world. It has the power to inspire. It has the power to unite people in a way that little else does. Sport can awaken hope where there was previously only despair. Sport speaks to people in a language they understand.*
> **Nelson Mandela**[11]

The key phrase in that oft-quoted sentiment, articulated by one of the most widely admired human beings of this or any other era, is not so much "the power to change the world" or "the power to unite" as "in a language they understand". Sport is our lingua franca. Young males boast about "getting to first base"; Elton John lauds David Bowie as "game-changing", a group of journalists is a "media scrum". In the Emmy-hoarding HBO series *Mad Men*, Herman "Duck" Phillips sympathises with Pete "Bastard" Campbell for being on a "sticky wicket" – a comment all the more surreal for being uttered on an American TV show set in New York. During a 2012 hearing of England's Treasury select committee, John Thurso MP proffered an acidic rejoinder to the stonewalling tactics of Bob Diamond, the American who had recently quit as Barclays Bank chief executive after revelations of rate-fixing had seen him fined £290m: "If you were a cricketer you would be Geoffrey Boycott. You've occupied the crease for two and half hours… and I'm not sure we're much further." On this occasion, being American was no excuse whatsoever for not getting the drift.

But let's not be coy. Sport is largely a boy thing – and, hence, by very definition, not an entirely healthy thing. In the beginning it taps into our love of games, not simply as a distraction and relief from more humdrum activities, but because they help us measure ourselves – though measuring ourselves by our ability to move a wooden horse around a board, pick up an ace of hearts or bankrupt the opposition for daring to land on our property is hardly an unambiguous sign that one has an ideal sense of proportion.

The pursuit and enjoyment of games requires at least one of two things: an ability, regardless of its perceived value, to glean pleasure and satisfaction from the activity itself – its demands on brain and/or body and the sensations these generate – and a thirst for, if not victory, then certainly competition. Asked what it felt like to play Robert Miller, a fictional hedge-fund manager in the 2013 movie *Arbitrage*, who defrauds his own company then covers up a car crash that kills his mistress, Richard Gere homed in on the timeless universal masculinity of that desire: "I do think there is something unfinished about these guys. They have got all the suits, the cars, the grey hair, but there is something unfinished. They are boys. They are still playing. It is not the money or the stuff it buys. The money is just the marker of who won the game."[12]

What, then, can we say of those who merely watch, who sustain pain and obtain thrills sitting down? Well, the watchers are playing as much as the players: playing at caring. Caring who wins; caring who gets hurt and who cheats; caring so much you get into a bitter argument with your opponent-in-caring, or beat him senseless; caring so much it hurts. In October 2012, two young Sri Lankans hanged themselves after the national cricket team had lost the World Twenty20 final. That they were merely the latest sporting "tragics" (© John Howard, ex-Australian PM and self-confessed "cricket tragic") to have loved anything but wisely, and far too well, did nothing to dilute the overwhelming sense of needless, mindless tragedy. How disproportionate could our values possibly get? And the players we watch the most, of course, are not really playing at all. For them it's always work.

In the broadest terms, this book seeks to tell the tale of these professional sportsfolk, and the context in which they have plied their trade – or been prevented from doing so. It aims to explore and reflect how sport has developed, seeping into and often enriching lives from Afghanistan to Zambia. How, as a field of dreams, its fertility came to be symbolised by the principal owner of its most ardent promoter, the imperial media artiste otherwise known as ESPN: namely, Walt Disney, that globally-renowned home of fable, fantasy, fabulous profits and happy endings (even if the chap behind it all was a good deal less loveable than Bambi or Dumbo).

In praise of disproportion

Of course we could go the whole hog and use the b-word. Millions talk about the music business and the movie business, but why not the sport business? If such a phrase shocks – probably because relatively few ever write still less utter it – the reasons will soon, I trust, become apparent. Suffice to say that, given some of the evils perpetrated in the name of bottom lines – whether through exclusion, exploitation, fraud or good old-fashioned cheating – and notwithstanding the fact that only a tiny minority of the ringmasters ever own up to it, spectator sport is as efficient a profit machine as any yet devised.

Consider, too, the inherent conundrum. "Quite simply, sport matters more than it did," declared Matthew Engel, the much-travelled journalist, author and distinguished erstwhile editor of *Wisden Cricketers' Almanack*, the planet's second-most famous annual sporting publication behind the *Sports Illustrated* Swimsuit Issue. "And more," he added, "than it should." When he made that assertion during his inaugural lecture as a visiting professor at Oxford University, no student present could have been left in any doubt that he was referring to the sports we watch rather than those we play.

Engel is alone, to my almost certain knowledge, in having reported from Olympic Games, World Cups, general elections, battlefields and the South Pole while writing wittily incisive books about hardy British institutions (the tabloid newspaper, the second-class railway carriage and, coming soon, the county). I freely confess that, along with his then-*Guardian* teammate, Frank Keating, he inspired me to believe that writing about bats and balls could mean spending one's days lionising the good guys, exposing the bad 'uns and earning a decent crust in the process; I should also add that Matthew and I are now close friends. All bias aside, nevertheless, those two sentences articulate perfectly the balancing act we must all perform if we are to understand how we reached a point where we are less likely to know how wars are faring than be able to name the Manchester United centre-forward or the winner of the 3.25 at Market Rasen.

The chief lesson of the Vietnam War, reckoned Engel, "was not, as you might think, to avoid foreign entanglements unless they have clarity of purpose and an assured outcome – but to keep proper control of the information stream." It is impossible, he lamented, "to follow accurately the progress of the war in

Afghanistan, even if we could be bothered to do so, because the Ministry of Defence's public relations officers control access to the front line even for the press. Especially for the press." On the other hand, the sporting world is a comparatively open book. "If you were sleepless at 4am this morning, knowing you could catch up by having a zizz at this lecture, you could – without getting dressed – have watched any one of the following…" Whereupon he listed 16 separate televisual attractions for the sportily inclined, ranging all the way from the all-inaction All-American Bass Fishing Championships (worth – brace yourself – $120,000 to the winner) to the decidedly unplayful Cage Wars 8.

At length, though, Engel asked the inevitable question, one that anyone should ask who does not regard spectator sport as – in the words of the flair-free French left-winger Jean-Marie Brohm – "a prison of measured time". Namely, do we value sport out of proportion to its significance? There is no correct answer to this question, merely opinion, educated and gut.

* * *

A couple of days after the end of the 2012 Paralympics had left Britain patting itself on the back for supporting such a noble venture with such gusto, Matthew Syed struck a blow for killjoys/commonsense (take your pick) by assailing what he dubbed the "Olympivangelists". Beneath a black-and-white photo of that courageous African-American desegregationist, Rosa Parks, he listed some "hard facts" about Britain's normal attitude to the disabled: only half its railway stations were accessible to wheelchair users; 70% of polling stations were difficult to access; the disabled were less than half as likely as their more fortunate countrymen to hold a qualification after the age of 19; barely 50% of them, moreover, were in work, and were far more likely than the able-bodied to experience unfair treatment.

A letter published in *The Guardian* – from Ivor Tittawella in Sweden – took the point a stage further: "Should not the money [spent on the Paralympics] be spent instead on encouraging greater confidence and creativity in the physically disabled? Physical disability need not remove the competitive spirit, but why pitch this disability against another's in combat, knowing that the records achievable would nearly always be below those achieved by the able-bodied?"[13] Syed also poured a bucket of harsh reality on the euphoria felt by Australia after Cathy Freeman, an aboriginal, won the 400 metres gold at the 2000 Sydney Olympics: far from being the moment that "healed the nation", it had failed (thus far) as a catalyst – alcoholism and unemployment among the benighted minority had gone up. Healing, though, is not about clicking fingers.

"A similar thing could happen here," Syed mused, referring to Mo Farah's victory in the Olympic 5,000m. The "unifying sense of Britishness" had been intoxicating when Farah was cheered to the rafters despite having spent his formative years in Somalia, demonstrating, surely, wonderfully, that "patriotism is capable of trumping xenophobia"; unfortunately, he added, "racism didn't die when Farah crossed the line". The Olympics, Syed acknowledged, "have been wonderful and uplifting", but "in the hands of the Olympivangelists they have been hymned beyond reason and dulled our political senses".[14]

I am a staunch admirer of Syed – as his frequent appearances in this book will testify – but on this score we are at extreme loggerheads. It goes without saying that the Olympics should be regarded as a passing show, a circus of distraction; of course other, weightier matters demand our attention. And yes, while allegations of racism have become as much a media *cause célèbre* as over-the-top tackles were a generation ago, white Britons still find it easier to obtain bank loans than their black counterparts. Yet even a devout Olympifusenik, such as myself, or someone with a PhD in applied curmudgeonry, would have been reluctant to cheer Syed's sentiments. Sport can distract us, obsess us and brighten our lives, but no, it cannot change the world. It never claimed it could. It can, however, nudge it in the general vicinity of the right direction, as this book aims to demonstrate.

* * *

Before we go any further, let's dispense with the trickiest bit. What do we mean by "sport"? "Comedy is tragedy plus time," declares oh-so-pompous Alan Alda in *Crimes and Misdemeanours*, for this undisinterested judge the most successful merger of laughter and gloom achieved to date by Woody Allen (henceforth, since we will be bumping into him again and can therefore justify a spot of over-familiarity, to be referred to as The Woodster). Sport is a more complex equation: something along the lines of practice + luck + decent weather + tradition + alcohol + tragidramedy, divided by idiocy then multiplied by the square root of time. Boxing may be classified as such, but "sport" must surely be preceded by the word "play". Hunting is a field sport, but is of course incontrovertibly one-sided. Does "sport" incorporate bridge or chess, for which the physical demands extend as far as the ability to remain seated for hours on end while occasionally moving a hand? What of those activities that exist below the media radar such as parkour, wherein competitors leap from small buildings to smaller buildings in a single bound? What of motorsports and sailing and equestrian events? While undeniably searching examinations of flesh, bone and brain, all rely at least as much on machine or beast as human capacity and will.

As much as I could prattle on for England about boxing's moral complexities, let's content ourselves, for now, with applying the description to those activities involving physical movement, skill, competition and persistent proximity to failure and injury. Courage, too, not only physical, but mental and spiritual. That's why we recoil at artificial aids, hence the recent ban on anchored putters. Sure, we accept the need for armour – from helmets and scrum caps to arm guards and shoulder pads, even shin pads. We also tolerate the steady flow of ever more helpful equipment – bouncier, swervier footballs; thicker, meatier cricket bats; even tennis rackets strung with spin-friendly technofibre (though Pat Cash's disgust did lead him to claim that, at 48, he would beat the Pat Cash who won Wimbledon at 22).[15] But an implement whose sole purpose is to calm jittery hands? Next thing you know, marijuana will be mandatory.

The daily fix

Mission statement Part 2. It is easier to say what this book isn't. It isn't a definitive account of every sport that has ever been played. The anticlimactic fact, after all, remains: once the big top had been dismantled and the Olympic circus left town, media and public attention for individual endeavour and ball-free activity faded in a hurry: for the majority of the planet, it is balls and full-time pros that do most to persuade us to part with our money, our loyalties and our sense of proportion.

The prime focus here is on those sports that belong to our daily routine, those we buy season tickets and memberships and satellite dishes to follow, drawn by plotlines that twist and turn and thrum, stretching out over decades, even centuries, often resisting a final score, much less closure: let's call them spectator sports. Yes, a triathlete faces an unimaginable trial (to 99.99% of us) of strength, skills, discipline and willpower, but the pressure imposed by tens of thousands of people shouting, screaming, cheering, booing and abusing – let alone the millions who might be watching further afield – is unfamiliar if not quite a total stranger. This external pressure, amplified by the increasingly glittering prizes, is impossible to quantify, but the terror induced by stage fright is an omnipresent threat. Pity poor I.K. Kim. Confronted by a one-foot putt to win the Kraft Nabisco Championship, the first women's golf major of 2012, she struck the back of the hole and saw her ball rebound away like a frisky puppy, forcing a playoff which the stunned South Korean lost. Us old hands recalled Doug Sanders missing from four feet on the final hole of the 1970 British Open and winced all the more.

In other words, the subject of this book is those sports where the result reverberates beyond the field; where, because they are vulnerable to the unique burdens imposed on those who do their job in full, jaundiced and vicious public view, the stars are performers as well as competitors, where the watchers, too, are participants. Sports where the show almost always goes on (weather permitting) and the game most readily reflects life – and sometimes even improves on it.

Even then, in most cases, we must narrow our gaze further, to team sports, those that value the collective above the individual, reflect our need for shared experience and hence attract, more readily and regularly, the sporting team's soul twin – a mass partisan following. Of the 44,000 or so hours and 1000-plus live events screened by Sky Sports in 2010, the leading four sports were football (more than 500 live matches and 6,226 hours), followed by golf (4,430 hours, 218 tournaments), cricket (223 matches, more than 3,500 hours) and rugby (360 league and union games). The following year the gap between football and its pursuers had widened. If we include support programming, 3D and live coverage (but not simulcasts on HD and interactive programming), the sports receiving the most coverage on the broadcaster's four main channels in 2011[16] were as follows (in hours):

Football	6,912
Golf	4,532
Cricket	3,779
Rugby Union	1,670
Motorsport	1,544
Tennis	1,398
Rugby League	1,308
Boxing	948
NFL	874
Darts	844

Across the Atlantic, the emphasis is no different. The ESPN America schedule from 7am on 26 May 2013 to 7am the following morning comprised baseball (16½ hours), lacrosse (4), drag-racing (2½) and basketball (1½). The previous day had been almost identical, with boxing displacing drag-racing as the lone individual contest.

* * *

Many, of course, have already sought to navigate these treacherous seas. Whether running the gamut of sports or focusing on one, some have done so with oceans of devotion, considerable acumen and astute judgement, most notably – in my experience – a sedulous septet of scholars: Derek Birley, Allen Guttmann, Dave Russell, Dick Holt, Tony Mason, Harold Seymour and Peter Wynne-Thomas. Hats off, too, to those who have dared to compress and distil centuries into a single volume, principally John Arlott, with *The Oxford Companion to Sports and Games*, and, more recently, Tim Harris, who in entitling his gargantuan effort *Sport: Almost Everything You Ever Wanted To Know* explicitly acknowledged the impossibility of achieving what amounts to the literary equivalent of reeling off a 147 break without allowing your opponent to come to the table.

Like Holt's volumes on British sport, this one places less emphasis on strict chronology than recurrent themes: the impermanence of "truth" and the timelessness of history's lessons; the role of privilege and class, gambling and corruption; the prescience and misguidedness of rulers; the rise of commercialism and internationalism, of professionalisation and players' rights; the influence of politics and prejudice, whether in terms of governments, governing bodies, corporations, race or sex. There may be times when you wonder why a favourite story of yours has been omitted: be patient. Since many illustrate more than one of these themes, it might be lurking in a subsequent chapter. Nor is the batting order in any way hierarchical, as may readily be ascertained from the tail-end presence of those addressing racial and sexual prejudice. You don't have to speak fluent ballish to get the most out of all this – or even know "offside" means entirely different things depending on whether you insert a hyphen – so long as you know your American football from that up-and-coming Limey concoction and are familiar with the other rudimentary stuff, you should get the gist.

It is unlikely to elude your notice that many other important themes have supporting roles at best – the evolution of rules, customs and tactics, the role of managers, coaches and the media, the impact of violence or other forms of villainy. Nor, speaking of the last, will we dwell – despite the indications thus far – any more than absolutely necessary on illegal performance-enhancement; the reasons, I trust, can be gauged from the aforementioned Usain Bolt conundrum. This should in turn explain why there is only fleeting mention of L**** A********* and barely a nod to the sport he did more than anyone to bring into possibly terminable disrepute. Ideally, I would have had more pages at my disposal to remedy those other omissions and passing mentions, but what you have in your hands was supposed to be a third as fat as it is. Feel free to blame the publisher's innate grasp of the demands one can make on you, the reader, without risking accusations of having accepted bribes from the opticians and optometrists' union.

Nor, at the risk of sounding lazy, does this book try, doomed as such enterprises almost invariably are, to submit an incontrovertible answer to the question of how each and every one of these activities began. What it will do is analyse the whys and the hows as well as the whos and the whats. What were the social conditions that encouraged their evolution? What were the key tipping-points? Who were the catalysts, the makers and breakers? Why and how did some sports take the lead and others follow? How has sport held a window up to society, even influenced it? What, above all, have been the common threads that continue to bind goalkeepers to goalminders, tight-head props to tight ends, middle-order batsmen to middle relievers, knuckleballers to knuckle-throwers? The chapter titles reflect these questions.

Stories we could tell

While spectator sport does not inspire untrammeled joy by any means, it does not seem excessive to toast it as our most reliable source of post-Grimm fairytales and fables. Few sporting tales are quite as inspirational as that of Bernhard Carl Trautmann. Barely a decade after the defeat of Nazism, this erstwhile Luftwaffe pilot and Iron Cross-winner became a hero to the blue half of Manchester.

Commonly addressed as Bert, Trautmann was the son of a Bremen dockyard worker, a tall, blue-eyed blond, recalled Brian Glanville, "the very picture of the ideal Aryan".[17] He volunteered for Hitler Youth at 17. "People say 'why?', but when you are a young boy war seems like an adventure," he told *The Guardian*'s Louise Taylor in 2010, three years before his death. "Growing up in Hitler's Germany, you had no mind of your own." He served as a paratrooper in Russia, hence the title of his autobiography, *Steppes to Wembley*. "You didn't think of the enemy as people at first," he reflected. "Then, when you began taking prisoners, you heard them cry for their mother and father. When you met the enemy, he became a real person."[18]

Fortunate to survive being blown up as the Nazis retreated, he was captured on the Russian front, escaped to France and survived being buried in rubble in a bombed building. Then he eluded the Americans before, finally, the British recaptured him, interning him in a prisoner-of-war camp near Ashton-in-Makerfield, Lancashire, where he learned English and acquired a Lancastrian accent. It was while acting as a driver for a Jewish officer, Hermann Bloch, that his view of Hitler's *bêtes noir* changed. "I quickly came to see Bloch, and every other Jew, as human beings," he told Taylor. Until then, "deep down", he had clung to the grubby moneylending stereotype.

Sport supplied redemption. Declining repatriation, he performed net-minding service for non-League St Helens Town, whose secretary he would marry. When he joined Manchester City, unsurprisingly, this did not sit well with the city's strong Jewish community; objections were strenuously vented. "My parents were certainly of that persuasion," recalled Colin Shindler, the Mancunian-Jewish writer and broadcaster. "It fell to Dr Alexander Altmann, Manchester's communal rabbi and a German himself, to urge an opening of hearts. How in all conscience, he demanded, can we punish an individual for the sins of a nation?"[19]

"Thanks to Altmann, after a month it was all forgotten," Trautmann would reflect. "Later, I went into the Jewish community and tried to explain things. I tried to give them an understanding of the situation for people in Germany in the 1930s and their bad circumstances. I asked if they had been in the same position, under a dictatorship, how they would have reacted? By talking like that, people began to understand."[20]

As lithe and dauntless as he was between the posts, Trautmann was never capped by Germany because he was playing in England – though his countrymen did ultimately make use of him as a liaison officer during the 1966 World Cup, where the final was played at Wembley, scene of his gallant entry into football folklore. Ten years earlier, he had helped City beat Birmingham City in the FA Cup final despite suffering a horrendous injury diving at the feet of an opposing forward, Peter Murphy, an act typical of his unblinking commitment. With substitutes still a decade away, he stayed on, playing the last 16 minutes in searing pain; only afterwards, when he was X-rayed, was it discovered that several vertebrae in his neck had been broken. The Football Writers' Association duly voted for their most improbable Player of the Year.

"When the time came for him to say farewell at the grand old age of 41, though we could see he wasn't the great goalkeeper of times past, the outpouring of emotion in Moss Side was almost tangible," wrote Shindler. "Before the end of his testimonial game the pitch was invaded – not by hooligans but by a crowd who want to touch him, to embrace him, to cry like my six-year-old self at the cruelty of the passing of the years that would take him from us."

Returning to Germany in the Sixties to manage Preussen Münster, Bert then went to live in Spain, helped the German FA promote the game in Africa and Asia, and in 2004 was awarded an OBE for services to Anglo-German relations (having launched his own sport-focused foundation with that same aim). Following his death in July 2013, the City players wore black armbands for the opening fixture of the new season and a minute's silence was observed. A statue of him, plunging low to save, can now be seen in the club's reception. Glanville may not have been wholly mischievous in inferring that, had he played for his nation of birth at Wembley in 1966, England fans would be lamenting nearly twice as many years of hurt.

* * *

Stories such as these are the lifeblood of sport, and this book. Because they mostly symbolise struggle, not all of them are even half-happy. Some are incredibly depressing. Some will make you want to emulate Peter Finch's unforgettable battle-cry in *Network*: "I'm mad as hell and I'm not going to take it anymore." Some I knew about before starting my research, if not in sufficient depth; others I dug up along the way. I now know a lot more, and understand even more, than I did when those nice people at Bloomsbury gave a 40-year ambition the green light. A warning, though, is imperative: such is history's way, just as it changed course during my research, some of the "facts" stated in this book could well be outdated by the time you read it.

Some of these stories, perhaps many, will be familiar but in need of fuller telling, context and clarity, ideally with a few more grains of truth than you may have read elsewhere. Some will be unfamiliar because the further we get from their birth and the more deeply they are immersed in folk memory, the less we bother to question their veracity. Before seeing Steven Spielberg's *Lincoln*, I had always assumed that the Gettysburg Address was a lengthy, even interminable speech: how else could it have attained such gravitas? In actuality, having been stirred to read it by Daniel Day-Lewis's mesmeric performance, I discovered that it encompassed a mere 278 words. Even if every sentence was enunciated with the utmost care and deliberation and drawn out to ensure no syllable was left unheard, while still leaving plenty of pregnant pauses for applause and cheers, it would have taken Abe about five minutes tops. Not a major revelation, no, but a worthwhile lesson in the dangers of assumption.

Some of these stories will be unfamiliar because the full context took years, even decades, to come to light. Some will be unfamiliar because you're reading this in North Dakota, you haven't the foggiest clue about cricket other than that it's bad when it isn't and that it makes snail-racing look like the epitome of high-speed entertainment. Some will be unfamiliar because your concept of sporting villainy is Mike Tyson biting Evander Holyfield's ear or a centre-forward tumbling theatrically in the penalty area, so you probably have no idea that, to quite a few learned people I know, sport's all-time Public Enemy No.1 was a man who devoted his life to the Olympic movement and the purportedly noble aspirations of amateurism. Some will be unfamiliar because you have no time for women's sport or bat-and-ball games. Ultimately, this book is for anyone who, upon reading the words "Jackie Robinson was baseball's first black player", or "Jason Collins is the first active professional male athlete to come out", doesn't shake their head and sigh heavily.

Together, these stories constitute a modern Bayeux Tapestry: inspiring tales, thousands of threads, a goodly number of horses, all the triumph, disaster, pain and fury you could possibly want, and even more unfair play (did you see where King Harold *actually* sustained his fatal injury?). Every day and everywhere, sport transports us to Elation Street, Confused Junction, Misery Circus and all stations between, emotions stirred by the winning, the losing and, best of all, the drawing; best because life is more about the greys and beiges of the stalemate than the monochrome extremities of success and failure. Knowing the history, the context, accentuates those emotions.

A trivial pursuit?

So, why *do* stories about these sometimes savagely trivial pursuits mean so much, however disproportionately, to life in the 21st century? Why do such stories seem to say more, about ourselves and our predecessors, than any other branch of our cultural tree? Stories such as the singer Beyoncé Knowles's decision to pre-record her rendition of the American national anthem for President Obama's second inauguration. She had wanted to keep herself fresh, she explained, for her upcoming

Super Bowl gig, where she would be watched by a projected 160 million Americans – eight times as many as tuned in for Obama's address.

Well, for one thing, those pursuits are not all that trivial. Not unless you want to demean the masses who play and the multi-masses who watch, lionise and despair. Sport is both reflection and distraction. It reflects society and distracts from it, a newtopia where the same imperfections exist but, in the 21st century at least, the difference between success and failure, in general, has less to do than it once did with upbringing and parental wealth than physical aptitude and sheer hard work.

Professional sport is probably the closest civilisation gets to true meritocracy: a musician can hide behind a producer with a decent ear and an aptitude for knob-twiddling; a movie star can be saved by a canny director of photography and a skilled editor; a novelist buoyed by a supportive network of friends-cum-reviewers. Professional sportsfolk may don their armour, but in essence they stand naked. For them there are no second takes, no body doubles, proofreaders or CGI. Nowhere is the line separating success and failure so clear yet so gossamer-thin; nowhere is the role of chance so obvious; nowhere is the strength and fragility of human beings so visible. This undying respect for what they do should not, however, be interpreted as an unwillingness to emphasise the ways in which they, and their trade, fall short.

Spectator sport is confrontational theatre, a non-stop people's theatre where fellow thespians do their damnedest to make you muck up your lines. Drama, suspense and wonder are the ingredients that magnetise tens of millions of citizens and drive TV subscriptions, supplying us with the soap opera that makes professional sport the 21st century's most authentic reality show and – in probably far too many cases – a barometer of our emotional state. Spectator sport enhances and exaggerates our sense of "we" and "us" and "our", taps into our finest instincts (compassion, meritocracy, fairness) and our basest (physical aggression, deceit, *schadenfreude*). In doing so, as I hope this book demonstrates, it underpins so many of our moral and ethical debates.

* * *

It's the fantasy bit, of course, that complicates matters: that childhood-borne view of sport as a combination of school and dreams – the discipline imposed by rules, strategy and uniform, the exultation that comes with hitting that winning goal or home run or putt. As we grow older and more distant, so that world becomes a vessel for our finer aspirations, a symbol of what *should* be. And what better world could there be than one where the little guy frequently has a chance and losers can not only be more interesting than winners but can actually be heroes? If heaven really is "a place where nothing, nothing ever happens", as the Talking Heads song would have us believe, Planet Sport is miles more fun.

Here is a magical kingdom where giantkillers still roam the earth, where Greece's footballers can become European champions and an Ethiopian swimmer, Yanet Seyoumu, is hailed as a hero for finishing last in an Olympic heat; where the most successful bowler in 137 years of international cricket is not an Englishman, an Australian or an Indian but Muttiah Muralitharan, a Sri Lankan Tamil in a predominantly Sinhalese team unable since birth to flex the elbow that played such a significant part; where the winner of the 1908 Olympic marathon is immeasurably less renowned than Dorando Pietri, the Italian pastry chef disqualified after officials helped him across the finishing line.

As fate would have it, the almost pitifully weedy Pietri collapsed a few yards from the seat occupied by that keen cricketer and skier Arthur Conan Doyle, one of the 100,000 cramming London's White City (a million more spectators followed the race), stirring him to write the following for the *Daily Mail* as if guided by the hand of Sherlock Holmes: "It is horrible, and yet fascinating, this struggle between a set purpose and an utterly exhausted frame... Amid stooping figures and grasping hands I caught a glimpse of the haggard, yellow face, the glazed, expressionless eyes, the long, black hair streaked across the brow. Surely he is done now." So taken was Sherlock Holmes's creator with this story, the public outcry over Pietri's disqualification persuaded him to start a campaign to raise money for a gift to honour him. A few days later, Conan Doyle made a speech and his wife Jean presented Pietri with a gold cigarette case plus a cheque for £308 and 10 shillings.[21]

Two more short stories to keep the philosophical juices flowing. A lifelong rooter for the New York Knicks (in *Annie Hall*, he sneaks away from a pretentious cocktail party his wife is hosting to watch his favourite – as she puts it – "pituitary cases"), The Woodster has always seen sport as an antidote to the ephemera of Hollywood and showbiz. If the Knicks are playing, rehearsals and shooting schedules must adjust. Explaining his decision to play with his Dixieland band in preference to collecting his Oscars for *Annie Hall*, he ridiculed the notion of a "best picture". How can you be so categorical about something so ephemeral as taste? Winning races on a running track, as he had in his youth, felt infinitely more meaningful and satisfying: "At least I knew I deserved it."[22]

"There was a common denominator between us: sport." So said Gilad Schalit, a young Israeli soldier held captive for five years by Hamas from 2007 to 2011. By "us" he meant himself and his captors. "During the day I would play all kinds of games with them – chess, dominoes. There were moments when a kind of emotion would arise, a kind of laughter, when we watched a good game on television." *The Times* headline over that touching memory might well have been the most ringing endorsement yet of the competitive arts: "Love of sport got me through five years of Hamas captivity, says Israeli soldier."[23]

Past 1 Present 1
(after extra-time; replay Wednesday 7.45pm)
Jean-Baptiste Alphonse Karr, the 19th century French journalist, novelist and epigrammatist par excellence, was only fractionally

off-target with his best-known attempt on goal. *Plus ça change, plus c'est la même chose*? Let's tweak it a little: the more we appear to stay the same, the more we miss our own growth.

In terms of popular culture, in the west if not the east, the 20th century can be characterised as the advance of four apocalyptic horsemen: cinema, television, popular music and spectator sport. The first three developed at a rapid lick. The movies took a century to go from silent two-reelers to computer-enhanced extravaganzas via talkies, technicolour and in-your-face realism; television went from black-and-white squares to interactive 3D monster in the space of barely half a century; from the advent of the long-playing record in 1948, as technology and marketing fuelled ever-changing modes of delivery (vinyl, cartridge, cassette, compact disc and sundry variations), music surged from folk, blues and jazz to hip-hop, rap and ambient via rock 'n' roll, pop, R'n'B, soul, funk and all the myriad rocks: prog rock, art rock, jazz rock, country rock, punk rock, hard rock. The fourth horseman was different, defying time almost nobly.

One day last July, I informed Karen Bouchard, the smiley young woman of French-Canadian-Philippine stock then running the source of my morning coffee, Flint Owl Bakery, that I was off to Lord's that afternoon. "I went to my first game of cricket recently and I really liked it," she cooed. "It's soooo… civilised. At one point they all went off and it turned out they were going for tea. How civilised is that?" Given some of the boorish, brattish and downright bad behaviour it has witnessed down the years, that the game should still inspire that particular c-word surely says something extraordinary about the apparent timelessness of cricket's image, however assiduously it is buffed up.

Nearly 250 years after it was first run at Doncaster, the St Leger remains one of the jewels in English horse racing's crown; 14 decades after the inaugural Test match in Melbourne, cricket matches between England and Australia still bewitch millions; nearly a century and a half after the first All England Championships, the last week of June and the first week of July still mean Wimbledon, glamour, strawberries 'n' cream, ivy-clad walls and, oh yes, a spot of tennis – and by no means exclusively to Britons; nearly a century after Babe Ruth signed for the New York Yankees, there is still no more famous sporting club on the planet – unless it's Manchester United, an institution since Victorian times.

In the interim, the old world was steamrollered by the new: technology shrank the planet into a global village; communism and fascism rose and (for the most part) fell; the English finished on the right end of two world wars but lost an Empire (and finally stopped bossing the Irish, Scots and Welsh around too); the Germans lost two world wars yet rose anew as Europe's mover-and-shaper-in-chief; coal became yesterday's fuel, ships yesterday's transport.

And of course spectator sport has changed too, and in innumerable ways – good, bad, ugly and superficial. It is every bit as receptive and vulnerable as our other horsemen to technology, commerce and corruption (in fact, so easy is it now to watch our competitive artists without leaving the sofa – or even the office – perhaps we should redefine our subject as viewer sport?). Competitors are fitter, faster and stronger. Their weapons – bats, rackets, clubs – are better; their shields – helmets, gum shields, gloves – are better. Psychologists, dieticians and video analysts are now integral to the ever-growing backroom support. Yet while the lust and rewards for success have never been greater, a greater acceptance of the need to ensure elite sportsfolk are always in the right frame of mind – and that men should no longer be expected to be mere appendages to their family – means that players are now permitted to miss matches to attend births and funerals, even admit to depression. In 2013, we were apprised that the performances of the England cricket team had been aided by Sigmund Freud's protegé. The Myers-Brigg Type Indicator apparently furnished management with a guide to both personality traits and the ability to interact with teammates; in developing it, Isabel Briggs Myers and her mother Katherine had built on the work of Carl Jung.

Other tales of the unexpected abound, especially the geographically unexpected. Britain no longer rules the sporting waves, but then nor do the United States. Russia and Qatar are lavishing billions of roubles and petro-dollars on staging the FIFA World Cup; Kenyans have supplanted Finns as the runners with the most puff; Jamaicans are the fleetest; as I write, the number one male tennis player is Serbian, the world heavy-weight boxing champions are Ukrainian brothers and baseball's global champions Dominican Republicans. Meanwhile, the capacity of sport to override nationalist urges was encapsulated in 2012 when, in a survey[24] of Australians' attitudes and opinions towards more than 200 sporting icons, No.1, for the third year running, was Mr Switzerland, Roger Federer.

Yet in so many other ways spectator sport hasn't budged. Substitutes and extra-time and penalty shootouts notwith-standing, its most popular variation remains what it was when my father's grandfather left Russia: an 11-a-side contest lasting 90 minutes. Hole-in-ones and no-hitters still astound; it's still three strikes or ten wickets and out. Professionalism has made drivers, strikers, sluggers and smashers as rich as Hollywood's starriest but, just as they were in 1912, the highest-grossers of 2012, Manny Pacquiao and Floyd Mayweather Jr, were still obliged to fight for their supper (albeit not, sadly, each other).

After a century, little New Zealand's almighty All Blacks still dominate rugby union, albeit reinforced by the sons of the Pacific Islands; in cricket, play still stops for rain, likewise lunch and tea. And for all the advances in preparation and strategy, the trusty old standbys remain. Asked how Wales had found the wherewithal to achieve a late victory over France in the 2013 Six Nations Championship, Leigh Halfpenny, the triumphant fullback, went back to basics: "You looked across and the France players had their hands on their knees and their heads down."[25]

Empty victories and inspiring defeats. Touchlines, tramlines, finishing-lines – they're all still present, correct and immutable. The most radical addition? For freeing our pleasures from the tyranny of the sun, and thus defeating that inconsiderately intrusive beast we call the working day, it must surely be flood-lights – hence the title of this book. In one form or another, the often interchangeable lexicon is familiar to all ages, races, creeds and sexual persuasions, leaping vast oceans in a single bound.

Etymologists will tell you that the first reference to the word "goal" (or approximation thereof) can be found in *On the Trinity, Creation, the Existence of Evil, Devils, Adam and Eve, &c.*, an early 14th century work by the English poet William De Shoreham, vicar of Chart-Sutton, in which, as it happens, he spells it precisely as the Brazilians came to do – *Daz hy [God] nabbe ende ne for be gol*. Granted, it is difficult to imagine that such a pious soul was thinking of a bulging net at the time, but no matter. If not quite the king of words, it certainly seems to be the one most closely associated with absolute, undiluted delight: there is probably no more instantly recognisable sound on this planet right now than a football commentator exulting "goooooooal" at window-shattering volume.

Devout allegiance to the way we were, needless to add, can only ever be a flawed creed, obscuring as it almost invariably does the way we are, or should or could be. Because of its overt reliance on physical strength, mobility and masculinity, profes-sional sport is the last major citadel of male chauvinism, not to say the headquarters of homophobia. Perversely, Washington DC is home to both the Smithsonian's National Museum of the American Indian and yet still, unaccountably, the Washington Redskins. Ben Nighthorse Campbell, the first Native American senator in US history, told the audience at a Smithsonian symposium in 2013 that he asks people how they would feel "if the team was called the Washington Darkies". Not one person present defended the use of "Redskin" because, as one fan put it, "it really is defending the indefensible."[26]

By the same token, while tradition – as The Woodster contends – may be the illusion of permanence, some conven-tions survive because generation after generation perceive them to be worthwhile – or, at the very least, harmless; small but persistent reminders that time can be defeated: tossing a coin to decide who bats first; "seconds out, round one"; the three peeps of a referee's whistle that signify hostilities are over and hands must be shaken.

If life and art imitate each other, spectator sport, too, reflects and anticipates, telling us much about people we regard as very different to us and even more about ourselves. However, applying its values to everyday life, while often worthwhile, can offer simplistic answers to complex questions – look no further than those divisive and almost entirely unhelpful league tables for schools.

Three more brief but weighty stories, one from Japan, one from Sri Lanka and one from Somalia. The first began by accident, as historical developments so often do. At the World Table-Tennis Championships in Nagoya in 1971, with the Cold War raging and mutual mistrust rife between Washington and Beijing, one of the American competitors, Glen Cowan, accidentally boarded the Chinese team bus. The gasps were profound. How would the passengers react to the uninvited presence of a pot-smoking Yankee capitalist dog? Helpfully, Zhuang Zedong, a three-times former world champion and national hero, had detected a slight softening in Chairman Mao's rhetoric. Striding to the back of the bus, he gave Cowan a memento. When they reached their destination, word had got out and the paparazzi were waiting to snap them shaking hands. Mao learned of this the next day, and dispatched an invitation to the US team; before long, they became the first official delegation from America to visit China since the Long March, prompting Richard Nixon to pronounce it "the week that shook the world". Soon afterwards, Nixon dispatched Henry Kissinger to Beijing, and followed him there the following year. "Ping-pong diplomacy" they called it. Détente had been born.

A quarter of a century later, Sri Lanka, an island colonised for 400 years by the Portuguese, Dutch and British, now drowning in civil war, saw its cricketers overturn just about every odd and win the ICC World Cup. Kumar Sangakkara, a teenager at the time, destined not only to become one of his homeland's finest competitive artists but survive, barely, a terrorist attack on the team bus in Lahore, summed up the significance beyond the boundary:

> *The 1996 World Cup gave all Sri Lankans a commonality, one point of collective joy and ambition that gave a divided society true national identity and was to be the panacea that healed all social evils and would stand the country in good stead through terrible natural disasters and a tragic civil war. [It] inspired people to look at their country differently. The sport overwhelmed terrorism and political strife; it provided something that everyone held dear to their hearts and helped normal people get through their lives.*
>
> *The team also became a microcosm of how Sri Lankan society should be with players from different backgrounds, ethnicities and religions sharing their common joy, their passion and love for each other and their motherland. Regardless of war, here we were playing together. The Sri Lanka team became a harmonising factor.*[27]

In late 2012, it was announced that the national stadium in Mogadishu, touted by the Somali Football Federation as "the largest and most beautiful facility in Africa and the Arab world"[28], would be used once more for football. Built by Chinese engineers in 1978, it had been occupied for fully two decades by an assortment of soldiers, warlords and rebels. Since early 2009, the Islamist al-Shabaab group had used the stadium as a training base, and banned the playing and watching of football in areas over which it exerted control, but in 2011 it was driven out of the Somali capital by Amisom, the African Union peacekeeping force. At last the national team, then 188th in the FIFA rankings, would no longer be obliged to play all its matches on foreign soil. Football, argued the SFF secretary general, Abdi Qani Said Arab, could play a crucial role in disarming child soldiers and "creating friendship among people".[29]

Could there be a nobler calling?

Sorcerers and apprentices

At the height of my impressionable youth, a pair of maverick Celtic sorcerers left me spellbound: George Best and Barry John, walking billboards for the enthralling possibilities when physical dexterity combines with a creative and rebellious mind.

Best drove even the most measured reporters to flights of fancy. "With feet as sensitive as a pick-pocket's hands, his control of the ball under the most violent pressure was hypnotic," exulted Hugh McIlvanney. "The bewildering repertoire of feints and swerves, sudden stops and demoralising spurts, exploited a freakish elasticity of limb and torso, tremendous physical strength and resilience for so slight a figure and balance that would have made Isaac Newton decide he might as well have eaten the apple."[30] Brian Glanville was no less enchanted: "Best played like an angel. A football was almost too ludicrously large to test his skills."[31] And yes, he admitted it: beating a full-back gave him a sexual charge.

After Best's early, alcohol-fuelled and horribly miserable death, Alex Higgins, fellow Northern Irishman, snooker star and soul brother in self-destruction, launched a campaign to remove the three middle letters from Belfast and rename it "Best City". It failed, but the name now conjoined with Belfast City Airport isn't C. S. Lewis, Van Morrison, Mary Peters or Edward Carson, but Best. Nobody made that benighted city smile quite like Georgie.[32]

Barry John played a tougher, rougher sport – rugby union. If anything, he was even more unstoppable. "He had poise and balance and he played on impulse," asserted Gerald Davies, his teammate in those wonderful Welsh XVs of the late 1960s and early 1970s, as perceptive a writer as he was lethal on the wing.

He had the allure of a ladies' man, slim and attractive, a touch of feminine delicacy in his every movement… If there were titans in his day with bodily harm in mind, he dismissed them with a mischievous wink – as was truly his wont – as he glided beyond their threatening arms. No snarling back-row forward,

or anyone else for that matter, could enslave him, such was his
faith in that he could do what he wanted to do. He left the field of
play with his kit hardly needing to be laundered and with a smile
and an insouciant shrug. But such a style should not disguise
the sharp determination of the sliver of ice beneath. He was a
confidence trickster, readjusting his shape and position so as to
make the other side look heavy-footed and clumsy and whose
upper bodies had been persuaded to go one way while the lower
half would be speeding in the opposite direction, leaving the face
looking bewildered.[33]

The rules, nature and tempo of John's sport, thanks primarily
to the advent of professionalism, have changed so drastically
that it can seem almost impossible that we should ever see such
unfettered freedom again, but in this respect it is an exception.
The other major spectator sports, especially those with a less
snobbish approach to financial remuneration, have been more
blessed. Britons who thought they would never again clap eyes
on a footballer of such abundant and extravagant skills as Best
soon found themselves astounded by Kenny Dalglish, then
Paul Gascoigne, and then, when the overseas raiders began
flooding over, Eric Cantona, Gianfranco Zola and Dennis
Bergkamp, then Cristiano Ronaldo. Atop the global podium,
Pelé was succeeded by Johan Cruyff, Cruyff by Diego Maradona,
Maradona by Zinedine Zidane, Zidane by Lionel Messi. Michael
Phelps outswam Mark Spitz; Barry Bonds broke more than one
of Babe Ruth's most unbreakable baseball records; Federer and
Rafa Nadal have dared us to demote Rod Laver, Bjorn Borg and
John McEnroe in the tennis pantheon. Garry Sobers's deeds
on a cricket field have been matched by Jacques Kallis (albeit
not with the luminously effervescent spirit with which he
perpetrated them); Carl Lewis not only emulated Jesse Owens
but outran and outjumped him (if not with the same seismic
impact). A critic recently remarked of *Manhattan*, another of The
Woodster's finest 90 minutes, that, being shot in 1979 in black
and white, it created "nostalgia for the present"; spectator sport

makes nostalgia more or less redundant. Again and again and again, its performers confound us with their ability to reinvent, re-inspire and re-enchant.

Still, enough of my verbal diarrhoea (there's plenty more where that came from). The final words, for now, belong to two masters of another kind of moving image. Describing his enduring devotion to the cinema-going experience, and hence his capacity to keep nourishing it himself, Steven Spielberg invoked a sporting crowd: "All of us go into a kind of lock step where, if you were watching a tennis match, you'd see that perfect synchronicity of heads going left-right, left-right. The same thing in a movie theatre, when the movie is working and the audience is just galvanised, almost hypnotised, all watching the same things, all knowing where to look at the exact same time... it's a wonderful thing. There is nothing greater than that."[34]

But back to The Woodster. Asked whether he would rather give up watching movies or sport, Allen, a septuagenarian so besotted with work, craft and art he had written and directed a story for celluloid every year since 1967, responded without a moment's pause: movies. Sport, he reasoned, is still "thrilling".[35]

1 The Sound (and Fury) of the Crowd: Sport and Spectators

People come back from a game saying, "We won, we won."
No, they won, you watched.

Jerry Seinfeld

Welcome to the wild and wacky world of the spectator, without whom this book would be about as useful as secondhand toilet paper. Spiritually as well as economically, it is the presence of the watcher-participants that transforms a merely enjoyable or even popular activity into a spectator sport. Television and the internet may have wreaked havoc with orthodox perceptions of what constitutes attendance and involvement, but "being there" retains much, if not all, its attraction. Much of that appeal can be traced to the sort of misguided fervour apparent at an *amateur* football match in north-eastern Brazil in 2013, wherein the referee fatally stabbed a player who had refused to leave the field after reportedly hitting him, whereupon spectators decapitated and stoned the official, then tied him up and cut off his hands and legs.[1]

On the infinitely brighter side of the same coin, we are blessed with the shining example set by all those community-owned clubs, from the recently reconstituted Portsmouth FC, where revolution was deemed necessary to throw off the uncaring and reckless yoke of foreign investors, all the way up to hard-boiled, money-spinning collectives such as Barcelona and Wisconsin's very own Green Bay Packers, a franchise "woven into the tapestry of that city", rejoices Dave Zirin in *Bad Sports: How Owners Are*

Ruining the Games We Love, "that makes you think you're travelling back to a perhaps fictional time when fans came first."[2]

Shortly before *Bad Sports* was published in 2010, the Packers' 4,750,934 shares were owned by 112,015 stockholders drawn from 50 states as well as Guam and the Virgin Islands, not one of whom reaps any dividend from their initial investment. When shares were offered during 1997 and 1998, more than 60,000 were snapped up by Wisconsin residents. "The important thing is that they can never move," Jess Zarley, a proud son of Wisconsin, told Zirin. "Because it's publicly owned, the Packers can't ever pack their bags and leave the State of Wisconsin. That's the beauty of it. An owner can't extort concessions from local communities. There's no greedy owner demanding news stadiums with public funds who can move if he's turned down."[3] Call it The Us Syndrome.

* * *

As should be abundantly clear by now, this book is concerned more with competition and consumption than participation – though the second of those particular c-words may be deceptive. It is less concerned with assessing access or value for money than addressing the obstacles that bar the way to consuming sport at its most uplifting: fair sport, equal sport, genuine sport – sport for all. Still, it would be remiss, in a chapter about spectatorship, not to touch on the changes in the way we consume it, bringing us ever closer to the action in a visual sense while simultaneously adding to the bricks in the wall separating watchers from watched.

Clicking through the turnstiles, armed solely with a teamsheet and a preview from the local paper was once the only way to consume a match; then we started listening to it; then we started watching it via newsreel on a big screen while waiting for the latest Charlie Chaplin movie to begin; then it started coming to *us*, into our front rooms, wrapped in a box. Then we started watching it on video recorders, in our own time, at our own pace. Then we resumed watching it on big screens again, even bigger screens, in parks and fanzones, even in our team's home stadium when they were playing somewhere far away.

Then we started buying tickets with credit cards, online – much more convenient than queuing in the rain overnight with a handful of damp fivers or collecting coupons for an entire season or hanging on the phone for 45 minutes at peak-time while your ears are being force-fed the kind of demonic, stomach-churning elevator music that drove Randall P. McMurphy over the edge in *One Flew Over The Cuckoo's Nest*. Then we started clicking through the turnstiles again, spending the whole match craning our necks, missing everything in the penalty areas and repeatedly having to ask the not-terribly-nice bloke in front to sit down for three consecutive seconds. So we went home and watched the highlights in High Definition and 3D. By then, however, the process was beginning to reverse, leaving us happy watching it on ever-shrinking computer screens, so long as it was live and, preferably, exclusive. Next up, apparently, is 4D. Sensurround might not be too far behind.

Not that geography matters terribly much anymore. On 17 June 2012, the *Sunday Times* sports section led its letters page with a simmering missive bemoaning the ludicrousness of England hosting Australia in a five-match one-day international series while the subsequent Test rubber against South Africa, a tussle between the circuit's top-two ranked teams, spanned only three games; the bemoaner was Parimal Vandra, from Santos, Brazil. The following weekend the paper ran a double-page spread on England's European Championship football match against France. To find any mention of Donetsk, the venue, or Ukraine, the host nation, you had to wade through five factboxes and three lengthy stories before stumbling across them in the least prominent one. The only conventional fixture listing on the spread (Euro 2012, France v England…) displayed the kick-off time and the relevant TV schedule but again, not the venue. So massive is the proportion of sportswatching we consume via the cathode tube, the venue is immaterial: *almost* being there is often good enough.

So how do we explain the Indian Premier League? Continuing a trend discernible since the competition first ran in 2008, TV ratings were down in 2012. While the goggle box still accounted for the lion's share of income, the overall tournament rating was 3.45, with a cumulative reach of 162.93 million, down from 3.51 and 162.28 million respectively in 2011. Going in the other direction were the crowds, apparently, with Kolkata Knight Riders claiming a 25% surge and Kings XI Punjab claiming an increase in families attending. "The stadium experience is still unsubstitutable," insisted Santosh Desai, a social commentator and managing director of Future Brands. "The TV experience is substitutable. That is the fundamental difference. The television challenge is: how do you sustain viewership in the absence of the freshness of an on-ground experience?"[4]

While televised sport may be an infinitely superior experience to seeing theatre or opera at the cinema or online, it is hard to foresee a time when it will ever fully replace the real thing. Those Ancient Greeks and Romans certainly knew they were onto something when they started erecting stadiums with all that handy slave labour.

Home sweet home

Sport compels us to consider the difference between favourable and unfavourable conditions, between familiar and hostile, between "home" and "away". Academics have conducted any amount of research into the benefits of home advantage. Local conditions can be critical – especially so in cricket, where playing surfaces, the key to everything, vary vastly from continent to continent – but it is the sheer volume of spectators, in terms of both numbers and wattage, which exerts the greatest influence. Not for nothing did the BBC commentator Andrew Castle assert, as Andy Murray rallied to take the third set of his 2013 Wimbledon semi-final against Jerzy Janowicz, that the Scot was "feeding off the crowd".[5] Paul Ackford, the England rugby union player turned journalist, recalled a match in Cardiff, "when Anglo-Welsh hostilities were at their peak," when the England players returned to their changing room "to find their blazers peppered with globules of spit provided by Wales supporters, standing either side of the tunnel, who weren't too impressed with anything English."[6] Yet David Runciman, a renowned political scientist who teaches political theory at Cambridge University, argued in 2008 that players, fans and media alike "have merely bought into a myth of their own relative power or powerlessness, one that fits what they want to believe." The factors that count, he says, "are the ones that usually count in sport: skill, luck and changes of circumstance."[7]

Hence the consistency of the figures produced in their 2011 book *Scorecasting* by Tobias Moskowitz, a University of Chicago behavioural economist, and *Sports Illustrated*'s L. John Wertheim. According to their research, home teams, historically, had won 54% of Major League Baseball games, nearly 58% of NFL games, 59% in the NHL and 63% in the NBA; in 43 professional leagues in 24 countries covering more than 66,000 games spanning Europe, South America, Asia, Africa, Australia and the US, the share was 62.4%. In international cricket it was 60%, in international rugby union, 58%. "As radically as sports have changed through the years… the home field advantage is eerily constant through time. In more than 100 baseball seasons, not once have the road teams collectively won more games than the home teams. The lowest success rate home teams have ever experienced in a baseball season was 50.7% in 1923; the highest was 58.1% in 1931."[8] Only once, in 1968, have the away teams won more often in the NFL; this has yet to happen in the NBA, the NHL or the international soccer leagues.

Travel considerations, of course, are the conventional determinants of attendance: sportsfolk are far more likely to elicit inspiration from the energy and support of their followers when those cheerers and boosters and hooters are from the same town/city/state/nation, fostering mutual identification, the sense of a collective opponent.

As long ago as 1971, Harold Seymour, a Brooklyn Dodgers batboy in the 1920s and later unofficial major league scout, expressed a now familiar international lament. "Perhaps nostalgia blurs the recollection," the author of the first doctoral dissertation to take baseball as its subject acknowledged in *Baseball: The Golden Age*, the second volume of his magisterial history of the game, "but… I am left with a deeper sense of the emotional attachments and less inhibited loyalties of fans of those times. Parks were smaller and more intimate. Fans felt closer to the teams and players. Dyed-in-the-wool regulars knew the players by sight. Players lived in the neighbourhood adjacent to the park instead of in the suburbs, so they were often seen and recognised on the street or in some favourite saloon, such as the one on Tilden Avenue in Brooklyn."[9]

During those long-gone summers, Zack Wheat, "possibly as great a baseball idol as Flatbush ever had", lived with his family around the corner from the Seymour clan. Puffing a thick black cigar, Burleigh Grimes, another much-loved Brooklyn Dodger, would occasionally take his evening stroll past where Seymour and his pals were still playing something Seymour identified as "punch ball": "It was a thrill to be able to recognise him and say, 'Hiya Burleigh!' and have him reply, 'Having a workout, son?' This simple exchange imparted the feeling that we, too, belonged to the wonderful world of baseball, even though on a different level. Too much familiarity may not be conducive to hero worship, but too much distance breeds alienation."

By then, noted Seymour, groups of fans had begun heading south or west for their spring vacations expressly to watch their team in training. As winter vacations became increasingly popular, so these expeditions multiplied. "In these surroundings the conditions of the past are recaptured. Fans can watch the players close up, see the expressions on their faces, hear their voices, talk to them, collect autographs, and snap pictures. Hero worship includes bestowing offerings, and fans regularly brought presents to their idols. The usual gifts were gold watches, autos, and cash."

For Englishmen playing the English summer game, the largesse of supporters was vital to their future well-being. For county stalwarts of the Victorian age, noted Ric Sissons in his marvellous social history of the professional cricketer, *The Players*, an end-of-career benefit match could lead to financial security: the proceeds flowed directly – or so they hoped – from the pockets of generous followers into their own. "Although the benefit was often spoken of in terms of an old-age pension – at that time the state had no such provisions – it was, in effect, a deferred payment against a minimum of 10 years consecutive service, and usually against the player's entire first-class career."[10]

The benefit season also bought loyalty, and continued to do so throughout the 20th century. It also hurt solidarity. When seven Nottinghamshire professionals went on strike in 1881, they demanded that the club committee guarantee a benefit to any player completing 10 years' service, which was rejected out of hand. "For the Notts Committee to guarantee or even [assent] to a benefit would have been a concession that removed its disciplinary aspect," reasons Sissons. "It was hardly surprising that the only senior Notts professional who did not join the strike was William Oscroft, who had been promised his benefit in 1882."[11]

Advances in transport, cheap air travel especially, have strengthened those bonds. Exemplified by arch-loyalists such as England's Barmy Army and India's Bharat Army, who follow their national cricket team to distant territories year after year, distance is no longer remotely such a deterrent. The benefits to local economies, moreover, can be considerable. According to FIFA, live attendances for the 2006 World Cup in Germany totalled 3,359,439[12]; in South Africa four years later, the figure was slightly down at 3.18m. Compare those figures with the turnout for the previous World Cup in Germany 32 years before – just under 1.87m – let alone those in the 1950 tournament in Brazil, nearly 1.05m, or the 363,000 in Italy in 1934 (stunningly, nearly 600,000 turned up for the inaugural tournament in 1930, when Uruguay's population was 1.72m[13] and long-haul air travel was a concept familiar only to Charles Lindbergh, who had made the first Transatlantic flight just three years earlier). This is not, assuredly, about population growth alone: pockets are deeper; the world has shrunk.

Less welcome could be the deleterious long-term impact on that historical home advantage. The end game is not one to which Runciman is looking forward. "If new technology, ease of travel and the pursuit of money, wherever it is to be found, are hastening the day when the best football team always win, then they are also hastening the day when the sport will finally lose its appeal."

Let there be lights

"The idea that the poor should have leisure," Bertrand Russell once observed, "has always been shocking to the rich." Which may go some way toward explaining why it took so long for those running the show to tackle nature head-on and extend the sporting day. Granted, the invention of electricity was unquestionably the principal determinant, not to mention the hefty costs associated with illuminating large tracts of land, but that should not let the authorities off the hook. When Arsenal's Herbert Chapman installed floodlights at Highbury in the 1930s the Football League refused to sanction them. Yet such fixtures had been staged as early as 1878; with Nikola Tesla's induction motor still a few years away, the Neptune Bank Power Station in Newcastle nearly a quarter of a century distant and the national grid not due until 1926, those bright sparks at Darwen FC were obliged to rely on batteries and dynamos, as did emulators in Sheffield and East London.

Baseball and American football also experimented with primitive lighting in the final quarter of the 19th century, and the former began staging regular night games at minor league level in the late 1920s. In 1930, the Kansas City Monarchs, one of the Negro Leagues' leading lights, had engaged in a few illuminated encounters with the House of David, an eccentric troupe manned exclusively by chaps in beards who travelled to games in a bus accompanied by a truck stuffed with portable lights. Thanks to the entrepreneurial savvy of Larry McPhail, the Cincinnati Reds' general manager, Crosley Field became the venue of the first major league night game on 24 May 1935 when President Franklin Roosevelt, as that sterling *New York Times* servant George Vecsey commemorated in his engrossing history of baseball, "pressed a telegraph key, made of Alaskan gold, a gift to President William Howard Taft many years earlier."

"Dire results were predicted," writes Vecsey of the build-up to the game between the Reds and the Philadelphia Phillies. "Fans would go blind. Players would be maimed. Morals would tumble. Crimes would be committed."[14] Joe Bowman, the Phillies' losing pitcher, was pleasantly surprised to survive unharmed: "There was a lot of talk about how you weren't going to see the ball, how you'd only see half the ball, and so on. I didn't have trouble."[15]

The cost goes a long way toward explaining why the Limeys lagged so far behind: the light towers, whose 632 bulbs required more than a million watts of electricity, ran to $50,000.[16] Not until 1956 did the Football League consent to Portsmouth hosting the first floodlit game under its auspices. No club relished this freedom more than Torquay United. Summer months found the Devonian club, which installed lights in 1954, starting Saturday fixtures at 7.45pm, enabling holidaymakers to while away their evenings at Plainmoor – when, that is, they weren't being assaulted or insulted by Basil Fawlty.

The wheel, though, has come full circle. In 1971, evening starts came to baseball's World Series, and within two decades afternoon games were, apparently, history. Detroit's Tiger Stadium held the most recent such event outdoors, in 1984, though there was a last blast in 1987 at the home of the Minnesota Twins, aptly nicknamed "The Thunderdome": so noisy was it inside the Hubert Humphrey Metrodome, many spectators wore earplugs. In 1986, eager to improve its Nielsen rating, Major League Baseball decreed that all that season's World Series games should be played at primetime, the better to woo the armchair audience than the turnstile-clickers. The trade – a reduction in opportunities to create heroes for the young – grows increasingly less problematic as bedtimes recede ever deeper into the night and SkyPlus and Tivo make TV schedules redundant.

Grace and favours

The relationship between watchers and watched is both umbilical and turbulent. In 1974, when that wonderful Scottish striker Denis Law gave Manchester City victory over Manchester United with a nonchalant, seemingly thoughtless backheel, the look on his face suggested he had just mistakenly murdered his mother. After all, here was an Old Trafford idol, one-third of the Euro-beating Best-Law-Charlton triumvirate at the heart of the side Matt Busby had reconstructed in the wake of the 1958 Munich air tragedy. The sense of disloyalty was natural. Worse, his goal had sentenced United to relegation, multiplying the guilt.

At the other extreme is the abuse that so often greets the return of a former favourite, especially now freedom of contract and movement permit players to exercise their human rights by trading up their talent. Once it had emerged that Ashley Cole not only wanted to leave Arsenal for their London neighbours Chelsea but for more money (a lot more money), he was guaranteed fearful earfuls of abuse every time he returned to play against the Gunners. Whether he deserved sympathy is a matter of taste (and Cole has seldom sought to endear himself to those who contribute so weightily to his wages). It surely says a great deal more about society that our behaviour towards our fellow human beings – or at least those we see as representatives of our community – can so easily be swayed by a change from red shirt to blue.

No less complex, mind, are the relationships in individual sports, which lack the easy connections and the soap opera dynamic of team disciplines. After Murray had beaten Roger Federer to win the Olympic gold medal at Wimbledon in 2012, John McEnroe, the tennis artist formerly known as Superbrat but now a dignified BBC pundit, asked the victor whether he, like him, felt that the crowd had played a critical, even decisive role. He could hardly do otherwise. For once, the American argued, Federer had lacked any significant support. Even when he met Murray in the annual Centre Court showpiece 28 days earlier, there had been no end of vocal encouragement for the Swiss, who won easily. As there was four months later, almost unfathomably, in the semi-finals of the end-of-season ATP show at London's O2 arena: even though just a few weeks had elapsed since Murray had become the first Briton since Fred Perry in 1936 to win a grand slam title, it was again Federer who drew most of the favours of the packed gallery.

Two reasons for this unexpected bias suggested themselves: the stature and style of Federer, arguably the greatest of all professional tennis players, but also the way he conducted himself – or, rather, the stark contrast this drew with Murray's grumpy demeanour, self-flagellation and occasional tantrums. Which, in itself, speaks volumes for the lack of hometown bias. Driven by the overtly nationalistic flavour of the Olympics, nevertheless, the patriotism was overwhelming.

From a more extreme end of the spectrum came a sobering interview in 2012 with Tom Henning Ovrebo, the Norwegian referee ardently blamed by Chelsea fans for the club's loss to Barcelona in the 2009 Champions League semi-final. Yes, he readily confessed, he had made a number of key errors, but had that really justified the stream of threats that had been hurled at him ever since? Now a consultant psychologist with the Norwegian Olympic team, Ovrebo said he was using the experiences gleaned from that bitterly overheated contest as an example of how to cope with stress and learn from mistakes. However, he revealed, he had been sitting in his Oslo office just two days earlier when he received an email from a supposed Chelsea follower, vowing retribution. It was nothing if not succinct: "On 18 April I will come and slaughter your family." Across the city, Anders Behring Breivik was standing trial for 77 murders.[17]

The "destitution of fandom"

Watching the watchers has become an increasingly fertile field for analysis. I spent much of 1993 and early 1994 schlepping the

length and breadth of England to investigate this spectating life –
strictly in practical terms – on behalf of *The Independent on Sunday*:
in addition to the usual suspects – Lord's and Wimbledon – I
sampled Highbury for the footie, Newton Abbot for the gee-gees,
Wentworth for the fairways and Wakefield for the rugger. How
accessible and costly were the nation's favourite sporting fancies?
How were the watchers sheltered, fed and watered? What if you
were disabled? Having spent a fair amount of time going to baseball grounds in the US, where keeping the customers satisfied
appeared to be so much more of a priority, the abiding memory
is far from pleasant. True, the early spectator's unpleasant fate
was long gone – there were seats and toilets, protection from
rain, snow and sun. At some venues more strenuous efforts were
being made, but my time in the insulated, privileged pressbox
had not blinded me to any radical improvements in the English
punter's comparatively rotten lot. Value for money was the rarest
of commodities. The burgers were certainly not getting any less
rubbery; if anything, the tea was even pishier.

In 2010, Patrick Collins, the illustrious long-serving chief
sportswriter of the *Mail on Sunday*, went a lap or two further,
spending a year scrutinising "the people who make our sports
both possible and pleasurable". The resulting book, *Among The
Fans*, was a humorous and soulful travelogue that whisked
him from the traditional temples (Wembley, Wimbledon,
Cheltenham) to the comfortingly modest (Eastbourne, Hove,
Canterbury) to the modern (the FIFA World Cup in South Africa)
and the distant (the Ashes in Australia). Beneath the overcoat
of booze, still-dreadful food and sometimes boorish laddish-
ness, he found devotion: "And yet they return, again and again,
because they adore the experience, they relish the entertainment
on offer, and because they seek the Holy Grail, when extraordinary achievement unfolds before their eyes and when pride and
pleasure coalesce in a memory to endure down the years."[18]

Eduardo Galeano, the Uruguayan football writer, is more
intrigued by the obsessives. To him, a "fan" is "invariably
hopelessly at sea... His mania for denying all evidence finally

upended whatever once passed for his mind, and the remains of the shipwreck spin about aimlessly in waters whipped up by a fury that gives no quarter."[19]

A delicate deal

I sometimes sit and stare out the window and wonder, "What could I have done with my life if I had not spent all this time on the Red Sox?" Might I have completed this novel I've been working on for the past 25 years? Might I have done something else? But what it becomes in the end is like raising your children. If you raise them well and they love you and you love them back, at the end of the day you know that when you leave this life your children won't be thinking about "Oh, what a great column he wrote in October of 1972." They'll be thinking of the time they spent with you as a father. That's how I think of the Red Sox.

Thus did Mike Barnicle, an American journalist, rationalise his passion for the Boston Red Sox in the final episode of Ken Burns's monumental *Baseball* documentary. Mind you, Barnicle did lose his longtime job at the *Boston Globe* because of plagiarism, so we should perhaps take this particular expression of a far from uncommon romantic view with a dash of salt.

After David "Big Papi" Ortiz and his teammates had beaten the New York Yankees in the concluding encounter of 2004's American League Championship, thus becoming the first side in the history of North America's principal professional ballgames to overhaul a 3-0 deficit in a best-of-seven series, came a confession from a more celebrated Red Sox follower. Habitually a fretful fan prone to excusing herself from watching the miserable or nervier moments, the historian Doris Kearns Goodwin found herself so intoxicated and emboldened by the players' resolve and assurance that she watched every single pitch of the World Series. "How," she wondered to herself a few years after the Red Sox had swept to the title with four straight wins, "could we not believe in them?"

As spectators and especially supporters, we immerse ourselves, if not unconditionally then often beyond reason and restraint. Following sport, after all, is supposed to be a safe outlet for emotion, even aggression. Regrettably, if sometimes forgivably, proportion eludes us. The comedian Jerry Seinfeld summed up the illogic of devoting oneself to a team. "We're supporting the clothes," he reasoned. Woe betide a player if he leaves and returns in another club's kit, "this *exact* same human being!"

"Football is a brothel for intolerance," opined Simon Barnes. "Just as in the ordinary kind of brothel, you can go there for what you can't get at home, for what you can't get away with anywhere else. Normal rules are suspended."[20] Which is why fans of the Boston Red Sox and the New York Yankees, in common with those of Barcelona and Real Madrid, and Celtic and Rangers – to cite merely three of the most traditionally antagonistic tribes – give themselves licence to despise and detest, even hate and kill. Call it artless, call it heartless. OK, just call it fandom.

Football started as an expression of community, yet even in the 21st century, by when globalisation and multiculturalism had dissuaded major and even minor teams from drawing on (often more expensive) local talent, fandom could coax the worst from otherwise decent people. Sometimes the hostility is synthetic, the loathing contrived: tribalism is all. In 2012, a Tottenham Hotspur fan was stabbed in a Rome bar by a Lazio fan. A couple of weeks later, when West Ham came to White Hart Lane, the chant from the away supporters reverberated far beyond the touchline: *Can we stab you every week?* Close behind came a collective hissing and another song directed at the so-called "Yids": *Adolf Hitler, he's coming for you...*

Those West Ham fans weren't anti-Semitic. They knew full well that, while Tottenham may have long been perceived and characterised as "The Yids" – even though, if any English club has ever truly warranted such a racist label, it was Leeds United in the 1960s and 1970s – their own club not only had Jewish fans but Jewish directors. "Fans probably feel disinclined to mete out these insults in any other context," argues Paul Davis, a sociologist at the University of Sunderland. "But since fandom desperately seeks reasons to loathe the other, morally regressive sentiments are legitimated, and even required." The problem is not Glasgow, alcohol or slums, he added, referring to Britain's most notorious warring fans, "it is fandom".[21]

In this respect, there is an obvious disparity between individual and team sports. While the latter promote tribalism, the profoundly middle-class milieus of golf and tennis have always prided themselves on politeness and generosity; by and large, it is only in their collective, international incarnations – the Ryder Cup, the Davis Cup – that contests are discoloured by boorishness. Some sports, nonetheless, simply do not lend themselves to raucousness. Sporting cultures, suspected Matthew Syed, "are rather more entrenched than they seem"; any attempt to meddle with the traditional formula or redefine custom, therefore, can have unedifying consequences. Take 2010's "Power Snooker" event at the cavernous O2 arena in South London, regular scene for rock concerts and other relatively genteel crowd-gatherings. "The MC consistently incited the crowd to 'get involved' and to 'shout, cheer and even boo'. 'This is not a church service,' he intoned. Alcohol was liberally consumed." The results, Syed warranted, were "hideous".

> *Obscenities were shouted from the balcony, the (female) referee was insulted and the players were not sure whether to smile grittily or storm out in anger. It was a car crash. Nothing that was said, or done, by the crowd was much different to what you would expect at any Saturday football game. But it just didn't translate. The mêlée was not consonant with snooker's cerebral milieu or its history as a subterranean pursuit in gentlemen's clubs.[22]*

Box-office gold

So, how popular has sportswatching been? Stand by for some heavy-duty number-crunching. As Dick Holt relates in *Sport and the British*, the early Classic races, the first mass spectator events, were run at non-enclosed courses with no admission charged.

But by the end of the 19th century, "the concentration of population into large units created a market for mass entertainment on a new and hitherto unprecedented basis." English football clubs were quick out of the blocks: "Just as taverns with a tradition of singing were turned into music-halls with paid entertainers, so successful football teams were tempted to fence off their pitches and charge admission to the crowds that collected to watch them."[23] This culminated in an almost feverish addiction either side of the Second World War: as of 7 January 2012, two decades after the Taylor Report recommended all-seater stadia on safety grounds, diminishing capacities, no fewer than 51 extant club attendance records for a single match had been recorded between 1927 and 1955.[24]

The second quarter of the 20th century was unquestionably boom time. It produced the record attendance for *any* professional match revolving around ball and feet (of which more anon) as well as several other longstanding attendance peaks. The biggest international crowd in British football annals came during this period – 149,415 for the 1937 Scotland-England match at Glasgow's Hampden Park. In 1927, an estimated 117,000 jammed into Chicago's Soldier Field to see Notre Dame tackle the University of Southern California; 20 years later, 105,840 attended an exhibition game on the same turf between the Chicago Bears and a college all-star team. In 1934, 115,000 Tokyo baseball converts reportedly watched Babe Ruth and his fellow major league All-Stars.

Boxing, especially, would never have it so good again. For the first world heavyweight title collision between Jack Dempsey and Gene Tunney, at Philadelphia's Sesquicentennial Stadium in 1926, more than 126,000 filled the seats – a record that would survive for 66 years, until 132,274 paid to watch Julio César Chávez defeat Greg Haugen in a WBC light-welterweight title bout at the Azteca Stadium in Mexico City, though 136,274 is the more commonly quoted figure.[25] The next seven best-attended fights, before promoters turned increasingly to indoor venues, all occurred between 1921 and 1935.[26] In 1941, 135,132 punters were admitted free to see middleweight Tony Zale knock out Billy Pryor at Milwaukee's Juneau Park as part of the city's Midsummer Festival[27], although numbers of that ilk have been dwarfed by more regular non-paying events: an estimated 1m annually line the 26-mile route of the London Marathon, while the Boat Race between Oxford and Cambridge attracts up to 250,000 spectators to the banks of the Thames[28].

Because it no longer attracts mass-market broadcasters to the same degree, especially in Britain, horse racing is one sport that has lately enjoyed a substantial revival as a live attraction, with record crowds flocking to long-established events (though the decision by *The Guardian* in March 2012 to shift racecards from print edition to website was assuredly a sign of the times). True, Epsom's Derby no longer draws upwards of half a million (since so many watched from unenclosed public land, for which there was no entry fee, a *Racing Post* historian assured me that "there has been no accurate method of calculating their numbers"[29]), but the 2004 flat and jump-racing seasons combined to attract a record 6.1m spectators[30] and in 2011, according to Paul Bittar, chief executive of the British Horseracing Authority, the aggregate tally was 6.15m, a third consecutive rise.[31] Aintree claimed that a modern-day record of 153,583 turned out for that year's three-day festival of steeplechasing;[32] even though admission prices ranged from £29 to £90 and the house champagne bordered on £50 per bottle, the five days of Royal Ascot drew a smidge under 300,000.[33] In the same year, the 137th running of the Kentucky Derby, North America's most popular flat race, attracted a record 168,858 for the 13-race card, edging out the peak set at the event's 1974 centenary. That said, while the Tokyo Racecourse, completed in 1933 and home to the Japan Dirt and Turf Cups as well as the Nippon Derby, drew 196,517 in May 1990, it has been lucky to get half that this century.

Live audiences for boxing, the first sport to fully exploit television's potential, have waned – alarmingly for some, quite properly for others. In 1953, the inroads made by the ruthless invader were such that *The Ring* magazine reported that 51%

of the fight clubs in operation the previous year had ceased trading; even the bigger venues struggled to attract four-figure crowds. Although it boosted receipts and paved the way for pay-per-view, this decline only steepened with the advent of closed-circuit TV in cinemas and theatres. The 1951 world middleweight fight between Randolph Turpin and Sugar Ray Robinson marked the first time cinema exhibitors had outbid the broadcasters for exclusive rights.[34] Nine years later, the second chapter of the world heavyweight trilogy between Floyd Patterson and Sweden's Ingemar Johansson became the first such inter-city affair.[35] When Muhammad Ali knocked out Sonny Liston in Lewiston in 1965, the farcical events were followed in Europe, blow by fleeting blow, courtesy of the Early Bird satellite; barely 2,000 attended the fight itself.

The length of the contest, not unnaturally, tends to bump up attendance. The five Tests of the 1936-37 Ashes series drew 943,000; three successive such encounters in 1948 saw Australia draw record aggregate gates to a Test in England, culminating in 158,000 at Headingley, all of them bent on catching a last view of their incomparable 40-year-old captain Don Bradman. In their three home games in the 1959 World Series, the Los Angeles Dodgers set the three highest attendances – still a record – for baseball's showpiece, drawing 92,000-plus each day.

In seasonal terms, nothing matches the six-month American baseball regular season: with the 30 franchises each staging no fewer than 81 home dates, a record 79.5m tickets were sold in 2007. In terms of average attendances, the runaway market leader has long been the NFL, whose shrewd and brief schedule – 16 regular-season games per club – yielded a mean of 67,394 in 2011 and 68,840 the previous year; Germany's Bundesliga (42,673 and 42,565 respectively) was the closest pursuer, followed by the Australian Football League, which topped 36,000 every year from 2007 to 2010. It says plenty for the sport's allure that the largest crowd to watch any NFL game to date was 112,376 in a *pre-season* matchup between the Dallas Cowboys and Houston Oilers in 1994 – in Mexico City. By way of underlining the transportable nature of such contests, the annual NFL game at Wembley Stadium has pulled in some of the biggest gatherings of the British sporting year, headed by the 84,254 who saw the New England Patriots beat the Tampa Bay Buccaneers in 2009.

The biggest crowds for an annual non-international representative fixture are almost invariably the property of the NFL Pro Bowl, which drew 70,697 in 2010, the second-most to date, though the decision to take the 2012 game to Honolulu resulted in a relatively meagre 48,423, the second poorest yet; Australia's three State of Origin rugby league clashes drew a total of 186,607 in 2011. Multinational events, nonetheless, remain a vibrant drawcard. At 68,995 per game in 2012, rugby union's Six Nations Championship boasted much the highest average attendance of any annual team event. (Indeed, the 15-a-side code, recharged by the advent of over-the-counter professionalism and a more competitive league structure, bucked the general trend in the 21st century: Croke Park in Ireland set a world record for a club or provincial match in 2009 when 82,208 saw the all-Irish Heineken Cup semi-final between Leinster and Munster, a figure eclipsed by the Harlequins-Saracens affair at Wembley in 2014, watched by 83,889.)

Between 1962 and 1979, aggregate attendances at the four-day British Open golf tournament soared from 37,098 to 134,501[36]: how it helps when the show goes on all day. As was reinforced with a vengeance in 2008, when the final round of the FBR Open in Scotsdale, Arizona, was watched by 170,802. India's all-consuming passion for cricket, meanwhile, saw an estimated 465,000 jostle for elbow-room in February 1999 over the five days of the Test against Pakistan in Kolkata (then Calcutta), during the course of which the format's only single-day throng of 100,000-plus was recorded (the same venue, Eden Gardens, has also hosted cricket's five other six-figure crowds, all for one-day internationals).

Breadth, too, is a factor: the most crowded events are those played beyond the confines of a single stage. Pierce O'Neil, the US Tennis Association's chief business officer, claimed in 2005 that the multi-court US Open was drawing upwards of 625,000 spectators for the event's two-week duration, making it, or so he contended, "the highest attended annual sporting event in the world". In 2007, the total attendance was cited as a record 721,087 (in 2012, the Australian Open broke its record with 686,006; Wimbledon, Britain's most heavily attended annual sporting event, broke the house record in 2011 with 494,761[37]). That, though, pales beside the Tour de France, which covers thousands of miles and spans 21 days, for which the organisers have claimed total crowds as high as 15m. When the Tour came to southern England in 2007, according to official research, more than three million lined roads in London and Kent.[38]

And then there's the Olympics, which for London 2012 spanned 26 sports at 33 venues in 17 days; Beijing boasted 38 events over the same span at 37 venues, including Hong Kong. Throw in the Paralympics, the second half of the English double-bill (20 events), and we're clearly talking about something rather bigger than a game of squash. On 11 August 2008, according to the organising committee, 186,037 trooped in for the myriad events in Beijing.[39] In 1956, 1.153m saw the 15 days of the Melbourne Olympics held at the city's cricket ground. In July 2008, the Beijing ringmasters announced that their entire allocation of 6.8m had been taken up, making it the first Olympics to sell out. Small fry, according to the *Guinness Book of Records*, compared with 40 years earlier, when 8.3 million tickets were sold for the Atlanta Games. Then again, as we shall see, paid-for seats and occupied seats can be two different statistics altogether.

There can also be a chasm separating official and actual figures. For decades, the largest-ever attendance at a football match was routinely quoted as the 199,854 people (rounded up to 200,000) who crammed into Rio de Janeiro's spanking new Maracana Municipal Stadium for the final match of the 1950 FIFA World Cup; as distinct, that is, from the adjusted figure of 173,830 of *paid* attendees. And while the first FA Cup final at Wembley Stadium drew an official gate of 126,047, contemporary estimates claimed there to have been more than 200,000 inside the ground, perhaps – if folklore can be trusted – as many as 300,000. Spectators spilled onto the pitch, forcing the kick-off to be delayed by 45 minutes.

Then there are the *extremely* rough figures. Before World War II, track officials routinely claimed that 300,000-plus watched motor racing at the dreaded Nurbürgring, a dubious figure, believe many, considering that this was during the Great Depression, when the country also happened to be neck-deep in postwar reparations and few inhabitants even owned a car. In more modern times, it was claimed that 250,000 spectators regularly attended the annual German Grand Prix there. When Chris Economaki, the highly respected American motorsports expert, covered the race for *National Speed Sport News*, he and a few fellow reporters decided to investigate. "We came to the conclusion," he said after talking to crowd-control officials and monitoring the crowds, "that the two-lane country roads around the place would be hard-pressed to handle more than 100,000 spectators."[40]

More recently, there has been the maze of the IPL. After the competition's first season, it was claimed that 3.422m spectators had filled the grounds at an average of 58,000 per game – only the NFL, purportedly, was a bigger draw that year. The league, however, had declined to distribute any breakdown of the figures to the media, a practice that still persisted as the fifth edition got underway in 2012. Belief, therefore, was in short supply among those who pointed out that even if every game had been sold out, the capacities of the grounds would have made the total and average figures most improbable. In addition, many Indian reporters suggested that a good deal of the seats had been filled by offering free admission, the better to sell the event to advertisers.

Organisers of the Australian Grand Prix in Melbourne's Albert Park, meanwhile, have faced accusations of inflating figures. Responding to confident forecasts that the 2012 race would be attended by more than 300,000, Peter Logan, a spokesman for the Save Albert Park campaign, was quick to express scepticism: "Ticket sales in last year's audited account indicated only about 60,000 paying customers – so please explain. The place is nearly empty on Thursday and Friday. They have never used turnstiles or barcode ticketing. You just can't believe them." The revenue figures diverged no less appreciably. While a race spokesman claimed sales revenue in 2011 had surged from A$24m to A$26.46m, Logan asserted that it had actually slumped by more than $11 million.[41] In the event, the "official" attendance relayed to the media was 313,700, the highest since 2005, with 114,900 congregating for the race.

By dint of both the necessary size of the venues and the global penchant for speed and fumes, motor sports still occupy a lofty perch on this particular tree. The largest attendance to date for the Le Mans 24-Hour race has been 250,920 in 2007. The planet's most accommodating sporting venue, the Indianapolis Motor Speedway, opened in 1909, has a permanent seating capacity of more than 257,000; infield seating has swollen crowds to 400,000. In 2007, a record 140,300 attended the Spanish Grand Prix. Even amid this testosterone nirvana, however, decline set in.

The most recent Australian Grand Prix to be staged in Adelaide, in 1995, saw 520,000 watch the practice laps and race proper; shifting the race to Melbourne saw crowds drop from 401,000 in 1996 to 305,000 in 2010. As demand at traditional venues began to stagnate at best, reflecting excessive ticket prices, new venues plugged the gap, albeit nowhere near enough to de-furrow president Bernie Ecclestone's brow. Crowds of 65,000 were reported for the Malaysian GP (2011), 85,000 for the Chinese GP (2010), 94,800 for the inaugural Indian GP (2011) and 106,000 for the Hungarian GP (2008), but the early enthusiasm slackened, and fears for the future of the Shanghai race in particular, first run in 2004, saw admission prices slashed for 2011.

A similar picture emerged in Moto GP, Formula 1's kid brother. Authorities reported raceday gates of 155,000 in the Czech Republic (2011), 150,000 in Jerez, Spain (2007) and 134,000 in Italy (2008), but more indicative of the spectators' disposable income was the precipitous decline in Indianapolis: while its inhabitants may love the smell of petrol in the morning, crowds dwindled from 91,064 in 2008, the first time the race was staged there, to 62,974 two years later before inching up to 64, 151 in 2011. While this underlined the more robust appeal of the four-wheelers, the economic crisis was weighing on pockets everywhere. Thanks to TV and live internet streaming, being there now took second place to virtually being there.

Hooliganism

I know of no excitement greater … Being in a crowd. And – greater still – being in a crowd in an act of violence. Nothingness is what you find there. Nothingness in its beauty, its simplicity, its nihilistic purity.

Bill Buford, *Among the Thugs*[42]

Because the spectator cannot experience what the athlete is experiencing, the fan is seldom a good loser.

George Sheehan, *Running and Being: The Total Experience*[43]

Why do young males riot? Thus pondered Bill Buford, an American journalist who spent eight years following English football hooligans and wrote a rivetingly insightful book about the experience. "They do it for the same reason that another generation drank too much or took hallucinogenic drugs or behaved rebelliously. Violence is their antisocial kick, their mind-altering experience."

It would therefore be naïve in the extreme to imagine that antisocial behaviour in a sporting context began in the Sixties, an age when hooligans started turning football terraces, high streets and trains into battlegrounds and the likes of Upton Park and Stamford Bridge became recruiting grounds for right-wing extremists. It was also more than mere coincidence that the so-called "English disease", which would infect Italy, Holland and Turkey most visibly, should reach its nadir in Britain the following decade. For Britons, after all, the 1970s was the decade the postwar bubble burst and the full reality of post-imperialism dawned – a period of economic strife, high unemployment, low collective self-esteem, waning international status and confused and morally dubious leadership.

If you are looking to trace football's violent roots, 1314 is the year most popularly cited. That was the year Edward II banned the game in England, fearing that the disorder surrounding inter-village contests of pig's-bladder hacking might lead to social unrest or maybe even treason. The Synod of Ely followed suit 50 years later, prohibiting the clergy, and Edward IV and Henry VII had both emulated Edward II before the 15th century was out.

A handy list of subsequent disturbances can be found in a valuable 2005 primer, *Football Hooliganism*, written by Steve Frosdick, principal lecturer at the Institute of Criminal Justice Studies at the University of Portsmouth, and Peter Marsh, a psychology lecturer and director of the Social Issues Research Centre who was previously co-director of the Contemporary Violence Research Centre at the University of Oxford. In a 1579 match against Cambridge University students, residents of Chesterton assaulted the opposition with sticks, driving them into the river. A 1740 match in Kettering degenerated into a food riot during the course of which a mill was destroyed then looted. When Preston North End met Sunderland in 1843, 200 soldiers and 50 policemen patrolled the ropes; at the end of a game 41 years later, Preston followers attacked the Bolton Wanderers players and spectators.[44]

The most troublesome spectators at early baseball games, by utter contrast, were the so-called "boosters", attested Harold Seymour. "They harassed the more 'sedate' spectators with their organised rooting, megaphones, fish horns, and other 'nerve-racking and ear-splitting devices'. The more orthodox among the faithful, who believed that rooting should be spontaneous, condemned 'bidders for publicity' for turning the sport of the people' into a 'sideshow for rehearsed exhibitions'. After the games, bands of city urchins waylaid the players as they left the parks and tried to get their autographs."[45]

John R. Tunis, the American sportswriter, recalled queuing up as a boy to see the 1903 World Series between the Pittsburgh Pirates and the Boston Americans (later the Red Sox). Suddenly, wrote Seymour, "the sound of distant music signalled the approach of Boston's Royal (or Loyal) Rooters. At last the marching men came into sight, in their best black suits and high white collars, blue rosettes pinned on their lapels." Each man, Tunis told him, "had his ticket stuck jauntily in the hatband of his derby".

At the head of the Rooters was their leading spirit, Mike "Nuff Ced" McGreevy. A forceful, outrageous figure who ran a Boston bar, the 3rd Base Saloon, from where the Rooters would march on matchdays, the nickname stemmed from his habit of pounding the bar with his fist whenever a dispute broke out between fans of the city's two major league baseball teams, the Americans and the Braves, whereupon he would settle the matter by declaiming "Nuff said!"

Another eminent leading Rooter was the city's mayor, John "Honey Fitz" Fitzgerald, who led similar parades when the Red Sox won the Series in 1912 and 1916. Nearly half a century later, recorded Seymour, his grandson, President John F. Kennedy, reportedly delayed an appointment with the Laotian prime minister so that he could stay until the end of Washington's opening game.[46] The Rooters' theme song was "Tessie", originally sung to a pet parakeet in the musical *The Silver Slipper*, which had ended a lengthy Broadway run in 1903. The Rooters' rousing rendition in the deciding encounter of that year's Series against the Pirates was held to have intimidated the opposition and inspired their favourites' first such success. A punky 2004 version by the Dropkick Murphys would become the official song of the Boston Red Sox' triumphant postseason progress to victory in the 2004 World Series.

The Old Firm

Desmond Morris, "that illustrious watcher of mankind"[47] according to *New Scientist*, was one of the more thought-provoking analysts of football during the last quarter of the 20th century. A zoologist, ethologist and author of *The Naked Ape* and *Manwatching*, he was so fascinated, and disturbed, by the game and its supporters that he not only became vice-chairman of Oxford United but wrote a book about them, *The Soccer Tribe*, published in 1981. Endorsing the oft-touted view of football as a tribal activity, a replacement for the wars that once bedevilled Europe, he discussed hooliganism with due compassion:

> *Sociologists studying the background of the offenders have found that, time and again, it is the young men from the more deprived areas of the city or town, living out their daily lives in crowded slums or boring, soulless council estates, who are the typical offenders. Their outbursts of violence have little to do with the Soccer Tribe itself, which merely acts as a dramatic stage on which they can perform. Since society has given them little chance to express their manhood in a positive or creative manner, they take the only course left to them apart from dumb subservience, and strike out in a negative and destructive way. They know that at least they will not then be ignored and that they will be able to make their mark on society, even if it is only a scar on somebody else's body.*[48]

For sheer weight of ruthlessness, corruption and violence, you would have to go a mighty long way to find a more devoted tribe of football followers than the Argentinian gangs, aka *barras bravas*, characterised by Simon Kuper in his lively and exemplary study of global fandom, *Football Against The Enemy*, as "a kind of Argentinian KGB". They scalp tickets provided by the clubs, run merchandise and food concessions, and control parking at the stadiums. They are also employed by club directors to carry out violence and blackmail, their tactics the stuff of urban myth and plenty of solid, sordid, horrid truth. According to Gustavo Grabia, a reporter with the sports daily *Ole* and author of a book about *La Doce*, the hooligans of Boca Juniors, the top half-dozen *barras* leaders at Boca Junior or River Plate were earning, in 2011, around $80,000 per annum – roughly 15 times the national minimum.[49]

"There are three important things in football," Amilcar Romero, who has written widely about football-related murders in Argentina, told Kuper. "Violence, information and money. The gangs have violence and information. The directors have money."[50] The *barras* are even said to control the players to an extent, supplying them with drugs and informing cuckolded girlfriends about their partners' sexual antics. Following a mid-1990s boardroom row over his capabilities, Daniel Passarella, Argentina's 1978 World Cup-winning captain and by now managing River Plate, was beaten up by representatives of one of the dissenting directors. "Part of business," shrugged Romero, *"a guerre de boutique."*[51]

Even so, for sheer longevity and savagery *between* fans, it is hard to imagine anything worse than the seemingly perennial mayhem in Glasgow, home to the sectarian football wars between Catholic Celtic and Protestant Rangers, the so-called Old Firm. Until the latter's financial tribulations prompted demotion by three divisions in 2012 and thus an unplanned cessation of hostilities – at least for League fixtures – derby day, sometimes half a dozen of them in a single season, would see the stands brimming with Union Jacks and Irish tricolours; here, religion, as Andrew Davies warrants in the journal *Irish Historical Studies*, is "inextricably bound up with nationalism".[52] Even so, as Tom Gallagher has testified in *Glasgow: the uneasy peace: religious tension in modern Scotland*,[53] allegiances tend toward the tribal rather than the doctrinal. The backdrop of squalid living conditions and social deprivation has not been all that dissimilar to The Troubles that beset Northern Ireland for the majority of the last century, inflaming hatred on the (theoretically) safe side of the Irish Sea, from where, as we shall see, it bounced back. "I've always felt we were the underdogs in this country," said Billy McNeill, who captained Celtic to the 1967 European Cup, a triumph made all the more remarkable by the fact that the entire winning team had been born within 30 miles of Parkhead. "The bulk of the population will always be more inclined to be Rangers orientated than Celtic."[54]

Of the Irish immigrants to Glasgow in the late 19th century, it is estimated that Roman Catholics outweighed Protestants by three to one. Rangers were founded first, in 1873, as a Protestant boys' club; Celtic emerged 15 years later, expressly for Catholics, spurring Rangers toward a Unionist identity.[55] It has been claimed that, up to 1912, there had been no serious strife between supporters, suggesting that the arrival of Irish shipbuilders in Glasgow was significantly divisive. That was not only the year James Craig and Edward Carson established the Ulster Volunteer Force but also the year Rangers elevated to club president John Ure Primrose, whose predecessor, James Henderson, had been respected in the city's Catholic communities. Primrose pledged Rangers to the Masonic cause and became an active West of Scotland Unionist, often spouting anti-Catholic invective. A rivalry with Celtic, he realised, was rich in financial promise; by extending it along clearer religious lines, it could not only be accentuated but perpetuated on moral grounds.

Trouble, though, had begun much earlier. By 1896, reported *Scottish Sport*, there was "bad blood" between the fans; two years later came the first brawl, causing the New Year's Day match to be abandoned. The same newspaper characterised the crowd as "the scum of the city, drunken and brutal in their behaviour and language".[56] The second of 1905's two pitch invasions bred another abandonment: Rangers were leading 2-0 with eight minutes left when Jimmy Quinn, Celtic's vaunted centre-forward, was sent off for kicking Alec Craig, whereupon spectators invaded the field and assaulted the referee with iron spiked palings.

The two most tragic episodes owed nothing to intentional ugliness, yet both illustrated the enmity. On 5 September 1931, Celtic's John Thomson, the so-called "prince of goalkeepers", died after diving at the feet of a Rangers forward, Sam English. Upon realising the possible gravity of the collision, Davie Meiklejohn, the Rangers captain, implored his supporters to stop baying and singing their sadistic approval. Players from both sides carried off the stricken Thomson; humanity prevailed. To this day, Celtic take the pitch for home games accompanied by *The Celtic Song*, rejigged by supporters to accentuate both the enduring despair for Thomson and the continued pride in his courage and devotion:

> *For it's a grand old team to play for*
> *For it's a grand old team to see*
> *And if you know your history*
> *It's enough to make your heart go oh-oh-oh-oh.*

On 2 January 1971, at the end of the New Year derby, 66 Rangers fans were killed on a stairway; 147 more were injured. The theory most commonly espoused is that when Jimmy Johnstone put Celtic ahead with moments remaining, many Rangers followers began leaving their section of the segregated stadium, an 80,000 packed house, and were heading down stairway 13 only to turn back upon hearing the acclaim for Colin Stein's equaliser a minute later. When the final whistle followed shortly afterwards, thousands of other fans, it was said, started heading down the same stairway; the fatalities were the consequence of the ensuing crush. The police report referred to six-foot-high stacks of bodies.

Even though differing accounts were rendered and the Fatal Accident Inquiry found no convincing evidence, this version stood firm. The inquiry's conclusions, together with a case brought against Rangers by a relative of one of the deceased, indicated a "much more probable" cause, according to Graham Walker's reading in *Soccer and Disaster*: "someone stumbling and falling almost halfway down the staircase, precipitating a surge forward by a densely packed crowd."[57] Of the many witnesses, some of whom recalled seeing someone fall, only one claimed to have seen the supposed crush. The upshot, four years later, was the Safety of Sports Grounds Act. By 1981, in a foretaste of the measures that would change British football as a whole, Ibrox was predominantly seating-only.

Yet even that unspeakable incident did little to temper Old Firm hostilities, in Scotland or even Northern Ireland, from where, estimated *The Belfast Newsletter*, 2000 fans had come to attend the match. In the same month as the Ibrox disaster, on Belfast's

Upper Springhill Road, a Catholic mob taunted Protestants with the cry "Rangers 66 Celtic 0". During a battle between rioters and troops on the Shankhill Road the following week, the Rangers supporters club building was razed to the ground.[58]

And yet, and yet… the greatest Celtic manager was without question Jock Stein, a Protestant. Indeed, Paul Davis argues that the vast majority of Scots "do not care or pretend to care about Catholics and Protestants, or Loyalists and Reds, any more than they care about the Great Pumpkin". As Lawrence Macintyre, head of safety at Ibrox Park, elaborated: "It is called a 90-minute bigot, someone who has got a friend of an opposite religion living next door. But for that 90 minutes they shout foul religious abuse at each other."[59]

* * *

In 1963, during the minute's silence for the assassinated President Kennedy, a Catholic, Rangers fans jeered. According to Ralph Brand, as yet, there was no antagonism between the players. "Having been born on the east coast, I never knew anything about it [the sectarian issue]," the former Ibrox forward recollected in 2011. "I went through there and was sitting [in a dressing room] next to all my football heroes. It was all chit-chat, it was all in fun. It was not serious. You had a joke and when it came to the game, you wanted to beat them [Celtic] so much. But that's where it ended."[60] Following his transfer to Manchester City in 1965, nonetheless, Brand publicly stated what had long been suspected, telling the *News of the World* that the Ibrox club operated a sectarian policy. Two years later, when vice-chairman Matt Taylor was questioned about this, he replied that it was "part of our tradition". To change now "would lose us considerable support".[61]

Playing for both clubs had long since been unthinkable. Not until 1977 did Alfie Conn become the first postwar player to don both the dark blue shirt and the green-and-white hoops, and there was much politicking behind the scenes before Maurice "Mo" Johnston, joined Rangers from Celtic in 1989. "It has been suggested that the rationale behind the transfer was that it would remove any inhibitions of clubs in Catholic countries such as Italy and Spain regarding the admittance of a perceived anti-Catholic institution into a future European League," wrote Dan Burdsey and Robert Chappell in the journal, *Sociology of Sport,* drawing extensively and correctly on Bill Murray's searching and balanced 1984 book *The Old Firm: Sectarianism, sport and society in Scotland.* In protest, the Shankhill branch of the Rangers supporters club in Belfast folded. "COLLABORATORS WILL BE KNEECAPPED MOJO" was but one example of graffiti on Glasgow walls paralleled with paramilitary violence in Northern Ireland.

Although as many as 15 Catholics had previously turned out for Rangers, the backlash that followed Johnson's perceived defection – to a club he would help match Celtic's record streak of nine consecutive Scottish League titles – was still reverberating two decades later. McNeill, the manager Johnston left slack-jawed at Celtic, pulled no punches: "I can't forgive him and I don't think the Celtic fans ever will. He disrespected us all." Last seen living in London, reported Ewan Murray in 2009, "Johnston has no plans to return to Scotland, unwilling to subject his children to the potential ramifications of the most controversial transfer the country's football scene has ever witnessed."[62]

It will surprise few that, in the wake of their savage battle on the Hampden Park pitch at the end of the 1980 Scottish Cup final, the Old Firm paved the way for the banning of alcohol at football matches in Scotland. On the other hand, it is also a rivalry estimated by the University of Strathclyde's Fraser of Allander Institute to have been worth £118m to the Scottish economy in 2005, three times the amount generated by the Edinburgh festivals. In addition, it had created more than 3000 jobs, primarily in hotels, pubs and catering, 876 of them at the two clubs.[63]

One night in Luton

As terrifying as their bigger and wealthier cross-London rivals were, no set of English club loyalists induced quite as much fear as those of lowly Millwall, whose defiant unofficial motto said it all: "No-one likes us, we don't care". That they would contribute mightily to the era's most catalytic outbreak of hooliganism was nothing short of inevitable.

Around 10,000 Millwall fans travelled to Bedfordshire on 13 March 1985 for an FA Cup tie against Luton Town at Kenilworth Road. Before kick-off, George Graham, Millwall's laconic Scottish manager, pleaded for order, urging his fans, some of whom had already invaded the pitch, to return to the away end. One of the more peaceful visiting supporters, Tony Cascarino – who would go on to play for, among others, Chelsea and the Republic of Ireland – recalled two further invasions in the first half, during which the referee called the players into the dressing room for around half an hour while police and stewards battled to restore order. Missiles rained down on Luton's players; seats were hurled into a stand occupied by local families, even billiard balls. Cascarino remembers fans "baying to get at the home support".

It would get worse. At the final whistle, thousands of Millwall fans ran onto the pitch to fight the police. "There were running battles," remembered Cascarino. Dogs were unleashed, more missiles thrown. Then the rioters charged the home end, "trying to spark them into retaliation". There was "a nasty mood even among the away fans, a divide between those who wanted to get out and those who were relishing the chaos". Cascarino felt stuck. "I had no intention of going anywhere near the pitch. All I could think was that I shouldn't be there. I didn't need to be there. I don't know how long I had to wait, with my friends, before we could get out. The scene outside was hardly better. The streets looked like a battleground. There was fighting everywhere, shattered glass scattered across the pavement, shop windows put through."

The toll was heavy. There were 47 injuries and 31 arrests; one policeman was struck by a concrete block and had to be resuscitated. The cost of the damage to the ground amounted to £20,000. Millwall were fined £7,500 but appealed successfully, accentuating the governmental backlash. Alcohol was banned from grounds; fans were searched upon arrival; segregation of home and visiting fans was improved; police became ever more sophisticated in their vigilance, not least through the deployment of close-circuit cameras. Having backtracked on a plan to erect fences, Luton became the first club to ban away fans, and paid for it the next year when they were expelled from the League Cup for refusing to admit Cardiff City supporters, a decision Margaret Thatcher, the prime minister, openly abhorred. The match had been televised live, enabling her to witness the running battles that would spur her to propound the view (which, happily, never quite translated into law) that the only solution to hooliganism was identity cards – Big Brother incarnate.

Even more extreme was the Chelsea owner, Ken Bates, a brusque, brash, publicity-hungry success in the business world who wanted fans penned behind electric fences. When I interviewed him in his office a few months after the Kenilworth Road episode, the wall behind his desk was dominated by a framed copy of a newspaper cartoon published at the time, gently satirising his proposal. His pride in such notoriety was immense. Yet in some ways it was possible to see his point. After all, he had had to put up with no end of crowd disturbances. It was at his Stamford Bridge stomping-ground the previous year, indeed, that I had had my own Damascene moment.

It was an evening when the home fans were livid; not only that their team, *our* team, were losing a League Cup semi-final against Sunderland, but that the matchwinner, Clive Walker, had once graced that royal blue shirt. In a blatant attempt to get the game abandoned – Newcastle United's followers had set that crafty precedent in a 1974 FA Cup tie against Nottingham Forest – those standing up invaded the playing arena; those sitting down uprooted their metallic-framed seats and chucked them onto the field, further endangering the players. By now, mounted police had rumbled onto the pitch, though play, surreally, carried on. All I felt was shame and disgust. Never again would a football club command my loyalty.

"I would have been unhappy if we hadn't protected each other"

Given what they have to put up with, it is a wonder so few sports-folk react intemperately to criticism from the stands. That's why the generations who witnessed the exceptions recall them so vividly. In 1912, Ty Cobb, the troubled, turbulent high priest of early 20th century baseball, assaulted a one-armed spectator who had had the temerity to call him a "half-nigger"; nearly threequarters of a century later, Inzamam-ul-Haq, the strapping Pakistani cricketer and future national captain, waded into the crowd in Toronto, bat in hand, to settle the score with a fan who had cast unkind and needless aspersions about his bulk.

In May 2000, in the timelessly enchanting ivy-clad setting of Wrigley Field, intimate home to the Chicago Cubs and my favourite sporting arena, came one of the most grievous outbreaks of vengeful player-itis. Chad Kreuter, the LA Dodgers' backup pitcher, was sitting in the bullpen in the ninth inning of a nip-and-tuck game when he felt a blow to the head and was relieved of his cap. Looking to my right from behind home plate, discerning what happened next was next to impossible, but the media bulletins filled in the grisly details. Supported by coaches as well as teammates, Kreuter clambered up into the grandstand seats occupied by the taunting Cubs followers, fists flailing; the brawl lasted nine minutes. "I would have been unhappy if we hadn't protected each other," Kevin Malone, the Dodgers' general manager, said afterwards, adding that Kreuter's assailant had been inspired by "intoxication and over-indulging in alcohol". Nineteen Dodgers were suspended for three weeks up to the eight slapped on Kreuter; most had their sentences reduced.

England's most infamous such episode had come five years earlier, when Eric Cantona, Manchester United's flamboyant French striker and self-styled philosopher, waded into the throng at Selhurst Park to launch a kung-fu kick at Matthew Simmons, an abusive Crystal Palace supporter. "As a ten-year-old, it was difficult to see what exactly was happening," remembered

Darren Richman in his blog, The Republic of Mancunia. "There was a good deal of swearing and a palpable tension in the air. We were about fifty yards to the right of the man in the awful leather jacket and the adults in our party could see something wasn't right. As it transpired, Matthew Simmonds had rushed down eleven rows of the stand to hurl abuse at the departing genius. He memorably informed *The Sun* his exact words were: 'Off you go Cantona – it's an early bath for you!' More reliable witnesses have suggested it was closer to: 'Fuck off, you mother-fucking French bastard'."[64]

The most shocking reaction came from Richard Williams, quite possibly the most admirable media all-rounder England has ever produced, as apt to comment with acuity and percep-tiveness about Steven Spielberg, Miles Davis and Stevie Wonder as Ayrton Senna and football's greatest No.10s; a writer of the highest order and a fair-minded, pacifist son of a country vicar. His spite for Simmons could not have been more atypical: Cantona's only crime, he averred in *The Independent on Sunday*, "was to stop hitting him".[65]

"The tragedy that dares not speak its name"

For many, though, English football's most spiteful night, one that did not involve the players, came two months after that foul one in Luton, at Brussels' dilapidated Heysel Stadium. Before the European Cup final between Liverpool and Juventus, the English club complained to UEFA about the state of a venue that had been built in the 1920s and had already been condemned, just a few years earlier, for failing to meet safety standards; their impreca-tions fell on blinkered ears. Come the evening itself, Liverpool fans charged at their counterparts before kick-off, easily over-coming the constraints of a flimsy fence: when the innocent tried to flee over a wall, it collapsed. The ensuing stampede left more than 400 injured and 39 dead – 32 from Italy, four from Belgium, two from France and one from Northern Ireland. And still the show went on. Here, as Oliver Kay put it so memorably in *The Times*, was "the tragedy that dares not speak its name".[66]

Liverpool immediately withdrew from the following season's UEFA Cup, though chairman John Smith and two Merseyside councillors would blame National Front infiltrators from London for the carnage. Hours later, in what its chairman, Bert Millichip, acknowledged as a "pre-emptive move", the FA banned English clubs from participating in European competition, a move urged by Mrs Thatcher. Not long afterwards, as anticipated, UEFA imposed a ban that would extend for five years (six in the case of Liverpool, punished additionally for Heysel). "It felt as if Liverpool had let English football down, when for 20 years they had been its finest ambassador," Phil Neal, the club's hardy full-back, would reflect. "That's what really turned our stomachs, the feeling that the club's impeccable record over two decades in Europe had ended in something so horrific."[67]

The punishments now seem criminally light. Twenty-seven Liverpool fans were arrested and 26 charged with manslaughter. In 1989, a five-month trial in Brussels found that 14 of those in the dock had been guilty of involuntary manslaughter: each served around a third of their three-year prison sentence (half of which was suspended anyway); the remaining dozen were acquitted, though a few had their bail money, £2,000, confiscated for not having attended the entire proceedings. The Belgian Football Union and the convicted supporters were ordered, provisionally, to pay £5m in civil damages to the bereaved. "You never hear of this," attested Kay, "because the tragedy is taboo." Albert Roosens, the erstwhile secretary-general of the BFU, received a six-month suspended jail sentence over the ticketing arrangements; Johan Mathieu, responsible for marshalling the police presence in the stands, was similarly dealt with after being described by the judge as "far too passive"; Jacques Georges and Hans Bangerter, respectively UEFA president and general secretary at the time, were threatened with incarceration but received a conditional discharge.

For many years, Liverpool kept its distance from it all. Recognition – of the tragedy and the legacy – took an unconscionably long time; now there is a plaque at Anfield commemorating the dead, and a tribute every May. The lasting mystery, believes Kay, is that Heysel "is even more of a taboo in Turin", where 1985 is associated immeasurably more readily with Juventus' first European Cup triumph. On the club website in 2012, the events of that dreadful evening were shunted into an article headlined "Juventus wins everything", wherein the tragedy was deemed worthy of precisely 106 words. Succinctness can seldom have been more ably or coldly personified. "No wonder the Association for the Victims of Heysel has felt hurt by Juventus's reluctance to acknowledge what happened," reckoned Kay. The families, he surmised, do not want their lost ones to become a cause célèbre in England, where the purpose is solely to score points on the terraces. "A little recognition closer to home is what they want."[68]

Keeping the customers dissatisfied

Indefensible as the violence was and remains, it ill-behoved the game's authorities in the 1980s to accuse the troublemakers of lacking respect. Spectator comfort and safety, after all, had never been of paramount concern. During the 1902 Scotland-England international, the first to be played between wholly professional teams, heavy overnight rainfall led to the collapse of Ibrox Park's new state-of-the-art, wooden-terraced West Tribune Stand, constructed at the heavy cost of £20,000. Fans leapt 40 feet below: 25 died, 517 were injured. "Wooden joists snapped clean through in what is now the Broomloan stand," recollected *The Herald* in 2008.

> *They'd been laid on a steel frame-work, supporting wooden decking, but a hole some 20 yards square opened up. Hundreds of spectators plunged up to 40 feet to the ground. Rescuers found "a scene of indescribable horror and confusion ... a mass of mangled and bleeding humanity, the victims piled one above the other ... enough to unman the strongest." The resources of the city's hospitals were over-stretched. Doctors in the crowd lent immediate help, but at Govan police station, cells were called into service as a casualty clearing station.*[69]

William Robertson's father went to the Western Infirmary after the match in the hope of finding his 25-year-old son. Unable to find him among the injured, he was shown to the mortuary where he identified a body as being William's. He was arranging the funeral when William arrived home. According to *The Herald* report on the Monday, there was barely any debris at the scene on the day after the match: almost all the timber and sheets of corrugated iron had been deployed as makeshift stretchers. No more would wooden terracing be supported on steel frames; earth embankments or concrete terracings became *de rigueur*. The contractor was prosecuted and acquitted.

There were no further significant safety measures in Scotland until the wake of the 1971 disaster at the same ground. This begat the Wheatley Report into safety at British sports grounds, which echoed the recommendations of the Moelwyn Hughes Report into the 1946 tragedy at Bolton's overcrowded Burnden Park, when 33 died under similar circumstances: namely, a licencing system to ensure safer grounds. Wheatley noted with understated scorn that such a proposal had been "mooted" for almost 50 years.

Nor was Britain alone in its negligence and suffering. During a 1964 international in Lima between Peru and Brazil, protests at a disallowed home goal two minutes from time erupted in a riot: 318 were killed and more than 500 sustained major injuries. In Buenos Aires four years later, 74 deaths ensued after spectators erroneously headed towards a closed exit after a first division match. Those at the front were crushed to death against the doors by others ignorant of the closed passageway at the back. In 1982, during a European Cup tie in Moscow, 340 supporters reportedly died in a replica of the original account of the 1971 Ibrox tragedy: police were said to have driven fans down a slender, icy staircase only for a late goal to send thousands surging back into the ground, crushing those trapped in the middle. Russian officials attempted to claim the official casualty loss was only 61 and that the police were not responsible for the disaster. Few were convinced. The havoc even extended to

Kathmandu, in Nepal: in 1988, 93 spectators died fleeing a hailstorm only to find the stadium doors locked. No less horrendous was the stray unextinguished cigarette that set alight a stand at Bradford City's Valley Parade in 1985, killing 56. The terracing was wooden.

Responsibility for the safety of spectators, insisted Lord Wheatley,

> *lies at all times with the ground management. The management will normally be either the owner or lessee of the ground, who may not necessarily be the promoter of the event. In discharging its responsibility, the management needs to recognise that safety should not be seen as a set of rules or conditions imposed by others, but rather as standards set from within which reflect a safety culture at the sports ground. A positive attitude demonstrated by the management is therefore crucial in ensuring that safety policies are carried out effectively and willingly.*[70]

As the police exerted ever stricter control at the height of hooliganism, Lord Wheatley's message would be ignored with progressive ease.

Hillsborough

Throughout those pitiful times endured by the British in the 1970s, instead of the corrupt politicians or crooked businessmen or bent coppers, it was the working classes, the traditional rump of football supporters, who were most persistently demonised in the media. Not merely for beating each other up and vandalising trains and terrorising town centres, but for having the audacity to fight, individually and collectively, for their rights; for joining unions that dared to strike over repressive working conditions, paralysing industry and leaving streets strewn with piles of rubbish bags; for transforming gleaming new tower blocks into graffiti-scarred palaces of alleged filth and depravity. In his vivid and unsparing *Red Riding* novels, David Peace, a Leeds United supporter, chose his native Yorkshire as the scene for a study of shocking malevolence and endless suffering, its most fiendish villains not the perverted priest or the vicious businessman but the boys in blue: the West Yorkshire Police. Yet not until 2012 would the extent of the county constabulary's greatest crimes be officially acknowledged.

* * *

The South Yorkshire Police's ignoblest hour began on the afternoon of 15 April 1989. I was with my best friend Jed in Amsterdam that day, on a two-man stag weekend. Around 5pm we returned to our hotel room to watch the BBC's coverage of the FA Cup semi-final between Liverpool and Nottingham Forest, broadcast live across Europe from Sheffield Wednesday's Hillsborough stadium. Awkwardly, the poor signal on the TV set left the volume muted, but neither of us, having sampled the spiffing local smokables, could be bothered to do anything about it. The sight of the pitch laden with spectators after the scheduled kick-off time sowed the seeds of confusion, followed by a gut reaction born of contemptuous familiarity.

In the 1980s, for a sensitive Englishman, football was the love that dared not speak its name. Having spent my teens falling out of love with the game because of the shame I felt in following a club, Chelsea, whose more extreme "supporters" felt an obligation to beat up and maim rival "supporters" in the interest of local supremacy, having reported on riots at Millwall and Chelsea, having spent five years as a full-time sportswriter trying with limited success to cover football matches without the need to scribble the word "crowd" and follow it with "trouble", only one possibility crossed my mind at that moment: it *must* have been the work of the hooligans. Disgusted, we gave up and turned off. I'm not sure when we discovered that 95 people had been killed in the crush at the Leppings Lane end – the final toll would be 96 – but the following Wednesday the front page of *The Sun* appeared to confirm our worst prejudices. "THE TRUTH" avowed the headline. Beneath ran three subheadings that tapped expertly into the popular perception of football supporters: "Some fans picked pockets of victims…

Some fans urinated on the brave cops… Some fans beat up PC giving kiss of life."

The Sun version took root. "My eye-witness version – with its broken and twisted limbs and young people dying in the sunshine – was discounted as Scouse revisionism," attested Tony Evans, a Liverpool follower writing 23 years later as football editor of *The Times*. He was also an active supporter of campaigns by the bereaved families to drag into the public domain the *actual* truth: "After these conversations I would often wake from gruesome nightmares and howl with rage."[71]

Context, again, is all. It says much for the power of tradition, and the fury they rouse, that London's warring national newspapers continued to be known, collectively, as Fleet Street and "the Street of Shame" long after their relocation to the concrete-and-steel towers of Canary Wharf and the aircraft hangars of Wapping, a process which began in the 1980s. It is the breadth and depth of coverage offered by these papers that has defied all efforts to successfully launch an English *L'Equipe* or even *Sports Illustrated*. They also operate in a uniquely competitive market that has wrung the best and worst from journalists and journalism. The very worst, because it disdained any sense of the responsibility that comes with power, was that front page of *The Sun* on 19 April 1989.

The basis for "THE TRUTH" was unsubstantiated allegations made by South Yorkshire police "sources". The chief cause of fury was the headline, not the allegations themselves; they had already been published elsewhere, even in Liverpool's own *Daily Post*, which ran an article headlined "I blame the yobs".[72] While many of the allegations were first reported in the *Sheffield Star* the previous day, and were carried in many other media outlets, millions bought *The Sun* every day. For all the groveling apologies and cap-in-hand pilgrimages to Liverpool made over the ensuing decades by *The Sun*'s executives, the boycott of the country's bestselling daily by the city's inhabitants is still going strong.

Yet *The Sun*, of course, was only the messenger. The official verdict was accidental death but the bereaved families never accepted that. When Lord Justice Taylor published his interim report to the Home Office in August 1989, he begged to differ with Lord Wheatley, citing the constabulary as being ultimately responsible for crowd safety. More creditably, he took a highly unpopular line, blaming inadequate police control and safety provision. He also brought an unlamented (initially at least) end to standing at grounds. "The ordinary provisions to be expected at a place of entertainment are sometimes not merely basic but squalid. This not only denies the spectator an essential facility... [but]... directly lowers standards of conduct. This crowd conduct becomes degenerated and other misbehaviour seems less out of place."[73]

Thereafter, the bereaved fought tooth and nail for the real truth, forming action groups renowned for their resilience, unbounded optimism and absolute refusal to be denied. The toll, inevitably, was crippling, soul-destroying. "Thousands of people witnessed unspeakable sights. Even now, suicides, breakdowns and alcoholism abound as people still struggle to cope with their experiences," Evans would relate. In 2011, Stephen Whittle told a doctor he had sold a ticket to a friend who had died in the Leppings Lane end, then proceeded to jump in front of a train. Yet compassion gave way to indifference and even ridicule: Manchester United fans thought nothing of taunting their arch-rivals with chants such as "You killed your own fans" or "If it wasn't for the Scousers we could stand".

Not for 23 years, until September 2012, were the smears and cover-ups and callous untruths confirmed in a report by the Hillsborough Independent Panel under the aegis of an eminent religious leader, the Bishop of Liverpool, who had pored over 80 documents and some 450,000 pages of evidence. Suddenly, just as David Cameron was bathing in the reflected glow of the London Olympics, England's first minister found himself pitchforked into a more sobering side of this sporting life.

Rising in the House of Commons, Cameron apologised to the bereaved and described the panel's findings as "deeply distressing". The Taylor Report had been informed by an inquiry, he acknowledged, that "didn't have access to all the documents that have since become available". Nor did it "properly examine the response of the emergency services". It was followed, more-over, "by a deeply controversial inquest and by a media version of events that sought to blame the fans". As a direct result, "the families have not heard the truth and have not found justice".[74] The bottom line? Two statistics that defy all adjectives: no fewer than 116 of the 164 police statements identified for "substantive amendment" had been "amended to remove or alter comments unfavourable to" the South Yorkshire Police; no fewer than 41 lives, meanwhile, could have been saved had the emergency services done their job.

In December 2012, the verdict of accidental death was finally quashed and the home secretary, Theresa May, announced a new inquest. The following May brought a *Panorama* documen-tary, *Hillsborough – How They Buried the Truth*, which drew on CCTV and BBC footage to claim that witnesses were leant on or discredited, including a respected SYP officer and a senior doctor. From the grave came the remarkably calm if damning video perspective of Anne Williams, whose 15-year-old son Kevin had died that dreadful April afternoon. "My son did not die in an accident and neither did the 95 with him," said this most indefatigable of Hillsborough campaigners, who had died from cancer the previous month. "So at least we have got rid of that because that accidental death verdict used to really, really upset me because it let them off the hook, didn't it?" Williams said she had long distrusted the verdict of the original coroner, Stefan Popper, who pronounced that the victims were all dead by 3.15pm; she believed that it was part of a cover-up to distract from the culpability of the police and emergency services. The film claimed that the inquest suppressed the evidence of a key witness, Derek Bruder, an off-duty policeman who had tried to resuscitate Kevin Williams and had always insisted that, by then, it was well after 3.15.[75]

It had been a measure of public feeling that the UK's Christmas No.1 for 2012 was a cover of The Hollies' *He Ain't*

Heavy, He's My Brother by The Justice Collective, an ad-hoc collection that numbered Sir Paul McCartney as well as other acclaimed Liverpool musicians: it had been recorded to raise funds for the court case. The song was chosen by Margaret Aspinall, chair of the Hillsborough Families Support Group, whose teenage son had bought her a copy of the original five months before he lost his life at the Leppings Lane end. [76]

* * *

Only in extremely recent times has being a spectator at a sporting event become widely associated with comfort and convenience, i.e. respect. In Ancient Greece, those teeming into Athens from Corinth and Sparta and further afield saw only one hotel, the Leonidaion, and only if you were an ambassador or official could you enjoy its plushness. Everyone else had to make do with extremely basic facilities while sleeping in tents and makeshift barracks. One slave was said to have been subjected to an odious threat by his master: a visit to the Olympics. "For 16 hours spectators would be on their feet, their bare heads exposed to the endless sun and dramatic thunderstorms, while itinerant vendors extorted them for suspicious sausages and dubious cheese," Tony Perrottet wrote with arresting vividness in *The Naked Games: The True Story of the Ancient Olympics*. "Most excruciating, there was no reliable water supply so dehydrated spectators would be collapsing in droves from heatstroke." More than 2,000 years later, Sheffield Wednesday, the FA and the SYP showed that nothing much had changed.

The safety of the crowd at Hillsborough, decided the Hillsborough panel, damningly, was "compromised at every level".

David Bernstein, the FA chairman, received a torrent of criticism, and properly so, when the initial statement welcoming the report somehow contrived to omit the word "sorry". Bernstein's insensitive lapse was corrected a few hours later by an "unreserved apology" but Tony Barrett told *Times* readers he was far from convinced. "This was an organisation that 23 years earlier had put Liverpool supporters in the death trap that was the

Leppings Lane terrace and then failed to accept any culpability for what followed. That this was done despite the pleadings of Peter Robinson, then the Liverpool chief executive, who beseeched them to switch the semi-final to Old Trafford, makes the decision all the more inexcusable."[77]

Hillsborough, after all, had been deleted from the list of FA Cup semi-final venues after a near-tragedy in 1981 when, on the same treacherous terrace, Tottenham fans were being crushed: on that occasion, the police had had the good sense to unfasten the gates, sparing 500. Today, the FA's priorities are money, money and money; in 1989, they put security before both safety and respect for the customer. Greed, though, was still a common and crucial ingredient: the root cause of the deadly crush was the decision to sell too many tickets. One of the unsung benefits of a seating-only policy is to make this impossible – in theory.

For those of us who lived through the most toxic period of the English disease, nonetheless, it was difficult to read a letter published in the *Sunday Times* without an involuntary nod of the head. "Throughout the 1970s and 1980s, away fans were met at railway stations by police with Alsatians," recalled Jon Anderson from Manchester, shortly after the Hillsborough verdict. "They were then 'kettled' and walked en masse to the home ground by officers with horses and dogs and placed in fenced-off areas, usually with a large empty terraced area between rival fans. If such measures were necessary to ensure safety at football matches, then the sport should not have been allowed to be played. It is the Establishment and the game's authorities, in neglecting to deal with the problem of football violence, that allowed tragic deaths to occur in stadiums where merely to be present was to place oneself, or one's family, in harm's way."[78]

What made the original "Truth" about Hillsborough so easy to swallow was the fact that that same Establishment and those same authorities were so utterly unwilling to distinguish between those who saw sport as a safe outlet for emotion and the minority to whom it served as a vehicle for the expression of something a good deal more complex. Behind the Hillsborough disaster lay sneering, undiscerning contempt for both.

Hitler, Stalin and Walter O'Malley

When Pete Hamill met Jack Newfield, another esteemed journalist from Brooklyn, he suggested Newfield jot down the names of the three 20th century figures he most detested; Hamill did likewise. The lists were identical: Hitler, Stalin and Walter O'Malley. This in turn led to a 2005 documentary, *Hitler, Stalin and Walter O'Malley*. To be bracketed in such satanic company plainly takes some doing, and clearly Hamill and Newfield were allowing hometown bias to obscure the vastly more blatant misdeeds of Henrik Verwoerd and Pol Pot (and when they made those lists, Simon Cowell, to be fair, was still at school). Yet all the logic in the world will never stop Brooklynites born in the first half of the last century spitting eye-bulging hatred at the slightest reminder of the man who stole their beloved Dodgers.

O'Malley was not the first owner of a sporting franchise to wrench it from fanbase and roots. Just two years after becoming the first professional baseball team in 1869, the Cincinnati Red Stockings reacted to a dip in attendance by upping sticks for Boston. In 1902, Milwaukee's Brewers were shipped off to St Louis, where they became the little-loved, lame, pathetic Browns. Indeed, the most famous of all American sporting teams came as a direct consequence of such a move: in 1903, the Baltimore Orioles morphed into the New York Highlanders and thence, 10 years after that, the Yankees. It is also true that, when the Dodgers vacated Ebbets Field and upped sticks for Los Angeles in 1957, the New York Giants, hitherto bedded down at Manhattan's Polo Grounds, bolted for San Francisco. Yet while the name of their owner, Horace Stoneham, generated few ripples beyond the Big Apple, no territorial shift has stirred the degree of heartfelt loathing felt to this day towards O'Malley. The easiest explanation is to have a sense of what it was like to live near Ebbets Field in the mid-1950s.

To appreciate the full impact of a sporting team on a community, the best time and place to start is 1957 and the city-borough of Brooklyn, then home to 2m inhabitants and increasingly unrecognisable to its older denizens. The *Eagle* newspaper was no more; nor the trolleybus. With postwar prosperity had come new highways and the all-conquering automobile, enabling residents to pay $300 down, buy a Studebaker or a Ford and head anywhere they desired. As another erudite Brooklyn sportswriter, Roger Kahn, observed in *The Boys of Summer*, his elegiac 1972 homage to the Series-winning, city-lifting Dodgers of 1955 – and one of the very finest books ever written that is even vaguely about sport – old families, primarily white, left town, to be displaced by new ethnicities, mostly black and, as *West Side Story* would testify, Puerto Rican. "The flux terrified people on both sides. Could Brooklyn continue as a suitable place for the middle class to live? That was what the Irish, Italian and Jewish families asked themselves. Are we doomed? wondered blacks, up from Carolina dirt farms and shacks in the West Indies. Was black life always to be poverty, degradation, rotgut? The answer, like the American [suburb] itself, is still in doubt."[79]

Hopeless between the world wars, long the butt of endless jibes, the Dodgers, aka "Dem Bums", had been enjoying a remarkable renaissance since Jackie Robinson integrated major league baseball in 1947, dominating the National League and, in that unforgettable October of 1955, finally winning the World Series for the first time. Better yet, they bested their nauseatingly dominant neighbours, the Yankees. In the Dodger Sym-Phony, a band of inept but enthusiastic and jolly musicians, and Hilda Chester, a bell-ringing cheerleader as loud as she was diminutive and prone to proffering advice to managers via handwritten notes, Ebbets Field flourished national symbols of devotedly eccentric fankind. Yet O'Malley, the president and majority shareholder, was far from satisfied.

Walter Francis O'Malley was the son of a controversial New York politician, a lawyer by trade. Bulky, bespectacled, outwardly wise and respectable, he was a wolf in owl's clothing. Journalists liked him. "An engaging person is the president of the Dodgers, a man of charm and amiability," enthused the *New York Times*' Pulitzer Prize-winning Arthur Daley, who had been the first sports reporter sent on an overseas assignment by the paper when he covered the 1936 Berlin Olympics. "Few men in base-ball are as delightful and likeable as he. And none more clever."[80]

The man referred to by Daley as "The O'Malley" was making money from the Dodgers, just not enough. Seasonal atten-dances at decaying Ebbets Field, having topped 1.6m in 1949, were hovering around 1m; in 1957, even the hitherto hapless Braves, having relocated from Boston to Milwaukee, were easily out-pulling the Dodgers. O'Malley wanted a new stadium and a much bigger parking lot. Meanwhile, he was sniffing the money in that California air, a tonic he would seek to convince Stoneham, owner of the Dodgers' fiercest rivals, the similarly troubled Giants, might just work for him too: major league base-ball had yet to venture that far west.

These were also troubling times for baseball. Even the Yankees were feeling the pinch: attendances at The House Ruth Built had swooned from 2.3m in 1948 to under 1.5m in 1954. And it goes without saying that, if New York's clubs were suffering, this merely reflected the game's overall box-office decline: gates had plummeted by a third since 1947, paralleling a similar fall-off in English football and cricket in the wake of the postwar surge. In the space of 20 months, three cities had had their MLB representation halved from two to one, leading to three new franchises in fresh locations. Whoever began the march west, nevertheless, it was unthinkable that it could be one of the New York trio, bound umbilically as they were to their communi-ties. But why on earth would the 16 franchise owners – whose approval was required – blithely hand over such potential riches to an interloper?

And so, in 1954, the rumours began to swirl around the Dodgers and Giants. Stoneham felt obligated to soothe Manhattan breasts by public proclamation: the Giants would not, repeat not, be leaving town; Brooklyn's junior chamber of commerce launched a campaign to keep the Dodgers. If either departed, an economically necessary feud would be lost: as Stoneham stressed, a third of all the tickets he sold every year were for games against the Dodgers. How, he wondered, "could we possibly build such a strong rivalry" in California?[81]

O'Malley had ambitious plans: a slum redevelopment project incorporating a new railway station in addition to a new stadium and as much parking as he could handle. The latter was especially crucial, as he seldom tired of reiterating: the current lack of vehicle space, he claimed, was crippling attendance. In September 1955, with the Dodgers progressing towards that triumphant World Series, O'Malley outlined his masterplan to a *New York Post* reporter. When the editorial columns of the *New York Times* supported him, calling on Mayor Robert Wagner to play his part, Wagner quickly ushered O'Malley to his mansion, along with two of the city's heaviest hitters: John Cashmore, the Brooklyn borough president, and Robert Moses, the city's parks commissioner and head of the Triborough Bridge and Tunnel Authority, Construction Commission and Slum Clearance Committee.

In announcing that he was willing to sell Ebbets Field to anyone prepared to offer him a two-year lease, O'Malley made it abundantly clear that the next step would be relocation to the new home he envisaged. He would put up $6m, he said, provided the city ensured the land was available. He also upped the ante by reminding Wagner that Stoneham was equally dissatisfied with his lot and that New York stood to lose two clubs in one fell swoop.

Moses would become O'Malley's nemesis. Both incited extremes of opinion. According to Robert A. Caro, an acclaimed biographer of US presidents, in his masterly 1975 dissection of mayor and city, *The Power Broker: Robert Moses and the Fall of New York*, his subject entered service "in the very year in which there came to crest a movement – Progressivism – that was based, to an extent greater perhaps than any other nationally successful American political movement, on an idealistic belief in man's capacity to better himself through the democratic process."[82] To

Moses, however, democracy was merely a means to a dictatorial end. "New York had never seen a political creature quite like Moses," averred the journalist Michael Antonio. For decades he had promoted himself as "uniquely competent, visionary, moral, and wise" but in fact had "secretly used this money to enrich politically connected attorneys, developers, banks, and others who, in exchange, lent him their loyalty. By all evidence, he never lined his own pockets, but this didn't mean he wasn't corrupt."[83] Through power he could express his vision for the city's future: a concrete future, a future full of roads. While his "manipulations" received plentiful coverage, wrote Caro, "his triumphs were on page one". Serenely surfing press revelations that would have obliterated the careers of his colleagues, Moses "killed, over the efforts of O'Malley, plans for a City Sports Authority that might have kept the Dodgers and Giants in New York".[84]

On 2 June 1957, O'Malley told Mayor Wagner he had received some tempting offers from California but would spurn them if he could buy the rights to the Long Island Railway Station on Atlantic Avenue and Flatbush Avenue, and thence build a new, domed ballpark. There was no way, bristled Moses, that he would permit a baseball stadium in downtown Brooklyn: just think of the traffic. Instead, as Kahn relates, he offered a "lovely parcel" of land in Flushing Meadow at the site of the World's Fair, in the borough of Queens. "If my team is forced to play in the borough of Queens," retorted O'Malley, "they will no longer be the Brooklyn Dodgers."[85]

Hindsight being the impeccable tool it is, it is all too easy to side with those who assert that O'Malley – who persuaded Stoneham to join him in California – never had the slightest intention of keeping the Dodgers in Brooklyn. He had convinced many, Daley included, that he had "sincerely" been seeking a new site in Brooklyn. "But once Los Angeles began the siren song The O'Malley was so beguiled that he was lost. The City of the Angels offered him more than the keys to the city. It gave him the keys to the kingdom. New York balked at twelve acres. Los Angeles enthusiastically proffered 300 acres. This is the biggest haul since the Brink's robbery – except that it's legal."[86] Other teams, Daley pointed out, "were forced to move by apathy, or incompetence. The only word that fits the Dodgers is greed."[87] Before he could consummate his relationship with LA, nonetheless, O'Malley would come close to bankruptcy.

That last night at Ebbets Field, 24 September 1957, is engraved on the retinas of fewer first-hand witnesses than one might imagine: fewer than 7,000 turned up, which rather diminishes the sense of communal loss, though as D'Antonio writes, it was a sombre occasion. "Most sat in the lower level, behind home plate, and along the baselines. In the big empty sections of the grandstand a light autumn breeze blew paper cups and empty peanut bags down concrete aisles and against rows of old slatted chairs. On the field, players moved with the extra weight of knowing that this time there would be no 'next year'. After many seasons of joy – in the face of Jackie Robinson, in the bellowing voice of Hilda Chester, and in the roar of standing-room-only crowds – Ebbets Field had become a desolate and unhappy place. The Dodgers beat the Pirates 2-0. Organist Gladys Goodding played 'Auld Lang Syne' as the grounds crew raked the infield and, out of habit, spread a tarp over the pitcher's mound. Emmett Kelly, the sad-faced clown who had performed his acts before Dodgers games through the season, would recall seeing many women – and a few men – crying as they left Ebbets Field for good."[88]

Brooklyn would neither forget nor forgive. Indeed, when O'Malley was posthumously elected to the Baseball Hall of Fame in 2007, Hamill employed the damning phrase "Never forgive, never forget", declaiming that O'Malley's ascension removed every vestige of morality from the honour. In *Blue In The Face*, an entertaining, partly improvised 1995 Wayne Wang movie set on a Brooklyn street corner and scripted, so far as it went, by that thought-provoking writer Paul Auster, the ghost of Jackie Robinson walks noiselessly into Augie Wren's smoke shop. As the puffers and draggers drift in and out, much heated discussion ensues about the loss of the Dodgers and the destruction of Ebbets Field, and the pain still endured by Brooklynites.

Yet in causing that pain, O'Malley had done more than anyone to make major league baseball a truly national game. In LA, moreover, the Dodgers' success (starting with World Series triumphs in 1959 and 1963) saw him toasted as a hero before his death in 1979. On the 50th anniversary of the Dodgers' arrival, a five-foot bronze frieze of his image joined those commemorating Jesse Owens and Jackie Robinson at the Memorial Coliseum Court of Honour, all of them sporting figures who had contributed to the city's "growth and glory".[89]

* * *

O'Malley's legacy would endure. He inspired a new wave of carpetbaggers: from Baltimore to Indianapolis, LA to St Louis and even French-speaking Montreal to jargon-spouting Washington D.C., no leap has been too far, in any US team sport.

Witness the 2012 NBA finals, whose inner plot revolved around a good deal more than a pair of thrilling young teams.

In the blue corner, Miami Heat, "scorned", attested Dave Zirin at the time, "for being built around a hastily assembled group of free agent All-Stars" – Dwayne Wade, Chris Bosh, and LeBron James.[90] In the red corner, by contrast, sat Oklahoma City Thunder, "a small market franchise beloved by the sports media and fans for 'doing it the right way'. They drafted beautifully and evolved organically toward greatness. They are also led by Kevin Durant, the NBA's most endearing superstar. The 'Durantula' is only 23 but already has three scoring titles and he absolutely lusts for the big moment. He also, unlike LeBron, signed a long-term contract to stay in a small market because he wanted to take the team that drafted him to a title." How we choose to see the Heat and Thunder "is a litmus test"; one that "reveals how the sports radio obsession with villainising 21st century athletes blinds us to the swelling number of villains who inhabit the owner's box. And in Oklahoma City, we have the kinds of sports owners whose villainy should never be forgotten."

The Thunder may have been praised for doing things "the right way", but, argued Zirin, no franchise is more "caked in original sin" than the Oklahomers, a team stolen from the people of Seattle "with the naked audacity of Frank and Jesse James". The villains were the owners, Clay Bennett and Aubrey McClendon, and David Stern, the NBA commissioner, architect of the game's palace of riches. Bennett and McClendon are Republican moneybags who fund anti-gay referendums; Stern, a political liberal, has sat on the board of the National Association for the Advancement of Coloured Peoples. The trio, nevertheless, are "united in their addiction to our tax dollars".

> *While Bennett said all the right things about keeping the Sonics in Seattle, a team executive dinner on Sept 9 2006, tells you all you need to know about the man and his motives. On that fine evening, the Sonics management, all held over from the previous ownership regime… gathered in Oklahoma to meet the new boss. Bennett made sure they were sent to a top restaurant, and picked up the bill. As the Seattle execs sat down, four plates of a deep fried appetiser were put on the table. After filling their mouths with the crispy goodness, one asked the waitress what this curious dish with a nutty flavour actually was. It was lamb testicles. Bennett laughed at their discomfort and the message was clear: the Sonics could eat his balls.[91]*

Understandably, merely contemplating victory for the Thunder made Zirin shudder: America would lionise Bennett and Stern. The theft of the Sonics would be justified and cities involved in stadium negotiations threatened with being "the next Seattle" if they refused to acquiesce to "the whims of the sporting 1%". A championship for the Thunder would be "a victory for holding up cities for public money", a victory "for ripping out the hearts of loyal sports towns" and a victory for "greed, collusion, and a corporate crime that remains unprosecuted".[92]

When James led Miami to victory instead, a goodly number of those whose instinctive inclination is to back the underdog breathed easier.

When seats no longer need bums

For a century and more, attendances were measured strictly by clicks of the turnstile. In the final quarter of the 20th century this changed as ticket agencies, corporate sales, block bookings and resales barged their way into the sporting lexicon. "How many people actually come to the game is not nearly as important as whether there are tickets sold," argued Maury Brown of *Forbes* magazine. "Sure it matters who goes, but ticket sales, especially in advance, gives cost certainty."[93] In the televisual age, nonetheless, there is an increasing awareness among broadcasters of the cost-ineffectiveness of empty seats.

"Our biggest challenge going forward," Roger Goodell, the NFL commissioner, declared in 2012, speaking for administrators the world over, "is how do we get people to come to our stadiums because the experience is so great at home. When you turn on (a football game), you want to see a full stadium."[94] Hence the creative decision by Australian cricket authorities to deploy yellow and green seating: from a distance, they look occupied even when they aren't. And hence, perhaps, the IPL's alleged generosity with tickets and purposeful exaggerations of attendances, all in the name of marketing its product to the spectators who really matter: those viewing from the comfort of pub or club or hearth and home; the ones who do most to reel in advertisers and sponsors.

In the NFL, where most competing sides are fortunate to play as few as 16 games per season, clubs are threatened with broadcasting blackouts – fans in the home city cannot watch live, as happened in cricket for many years in Australia – if the game is not sold out (although the price actually paid for tickets is deemed irrelevant, discounts and freebies count in the NFL, the NBA and the NHL). In 2010, Russell J Salvatore, a restaurateur, was hailed as a local hero after shelling out for the remaining 7,000-plus tickets at the last minute, ensuring the Buffalo Bills' armchair fans would be able to tune into the campaign's final game.[95] Baseball's Florida Marlins sold 3,500 tickets of a game that had already been played: Roy Halliday's historic "perfect" game for the Philadelphia Phillies against their team in June 2010 roused thousands to buy mementoes; all counted as sales.

So creative is the accounting, *Forbes* recently offered 13 trusty ruses:

- *Sell standing-room only tickets first at a reduced rate to reach a sellout threshold before selling seats in the bowl.*
- *On season tickets, deeply discount tickets, offer "Buy 2 get 2 deals" or offer pay-as-you-go season tickets. Tickets are tickets. Getting you to close the deal is imperative.*
- *For group tickets, offer 50 to 70 percent off weekday early season.*
- *Sponsors get tickets. Each team has 50 to 100 sponsors times 4 to 8 tickets each is 200 to 800 potentially paid season ticket buyers.*
- *On those sellouts, employees get comps. The front offices have 75 to 150 full-time employees plus innumerable number of part-time staff that could potentially "comp out" 300 to 2000 seats a night.*
- *Player coaches and retired player comps.*
- *Visiting team comps – 4 times 35 players per game whether used or unused.*
- *Umpire comps – 4 Umps equals 16 tickets per game per Umps contract.*
- *Commissioner's Initiative – requires each team to donate 50 or 100k tickets per year to lower income charities. While this doesn't impact paid attendance, it can push the needle up for sellouts.*
- *Voucher redemption – offer free or virtually free discounted tickets through sponsor store or product.*
- *Team charities – The league sends out thousands of tickets to games to local charities via team, seats sold to charity at pennies so they are sold then written off by team.*
- *Internet – Similar to groups like Travel Zoo, Groupon, etc. Offer deep discounting on 3rd party website to push inventory.*

- *Military Night – Many are offering free tickets, which is a great gesture as it doesn't count as paid attendance. But, not all. For example, the [Baltimore] Orioles just announced a $3 discount deal off all tickets for all military (active, retired and reserve) and their families, which bumps up paid attendance.*[96]

Taking over the asylum

In the early days of professional football, warrants John Williams, expressing fandom "outside of match attendance and local connections was deeply problematic: there was simply no substitute for 'being there'." Some supporters, indeed, often raised the cash required to help build new stands and improve facilities. These days, they are "rather more likely to raise money for celebration and nostalgia; for the erection of commemorative football monuments and statues. But this arrangement, in which being a fan meant being local and physically present at matches, also worked culturally, in terms of providing opportunities for working people to generate a sense of meaningful collective place and identity, and to engage directly with the sport and its stars – most of whom were still within touching range of their followers. Things have changed." Indeed, "the recent loss in developed societies of the social anchors that once made identity seem 'natural' and 'non-negotiable' has meant a desperate search for a 'we' experience through football club support."[97]

This, it is worth reiterating, is the age of the virtual fan. Being a follower of the competitive arts in the 21st century can mean cheering on Chelsea from Chile, the Boston Celtics from Bulawayo or the Indian cricket team from Inverness. It has been claimed that Manchester United have close to 350 million fans, around 10m of them via Facebook. In January 2007, while 75,000 congregated at Old Trafford to see Alex Ferguson's side take on Arsenal, up to eight million more watched the Sky Sports feed; all told, it was broadcast in 201 countries, potentially reaching 613m homes. As Libya erupted at the end of Colonel Gaddafi's painful era, rebels marched on Tripoli wearing English Premier

League and Italian La Liga replica shirts. (On a personal level, I have often given lectures in a replica of Pakistan's Lincoln-green 2003 World Cup shirt, albeit strictly out of sympathy for that benighted nation).

Technology – primarily television, the Internet and the mobile phone – has done its best, and worst. Message boards, fan blogs and fanzine forums abound, a haven for the casual and the tragically smitten but also for those seeking displacement activities and in urgent need of anger management sessions. Those who see the game as site of conflict now vent their spleen away from the cameras, in lower divisions and outside grounds, though social media and websites offered a ready release for loathing. Despite the marginalising of English hooligans ("by price, by video technology, and by the new safety cultures of all-seated stadia, as well as by police intelligence gathering and even new 'dialogue and facilitation' approaches to managing hooligan gangs", as Williams puts it[98]), hooliganism thrived in southern and eastern Europe; in the latter, racist abuse of players was reported with rising frequency, most notoriously during an Under-21 match between Serbia and England in 2012, when members of the visiting squad were hit and manhandled; that this led to a cursory fine and ban from UEFA enraged many.

"In the Balkans and in parts of the old Eastern Europe… the strains of new nationhood, high unemployment and the re-emergence of old ethnic divisions in extremist political clothes both dramatise and feed hooligan outbreaks," attested Williams.[99] In Poland, youth alienation was blamed. In October 2010, a Euro 2012 qualifier between Italy and Serbia was abandoned in the wake of nationalist-inspired violence and Albanian flag-burning by Serbian hooligans and agitators. Eleven months later, Turkey "inventively highlighted the problematic masculinities that continue to lie at the heart of football hooligan cultures all over the world". Following crowd trouble at Fenerbahce, the Turkish FA banned adult males from the next home match – which attracted "an enthusiastic, well-behaved" crowd of 41,000 women and children. Maybe, mused Williams, "there was an alternative, after all, to stadium Disneyisation, ticket price rises and intensive video surveillance". Nonetheless, the stabbing of that Tottenham fan in a Rome bar did nothing to reassure those who felt a widespread sense of proportion remained elusive.

Some contend that Europe's major football clubs are playing a significant role in building a network society, which is hardly a bad thing. That sense of "us" led SV Hamburg followers to establish a supporters' cemetery just 50 metres from the club stadium. As stonemason Uli Beppler put it, "If you think about people supporting a club for 30, 40, 50 years, it's part of their life, so why shouldn't it be part of their death?"[100] It can also prompt some to start their own club when the old one goes awry.

When MK Dons met AFC Wimbledon in a cup tie in late 2012, the battle lines were clearly drawn: in 2002, citing waning crowds, Charles Koppel, the owner of the town's original representatives, Wimbledon AFC, had hauled the club off to Milton Keynes, a long way up the M1; unhappy supporters formed AFC Wimbledon. It was the first time a Football League club had followed the trail blazed by Cincinnati's Red Stockings. Paul Doyle's match report in *The Guardian* captured the collision eloquently:

> *Ahead of a meeting for which the fans had pondered their tactics as much as the managers did theirs, most AFC Wimbledon supporters decided to attend the match, more than 3,000 of them choosing to pour into the away end and pour out their bile for the club they accuse of hijacking their heritage.*
>
> *While MK Stadium may be an insult's throw from Bletchley Park, there was no need for codebreakers to decipher the messages emanating from the crowd, chants such as "You know what you are, you franchise bastards" getting straight to the point. "We're keeping the Dons …. Get over it" declared one large banner in the home end, while visiting supporters had a prepared retort, holding aloft placards declaring "We are Wimbledon". Whether any of the home fans could read that reply is doubtful as the placards were impractically small, lending a certain Spinal Tap vibe to the protest.*

While the atmosphere was raucous there was no sign of the strong sentiments spilling over into violence.

In arguably belated response to Barcelona and the Green Bay Packers, supporter trusts are emerging, "a potentially progressive new dynamic and a local community focus" believes Williams, yet vulnerable to the accusation that they wind up being "incorporated into the commercial activities of the club hierarchies they seek to replace".[101] In England, the corporate invasion has not been met meekly, especially when American tycoons are involved. The global recession helped end the much-unloved ownership regime at Liverpool, but so did supporters calling themselves, collectively, "the Spirit of Shankly", an homage to the club's best-loved manager. Similarly angered by Stateside owners, a group of Manchester United fans broke away to form a new club, FC United of Manchester.

A radical departure came in 2007, in the shape of the MyFootballClub website. Football fans the world over were offered direct involvement in the management of the non-league club Ebbsfleet United, based in Gravesend, Kent. Initial subscriptions amounted to around 32,000 members drawn from 70 countries; digital media proved a handy tool, allowing the club to "camp in [their] front garden".[102] Unfortunately, come 2011, membership had dwindled to little more than 1,000. An idea ahead of its time? Possibly.

Nevertheless, as Williams asserts, "for the 11 heroes on the field to consider playing *without* their fans in the stands in the future is really like dancing without music."[103]

Fandom as tragedy
In August 1934, Lou Gehrig, the New York Yankees' "Iron Man" fouled a pitch into a screen. When a teenager named David Levy attempted to retrieve it he was attacked by over-zealous ushers and suffered a fractured skull. Three years later, a federal court awarded him $7,500 and spectators were informed that they could henceforth keep any ball they could

reach so long as it didn't interfere with the game. Fast forward to Wrigley Field, 14 October 2003, to game six of the National League Championship Series between the Chicago Cubs and the Florida Marlins. Chasing their first World Series appearance since 1945, the Cubs led 3–0 and were just five outs away from their holiest goal when Steve Bartman, one of their most devoted fans, reached for a foul ball hit by the Marlins' Luis Castillo; in so doing, he unintentionally destroyed any chance the home outfielder, Moisés Alou, had of catching it. The Marlins scored eight times in the inning and went on to not only win the playoff but the World Series.

Alou refused to blame Bartman – "We just got beat by a better team" – but the crestfallen fan was pelted with drinks, peanuts and other debris and had to be escorted from the stadium for his own protection. Once outside, he became the subject of a manhunt and subsequently received death threats, as an upshot of which police were assigned to watch over his home. Thereafter, he hid. "He isn't on Facebook, though his fake profile and a fan club for him are," reported the *Chicago Times* in 2010. "He doesn't Tweet, at least under his name. He never did the talk show circuit, cashed in any of the lucrative financial offers thrown his way or accepted the official overtures to return as a VIP to his beloved Wrigley Field. Instead, Steve Bartman disappeared."[104] In 2005, an ESPN.com reporter followed Bartman to his office car park and waited 10 hours for him to re-emerge; Bartman refused to break his silence other than to scold him for stalking.

Erica Swerdlow, managing director of Burson-Marsteller, a public relations firm specialising in crisis management, lived in the same suburb as Bartman's parents; she remembered "screaming at the TV" when Bartman's brother-in-law read out a statement on his behalf. "He should've put everybody in his shoes. He was very apologetic. He said he was a big Cubs fan. But he should've said, 'I believe I did something every single fan would've done if they had been sitting in that seat.' It would've made all the haters stop and say, 'It's not his fault. It's just another bad luck thing for the Cubs.' That doesn't work in every case. Tiger Woods couldn't say, 'A lot of people cheat on their wives.' But in this case, it was an honest mistake."[105]

Catching Hell, an ESPN documentary about this pathos-riddled episode directed by Alex Gibney, premiered in 2011 at the Tribeca Film Festival in New York. At one point, as Bartman leaves the so-called "Friendly Confines" with a jacket over his head, we see and hear one aggrieved fan urging him to blow his own head off with a shotgun. "He's still called the most hated man in Chicago," insisted Michael McCarthy in *USA Today*. "His face adorns dart boards. One fan compared his 'evil' to that of the September 11th hijackers. He stayed in the Chicago area but has lived as a semi-recluse ever since becoming, as one interviewee says, the 'J.D. Salinger' of Chicago. The saddest part? Out of everybody involved, from Alou who egged on fans with his reaction to Fox broadcaster Steve Lyons to the TV producers who showed his face over and over, Bartman's acted the most honourably. He's never tried to cash in on the incident although he's been offered hundreds of thousands of dollars to tell his story."[106]

Of all the images in Gibney's disturbing film, none are more compelling nor poignant than the repeated shots of Bartman in the immediate aftermath of his mistake: the eyes are dazed and glazed, the expression blank, cheeks stained with tears, the enormity of what he has done sinking ever deeper into his heart and mind, destroying his sense of self: of what it means to be a supporter.

Ultra prejudice

Soccer stadiums in the Middle East and Africa, according to James Dorsey, Senior Fellow at the Rajaratnam School of International Studies in Singapore, "are a symbol of the battle for political freedom; economic opportunity; ethnic, religious and national identity, and gender rights." Until the Arab Revolt of 2010, the football stadium was, alongside the mosque, "the only alternative public space for venting pent-up anger and frustration". It was here, moreover, that fiercely partisan fans in Egypt and Tunisia "prepared for a day in which their organisation and street battle experience would serve them in the showdown with autocratic rulers". Matches in such countries, Dorsey summed up, were a "high-stakes game of cat and mouse between militants and security forces and a struggle for a trophy grander than the FIFA World Cup: the future of a region".[107]

Anyone wondering why Egypt's President Mohamed Morsi declared a state of emergency in January 2013, or why the country's defence minister felt compelled to warn that the state was in danger of collapse, can only benefit from Dorsey's comments, explaining as they do why football fans, aka "ultras", played such a significant role in the 2011 revolution that toppled President Mubarak. "Under Mubarak's three-decade kleptocratic rule," wrote Dave Zirin, "the hyper-intense ultras – made up almost entirely of young Egyptian men – were given near-free rein to march in the streets, battle the police, and of course fight each other. This has been a common practice in autocracies across the world: don't allow political dissent but for the young, male masses, allow violent soccer clubs to exist as a safety valve to release the steam. Mubarak, surely to his eternal regret, underestimated what could happen when steam gets channeled into powering a full-scale revolt."[108]

Crucial to all this were the ultras of Al Zamalek, a club created by British colonial administrators and their Egyptian allies and monarchists, and those of their Cairo rivals Al Ahly, founded more than a century ago as a focus for anti-British republican nationalism. Setting aside their deep-seated mutual hatred, they joined forces, first against Mubarak, then against the military. They helped secure Tahrir Square, setting up checkpoints and fighting off the police, thus playing, warranted Dorsey, "a key role in breaking the barrier of fear that had prevented Egyptians from protesting en masse".

When Mubarak was removed from power and succeeded by a military junta, the ultras continued to push for meaningful and lasting change. Then, on 1 February 2012, came tragedy. Following a match in Port Said between Al-Masri and visitors

Al-Ahly, the home fans rushed the field after a 3-1 victory, resulting in a clash between the bitterly antipathetic supporters and a host of stabbings and beatings. The majority of the 74 fatalities that day, however, were caused by asphyxiation as Al-Ahly fans were crushed against locked stadium doors. Video evidence confirmed the view that, through inaction at the very least, the military and security forces were complicit in these deaths. According to Dorsey, the incident was "widely seen as an attempt that got out of hand by the then military rulers of the country and the police and security forces to cut militant, highly politicised, street battle-hardened soccer fans or ultras down to size".[109]

"There was something planned," claimed Diaa Salah, then working for the Egyptian Football Federation. "Our security knew about it. People were tweeting before the match. I saw a tweet with my own eyes 13 to 14 hours before the match in which a Masri fan was telling Ahly supporters: 'If you are coming to the match, write your will before you come'. The government is getting back at the ultras. They are saying, 'You protest against us, you want democracy and freedom. Here is a taste of your democracy and freedom."[110] Shortly after this, Salah resigned, hours before the government dismissed the Federation's board of Mubarak appointees.

The court verdict on the Port Said deaths brought further catastrophe: 21 people were sentenced to hang but not a single member of the state and security forces; the ensuing riots brought more than 30 deaths and 300 injuries. The violence, wrote Dorsey, "was the latest in a seemingly endless series of confrontations between the disparate forces of the revolution and the still-unreformed institutions of the Egyptian state".[111]

The Barmy Army

In addition to being intimidatingly good at his job, Patrick Collins is also one of the calmest and most courteous journalists I have ever met. Yet even he has his bêtes noir and blind spots. Before embarking on the global trek that resulted in *Among The*

Fans, he listed the questions he wanted to address: "What are they doing here? What are they given? How do they behave? How has it changed? How much does it mean?" and so on. The most intriguing, for this reader, was "Are they there to see, or be seen?" In his answer, he made no attempt whatsoever to disguise his hearty contempt for the Barmy Army, that travelling band of cricket followers who divide opinion even more efficiently than Moses supposedly parted the Red Sea.

"Wade through their website and you will discover that they actually possess a set of rules, a Boy Scout's charter which includes: 'Have fun – good, clean and entertaining fun… Show Respect – for all players, officials, fans and grounds rules and regulations… Give Consideration – to people's views, beliefs and cultures.'"[112] Whereupon Collins avails us of a couple of the Army's songs, including the following shining example of sensitive wordplay:

> *Ponting is the captain*
> *Of the Aussie cricket team*
> *But once the match is over*
> *He is a gay drag queen.*

That the Army has long had its harrumphing detractors is partly attributable to that brazen, unblinking hypocrisy (though chants of that ilk have now been mercifully mothballed), but mostly because its troops are such an easy target for the primarily middle-class English media – and it all starts, of course, with that self-mocking name. Barmy, after all, is another take on "loony", "bonkers", "potty" and sundry other deliciously wry English words denoting a lack of mental mettle. Happily, as Paul Winslow affirms in *Going Barmy – Despatches From a Cricketing Foot Soldier*, his wry, perceptive and winningly-written travelogue of life on the road "chasing the cricket dragon", the brand of looniness favoured by foot soldiers such as himself is not only almost entirely benign (Ricky Ponting doubtless disagrees) but, in its way, rather beautiful. In a sweet, sweaty, bromantic sort of way.

Until fairly recently, among the English media, the consensus was both unequivocal and unshiftable: not only was the average Barmy rude, crass and never knowingly sober, he (and they were always "he") possessed a few thousand cells too few for an operable brain, not to mention having far too much in common with his footballing counterpart. In the *Daily Telegraph*, that master of the provocative look-at-me tirade, Matthew Norman, urged someone, somewhere, to "round the lot of them up, press-gang them into signing enlistment papers and put them on the first RAF transport to Helmand province." He also had the brass balls to claim that, unlike the Barmy Army – "that coalition of saddoes… the only faction of any sporting audience in history whose primary motivation for attending games is not to watch but be watched" – football thugs "had integrity".[113] Winslow neatly and thoroughly demolishes this assertion for its intergalactic remoteness from fact. The image, nonetheless, was set in stone and ink: a bloody national disgrace.

This has always struck me as profoundly snobbish, not to say grotesquely unjust. After all, what national team, in any sport, can command such a devoted caravanserai, such a loyal source of lungpower and lusty encouragement without feeling any compunction to duff up the opposing ranks? Even now, the most damaging and regrettable incident involving an England cricket fan dates back to Perth 1982, a dozen years before the first Barmy Army t-shirt went on sale, when Terry Alderman dislocated a shoulder bringing down a pitch invader. Consider, too, those endless allegations of self-aggrandisement. A recent browse through the Army's website forum revealed 1,685 posts for "Barmy Army Chat" and 19,408, more than ten times as many, for "General Cricket Chat".

The main difficulty, attests Winslow, lies with perceptions and, in particular, the Army's "schizophrenic identity issues". "Those who have been involved in shaping it, maintaining it, developing it and caring for it have a clear definition of what it is, but those who write about it, those who join it without realising what it stands for and even those who are not involved at all can both skew public opinion and have a damaging effect on its reputation." Yet even that definition – cricket-loving patriots – falls short: sure, there's the hardcore group that flew steadfastly to India after the 2008 Mumbai bombings but then there are those who turn up for a couple of Tests in the more attractive cities. "Even to us the Army can be a different beast every day, and some days we like it more than others."

It is impossible to quantify how much Andrew Strauss's team benefited from Bill Cooper's rousing trumpet or those endless renditions of "Everywhere We Go" and "Jerusalem" on their triumphant Ashes tour of 2010-11, but no psychologist worth his salt could have denied that their impact was positive. In the wake of the urn-clinching victory in Melbourne, as the Barmies dipped into their Beatles repertoire ("Yesterday, Ponting's troubles seemed so far away..."), even Norman, surmised Jim White, his *Telegraph* teammate, "must have put aside his distaste".

Chaps of undistinguished dentistry and ruddy complexion queued up to tell the cameras that this was a moment they never expected to see. One man had followed England's defeats for more than 20 years, and wasn't quite sure what to do now. Though you suspect alcohol might have been involved.

This is the glorious point of the Barmies – indeed, of this nation more generally. Lovely as triumph might be, the purpose is not the pursuit of winning. The blokes pinking up in the Victoria sun represented a strain of sporting support that is gloriously, wonderfully and uniquely British.

Only among our fans is there such stubborn insistence on maintaining loyalty in the face of defeat. Only our followers exhibit such levels of wilful masochism. It was evident throughout the World Cup in South Africa, where English football supporters – once the game's hooligan pariahs – astonished the hosts with their good-natured backing of a team that was so supine in its uselessness it would have drained the resolve of Hercules.

No one else does it like this. In Italy, Argentina, Brazil they turn on their failed sportsmen in an instant. Even in Melbourne,

the heartland of a country largely defined by its sporting
prowess, the stands drained of home support the moment things
started to turn against the Aussies. For the Barmies, it would
have been the time to up the volume.[114]

The deal-breaker? I'll settle for the view propounded by Graeme
Swann in his foreword to *Going Barmy*. "They are not hooligans,
they are not troublemakers, they are just cricket nuts who fly the
flag for this brilliant country we live in," declaimed the England
spinner. "They are the very heartbeat of our Test team abroad.
And I love them for it."

The Twittering Classes

By the second decade of the 21st century, social media had
captured the imagination of a generation to whom patience was
no longer virtuous, loosening still further the grasp of the more
venerable media. Television and the English Premier League,
inevitably, were the drivers-in-chief.

By 2013, nearly 98% of Premier League matches were being
watched beyond Britain. In October 2012, the league signed a
six-year deal with Super Sports in China, giving the latter's 1.3
billion inhabitants potential access to coverage – according to
data published by the respected fortnightly online newsletter,
TV Sports Markets – on no fewer than 21 different free-to-air
TV stations. On the Indian subcontinent, the value of the latest
rights had surged by 200 per cent; respectively, the increases
in Vietnam and Thailand were 300% and 450%. In Africa,
SuperSport's 14 channels were showing 95% of each season's
games live, with the remaining 5% broadcast in full on delayed
transmission, and further growth anticipated. In securing the
US rights from 2013 to 2016, NBC had announced that live
matches on their main channel as well as Telemundo, their
Spanish-language network, would be available to more than
115m American homes, while games on NBC Sports Network
and NBC's other cable platforms would reach more than 80m
homes (by illuminating comparison, live Premier League

matches broadcast by Fox and ESPN were drawing an average weekly audience of 140,000).[115]

The Facebook Generation needed no second invitation. Come the end of 2012, Liverpool had launched native-language Twitter accounts in Indonesia and Thailand; come the following February, the Anfielders were attracting 38,000 Indonesian followers and 16,000 Thai. By then, Chelsea and Manchester City, too, were focusing on a range of digital and social media.

"Social media works effectively to bring American supporters together and connect us with fans from abroad," Kyle Diller, director of social media for One United USA, the official Manchester United Membership and Supporters' Club of America, told Jonathan Dyson. "On Facebook, Manchester United have an official supporters' group page for fans in the US where we can connect and talk about the club. On Twitter, from my personal account, I've been able to connect with numerous Manchester United fans from around the world, many of them from Manchester. The last time I travelled to watch a match, I actually stayed with a fellow fan I had met from connecting with United fans on Twitter. It just makes you feel more connected to the club through fellow supporters. You feel like a part of the fan base even though you can't attend matches regularly. Every supporter I've met via social media has made me feel welcome as a supporter, which just reinforces that feeling as a fan."[116]

How proud Peter Gabriel must be that his second-biggest hit has found its post-modern context. *Jeux sans frontières* indeed.

2 Class Wars: How Spectator Sport Began

*For the aristocracy and gentry, who had once seen it as voca-
tional training, sport had become a dream world, a refuge from
the harsh pressures of the real one, in which first capitalism
and then its accidental by-product democracy were gradually
undermining the old order. On the other hand, the dream world
was open to all, and sporting values, especially when gambling
was involved, were potentially anarchical: given the chance Jack
often turned out to be not merely as good as but better than
his master. Beyond all this, however, people of all classes saw
the sporting spirit as a vital ingredient in the British make-up,
fostering qualities of character that fitted them uniquely well for
the task of governing the vast empire they had acquired, and for
defending it against lesser nations.*

Derek Birley, *Land of sport and glory*[1]

To earn a place at the Olympic table a sport has to jump through
39 hoops. Such is the number of criteria that must be met,
covering eight categories ranging from history and governance
to finance, popularity and universality. Inevitably, qualifying
for that elite 25-sport roster is far more taxing than dropping off,
as those who have been pushing squash's credentials down the
years will grudgingly testify. In February 2013, nevertheless, the
IOC's executive board voted to remove Greco-Roman wrestling,
one of the nine founding sports of the modern Games. At the UN,
the ensuing widespread fury achieved the not inconsiderable
feat of uniting Russia, the US and Iran. Even modernists were
aggrieved. Already peeved, and justly so, that golf was about to
join tennis as a wholly inappropriate and unnecessary dish on

a menu dominated by sports that are only ever widely watched every four years, Simon Barnes implored the 15 members of the executive board to think again:

> *The initial idea of the commercial Olympics was that the Games ensured their own survival by becoming self-sufficient. Alas, it didn't stop there. The Olympic Movement slowly and subtly converted itself to the belief that if the Games could make money, they should make money. At first money mattered because it made the Olympics possible. Now the Olympic Games matter because they make money... The Olympics is the jewelled setting for these ancient and atavistic fields of endeavour. Lose their link to the past and we lose the point. Lose wrestling and we lose the Games.*[2]

The international wrestling federation duly implemented reforms and simplified regulations, whereupon, three months later, the sport was shortlisted for inclusion at the 2020 Games. At the IOC board meeting in St Petersburg the reprieve was acclaimed by a resounding cheer.[3] To no great astonishment, a comeback was duly approved, at the expense of baseball, softball and, to widespread chagrin, squash.

* * *

Being bound up in legend and myth as all the best stories are, the history of sport is an especially hazardous topic. This is in good part because, in my experience of working for most of the titles on what is still termed Fleet Street as well as sundry overseas publications, those seeking enlightenment come armed with more knowledge than those inquisitive about other cultural phenomenon. Tracing the precise time and place where the various forms of athletic spermatozoa first saw daylight, moreover, would almost certainly require at least one lifetime – "and not, I suspect, a particularly enjoyable one", as Tim Harris acknowledged in the introduction to *Sport: Almost Everything You Ever Wanted To Know*. A former advertising copywriter and creative director, as his Random House author's bio states, his motivation for tackling such a gargantuan task was rooted in a pub argument "about why football shirts tend to be striped and rugby shirts hooped", a question I feel obliged, in the circumstances, to let him answer. "I hope that every falsehood has been detected and every myth exposed," he added, "but I doubt it."[4]

Whether this matters is moot. How we begin life, after all, runs a distant second to how we tackle it, however much that might mean defying any disadvantage bestowed by the circumstances of that birth. Still, regardless of any and all evidence to the contrary, who doesn't love a good creation myth? As Professor Lincoln Allison warranted in a lecture to sports journalism students at the University of Brighton in 2012: "That Romulus and Remus founded Rome or that St. Peter founded the Roman church are beliefs which have happily co-existed for long periods with research which casts severe doubt on their essential and literal truth. Myths in sport have proved especially durable, not least because for most of the history of modern sport there has been little or no scholarship to contradict them."[5]

"Football's coming home" rejoiced The Lightning Seeds in 1996, a cry taken up with gusto by England supporters when their country staged that year's European Football Championship. But was it? The annual inter-village Shrove Tuesday battles are rightly cherished as evidence of the country's contribution to the game's medieval pre-history, but as Dave Russell asserts in *The Cambridge Companion to Football*, the "desire to kick, throw or run with a ball, whether the inflated pig's bladder that gave its name to the Irish game *Caird* or the stuffed leather skin of the Chinese Han dynasty's *Cuju*", goes back millennia. Ball games were a feature of the Mayan civilisations of Mesoamerica for at least 3,000 years; Native Americans, Aboriginal Australians and the Pacific islanders of Micronesia and Polynesia all enjoyed games with perhaps even longer histories.[6]

Cricket? Similar longstanding theory exists about English foundations, but learned Frenchmen will assure you that *les soldats Rosbif* picked it up in their country before a derivation of the word cropped up in the household accounts of Edward I, for whose brutal warmongering the phrase "not cricket" might have been invented. According to a document from the Archives de France, *criquet* was played in Northern France in 1478 – 120 years before a court report quoted the recollections of one John Derrick, whose boyhood memories encompassed playing "cricket" in Guildford, Surrey.

Hambledon, in Hampshire, was long touted as the "cradle" of the game, but Major Rowland Bowen, a military man turned historian whose worldview had been broadened by service in the Indian Army, politely rubbished that in his groundbreaking 1970 tome *Cricket: A History of its Growth and Development Around the World*. "One does not," he argued, "put a lusty young man into a cradle." He also reinforced the French connection, suggesting that the evolution of the 11-a-side game may have been influenced by an area of Northern France "extending roughly from the Seine and on into Flanders", where a foot comprised 11 inches and each of those was sub-divided into 11 *lignes*.[7]

Tennis? During the Middle Ages, French monks were partial to a spot of *jeu de paume* (palm game), which involved hitting balls with their hands over a rope extended across their cloistered quadrangles. This apparently evolved into "tennis" because the server started each point by shouting "*Tenez!*" – broadly speaking, "Take it!"

Rugby? Museums and books will insist that it all began when William Webb-Ellis, playing football at Rugby School in 1823, left all and sundry flabbergasted by picking up the ball and running with it. Just as the Duke of Wellington's fabled assertion that the Battle of Waterloo was won on the playing fields of Eton did not surface until after his death, so the Webb-Ellis legend appears not to have emerged until a good while after the purported fact, in the 1870s. Yet so relentless and durable has been its grip on our imaginations, when Jean Dujardin was presented with the BAFTA best actor award in 2012 for his mesmerising lead role in *The Artist*, he declared his pride in receiving such a salute, not from the home of Shakespeare, Dickens or The Beatles but "from the land of Webb-Ellis". Nevertheless, as the journalist and sports historian Huw Richards points out, no contemporary account exists of Webb-Ellis's impromptu intervention. "Impossible to disprove," he reckons, but not actually grounded in substantive fact. Allison elaborated on this after noticing that the story told by Rusty MacLean, chief librarian and archivist at Rugby School, on guided tours of the school, jarred so utterly with the legend. The result was a paper written in conjunction with McLean; it might have made both a few enemies:

"Actually, it is not so much false (which it isn't, necessarily or completely) as preposterous in its assumptions and implications and derisory in its provenance. The plaque says that Webb Ellis was a boy in 1823, 'who with a fine disregard for the rules of football as played in his time took the ball in his arms and ran with it thus originating the distinctive feature of the rugby game'. If the statement is put into the context of Rugby School in 1823 it reads very oddly, as if designed to mislead. That he 'took the ball in his arms' has to be understood in the context that the right to handle the ball fully was an undisputed convention of all forms of 'football' played in both the area and at the school. The incident precedes the Association (or 'soccer') code of the game by forty years. Read by a less informed and more recent reader it might be understood that they were playing 'soccer' – or something very much like it – at the time.

"The idea that he then 'ran with it' is missing an important detail. The crucial missing word is 'forward' because a player could run backwards or sideways after making a mark. What was in dispute was whether he could gain ground simply by running forward carrying the ball. Among the descendants of the game in the twenty-first century this is allowed in the American code, but not in the Australian.

"Thus the reference to 'the rules of football' is also anachronistic. There were conventions and there were disputes, but no rules as such. Among the most disputed issues were, whether one could 'hack' opponents, how one could pass the ball and the circumstances under which one could run carrying the ball. Webb Ellis may have been one of those who favoured carrying, but he was not the only one and there is no evidence that he was particularly influential."[8]

Baseball's early rulers turned such liberty-taking into an art form, fabricating what Allison calls "a manipulated myth". General Abner Doubleday, a Civil War hero, was the central figure in this elaborately woven yarn, one with no discernible respect for fact.

The first reference to America's national pastime, records the baseball scholar David Block in *Baseball Before We Knew It*,[9] can be traced all the way back to John Newbery's *A Little Pretty Pocket-Book*, a children's title published in London in 1744 containing the following lines:

B is for Base-ball
The Ball once struck off,
Away flies the Boy
To the next destin'd Post,
And then Home with Joy.

Half a century later, in his less than snappily-titled book *Games for the Exercise for the Recreation of the Body and Spirit for the Youth and His Educator and All Friends of Innocent Joys of Youth*, Johann Christoph Friedrich Gutsmuths mentions an 18th-century German ballgame as well as "English Base-ball", aka "Ball with Free Station", one in which runners could be out in various ways, such as throwing a ball to a base and shouting "Burned!"[10] Still, as we shall see, the very last thing those determined nationalists responsible for devising the Doubleday myth wanted to do was to permit it to be polluted by association with Germans, much less those imperialist English swine.

Now take ice hockey. Have a peek at the relevant chapter in the *Oxford Companion To Sports And Games*, last published in 1977 and as admirable and exhaustive a work of sporting reference as one could ever wish to read. John Arlott, best known as a poetic *Guardian* journalist and the most respected of all BBC cricket commentators, traced its origins back as far as the second century, even though it was then generally recognised to have stemmed from a game played in 1860 by English soldiers on the frozen expanse of Kingston Harbour, Ontario. That, he warranted, was the first time a puck was used, as opposed to the ball deployed in what North Americans call "field hockey", a distinction that may strike you as presupposing that the latter emerged afterwards even though a version has been traced back to Ancient Egypt.

Refreshingly, in seeking to establish the sport's roots, the Society for International Ice Hockey Research acknowledges it as a question that "may never be conclusively answered". Not that it fails to proffer some suggestions. The first written reference to the word "hockey" in relation to ice, it claims, was in 1825, in a letter from the Arctic explorer Sir John Franklin to Roderick Murchison, dated 6 November, which stated: "Till the snow fell the game of hockey played on the ice was the morning's sport."[11] However, the society also concedes that "there is no clear evidence that the people playing 'hockey for the morning sport' were wearing skates." This is believed to have been a game of field hockey, which took place while Franklin and his men were wintering at Fort Franklin in what are now known by Canadians as the Northwest Territories. According to www. birthplaceofhockey.com, however, the sport "originated around 1800, in Windsor, where the boys of Canada's first college, King's College School, established in 1788, adapted the exciting field game of Hurley to the ice of their favourite skating ponds and originated a new winter game, Ice Hurley." Which in turn begat ice hockey. What cannot be disputed is that it was Lord Stanley, Canada's governor general, who donated the Stanley Cup.

But what of the Dutch factor? Bandy, a popular winter pastime in northern Europe which differs from contemporary ice hockey in using a ball, is said to have originated in Russia, where it has been played for upwards of two centuries. The first recorded mention of a bandy club, Bury Fen, dates back to the frosty English winter of 1812-13; Nottingham Forest FC were initially formed in 1865 as Nottingham Forest Football and Bandy Club. Yet a number of 16th century Dutch paintings depict people striking a ball on ice with stick-like implements; in particular, Pieter Bruegel the Elder's *The Hunters* shows warmly-wrapped folk doing so on skates.

Games on

When John Cleese, Terry Jones, Michael Palin and Terry Gilliam announced their intention to revive *Monty Python's Flying Circus* in 2014, it was tempting to wonder whether they might soup up their act with a new question: what did the ancient Greeks do for us? Every bit as much as the Romans, actually. Apart from digging the foundations of Western art, drama, science, philosophy and geometry, we can also thank them for conceiving our passion for sport, as activity and spectacle. They also invented the gymnasium, built next to the academies of learning and whose purpose was to improve body as well as mind, "a place", noted Robin Harvie in *Why We Run*, "to retreat to from the demands of the day and to address the Socratic issues that would have been as refreshing to the mind as cold water to aching limbs."[12] And it was here, for 10 months of the year, that aspiring Olympians would train.

Homer observed in *The Odyssey* that there "is no greater glory for any man alive than that which he wins by his hands and feet", a philosophy that underpinned Hellenic education. To an extent, he found vindication in the original Olympics, for all that they were confined to the social elite. Commencing in 776 BC as a single event, a 210-yard dash won by a cook named Koroibos, the ancient Olympics, as we now refer to them, first flowered as a series of foot races and pounded on for the next 1,170 years, uninterrupted by invasion or inter-state squabbles. Indeed, all warfare was banned for the duration of each Games, by edict of Zeus himself – though an attack on Olympia itself in 364 BC suggests the so-called "Olympic truce" was not universally observed.

The last of these 293 Olympiads was in AD 393, whereupon Emperor Theodosius and Christianity did for them. The success of the Ancient Greeks, nonetheless, could be traced to the national zeal for competition, or so argued Jacob Burckhardt, the Swiss historian, art aficionado and Renaissance expert who taught alongside Friedrich Nietzsche at Basle University. Politics, mathematics, science, philosophy, poetry – you name it, the Greeks wanted to be the best at it. That hero-hungry spectators from the Mediterranean to the Black Sea flocked to see the athletic encounters in Athens testifies to the historic box-office appeal of the competitive arts.

* * *

Along with music and theatre, spectator sport emerged as one of the earliest branches of popular culture and shared experience, yet their paths have progressively diverged. Given that so much about the competitive arts remains the epitome of continuity, might this explain a good chunk of their extraordinary appeal to the tradition-fixated English? "In the history of the British Empire, it is written that England has owed her sovereignty to her sports,"[13] proclaimed J. E. C. Welldon, who played in the 1876 FA Cup final before becoming headmaster of Harrow School – the chief nursery, along with his alma mater Eton, for budding English imperialists. These establishments were cultural imperialism incarnate. Three team games in particular, cricket, football and rugby, built a strong international base; it helped having an empire that would grow to around 40% of the earth's surface. Lawn tennis, too, flew far and wide. As sport evolved into a secular religion, so Lord's and Wimbledon in particular, and later Twickenham and Wembley, became its most prominent early cathedrals.

"Giles Whittell is right to note that it was Britain which gave the world the sportsmanship we have seen on show during these Olympics."[14] So claimed Patrick Derham, headmaster of Rugby School, another exclusive English educational emporium inextricably linked to sport, in a letter to *The Times* during the 2012 Games. He was referring to the values so admired by the man who would revive the Olympics, Pierre de Frédy, Baron de Coubertin, who like two fellow Frenchmen in the early 20th century, Henri Delaunay and Jules Rimet, would look to Britain for inspiration. In the penultimate decade of the 19th century, De Coubertin visited Rugby School, where Thomas Arnold, the revered former headmaster, had instituted a physical education programme; he was influenced by Arnold's emphasis on "courage, excellence, determination and fair play", of which more anon. As Tony Perrottet noted in *The Naked Olympics*, the modern Games "might never have occurred without the efforts of the British, particularly a group of upper-crust Victorians who were obsessed with sports, the classics, and the idealised male form in Greek art".[15]

"The British tried their hands at everything, and prided themselves on inventing, improving or at least bringing a sense of order into most of the world's athletic pleasures,"[16] claimed the late Sir Derek Birley, the notable social historian and former vice-chancellor of the University of Ulster. As the journalist and Emmy-winning scriptwriter Julian Norridge also attests in his wide-ranging, informative and hugely entertaining 2008 book *Can We Have Our Balls Back, Please? How the British Invented Sport (And then almost forgot how to play it)*, the development of sport in these islands can be divided, roughly, into two stages. Spanning a century and a half, the spurs included industrialisation, Empire expansion, mass migration from countryside to cities, the emergence of international trade and the middle-class. With some justification, Arlott, Birley and Norridge alight on more than a score of still-popular spectator sports conceived, revived or remixed by Britons. In addition to a motley crew of pub games headed by darts, this roll of patriotic honour includes baseball, boxing, horse racing, cricket, golf, rowing, lawn tennis, badminton, swimming, sailing/yacht racing, association football, rugby (and hence variations such as rugby league, Australian Rules and American football), hockey and, according to Norridge, "maybe even" ice hockey – although, as we have already seen, Americans will dispute the baseball theory for evermore while the last claim is more than a little fanciful.

In the second phase of development, from the mid-to-late 19th century, the focus was internationalism: spreading the gospel of Englishness (as opposed to a more collective Britishness); we shall return to this. Coming in the wake of the Industrial Revolution, the first stretched from the mid-to-late 18th century, a period that saw communications improve markedly, thanks in good part to the canal network started in 1759 – as Birley celebrated – by "the entrepreneurial enthusiasm of the Duke of Bridgewater and the engineering skills of an illiterate genius, James Brindley".[17] This in turn helped exports surge from about £14 million between 1760 and 1780 to £23.7m by 1792. To Birley, who credited aristocrats and entrepreneurs for sport's expansion, the "great levellers" of the age were sex and sport,[18] with Prince Frederick, the Duke of York, sparking headlines for both his exploits between the sheets and his tribulations as a stable owner at Newmarket.

It was also a period during which, as another social historian, Harold Perkin, observed with perhaps only mild exaggeration, "the English ceased to be one of the most aggressive, brutal, rowdy, outspoken, riotous, cruel and bloodthirsty nations in the world and became one of the most inhibited, polite, orderly, tender-minded, prudish and hypocritical."[19]

To the death (I)

A World Cup evening at Wembley and the questions came crowding in. Why did the FA declare the match a sell-out when there were empty seats all over the stadium? What was the point of that? And why was kick-off delayed so that a Royal Marine could abseil from the roof with the match ball? What was that all about? Year upon year, we become a little more like the Americans in our obsession with the military. With the greatest respect to the armed forces, there are times when Wembley feels like the Royal Tournament.[20]

Patrick Collins deserves admiration, not simply for expressing such sentiments but for daring to express them in the *Mail on*

Sunday, a newspaper scarcely inclined to publish anti-armed forces rhetoric. In questioning sport's celebration of the military, of course, he was questioning a link that goes directly to the heart of the competitive arts. The Royal Engineers Cricket Club have been playing since 1862, their naval counterpart only a year less; the first Army v Navy rugby union match was in 1878; likewise the first such encounter between US Army and Navy on the gridiron; the British Army XI played first-class cricket for much of the second and third decades of the 20th century, the Combined Services for a large chunk of the middle. But all that enthusiasm, to be honest, is beside the point.

Spectator sport stems from our base instincts – or, rather, the baser ones. While it does not rely entirely on humanity's penchant for hitting – people or, when they're unavailable, inanimate objects – most of its most popular variants certainly do: boxing, football (both American and unAmerican), cricket, rugby, baseball, hockey and tennis. Indeed, sport as a whole has often been justified as an acceptable outlet for aggression in testosterone-woozy men and, latterly, women.

The origins of spectator sport have been traced to several sources, most of them military and barbaric. The year 264 BC, claimed the Romans, saw the first gladiators – slaves instructed to fight to the death at the funeral of a distinguished aristocrat, Junius Brutus Pera.[21] "Gradually gladiatorial spectacle became separated from the funerary context, and was staged by the wealthy as a means of displaying their power and influence within the local community," notes Kathleen Coleman, a Harvard professor. These combatants can be seen alongside the Grecian Olympics as the forerunners of all professional sportsfolk.

Living together in barracks, they received rigorous training and the best medical attention, subsisting on high-fibre diets. After all, so far as their masters were concerned, they were an investment. As Coleman points out, adverts for gladiatorial displays have survived at Pompeii, the handiwork of professional sign-writers – "on house-fronts, or on the walls of tombs clustered outside the city-gates". The number of gladiators billed was crucial: "the larger the figure, the more generous the sponsor was perceived to be, and the more glamorous the spectacle." Precious few questioned the morality of it all; the gladiators' own epitaphs "mention their profession without shame, apology, or resentment".[22]

The original crowd-puller, nonetheless, was chariot racing, immensely popular in Ancient Greece and later Rome, where capacity at the vast Circus Maximus had to be increased to accommodate the hundreds of thousands who wanted to revel in the bloodthirsty spectacle. In Athens, contestants in the *apobates* set the trend by donning full armour. Evidence of this rugged sport can be found on the frieze around the Parthenon, dated c. 440 BC. "The military nature of the contest is certainly paramount but it also ranked as an equestrian event in the programs of the festivals," related Nancy B. Reed in the *Journal of Sport History.*

> *Ancient equestrian events were varied, including horse races as well as chariot races of two- and four-horse teams, but all have a common basis. The considerable expense involved in owning race horses, operating stables, and entering competitions placed equestrian events in the hands of wealthy aristocrats... It is generally held that the contestants (the* apobates*) mounted the chariots when they were at full speed and then dismounted, apparently at regular intervals as the charioteers drove toward a finish line. Dionysios of Halikarnassus records that at the conclusion of the chariot races "those who have ridden with the charioteers... (the apobates)... leap down from their chariots and run a race with one another the length of the stadium."[23]*

Then there was boxing. According to Olympic.org, the official website of the Olympic movement, the earliest evidence of men punching each other sportily dates back to Egypt, circa 3000 BC. Other sources suggest it goes back further still, to Ethiopia: images have been traced to Sumerian relief carvings from the third millennium BC. The sport was introduced to the ancient

Olympics in 688 BC; for protection, competitors' hands and fore-arms were bound with soft leather thongs, replaced in Rome by metal-studded leather gloves/thongs. Neither, mind, was of much help to the protagonists: fights usually ended with the death of one or the other.

Although the Emperor Constantine banned gladiator fighting in AD 325, according to the ancient Roman historian Ammianus Marcellinus, who recoiled at the prevailing "gluttony and gross immorality" of the age, the Caesar Gallus encouraged and took disturbing delight in such contests, boxing too: "Another plain and obvious indication of his cruel nature was the pleasure which he took in gladiatorial shows; he sometimes watched as many as six or seven fights with fascinated attention, and was as happy at the sight of boxers killing one another in bloody combat as if he had made a great financial coup."[24]

* * *

In AD 383, Rome abolished boxing on account of its alleged excessive brutality. This apparently brought a lull until 17th century England.[25] In 1681, reported the *Protestant Mercury*,[26] London was the scene of a formal bare-knuckle fight; by the end of the century, the Royal Theatre was hosting regular bouts for size-able purses. Punching and wrestling were both permitted: few if any holds were barred. James Figg, said to be the son of poor Oxfordshire farmers, developed his skills under the tutelage of Timothy Buck, the so-called "Master of the Noble Science of Defence", and rose to champion of England. After an estimated 270 fights, he retired undefeated; Jack Broughton, the second of his successors as champion, would be hailed as the "Father" of English boxing.

Meanwhile, in the third decade of the 17th century, Richard Dover, a lawyer besotted with history, emerged as the engine behind the first revived "Olympick" festival, staged near the village of Chipping Campden amid the decidedly un-Greek hillsides of the English Cotswolds. This was an age when the nation's rural festivals – which had long celebrated drinking and gambling, not to mention all manner of lewd antics and pagan fertility rites such as dancing around the maypole – were under attack by the fun-loathing Puritans.

Among the sporting treats available to the ale-quaffing spectators at the Cotswold Olympicks – according to a 70-page booklet published in 1636 and sold at auction in 2013 – were bear-baiting, "fighting with cudgels" (an unintentional nod to the goriest of ancient Greek contact sports, the pankration), dwile flonking (dodging beer-soaked rags) and shin-kicking, the last of which is still practised with considerable expertise in stadiums the world over. One poet proclaimed Dover, whose intention was to improve fitness for armed service, "an Hero of this our Age"[27]. Festivities were soon halted by the outbreak of the Civil War but revived after the Restoration, and kept going until 1860, by when proceedings had degenerated into a drunken brawl. Restored a century later, competitions in the May celebrations now include gurning.

Bats, clubs, horses and fists

"Public hangings were the Arsenal versus Chelsea of the day, popular with all classes, but more fun because they hanged the star."[28] Thus, in his vivid study of Tom Cribb, the legendary bare-knuckle fighter, does Jon Hurley, the Dublin-born novelist and author, characterise London at the turn of the 19th century. "Cheering, praying, swearing, wildly gesticulating fans ate hot dogs and drank ale while someone, often innocent, it mattered little, twitched in front of them. White collar crime, properly, drew the biggest crowds and the direst penalties. The poor loved nothing better than to see a gent dangle and froth. When the forger Henry Fauntleroy was despatched in 1824, his audience was 100,000, with front row, scaffold-adjacent seats changing hands at a guinea a time. Many a bloated, gem-encrusted oligarch would love such an audience." Rat-killing, a popular medium for betting, was another of the period's big draws.

Since around 1680, bare-knuckle prize-fighting had been technically illegal yet patronised by Royals, by Government ministers, by artists such as Blake, Hogarth and Turner, and by illustrious word-spinners such as Byron, Cobbett, Keats and Swift – and even one or two women. As Hurley observed, it "was a poor man's escape hatch". Fights were staged, in the main, in or near the capital. The blue-blooded, needless to add, always nabbed the best seats.

Part of the attraction, of course, was that they were watching a two-horse race. It might be an exaggeration to suggest that the evolution and growth of spectator sport was entirely attributable to man's fondness for a punt, but barely. The next chapter addresses this in detail.

Kings and commoners

History never stands still. At least one historian has identified "Joseph of Exeter" as the source of the first reference to cricket: writing in Latin, his couplet was translated as: "The youths at cricks did play/Throughout the merry day." More widely and famously cited is the mention of "creag" in the wardrobe accounts of Edward I (circa 1300). These and other claims, however, have been given short shrift by both Bowen and his former assistant, Peter Wynne-Thomas, who emerged from the major's shadow to become one of the game's most devoted and questioning chroniclers ("I knew Bowen from 1963," he recalled to me in 2013, "went to his house in Eastbourne and lunched with him in London, also receiving letters from him two or three times a week – he always replied by return of post. He taught me how to look at and research cricket history."[29]). Not that the pupil lost much, if anything, by comparison: Wynne-Thomas was sufficiently authoritative and respected to dare to call his 1997 tome "The" as opposed to "A" history of cricket.

As Wynne-Thomas sagely put it, "it is debateable whether many, if any" of these claims refer to cricket. As with Bowen, the first "authentic" reference to the game he cites dates back to 1598 and John Derrick, who as a witness in a Guildford court case over land, recalled playing "creckett" on the disputed territory 50 years earlier.[30] Eerily enough, by the time Norridge began writing *Can We Have Our Balls Back, Please?*, the plot was occupied by a Multiyork furniture store, whose area manager just happened to be the father of Matt Prior – who is still, as I write, England's wicketkeeper.[31]

The most ancient football in existence has been traced to the late 15th century. Made of cow leather and a pig's bladder, it was discovered in 1981, in the Queen's bedchamber in the roof of Stirling Castle in Scotland. According to Michael McGinnes, collections manager at the local Smith Museum, it may have been given to the future Mary Queen of Scots by her father King James IV, whom documents suggest paid two shillings for a bag of "fut ballis" in April 1497. Here, to Richard McBrearty, curator of the Scottish Football Museum, was a rejoinder to those still propounding the traditional notion that the game as we know it was born in the early 19th century.[32]

The birth of golf, meanwhile, has its roots in political symbolism. "The Royal and Ancient Game of Golf has ample justification for its historic title," declared Robert Browning M.A., LLB and editor of *Golfing* magazine from 1910 to 1955. After all, from the Peace of Glasgow in 1502 until the Scottish hold on the English throne was terminated by the somewhat overrated "Glorious Revolution" of 1688-89, every Stuart monarch played a primitive form of the game – four kings of the United Kingdom, two kings and one queen of Scotland. "Yet golf is something more," insisted Browning, "than the favourite pastime of the Scottish royal house; it is the outward and visible symbol of the union of England and Scotland."[33]

While the auld enemies spent much of the first half of the second millennium doing all sorts of beastly things to each other in glens, on moors and assorted other battlefields, the game was banned in its land of purported origin in order to focus minds on military training. Indeed, the first official documented references to golf in Scotland can be traced back to 1457, when James II ("James of the Fiery Face") decreed that "the futeball and golfe be utterly cryed downe and not be used".[34] His son and grandson both renewed the ban. The 1502 peace treaty – sealed the following year by James IV's marriage to Princess Margaret, daughter of Henry VII – freed them to indulge anew. There is even an indication, suggested Browning, that these events made James's sporting passion fashionable down south. A letter written by Catherine of Aragon, first wife of Henry VIII (whose fancy was tennis), includes the following: "And all his [i.e. her husband's] subjects be very glad, Master Almoner, I thank God, to be busy with the golf, for they take it for pastime."[35] A licence to play "golf, football, schueting at all gamis with all other manner of pastime", dated 25 January 1552, reckoned Browning, was the earliest documented evidence of the game being played at its purported spiritual home, St Andrews.[36] Half a century later, another Scottish monarch, James VI, transported the game with him to London after inheriting the English throne.

The first clubs began emerging in the mid-18th century, around the time Thomas Mathison penned *The Goff*, a "mock-heroic epic" and reportedly the first slice of golfing literature ever published, in Edinburgh in 1743.[37] The following year, a petition signed by "several Gentlemen of Honour, skilfull in the ancient and healthfull exercise of Golf" was dispatched to City of Edinburgh magistrates requesting the provision of a silver club for annual contests on the Links of Leith. The majority of the dozen entrants to this, the first golfing competition (only 10 actually teed off), were mentioned in Mathison's poem.[38] In Browning's view, the first club sprang from this – the Honourable Company of Edinburgh Golfers. On 14 May 1754, twenty-two "Noblemen and Gentlemen, being admirers of the ancient and healthful exercise of the Golf",[39] convened to subscribe for another silver club, the prize for what would in Browning's time have been referred to as an Open Scratch competition, establishing the St Andrews Golf Club, where strokeplay – as an alternative to matchplay – was introduced in 1759.

* * *

The king nobody ever called Jimmy to his face also had a sizeable hand in ensuring that horse-racing, too, was out of the stalls early. There are records of such events during Roman times, and on public holidays in the 12th century, at Smithfield in London and at Chester, the latter the scene of Shrove Tuesday races;[40] it was in the same century, moreover, that soldiers began bringing back remarkably fleet Arab horses from the Crusades. A keen hawker and hunter as well as golfer, James VI is nevertheless credited with bringing the sport to England shortly after succeeding Elizabeth I on the southerly throne in 1603, when an East Anglian market town, Newmarket, caught his eye. He bought a permanent base there in 1609 in addition to the Swan Inn, later the headquarters of the Jockey Club.[41] The first recorded race at Newmarket took place on 18 March 1622 – a match race between two horses belonging, respectively, to Lord Salisbury and the Marquis of Buckingham: the latter won his owner a prize worth £100.[42]

James's heir, Charles I, raced keenly before quite literally losing his head. Although Oliver Cromwell's Puritanical attitudes prompted horseracing to be banned from 1649 until the Commonwealth interlude ended in 1660, Charles II made up for lost time with brio. In that same year "The Merry Monarch" embarked on what became biannual visits to Newmarket; once a year he would move his entire court there. In 1661, he also attended a major race at Epsom. In 1665, the first governor of New York, Richard Nicolls, a Royalist who had fought in the English Civil War and helped Charles secure "New Netherland" from the Dutch, established the first race held in America, staged every May at a course named, with appropriate respect, Newmarket. In the same year, Charles decreed, via an Act of Parliament, that, as from 1666, the Town Plate would be run at the original Newmarket every October – the first equine race run under written rules.[43]

Interlude: The game that shrank

That athletics' first official world championship did not arrive until 1983 says much for the tyranny of the Olympics – and hence the supposed amateur principles propounded and upheld with such devoted zealotry by Avery Brundage, IOC president for almost the entire third quarter of the 20th century. That was four years before rugby union but a fair time after badminton (1977), cricket (women 1973, men 1975), ice hockey (1969), squash (1967) and rowing (1962)[44], much less rugby league (1954), golf (1953), basketball (1950), motor racing (1950) and motor cycling (1949), let alone soccer (1930), cycling (1927), ski-ing (Nordic 1926, Alpine 1931) and table tennis (1926). Best not to dwell, therefore, on boxing (1882). All the same, the identity of the sport that gave us the first world championship may surprise. The distinction fell, in 1740, to what we now call real tennis, the original racquet sport. Originally known as royal tennis in England and Australia, and as court tennis in the US, in France it was called *courte-paume*, a variation of *jeu de paume*. And yes, inevitably, it had the royal assent.

Tennis courts became all the rage in 14th century France. It was the place for European aristocrats to be seen. Precisely when the game crossed the Channel is unknown, but in *Troylus and Crysede*, written circa 1380, Mr Canterbury Tales himself, Geoffrey Chaucer, mentions tennis. In 1414, according to the story told to untold millions of English schoolchildren down the years, Henry V was presented with a gift of tennis balls by the heir to the French throne, the Duke of Touraine – not that that stopped the young English king from ordering his longbowmen to terminate the French army with extreme prejudice at Agincourt the following year. Still, as Shakespeare reports in that inimitable way of his, Henry was certainly partial to a spot of racquets and balls:

> *We are glad the Dauphin is so pleasant with us;*
> *His present and your pains we thank you for:*
> *When we have match'd our rackets to these balls,*
> *We will, in France, by God's grace, play a set*
> *Shall strike his father's crowd into the hazard.*
> *Tell him he hath made a match with such a wrangler*
> *That all the courts of France will be disturb'd*
> *With chases.*[45]

François I was an early 16th century enthusiast, not only commissioning courts at three of his palaces but also, it was said, on his modestly-named flagship, *La Grande François*. Pierre Gentil, reportedly the game's first professional (or *Maître-Paumier*), earned a salary of 500 francs coaching François' successor, Louis XIII (aka Louis The Just). These revered practitioners had had their own guild since the early 14th century, protected by Royal patent from unauthorised sellers of balls and racquets. Come 1571, Charles IX had granted statutes to a Corporation of Tennis Professionals, one of whose members codified the rules in 1592.

By then, racket and ball guilds had emerged in Venice and Florence, and it was an Italian, Antonio Scaino, who wrote *Tratta del Giuoco della Palla*, characterised by Arlott as "a philosophical treatise". Published in 1555, it was dedicated to the monk's patron, the Duke of Ferrara. "The pretext was to settle a dispute which had arisen when the duke was playing one day, but the work goes deeply into the game and reveals how seriously it was regarded. From Scaino we learn that the size of the court, the method of scoring, the imparting of cut to the ball, and many other features of real tennis as it is played today, were well established more than 400 years ago... From Scaino we gain confirmation, too, that what was known as a tennis court was often a town square or a section of street."[46]

Another eager early proponent was Henry VIII, François I's sport-potty English counterpart and rival. With energy, power and money to burn, he slaked his thirst for sport by equipping royal palaces up and down the Thames, converting them, as Harris relates, into the nation's first permanent sports centres, complete with hunting parks, bear pits, cockpits and spaces to practise athletics, wrestling and, inevitably, swordplay. Henry also had tennis courts constructed at Hampton Court, Whitehall and St James's. Having assumed control of Hampton Court Palace from Cardinal Wolsey, he re-roofed and remodelled its open court, even installing a viewing gallery for spectators.[47] It was claimed that Anne Boleyn, one of his least fortunate wives, was playing there when she was arrested; and that the king himself was playing when he received the welcome news that she had been safely beheaded.

By the start of the next century, France boasted of a reported 18,000 courts, though many, suggests Harris, were probably simply "outdoor spaces for playing the simpler game of *longue paume*".[48] By then there were 14 real tennis courts in London, though as Arlott deduces, there must have been "many humbler courts" in England: by 1558, a French visitor could recall seeing "hatters and joiners… playing tennis for a crown, which is not often to be seen elsewhere, particularly not on a working day".[49] It would be wrong, however, to assume that this essentially regal world lacked nothing in manners and decorum. The future King Louis XII had his ears boxed on court by the Duke of Lorraine; when a disputed point provoked the Earl of Essex beyond endurance, he clobbered Henry, then Prince of Wales, on the head with his racquet; Caravaggio, the painter, killed an opponent and was forced to flee Rome.[50]

In 1635, a court was built in London's James Street, now Orange Street. It was there that William Whitcomb, whose name is commemorated on the street with which it shares a corner, founded the Hand and Racquet brewery, which became a pub and thrived for more than 300 years. After moving from No. 21 to No. 48 Whitcomb Street it became a mecca for postwar British comedians. It was here that Tony Hancock's co-writers, Ray Galton and Alan Simpson, staged so many episodes of the much-loved BBC comedy *Hancock's Half-Hour*. It was also here, when the bar was divided into two, that another beloved comic, Tommy Cooper – somewhat tight-fisted when it came to buying his round – would use his height to peer through the windows, to spot anyone he knew; unfortunately, his trademark fez gave the game away, encouraging people to follow him inside.

That inaugural world real tennis championship was won by a Frenchman, Clergé the Elder, who hung on to it for a quarter of a century. The game's inability to fully transcend its elitist roots and widen its constituency can perhaps best be summed up by Robert Fahey: when the Tasmanian won the first of his 11 successive championships between 1995 and 2012, he became just the 24th holder. The painting of him shortlisted for the 2012 BP Portrait Award is the handiwork of Rupert Alexander, whose other sitters, aptly enough, have included Elizabeth II and the Duke of Edinburgh.

Turf wars

The 18th century witnessed all manner of sporting firsts: the first inter-county cricket match – Kent v Surrey at Dartford, for a purse of £50 (1709); the first Laws of cricket (1744); the first recorded women's cricket match (1745); the turf's first governing body, the Jockey Club (1750), and the first "Classic" – the St Leger race (1776). In 2013, Beverley racecourse said it would honour two 246-year-old free tickets for the last of these, which had been snapped up at auction in Yorkshire: in 1767, these and 328 other silver tickets had been sold to fund a new stand.[51]

Doncaster was the stage for the inaugural St Leger for extremely practical reasons: it was conveniently close to the Wentworth Woodhouse estate in Yorkshire belonging to the Earl of Rockingham. Briefly Chief Minister and a racing lover, his Lordship was the principal sponsor of a 25-guinea sweepstake for three-year-old colts named not after some mysterious long-neglected saint, but the race organiser, Colonel Barry St Leger. Three years later, the Countess of Derby leased The Oaks, a country house in Epsom, Surrey, from her uncle, General Burgoyne, infamous for leading the Redcoats to defeat in the critical Battle of Saratoga during the American Revolution. As Birley related, Epsom, an old spa town, "had fallen behind the fashion when Bath and its imitators developed their Assembly Rooms and refined entertainments, and its magnificent Downs had not hitherto staged any races of distinction."[52] At one of Lord Derby's "roystering" house parties, a counterpart to the St Leger was proposed – a sweepstake for three-year-old fillies over one and a half miles, called The Oaks, to be staged at Epsom. It was repeated the following year, 1780, when it was joined by another event open to all three-year-olds; that this one wound up being named in honour of Lord Derby was a consequence – or so legend has it – of a coin-toss with Sir Charles Bunbury. Still, if there was to be no Bunbury Stakes, at least Sir Charles had the satisfaction of owning the first winner, Diomed.

Respectful imitations would follow. Initiated in 1836, the French Derby, aka The Prix du Jockey Club, was named in homage to the Jockey Club. After a stuttering start in 1817 and resumption in 1848, the Irish Derby as we know it began life at The Curragh in 1866. Known interchangeably as "The Most Exciting Two Minutes In Sports" or "The Fastest Two Minutes in Sports", the Kentucky Derby, first run in 1875, followed a taste of Epsom Derby Day enjoyed three summers earlier by Colonel Meriwether Lewis Clark Jr., whose grandfather, William, had formed one half of the fabled Lewis and Clark expeditionary team.

Bunbury had previously thrown his considerable clout behind the stout efforts of a Newcastle lawyer, James Weatherby, to publish a *Racing Calendar*, which bore fruit in 1769, albeit only after a five-year wrangle. Here could also be found, as Birley put it, the sport's "increasingly elaborate" rules. While Weatherby stormed up the Jockey Club ranks – from editor to secretary to solicitor to treasurer – Turf accomplishments counted for little when it came to being granted admission to that snobbily elitist enclave. Dennis O'Kelly, a professional gambler of Irish stock married to a successful prostitute, made a pile and a half from his exploits, most notably through his purchase of Eclipse, bred by the Duke of Cumberland; it became the century's most celebrated racehorse (the Eclipse Stakes and the annual American thoroughbred awards are both named after him; in 1970, indeed, the Royal Veterinary College declared that close to 80% of thoroughbreds were descended from him in some shape or form). This enabled O'Kelly to scurry up the social ladder, even trading his Epsom home for a house on the grand Middlesex estate of Lord Chandos. "That none of this secured him membership of the Jockey Club was nothing to do with morality," reasoned Birley, "but everything to do with belonging to the right circles."[53]

Lord's (but no ladies)

This was also the century that brought an early lawsuit involving two cricket teams (Rochester Punch Club Society and the London Gamesters, 1718), and the first recorded charge for admission to a cricket match (1744). The last of these dates is also regarded as the latest year that could have seen the birth of the institution now known as Marylebone Cricket Club, which would run English cricket until deep into the 20th century and still remains the custodian of the game's laws. To Wynne-Thomas, 1787, the year most reference books give for the birth of MCC, was "almost certainly" merely the year a new London cricket ground was born. While the name disguised more plebeian origins, it quickly came to reflect the venue's nose-bleeding berth in the English social hierarchy: Lord's.

In its formative years in England, as we have seen, sport was rooted in privilege. And nowhere, beside real tennis, was this more visible than in cricket. Women may be allowed into the pavilion these days (albeit only since 1999) but it remains a bastion of masculinity, propriety and privilege. In 2012, following complaints about slipping standards, MCC members were issued with cards containing photographs illustrating what was "acceptable" and "unacceptable" to wear, not only in the pavilion but in the more casual enclosures for members' friends. That sense of constancy was captured by Magnus Linklater – a sagacious Scotsman and my first newspaper editor. Along with Elizabeth Windsor, David Cameron, Sir Mick Jagger, Russell Crowe, Sam Mendes and countless other notable personages, he attended an Ashes Test there in 2013:

> *Privilege yesterday was standing in the Long Room at Lord's, watching the play from behind the bowler's arm, before slipping next door to squeeze in an ice-cold Chablis. Privilege on Thursday was clapping Ian Bell on the shoulder as he ran into the pavilion, sweat pouring, after his century. Privilege was simply being there, in cricket's inner sanctum. Belonging to MCC conjures up visions of crusty old men in frayed*

bacon-and-egg ties, with battered panamas, slumped in the front row of the pavilion, dozing gently in the sun. The visions are entirely accurate.[54]

All of which made his subsequent sheepish confession all the more surprising: "But just for a few days, to be among them was heavenly."

Without privilege, Lord's would not be Lord's. At a "Fine Silver Sale" in 2012 organised by Bonhams, a pair of silver sauceboats went under the hammer, estimated to be worth between £3,000 and £4,000. They were originally the property of George Finch-Hatton, who doubled up as the 9th Earl of Winchilsea and 4th Earl of Nottingham. Making up amply in enthusiasm for what he lacked in talent, His Lordship travelled immense distances to play cricket, earning him the reputed distinction of having participated in more fixtures than any other 18th centurion.

Finch was a fiery opponent of the Duke of Wellington, opposing the latter's advocacy of Catholic emancipation so strenuously that the pair fought a duel at Battersea Fields in 1829 (both survived). While playing for the White Conduit Club at White Conduit Fields, a public space in Islington, he and another regular, Colonel Charles Lennox, decided to seek greater privacy; this led them to commission one of the team's professionals, an enterprising Yorkshire wine trader named Thomas Lord, to find a new ground, for which they would underwrite the cost. Lord leased some land in Dorset Fields (now Dorset Square) and in 1787 Conduit Club played their first match on what was originally called The New Ground. The name was soon revised to Lord's Cricket Ground; since they were now playing in Marylebone, the WCC was reborn as MCC. Lord opened his gates to archers as well as cricketers; in 2012, cricket paused to allow the ground to host the Olympic archery competition.

In 1811, Lord found a new home for Lord's at North Bank, and three years later relocated to the current premises in St John's Wood. It remains one of sport's most resplendent stages. A combination of award-winning modernist architecture (the media centre bears a strong resemblance to an over-plump pickled cucumber) and near-125-year-old pavilion (plus 170-year-old rackets court)[55] makes it at once an ancestral seat and signpost. In 1825, the original fixtures, fittings and score-books were lost in a fire, but the turf – excavated during the relaying of the outfield in the winter of 2002-03 – can now be purchased by members and visitors. Some of the sods have been put into paperweights for sale in the club shop; another lump can be found in the museum. However, the evidence that Lord moved the turf from ground to ground – as submitted a century later by F. S. Ashley-Cooper and Lord Harris in *Lord's and the MCC* – appears to be strictly anecdotal. Not least since the MCC archives feature photos taken in the mid-20th century showing turf being replaced on the outfield.[56]

MCC bought Nathaniel Dance's 1771 portrait of Finch at Christie's in 1989; a few years later the circle was complete. Marriage links the Earl's family to A. J. Drexel, a native of Philadelphia, spiritual home to cricket in North America; Drexel was a friend of Junius Morgan as well as mentor and business partner to his son, J. Pierpont Morgan, founder of the epony-mous merchant bank, now one of the main sponsors at Lord's.[57]

What, then, of the wine trader who benefited from the Earl's motivation and largesse? We do know that Lord came perilously close to ensuring that his ground was demolished: encouraged by the royal masterplan for Regent's Park then being worked on by the great architect John Nash, he sought to sell it to devel-opers; it took no less than the governor of the Bank of England, William Ward, to step in and secure the lease in 1825. We also know that Lord maintained an outlet at the entrance to Lord's – dispensing, among others, the South African wines on which duty had been reduced that year by sixpence a gallon; one assumes he was not all that dismayed when the wine cellar was destroyed in the pavilion blaze. Overall, however, Adam Chadwick, the MCC curator of collections, asserts that "much" that is known about Lord was "conjecture". He may be credited with Jacobite roots and a passionate love for the game of cricket, "but there is no proof of the former and he was quite ready to sell off Lord's for development to fund his retirement".[58]

In *Breakfast at Sotheby's*, published in 2013, Philip Hook, the senior specialist at the renowned auction house, amplified the social importance of cricket and horse racing: the mere presence of a bat or a well-bred filly, he claimed, would hoist the contemporary price of an 18th century painting.[59]

For "the idle and disorderly"

"Anyone entering the social and mental world of eighteenth-century English men and women is immediately struck by [a] kind of overlapping between old and new," observed the historian David Underdown. "On the one hand was a very traditional kind of culture, expressed in the village feasts and festivals of the old agricultural and church calendars... But at the same time new kinds of leisure were becoming available as inn- and tavern-keepers responded to the beckoning lure of profit, and began to promote sporting contests at or near their hostelries, attracting, they hoped, throngs of thirsty customers. Some of these pub-sponsored affairs were connected with the traditional festivals – Whitsun week, for example – but others were straightforwardly commercial."[60]

Some were encouraged, some not. In 1767, justices of the peace in Hampshire complained of the "pernicious practice" whereby publicans could "advertise and encourage revels and such like unlawful meetings of idle and disorderly persons... for their private gain and advantage". Given that the "idle and disorderly" were "the lower sort of people... seduced from their respective labours and employment", the JPs declared that they would no longer award licences to pubs and inns staging such activities.[61]

Cricket, Underdown discovered, was a major feature of these festive occasions. Helpfully, public holidays abounded. In addition to Christmas, Easter and Whitsuntide, Thomas Marchant, a wealthy Sussex yeoman, noted in his early 18th century diaries that his labourers also "kept holiday" on Ascension Day and

Midsummer Day; sometimes he would also discharge them of their duties for Candlemas, Michaelmas, Restoration Day, Gunpowder Treason Day, Lady Day, All Saints' Day, St George's Day and St Andrew's Day. Local fairs were not the sole attraction: Marchant made 18 references to inter-village cricket in his diary between 1717 and 1727. A few years later, in 1735, came an early indication of the power the elite would exert: the Prince of Wales and the Earl of Middlesex chose the London and Kent teams for a match to be played – or so it was advertised – for a purse, massive for the era, of £1000.

"The patronage of popular sport and entertainment," argues Rob Light, a member of the Cricket Research Centre at the University of Huddersfield, "played an important role in reinforcing relationships that underscored the eighteenth-century social structure of Britain."[62] Horse racing, the so-called "Sport of Kings", and cricket, that self-billed barometer of gentlemanliness, were especially popular in this respect. In staging "lavish events", notes Light with due scepticism, the aristocracy "aimed to attract a wide audience in order to court popularity and emphasise the importance of a common English culture that crossed class divisions. Such displays of wealth or power were also a means of demonstrating economic and social standing through which the position of the aristocracy at the head of society could be reinforced."

Typical was a cricket match played in 1725 near Arundel, Sussex, between two sets of "Gamesters" led by the Duke of Richmond and Sir William Gage, "Bart and Knight of the Bath", watched by "a vast concourse of people" numbering the Duke of Norfolk, who obligingly held a ball that night at his neighbouring castle.[63] Not that crossing social divisions would ever be easy. Witness two of this country's most hallowed sporting leaders and knights of the realm: East London's Alf Ramsey, the managerial nous and tactical brains behind the FIFA World Cup triumph of 1966, and Yorkshire's Leonard Hutton, the captain and master batsman who in the previous decade regained then retained The Ashes for England after two humbling and occasionally humiliating decades. Long before ascending such heights, both would feel obliged to take elocution lessons.

"An Indian game accidentally discovered by the English"

Thanks to the extensive tentacles of the British Empire, cricket spread with some rapidity, initially, if tentatively, to continental Europe. In 1676, Henry Teonge, a chaplain aboard the *Assistance*, a naval vessel moored in the Eastern Mediterranean, recorded in his diary: "This morning early (as it is the custom all summer long) at the least 40 of the English, with his worship the Consull, rode out of the city (Aleppo) about 4 miles to the Green Platt, a fine valley by a river side, to recreate themselves. Where a princely tent was pitched: and we had several pastimes and sports, as duck-hunting, fishing, shooting, handball, krickett, scrofilo; and then a noble dinner brought thither…"[64]

North America was another early convert. In 1709, a Virginian, William Byrd, wrote in his diary: "I rose at 6 o'clock and said my prayers shortly. Mr W-L-s and I fenced and I beat him. Then we played cricket, Mr W-L-s and Mr Custis against me and Mr Hawkins, but we were beaten."[65] Wynne-Thomas sounds a characteristically scrupulous and wary note: "If viewed in isolation this can be taken as the English game of cricket, but a careful reading of all the references in context reveals that the game played was a version of 'old two-cat', which involved four players and was still occasionally being played in the United States in the 19th century."[66] Besides, despite maintaining a detailed diary on his trips to England, wherein he visited some of the game's "early authentic homes", Byrd omitted any mention of cricket. More credibly, Wynne-Thomas cites a 1751 report in a New York publication, *Gazette and Weekly Post Boy*, of a match between "eleven Londoners" and "eleven New Yorkers".[67]

According to another cricket historian, Deb K. Das, some of the Founding Fathers were said to be avid players. In the decade following independence, indeed, John Adams asserted in Congress that, since leaders of cricket clubs could be called "presidents", there was no reason he could see why the nation's leader could not be called the same.[68]

Then there was India. In 1721, Lieutenant Clement Downing made the first mention of a game there: a match between English sailors of the East India Company, most likely at Cambay, 30 miles west of Baroda.[69] Not until the end of the century, though, did the subcontinent give birth to its first known club, the Calcutta Cricket Club. In 1915, Madras hosted the first Presidency match, played between Indians and Europeans, a fixture that would endure until 1952 and one born, according to V. Ramnarayan, of a "desire to meet the Englishman on equal terms on the cricket ground, and to try and vanquish him"[70] – a desire that, more often than not, was fulfilled. "The English have always ridiculed us as 'effete'," stressed the Maharajah of Natore, an eminent if unorthodox nationalist of the early 20th century. "It is on the sporting field that we may counter such allegations."[71] Not for nothing would Boria Majumdar entitle his cliché-shattering social history of Indian cricket *Twenty-Two Yards to Freedom*.

Yet as the game spread throughout that colossal land, whether seen as a means of self-expression, social advancement or nation-building enterprise – or all three – not all arms would fling open. In a 1950s speech, the so-called "Guru of Hate", M. S. Golwalkar, who for three decades led the right-wing Hindu nationalist group Rashtriya Swayamsevak Sangh, contended that "the costly game of cricket, which has not only become a fashion in our country but something over which we are spending crores of rupees, only proves that the English are still dominating our mind and intellect."[72] Rather better known is that oft-quoted claim by the cultural theorist Ashis Nandy, who declared in *The Tao of Cricket*, tongue perhaps only scraping cheek, that cricket is "an Indian game accidentally discovered by the English".[73]

Maintaining social order

It was the Industrial Revolution, expanding employment, determining the working day and week anew, that spurred the development of sport as entertainment, something to watch as well as play – notably in the post-revolutionary United States. "As the nineteenth century dawned," writes Nancy L. Struner of the University of Maryland in a review of Patricia Click's *The Spirit of the Times. Amusements in Nineteenth-Century Baltimore, Norfolk, and Richmond*, "ministers, other middle-class conservators of public morality, and the traditional southern elites were overtly suspicious of amusements. This negative view was not to last. By mid-century, and even more so after the Civil War, not only were amusements no longer objectionable but they were also accepted entertainments. By the 1870s, as well, many people even believed that a city without entertaining amusements was more than just a dark horse in the arena of inter-urban competition; it was actually in the dark ages of civilisation."[74]

Underpinning this stunning reversal of attitudes, contends Click, "was the reconciliation, though not quite the resolution, of two 'tensions', or intellectual dilemmas. The first problem involved the nature of amusements: did such activities have to serve some useful purpose or could they just be entertaining? The second issue involved the relationship between the organisation of society and the place of amusements therein. How could amusements proliferate and entertain, especially among labourers and immigrants, without upsetting the social order and destabilising society?"[75]

Upsetting the social order was even lower on England's list of priorities. Having so much more time for leisure than most, public schoolboys and students now led the way. In 1827 came the first Varsity cricket match between Oxford and Cambridge University; two years later, the same institutions scrapped for supremacy in the inaugural Boat Race. Croquet, lawn tennis and polo, on the other hand, were all products of the new Victorian leisured class, emerging as popular amusements on country estates during the prosperous 1860s and 1870s.

Polo was a male-only pursuit; croquet, a bland game involving ball, mallet and hoops, derived from an Irish game, crookey, soon grew tiresome. By contrast, Major Walter Clopton

Wingfield's invention, sphairistikè (Greek for "ball games"), played on a grass court, caught on with both sexes. In 1873, this aristocratic Welsh hustler patented nets for a new variation on an ancient bat-and-ball game; two years later, the MCC Tennis & Racquets sub-committee revised Wingfield's scoring system while the All England Croquet Club laid out courts – rectangular (20 yards by 10) and divided by three-foot-high nets. The more logical name of "lawn tennis" was adopted. No fewer than 7000 copies of the new rules were sold.

The game's most important facilitator was nonetheless cited as the American Charles Goodyear, who in 1839 mixed gum and rubber to produce vulcanised – and hence weatherproof – rubber. There were no inventor's spoils for him, and he died more than $200,000 in debt, but in addition to bequeathing the automobile industry, the man now commemorated by the planet's biggest rubber company had also created a ball that would bounce on grass.[76] However, the true, vastly earlier source appears to have been the Ancient Mesoamericans, who harvested latex from *castilla elastica*, processed it using liquid extracted from *Ipomoea alba* (a species of morning glory vine) and fashioned hollow rubber artefacts from the resulting material, including rubber balls.[77] No wonder they are believed to have been playing their own ball game, *ōllamaliztli* (think racquetball), nearly three and a half thousand years ago.

Wakefield soon found himself flogging boxes of racquets, balls and nets to the bluest of blood: the Princess of Prussia, Edward, Prince of Wales, Prince Louis of Hesse, more than 50 dukes and earls and countless viscounts and marquises. The social restrictions were plain in the name: who else but the privileged and wealthy had a lawn in the first place? "It was an athletic form of conspicuous consumption; only golf requires more land per person,"[78] reflected Stephen Tignor, a leading contemporary American tennis columnist and author. Across the Atlantic, it was embraced as "a society fad" in the summer retreat of Newport, Rhode Island, eventual venue for the inaugural US Championships in 1881. In France it had that

Riviera touch; in Australia, news that the game had received the Prince of Wales' seal of approval rapidly aroused enthusiasm in Melbournians and Sydneysiders seeking to emulate royalty; Germany's leading exponent in the first half of the next century would be Baron Von Cramm; in Russia it was lapped up by the nobility, and withered after the 1917 Revolution.

* * *

England, in the main, remained split between the landed gentry and the working-class, but the advent of the middle-classes queered the pitch. Cue, in 1806, the inaugural Gentlemen v Players match at Lord's, a fixture that would endure until 1962 and come to be seen as sport's most withering reflection of the English class system. "For the rest of the 19th century and beyond," wrote Wynne-Thomas, "members of the middle classes had to decide whether they were Gentlemen [amateurs] or Players [professionals]."[79] So dominant were the Players, "numerous devices had to be experimented with in order to make a proper match". One match saw 11 Players take on 18 Gentlemen; another found the former defending larger sets of stumps; sometimes the latter borrowed one or two Players. MCC members turned up in sufficient numbers "to keep the bar receipts healthy".

Less work, more play

Eighteen eighty-four was a pretty good year for firsts: the first eight-hour working day, the first local anaesthetic, the first automatic rifle and the first edition of *The Oxford English Dictionary*. The world's first practical automobile, though, was still a year from being unveiled; the first electric trains, on what is now the Northern Line in London, were a further five away, the invention of radio more than a decade distant, the first TV broadcast nearly four. By 1884, though, new traditions had already taken root. The FA Cup final, Wimbledon, the Ashes and the British Open were already up and running when, in December 1882, England beat Wales by two goals (i.e. two converted tries) in Swansea to kick off rugby's International Championship.

Shortly before this, the four British FAs had met in Manchester to agree on uniform rules, forming the International Football Association Board to authorise the changes; this paved the way for the inaugural Home International Championships, kicked off by Scotland and Ireland in January 1884.

Two critical factors in the growth of spectator sport in Britain were transport and changes in labour practices. In 1837 there were 1500 miles of railway track; by 1870 this had increased to 15,600; 20 years later, this had been augmented by 4,400 miles of branch lines. By then, safety bicycles had emerged, the motor car had arrived and migration from countryside to city, triggered by the Industrial Revolution and reignited when agricultural prices began to collapse in 1877, had fuelled a surge in the ranks of the suburban- and urban-dwelling white-collar middle-classes. Courtesy of the reduction of the working week to 55 hours and the introduction of a fourth bank holiday, even factory workers now had more leisure time. Other helpful developments included the first patent for a lawnmower, taken out in 1830.[80]

In a Christian country where Sundays were roped off for more pious pursuits, the rise of Saturday as a day for Britons to watch sport can be traced to the advent of the Saturday half-holiday in the late 1840s and, in particular, the rash of work-place closures in the early 1870s, spurred in part by legislation but also by trade union pressure. The potential for shared experience was realised by a 30%-plus rise in real wages between 1875 and 1890. In terms of football's swooping capture of native hearts, transport advances were highly significant, alongside, as Dave Russell points out, the granting of the vote to the working classes, rising literacy levels, an expanding press and a cheap postal service.[81]

A handful of durable sporting events kicked off in the first half of the 19th century – world rackets championship (1820), Grand National (1836), Henley Regatta (1839) – but by way of underlining how rapidly spectator sport mushroomed after 1840, consider the following lists. First, the foundation-stones:

1843: *Formation of first rugby club – Guy's Hospital*

1848: *First (association) football rules drawn up at Cambridge University*

1855: *Formation of Sheffield, oldest football club still in existence*

1863: *Formation, in London, of the Football Association, the game's first governing body*

Now the showpieces and international growth:

1840: *First Jockeys' Championship (flat racing)*

1851: *First America's Cup (sailing)*

1857: *First golf championship (in Scotland)*

1858: *First sporting league: the National Association of Base Ball Players (USA)*

1859: *First overseas tour (English cricket team to North America); first Australian football club – Melbourne FC, founder of Australian Rules*

1860: *First major international tournament (golf's British Open)*

1861: *First tour of Australia by an English cricket team*

1862: *Formation (purportedly) of first football club outside England – Oneida FC, Boston, USA*

1864: *First County Championship (cricket)*

1867: *First Belmont Stakes (US horse racing)*

1868: *First Australian cricket tour of England*

1869: *First American college football game – Rutgers v Princeton; first professional baseball team (Cincinnati Red Stockings)*

1871: *First rugby international (England v Scotland); first professional league (National Association of Professional Base Ball Players) and baseball game (Cleveland Forest Cities v Fort Wayne Kekiongas)*

1872: *First football international (Scotland v England); first FA Cup final*

1873: *First Scottish FA Cup; Rangers FC formed*

1876: *First European football club formed outside Britain – Denmark's Kjøbenhavns Boldklub; first professional* baseball league formed – the National League of Professional Baseball Clubs

1877: First Test match (cricket); first All England Tennis Championships

1882: British FAs agree on uniform rules and form International Football Association Board; first world boxing champion – John L. Sullivan (heavyweight)

1883: First Home International Championship (football) and International Championship (rugby union)

1884: First Wimbledon women's singles championships

1885: First football international not involving British teams – USA v Canada

1888: First Football League season; first British Lions tour (to Australia and New Zealand)

1889: First Football Associations formed outside Britain (Denmark and The Netherlands); first rugby union county championship

1890: First Iroquois Cup (lacrosse)

1891: First French Championships (tennis); first middle-weight, bantamweight and featherweight world boxing champions

1892: First professional American footballer – William "Pudge" Heffelfinger, paid $500 to play for the Allegheny Athletic Association against the Pittsburgh Athletic Club; first Sheffield Shield season (Australian cricket)

1893: First Stanley Cup (ice hockey)

1895: First US Open (golf); first professional game of American football

1897: First Victorian Football League (VFL) season

1900: First Davis Cup (tennis)

1901: First football international in South America: Uruguay 2 Argentina 3

1902: First Rose Bowl (US college football)

1903: First Tour de France, World Series (baseball), world gymnastics championships

In the space of 60 years, in other words, much of the sporting world as we know it had already left a hefty footprint. It does not seem excessively reductionist or simplistic to suggest that the subsequent century brought merely refinement and a less hypocritical approach to money.

School of Sport

Thomas Arnold, whose mid-century reforms spread to other leading schools, was guided by three ideals – "religious and moral principle, gentlemanly conduct and intellectuel [sic] ability": the cornerstones of what he famously called "muscular Christianity". As he saw it, being headmaster was less about running a school than encouraging students to become free-thinking and freely-functioning individuals – the better, while they were at it, to perpetuate the rigorous hierarchy in the class-room and beyond. This hierarchy is captured in *Tom Brown's School Days*, the classic tale of public school japes written by Thomas Hughes, an Old Rugbeian whose statue can be found at the back of the school's capacious one-roomed hut, "The Green Pavilion", cited by some as the most elderly purpose-built cricket pavilion still standing. Here was a self-sustaining, hermetically sealed world populated by masters, prefects and frightened fags – young boys who faced various vile varieties of corporal punishment should they fail to satisfy their elders' every whim. Hughes justified "the fag system", conceded George P. Landow, Professor of English and Art History at Brown University, by suggesting it "provided a practical embodiment of the idea that if one were to become a leader, one first had to become a follower and obey orders from those of higher status".[82]

On the bright side, Hughes hymned the praises of team sport as a path to friendship, co-operation and selflessness – and hence a finishing-school for empire-builders. In one famous passage, Tom and a master discuss cricket's virtues:

> "The discipline and reliance on one another which it teaches is so valuable, I think," went on the master, "it ought to be such an

> *unselfish game. It merges the individual in the eleven; he doesn't play that he may win, but that his side may."*
>
> *"That's very true," said Tom, "and that's why football and cricket, now one comes to think of it, are such much better games than fives or hare-and-hounds, or any others where the object is to come in first or to win for oneself, and not that one's side may win."*[83]

"Cricket bats, fishing poles, footballs, and other sports equipment clutter every corner" of *Tom Brown's School Days*, wrote Landow. "Appropriately so, for Hughes believed sport, particularly of the collective variety, played an important role in secondary schools for exactly the same reasons that they often receive support today: First of all, they give the student (like Tom Brown) with average, or below average, academic interest, ability, and accomplishment something in which to take pride, even to the point of providing a reason to work hard enough to remain in school. Another value of such activities, as the headmaster of a boarding school explained to me more than a half century ago, is simply that it keeps students busy and therefore out of trouble — a point that I am sure both Thomas Hughes and his idol, Thomas Arnold, were well aware."[84]

Is Rugby School the most important sporting cradle? The case is strong. It certainly boasts an illustrious lineage of influential old boys, extending all the way to Chris Brasher, who founded the London Marathon in 1981. Indeed, Lincoln Allison's work on the Webb-Ellis myth was motivated in part by a desire to prove that J. A. Mangan, another respected sports historian, had been wrong to conclude the very opposite: that Rugby School was of no import whatsoever because Dr. Arnold had little or no interest in sport. Headmasters at private schools were too busy pleasing the parents who funded them to bother with such trifles; it was the boys themselves who organised the games.

Yes, Arnold was largely indifferent to sport, but he was receptive when the students themselves came up with a fourth ideal – "athletic proficiency secured through compulsory organised games", as John A. Lucas, associate professor at Pennsylvania State University, put it. "This new branch of pedagogy was never described as such," reasoned William Milligan Sloane, an eminent American history professor and charter member of the IOC, referring to the importance placed on athletic endeavour at Rugby, "because sport is its own impulse, and the out-door life its own exceeding great reward."[85]

Dick Sykes, from Stockport, emigrated to the US, where he founded five towns in North Dakota; it was he who organ- ised the first football game in Liverpool, started the city's first club and for good measure helped launch Manchester's too; he also introduced football, golf and rugby to Americans. Other Old Rugbeans busied themselves transporting sports back to their native land. H. H. Castens, who rose to government secre- tary in Southern Rhodesia, excelled in cricket and football at Rugby and Oxford, captained South Africa at both, then – so loose were the qualification rules – captained and managed the first British Lions tour there in 1891. Tom Wills returned to Australia and organised games in Victoria where, in 1858, he helped arrange a 40-a-side game between Scotch College and Melbourne Grammar School, conducted according to "the Rugby regulations". The following year, he chaired the meeting that modified these into the rules of Melbourne Football Club, devising "a game of our own": thus was Australian Rules codi- fied.[86] That said, until recently, historians had downplayed Wills's contribution.

Those seemingly elasticated tentacles also stretched to India: Arnold ended his short life there in 1859 while in charge of education in the Punjab. "Globalisation," avers Allison, "was not something that would wait for internal processes to be completed nor did it depend on official channels. It occurred instantly and personally and pre-dated the official gospel of games."[87]

Mike Marqusee, a New Yorker transplanted to London in the 1970s, was not being unjustly contrary when he examined cricket's wistful relationship with its origins. "Cricket's obses- sion with the past, its status as something of a national relic, its association with the village green are not accidental or even incidental. Yes, cricket boasts a longer history than other sports, but there is more to it than that. Cricket is what it is because of its origin as a modern sport in a particular time and place: late eighteenth-century England. From that point of origin, everything flows."[88]

* * *

The inextricable links between English cricket and private schools are as plain today as they were then. By 1993, nine members of the England XI in the first Test against Australia had attended a state school, but the selling-off of playing fields, under Conservative and Labour governments alike, meant that, come the tour of New Zealand in early 2013, only a third had done so. Nor was there much promise of improvement: Joe Root, Jonny Bairstow, Joss Buttler and James Taylor, the four fastest-rising young batsmen, had all been privately educated.[89] A survey of the 413 county professionals in England and Wales that same year found that while half (207) were educated in the state sector and 21% (87) overseas, 29% (119) had attended an independent school – four times higher than the total proportion of children in private establishments. Hence the foundation, in 2005, of Chance To Shine, a laudable programme designed to encourage a revival of cricket in state schools, fewer than 10% of whom played the game. Encouragingly, the target – taking it to a third of such schools – was reached two years ahead of schedule, but the contrast with Australia remained stark: the proportion of children attending private schools there may be five times that in England (35% to 7%) but of the 12 players voted the nation's best of the 20th century, eight had a state education. Indeed, the media painted Ed Cowan, a graduate of an elite private school in Sydney who played in the 2013 Ashes series, as "disadvantaged".[90]

"Socker"

In the opening pages of his novel *The Good Companions*, published in 1929, J. B. Priestley distilled the significance of football to communities in the north of England during that decade: this was a world where "your shilling for the match at Bruddersford United Association Football Club turned you into a critic… a partisan… a member of a new community".[91]

Despite being perpetually at the mercy of the inclement English weather, cricket, the summer folly, was the first team game to attract crowds and patronage. By the second half of the 19th century, the tussle for the honour of becoming the nation's chief winter tipple found football and rugby in opposition. As late as 1880, *The Times* would claim that enthusiasts of the latter were "probably twice as numerous", but since the middle of the previous decade the identity of the winner had been becoming increasingly inevitable.

It was during the 1880s, as Russell relates, that soccer began to pierce rugby's territories. "Differing attitudes to cup (and, later, league) tournaments were crucial here, the FA encouraging them, the RFU hostile lest the game's social tone and sense of class exclusivity be compromised. Interestingly, where rugby enthusiasts ignored the centre and encouraged cup football, the game often became a part of popular culture. Where they did not, it remained a middle-class pursuit and left the field open to its rival." When the Lancashire FA was founded in 1878, the 28 members came from just six neighbouring towns in and between Bolton, Darwen and Blackburn. Stimulated by the FA and Lancashire Cups, clubs such as Preston North End and Burnley exchanging rugby for football. In 1888, while nearly half the 12 founder members of the Football League came from this "expanded heartland", the Lancashire RFU, which scorned "pot-hunting", saw rugby "become almost moribund within it".[92] In the next chapter we will see how this led to a split that has still to heal.

Association football's development has stoked intense debate, especially its debt to the public schools. "An increasingly influential body of work now challenges established narratives placing public school football and ex–public schoolboys at the heart of the game's codification and dissemination ['association football' soon became 'socker' in old boy slang]," acknowledges Russell. While not completely rejecting this, recent revisionist texts "suggest a far greater role for Sheffield than allowed by London-centric interpretations and argue that public schools' insularity and status-consciousness may have actually retarded football's diffusion as much as facilitated it".[93]

Russell's research led him to young men from "a rather more generously defined elite". Football in Liverpool, for example, owed much to some half-a-dozen Cambridge University-educated curates, themselves the products of minor private establishments and grammar schools, who introduced the game to their urban congregations from the late 1870s. Former grammar school-boys were also responsible for establishing a number of teams, including Blackburn Rovers, Chester City and Leicester.[94] In the 1870s, Old Harrovians returning to the Lancashire communities of Turton and Darwen formed sides among local workers. Many others sprang from that deep well, from church and chapel too, though the largest single springboards could be found in working-class communities. "Again, religious and works teams were often the result of initiatives at the grass roots rather than from higher up the social scale. The history of association football, as with that of popular recreation more widely, also offers powerful evidence of working-class resistance to attempts at middle- or upper-class cultural domination. Christ Church FC, Bolton, eventually Bolton Wanderers, split from the parent body in 1877 when the vicar proposed compulsory church attendance as the price of his continued support."[95]

Football's working-class appeal has seldom been more winningly bottled than by Harry Pearson, who in *The Far Corner*, a book published in 1994 characterised by Peter Stead as "a bleak, sardonic and amusing tour" of north-east English grounds, contended that, for manual workers, the game was "a means to show they were capable of more than their jobs allowed: of brilliance and creativity… where sport was not an education in reality but an escape from it… a glimpse of something better".[96]

Baseball 1 Cricket 0

Baseball is Greek in being national, heroic, and broken up in the rivalries of city-states. How sad that Europe knows nothing like it! Its Olympics venerate anger, not unity, and its inter-state politics follow no rules that a people can grasp. At least Americans understand baseball, the true realm of clear ideas.[97]

The thoughts of Jacques Barzun, an American cultural historian who died in 2012 at the admirable if not necessarily enviable age of 104. As an observer of the competitive arts, he is best-remembered for the slick one-liner that preceded his Grecian comparison: "Whoever wants to know the heart and mind of America had better learn baseball." Which brings us back to the question that has exercised so many minds – why did North Americans spurn cricket in favour of baseball? Blame it on burgeoning nationalism. "If one had been asked the question 'Why baseball?' in the 1840s and 1850s," wrote John Thorn, the historian and senior creative consultant on Ken Burns' masterly documentary series *Baseball*, "the answer would have been this: first, the novelty and excitement of play, a rebellion against puritanism; second, the opportunity for sallow city clerks to expend surplus energy – the sort that impedes hard work at a desk – in a sylvan setting, communing with an American Eden of the mind; and third, the assertion of a binding national identity, independent of John Bull."[98]

In that original 1751 game we have already mentioned, the *New York Gazette* reported that it was "play'd according to the London Method; and those who got most notches in two Hands, to be the Winners."[99] The "London Method", believes Beth Hise, whose sterling work linking baseball and cricket has been of immense value in augmenting the ranks of those who appreciate the strength of the connections, "highlights just how recognisable and increasingly widespread the formalised 1744 version of the game had become; yet it would be another full year before the laws were printed in the *New Universal Magazine* and another four before they would become available in pamphlet form."[100]

Hise also notes two key if contrasting similarities between the 1744 cricket laws and the first rules laid down in 1848 by the New York Knickerbockers: umpires were the ultimate, unchallengeable arbiters and the toss of a coin decided who batted first. And just as bowlers progressed from simply tossing up the ball for the batsman to hit to developing ever craftier twists and deceptions, so pitchers travelled the same journey from meek servitude to self-assertion.

One fact should be noted with some pride by Americans, and no little consternation by those accustomed to the Anglicised take on sporting history. Granted, the National Association of Professional Base Ball Clubs was blighted by low attendances, incomplete schedules, allegations of fixed games, widespread mismanagement and the unyielding dominance of a single club, the Boston Red Stockings, and thus only lasted from 1871 to 1875; yet it was still baseball that did the trailblazing in terms of professional leagues, while cricket and football did the emulating. Indeed, as a corrective to Rowland Bowen's theory that, but for the Civil War, Americans, rather than Australians, would have been England's natural cricketing bêtes noir, it is a fair bet that, without that bloody and divisive interruption, baseball would have organised itself even earlier. After all, its first convention, attended by 15 clubs, was held in 1857, while the following year saw the first annual National Association of Base Ball Players convention held in New York. Although all 22 clubs in attendance were from the city, the 1859 convention saw membership spread to New Jersey and attendance more than double; by 1863, unsurprisingly, inter-state hostilities had cut that to 28.[101]

On the other hand, but for the Civil War, would baseball have seized the national imagination as it did? "It received its baptism in the bloody days of our Nation's direst danger," claimed Albert Spalding, a famed sportsman, sports goods manufacturer and publisher of *Spalding's Baseball Guide* as well as the game's loudest and most industrious early promoter. "It had its early evolution when soldiers, North and South, were striving to forget their foes by cultivating, through this grand game, fraternal friendship with comrades in arms."[102]

Come 1866, the year after the end of the Civil War, no fewer than 202 clubs were turning out for the national convention. By then, added Thorn, "cricket in this country had been reduced to a diversion for a shrinking band of Anglophiles, while the New York game of baseball was spreading across the landscape like dandelions, courtesy of returning veterans whose first exposure to the game might have come in a prisoner-of-war camp. Actually, cricket was doomed in this country regardless of England's actions in the Civil War. The pace was too slow and, more importantly, the requirements for field maintenance were too great for it to be played by soldiers forever on the move. What America did to cricket was what it does to all exogenous innovation – repackage it to suit its own tastes. Baseball borrowed much of cricket's nomenclature, its copious record-keeping, its style of play and, most significantly, its emblematic relation to its nation of origin."[103]

The Doubleday Myth

Baseball, wrote Harold Seymour, was "ingrained in the American psyche", its importance in the early 20th century "astonishing". Every city, town and village had its "ball team", claimed the St Louis *Globe and Commercial Advertiser* in 1905. Around that time, another observer claimed that his country had five seasons: "Spring, summer, autumn, winter, and the baseball season."[104] Seymour commends the explanation submitted by Zane Grey, the popular author of western fiction who idealised the history of the American frontier and played baseball at university: to him, the game "fulfilled the American need for expression because it was open and manly, and full of risks, surprises, and glorious climaxes".[105] And as Grey also put it, "Every boy likes base-ball, and if he doesn't he's not a boy."[106] And it was 1905 that saw a highly dubious study commissioned by Spalding, whose aim was to prove that the game was an entirely American invention rather than a composite descendant of rounders and cricket, a couple of Limey inventions, as claimed by Henry Chadwick, the Englishman dubbed "The Father of Baseball".

An émigré from Exeter who arrived in Brooklyn in 1837, Chadwick may not have quite been the game's first chronicler, but as the sports historian Bob Carroll put it, "he was without doubt the most knowledgeable, ubiquitous, and influential baseball writer of his day".[107] Chadwick invented the first scoring system and the box-score (cribbing liberally from cricket's scorecard), composed the first instructional guides and devised statistical terms such as earned run average; throughout the second half of the 19th century he resided unchallenged as the game's most eminent authority. Like many Americans, John Montgomery Ward, founder of the first baseball players' association, resented this intruder, not to mention those "who believed that everything good and beautiful in the world must be of English origin".[108]

"I have been fed this kind of 'Rounders pap' for upward of forty years, and I refuse to swallow any more of it without some substantial proof sauce with it,"[109] Spalding scoffed while speaking at a YMCA in Springfield, Massachusetts, one of a succession of public speeches he gave in 1904 in a zealous effort to denounce Chadwick once and for all. Having set out his stall in an article for the *Boston Journal* published on 3 April 1905, headlined "The Origin of the Game of Base Ball", Spalding set up a committee to establish and certify the game's American origins. What evidence was gleaned relied heavily on the word of an elderly mining engineer, Albert Graves, who had read the *Boston Journal* piece and came forward to claim that he had been there to see Doubleday create the first diamond in 1839 in Cooperstown, a village in upstate New York.

The ensuing Mills Commission Report was published to wide acclaim and no little patriotic relief; significantly, it was compiled not with the aid of the non-compliant octogenarian Chadwick but by Spalding's supporters, chums, business acquaintances and even an employee – among them two senators and two former National League presidents as well as Al Reach, the owner of the Philadelphia Phillies and a fellow sports goods manufacturer, who in response to the Duke of Wellington's alleged assertion that the Battle of Waterloo had been won on the playing fields of Eton (the role of the playing fields of Prussia was presumably overlooked), insisted that the Spanish-American War of 1898 had been won through American training at baseball.[110] Carroll likened it to "sending the mice to investigate the curious disappearance of the cheese".[111]

Drawing on the reminiscences and unsubstantiated claims of other early players, the report patriotically ignored the two other games completely. Ward asserted that baseball descended from "cat-ball" – an English invention had he but known it. In Spalding's view, sundry variations of cat-ball, with its four-base infield, bred town ball and thence baseball, though cat-ball and rounders, recollected Henry Sargent – who had played a Massachusetts mix, round-ball – were in fact indistinguishable.[112] In his 2008 biography of Chadwick, Andrew J. Schiff quotes the dynamic Devonian thus: "There is no need of presenting any arguments in the case, as the connection between rounders and baseball is too plain to be mistaken."

"Never mind the fact that Doubleday had never discussed the sport he had supposedly invented in any of his diaries," reasoned David H. Martinez in *The Book of Baseball Literacy*. "Spalding wanted an American genesis, and he got one."[113] What would prove even harder for Spalding to stomach was the claim, emanating from Canada, that the first recorded account of a baseball game there concerned one that took place in Beechville, Ontario, in 1838 (though this did not come to light until 1886, when a detailed letter by Dr Adam E. Ford appeared in the publication *Sporting Life*).

In their acclaimed book *Diamonds in the Rough: The Untold History of Baseball*, Joel Voss and John Bowman suggest why such a myth should have exerted so seemingly unshakeable a grip on American imaginations:

> *One of the most endearing qualities of baseball is its role in human imagination. Very few of a club's most devoted fans ever*

get to attend even one tenth of its games, which means that for most people, baseball is experienced primarily in the newspapers, through writers' interpretations; on the radio, which leaves everything to the imagination; or on television, which creates its own reality. As such a product of the imagination, baseball very easily takes on the attributes of a mythological system, and as Civil War historian Bruce Catton has pointed out, baseball's legends "are, in some ways, the most enduring part of the game. Baseball has even more of them than the Civil War, and its fans prize them highly." In the United States, which as a nation is largely defined by its lack of any sense of history or tradition, the citizens turn to myths for continuity, and to sports for myths. Baseball is not only America's oldest popular team sport, but one of the oldest institutions in American society.[114]

"The fundamental reason for the popularity of the game," reinforced Allen Sangree in *The New York World* in 1907, "is the fact that it is a national safety valve… [A] young, ambitious and growing nation needs to 'let off steam'. Baseball… serves the same purpose as a revolution in Central America or a thunderstorm on a hot day… A tonic, an exercise, baseball is second only to Death as a leveller. So long as it remains our national game, America will abide no monarchy, and anarchy will be too slow."[115]

To the death (II)

Some sports have endured far longer than envisaged. Witness the hammer throw. After all, whirling around like some amphetamine-powered dervish to propel a cast-iron ball attached to a chain and handle hardly scores too many points for everyday usefulness or inspiring athleticism. Then there are those jolly ancient pastimes that continue to lurk and flourish beneath the spotlight despite being largely – and justly – illegal, such as cock-fighting and dog-fighting. Some persist despite the blatant and perennial potential for fatalities: boxing, steeple-chase races, motorsports. Attempts to ban the first have been far from uncommon – indeed, Sweden imposed one in 1969, and

Norway followed in 1982, though the former would recant four decades later. Perhaps the most mysterious survivors are the Isle of Man Tourist Trophy and Manx Grand Prix.

The TT was first run on the dauntingly undulating course in 1907, the start of a surge in motorsport that saw the Monte Carlo Rally and the Indianapolis 500 both line up on the grid in 1911. The annual Manx bloodbath (there seems no more apposite term) became even more arduous four years later when, in what Arlott portrayed as "the most significant development" in the history of motor-cycling (albeit in 1976), riders were obliged to contend with a stiff new climb: Victor Sturridge became the first fatality – the first Manxman, in fact, to be killed by an automobile. By the end of the 2011 race, the unforgiving circuit had claimed nearly 250 more victims, including three during unofficial testing, five race officials and even two riders on the parade lap. That just two spectators and one bystander had lost their lives was a medium-sized miracle.

"What drives men and women to do something as dangerous as the [TT]?" wondered Rick Broadbent. He solicited an aptly chilling insight from Guy Martin, "a lupine, tea-drinking maverick", in the wake of the crash that nearly killed him: "If it was dead safe I wouldn't do it. And I do get off on the pain. I look back on my crash and yeah, it did hurt. I had to dig my teeth out of my nose. My chest was caving in and they put this drain in, threaded it through so you could feel it moving around your innards. Hey, hey. That's life." It was, as he put it, "that near-death thing".[116] Those sentiments inspired Broadbent to write a book, *That Near-Death Thing: Inside the TT, the World's Most Dangerous Race*. The story of the Dunlop clan loomed large. In 2000, Joey Dunlop was killed while racing in Estonia; eight years later, brother Robert died practising for an event in Northern Ireland. Next day came the wake. The day after that, Michael, Robert's son, left the house and his father's corpse, and got back on his bike. "Some dickhead in a suit said I wasn't mentally right," he recalled. "I said I'd never been mentally right." He won the race.[117]

Martin submitted his own, arguably rational, explanation. "It's so fast and long, the thick edge of 200mph, sucking rabbits out of hedges. I saw a guy about my age, in a people carrier, kids in the back, steam coming out the engine, wife giving him all that. What's he do at the weekend? Mow the grass? Wash the car? How can I explain something like this to someone like that? It's just not in his DNA."[118]

The American version

In 1827, a tradition known as "Bloody Mondays" began to flower among the bloom of American privilege at Harvard University, pitting freshmen against sophomores. The style of play, such as it was, was likened to a mêlée: scores of young men pushing and shoving and grappling to manoeuvre a ball across a field. Injuries and even death were not uncommon, persuading Yale to ban all types of football in 1860; Harvard followed the next year. Not that that put a stop to Bloody Monday.

"'Bloody Monday' night was celebrated at Harvard tonight with a fierce rush between the freshmen and the sophomores," reported the *New York Times* in October 1903. There was also "a score of damaging fights between upper and lower classmen, a bombardment with eggs of a whole line of Harvard Square store windows, and the arrest of two students, who were held on $100 bail to await trial for riotous conduct tomorrow morning. Despite the superior forces of the freshmen, the rush was led by the sophomores, who tore up things generally. Clothes were torn in shreds from the backs of the contestants, black eyes and bruises were seen everywhere, and every one received a liberal smudge of mother earth, which was worked into a fine paste under a thousand feet."[119] What better metaphor for the organised, military-style chaos of North America's very own brand of football?

Even more than baseball, this similarly canny spin on a well-spun theme is seen as the personification of American sporting exceptionalism. Not for its makers a nationalist-fired self-determinism predicated on fantasy. Despite owing an even more blatant debt to established games (rugby most palpably), those who concocted the national football code were clear-minded in their resolve to distance the game from its forbears through ingenuity. If nothing else, the invention of the forward pass made the quarterback the single most influential onfield position in team sport, and hence at once the most coveted and most invidious. For every successful "Hail Mary", for every fourth down converted with 10 to go, a world of pain awaits.

What is constantly cited as the first intercollegiate game of "American football" – Rutgers 6 Princeton 4 on 6 November 1869 in New Jersey – was actually, to all intents and purposes, a soccer match. Played under modified London Football Association rules – players could only kick the ball, each score was a goal – the chief difference was the presence of 25 men per side. The game spread to other Ivy League institutions but Harvard took exception, favouring running with the ball and preferring to adapt the rules of rugby. This led to a pair of contests against Montreal's McGill University which, in due course, saw Harvard's preference win the day. The meeting to standardise regulations, known as the Massasoit Convention, produced a code firmly based on the one adopted by the RFU. The key mover was a former Yale student, Walter Camp, whose changes were gradually absorbed: establishing the line of scrimmage; awarding six points for a touchdown and three points for a field goal; slashing participants to 11 a side.

In their brief but fascinating history of sport in Pennsylvania, Jeff Silverman and Charles Hardy III of West Chester University address the new sport's intrinsic appeal:

> *The collegians added structure, discipline, and regimentation to the controlled mayhem they had inherited, as the game came to reflect America's emerging industrial economy and society. Like baseball, the game fostered competition and teamwork, two essential qualities advanced by industrial capitalism. But in football, players divided into skilled and unskilled positions, the game was run by clock, and each play, designed to drive deeper*

into the opponent's territory, was like a new work shift. Fearful
that the modern world was softening American manhood,
middle-class and elite Americans embraced football's aggressive
nature and the courage and muscular vitality it required.[120]

Rugby's influence cannot be underestimated, as the Professional
Football Researchers Association readily concedes. Yet in one
crucial respect the junior code was ahead of the game, as the
two Bobs, Braunwart and Carroll, elaborate in *The Journey
to Camp: The Origins of American Football to 1889*. "In the fall
of 1876, Yale was in the throes of learning a new game. The
beating they'd been handed by Harvard the year before still
smarted, and [they] were determined to see it didn't happen
again. No more halfway, concessionary rules! Yale planned on
playing straight rugby and knocking the hell out of Harvard.
Rugby was the new deal at Princeton, too. In fact, the Tigers
had much to do with the nearly overnight conversion to rugby
all across New England. W. Earle Dodge and Jotham Potter, the
pair of Princetonians who watched Harvard lick Yale in 1875,
had succeeded in selling the rugby game to their own campus,
a feat only slightly inferior to selling refrigerators to Eskimos.
As Princeton went, so should everybody else, figured Messrs.
Dodge and Potter. They fired off invitations to Harvard, Yale,
and Columbia, inviting them to Springfield, Massachusetts, so
they could all sit down and decide to play the game the way
Princeton wanted to."[121]

On 23 November 1876, a brace of representatives from each
school convened at Massasoit House: Yale favoured 11 per side
– a complement picked up from the even posher Eton College
in 1873 – but otherwise disputes were minimal and the RFU
code was filched more or less verbatim. The one prolonged
argument involved touchdowns: again echoing the RFU line,
Columbia and Yale objected to counting them; Princeton and
Harvard disagreed, the latter with especially good reason. Just
five days earlier, shortly before taking on Yale, Harvard had
assented to a request to play 11-a-side and ignore touchdowns,

whereupon Harvard achieved three but missed all the ensuing goal attempts; Yale's lone successful kick thus proved decisive. Not unnaturally, this hardened Harvard hearts, leading to a compromise: matches would henceforth be decided by "a majority of touchdowns". A goal would equate to four touchdowns, but in the case of a tie, "a goal kicked from a touchdown shall take precedence over four touchdowns".[122]

The Massasoit Convention saw Princeton, Harvard, and Columbia form the Intercollegiate Football Association; Yale backed off for a couple of years, striking individual agreements with opponents to play 11-a-side and/or ignore touchdowns, but relented in 1879. However, echoing the way soccer transcended its public school gestation and found enthusiastic disciples in the industrial communities of Lancashire and Yorkshire, professional gridiron, as we shall see, was rooted in the mining communities of western Pennsylvania and in Ohio, described by Chris Willis in his oral history of early professional football in the state, *Old Leather*, as "the geographical centre of professional football".[123] Collegiate sports continued to grip the attention of white-collar enthusiasts in the East, the businessmen and lawyers of New York and Boston; those blue-collared sorts more accustomed to dirtying their hands (in the most literal sense) desired something a mite more... rugged.

The lone exception

In terms of its roots, it can be argued that basketball offers us the prime T-bone case of American sporting exceptionalism. Here, after all, is the only one of the nation's major sports that can confidently rebut all charges of plagiarism, being utterly free of British roots. That its inventor, Dr James Naismith, hailed from Scottish stock and spent his youth in Canada hardly dilutes the sense of a fully-fledged in-house creation – and a weatherproof one to boot. As even those of us who find that the incessant click of the scoreboard militates against enjoyment will happily rejoice, Naismith's brainchild, however unintentionally, has done more than any other sector of the competitive arts to encourage

African-Americans to express themselves, and be suitably appreciated, by *all* races.

At the time of his eureka moment, Naismith, then 30, was a clergyman working as a PE instructor at the School for Christian Workers in Springfield, Massachusetts – now home to the NBA Hall of Fame. While studying at McGill University in Montreal he was twice voted the college's best all-round athlete, playing rugby, soccer and lacrosse in addition to running for the track team. A proponent of muscular Christianity, he is understood to have enrolled on a course in Springfield with the aim of becoming a physical director, and wound up staying on for the 1890-91 academic year as an instructor, teaching boxing, canoeing, swimming and wrestling. Had he followed the usual path and instead relocated to a local YMCA as physical director, notes Robert W. Peterson in *Cages To Jumpshots: Pro Basketball's Early Years*, "there might be no basketball today".[124]

Instead, it was conceived while Naismith was labouring forlornly with a class of general secretaries (or, as he put it, "incorrigibles"). Growing ever more disheartened as game after game failed to engage the students – who spurned them as either too rough or too tame – and with one day to go before he was due to report to the faculty on how the class was progressing, he approached the conundrum systematically. If he was going to manufacture a new, more attractive game, to stimulate young minds and bodies, there would have to be, he decided, certain prerequisites, first and foremost a ball. After all, every popular team sport had one. But should it be big or small? Since the latter would necessitate equipment – a bat, a racquet, a stick, a club – and his aim was simplicity, big it was.

"Naismith believed that the most interesting game in those days was rugby, which was gradually evolving into American football," relates Peterson. But you couldn't very well play it in a gym, could you? So if you couldn't run with the ball, Naismith concluded, why not pass it? His memory of that eureka moment was burned into his frontal lobe: "I can still recall how I snapped my fingers and shouted, 'I've got it!'"[125]

Ah, but how would he score it? Abhorring the notion of rough stuff in the gym, his first move was to resist the temptation to emulate popular contact sports and eschew ground-level goals. Peterson picks up the thread: "He thought back to his Canadian boyhood and the game of Duck the Rock and remembered that the most effective way of knocking off the duck was to throw one's own rock in an arc so that it would not go far if it missed the guard's rock. So, he reasoned, if the goal in his new game were horizontal, finesse rather than force would be desirable. Furthermore, if the goal were above the players' heads, the opponents could not mass around the goal to prevent a score. James Naismith went to bed that night with an untroubled heart for the first time in two weeks."[126] The following morning he went to the school janitor and requested two boxes approximately 18 inches square. The janitor couldn't oblige, but he did have a couple of old peach baskets in a storeroom. "Thus," chuckles Peterson, "did the game miss being called boxball."

Before the first game, Naismith posted 13 rules on a bulletin board and prepared the gym by nailing two baskets to balconies on either end of a court. "I busied myself arranging the apparatus all the time watching the boys as they arrived to observe their attitude that day," he wrote in his diary, one of a slew of documents and mementoes his grand-daughter, Helen Carpenter, found in her basement in 2006, among them a type-written page of regulations. "I felt this was a crucial moment in my life as it meant success or failure of my attempt to hold the interest of the class and devise a new game."[127]

The exact date of the game, Peterson concedes, remains unknown, but it seems likely that it was in December 1891: "By the time the school's Christmas break began, the secretaries were hooked on the new game and many apparently introduced it in YMCAs back home during their vacation."[128] When they returned, Frank Mahan, the most vocal of the incorrigibles, who had originally pooh-poohed the new game, proposed that it be named "Naismith ball". The honoree was tickled: "I laughed and told him that I thought that name would kill any game." To which Mahan, he said, replied: "Why not call it basketball?"[129]

The following year, Senda Berenson, a physical education instructor at nearby Smith College, having read an article on basketball, adapted it for her female students, prioritising greater gentility. Cue netball.

British rejectionism

Yet another expression of sporting exceptionalism lies in the resolution of these games. The draw has no place in the US sporting lexicon, and ties, the equivalent, are exceedingly rare. Professional baseball is steeped in the addition of extra innings; overtime was introduced to basketball once leagues began to be formed, initially as sudden death tie-breaks and, from the 1960s, as a specified period; overtime came to the gridiron in 1940 for divisional tie-break games, six years later for championship games, in 1958 for the postseason and in 1974 for the regular season; ice hockey followed suit in 1983.

But if we find fault with American exceptionalism, what of British rejectionism? While all four pre-eminent North American sports are played across the UK, it would be stretching a point to suggest they have been embraced, with only ice hockey enjoying prolonged spells of professional prosperity.

In 1908, Britain became a founder member of the International Ice Hockey Federation, and the game was the most popular indoor spectator sport there either side of the Second World War (1935-1954), albeit utterly dominated by Canadian imports destined for the NHL. In 1936, to widespread astonishment, Great Britain won the triple crown of Olympic, World and European titles, but the British National League, formed in 1954 as a merger of the English and Scottish leagues, was beset by the double-whammy of falling gates and rising wages, collapsing in 1960. The modern revival began with the formation of the English Ice Hockey Association in 1982, accompanied by unprecedented rink-building; today, with 10 teams competing in the Elite Ice Hockey League, it claims to be Britain's third-largest winter spectator sport, its prizes commemorating a more lustrous past. Five teams compete in the Erhardt Conference, named after Carl Erhardt, who captained Great Britain to that lone and distant Olympic gold; five more compete in the Gardiner Conference, named in honour of Charlie Gardiner, the Edinburgh-born netminder who captained the Chicago Blackhawks to the Stanley Cup in 1934.[130]

Baseball gained traction, too. In 1890, it was introduced to the UK by Albert Spalding and Francis Ley, who had returned full of enthusiasm to his native Derby from a Stateside trip. Derby County Baseball Club easily won the inaugural National Baseball League that year but were immediately forced to drop out following complaints about the number of American players on their roster. The club remained a going concern long enough for Derby County FC's home ground to be named The Baseball Ground in 1895. The game peaked in the 1930s, popular enough for clubs to share grounds with their footballing counterparts and attract five-figure crowds; Britain, furthermore, actually won the inaugural World Cup in 1938, stunning their US opponents in what was, admittedly, a strictly amateur, two-team event. A professional league, however, remains a step too far.

Inevitably, given its proximity to rugby, American football found the fewest converts. The British American Football League lasted from 1998 to 2010; staffed mainly by the NFL's so-called developmental players, the London (later England) Monarchs were one of three European teams in the inaugural World League of American Football but managed just five seasons (1991-92 and 1995-97) and just one in the revamped NFL Europe (born 1998, died 2007). Yet NFL teams have often played to sold-out crowds in London. Indeed as I write, there are ongoing talks about an English franchise.

Basketball crossed the pond far more speedily. In 1892, having discovered the game in Canada, C. J. Proctor, president of Liverpool's Birkenhead YMCA, tried to enthuse his young members; two years later, Mel Rideout, who had played in that trailblazing game in Springfield, sought to spread the word at a YMCA convention; but although hoops and baskets found favour in the Birkenhead area, it was not until 1911 that the game was taken up elsewhere, in Birmingham. A six-team national league began in 1939 whereupon war intervened, but although US forces exerted a protracted influence, it was not until 1987 that the British Basketball League was born. It may, nonetheless, be a sign of things to come that London staged the first NBA regular-season game in Europe, a brace of sold-out contests in 2011 between the Toronto Raptors and New Jersey Nets at the O2 Centre. Here, more than the other imports, it is easy to envisage growth among a generation captivated by TV coverage of the NBA.

Pupils turned masters

Britain would not rule the sporting world for long. Granted, it was an Anglo-Scot in Brazil, Charles Miller, and an Englishman in Vienna, Jimmy Hogan, who did much of the teaching, but football's technical development, for example, owed much to the way the waning Austro-Hungarian empire responded. Indeed, two of England's first three defeats at international level by non-British opposition would come at the hands of Austria (Vienna 1936) and Hungary (Wembley 1953). As Huw Richards observed in *The Cambridge Companion to Football*:

> *What made the great cities of the late Austro-Hungarian empire – Vienna, Budapest and Prague – so receptive to football is as much a matter for anthropologists as historians of sport. While a stream of British teams visited from the 1890s onward, these would-be missionaries were not heading into a vacuum. They needed aspirant natives to issue invitations and provide opposition. The Empire might have looked a palsied relic, but its great cities were places of intellectual and economic vigour. Vienna was host to the talents of Arnold Schoenberg and Sigmund Freud and a political culture that would generate the interwar phenomenon of Red Vienna. Budapest, one of the fastest-growing cities of the second half of the nineteenth century, was home to the continent's first underground railway, Béla Bartók*

*and, in 1919, a short-lived experiment with Communist govern-
ment. Prague had two satirical literary giants, Franz Kafka and
Jaroslav Hasek, both born in the same year.*[131]

In fact, while the First World War would spell the end of the
Austro-Hungarian empire, the ensuing trauma has been cited
as a spur for football in Budapest and Vienna, home – along
with Prague – to the Mitropa Cup, Europe's first major continental club tournament. In 1914 Austria had boasted 14,000
registered players; by 1921 there were 37,000, the majority in
Vienna. Crowds followed suit. In 1914, 24,000 saw Austria play
Hungary; eight years later the attendance was 65,000. "More
than a pastime for boys, football became an export product for
these capitals without hinterlands," wrote Pierre Lanfranchi.
"The endemic economic crises which characterised the nations
of Central Europe in the twenties, the weakness of the markets
and the difficulties which these 'new little nations' encountered
on the international scene, further accentuated the importance
to them of football."[132] In 1924, the same year professionalism
officially came to Austria and Hungary, the *Neues Wiener Journal*
proclaimed Vienna the "football capital of the European continent". This journalistic effusion, warrants Richards, was "an
unmistakeable foretaste of the most vital of modern city-state
sporting cultures, Australian football in Melbourne". Where
else, wondered the journal, "can you see at least 40–50,000 spectators gather Sunday after Sunday at all the sports stadiums, rain
or shine? Where else are the majority of the population so interested in the results of games that in the evening you can hear
almost every other person talking about the result of the league
matches and the clubs' prospects in the coming games?"[133]

The pupils had long been biting back elsewhere. Just as
Scotland's footballers took no time establishing the upper hand
in their annual fixture against the reviled Sassenachs, winning
11 and losing just two of the first 16, and just as Wales beat
England's finest on a rugby union field 10 times between 1899 and
1909 without suffering a single reverse (the Scots enjoyed an 8-2

advantage over the same span), so the purported masters quickly found that playing games with colonials, too, would not be an uninterrupted showcase for English command and discipline.

In cricket, Australia soon established Ashes parity, moved ahead in overall victories in 1921 and built a comfortable statistical superiority that persists to this day. In rugby union, by the early 20th century, the British Lions had lost Test series in New Zealand and South Africa; thereafter, defeat was the bruising norm. Britain won four of the first six Davis Cups (1903-06) but as the opposition expanded beyond the US so fortunes declined: as of 2012, 12 nations had won the trophy since 1936 but not the home of lawn tennis. Indeed, as has often been stated in not so many words, while the global spread of sport can be attributed to the English fervour for playing games with those from their own class, the principal function of international sport has really only ever been about bashing the Poms.

Final score

"From the British Isles, modern sports went forth to conquer the world," declared Allen Guttmann, Emeritus Professor of English and American Studies at Amherst College and author of *Games and Empires: Modern Sports and Cultural Imperialism.* But after World War Two the baton changed hands and the United States became "the primary agents in the diffusion" of modern sport.[134]

The development of spectator sport can indeed be seen, primarily, as a struggle between one ex-Empire and one exceedingly modern if no less tyrannical one. Come the 1950s, pink expanses no longer proliferated on the global map; by then, while pursuing a political policy of isolation and exceptionalism, and valiantly keeping its distance from international team competition whenever possible, the US had become the epicentre of the sporting universe. If you boxed, played gridiron, baseball, basketball, golf, ice hockey or tennis, your holy grail was New York, Chicago or Pittsburgh, Madison Square Garden, Yankee Stadium or Augusta National. Old world and new had both exported sport, but whereas the British missionaries were motivated in part to find opponents worthy of humbling on the field, their imperial successors were keener on replenishing the till. As resoundingly successful as it has been in becoming sport's most consumed multinational product, the Premier League is merely one of a number of major European football competitions vying for the services of the finest foot artistes; on the other hand, there is room for only one set of presiding sporting acronyms, one NBA, NFL, NHL or MLB; one highest bidder.

The NFL's European league might have been shortlived but, as we have seen, the home of afternoon tea and bath buns has hosted NFL and NBA games; since 1999, MLB campaigns have opened in Australia, Japan, Mexico and Puerto Rico. County cricket recently started kicking off its season in Dubai, and there has been talk of combatting Britain's recent spate of vile springs by playing more such fixtures overseas (the reaction among club members could in no way be described as keen). On the other hand, a proposal that each Premier League club play a 39th match in foreign climes received brutally short shrift. It was a measure of how much the Indian Premier League has learnt from North American sports that, when the national elections precluded the 2009 edition from being held in India, the switch to South Africa was a roaring success.

* * *

If Imperialist Britons gave spectator sport life, meaning and order, Imperialist Americans introduced innovation, business savvy and electricity. Where Britons were evangelists, Americans laid on what became a never-ending party, hired the finest caterers known to man and invited the entire world. That refusal to follow the British-led pack can be viewed as evidence of both a search for identity and what Oliver Stone likes to call his country's "capacity for self-love".[135] All the same, the planet's most avidly followed single-discipline events are the FIFA World Cup, the UEFA Champions League and the ICC World Cup; Formula 1 is a bigger televisual draw than NASCAR.

As for tomorrow, sheer population size points unerringly to China and India as the most influential spheres. Indeed, the latter's gusto has already ensured, and perhaps even insured, the medium-term future of that most overtly anachronistic of spectator sports, cricket. According to *The Cricketer* magazine's "Rich List", six of 2012's eight highest-earners were Indian.[136]

Come the following year, far more unexpectedly, cricket was part of the school curriculum not only in France but also, in a major push to embrace *shen shi yun dong* ("the noble game" was introduced by the Asian Cricket Council in 2005), nine Chinese provinces. Game, set and match to the Limeys? Time and fashion will tell.

3 Odds and Sods: Sport and Gambling

It is two years to the day since Tony, my best friend, died. The post mortem blamed a weak heart but missed the shadowy presence in the background that was also responsible. Gambling. By the end, he had no money left, the strain of wishing to repay the handouts from his friends more intolerable than any pain. His life force seemed to vanish in those last days... [His] desperation towards the end was harrowing, doubling up to get out of the mess. The vicious circularity of the gambling addiction is like a stranglehold, cutting off oxygen even as it offers false hope. Sport is not just one of the portals into gambling, it is also one of its most lucrative markets.

Matthew Syed was not referring exclusively to the ancient art of wagering when he typed those angrily mournful words. He also fixed both barrels on the prime economic source of all that Olympic medaling and national joy during the summer of 2012 – the National Lottery. "The Olympics were a cultural blessing in part because they reacquainted us with an authentic notion of success. Medal-winners looked into the camera and shared a story of dedication, years of hard work, and the sacrifice of parents and coaches... an empowering metaphor for any young person wondering how to fulfil their potential... If you want to get something out of your life, you need to put something in. The Lottery connives at a rather different message. It silently promotes the idea of getting rich quick, not on the basis of effort, merit or dedication, but as a consequence of a mindless, utterly capricious draw. It doesn't even have the virtue possessed by sports gambling that knowledge and information can increase your odds of success."[1]

Not all that long ago, British bookmakers operated under the eminently respectable guise of "turf accountants". It is some small consolation for the suffering they facilitate that they no longer have the gall to do so. In 2012, there were four times as many betting shops and fixed-odds betting terminals in the 50 English constituencies with the highest unemployment levels than in the 50 at the other end of the spectrum (the respective figures were 1,251 and 4,454 to 287 and 1,045). Poor people "put getting rich down to luck and think they can take a gamble," claimed John Redwood, Conservative MP for Wokingham in Berkshire, home to three betting shops. "It's a business model which sucks money from the poorest communities," lamented Diane Abbott, Labour MP for Hackney North and Stoke Newington, where almost £200m, she said, had been spent on betting that year.[2] On average, the gambling machines reaped a profit of £900 per week, driving bookmakers to bypass restrictions (four per shop) by opening more branches in poorer areas, where rents, inevitably, were lower.

In that same year, 855 complaints were made to the Advertising Standards Authority about 357 adverts for gambling seen, heard or read, up from 148 complaints in 2011. Not that these were exclusively targeted at William Hill, Paddy Power or those mushrooming online poker sites. An ad for one of the more family-friendly bets, the Health Lottery, "Mortgage? What mortgage", was accused by the ASA of irresponsibility because of the implicit assertion that playing the lottery is "a way of solving financial concerns or achieving financial security".

"We are the only country in the English-speaking world that does not require a helpline number on adverts for gambling," said Anthony Jennens, chief executive of the charity GamCare. Can we be the slightest bit surprised that, over those 12 months, according to data collected by H2 Gambling Capital, gamblers in Britain collectively lost the unseemly sum of £9.5 billion?[3] So heavy were the losses suffered by online gamblers, in 2013, by way of further affirmation, the value of each of the top 10 British internet betting magnates in the *Sunday Times* Rich List exceeded £100 million, with the Coates family behind Bet365 boasting an estimated combined wealth of £925m.[4] Sport's complicity in all this was everywhere, from Paddy Power outlets at Royal Ascot to the BetFair blimp hovering overhead at Lord's and football's SkyBet League: a perpetual thumbs-up for the fun of the flutter.

* * *

Gambling courses through the arteries of spectator sport. In many respects, it can be seen as driving it, plainly so in horse racing and boxing but also cricket, where codification came about as a means of settling betting disputes, and, long before that, real tennis. On 22 October 1532, records John Arlott, Henry VIII paid out the fairly princely sum of 46 pounds, 13 shillings and fourpence to settle wagers with two opponents.[5] Not that the participants were alone in staking bets; so did spectators. In betting on individual points, they anticipated spot-fixing.

The shadow cast by gambling is long, bleak and unending. In *The Great Gatsby*, F. Scott Fitzgerald utilised the 1920 "Black Sox" scandal as a metaphor for his nation's decay; it is with some admiration, indeed, that Jay Gatsby introduces the shady Meyer Wolfsheim to Nick Carraway as "the man who fixed the World Series back in 1919". This staggers Nick. "It never occurred to me," he reflects, "that one man could start to play with the faith of fifty million people." Is there any gloomier glory than Bangladesh's greatest sporting feat, victory over Pakistan at the 1999 ICC World Cup, continuing as it does to be shrouded in allegations of match-fixing at worst, complicity at best, none remotely proven? Is there any uglier juxtaposition than that between Sky Sports' exemplary and highly ethical coverage of cricket and those inter-over adverts informing viewers that "It matters more when there's money on it"?

Resolving outcomes in advance may be entirely acceptable to novelists, playwrights, scriptwriters and musicians, but without uncertainty, spectator sport is meaningless and fraudulent. The final result should always, in the words of Mike Brearley, probably the brainiest man ever to captain an international cricket team, be "morally appropriate". That's why match-fixing is perceived in some quarters as the most grievous of all sporting sins. Shortly before Christmas 2013, an email popped into my inbox from the International Cricket Council headlined "ICC confirms investigation into former New Zealand cricketers". Usain Bolt couldn't have beaten it to the recycle bin.

In his captivating book *Gambling*, Mike Atherton, the insightful former England cricket captain turned award-winning sportswriter, describes match-fixing as "the natural and inevitable consequence of the commercialisation of gambling, the professionalisation of sport and human nature."[6] The first recorded instance was in 388 BC, when Thessaly's Eupolus bribed three boxers to throw fights against him. The fines meted out to subsequent miscreants were used to fund statues with anti-corruption inscriptions such as "You win at Olympia with the speed of your feet and the strength of your body, not with money."[7]

It was on his travels during the expansion of the Roman Empire, relates Atherton, that Tacitus observed "the earliest forms of the concept of chance" in the ancient process of divination followed by tribes in Germany, who arrived at collective decisions by drawing lots. And what better vehicle to profit from chance than the purported uncertainty of a sporting contest? In 2011, the IOC president, Jacques Rogge, acknowledged that performance-enhancing drugs had a partner-in-crime. "We have made doping a top priority, now there is a new danger coming up that almost all countries have been affected by and that is corruption, match-fixing and illegal gambling," Rogge asserted while in Tokyo for the 100th anniversary of the Japanese Olympic Committee. Recent non-footballing exhibits included the national shame that followed the arrest in Japan of 25 sumo wrestlers who had been complicit in voluntary defeats. "This is the new fight we have to confront. Today, you can't open up a newspaper without finding examples of this so we have to fight against it and this has to be waged by sports movements together with traditional and state authorities."[8] While this represented a welcome and considerable step for sportingkind, it was also an exceedingly unpunctual one.

* * *

This, though, is both a social and a sporting problem. A police wire-tap that enmeshed some of Turkey's most powerful in 2012 led to cumulative sentences totalling more than 42 years being handed down to 93 officials, players and agents for match-fixing, bribery, extortion and membership of a crime syndicate. The extent of the investigation, perhaps even more disconcertingly, was just 17 games, of which 13 were proven to be corrupt. True, there was no evidence of illegal betting, but the links established to organised crime bosses made it difficult to credit that gambling played no part. "Once you find out everything is set up," reasoned Yusuf Reha Alp, a member of the Turkish Football Federation's disciplinary committee, "there is no point in watching it."[9] A year on, nonetheless, Western politicians, the IOC and UEFA alike were all still courting Istanbul; having lost out to Japan as Olympic hosts for 2020, the city may still stage the final of football's European Championships that year.

* * *

There comes a time in boxing when the robberies, controversy, call it what you may, stop being a surprise... it merely becomes a matter of measuring the size of the outrage.[10]

That Ron Lewis should have expressed those sentiments in 2012 – Timothy Bradley's split-decision points "victory" in Las Vegas over the planet's foremost pugilist, Manny Pacquiao, had left him virtually speechless – demonstrates how much those afflicted with a sporting passion can delude themselves. Of all the spectator sports, the history of boxing has been the one most readily linked to the bent and the crooked. Temptation is always that much harder to resist when there are only two competitors.

As the most iconic of the weight divisions, world heavyweight bouts have attracted no end of conspiracy theories, albeit none proven. In 1915, to cite one of the most popular, Jack Johnson's knockout by Jess Willard was seen by the *Sioux City Journal* as a case of man accepting his own mortality: "There is much discussion tonight, and probably will be for a long time, among the followers of the fighting game as to whether Johnson was really knocked out. In the sense of being smashed into unconscious-ness… opinion is that Johnson expected and knew that there was no hope of winning; so when knocked down he chose to take the count rather than rise and stand further punishment."[11] Others tended to believe Johnson's own explanation: he had done the gamblers' bidding. Look at how he had had the presence of mind, as he lay on the canvas, to shield his eyes from the sun.

Even if a tenth of the suspect bouts were bent, the *Encyclopedia Britannica* would still have to give over a fair chunk of its volumes to cover them. Plucking examples from that prickly tree serves little purpose.

"Like dancing without sex"

Betting, as Atherton rightly testifies, has always been the "*raison d'etre*" of horse racing. "A minority might argue that they go racing to pay homage to the thoroughbred at its most refined, that rare mixture of stamina, speed, class and courage which defines the great horses; some might even say that they go to marvel at the bravery of the jockeys as they go hurtling towards a six-foot fence. A minority might say all that. The majority come to bet. In any case, it's a whole lot more fun to have a financial interest. As Simon Barnes noted, 'Racing without betting is like dancing without sex.'"[12]

In the early 18th century, before cricket laid out the first formal set of standardised rules for spectator sport, match-specific Articles of Agreement would often be drawn up for the bigger contests to accelerate the settlement of disputed wagers. One such, for a 1727 encounter between the Duke of Richmond's XI and Mr. A. Brodrick's XI, stipulated that "twelve gamesters shall play on either side; that each match should be for twelve guineas of each side". It also stated: "'Tis lawful for the Duke of Richmond to choose any Gamesters who have played in either of his Grace's last two matches with Sir William Gage; and 'tis lawful for Mr. Brodrick to choose any Gamesters within three miles of Pepperhowe." In 1744, the year the game's laws came into force, the *Morning Chronicle* railed about the "excessive gaming and public dissipation" and that "cricket matches are now degenerated into business of importance".[13]

If you wanted to place a bet at Lord's after it opened for business in the early 19th century, all you had to do was head for William Crockford and John Gully, who traded under the pavilion. In 1823, Mary Russell Mitford could still be justified in expressing her scorn for men who "make the noble game of cricket an affair of bettings and hedgings and, maybe, of cheatings."[14] By then, though, the game had already endured its first match-fixing crisis.

Even the upper echelons of the upper crust were not above a spot of scriptwriting. Witness that duel between the Duke of Wellington and the Earl of Winchilsea at Battersea Fields in 1829. As the King's College archive relates:

> *Wellington raised his pistol and fired on the command. Accounts differ as to whether Wellington came close to killing his rival. The Duke declared that he deliberately shot wide when Winchilsea remained motionless; other contemporary reports, perhaps more sympathetic to Winchilsea and anxious to prevent Wellington claiming the moral high ground, claimed that the ball tore through the Earl's lapel and that he had aimed to kill. Whether an intentional delay on the part of the Duke or the result of his being a notoriously poor shot, Winchilsea remained standing with his arm by his side.*
>
> *Quite deliberately, he then raised it vertically and discharged the pistol harmlessly above his own head – a gesture of submission known in the duelling world as delopement. A witness describes how the Earl wore a pensive expression on his face and was "steady and fearless" in receiving the Duke's fire without*

moving, but having fired his pistol he smiled, "as if to say, 'Now you see I am not quite so bad as you thought me.'"

What is almost certain is that Winchilsea and Falmouth had both agreed on their course of action beforehand, a fact evidenced by their prior drafting of a written apology that Falmouth now presented to Wellington and Hardinge.[15]

The fine art of horseplay

Some gamblers go in with eyes wide shut. In the 1930s, Dorothy Paget, an erratic sleeper better known as the profoundly blue-blooded aristocrat and highly eccentric owner of the five-time Cheltenham Gold Cup winner Golden Miller, was allowed by bookies to ring up at night and bet on races run hours earlier – she usually got it wrong and ultimately lost around £3m; mind you, given that she often bet in the millions, this was no great hardship.[16] Others leave less to chance.

Nobbling, ensuring that a horse cannot win, is one of the most time-dishonoured of the competitive arts' dark sciences, as Jamie Reid was merely the latest to relate in *Doped*, the 2013 William Hill Sports Book of the Year, a ripping, gripping yarn telling the grimy, unsavoury tale of an English doping ring in the 1960s that targeted favourites, doped them and bet against them. As noted by the perceptive racing writer John Cobb: "There is no do-it-yourself manual, complete with free syringe, circulating in underworld circles to help the would-be doper, but then stopping a racehorse from running its fastest is easy. A trainer has a hundred ways to prevent his horse from winning and they are all pretty simple, ranging from fitting its shoes too tight or giving it a belly-filling bucket of water, but more usually running it on firm ground when it needs soft, on a left-hand track when it prefers to race right-handed, or just letting it take part when it is too fat and unfit to do itself justice."[17]

Sometimes, related Cobb, the aim is to deceive the official handicapper and the betting public about the horse's quality, "saving it for a day when it has a lighter weight to carry and the money is down". A different path must be pursued by the dopers, who have a different and even more disreputable aim in mind. "The doper is aiming either to slow a horse down so that he can back others in the race or, if he is a bookmaker, so that he can take bets on the doped horse without fear. The prospective doper requires access to the right drugs and access to horses at the right time." The favoured drug of the 1990s, for instance, was "frighteningly easy to obtain" and could be found in every racing stable in Britain: Acetylpromazine, or ACP, a fast-acting, mild tranquilliser used to sedate a horse when, for instance, it is having its coat clipped. Obtainable only from vets, it became so ubiquitous it was widely kept in abundance in stables – "and not necessarily under lock and key".

In 2013, the British Horseracing Authority decreed that three leading English footballers, James Coppinger, Mark Wilson and Michael Chopra, the last a young man beset by well-chronicled problems with gambling addiction, were guilty of offering bribes to Andrew Heffernan, an apprentice at the time of the crime.[18] Along with five other defendants, the trio were banished from racecourses, in their case for 10 years apiece; found guilty of not riding three horses as hard as he might, Heffernan had his licence suspended and was disqualified for 15. For a truly sophisticated betting coup, however, the 1844 Epsom Derby still takes some beating.

It had everything: subterfuge, substitutions, false age declarations, nobbling, horse-napping and, when the case came to trial, perjury and witness-tampering – all in the name of ensuring a four-year-old steed, competing under the name of Running Rein, won a race restricted to three-year-olds. In fact, the winner's true identity was Maccabeus, a four-year-old, owned, like the real Running Rein, by one Abraham Levi Goodman, the leader of the conspirators. This right royal scam appears to have been something of an open secret in racing circles, yet while stewards were alerted in writing, in *advance* of the off, they did nothing; in the interest of tucking it all safely under the carpet, they simply crossed their fingers that the horse would not win.

The most rounded portrait of the ins and outs, indeed, emerged by accident: Georgina Byles was working in the marketing department at Newmarket when, seeking storage space, she found an outhouse where she chanced upon a brown manila envelope bulging with newspaper cuttings, letters and case notes pertaining to the scandal. She handed them on to her father, Tony, inspiring and informing his 2011 book, *In Search of Running Rein: The Amazing Fraud of the 1844 Derby*. In it, he characterises Francis Ignatius Coyle, who helped abduct Running Rein/Maccabeus from his trainer's yard before the trial, as "probably the most unutterable of all unutterable scoundrels ever to have disgraced the Turf". The competition has been nothing if not fierce. Intriguingly, the seventh-placed finisher was Akbar – the same name given to a handy 21st century horse owned by the Aga Khan.

"An unmitigated scoundrel"

For all their claims to represent the best of the nation that served as their cradle, cricket and baseball, the first two major team sports, have similarly shabby tales to tell. At the beginning of the 19th century there was no more formidable sporting villain than Lord Frederick Beauclerk, a thoroughly objectionable sort most famously described as "an unmitigated scoundrel". The son of the Duke of St Albans and purportedly a direct descendant of Charles II and his fruit-selling lover Nell Gwynn, he emerged as the best amateur batsman of his day, a man so contemptuous of certain bowlers he would hang a valuable gold watch from his middle stump, daring them to hit it. Foul of mouth, short of fuse and unencumbered by decency or fair-mindedness, he rose to become the second MCC president but was widely detested – not a common complaint for a vicar. Even Daniel Dawson, a notorious lowlife who would be hanged for horse-poisoning, refused to share a carriage with him, so offended was he by his Lordship's filthy vocabulary. By his own account, Beauclerk made 600 guineas a year from gambling on matches. The lengths he went to in order to secure his winnings were legendary. Once, after losing a single-wicket game, he merely asked the press not to publish the details.

Beauclerk was also a compulsive match-fixer, and his bitter rivalry with George Osbaldeston triggered one of the scandals of the Regency era. In 1817, Sussex's William Lambert became the first man to score a century in each innings of a match; not for 76 years would anyone emulate that feat. Later that summer, he was banned from Lord's, and the game, for not trying. He was Osbaldeston's man.

The start of the century had found cricket mired in a trough of corruption. Single- and double-wicket matches, involving two or four players and hence far easier to fix than 11 v 11, were highly fashionable; bookmakers swanned around grounds, operating openly. "Silver Billy" Beldham, among the most highly-rated of the early batsmen to emerge from Surrey, painted a vexing picture for the game's first historian, the Reverend James Pycroft:

> *Matches were bought and matches were sold and gentlemen who meant honestly lost large sums of money, till the rogues beat themselves at last. Many a time I have been blamed for selling when as innocent as a babe. In those days, when so much money was on matches, every man who lost his money would blame someone.*[19]

MCC resolved to clean the game up, and alighted on Lambert as the fall guy. Osbaldeston, a graduate of Eton and Oxford, was a well-bred fast bowler known as "The Squire" who despised sporting parsons in general and in particular Beauclerk, whose title he envied. In 1810 Osbaldeston hired Lambert for a 50-guinea, double-wicket match at the original Lord's against Beauclerk and his partner. When Osbaldeston fell ill, Beauclerk insisted the contest went ahead, whereupon Lambert won the pot for Osbaldeston by outsmarting Beauclerk, in good part by bowling wides (then legal, though Beauclerk would soon change that). Lambert was seen leaving Dorset Square with a brown-paper parcel, allegedly bulging with banknotes.

In 1817, Osbaldeston arranged a match between "England" and Nottingham, employing Lambert again. This time, both sides were on the take, having accepted bribes to lose. Beauclerk saw the mindless swipes and dropped catches and seized the opening. Thirsting for revenge on Osbaldeston but knowing full well it really wasn't done for him to be seen to be exacting vengeance on a fellow gentleman, he persuaded his MCC underlings that Lambert had failed to give his all: the Sussex man was banned, his career effectively finished. The unprivileged always did suffer for the sins of their alleged social superiors.[20]

Nor would the international game prove immune to what the early cricket historian John Nyren called "tricking and crossing". On Boxing Day 1873, W. G. Grace and 10 other Poms commenced battle against Victoria at the Melbourne Cricket Ground, stage for the inaugural Test match four years later. The three-day game would be watched by 40,000, each paying a whopping two shillings and sixpence; the takings amounted to £5,000, which would still stand as the ground record come the end of the century. Shockingly, Grace and his illustrious company were trounced by an innings, yet the mood was cheery as the champagne flowed freely. "Grace," as his biographer Simon Rae put it, "had proved his commercial value."[21]

According to a scrapbook kept by one observer, George Arthur, the gamblers were livid. "They argue that the gentlemen of the grandest nation on the earth have sold themselves for lucre, and given away a match they could have won as easily as it was lost… Mr Grace and his coadjutors have been wilfully and dishonourably dishonest." In fact, attested Mr Arthur, they were "a bookmaker's dream" more than happy to swindle the Australian public. Word had it that Grace had deployed the MCG's newly installed telegraph to warn his London friends not to bet on the tourists because the match was destined to be lost.[22]

"I am dumb, Harry"

In 1877, the Louisville Grays, in irresistible form at the start of the major league baseball campaign, suddenly lost seven games in a row. Fielders misfielded, runners were sluggish. "It is not known whether the players have been dissipating, keeping late hours, and having a jolly time, generally," wrote the editor of the city's *Courier-Journal*, whose suspicions had been inflamed, "but tight or sober, they should realise the fact that they have run afoul of a most humiliating set of reverses."[23] In the wake of these defeats, they were spotted sporting diamond accoutrements.

Gamblers, it transpired, had purchased the services of four players billed in the newspaper (with epithets to match) as "Gentleman George" Hall, Bill "Butcher" Craver, Al "Slippery Elm" Nichols and Jim "Terror" Devlin. "Gamblers were a standard part of baseball scenery in the 1870s," attested that scabrously witty author, screenwriter and sports journalist Ring Lardner Jr. "Devlin and Hall made an arrangement with a New York operative named Mcleod, throwing games for him whenever a signal telegram contained the word 'sash'. Devlin's price per game was $75, and Hall's was $25, giving rise… to a bon mot of the period, 'You can hire a Hall fairly cheaply these days, for only $25.'"[24] Confessed Devlin:

> *Was introduced to a man named McCloud in New York who said when I wanted to make a little money to let him know… We made a contract to lose the Cincinnati game, McCloud sent me $80 in a letter and I gave Hall $25 of it… Helped McCloud throw a game in Indianapolis… Received $100 from McCloud for it… Gave it to my wife.*

The corrupt quartet claimed they had accepted the bribes because the Grays' owner had refused to pay their salaries. Not that this tempered the authorities' fury – they were all banned for life by William Hulbert, owner of the Chicago White Stockings and driving force behind the creation of the National League – or that of the *Courier-Journal*, which painted them, rather lyrically, as "eels of a superlative degree of lubrication". The following February, Devlin, one of the league's most formidable pitchers, wrote to Harry Wright, the English-born son of a famous cricketer, owner of the Boston Red Stockings and the pathfinder hailed by no less an authority than Henry Chadwick as "the father of professional ball-playing".[25] Devlin's handwritten communiqué was as plaintive as it was illiterate:

> *Dear Sir,*
> *As I am Deprived from Playing this year I thought I woed write you to see if you Coed do anything for me in the way of work I Don't Know what I am to do... I Can asure you Harry that I was not Treated right and if Ever I Can See you to tell you the Case you will say I am not to Blame. I am living from hand to mouth all winter I have not got a Stich of Clothing or has my wife and child You Don't Know how I am Situated for I Know if you did you woed do Something for me I am honest Harry you need not Be afraid the Louisville People made me what I am to day a Begger... I am Dumb Harry I don't know how to go about it So I trust you will answear this and do all you Can for me...*[26]

Though Wright proved unmoveable, Hulbert agreed to see Devlin, pressed a $50 note into his hand, then made his feelings abundantly plain: "Damn you, Devlin, you are dishonest; you have sold a game and I can't trust you. Now go, and let me never see your face again; for your act will never be condoned so long as I live." For five years Devlin hung around corridors while the National League owners convened, and eventually found employment on the purportedly safe side of the law, as a policeman, before dying of consumption in 1883. His early passing, proclaimed the *Courier-Journal*, was an illuminating example of "the fruits of crookedness".[27]

Shallow Hal

Hal Chase made William Lambert seem like an ingénue. Baseball's premier first baseman, he was publicly denounced in 1908 for under-performing, allegedly out of pique after having been bypassed in favour of Kid Elberfield as manager of the New York Americans. Teammates and journalists began accusing Chase of deliberately throwing games so as to undermine another manager, George Stallings, who was fired after casting the same aspersions. Defended to the hilt by Ban Johnson, president of the American League, Chase was appointed in his stead but didn't last long either, then went to war with his successor, Frank Chance.[28]

After one defeat, related the sportswriter Fred Lieb, Chance "stormed over to the pressbox... and asked, 'Did you fellows see what was going on out there? Chase has been throwing games on me.'" Lieb's editor deemed it inappropriate to publish this outburst, but another journalist, the vaunted Heywood Broun, filed it as a note to the *New York Tribune*.[29] The next day, Frank Farrell, owner of the New York Americans, took Broun to task, claiming his manager had never said anything of the sort, then promptly traded Chase to the Chicago White Sox.

Chase was not long for the American League, where his chance of acceptance was likened by the *Sporting News* to that of "a nihilist in Russia". Baseball, though, did not neglect his more orthodox talents, and by 1916 he was back in the majors, in the National League, with the Cincinnati Reds. Now he spread his wings, not only throwing matches himself but persuading others to do likewise, collecting commissions on bets placed by others on games he had fixed. In August 1918, the Reds' manager, Christy Mathewson, the peerless ex-pitcher and so-called "Christian Gentleman", bowed to pressure from the rest of the dressing room and suspended Chase without pay for the remainder of the season for "indifferent playing" – shorthand, Chase revealed, for betting on games and trying to bribe a pitcher, Pol Perritt of the New York Giants, to throw one.[30]

Chase denied all, suing the club for $1,650 in back salary. The following February he was cleared; whatever he had supposedly said, it had been in jest. Not only did he avoid even so much as a reprimand, he was quickly signed by the Giants, even though the manager who signed him, John McGraw, had testified against him. To make matters even more surreal, Mathewson left the Reds to coach the Giants. Not that this dissuaded Chase from carrying on regardless, fixing games and corrupting teammates. In September 1919 he and Heinie Zimmerman were dropped by McGraw, who refused to explain to the press that the evidence against them was such that the Giants' owners had been informed. Neither player darkened a major league diamond again.[31]

"I gave my all"

Professional football's first reported fix dates back to 1900, when Jack Hillman, the Burnley goalkeeper, was banned for a year. Burnley needed to win the final League fixture of the season against Nottingham Forest to avoid relegation but lost 4–0. After the game, the Forest captain, Archie McPherson, alleged that Hillman had tried to bribe his team to lose. The FA refused to believe Hillman's claim that he was only joking and he was banned for 12 months, costing him not only his salary but a £300 benefit.

The English game's most unsavoury episode did not enter the public domain, however, until 1964. The credit for exposing it went to a Sunday newspaper, *The People*: having financed a year-long investigation, it revealed that a group of Football League players had pulled off a betting sting to capitalise on the enticing new Treble Chance, where substantial winnings could be gleaned by forecasting the number of draws. This marketing device had recently been instituted by the pools companies, led by Littlewoods, whose owners, the Moores family, controlled Everton FC and would make a similar investment in their Merseyside rivals Liverpool.

Jimmy Gauld, the ringleader, and his accomplices were banned *sine die* and imprisoned. Also implicated, jailed and declared persona utterly non grata were Tony Kay, Peter Swan and David "Bronco" Layne: they had bet on their own team, Sheffield Wednesday, losing to Ipswich in what Kay insisted most forcefully had been an unrelated episode dating back to 1962. He was always equally quick to tell interviewers that *The People* named him man of the match; as he reasoned, "I gave my all."[32]

Layne approached me before the Ipswich game and said, "What do you reckon today?" I said, "Well, we've never won down here [Portman Road]." He said: "Give me £50 and I'll get you twice your money." I thought that was a good deal. The story of my bet eventually came out after I was transferred to Everton. I was in a Liverpool nightclub one Saturday night [in 1964] and a friend said to me: "You're all over the front page of the Sunday People *about the Ipswich game. They're saying you bet on the match and the bookmakers have been screaming because they lost £35,000 that week." I felt awful...*

I think [Gault] wanted to sell his story for one last payday. There had been rumours for ages about match-fixing in football, but no-one had ever proved it. Gauld knew Layne, who had been at Mansfield and who before the Ipswich match had acted as the go-between. I had never met Gauld but then one day he turned up at my house in Liverpool and introduced himself as a friend of David Layne's. He said that he wanted to speak to me, so we went and sat in his car outside my house. He began to fire questions at me, trying to confuse me. He asked if I'd accepted money for fixing a game. I said: "I don't know what you're talking about." I didn't realise that he was recording our conversation. The tape of our conversation was used in court as evidence against me. It was one of the first times that this had ever happened. But even though the tape was incoherent and you could hear nothing, it still stood up.[33]

At the time of their crime, Swan and Kay were both England internationals. Thus did both lose their chance of immortality at the 1966 World Cup.

Italians seem to have had a stronger stomach for all this. "Operation Last Bet" was the fifth such scandal in their country since 1974, the year Polish players accused the *Azurri* of offering them money to lose a World Cup match in Stuttgart. In 1980, Paolo Rossi, the striker who would win his country the World Cup just two years later, was among 30 players arrested in what became known – after Italy's illegal football pools system – as

Totonero I, which saw AC Milan and Lazio relegated and five clubs have points docked. Cue the sequel, *Totonero II*, in 1986, which led to relegation or points deductions for no fewer than nine clubs; again, Lazio were among the sinners.

After a 20-year hiatus, the sordid business resumed with *Calciopoli*: accused of assembling a network of compliant referees and officials, Juventus were stripped of two league titles while punishments were also meted out to Milan, Fiorentina and – yes – Lazio. Half a decade later came *Calcioscommesse*, for which the 38-year-old midfielder Cristiano Doni, who had played in the 2002 World Cup, received a three-year ban for his role in a 17-man plot to influence results in Italy's second tier, Serie B. May 2012 brought the results of "Operation Last Bet", an investigation into match-fixing and illegal betting that saw Stefano Mauri, the Lazio FC captain, arrested and cost Domenico Criscito his place in Italy's squad for the impending European Championships; the national coach, Cesare Prandelli, decided that Criscito, who maintained his innocence, was "under a pressure no human can cope with". The defender had been photographed by police in May 2011 dining with a Genoa teammate, Giuseppe Sculli, two of the club's *ultra* supporters and a known Bosnian criminal.

The scale of football's gambling problems, though, was perhaps best exemplified in January 2013, when the power of the Asian betting market, an illegal one, was underscored in indelible ink. Europol, the European criminal intelligence agency, claimed that more than 680 top-level football matches dating back to 2008 had been fixed, including a Champions League match in England – a goodly proportion outside the continent. According to German prosecutors, around 150 of those fixtures had been targeted by a Singapore-based betting cartel suspected of bribing players and officials: 425 people from upwards of 15 nations were involved, the biggest bribe £135,000. Eighty-six search warrants were issued; a thrilling October 2009 Champions League match that saw Hungary's Debrecen clamber back from 4-0 down to lose by the odd goal to Italy's Fiorentina, was one of 47 games rigged by a ring led by Ane

Sapina, a Croat who had already been convicted for match-fixing. The fixmasters, though, operated primarily from Asia.

"So how do you fix a football match?" wondered Ed Hawkins, whose investigation into the Asian betting market resulted in an arresting book published in 2012, *Bookie Gambler Fixer Spy: A Journey to the Heart of Cricket's Underworld*. "Investigators believe that worldwide fixing yields $90 billion (about £57 billion) annually and that financial muscle and malevolence to cajole or threaten players are prerequisites. Mafia, who have plenty of both, step in and demand players manipulate the result or the number of goals scored." It is a myth, he claimed, that fixers will bet on the first throw-in or red card or number of corners. "The Asian betting market is dominated by two options: the Asian handicap and goals scored. The Asian handicap is, essentially, betting without the draw [thus ensuring a winner] but with the favourite giving a headstart of a quarter of a goal or more to the opposition… There is no match too big or too small which is not vulnerable." TV makes that possible, allowing legal bookmakers such as IBC Bet, licensed in the Philippines, to turn over £30m on a single match. Even a Scottish Under-18 game wasn't immune.[34]

Hansie

And so the wheel spun. As the 21st century dawned, match-fixing returned to the cricket pitch when Hansie Cronje, captain of South Africa and hitherto one of the most admired cricketers of his era, hauled it onto news bulletins across the globe. In the preceding weeks he had been the toast of sport: in becoming the first captain to forfeit an innings in a Test match, astounding those who regarded him as dour and breathing unexpected life into a match devastated by rain, he had delivered a dramatic climax and, even more generously – so far as the travelling supporters were concerned – a frantic English victory. He may have lost but hell, he'd done the right thing, a lovely, wonderful right thing; something pretty much impossible to imagine any contemporary doing in that context. To find the previous most talked-about exercise in philanthropy you had to go back to 1968, when Garry Sobers, the West Indies skipper, had declared in Trinidad, leaving England to meet an eminently gettable target. He claimed to some that he had done so out of pique: the opposition's defensive, go-slow mindset represented everything he detested and he simply had to take a stand.

In fact, the revelation that Cronje had accepted a gift from a bookmaker to revive the match at Centurion was strictly accidental: the Indian police had reportedly tapped his mobile phone by mistake and found him talking to a bookie, Sanjeev Chawla. The denials flowed, from Cronje and among his adoring public. Eventually, the truth came out – or a portion thereof.

The ensuing presidential inquiry, the King Commission, for which Cronje was granted immunity from prosecution, was characterised by the journalist Neil Manthorp in a 2008 Sky Sports documentary as "a very well-organised, well-presented circus... a cleansing tool for the government and the country", enabling Cronje to shoulder all the blame; a circus for which two key witnesses, Gary Kirsten and Jonty Rhodes, characterised by Manthorp as being "pathologically incapable of telling a lie" as well as Cronje's closest friends in the South African team, just happened to be overseas. Cronje did confess on the stand, and apologise, but most South Africans remembered his tears and felt for him. Related *Wisden*: "A born-again Christian who wore a bracelet with the initials WWJD – What Would Jesus Do? – he talked of how Satan had entered his world when he took his eyes off Jesus and his 'whole world turned dark'. There was something pre-Christian in this, an echo of Greek heroes blaming the gods rather than themselves for their misfortunes."[35]

He was duly banned from the game for life, yet talk of him being allowed to coach was already bubbling when, a year later, he died in an air crash, on a flight he had only booked at the last minute, affirming his place on the pedestal constructed for him by white South Africa in general and his own Afrikaaner community in particular, where his ghost still hovers. Not until 2013 would the police file the charge-sheet in a Delhi court.

The *Wisden* view of the funeral fought hard to be balanced and almost succeeded: "The divisions were forgotten as South Africa, a nation rebuilding on forgiveness and reconciliation, mourned, in Gary Kirsten's words, 'a great cricketer, a great performer and a great on-field leader of his country'. It was elsewhere that cricket would still consider Hansie Cronje a tarnished hero."

Prejudices and illusions died hard. During the opening ceremony for the World Cup, held in South Africa the following year, punters could buy "The Hansie", a humungous and somewhat grotesque roll jammed with ham, tomato and chips: its original name had been "The Gatsby". In their mutual preference for lucre over honour, Cronje and Scott Fitzgerald's anti-hero had much in common.

When the South African Broadcasting Corporation conducted a survey to discover the hundred "Greatest South Africans" – given that email responses were the norm, it was clearly biased towards the white minority – Nelson Mandela emerged on top; Henrik Verwoerd, the architect of apartheid, finished 14 places higher than Walter Sisulu, who helped detonate it; in 11th place, just behind then-President Thabo Mbeki and the endlessly admirable Archbishop Desmond Tutu, was Cronje.[36] All of which, in 2012, was still bewildering Mike Atherton, who had led England against South Africa while Cronje was in charge and who recalled feeling "uncomfortable" when the latter made his undivine declaration at Centurion: he was accustomed to Cronje's conservatism. "There's no worse thing you can do as a captain," he raged, "absolutely none."[37]

That, though, wasn't the half of it. Cronje's tragic flaw was as ancient as time itself: greed. In 1996, he had accepted a bribe to engineer a betting coup during a one-day international against India. He had sought to engineer similar deals before but failed to persuade any teammates to join him. This time the web he cast drew in the most inexperienced and vulnerable members of his side: Henry Williams, a black fast bowler grateful for his belated chance, and Herschelle Gibbs, the gifted but scatter-brained young coloured batsman. The former agreed to bowl wides, the latter to get out before he reached 20: Williams kept to the script; Gibbs forgot his lines, or so he claimed (that Williams stated in 2013 that the precise offer his captain had made him had been a fiction, encouraged by his lawyers, did little to dispel the bitter aftertaste). Thus it was in 2001, when Cronje confessed some if not necessarily all, that the world learned all about the new game in town: micro-fixing, aka spot-fixing. Nourished by the Indian obsession with cricket, which in turn underpinned a flourishing and highly illegal betting market, it soon became the clever fixer's weapon of choice.

For Pete's sake

Pete Rose once said he would "walk through hell in a gasoline suit" to play baseball. His enthusiasm for a wager was no less unbridled, and it saw him banned from the game *sine die*. Should this arch-competitor's obsession bar him from the Hall of Fame, an honour his feats do not so much commend as demand?

Posted in every major league clubhouse, the regulations (Rule 21, Clause D, BETTING ON BALL GAMES) could scarcely be any clearer: "Any player, umpire, or club official or employee who shall bet any sum whatsoever upon any baseball game in connection with which the bettor has no duty to perform shall be declared ineligible for one year. Any player, umpire, or club or league official or employee who shall bet any sum whatsoever upon any baseball game in connection with which the bettor has a duty to perform shall be declared permanently ineligible." In August 1989, Rose, then managing the Cincinnati Reds, in whose colours he had so distinguished himself as a player and whose record for the most major league hits still stands, was found guilty of breaching that clause and banned for life by A. Bartlett Giamatti, the baseball commissioner; the stress he endured while coming to that decision was such that he suffered a fatal coronary shortly afterwards.

Giamatti's statement still resounds with the sombre timbre of betrayal: "One of the game's greatest players has engaged in a variety of acts which have stained the game, and he must now live with the consequences of those acts. By choosing not to come to a hearing before me, and by choosing not to proffer any testimony or evidence contrary to the evidence and information contained in the report of the Special Counsel to the Commissioner, Mr. Rose has accepted baseball's ultimate sanction, lifetime ineligibility." Yet a *Washington Post* poll conducted shortly after Rose had been formally accused found nearly half the respondents railing against the game's post-1919 zero tolerance. Fanning the flames further, Carl B. Rubin, a District Court judge in Ohio, claimed there was "evidence of a vendetta" against Rose.[38]

Not that any of this prevented Rose from bidding for another title: baseball's autograph king. By 2013, at the age of 72, it was estimated that, in exchange for signing anything from balls to photos, his annual earnings were upwards of $1m. In 2007, sales reached $3.6m. He was still gambling, albeit not on the game he divided. "That cost me too much," he acknowledged. Meanwhile, Bud Selig, the MLB commissioner, had still not responded to Rose's 1997 application for reinstatement. Asked whether he planned to make a ruling before his term ended in 2014, Selig ducked the bouncer with disdain: "I keep saying it's under review, and that's where it is. I'll let you draw your own conclusions."[39]

Jimmy Carter was as firmly in Rose's corner. "One of society's most difficult decisions is whether to extend forgiveness to someone who has committed a crime or made a serious mistake," the former US president wrote in *USA Today* in 1995. "In international diplomacy, it is often necessary to grant amnesty to former oppressors and corrupt officials in order to reconcile antagonists and bring peace, justice, and respect for human rights to a troubled nation. U.S. presidents are responsible for the ultimate decisions about pardons and paroles for convicted criminals who have served a portion of their sentences. A most difficult decision for me was amnesty for draft avoiders to help heal the trauma of Vietnam. President Gerald Ford made the politically costly choice of pardoning President Nixon to address the national wounds of Watergate. In every case, it is necessary to assess the offence, extenuating circumstances, evidence of reform or restitution, and the willingness of victims to forego continuing punishment of the guilty."[40]

In Carter's view, it is an enormous pity that journalists nominate candidates for the Hall of Fame. Forgiveness, after all, had apparently already arrived from the most crucial quarter: Rose's primary victims, "the millions of dedicated fans who support baseball and are very protective of the game's reputation and integrity". A 1994 article in *Sports Illustrated*, Carter pointed out, had reported a telephone poll in which 97% of respondents contended that Rose should be in the Hall of Fame. Come 1999, fans would vote him into the MLB All-Century team. Half a decade on, in an extract from his autobiography *My Prison Without Bars*, he finally came clean: despite repeated assertions to the contrary, he confessed that he *had* bet on baseball, and the Reds – though never, he insisted, to lose.

"In the summer of 1989, I'd sit in the manager's office in Cincinnati's Riverfront Stadium and listen to Pete Rose lie," recalled the former *Cincinnati Enquirer* reporter Paul Daugherty, likening Rose to Roger Clemens: the meanest and most formidable of modern pitchers, Clemens had repeatedly repudiated allegations that he had used performance-enhancing drugs, convincing few. "The same traits that made Rose who he was — the drive, the arrogance, the boundless determination – contributed to his demise. I look at Clemens – puffing his chest with Mike Wallace on *60 Minutes*, offering plausible earnestness before Congress, repeating the same lines again and again – and I see Rose."[41] Tried for perjury, Clemens was eventually acquitted on all six charges; as yet, he, like Rose, has yet to be forgiven by sufficient numbers of baseball scribes.

"Pete Rose belongs in the Hall of Fame," charged Daugherty. "It's a museum. It has a front door, not pearly gates. Nobody got more base hits... Probably, no one ever will. Put him in the Hall. Give him a super-sized plaque, big enough for a detailed explanation as to why he told one story for 14 years and another in January 2004."[42]

The Black Sox

The best thing one can say about the most infamous fix in sporting history is that it so astonished and shamed its country of origin that, at the time of writing, the United States had never since suffered a major bribery scandal in professional sport. Even before its approaching centenary galvanised fascination anew, it was still informing the work of academics, journalists, movie directors (*Eight Men Out, Field of Dreams*) and even TV drama producers (*Boardwalk Empire*): an untouched, untouchable symbol of betrayal and lost innocence. In *The Godfather: Part II*, in a scene set in 1959, Michael Corleone sits watching baseball with Hyman Roth, his ageing rival mobster, whose comment echoed Jay Gatsby's introduction of Meyer Wolfsheim. "I've loved baseball," declares Roth, "ever since Arnold Rothstein fixed the 1919 World Series." The Don smiles; like Gatsby, both admire the sheer chutzpah.

The details vary from account to account, depending on perspective, but the essential plot runs thus. While the Chicago White Sox were comfortably the best team in the American League in 1919, disgruntlement had been growing, reaching mutinous proportions as their miserly owner Charlie Comiskey – "The Old Roman" – treated them like serfs. He instructed the manager, Kid Gleason, to bench Eddie Cicotte and hence deny him a promised bonus for winning 30 games; he even refused to pay for the players' kit to be laundered, hence the grubby team's new nickname: the Black Sox.

As the Series approached, Cicotte and six teammates fell into bed with gamblers and agreed to ensure victory for the Cincinnati Reds; Buck Weaver was also privy to the plot, but was too proud and principled to either under-perform or accept a dime. In the event, most of the sums promised by the intermediaries who shuttled between Rothstein and the players did not materialise, provoking the furious rebels into playing with their customary excellence, but the gamblers prevailed: before the eighth and deciding game, it is widely believed, Claude

"Lefty" Williams was advised in no uncertain terms that he should pitch badly or else his wife would be shot. His performance did nothing to contradict this.

* * *

The first person to draw public attention to the possibility of a fix was the journalist Hughie Fullerton, long a thorn in the side of the owners. Hinting at skulduggery the day after the Series ended, he predicted that, come the following season, seven White Sox players would be missing. Not unnaturally, Comiskey's denial was swift and certain, yet he also launched an investigation, offering a reward of $10,000 to $20,000 (reports varied) for "a single clue"[43] leading to any evidence of jiggery-pokery. This in turn prompted a furious editorial in the *Sporting News* that lacked little in derision or racist overtones: "Because a lot of dirty, long-nosed, thick-lipped, and strong-smelling gamblers butted into the World Series… and some of said gamblers got crossed, stories were peddled that there was something wrong with the games… Comiskey has met that by offering $10,000 for any sort of a clue that will bear out such a charge… [but] there will be no takers, because there is no such evidence, except in the mucky minds of the stinkers who – because they are crooked – think all the rest of the world can't play straight."[44]

In the event, Comiskey not only re-signed Cicotte and his co-conspirators but gave the key men – Cicotte, Oscar "Happy" Felsch, Williams and "Shoeless Joe" Jackson – chunky pay rises. Then, on 27 September 1920, a front-page headline in the Philadelphia *North American* thrust virtually a year's worth of conjecture into the foothills of fact – "Gamblers Promised White Sox $100,000 To Lose". The basis for this was an interview by James Isaminger with Bill Maharg, a boxer and semi-pro ballplayer turned two-bit gambler. Claiming that the Sox had intentionally blown the first two games of the 1919 Series, Maharg implicated, in ascending order of clout: "Sleepy" Bill Burns, a former major league pitcher whom Cicotte, Maharg charged, had initially approached; Abe "The Little

Hebrew" Attell, a former world featherweight champion boxer, and Rothstein.[45]

Eventually, a public trial opened on 27 June 1921. It resulted in a verdict of not guilty – strangely, the players' reported confessions to a grand jury had disappeared, though Harold Seymour has contended that they were signed under duress and thus might not have been credible. The upshot was a clean bill of health for the White Sox and the national pastime, which delighted Ban Johnson, Comiskey and all the other owners and officials. It also let Rothstein off the hook: after he was murdered in 1928 (for welching on a poker debt), affidavits were discovered in his files testifying to his having paid out $80,000 for the fix.[46]

On 28 June, nonetheless, the plotters, Weaver included, were banished for life by baseball's first, newly appointed commissioner, Judge Kenesaw Mountain Landis, who thus quickly displayed his ability to understand the essential requirement of his job: to protect the interests of the game, i.e. the owners. A slight man with as mountainous an ego as his name suggests, Landis "wielded not a sword of justice but an extra-large scythe", wrote Seymour. "He recognised no degrees of guilt but cut off from their livelihood seven ball players acquitted in a court of law and two others who were not even indicted. The same harsh penalty he gave to those assumed to have thrown the Series he meted out to a player who had appeared only briefly in it (McMullin), to another who probably only had 'guilty' knowledge (Weaver), and even to one who was not on the team but who had sat in on a meeting with gamblers (Gedeon)."[47] Even now, there are many prominent Americans, Jimmy Carter among them, who are still campaigning for a pardon for "Shoeless" Joe Jackson, the big-hitting, illiterate innocent immortalised in *Field of Dreams* as well as for the plaintive if ritually misquoted line an adoring schoolboy supposedly uttered to him on the courtyard steps: "Say it ain't so, Joe."

Any single, consensual "truth" remains obstinately elusive. As recently as 2006, Potomac Books published *Burying The Black Sox – How Baseball's Cover-Up of the 1919 World Series Fix*

Almost Succeeded, in which Gene Carney examined the efforts of Johnson et al to conceal the sordid chapter. Nearly the entirety of the following season had expired before the story entered the public prints. Carney unearthed the statements made to the grand jury by Jackson and Cicotte, and traced the former's bid to clear his name in court in 1924. "Jackson took the money," Carney concluded, "and he kept it; but if he kept it, maybe his team knew that and even instructed him to keep it. He apparently did not spend it on himself."[48]

Carney's summing-up was nothing if not measured. Vitally, it also underscored the mutable nature of history and the need to keep questioning it:

> *Many people have formed their opinions about the Black Sox scandal believing that they were looking at a butterfly. What is amazing is that even after historians and researchers and writers, starting with [author of* Eight Men Out, *Elliot] Asinof, have pointed out that there is no butterfly, only a potato chip – so many have continued to believe that the thing flew up here from Brazil. Possibly, we have all become sceptical of revisionists and prefer our old way of seeing things. We really do not want to have to dig things out ourselves and make up our own minds – and who has the time? Eight men out, that's all we need to know. I know this: that I have lived for many years with mistaken ideas about the Big Fix. Now I know that the more I learn about it, the more there seems to be to be learned. Certainty about things related to the fix and the cover-up is elusive. And perhaps that is not such a bad thing. It keeps our minds open and searching.*[49]

4 Ringmasters Inc: Sport and Governance

Sport's great problem is that it is run by power-crazed old fats in blazers who want to keep things as they are, on the grounds that any system that put them in charge has to be a good one. They are mostly horrible old white men who have lost the sport inside them, swapped it for power, knowing that the power you wield is directly proportionate to the thickness of your wallet. So they run sport to make money, not to pursue excellence.

Simon Barnes[1]

Russian businessmen and officials close to President Vladimir Putin have stolen up to $30 billion from funds intended for preparations for next year's Sochi Winter Olympics, according to a report released on Thursday by opposition leaders. Putin, who has staked his reputation on a successful Games, faces criticism over allegations of corruption and costs overruns that have pushed up the price tag for the event to $50 billion – more than quadruple initial estimates, making them the most costly Olympics ever. "In preparing for the Olympics $25 to $30 billion was stolen," Russian opposition leader Boris Nemtsov told reporters.

NBC News, 30 May 2013[2]

I don't recall an Olympics without corruption.

Jean-Claude Killy, head of IOC coordination commission for Sochi Games[3]

Come the 21st century, the balance of sporting power was as precariously balanced as a ballerina on tiptoes after a night on the tiles. In the thin ranks of sports where players' unions have some clout, most notably American baseball, basketball and football, some might say the players – and hence their agents – have a strong voice (of course, those adamant that sportsfolk should be grateful to have such a pleasant job will tell you that voice is far too loud and far too bolshie). Far more commonly, you might say power lay in the hands of the billionaire club owners, men (and they are always men) accustomed to getting their own way. Others would cite the broadcasters, who in exchange for colossal rights fees dictate the timing and reach of the events they cover, and sometimes even their nature and structure. Still others would plump for the politicians. Then there are those who are supposed to be running the store, the administrators who comprise the official governing bodies, the chairmen and directors and chief executives. All of which made the final part of *The Times'* "Sport Power 100" for 2012 an intriguing read.[4]

Compiled by a panel of journalists, the Power 100, explained the paper, "is a collective judgment on who matters most in British sport and why. It is a subjective view that ranks the depth and breadth of an individual's reach, gauging their ability to shape a sport or a number of sports, influence decisions or change the market." What it was not, ran the necessary rider, was "a judgment on the virtue or otherwise of this power". As unquantifiable and unscientific as this chart was (is power measurable in quantitative terms?), few would have argued heatedly about the composition of the top 10 (in ascending order of omnipotence):

10. *Jeremy Hunt – Secretary of State for Culture, Olympics, Media and Sport*
 9. *Sheikh Mansour – Owner, Manchester City FC*
 8. *Michel Platini – President, UEFA*
 7. *Boris Johnson – Mayor of London*
 6. *Jeremy Darroch – Chief executive, British Sky Broadcasting*
 5. *Sepp Blatter – President, FIFA*
 4. *David Bernstein – Chairman, FA*
 3. *Richard Scudamore – Chief executive, Premier League*

2. Jacques Rogge – President, IOC

1. Lord Coe – Chairman, London Organising Committee for the Olympic Games

Inevitably perhaps, administrators held sway, accounting for 50% of those names, though three of them (Blatter, Platini and Rogge) governed from overseas. The remainder encompassed two current politicians (Hunt and Johnson), a Conservative peer (Coe), a broadcasting executive (Darroch) and a club owner (Mansour). The next 10 included two other LOCOG bigwigs (chief executive Paul Deighton and vice-chairman Sir Keith Mills), another pair of administrators (Formula 1's Bernie Ecclestone and Manchester United's David Gill), a club owner (Chelsea FC's Roman Abramovich), a club manager (Harry Redknapp), another broadcaster (the BBC's director of sport, Barbara Slater, the only woman in the top 18 and one of just 11 all told) and another Sheikh (the Emir of Qatar). In 19th and 20th place, respectively, came two actual sportspeople – golfer Rory McIlroy and heptathlete Jessica Ennis.

In an Olympic year that saw London become the first city to host the Games three times, Coe's ranking seemed apt. The success of the bid, though, depended on government funding. One of its key pledges, therefore, was to increase participation in sport at all levels, in keeping with the (then) Labour government's belief that this could help alleviate the country's growing health problems, especially obesity. This in turn was a cue for investment decisions, such as £140m for free swimming. "Coe meets all the criteria regarding influence in *The Times* Power 100 list," affirmed Ashling O'Connor. "He has shown that he can mobilise opinion, get bums on seats, change government policy and drive huge sums of money into sport from the very top to the grass roots."[5]

* * *

All the same, finding spectators with something nice to say about sporting administrators is a tall order. In fact, it would be more accurate to say the competitive arts have prospered despite rather than because of their fitfully admirable efforts. While we have already witnessed plenty of their shortcomings, and are about to sample some more, it took an erudite Sri Lankan batsman and law student, Kumar Sangakkara, to highlight them as eloquently as any sportsman ever has.

"Those from within the team became involved in the power games within the board," he recalled at Lord's in 2011 after being invited to be the first active player to give the MCC Spirit of Cricket Cowdrey Lecture, referring to the aftermath of the improbable World Cup victory of 1996 that pitchforked war-riven Sri Lanka into the wider sporting consciousness. Inevitably, given the unfamiliarity of money and power, the teething problems were considerable.

"Officials elected to power in this way in turn manipulated player loyalty to achieve their own ends. At times board politics would spill over into the team, causing rift, ill-feeling and distrust. Accountability and transparency in administration and credibility of conduct were lost in a mad power struggle that would leave Sri Lankan cricket with no consistent and clear administration. Presidents and elected executive committees would come and go; government-picked interim committees would be appointed and dissolved. After 1996 the cricket board has been controlled and administered by a handful of well-meaning individuals either personally or by proxy rotated in and out depending on appointment or election. Unfortunately, to consolidate and perpetuate their power they opened the door of the administration to partisan cronies that would lead to corruption and wanton waste of cricket board finances and resources. It was and still is confusing. Accusations of vote-buying and rigging, player interference due to lobbying from each side and even violence at the AGMs, including the brandishing of weapons and ugly fist fights, have characterised cricket board elections for as long as I can remember."[6]

* * *

No such thing as bad art? Nonsense, harrumphed Robert Hughes, the hard-drinking, no-holds-barred university dropout who as the chief art critic of *Time* magazine would so gleefully and gloriously skewer his profession's pretensions. To him, "bad art" is anything combining "technical incompetence, a belief in one's own unassailable creative glory, and absolute sincerity". He might have said precisely the same of bad sports administrators. Or most of them.

Rules may be the backbone of any sport but of theoretically far greater import are those who decide and impose them. "Administrators", though, seems far too dry a collective title. "Ringmasters" feels much showier and infinitely more self-deluding: vastly more appropriate. Their principal function, in theory, is to administer, to organise and supply the best sport possible; the modern reality, of course, is appreciably less commendable, as borne out by a blithe willingness to demand too much of the players' bodies.

Before the headlong pursuit of money began to tighten its unshakeable grip and the right sort of blazer became secondary to the obsequious courting of broadcasters and sponsors, the Football Association of Wales encapsulated the motivation common among so many ringmasters. For the 1958 World Cup finals – the first and still, as I write, the only ones for which the national team have qualified – the squad comprised just 18 players, fewer than the number allocated to the hangers-on: among those 25, notes Phil Stead in his history of Welsh football, was the sister of the secretary of the Welsh FA.[7] Eleven years later, bound for a World Cup qualifier in East Germany, Gil Reece was left on the airport tarmac. Insufficient seats had been booked; the petite but elusive winger, being at the bottom of the list of players in alphabetic terms, had been bumped. Yet no fewer than 11 of the other berths were occupied by officials, one of whom had the bare-faced gall to go to the rear of the aircraft and remonstrate with the press for not giving up one of theirs.[8]

In early 2013, as global reaction to the noxious L**** A******** and his belated confession that he had persistently availed himself of performance-enhancing drugs reached an almost hysterical pitch, it became impossible not to feel some sort of awe, however grudging, at the bare-faced gall of Pat McQuaid, the Irish president of cycling's governing body, Union Cycliste Internationale. Here, after all, was a fellow who had somehow seen fit to hold on to the reins of power even though the world was fully aware of at least some of the ways in which he and his fellow ringmasters had conspired to keep the lid on Armstrong's infractions. Nor did he willingly step down when his term expired, applying shamelessly, if forlornly, for re-election. Then again, perhaps we should not have been the slightest bit surprised. As we have seen, the history of sport, professional and amateur, is not exactly light on unenlightened despots.

On the eve of Christmas Eve 2012 came a less widely publicised but equally sobering reminder of the balance of power. It began when Sangakkara's globally respected teammate, Mahela Jayawardene, in one of his final acts before voluntarily stepping down as captain of Sri Lanka for the second time, asked that the fee he was due from participating in the World Twenty20 be shared with the team's support staff as well as groundsmen and groundstaff, for working "closely and tirelessly with the team". This laudably considerate request was slapped down by the Sri Lankan board (Sri Lanka Cricket, to give these less-than-august gentlemen their correct collective identity): it had no intention of deviating from "standard practice". When this story found its way into the Colombo *Daily Mirror*, Jayawardene wrote a letter to the editor; to the paper's credit, it was published. "As the Captain of the National Team, I am disturbed and deeply disappointed that a confidential document handed over to Sri Lanka Cricket has been published in the *Daily Mirror* on December 19 causing much concern, embarrassment to players and other staff members," wrote Jayawardene. As a result of the story being leaked to the papers, he said he had "lost all confidence in dealing with SLC in the future".[9]

Jayawardene's problem was not so much that his planned philanthropy had been thwarted but that a private matter had been made public. Why his employers saw fit to act as they did prompts a number of conclusions, one more compelling than the others, none of them complimentary. Having not once but twice had the ingratitude to leave office of his own accord – a shortlived option at best for cricket captains and one taken only by a fortunate few even once – was this simply an act of revenge? At the very least it can be interpreted as a case of showing who's boss.

* * *

Beginning with the Football Association, Rugby Football Union and MCC in England, the ringmasters' hegemony soon spread, begetting international umbrella bodies such as the International Olympic Committee (1894), FIFA (1904) and the Imperial Cricket Conference (1909). While the FA, the RFU, the IOC and FIFA remain at the forefront of the competitive arts, the titular names would not always survive: the Australian Board of Control became the Australian Cricket Board and later simply Cricket Australia; the game's governing body retained its ICC acronym but evolved from Imperial Conference to International Conference (1965) to International Council (1993). Their essential functions, nonetheless, would be as recognisable in 1914 as they are now. It is these bodies that organise and market fixtures, devise, tinker with and enforce regulations, for matches and discipline. For the past half-century they have added enormously to their reach and income streams, and, more recently, promoted themselves via websites and Twitter. Yet the growth of such over-arching institutions did not necessarily mean they controlled their sport.

For all the recent non-stop arm-wrestling between FIFA, UEFA and the up-and-coming European Club Association, this is above all true of cricket. Even now, while the ICC is in charge of regulations for international contests, its verdicts handed down from Dubai, none of the game's laws can be changed without the say-so of MCC, the custodians. Nonetheless, it was assuredly a symbol of how far the game's administrative heart had come from its South African-financed, North London roots when I received an email announcing that the ICC offices would be closed for business on Sunday 17 June 2012, a public holiday to mark Isra Wal Meraj, "the night journey and the ascension of Prophet Mohammad".

Politicians, as we shall see in a subsequent chapter, needed little encouragement to meddle. The strenuous and tireless efforts of the ringmasters to keep professionalism at bay must also await examination. For now, let us toast some of the nobler members of that much-maligned tribe.

The father of modern sport

For all their catalytic influence, the role of public school old boys in the evolution of spectator sport should not be exaggerated, believes Russell, if only because "there simply were not enough to go round".

The game's most influential administrator, nevertheless, would be a man who had worn a boater to class. An Old Harrovian, Charles William Alcock had had the good fortune to attend a school where cricket and football had been compulsory since the early part of the century, inspiring a lifetime's devotion. James Catton, widely trumpeted as the first football reporter of consequence (though since he would have been only 15 when he filed his first report in 1875, this should on no account be regarded as gospel), dubbed Alcock "the father of association football"; that assiduous sports historian Dr Eric Midwinter hailed him as "the inventor of modern sport".[10] In choosing a title for his admirable if scandalously belated biography of Alcock – published as late as 2002, three years after his grave in West Norwood Cemetery was rededicated – Keith Booth plumped for *The Father of Modern Sport*.

Born in Sunderland in 1842, the son of a shipowner and later shipbroker and insurance broker, Alcock was one of nine children and had eight of his own; his other progeny are immeasurably better known. A talented and versatile sportsman, Alcock, together with his elder brother John, formed Forest FC in 1859;

four years later it was John who attended the inaugural meeting of the Football Association. Charles, though, soon outstripped him on the field: having co-founded Wanderers, a team of Old Harrovians, in 1863, he captained them in the inaugural FA Cup final; he also led the national football team to victory in an unofficial international against Scotland in 1875; as a cricketer, he not only played for the Gentlemen of Essex but once, surreally, skippered France against Germany. In addition, he refereed a Cup final and was the first president of the Referees' Association. Nevertheless, his most far-reaching contributions came as a journalist and, even more so, an administrator.

It was Alcock who stood astride English sport for most of the last quarter of the 19th century, as secretary, simultaneously, of both Surrey County Cricket Club (1872 to 1907) and the FA, a post he held from 1870, when he was just 23, to 1895, serving the cause for 17 of those years without accepting a penny. It was Alcock who initiated international football and Test cricket, organising the first England v Scotland encounter in 1870 and England's first meeting with Australia on home soil at The Oval in 1880; he also proposed the first major sporting knockout competition, and helped establish an official County Championship. As we shall see, he also navigated the treacherous waters of professionalism rather better than a good many others. For 35 years, moreover, he not only made the sporting news but reported it, founding specialist publications such as the *Football Annual*, *Football* magazine and, in 1882, the weekly *Cricket*: the first successful national magazine devoted to the sport, it anticipated an entire branch of the publishing industry, noted Dick Holt, by blending match reports, gossip and player profiles.[11] His influence, writes Booth, "spread beyond his own historical and geographical limitations and is still apparent today". His "management style and breadth of vision would certainly not be out of place in a twenty-first century boardroom."[12]

The best-known of his offspring remains the FA Cup. In proposing the planet's most famous knockout tourney at a meeting of the FA Committee on 20 July 1871 – in the offices of

The Sportsman, one of the many publications to which Alcock contributed – he was inspired, no doubt, by the Cock House competitions at Harrow, a format also familiar to pupils at Rugby and other schools. Just four years earlier, moreover, *The Field* had reported on a "prize cup", won by Hallam, under the auspices of the Sheffield Association; having played for London in representative matches against Sheffield, it seems eminently possible that he would have been party to talk of a national version. There is also a rather enticing possibility that the idea was fleshed out in discussion with W. G. Grace, whom Alcock counted as a close friend. From early in his career, after all, Grace had been alert to sport's commercial potential, hence his formation of the United South of England Eleven. "It may well be," writes Booth, "that Grace's organisational sense and commercial acumen and W. H. Gladstone's political mentality had some input into the idea." Even if Alcock's claim to have invented the FA Cup can be challenged, "there can be no doubt that he was primarily responsible for its development". Not for the first time did he "pick up the ball and run with it and develop an idea, irrespective of whether it was his own or not, to its maximum potential".[13]

It was "desirable", Alcock told his fellow FA committeemen, "that a Challenge Cup be established in connection with the Association, for which all clubs belonging to the Association should be invited to compete". Glasgow's Queen's Park FC, still the only amateur club in the Scottish League, were among the members who pooled their resources to pay £20 for a silver trophy. The handiwork of Martin, Hall and Co, the Football Association Challenge Cup stood less than 18 inches high. Its design is reproduced on Alcock's grave.[14]

Initially, involvement was more or less confined to southern clubs. In the inaugural 1871-72 season, the only exceptions to the 15 entrants, Scotland's Queen's Park and Donington School from Spalding in Lincolnshire, were drawn to play in the 1st round but could not agree a date. Both teams were awarded byes and then drawn together again in the 2nd round. Donington, however, apparently couldn't afford to travel to Scotland so Queen's

Park were given a walkover. After the Glaswegians had held Wanderers to a draw in their semi-final (both of these ties, like the final itself, were played on Alcock's home patch, The Oval), they, too, withdrew: another trip to London was out of the question. Wanderers overcame Royal Engineers in the final, played on 16 March and witnessed by a skimpy crowd of 2,000, though they did not receive the trophy until the following month, when it was presented to them at a special reception at the Pall Mall Restaurant. This capital monopoly, though, had not been the express intention. In order to maximise participation, notes Booth, there was "a built-in flexibility" in draws for the early rounds, "allowing concessions for provincial teams" to reduce travel.

The following season was unique, writes Booth, in being the only one in which the "pure 'challenge' principle was applied": having slogged their way through the first four rounds, Oxford University challenged the holders, Wanderers, exempt until the final, only to lose 2-1. In 1874 they made amends, beating Royal Engineers, who repeated the pattern by taking the trophy the next year; in 1876, by when the field had risen to 37 (albeit just four from the provinces), Wanderers embarked on a hat-trick of successes, which entitled them to keep it in perpetuity; instead, they chose to return it to the FA on the stipulation that nobody should ever be allowed to do so. Wanderers themselves would never lift it again: the reign of the amateurs, for all the glorious afternoons still to be enjoyed by Clapham Rovers, Old Etonians and the students of Oxford, was speeding to a close.

Non-chauvinistic nationalism

Some attribute the revival of the Olympic Games to the Greeks themselves, who staged several 'Olympic' festivals in the 19th century; others give equal credit to Dr William Penny Brookes, who in 1850 instituted a similar English celebration at Much Wenlock in Shropshire. Both, however, were strictly domestic affairs, which is why the name most commonly associated with the first modern Olympics, held in Athens in 1896, belongs to Baron De Coubertin.

The British were not alone in regarding sport as a means of civilising their colonies. So did their longtime protagonists, the French, whose empire stood second only to their own as the 19th century drew to a close. Even if you can't untangle the acronyms, consider the official names of 16 contemporary sporting governing bodies – particularly those running athletics, cycling, football and motor racing, but also aquatics, equestrianism, fencing, gymnastics, motor-cycling, pentathlon, rowing, ski-ing, volleyball and wrestling: a treasure trove for all Francophiles. Telling indeed was a speech made in 1884 by Jules Ferry, an arch-promoter of colonial expansion then serving the second of two terms as prime minister. The "higher races", he proclaimed, not only had "a right over the lower races": they had "a duty to civilise".[15] De Coubertin needed little encouragement.

Born into Parisian aristocracy, while his grandfather was a ranking military officer, both parents were artistic: his mother was a musician, his father a painter who was awarded the Légion d'Honneur, his country's highest decoration. The "impressionable young Coubertin"[16], as John A. Lucas depicted him, was 12 when, in 1875, he read a French translation of *Tom Brown's School Days*, in the *Journal de la Jeunesse*. He was also highly influenced by Hughes's other novels. As Allison attests, their themes of "manliness, sportsmanship, Christian duty and the importance of having the physical courage to stand up to bullies became a kind of moral and educational orthodoxy throughout the British Empire".[17]

De Coubertin graduated from the *Ecole des sciences politiques* in 1883 then headed to England, the better to taste life at its seats of privilege, the public schools – "in a desire to attach my name to a great pedagogical reform".[18] As his tour progressed, De Coubertin observed in the sports played there a capacity to "create moral and social strength". The impetus came from Rugby School, where he was shown around the premises by Henry Lee Warner, a former Rugby head boy now teaching there; the two forged a strong friendship, corresponding for the rest of their days.

De Coubertin soon came to realise that Rugby School was not preparation for adulthood but a microcosm of it. "Nowhere in France could he find its counterpart," wrote Lucas. "The social and political life at Rugby School, i.e. the associations, newspapers, elective government, not only were impossible without the binding force of athletics, but were the creation of this force. [De Coubertin] was convinced that the sports-centred English public school system of the late nineteenth century was the rock upon which the vast and majestic British Empire rested. In the recondite scholarship of Dr. Arnold and in the ensuing trend toward manly sport at Rugby and in England, Coubertin saw a catharsis, not only for the English, but for Frenchmen and eventually all mankind. The genius of Arnold had sown the seed."[19]

According to Lucas, De Coubertin's philosophical approach "combined the 'wholeness' of the Grecian spirit of antiquity with the extreme nineteenth-century moralism of Thomas Arnold". Focusing on the trinity of "character, intellect, and body", De Coubertin's concept of Grecian thought was "inexorably fused" with the school's "image of disciplined austerity and sportsmanship".[20] Holding especial appeal was the gymnasium, a training facility designed for intellectual as well as physical development. Yet as much as he admired the Greeks, De Coubertin espied flaws in their sporting fiesta, as can be gleaned from an inspection of his collected writings, *Olympism*.

He saw the layout of ancient Olympia as "chaotic… impractical and bothersome"; he feels for the spectators "packed together in rigid lines on their marble benches, broiling in the sun or chilled in the shade".[21] He does not appear to believe that ancient Greece was morally superior to his own era; nor did he think the Greeks were as sold on the value of athletic activity as generally thought: "The culture of sports in Greece, moreover, was never as widespread as we have believed… Many authors convey widespread notions of long-standing hostility on the part of public opinion with regard to physical exercises. Besides, those who engaged in exercise were not at all seen as models of virtue and continence."[22] The ancient Olympics owed their lengthy life, he further claimed, not simply to their encouragement of harmony between body and mind, but to "the spectacle, the hubbub, and the advertising"[23], and that corruption was the trigger for decay.

Ultimately, for the peace-loving De Coubertin, internationalism was the most human of grails. "In his early writings," notes Professor Norbert Müller of the University of Mainz, a member of the IOC Commission for Culture and Olympic Education who compiled *Olympism*, "he refers to international sporting encounters as 'the free trade of the future', seeing the participating athletes as 'ambassadors of peace' even though by his own admission he still had to take care, at the time of the founding of the IOC in 1894, not to say too much about this, not wanting to ask too much of sportsmen or to frighten the pacifists. With his ideas of peace, however, Coubertin associated an ethical mission which, then as now, was central to the Olympic Movement and – if it were to succeed – had to lead to political education. On the threshold of the 20th century, Coubertin tried to bring about enlightened internationalism by cultivating a non-chauvinistic nationalism. It is precisely the relationship between nationalism and international peace – a one-sided one hitherto, because invariably regarded as a contradiction in terms – that forms the challenging peace ethos and fascination of Olympism. From the beginning, Coubertin's sights were set upon interplay between nations united by enthusiasm for peace and an internationalism that would set a ceremonial seal on their peaceful ambitions."[24] A major influence was his friend Jules Simon, co-founder of the Interparliamentary Union, founded in Paris in 1888, and the International Peace Bureau, established four years later.

The IOC was formed on 23 June 1894, at a congress in Paris hosted at the world-renowned Sorbonne, one of the planet's first universities. Presided over by De Coubertin, it was attended by representatives of 13 nations (with 21 more sending written support), who passed a resolution to invite every country to unite in sporting competition every four years, on the lines of the original Greek Olympics. Over the next two years, aided by other friends such as William Milligan Sloane, Victor Balk and Demetrios Vikelas, De Coubertin organised the games of the First Olympiad in Athens, which opened on 6 April. Joining the Greeks were a disappointingly low number of visitors – Australia, Austria, Bulgaria, Chile, Denmark, France, Germany, Great Britain & Ireland, Hungary, Italy, Sweden, Switzerland and the US. The programme comprised nine sports – cycling, fencing, gymnastics, lawn tennis, shooting, swimming, track and field, weightlifting and wrestling.

The £36,000 budget proved puny. The original Olympic stadium having been wrecked, the stage for the running, jumping and throwing events was the 2,000-year-old Panathenaic, already rebuilt earlier in the century and now further reconstructed as a 70,000-capacity arena. This was financed at the request of Crown Prince Constantine, the president of the organising committee, by George Averoff, a Greek businessman and philanthropist whose statue still stands on the site. It featured a sand track laid at short notice by Charles Perry, later the groundsman at Chelsea FC's Stamford Bridge: the problems presented by a 333-metre oval circuit, observed Tim Harris, "included a turn so tight it forced runners down to walking pace", compelling the 200 metres to be abandoned. This, though, was the epitome of modernity by comparison with the swimming facilities: Averoff had only supplied a pier, obliging the swimmers to compete in the Bay of Zea, not noted for its warmth. The sailing and rowing were cancelled. "My will to live," Alfréd Hajós, the Hungarian winner of the 1,200m swimming event, would admit, "completely over-came my desire to win."[25]

"Such was the informality," warranted John Arlott, one British tennis player entered the tournament "simply in order to secure a court to play on", while several of the 500 entries "were merely tourists visiting Athens at the time".[26] Yet the venture was hailed as a success, with the Panathenaic accommodating the biggest crowds yet seen for a sporting event. This prompted a number of American competitors, in addition to King George

I of Greece, to urge that all future Games be held in Athens, but plans were already afoot to stage the next one in Paris; not until 2004 would they come home.

Henri the football engine

The first global football trophy was named after Jules Rimet, the son of a grocer who had qualified as a lawyer and founded Red Star Français (later Saint-Ouen) FC in 1897 as a haven for class-lessness. From there he rose to president of the French Football Federation and thence to FIFA head boy, a throne he kept warm for an unprecedented 33 years. Yet by rights this honour should have been shared with his compatriot and partner-in-internationalism, Henri Delaunay, as Huw Richards warrants in the *Cambridge Companion to Football*:

> While, as Bill Murray notes, "at times stormy", the Rimet-Delaunay double act was perhaps the supreme expression of France's contribution to the internationalisation of sport. As [Paul] Dietschy points out, "In the 1920s the majority of inter-national sports federations were based in Paris and, like FIFA, were headed by a Frenchman." Most of these sports were British-devised and it would be easy to depict the French assumption of international leadership as a shot in the age-old trans-manche rivalry. Easy, but wrong. The Frenchmen wanted to work with Britain, and were even prepared to defer to it – Robert Guerin only finally going ahead with the foundation of FIFA in 1904 after finding that trying to get the Football Association inter-ested was "like slicing water with a knife".[27]

It is fiendishly difficult to think of a more admirable admin-istrator than Delaunay. Born in 1883, he played football in the Paris suburbs, kindling a passion, notes Richards, "that survived even the trauma of, as a referee, being struck full in the face by the ball, swallowing the whistle and losing two teeth". His rapid progress through the ranks, from player to referee to administrator, was "characteristic of young sports". As Richards elaborates, he and Rimet were both sons of a French middle-class that had "turned to British examples and pastimes as a reaction to the decadence apparently revealed by the Franco-Prussian war of 1870". There was no more dedicated Anglophile among them than Delaunay, a fluent English speaker known, as Murray records, "as Sir Henry for his British airs, his pipe and his cocker spaniel, as well as his predilection for British names".

It was men such as Rimet and Delaunay, as Geoff Hare observed in *Football in France: A Cultural History*, who "helped move football beyond the national context to internationalise the playing and governance of the game, at times when its English inventors, with an insularity that went beyond the sporting domain, were reticent about the internationalisation of football and reluctant to be involved at the heart of European or world football until there was no alternative and most decisions were irreversible."[28]

Delaunay was appointed to the four-man committee, chaired by Gabriel Bonnot of Switzerland, set up in February 1927 to evaluate a possible competition, and it was his proposal for a quadrennial global cup that carried the day against rival clamour for an exclusively European and even amateurs-only tournament. It was also his resolution to stage it for the first time, in 1930, that was passed by 23 votes to five at the 1928 FIFA Congress in Amsterdam. But whereas Delaunay was primarily a technician, Rimet was the politician, persuading the French federation to send a team to Uruguay, thus ensuring the presence of at least one major European representative.

Delaunay's career was a long and continual stimulant. The founding secretary-general of the French federation as well as its forerunner, the Comité Francais Interfédérale, his joy at attending the 1902 FA Cup final begat a passion that led, 15 years later, to his country's first knockout cup, the Coupe Charles Simon, named after a keen sportsman who had died in the First World War. Delaunay was in his late 60s when he pressed for the creation of UEFA, the European regional federation, and beyond 70 when, in 1954, he became its first secretary-general.

He would die in 1955, shortly before the first conflab to discuss his long-nurtured ambition – a European Nations Cup; when the tournament began three years later, the trophy bore his name. Thus, albeit posthumously, did he enjoy the last laugh over Rimet: while the Henri Delaunay Trophy remains the prize for European's finest, the Jules Rimet Trophy was retired after Brazil's third victory in 1970, and lost in 1983.

"I am for the white race being on top of the black"

Notwithstanding the in-fighting and breakaways that begat the Alphabet Soup era, the ludicrous WBA-WBC-IBF-WBO Show that led to boxing's steep, agonising and seemingly irreversible decline, the trickiest spectator sport to run has been cricket, traditionally the most racially-divided and sheerly nationalistic of games, and hence the most discordant and disruptive. Which is why, as we shall see, its governance has changed in a manner no other sport has remotely emulated.

Formed in 1909, the Imperial Cricket Conference, the game's first approximation to an international governing body, was a white man's gang: England, Australia and South Africa. In effect, it was a two-nation operation: the first two, as "foundation members", could veto anything they pleased. That a governing body should arise from that first ICC meeting at Lord's, whose purpose had been to establish an international fixture schedule, was an undesigned consequence of the labours of a fascinating if not wholly likeable character by the name of Abe Bailey.

Bailey counted Cecil Rhodes as a mentor and Winston Churchill as a close friend. A South African of British parentage, he had played cricket for Transvaal and made a fortune from gold mining (and assorted other ventures) in Australia when he emerged as one of the game's principal patrons, underwriting reciprocal tours by England and South Africa in 1904 and 1905-06. Seeking a significant role for his own country, he had urged the South African Cricket Association to push for the creation of an Imperial Board of Control. Returning to his homeland, Bailey acquired the *Rand Daily Mail* as well as the *Sunday Times*, the country's biggest-selling newspaper. Come the summer of 1909, his long-running efforts to implement a de facto Test championship were about to come to fruition: Australian resistance was eventually overcome and a triangular tournament, bankrolled by Bailey, was approved at that inaugural ICC meeting and would commence three years later. Scepticism abounded, the *Sporting Chronicle* describing it as "the cock and doodle fancy of a millionaire".[29] Shrewd as well as fabulously wealthy, Bailey, who would be knighted two years later for his contributions to the Union of South Africa, had succeeded where so many had failed: he had managed to get on the right side of Lord Harris.

"He was certainly no liberal and his views on race were simply those prevalent at the time," warrants a sympathetic Patrick Ferriday, whose riveting and diligently researched investigation into the context of the triangular tournament was shortlisted for the 2012 Cricket Society Book of the Year award. Nor was Bailey apt to mince words, on one occasion stating: "I am for the white race being on top of the black."[30] Dame Fortune evidently disapproved: an unremittingly awful English summer and often pitiful crowds ensured the experiment has yet to be repeated.

Entirely dependent on agreement that the applicants were worthy of Test status, growth was slow, intentionally so: West Indies, New Zealand and India, in turn, played their first Tests between 1928 and 1932, Pakistan in 1954, Sri Lanka in 1982, Zimbabwe in 1992 and Bangladesh in 2000. Reconstituted for a second time in 1993, when England and Australia finally relinquished their much-resented veto, Sir Clyde Walcott, the former West Indies batsman, was appointed the body's first non-English, non-white president, whereupon, as Gideon Haigh put it, "it ceased to be an adjunct of MCC".

In 1993, the ICC's "headquarters" was an inconspicuous office at Lord's, opposite the nets at the Nursery End, next door to the mowers; all that changed in 2009, as Haigh illustrated:

Dubai, of course, is far from the obvious place to run an ancient English pastoral game, all soaring, twisting, massing, jutting, angling towers exploring every possible variation on the theme of the tall building. The low-key and well-finished three-storey headquarters occupied by the ICC since April 2009 are at least of a rather more human scale. Televised cricket plays on two screens in the sunny atrium, and a routine experience talking to ICC personnel is the way their eyes dart away every so often to check for messages on their Blackberrys from round the world – conversation resumes with their thumbs dancing busily.[31]

When Haigh paid a visit, the ICC boasted some 130 employees, ranging from management to development officers, umpires and match referees, its function to represent (and make money/supply funding for) not just the 10 full member nations, but getting on for 10 times that many associates and affiliates. Most significantly of all, the hands on the reins had changed complexion.

The art of monopoly

Woe betide those seduced by the Johnny-Come-Extremely-Latelys who sought to challenge the supremacy of the governing bodies, of whom those presiding over professional baseball were obliged to fend off more than their fair share. "Organised Baseball has engaged in more than a dozen trade wars during its turbulent history," outlined Harold Seymour. "The wars resulted from rival leagues' disregard for Organised Baseball's market monopoly, or its players' monopsony, or both. The arsenal of weapons used against such 'outlaws' has included boycotts, blacklists, salary duels for players' services, the use of conflicting schedules, price cuts, undercover agents, and the courts. The outcome has always been either the destruction of the competing league or its eventual absorption by the existing system. Someone once said that history is the propaganda of the victors. This epigram fits Organised Baseball."

The irony, as Seymour reinforces, is that the American League was once an outlaw too. In 1899, Ban Johnson, a former Cincinnati sports editor, and our old pal Charlie Comiskey traded in the six-shooter-and-ten-gallon-hat allusions of the

Western League for a more all-inclusive name; two years later they had barged their way into the palace hitherto occupied solely by the National League, propelled by Johnson's vision of a less rowdy game, more conducive to families. After two years of growling and grappling and mutual loathing, the American League persuaded the National League to share the wealth: each agreed to respect the other's reserve rights; each had a team in the major markets: Boston, Chicago, New York, Philadelphia and St Louis. The junior league had first exclusive rights to Cleveland, Detroit and Washington D.C., the senior to Brooklyn, Cincinnati and Pittsburgh; more than half a century later, these territorial alignments would still be intact.

Half a dozen of those revolts had occurred by 1903, leading, in the interests of harmonious governance, to the formation in that year of the National Commission. This three-man panel comprised the two major league presidents overseen by a chairman appointed by themselves, August Herrmann, the chairman of the Cincinnati club, who remained in situ until the commission folded in 1920. "This so-called Supreme Court of Baseball," explains Seymour, "interpreted and carried out the National Agreement by arbitrating disputes between clubs and was empowered to impose fines and suspensions for violation of the Agreement."[32] While excluding player representatives, the Commission regarded the protection of players as a duty and priority, subscribing to "the promotion of the welfare of ball players as a class by developing and perfecting them in their profession and enabling them to secure adequate compensation for expertness". A hefty fine of $500 would be levied on any club "that becomes party to a conspiracy to prevent a player from advancing in his profession, or in any way abusing the privilege of selection". This, argued Seymour, "did not deter the magnates, who employed more dodges to beat the rules than a sidewalk peddler without a license".[33]

"Pervasive" is the considered word Seymour deploys to describe the cover-up. "Before the drafting season began, half a dozen of Milwaukee's best prospects would find their way to

Chicago would then make the return trip the following spring. Both Comiskey and another of his minor-league friends, the New Orleans club, were fined for one of these bogus transactions." So, too, were Charles Ebbetts – Mr Brooklyn Dodgers – and his Philadelphia Athletics counterpart, Connie Mack, for whom the ideal season was a strong summer-long tilt at the pennant and a fourth-place finish: that way, the crowds came but there was no need for wage rises and bonuses.

Hovering over the players was the reviled reserve clause, whose economic impact, avers Marc Edelman, "was entirely to the club-owners' advantage...players had little leverage to negotiate their salaries and therefore benefited little from the game's growing revenues."[34] MLB salaries, as we shall see, appreciated little between the 1900s and the 1960s.

* * *

The time was ripe, then, for a new wave of interlopers. Cue the Pacific Coast League, targeted at the vast swathes of North America west of St Louis with neither a National or American League representative. Players were lured over by the kinder climate, loftier salaries and a longer season: in 1905, the San Francisco Seals, Joe Di Maggio's alma mater, played no fewer than 230 games (that the length of its fixture list still exceeds that of the competition explains why so many minor league records are still held by PCL alumni). As Seymour points out, even those who did not actually join the upstart league profited from it, using it, as one peeved owner put it, "as a bluff to get unreasonable salaries from us". This was cited as one of the reasons Rube Waddell, a brilliant but disturbed pitcher, kept his starter's job with the Athletics: fear of defection compelled Mack to be more tolerant than he might otherwise have been.[35]

In 1905, a year after the major leagues had negotiated a settlement with the PCL, one that permitted the latter to retain all contracted players, came the Tri State League, a predominantly Philadelphian operation, whose thievery led to a promise of lifetime bans for contract-jumpers. Within two years, however, the league was back in the fold and the blacklistees eventually rein-stated. Next up was the California State League; again, those jumping ship were banned, and although this, too, fell into line in 1909, it took three years for the offenders to be forgiven. There were other, smaller uprisings, such as the Tidewater League, the Atlantic League and the various Dixie leagues; the hubris-tically named United States League, launched by the mayor of Reading, Philadelphia, had two stabs: the first, in 1912, lasted around a month; the second, the following year, was history within days.[36]

It was also in 1913 that a band of amply-heeled businessmen took advantage of the players' discontent by starting up the Federal League, first as a minor league then, in 1914, as a direct rival to the major leagues. Behind it was John T. Powers, who had already demonstrated his ambition by trying to set up a Columbian League the previous year. Offering signees the chance to become free agents, he managed to attract 81 major leaguers to his new venture, enough to fuel teams in eight cities and help finance stadium construction and redevelopment. Wading into major league territory, he established outlets in Cincinnati, Cleveland, Pittsburgh and St Louis as well as his own base, Chicago; among the newcomers would be an arena on the north side of Chicago, which would rise to iconic status as Wrigley Field. Johnson used the same word to attack the boarders as had been applied to him when he conceived the American League, calling them "pirates".[37]

To stem the tide of defectors, Johnson and co raised salaries (that of Ty Cobb, the game's leading player, soared by two-thirds to $20,000) and consented, reluctantly, to recognise the players' union. They even agreed to pay for uniforms and have outfield walls painted dark green to aid the batters' sight of the ball and thus reduce injuries. The tide began to turn, prompting the Federal League owners, discouraged by modest attendances and rebuffed in their efforts to open the World Series to a third contender, to seek an antitrust injunction against the major leagues, whom they accused of restraint of trade via the reserve clause and the blacklisting of the defectors. "Do you realise," wondered Judge Kenesaw Mountain Landis, "that a decision in this case may tear down the very foundations of the game? Any blows at the thing called baseball would be regarded by this court as a blow to a national institution."

As the case meandered along, the franchise owners met in Chicago, where the plaintiffs withdrew their suit in exchange for $600,000, stock in several major league clubs, permission to sell players back to the American and National Leagues (without penalty) and the award of an American League franchise in St Louis to a Federal League owner. The peace treaty was signed in December 1915 but the extermination of the Federal League was quickly followed by the expiration of the players' union. Wages were slashed; even Honus Wagner, Cobb's equal in many respects and a man loved rather than loathed, took a cut. "When Ban Johnson turned the hose on the Fraternity," attested the New York *Sun*, "it vanished like old newspapers on the way to a sewer."[38]

The one club that refused to sign the agreement was the Baltimore Terrapins, who sued pretty much all concerned for conspiring to create a monopoly by destroying the Federal League. The defendants were ordered to pay damages of $240,000 but the verdict was reversed on appeal and the case went all the way to the Supreme Court, where Justice Oliver Wendell Holmes Jr decreed that "the business is giving exhibitions of base ball[sic], which are purely state affairs", and hence not subject to the Sherman Act. The ruling would be upheld in *Toolson v New York Yankees* (1952) and *Flood v Kuhn* (1972), to which we shall return.

Ain't no mountain low enough

Forget, for a moment, Cy Young, Babe Ruth and Roberto Clemente, if not Jackie Robinson. The case for Carl Mays to be cited as baseball's most significant professional is far from groundless. On 16 August 1920, Ray Chapman, batting for the Cleveland Indians, dug in against Mays, an unorthodox and often vicious New York Yankees pitcher whose "submariner" underarm action made him difficult to pick up at the best of times and who thought nothing of plunking the mighty – and mighty nasty – Cobb. The ball was grimy, the light indifferent. Chapman, leaning over the plate, found himself being followed by a rapid rising delivery and was struck so squarely over the left temple, wrote Grantland Rice, that the ball "dribbled down the third base line where Aaron Ward, thinking it a bunt, pounced on it and rifled to third baseman Wally Pipp".[39] Chapman froze then crumpled. The grisly aftermath was captured with no relish whatsoever by Robert Creamer, Babe Ruth's most measured and insightful biographer: "Aided by two teammates, he began to walk toward the clubhouse in center field. As he reached the outfield grass he collapsed again and had to be carried the rest of the way."[40] Taken to hospital, Chapman died the next day. To date, he remains major league baseball's only fatality.

The Boston Red Sox, Washington Senators and Cobb's Detroit Tigers all threatened to strike if Mays was allowed to pitch again, but he was reprieved after others rallied behind him, most helpfully Johnson. Muddy Ruel, the Yankee catcher, was adamant that, had the ball not hit Chapman – whose habit of crowding the plate, thus reducing the non-fleshy strike zone available to Mays, was widely seen as provocation – the pitch would have been called a strike. In the longer term, the upshots were considerable. The spitball – whereby spit was applied to the ball to make it behave erratically, Mays being just one of many unabashed exponents – was outlawed; any pitched ball that landed in the dirt, moreover, would now be changed for a new one, the sole downside of which was the expense: a single game might demand scores of new balls, a luxury fast bowlers would kill for. Yet Mays's reverberative impact on baseball history did not stop there. In fact, it had begun the previous season.

Enraged by what he regarded as his colleagues' inefficiency, Mays had stormed off the diamond during a 1919 game for the Boston Red Sox, vowing never to don the uniform again, but when Johnson refused to give his assent for a move to the Yankees, the club owners sued and Mays stayed. With the

Yankees, Red Sox and the White Sox all making high-wattage noises about jumping ship to the National League, the ensuing row almost wrecked the junior league. Cue a search for a baseball overlord to keep the warring owners from self-destructing, a solution first proposed by the National League, to whom an outsider would be nothing if not commonsensical. The eventual choice, beating the erstwhile President Taft, was Kenesaw Mountain Landis, the owners' saviour in the Federal League case. While despising alcohol, he was a far from sober judge. Instantly recognisable, a shock of bouffant white hair set off dark, blazing eyes; he was also a man with a marked fondness for exhibitionism.

Born in Ohio and named after Georgia's Kennesaw Mountain, site of a bloody Confederate victory during the Civil War, Landis was in his early 40s when he was appointed by President Theodore Roosevelt to sit on the bench of the Northern District of Illinois in 1905. Seymour memorably depicts him as a "hawk-visaged curmudgeon who affected battered hats, used salty language, chewed tobacco, and poked listeners in the ribs with a stiff right finger".[41] Characterised by a lengthy series of trials involving the Industrial Workers of the World, a union whose leaders had been accused of espionage, his judgements – as the Federal League case underscored – showed him to be no fan of the working man. Nor would he have any time for the second President Roosevelt's New Deal. In November 1920, not long after the Black Sox hearings but many months before the trial, he accepted the new post of commissioner for a seven-year term at a salary of $50,000 – minus, because he had no intention of giving up his gavel, his judge's salary of $7,500 – with one proviso: his power should be absolute.[42] For the next 24 years, it would be absolutely that.

"Landis had a deep affection for baseball and looked upon the players more as heroes than as employees," wrote Seymour. His foremost judicial flaw was that he "permitted his personal dislikes to warp his objectivity".[43] Shortly after his appointment, he made the statement that, in Seymour's estimation, "was to set the tone of his administration", saying of the Black Sox: "There is absolutely no chance for any of them to creep back into Organised Baseball. They will be and remain outlaws... It is sure that the guilt of some of them at least will be proved." A Federal judge, in other words, "was condemning men to the blacklist before they had been tried in a court of law and whatever the outcome of their trial".[44]

No less egregious was Landis's racism. "The first rumblings against the status quo began in the '40s," relates Peter Golenbock, "when black activist Paul Robeson confronted Landis, demanding to know why black men... were not permitted to play professional baseball. Robeson, who had been an All-American football player at Rutgers, told Landis that blacks played in football, track, and even professional croquet. Why not baseball? With great solemnity, Judge Landis told Robeson that there was no rule on the books prohibiting a black man from joining a major league team. It was up to the owners to hire whom they pleased. Landis could get away with such a cavalier statement because he knew that the owners weren't about to give a Negro the opportunity."[45]

Of Landis's few modern defenders, one of the staunchest is David Pietrusza, a former president of the Society for Baseball Research and historian who, in addition to an award-winning biography of Landis, has written acclaimed studies of a number of US presidents while being a regular contributor to that fount of right-wing tabloid unwisdom, Fox News. "Increasingly," he warrants, "modern observers have created the image of Kenesaw Landis as the George Wallace of baseball, standing in the doorway of every ballpark in the country, an unyielding racist who prevented the game's integration. It's a convenient image. Unfortunately, it oversimplifies the issue and – by shifting all or most of the blame to Landis – exculpates the rest of baseball for its actions, inactions, and attitudes. If truth be told, few in baseball wished to integrate, a fact revealed by the many teams that did not hire even token blacks until years following Landis's death."[46]

By the same token, it would be no less simplistic to bracket Landis with the pack. Without specifically banning integrated games, Landis did nothing to encourage and much to discourage them: major league teams, he resolved, would no longer be able to field their first-choice lineup against black opponents, nor wear their official uniforms in exhibition games, which could not be played, in any case, until after the World Series. Larry Lester, a historian and co-founder of the Negro Leagues Baseball Museum, called him "the monarch of segregated baseball".[47]

Nor did he soften. Come the late 1930s, and increasingly so after Pearl Harbour, segregation, in sport as well as wider society, was a topic of rising public interest. "Nationalism had at least briefly trumped racism when Joe Louis and Jesse Owens emerged triumphant against the Germans," avers Lester. "Within baseball, members of the media had loudly called for integration, which some major league managers, players, and even owners publicly supported. And as big leaguers went off to war, leaving behind diluted rosters and flagging attendance, calls for the signing of black players grew more persistent. In spite of these facts, some researchers contend that Commissioner Kenesaw Mountain Landis must be held blameless for extending the colour line; segregation, they argue, was a cultural wrong, and the time was not yet ripe to change it."[48] Yet Landis, in his view, "repeatedly disregarded calls for integrated play and in some instances acted to perpetuate segregation".

Only a "sort of gentleman's agreement", asserted Shirley Povich in 1939, was preventing integration – the accent less on "gentleman's" than "sort of".[49] Three years later, Lester Rodney, a sportswriter at the *Daily Worker* whose efforts to integrate the game would be as inexhaustible as they were noble, launched a campaign, "Can You Read, Judge Landis?" Other newspapers embraced the cause. "National Unity embracing all races, colours and creeds," read a statement that summer from Ford Local 600, the nation's largest trade union, "is particularly necessary at this point in order to win the war against Fascism."[50] In Manhattan, the League for Equality on Sports and Amusements, a group of Harlem activists, picketed repeatedly, brandishing signs carrying exhortations such as "IF WE

CAN STOP BULLETS, WHY NOT BALLS?" and "WE CAN PAY, WHY CAN'T WE PLAY?"[51]

The most acceptable counter-argument, as espoused by Landis himself, and a prescient one at that, was that integration would wreak havoc with the Negro Leagues, whose annual showpiece, the East-West All-Star game in Chicago, had drawn a record 50,256 spectators in 1941. Mused Ed Harris in the *Philadelphia Tribune*, a black-owned newspaper: "You get to wondering what the magnates of the American and National League thought about it when they read the figures. Did any of them feel a faint stir in their hearts; a wish that they could use some of the many stars who saw action to corral some of the coin evidently interested in them? Or did they, hearing the jingling of the turnstiles in this, one of the good seasons baseball has had, just dismiss the motion and reserve the idea of Negro players in the big league until the next time there is a depression and baseball profits began to decline?"[52]

All too instructive, moreover, was an exchange nearly two decades earlier between Landis and Andrew "Rube" Foster, the visionary entrepreneur behind the formation of the Negro Leagues in 1920. Livid that the commissioner had pulled the plug on a moneyspinning exhibition encounter in 1923 between the Chicago Americans, co-owned by Foster, and an "all-star" combination of white players, Foster confronted the judge. "Mr Foster," Landis explained, "when you beat our teams it gives us a black eye."[53]

In May 1941, a month before Rodney was drafted, an exhibition game was arranged featuring two sterling starting pitchers, "Dizzy" Dean and Satchel Paige, the Negro Leagues' No.1 hurler and the man after whom Woody Allen would name his first biological son. Rodney wrote Landis an open letter in the *Daily Worker* headlined "TIME FOR STALLING IS OVER, JUDGE LANDIS":

You, the self-proclaimed "Czar" of Baseball, are the man responsible for keeping Jim Crow in our National Pastime. You are the one who, by your silence, is maintaining a relic of the slave market long repudiated in other American sports. You are the one who is refusing to say the word which would do more to justify baseball's existence in this year of war than any other single thing. You are the one who is blocking the step which would put baseball in line with the rest of the country, with the United States government itself. There can no longer be any excuse for your silence, Judge Landis. It is a silence that hurts the war effort. [54]

Leo "The Lip" Durocher, the endlessly shrewd and proudly tactless Brooklyn Dodgers manager, ratcheted up the tension with a seemingly casual remark to Rodney: he would love to sign black players. Meanwhile, by mid-July 1942, a nationwide petition had climbed past a million signatures. And, as Rodney noted drily, "we didn't have a million Communists". The signatories, he warranted, "were people who were going to the ballpark and wanted to see justice".[55]

Landis finally issued a statement a few days later: "There is no rule against major clubs hiring Negro baseball players. I have come to the conclusion it is time for me to explain myself on this important issue. Negroes are not barred from organised baseball by the commissioner and have never been since the 21 years I have served. There is no rule in organised baseball prohibiting their participation to my knowledge. If Durocher, or any other manager, or all of them want to sign one or 25 Negro players, it is all right with me. That is the business of the manager and the club owners."[56]

The headline in the *Daily Worker* was celebratory: "Landis's O.K. on Negro Stars Is a Great Democratic Victory for All America". Others were more sceptical, among them Gordon Macker of the *Los Angeles News*: "What does that mean? Not a damn thing. [Landis] has merely stated that there is no rule against Negroes playing in organised baseball. There never has been any rule against them playing... The statement of the high commissioner is just a lot of words... just another case of hypocritical buck passing."[57]

Two franchise owners, William Benswanger of the Pittsburgh Pirates and Alva Bradley of the Cleveland Indians, promised to give trials to black players but none were signed. Writing in the *Baltimore Afro-American*, Sam Lacey, the first African-American journalist admitted to the Baseball Writers Association of America, homed in on the perversity of it all: "Baseball in its time has given employment to known epileptics, kleptomaniacs, and a generous scattering of saints and sinners. A man who is totally lacking in character has often turned up to be a star in baseball. A man whose skin is white, or red, or yellow has been acceptable. But a man whose character may be of the highest and whose ability may be Ruthian has been barred completely from the sport because he is coloured."[58]

Nothing had changed by 1944, when Landis died in office, having just been recommended for re-election. His contribution to baseball, reckoned Seymour, lay in having "kept its magnates in line to a greater extent than before – or since, for that matter". Better yet, "he provided a symbol that reassured the public of baseball's honesty and integrity, so much so that, even after the magnates recovered from their fright over the Black Sox and began having second thoughts about Landis and the commissionership, they found it expedient to maintain the status quo while he lived, for to alter it would appear to be casting virtue into the street."[59]

Only with Landis's passing, and the accession to the commissioner's seat of Albert "Happy" Chandler, would the world turn. Within a year, Branch Rickey had signed Jackie Robinson. "Landis had unlimited authority and tremendous influence, but the historical record makes all too clear that he lacked the fortitude to put a little soul into the game," concludes Lester, who also has the good sense to quote Voltaire:

Every man is guilty of all the good he did not do.[60]

Mission near-impossible

In October 1968, Dick Fosbury became Olympic high-jump champion by propelling himself over the bar backwards.

Flabbers were gasted from Tokyo to Toronto. Had you decided, then and there, to institute an all-time chart of daft ideas, the sudden disappearance of one obvious candidate might have impelled a tweak to the top 10, but nothing would have changed at the summit: selling un-American football to North Americans would still have ranked just below selling ice to the Inuit. Nobody expended more energy trying to tackle that improbable mission than Phil Woosnam. He may well have been the most courageous of all sporting administrators; he was certainly among the most determined and estimable.

The Woosnams are nothing if not a sporty bunch: Ian, Phil's cousin, was among the most successful professional golfers of the late 20th century, winning the US Masters; his uncle, moreover, was Max, hailed by some as the most gifted of all British sportsfolk – besides winning gold and silver at the 1920 Olympics, he captained England and Manchester City at football and Britain in the Davis Cup, won a Wimbledon doubles title, hit a century at Lord's and once even pulled off a maximum 147 break on the snooker table. Phil may have come a distant third in the family hall of fame in terms of athletic achievement, but as an influence on sporting history he beat them hands-down.

As it happened, a month before the "Fosbury Flop" entered the lexicon, the home of "saah-ker" had witnessed a seemingly significant breakthrough: the Atlanta Chiefs had become the inaugural champions of the North American Soccer League – the first national top division after 55 years of FIFA-authorised football. They were coached by Woosnam, who had traded in teaching physics in East London to distinguish himself as a creative inside-forward at West Ham and later Aston Villa, winning 17 caps for Wales between 1958 and 1962. Age, as ever, had sapped his legs; at 33, less able to evade the crunching tackles, he had decided to join the non-rush to the unrecognised National Professional Soccer League, signing for the Chiefs in 1966. From there he rose with alacrity, coaching the national team in 1968 before becoming the NASL commissioner. Undaunted as the league abruptly dwindled from 17 teams to five, he turned his attention to promoting the game, persuading investors to set up new franchises, negotiating TV contracts with the big-hitters, CBS and ABC, and overseeing expansion to the west. Enter the big-city likes of the New York Cosmos and the LA Aztecs, the former courtesy of the communications giant, Warner, the latter co-owned by Elton John.

It was also Woosnam who expanded the league to 24 teams, changed playing regulations, introduced innovations. The most imaginative and prominent – not to say notorious – of these was deciding games by shoot-outs to avert any of those silly draw-type thingies. Not via penalties but by giving the attacker, starting on the halfway line, five seconds to beat the goalkeeper by pretty much whatever method he saw fit. By 1974, average gates had doubled, albeit to just 7000, underlining the progress still required. A year later, the Cosmos signed Pelé and the world sat up. More sat down, too: the Brazilian diamond may not have been as dazzling as he had been at the 1970 World Cup, but New Yorkers turned up in scores of thousands to revel in his abiding genius. "The source of all [Woosnam's] ideas and the intensity with which he poured them out, I decided, was his Welshness coming through," said Paul Gardner, one of the first American sportswriters and broadcasters to take soccer seriously. "I saw it as an almost religious Welsh fervour, and marveled at it."[61]

Come 1978, with a network TV contract in Woosnam's pocket and entry fees standing at a cool $1m, the future looked bright. Losses, though, reached $30m, the Aztecs and the Washington Diplomats went bust and, in 1983, the franchise owners voted him out of office. Expansion had been too far and too fast, they believed, something, as *The Times* stressed, that "he could not have done without their approval".[62] The very next year the NASL collapsed.

As marketing controller of US Soccer, nonetheless, Woosnam continued to push the American game into the wider spotlight, doing much, crucially, to help secure the hosting rights for the 1994 World Cup, considered by many to be the last word in foot-balling sacrilege. "A true pioneer," insisted Bill Peterson, the commissioner of the NASL's latest incarnation, Major League Soccer, whose average gate for 2012, 18,807, ranked behind only baseball and gridiron among US team sports, and ahead of the game's top divisions in Argentina and Brazil. Without Woosnam, we would probably still be awaiting the foundation of LA Galaxy, let alone the arrival of David Beckham, much less the following tribute from *The Daily Beast*, a popular US website, shortly after he announced his retirement in May 2013: "No one hates David Beckham, which is odd for anyone who is estimated to earn in excess of $46 million a year, is married to a former Spice Girl, and has sold out more professionally, more extensively, and more successfully than any other soccer player in the history of the game." The headline was the story: "David Beckham is Retiring, But We Still Love Him".[63]

Woosnam "took soccer into uncharted waters", added Peterson, "and through his passion, carried the game on his shoulders."[64] Without him, the best-known expression of American exceptionalism might still be a standing joke.

Adi and Horst

The reason the Olympics are only every four years is because it takes them four years to count all the money. The problem is who gets a piece of the pie and who gets the crumbs.

John Carlos[65]

Relative to the clout it wields, the IOC does remarkably well to attract as little media attention as it does. Most of the unfavourable publicity and criticism it does receive revolves around vote-rigging for hosting rights. Writing in the *British Journalism Review* shortly before London 2012, the indefatigable Andrew Jennings explained why:

There's a private club of sports reporters who bring us the news and write about the Olympics. It is called the Olympic Journalists' Association. Run your eye down the membership list and you'll recognise many of the bylines from the sports

pages, radio, television and the wires: Mihir Bose, David Bond,
Paul Kelso and Ashling O'Connor – people who cover not just
the Olympics, but also FIFA and the other international sports
federations. But take a look at a membership list from 2009, the
year before the last Winter Olympics, in Vancouver. Hang on
a minute, here's Jon Tibbs. He's not a journalist. He's a sports
spin doctor out of Bell Pottinger and Hill & Knowlton, whose
eponymous consultancy, JTA, offers "strategic brand-building
and communications consultancy for clients in the interna-
tional sports movement". Tibbs has worked on Olympic Games
bids by Athens, Beijing and Sochi, helped clean up reputations
after the Salt Lake City Olympic bid sex-and-bribery scandal –
10 members of the International Committee were either expelled
or resigned – and played flak-catcher for the Glazer family,
unpopular owners of Manchester United.[66]

Jennings's exposés of the IOC and FIFA made him the ringmasters' Public Enemy No.1. Walking out on the BBC after the
corporation refused to screen an hour-long documentary about
the connection between Scotland Yard and cocaine, he wrote
a book about the subject then embarked on a series of uncompromising investigations into the hypocrisy and corruption of
the Olympic movement, whether solo or in cahoots with Vyv
Simson and Clare Sambrook. The first of these, *The Lords of the
Rings*, was retitled rather more bluntly in the US as *Dishonest
Games*. Jennings' reports and documentaries have won awards
from the Royal Television Society and at the New York TV
Festival; he has even received an "Integrity in Journalism"
award at the United Nations. "Of course," he assured me once,
"I am not a sports journalist – not since my stint on the *Burnley
Evening Star* in the mid-1960s. But I have strong views on how
sports journalists cover sports investigations – or rather don't."[67]

What, he asks, of Charles Battle, a Georgia lawyer turned
Olympic consultant who "suitcased thousands of dollars in cash
from the Caribbean to Florida to win an IOC member's vote
for Atlanta's bid to host the 1996 Olympics"? Or Jean-Claude

Schupp, another member of the Adidas team that, from the 1970s, intervened in leadership elections at the IOC, FIFA and the IAAF? Now consider Jean-Marie Weber, whom Jennings "door-stepped" while reporting for BBC's *Panorama*. "Weber was the bagman for the discredited ISL sports marketing company, handing over $100 million in bribes to top sports officials in return for multi-billion dollar marketing contracts for the Olympics and football's World Cup." Yet there he was, still an OJA member a year after coming clean in a Swiss court. "It was claimed that one of those bribes – for $1million – went to former FIFA president João Havelange. After our programme, the bribe was investigated by the International Olympic Committee's ethics commission. Havelange resigned from the IOC in a hurry."[68]

* * *

The thread here is supplied by a pair of German cobblers from Herzogenaurach, Adolph ("Adi") and Rudolph Dassler. One day the brothers rowed bitterly, and vowed never to speak again. Before long, they were establishing rival shoemaking outlets on opposite banks of the Aurach river – Adi and his wife named theirs Adidas; Rudolph went for Puma. At the 1936 Olympics, in a harbinger of reflected glory and profits to come, Jesse Owens won four gold medals clad in feet shod by Adidas.

The dispute divided the Dassler clan for decades, persuading Adi's son, Horst, to flee Germany for France, where he set up his own branch of his father's business. In the 1980s, having turned his father's legacy into a substantial fortune, he would set up a marketing arm, International Sport and Leisure. When the contract came up to handle the IOC's first formal marketing programme, ISL landed the gig.

It was Adi who, according to Patrick Nally, Horst's trusty right-hand man, "had started to see the importance of branding and the importance of the Olympics"; had seen to it "that it was becoming more and more important to get across the personalised imagery that only Adidas produced winners' shoes... In other words, if there was going to be a gold medal won, it was going to be won in Adidas shoes."[69] Horst picked up the baton.

"Dassler used Adidas France to build his own empire within sport," claim Jennings and Simson, who persuaded Nally to break his long-held silence. "Secretly, through the company, he built up a monopoly in the sports equipment market. He surreptitiously acquired other sports manufacturing companies and bought into other competitor shoe makers like Pony."[70] Nally understood the motivation better than most: "It wasn't just the Adidas brand that was Horst's. What he was doing was building up a second sports equipment group separate from the Adidas name just in case another fundamental split ever came. Then of course he could forget about Adidas, strengthen his base in France and take whatever he could with him."[71]

Horst Dassler, recalled Nally, was "in awe" of leading sportspeople. That's why he employed them. He hired Robbie Brightwell, Britain's leading contender in the 1964 Olympic 400m and husband of the women's 800m champion, Ann Packer. He also hired John Boulter, the former British 800m runner, who joined the powerful Adidas International Relations Team and later became, as Jennings put it, "a member of Lord Coe's hearts and minds persuasion squad" for the London Games.

"The Club"

Jennings and Simson write scathingly of "The Club", the self-styled "commissions" entrusted with organising the winter and summer Olympics in addition to dealing with finance, doping and sports medicine. When Don Juan Antonio Samaranch y Torelló, 1st Marquis of Samaranch, Grandee of Spain, assumed the IOC presidency in 1966, this elite corps had seven members; by 1992, on the eve of the Barcelona Games, there were 17. "These commissions alone eat up 4.5 million Swiss francs a year," noted Jennings and Simson. To further aggravate the authors' wrath, Ed Meyer, then chairman of the IOC's advertising agency, Grey, had described the Olympic movement as a "global brand".[72]

The late Ian Wooldridge, an oft-garlanded *Daily Mail* columnist, was an arch-proponent of the Olympic movement for more than three decades, yet he repeatedly expressed his contempt for Samaranch, lambasting "his self-styled Excellency's exploitation of the Games as his personal court, a shadowy chamber of furtive sycophants, dubious grace and dodgy favours".[73] On the eve of his final Games, the Atlanta Olympics of 1996, Wooldridge took enormous pride in being the 9,811th runner in the Olympic Torch relay chain, gleaning "a valuable insight into the sheer joy and enthusiasm that the Games can bring to a community", but remained unrepentant: "I have written as cynically as anyone about the commercialism and devious politicking of the Olympic movement in recent years and do not retract a word of it."[74]

For journalists, the path to any vestige of the truth is strewn with barriers. "The trouble is that FIFA don't put out press releases, and nor do the IOC for that matter – so you see nothing in the papers," explains Jennings, whose FIFA story was only seen in the *Mail*, between hard covers and on *Panorama*. "I had 2.9 million viewers for that, which is more people than buy the *Mail* every day, and not all of them read the sports pages. Which is why the bright young journalists are going into TV. The editors of papers aren't watching TV – they're busy putting the papers to bed and maybe having the big game on. The IOC have been better since Samaranch left. But who's asking questions about them? In mainland Europe yes, not England. The level of thievery in volleyball is huge. People think that if a sport isn't on Sky it isn't important. Editors have determined arbitrarily what the market is. During Colin Gibson's reign [as sports editor] at the *Mail* he pushed investigations with panache but nobody followed them up. Where are the sports editors to push them? I've got documents, half of which haven't been published yet."[75]

"We were told that Evangelisti had to get a medal"
In 1994, the IOC ruled that, in the course of its members' travels to see facilities and consider hosting bids, they were entitled to receive gifts up to the value of $150 – this did not so much

open Pandora's box as yank the lid off its hinges, resulting in the cash-for-votes scandal behind the 2002 Winter Olympics in Salt Lake City. Frustrated by four failed bids, Salt Lake officials had tried their level best, and plenty more besides, to ensure there would be no possible chance of rejection this time. IOC members were handed free credit cards; $19,991 was spent escorting three IOC couples to the 1995 Super Bowl; Intermountain Health Care provided $28,000 worth of free medical care to three people connected to an IOC member – care for hepatitis, cosmetic surgery and a knee replacement. Meanwhile, Mayor Deedee Corradini admitted the city had hired as an intern the son of David Sibandze, an IOC member. And that, notes Alicia Shepard in the *American Journalism Review*, was "just a taste of the largesse".[76] Resignations and expulsions duly followed, together with stiffer regulations, but although the US Department of Justice brought charges against the leading organisers, all were acquitted. If only because it actually affected the competitors, another chapter in the lengthy history of administrative corruption left an even sourer taste.

In 1987, The Club's third most powerful potentate – behind Samaranch and Havelange – was Primo Nebiolo, the IAAF president on whose watch occurred one of the more outlandishly flagrant slices of hometown sporting theft. The stage was those World Championships in Rome, where a gaggle of far from disinterested local judges helped Giovanni Evangelisti, the local hero, take the long-jump bronze medal behind Carl Lewis. The clincher was a last-round leap officially measured at 8.38 metres – albeit only after all the imprints in the sand had been prematurely and conveniently smoothed away. Competitors, spectators and experts alike were astonished; few if any believed the Italian had leapt as far as 8m; the Association of Track & Field Statisticians categorised the stated distance, generously, as "doubtful". Evangelisti's own reaction as he left the pit was certainly not that of someone optimistic that a medal was within the realms of possibility. "You must understand," Paolo Gionanne, the director of the championships, told Renato

Marino, chief coach of one of Italy's most prominent athletics clubs, "we were told that Evangelisti had to get a medal."[77]

Sandro Donati, the Italian sprint coach, pressed police to launch an inquiry and lodged a formal complaint with CONI, the Italian Olympic Committee. The following February, the truth was revealed, courtesy of an unmanned TV camera at the end of the pit. A single frame of the video obtained by *L'Espresso* could hardly have been more damning: with the aid of a handy optical prism he had secreted in the sand (during the medal ceremony that delayed the long jump), one of the judges, Tommaso Aiello, had recorded a measurement of 8.38m *before* Evangelisti had actually jumped. CONI declared the leap invalid. "If this is true," lamented Professor Arne Ljunqvist, Sweden's representative on the IAAAF council, "the athletes can no longer trust us."

Officially, the bronze now went to Larry Myricks, though Evangelisti had already given his ill-gotten medal away. Typically, Nebiolo boxed clever. First, he ensured that the only copy of the report shown to council members was in Italian. Then he spun the saga to emphasise how it demonstrated the unparalleled flexibility of the IAAAF: "We did what no other international body has done. We changed the result after watching TV. Did FIFA do this when Maradona handled a goal against England in the World Cup?"[78] How splendidly it suited Nebiolo, deduced Jennings and Simson, "to ignore the fact that Myricks and Evangelisti, two members of his 'athletics family', had been victims of a conspiracy by his own officials, not victims of a spontaneous foul."[79]

FIFA-fo-fum

International football, by comparison with the Olympics at least, has been a slice of battenberg. The balance, however, is entering a delicate phase. FIFA remains dominant, but the game's greatest riches lie in Europe, where UEFA now has to consider the wishes of the European Club Association; since its formal recognition by FIFA and UEFA in January 2008, this new force has represented 201 clubs from 53 member nations. It was an indication of its growing confidence when, in February 2012, it boycotted talks with FIFA over changes to the international calendar.

The previous September, the ECA had called for the number of friendly internationals per season to be slashed from 12 to six. Its president, the Bayern Munich chief executive Karl-Heinz Rummenigge, had emerged as a forceful rival to Michel Platini, the UEFA president and heir apparent to FIFA president Sepp Blatter; now he claimed clubs were sick and tired of losing players for "nonsense" fixtures. The ECA also wanted FIFA to take out insurance to pay for the salaries of players injured on international duty.[80] As an illustration of the power of the clubs, witness Bayern and Arjen Robben. Then playing on the wing for Bayern, the brilliant Dutchman was injured while on international duty in 2010. By way of compensation, not only did the German FA arrange a friendly with the Netherlands in Munich just 22 days before the 2012 European Championships, both managers were contractually obliged to select a full-strength side. As Oliver Kay noted in *The Times*, "what Bayern want, Bayern get".[81]

Much the same, still, could be said of FIFA itself. Its biggest challenge to date came in 1948. Thanks to the fruits of a surging economy and booming attendances, not to mention a government eager to distract attention from the country's bloody political and social unrest, the Colombian FA introduced the El Dorado league and began luring foreign talent with high salaries, including a number of prominent Englishmen such as Charlie Mitten and Neil Franklin but primarily players from the game's leading nations, Brazil, Hungary and Uruguay. In 1951, after the Argentine FA had complained of piracy, Colombia was expelled from FIFA. In the short term, the revolution was brief: it was not long before the *Pacto de Lima* saw Colombia readmitted to FIFA in exchange for the increasingly cash-strapped El Dorado agreeing to allow its imports return to their original clubs by 15 October 1954. In the longer term, this minor revolution certainly improved the lot of English footballers: the FA awarded two sizeable increases in the maximum wage before its repressive wage restraint was finally scrapped in 1961.

Yet only recently has FIFA come under any scrutiny, thanks primarily to Jennings' unstinting efforts. It is with justified pride that he published a revealing photo on his website, transperencyinsport.org: a banner hoisted by Internacionale supporters in Porto Alegre during a Brazilian league match, on which a cartoon of Jennings is flanked by the words "Andrew Jennings – Save the World Cup 2014". It was their way of expressing gratitude for his investigation of Ricardo Teixera, president of the Brazilian Football Confederation; in July 2012, a Swiss prosecutor's report had revealed that, during his tenure on the FIFA executive committee, he and Havelange, his ex-father-in-law and Blatter's predecessor, pocketed more than $41m in bribes in connection with the award of World Cup marketing rights to ISL.

Not that Brazilians were entirely surprised. The previous year, in an interview published by the magazine *piaui*, Teixera not only waved away the allegations but boasted of intending to do whatever he pleased when Brazil hosted the 2014 World Cup, whether that meant changing the match schedule on a whim or denying press accreditation to anyone who displeased him. So disdainful was his sense of impregnability, he used the word *caguei*, a Portuguese swear-word for the verb "to defecate": in other words, he couldn't care less.[82]

Fuelled by Jennings's assiduous pursuit of incriminating documentation, disquiet had been gathering momentum, over both corruption (to which the reaction from most members of the footballing fraternity had hovered between mild askance and complete apathy) and the nomination of Russia and Qatar to host the 2018 and 2022 World Cups respectively (the cases may not necessarily prove to have been mutually exclusive). By and large, nonetheless, FIFA has ruled with a rod of barely tempered steel.

* * *

As spokesman for the United States' failed bid to host the 1986 World Cup, Henry Kissinger's experience of Jean-Marie Faustin Godefroid Havelange made Richard Nixon's notorious former adviser feel "nostalgic for the Middle East". For a man of unprepossessing build, the Brazilian possessed an unexpected talent for intimidation. There was "such an aura about him", testified David Will, a Scottish lawyer and veteran FIFA committeeman, "people were actually physically scared of him".[83] To Guido Tognoni, a former FIFA media director, he was "a master of power" prone to convince you "that the sky was red when it was actually blue".[84]

Expanding the World Cup field (which doubled from 16 in 1970 to 32 in 2010) was Havelange's master-stroke. Representing a sea-change from the imperial figure of England's Sir Stanley Rous, his predecessor as FIFA president, he brought Africa and Asian nations out of the backwoods, ensuring their gratitude come voting time. Behind the scenes, Havelange was doing deals and gripping the reins, and not always with the highest regard for ethics or morals.[85]

Picking on a nonagenarian is seldom considered a virtue in polite or even philistine circles, not least when said elder has been nominated, however quixotically, for the Nobel Peace Prize. Then again, since our ringmasters almost invariably have to be dragged from their thrones kicking, screaming and ranting, many would argue that there are justifiable exceptions, and that Havelange, in particular, deserves every sling and arrow. Such is the pluralism of football realpolitik in the twenty-first century, however, there are also many, primarily but not exclusively from the Third World, who regard the Brazilian with respect and gratitude. To Hugh McIlvanney, he is "to moral leadership what General George Custer was to military prudence".[86] The only unanimity is that he will be remembered, whether fondly or bitterly, as the modern game's most influential mover and shaper.

It was Havelange who expanded FIFA from a shoestring operation to one he claimed, at the end of his reign, was worth around $250 billion; Havelange who, with his chums at Adidas and ISL, attested David Goldblatt, wise author of *The World Is Round*, an enthralling and astutely judged history of global football, "transformed FIFA from a penurious cottage industry into the owner of the world's greatest commercial and sporting spectacular"[87]; Havelange who wrested football's reins from Northern Europe, established lucrative partnerships with Coca-Cola and McDonald's, and globalised the game, giving Asia and Africa their say. It was Havelange, moreover, who eased Samaranch's passage into the Olympic fraternity and facilitated his rise. Havelange also saw himself as promoting world peace through football, waxing lyrical about the positive impact on East Asia of staging the 2002 World Cup in Japan and South Korea, and claiming to have helped bring China "into the world's economic and political embrace".[88]

It was also Havelange who hand-picked the profoundly unloved Blatter to succeed him, an election reportedly facilitated by kickbacks, vote-rigging, finance from the Gulf and undue use of FIFA resources. The honours, meanwhile, flew fast and thick – the Order of Special Merit in Sports (Brazil), Commander of the Cavaliers of the Order of Infante D. Henrique (Portugal), Cavalier of the Vasa Orden (Sweden) and the Grand Cross of Elizabeth the Catholic (Spain). The least warranted, and most revealing, was the Swiss Football Association's 1988 decision to nominate him for the Nobel Peace Prize, for turning FIFA into "a world power binding all nations".[89] It may have been pure coincidence, but the Swiss were contemplating a bid to stage the 1998 World Cup. During his successful campaign for the French presidency, however, Jacques Chirac claimed that Havelange, who voted for Barcelona ahead of Paris to stage the 1992 Olympics, had promised him France would be hosts, something FIFA's executive had yet to even consider. Countering the Swiss, President Mitterand awarded Havelange the *Légion d'Honneur*. Checkmate: the *Coup du Monde* went to France.

Somewhat tardily, the IOC began investigating Havelange in June 2011, nearly a decade and a half after he (theoretically) ceased calling the shots, stirred into action by Jennings's allegations on *Panorama* that he had accepted $1m in bribes, ostensibly on behalf of FIFA. An IOC member since 1963 and FIFA president from 1974 to 1998, the 95-year-old may have deserved gentle treatment on any other occasion, but his relationship with ISL could no longer be ignored.

Following the collapse of ISL in 2001, the Swiss liquidator Thomas Bauer informed Jennings that he had found evidence of "football-related" payments to FIFA officials to secure lucrative television and sponsorship rights contracts stretching back over two decades. Jennings claimed that the slush fund, channelled through a bank account held in Liechtenstein, was only discovered after a payment worth one million Swiss francs was accidentally sent to a FIFA executive in Zurich.[90] At the time, Jennings declined to name the official concerned, but on another edition of *Panorama*, screened in June 2006, he alleged that the recipient of the payment had been Havelange. In December 2011, with an IOC inquiry imminent, Havelange resigned from the committee; wary of the legal constraints, Keir Radnedge, chairman of the football arm of AIPS, the International Sports Press Association, contented himself with declaring it a "glaring coincidence".

In July 2012, Jennings' persistence was rewarded when court documents revealed that FIFA chiefs were fully aware that, between 1989 and 1998, ISL paid senior officials, including Havelange, a total of 122m Swiss francs in "commissions". FIFA offered compensation amounting to around 2% of that sum (£1.64m), but only on condition that criminal proceedings against Havelange and Teixeira were dropped. Now apparently doing Jennings' bidding by pursuing a policy of transparency, FIFA published the document on its website, though the accompanying *mea culpa* lacked finesse: "The finding that FIFA had knowledge of the bribery to persons within its organs is not questioned," reported Ashling O'Connor; "a certain payment made to Havelange... was mistakenly directly transferred to a FIFA account."[91]

Although Blatter was named, alongside Havelange, as a co-signee ("PI") of the ISL agreement, the report was adamant that he did not receive any kickbacks. The next day he admitted knowing about the payments – but why were Havelange and Teixeira permitted to stay in office if the then-secretary general was cognisant of the bribes? Because, he stressed, the past should not be judged "on the basis of today's standards" – back then, after all, "such payments could even be deducted from tax as a business expense."[92]

* * *

Teixera, Havelange and Blatter aside, the officials who bore the full brunt of Jennings' surgical probing were Jack Warner and Chuck Blazer – representatives, respectively, for the Caribbean and the US. "The FIFA career of Jack Warner began to unravel in May 2011," related Jennings, "when he was caught with $1 million in bribes, in envelopes each containing $40,000 in cash, for distributing to Caribbean football associations. The aim was to persuade them to vote for Qatar's Mohamed Bin Hammam, who was contesting the FIFA presidency against incumbent Sepp Blatter. Blazer 'ratted' on Warner to FIFA but was himself soon engulfed in documented corruption allegations."[93]

Jennings talks witheringly of the "culture of impunity created by the criminals controlling FIFA". This was encapsulated in that June 2006 *Panorama* when he asked Warner "how much profit he had made from his illegal World Cup tickets rackets". According to Jennings, the reply was a minimalist and earthy "Go fuck yourself". Blatter "was not moved to disavow this lowlife"; neither were "Havelange, Valcke, Blazer, Bin Hammam, Leoz, Teixeira, Hayatou, Makudi or the rest of the gangsters on the Executive Committee who we hope to see, one day, in shackles and manacles and orange jump suits being ushered by the Feds into a Manhattan courtroom".[94]

In May 2013, the net spread wider. The FBI confirmed that they were investigating "a major case" involving allegations of fraud and bribery at FIFA, with unofficial reports stating that

Warner's eldest son, Daryan, then domiciled in Florida, was co-operating as a witness. Nearly three years earlier, Jennings had been contacted by special agents from the Organised Crime and Racketeering Section of the Department of Justice in Washington as well as an FBI Organised Crime team in New York; his delight at this latest development was unconfined. "Daryan Warner was always the 'back office' money-man," declaims Jennings, "organising the laundering and concealment of bribes and profits from every kind of illicit football activity by his father – siphoning off grants, dealing in World Cup tickets and pocketing substantial bribes from countries hoping to host the World Cup."[95]

For once, Jennings felt encouraged. "The industrial-scale thieving of Warner and Blazer is woven into the fabric of FIFA. Repeatedly, the gruesome duo were encouraged to plunder grants and World Cup tickets. In return they delivered votes to keep Blatter in power. Football lovers must dream that the G-Men will find reasons to extend their investigations into Issa Hayatou's African empire and the rest of FIFA." The FBI investigation "should bring an end to three decades of institutional corruption", Jennings concluded, albeit with a surfeit of optimism all-too understandable in someone suddenly spotting a chink of light in an unremittingly dark tunnel.[96]

Bashing the BCCI

I think that the IPL is the best thing that has ever happened to cricket. The concept is superb. It engenders international and regional harmony. I would not like a return to the days when cricket was almost synonymous with xenophobia and fake nationalism.

Phil J Walton, email to Cricinfo, 26 May 2013

One might imagine that the highest aspiration of a sport's national governing body, in states where international sport is deemed important, would be to produce a strong national team. That this is no longer necessarily the case can be gleaned from the rise of the Indian Premier League, a venture stunningly rapid in its vaulting success yet as divisive as any in cricket history. Those who liken its organisers, the Board of Control for Cricket in India, to the United States are not unjustified. As with the NFL, the NBA and MLB, the IPL is a franchise-based competition; as with a succession of White House residents, bullying tactics are as common as fear of global disapproval is non-existent.

The BCCI's weapon-plaything is a game that has undergone facelifts galore over the past half-century, a reinvention unique among major sports. It was as inevitable as it was necessary. Being the most languid of ballgames, not to mention being so beholden to the vagaries of the weather, cricket is horribly ill-suited to modern temperaments and tastes: even to someone entering their teens in the 1960s, the notion that a match could last five or even six days and still not yield a winner was almost surreal.

The first tentative step into this brisk new world was the introduction in 1963 of the Gillette Cup, a knockout competition for the English counties wherein matches were condensed into 60 overs per side, and hence to a single day. Then, at Melbourne in 1971, the one-day international was born. In 1980 – the last year to witness more Tests than one-day internationals – the five-day game accounted for 54% of international fixtures. In 1990 that figure was 30%, then 26% in 2000, and 17% in 2010. While this switch in emphasis was encouraged by broadcasters as well as treasurers, and dismayed purists, there can be little doubt that it preserved the game.

Running parallel to this was a new cricketing world order. Bangladesh's admission as full members of the ICC in 2000 confirmed how far the balance of racial representation had swung, and hence (theoretical) power. As the new reality dawned, so envious and embittered references to an "Asian bloc" could be found in English and Australian newspapers on an almost daily basis. Fast-forward a decade and the Board of Control for Cricket in India accounted for an estimated 70% of the game's income, and, somewhat inevitably, was calling the shots in much the same way as England and Australia, having reluctantly surrendered their veto, once did.

The white cricketing nations were once the benevolent bad guys who saw themselves as benign dictators-cum-missionaries; now the colonials wore that hat, the Indians most swaggeringly of all – hence the decision by the Australian and South African boards to all but beg for a 50% stake (25% each) in the BCCI's Champions League tournament. The governance of spectator sport has seen no more radical transformation.

* * *

Beginning life in 2008, the IPL was the brainchild of the BCCI, an instantly profitable attempt to capitalise on the sudden explosion of interest in the Twenty20 format. Borrowing from the US model, the league, unlike the traditional states that had long competed for the first-class Ranji Trophy, comprised a range of city-based franchises owned by big business and Bollywood. With each team entitled to field four overseas players at any given time and with the salaries for six weeks' work superceding anything the game had previously had to offer, the best flocked in. Spectators, sponsors and broadcasters couldn't get enough; thus were the game's economics radically transformed.

Here, for the first time since the introduction of Test cricket, was a domestic event that not only challenged the sovereignty of the international circuit but threatened to destroy it altogether. The IPL auction not only turned players into millionaires but conceived a new breed: the freelance cricketer, a "have bat will travel", perpetually on the road warrior armed with a portfolio of contracts and no fixed abode (of whom more anon). So unprecedented were the rewards, leading players retired from official internationals or turned freelance, an increasing temptation as T20 tournaments mushroomed, not just in Australia and South Africa but Bangladesh and Zimbabwe. If that brought misgivings, the irresistible march of the BCCI saw it become a powerhouse of unseemly proportions, arousing anger as well as angst.

The advent of the IPL proved especially problematic for the England and Wales Cricket Board, not to say their employees. Because the English season runs from April to September (traditionally, those in all the other Test nations run either side), any county player wishing to compete in the IPL was contractually permitted to participate, at best, in no more than half of the tournament, thus reducing their marketability. Since the country's dozen centrally-contracted players were, at first, amply compensated, by 2013 even those pulling in around £700,000 per annum were looking in askance at their Australian counterparts, whose freedom to play in their own Big Bash League as well as the IPL had reportedly taken them well past that figure.

Needless to add, envy seeped in, oozing and polluting. Amid the ensuing corruption that came to light in 2013, which surprised exceedingly few, there would be no shortage of gloating. Even those who had championed India's toppling of cricket's old guard were hard-pressed not to join the relentless chorus of disapproval.

* * *

By 2011, the new broom had begun to lose its bristle, on the field at least: having reached the top of the ICC Test Rankings and won the World Cup for the first time since 1983, the Indian national team began slipping, a consequence of an ageing side and an increasingly onerous schedule dictated by the demands of the TV schedulers. On tour in England, they lost all four Tests and the one-day series. At the back end of the year they went to Australia and lost all four Tests, then failed to make the final of a one-day triangular involved the hosts and Sri Lanka. By then, though, many were convinced that the coffers of Indian cricket mattered far more than the success of the national XI.

Many likened the IPL to World Wrestling Entertainment, an accurately if shamelessly monikered enterprise that had sold its dubious pleasures to television through personalities alone, without any pretence of offering true competition. It seemed a reasonable comparison, as Sharda Ugra testified in the wake of the 2013 spot-fixing saga that saw Sri Sreesanth, a leading fast bowler, and Amit Singh, a player-turned-bookie, banned for life: "The IPL has always been sold to its audience as a marriage of cricket and entertainment; except in 2013, there came an accidental advisory – that there was a chance that parts of the 'cricketainment' could actually be pre-scripted."[97]

"As so often in India, the solutions are easy to state and hard to enact," conceded *The Economist*. "The government should legalise betting on cricket... The cricket board must also be regulated more tightly... It should start by cracking down on the alleged cheats – not, as in previous scandals, seeking to exonerate them after the dust has settled. Such reforms would be opposed by the same powerful people who aspire to run everything in India... International confidence in India's ability to uphold the rule of law and fight corruption is at an all-time low... its rulers should [clean] up their [favourite] game."[98] Shortly before the 2014 national elections, N. Srinivasan, the ICC president-elect, owner of Chennai Super Kings and the game's most powerful figure, was urged to step down as BCCI president by the Supreme Court; only then, it reasoned, could there be a full probe into the IPL spot-fixing scandal that had incriminated his son-in-law. That he had not done so to date was "nauseating". To say likewise of the English and Australian boards' willingness to accommodate his every whim would be to misjudge the realities of cricket realpolitik. Perversely, the IPL was exempt from conflict of interest claims. Ramachandra Guha, the eminent Indian historian, had already expressed his shame and contempt:

> *The IPL is representative of the worst sides of Indian capitalism and Indian society. Corrupt and cronyist, it has also promoted chamchagiri (sycophancy) and compliance. The behaviour of Messrs Lalit Modi and N Srinivasan cannot shock or surprise me, but I have been distressed at the way in which some respected cricket commentators have become apologists for the*

IPL and its management. Theirs is a betrayal that has wounded the image of cricket in India, and beyond. George Orwell once said: "A writer should never be a loyal member of a political party." Likewise, for his credibility and even his sanity, a cricket writer/commentator should keep a safe distance from those who run the game in his country.

What is to be done now? The vested interests are asking for such token measures as the legalisation of betting and the resignation of the odd official. In truth, far more radical steps are called for. The IPL should be disbanded. The Syed Mushtaq Ali Trophy, played between state sides, should be upgraded, making it the flagship Twenty20 tournament in the country. Then the clubs and state associations that have run our domestic game reasonably well for the past 80 years would be given back their authority, and the crooks and the moneybags turfed out altogether.[99]

"Own the Podium"

The late Christopher Hitchens, one of journalism's most wilfully provocative polemicists, donned his Orwellian hat in a *Newsweek* article on the eve of the 2010 Winter Olympics entitled "Fool's Gold: How the Olympics and other international competitions breed conflict and bring out the worst in human nature". Responding to complaints from Ron Rossi, executive director of the US luge team in Vancouver, about the hosts' "lack of sportsmanship" in trying to extract as much home advantage as possible, Hitchens sneered: "On the contrary, Mr. Rossi, what we are seeing is the very essence of sportsmanship. Whether it's the exacerbation of national rivalries that you want – as in Africa this year – or the exhibition of the most depressing traits of the human personality (guns in locker rooms, golf clubs wielded in the home, dogs maimed and tortured at stars' homes to make them fight, dope and steroids everywhere), you need only look to the wide world of sports for the most rank and vivid examples."[100]

Even in sane, nice, Michael Moore-approved Canada. In Vancouver a few days later, Nodar Kumaritashvili, a Georgian luger, died on a training run. One inescapable factor was that he had been denied adequate practice by Canada's determination, as the unabashed slogan stated, to "Own the Podium". Such was the name given to a five-year, $120m technical programme aimed at ensuring the host nation topped the medals table, more than half the cost of which was contributed by taxpayers. Everything possible was done to ensure the home competitors received every possible advantage. While this was firmly within the rules, what that says about those rules, much less those who enforce them, is anything but flattering.

Prior to that tragic practice, Kumaritashvili had confessed to his father that the course "terrified" him. By no means was he alone, nor remotely unjustified. Five teams dropped out following crashes, concussions and a cervical spine injury. Australia's Hannah Campbell-Pegg found self-restraint difficult. "To what extent are we just little lemmings that they just throw down a track and we're crash-test dummies?" she wondered. "I mean, this is our lives."[101]

There had been a hint of things to come during the build-up to the world speed skating championships in March 2009. Along with his charges, Kevin Crockett, a former Canadian Olympic medallist who coached the Chinese team, was escorted from the Richmond Oval, one of the sites for the 2010 Olympics. Bob de Jong, Holland's Olympic champion, was only admitted after being kept out for a day. The German team claimed they'd been denied access altogether. "We were there for three days and the only thing I could do was peek through the windows to look at the venue," said their coach Bart Schouten. "The Canadians are acting like this… is a fort that's being intruded upon," claimed the furious Crockett. "There's no fair play here, there's nothing like that."[102]

To attribute such outpourings exclusively to nationalism would be facile. In the aftermath of Kumaritashvili's fatal run, Rick Broadbent, writing in *The Times*, asked the most salient question: "Why, if the IOC was in 'deep mourning', as Jacques Rogge, the body's president said, was there not even a day of mourning after the nightmare before?"[103] Other awkward questions remained unanswered, such as: "If the track was safe, then why did the organisers move the start 580 feet lower down and add padding to the pillars at turn 16?"[104] Dave Zirin also blamed the IOC, "that sewing circle of monarchists, extortionists, and absolved fascists [which] likes to hide behind the pretense of nobility."[105]

On the IOC's website, there is a quiz: "The Ultimate goal of Olympism is to a) Organize the Olympic Games, b) encourage new world records, c) build a peaceful and better world through sport." It's perfectly understandable if you needed three tries to answer that correctly. The answer is, of course, c—although that would certainly be news to the family of Nodar Kumaritashvili. What trumps these grand "ethics" is the reality of what makes the IOC go 'round: television and corporate dollars. And if corporations can't come up with the money, then cities and host countries pay through the nose.[106]

* * *

In 2009, Australia's Labour government announced, to global astonishment, that it would be cutting Olympic funding. An infuriated John Coates, president of the Australian Olympic Committee and incoming member of the IOC's executive board, protested that, since Australia had declined to seventh in the medals table in Beijing (down to 46 golds, silvers and bronzes from 58 in Sydney 2000), the nation might even fall behind Italy come 2012 without an *additional* \$100m in taxpayer funding. In the *Sydney Morning Herald*, Richard Hinds took careful aim at Coates in particular and Olympism in general:

We are told Olympic success confirms our status as a nation of great athletes. But, if it is really our facilities, coaches, medics, sports scientists – the ones now being bought by other nations – and lavish grants that make the difference, are we not merely operating one of the world's great sports factories?

Which is not to say there should be no funding for Olympic sports. Indeed, those who need it most are those apparently endangered most by the Federal Government review – the archers and table tennis players, taekwondo-ists and others who don't attract the same endorsements or prize money as swimmers, track and field stars, basketballers and other professionals.

But it is not a bad thing to ask what we are getting in return. Beyond, that is, the rather pathetic bragging rights claimed by Olympic officials and politicians when our stack of expensive medals is bigger than yours.[107]

The UnAmerican Activity

"Some fans grumble that 'no player is worth a million dollars'," noted George F. Will in a nationally syndicated column for the *Washington Post* published in 1976, at the dawn of free agency.

But baseball owners are not running charitable organisations. If no players were worth that, no owners would pay it. In their forlorn attempt to roll back players' rights, some owners will argue, as the football owners argued, that a free market in player talent will mean a rush of superstars to rich teams. But that is another self-serving theory killed by facts. This year only twenty-four football players became free agents on May 1. The three richest owners – those of the Dallas, Houston and Kansas City teams – signed none of the top stars. Football owners fought tooth and nail, and unsuccessfully, against the players' union to prevent the emergence of something like a free market in talent. Every step of the way they argued that a free market would destroy "competitive balance", and that their only concern was "the good of the game". But sports businessmen are businessmen, which means they are neither irrational nor altruistic. None of them will spend themselves into penury by irrationally stockpiling expensive talent. And they are nimble at rising above principles: their passion for free market enterprise stops just a bunt short of the point where a free market might cost them money.[108]

To glean the full texture of such comments, context is required. Will is a syndicated columnist, author and rabid anti-pinko-commie-bastard, who has frequently propounded the view that, while society should adhere to the fundamental precepts of capitalism, he subscribes to the Marxist theory of labour when it comes to sport. Such a surprising confession surely strikes at the very heart of the contention that American sport, even at its biggest and brashest, mirrors universal perceptions of the American nation. And nothing punctures that thoughtless theory more conclusively than the fact that, in the cathedral of capitalism, team rather than individual sports are much the bigger attraction.

Will's analysis still stands up for its cold logic and unemotional reason. In US spectator sport, arguably the ultimate in sport-as-business, the key words are "competitive" and "balance". Although the richest, not unnaturally, tend to prosper more readily, baseball's ultimate honour, the annual World Series, was won by no fewer than 20 different teams between 1979 and 2010 – more than two-thirds of the average number of annual contenders (the 24 of 1976 had risen to 30 by 2010). As of the San Francisco Giants' victory in 2013, that unwieldy, virtually unhoistable trophy had been retained on just three occasions in 35 seasons. Compare that with the period stretching from 1947 to 1964, when the New York Yankees qualified for 15 of the 18 World Series, winning 10, while the Dodgers qualified for nine, winning three; no fewer than eight of those Series, moreover, saw the pair go head-to-head. Contrast this with the way Manchester United, Chelsea and Arsenal strangleheld the Premiership in England during its first 23 seasons, when only three times did one fail to secure the grail. The other major European football leagues are scarcely better. Yet the other two principal American sporting leagues have also been more democratic: 10 different teams won the SuperBowl between 1999 and 2012; seven divvied up the NBA title from 1996 to 2013.

The greater emphasis on a playoff-driven postseason is another key contributor to competitive balance; ditto the traditional refusal to countenance promotion and relegation (an exceedingly cartel-like philosophy). Another factor is the draft system, which rewards franchises in inverse proportion to the quality of their results. Yet another is that most un-American of activities, socialistic revenue-sharing. Art Modell, one of the NFL's more prolific dispensers of soundbites, summed it all up with admirable succinctness: "We are a bunch of fat cat Republicans who vote socialist on football."[109] Well, almost. It was Modell, after all, who held the reins and purse-strings at the Cleveland Browns before whisking them off to Baltimore and rebranding them as the Ravens.

Rejected by NBA owners, eventually copied by baseball, revenue-sharing was introduced in 1961 by its most efficient, profitable and even, dare one say it, wholesome disciple, the NFL. Television, again, was the spur. Commissioner Pete Rozelle persuaded the owners to surrender their local TV revenues in favour of selling them as part of a national package, from which the proceeds were evenly distributed. It helps, of course, when attendances for baseball are at an all-time high: 16 clubs drew a combined 17 million in the season Walter O'Malley decided to drag the Dodgers to LA; in 2012, the tally aggregated by those 30 clubs topped 74m.[110] In other words, 87.5% more franchises attracted around 350% more spectators. Even if we factor in the rise in games from 154 per season to 162, it remains a staggering statistic. Nor was this remotely a one-off: only four times had attendances ever been higher, all since the start of 2005. Throw in the vast profits and it is perhaps no surprise that the rest of sport's ringmasters look up with envy.

In 2012, when its 32 franchises pooled and shared two-thirds of over $9.5 billion in revenues, John Vrooman warranted that the NFL had over the past 50 years become "the most economically powerful sports league in the world largely because it has also been the most egalitarian". The underlying source of that economic strength had been "a survivalist 'league-think' mentality" that arose at the outset of the NFL-AFL "war" of 1960–1966 that preceded the birth of the NFC and the AFC.[111] How international cricket, dominated by four nations but serving dozens more, could do with a similar understanding of collectivism, a lament accentuated in 2013 by the reported desire of the less than starving Indian board (2012-13 net income $56.1m) for a chunkier slice of the ICC pie; it was duly granted.

Overall, the pros certainly seem to outweigh the cons. Yes, any number of institutions have left their communities or fallen by the wayside; yes, a great baseball team in the making, the 1994 Montreal Expos, were denied their due by a players' strike and then, 10 years later, renamed the Nationals and forcibly relocated to the American capital, not a city known for its Francophiles. On the other hand, small-market and often crowd-starved teams such as the Packers of Green Bay, Minnesota's Twins and even Pittsburgh's Pirates, who lost more games than they won every season from 1992 to 2012, have not simply been saved from the knacker's yard. The Twins have won more World Series than the Mets since the birth of the latter franchise in 1962, while the Pirates made the playoffs in 2013. As for the Packers, success, community adoration and collective ownership continue to set an example worthy of global plagiarism but heeded by far too few.

Productive collectivism? How Uncle Joe Stalin would have approved. As we shall see, however, with the sharing did not come caring.

"Mad King" Emanuel

We cannot conclude this chapter without some hearty jeers for Chicago's Mayor Rahm Emanuel, a rather extraordinary chap "who seems committed", reckoned Zirin in May 2013, "to win the current spirited competition as the most loathsome person in American political life". Mayor Emanuel, formerly Barack Obama's White House chief of staff, is a stark symbol of the way spectator sport has come to take precedence over matters of greater social import. Having overseen the closure of 54 schools and six community mental health clinics under the justification of a "budgetary crisis", he incurred the wrath of Zirin and many others by announcing that the city would be handing over more than $100 million to DePaul University for a new basketball arena, part of a mammoth redevelopment project "comprised", noted Zirin, "of a convention centre anchored by an arena for a nondescript basketball team that has gone 47-111 over the last five years. It's also miles away from DePaul's campus. These aren't the actions of a mayor. They're the actions of a mad king."[112]

One day, this distortion of social values may receive its comeuppance, though perhaps breaths should not be held.

5 The First Taboo: Sport and Professionalism

I. From "Gentlemen" to Shamateurs

It's "all about defying the limitations people put on you". So said Adebayo Akinfenwa, the 16st 7lb Northampton Town striker, in a 2012 interview with Barry Flatman of the *Sunday Times*, reciting with no little pride the mission statement for his HaHa t-shirt brand (slogan "Too big to play football. Ha ha."). Here was a clarion call for all: "Too big to play football. Too short to model. Too poor to ever be rich. Just because they can't doesn't mean you won't. A professional is just an amateur that didn't quit."[1] An amateur that didn't quit? There have been countless attempts to define the professional sportsman but that will do nicely.

When Gabriele Marcotti, one of Europe's leading contemporary football correspondents, was mulling over a title for his book about the game in his native Italy, he plumped for *The Italian Job* – and only partly in homage to the iconic 1960s movie, the much-loved crime caper responsible for the Michael Caine line "You were only supposed to blow the bloody doors off!", one that would endure as the back-window-sticker slogan on a million Minis. Playing football for a living may be a job like no other to the average teenage boy in Rome, Milan or Turin, but it is still a job. An alternative characterisation of professional sportsfolk, therefore, might be this: billions of people *play* sport; the elite, the ones we part with our hard-earned shekels to watch, work it.

The idea of being paid to play, however, was anathema to the large majority of those running spectator sport in its formative decades, and widely resisted for decades thereafter. Cricket and tennis in particular were adverts for the benefits of nature over nurture, of superior blood and aristocratic privilege: from wealth, after all, stemmed a healthier diet and more leisure time. The model for so many was Charles Burgess Fry. "Traditionally, the thing most admired in sport was effortless brilliance," as Simon Barnes attests. "You just had so much talent that you couldn't help winning. You imagine C. B. Fry handing his blazer and cigar to a friend to break the world long-jump record before going back to the cricket to score a century."[2] A late 19th century polymath – besides also playing for Southampton in the FA Cup final and for England at football as well as cricket, he was a politician, diplomat, academic, teacher, writer, editor and publisher – Fry attended two bastions of scholastic privilege, Repton School and Oxford University. "Charles Fry," attested Arlott, "could be autocratic, angry and self-willed: he was also magnanimous, extravagant, generous, elegant, brilliant – and fun... he was probably the most variously gifted Englishman of any age."[3] He was even said to have rejected an offer to assume the throne of Albania.

Heaven forbid that one's lack of effortlessness extended to hiring a coach or even training for the Olympics. Anyone who has seen the Oscar-winning movie *Chariots of Fire* will recall the story of Harold Abrahams, winner of the 1924 Olympic 100m. The son of a Polish Jewish émigré (which counted as two strikes against him for starters), Abrahams attended all the right educational emporiums – Bedford School, Repton, Cambridge – but when he deigned to employ the coaching services of Sam Mussabini he caused an almighty stink. It was the act of a bounder, an ungentleman; in essence, he was accused of cheating.

But while the professionalisation of sport amounted to the longest of kick-offs, and while it continues to be a source of interminable turbulence, this unintended by-product of sport-for-fun can still be seen as one of mankind's brighter ideas. Privilege, together with that attendant insistence on transparent effortlessness, limited the pursuit of excellence to the few. Once money was thrown into the mix, opportunities multiplied, launching sport towards the utopia of true meritocracy. Once again, Barnes has encapsulated this better than most:

If you were to design an activity for the pursuit of physical and mental excellence, you probably wouldn't come up with sport as we know it. Sport has changed its function and meaning across the years – but part of its meaning lies in its convoluted history and its bewildering and complex changes of use. But changes of use occur all the time. Dinosaurs developed feathers for insulation; by coincidence, they turned out to be ideal for flight. Feathers were never intended to make an eagle fly, but they do. Fish developed swim bladders to remain stationary in the water – in other vertebrates this structure turned out to be quite useful as lungs. Sport was once pretty good at demonstrating superiority of birth – it's now gloriously vivid at demonstrating the synthesis of nature and nurture in the pursuit of excellence. It wasn't what sport was invented for, but it's what sport is now, and it's pretty damned good at this secondary use.[4]

* * *

That Titian of the typewriter Roger Angell could never forget the day he first saw the chilling face of cold-blooded sporting professionalism. It was 1968, and it was personified by Bob Gibson, the St Louis Cardinals pitcher who had just thrown 17 strikeouts to beat the Detroit Tigers, a World Series record that, at the time of writing, still stood tall and invincible. A proud and unbending African-American and a fearsome, often ferocious competitor, in this context he was utterly colour-blind, happy to inflict pain on whoever stood in the batter's box. Never did he think twice about plunking a former roommate. Never did he fraternise with the opposition, even when playing alongside them during the All-Star Game.

When one writer asked him if he had always been as competitive as he had seemed on this day, he said yes, and he added that he had played several hundred games of ticktacktoe against one of

his young daughters and that she had yet to win a game from
him. He said this with a little smile, but it seemed to me that he
meant it: he couldn't let himself lose to anyone.[5]

"I didn't want to hang around and make friends," Gibson told
Angell a few years after he retired. "I don't think there's any place
in the game for a pitcher smiling and joking with the hitters. I
was all business on the mound – it is a business, isn't it? When
Orlando Cepeda was with us, I used to watch him and [Juan]
Marichal laughing and fooling around before a game. They'd
been on the [San Francisco] Giants together, you know. But then
Cepeda would go out and *kill* Marichal at the plate – one of the
best pitchers I ever saw – and when it was over they'd go to
dinner together and laugh some more. It just made me shake my
head. I didn't understand it."[6] The "basis of intimidation", the
way Gibson saw and practised it, was mystery. "I wanted the
hitter to know nothing about me – about my wife, my children,
my religion, my politics, my hobbies, my tastes, my feelings,
nothing. I figured the more they knew about me, the more they
might know what I would do in a certain situation. That was
why, in large part, I never talked to players on other teams. That
was why I never apologised for hitting anybody. That was why I
seemed like such an asshole to so many people."[7]

Gibson was acutely aware of how the colour of his skin
helped and hindered him: "As a black man, I was a member
of a race that had been intimidated by the white man for more
than two hundred years, in which we learned something about
the process. When one is intimidated, he resigns himself to the
backseat. He defers to his so-called superior, having no other
legitimate choice, and allows himself to be dominated. As a
major-league pitcher, I had the opportunity, at least, to push off
the mound in the other man's shoes."[8]

Yet Gibson was adamant that this had little bearing on the
way he went about his job. "There's no way to gloss over the fact
that racial perception contributed a great deal to my reputation.
I pitched in a period of civil unrest, of black power and clenched

fists and burning buildings and assassinations and riots in the street. There was a country full of angry black people in those days, and by extension – and by my demeanour on the mound – I was perceived to be one of them. There was some truth to that, but it had little, if anything to do with the way I worked a batter. I didn't see a hitter's colour. I saw his stance, his strike zone, his bat speed, his power, and his weakness."[9] Then again, as Tim Wendel observed in his engrossing account of the 1968 MLB season, *Summer of '68*, Gibson "knew as well as anybody that perception often becomes reality". And how he turned that fear to his advantage. "I'll never forget the look he gave me. It scared me to death," confessed Reggie Smith, a fellow African-American, after Gibson had all but beaten the Boston Red Sox singlehanded in the 1967 Series. "He sent a stare right through me, like, 'Who do you think you are?' I thought for sure there was a knockdown coming, but he fooled me with a slider."[10]

In many ways Gibson's ruthlessness personifies what spectator sport's Victorian forefathers found so repugnant about the notion of being paid to play. It was a question of attitude: should a *game* matter so much that a participant is prepared to forego what might in middle- or upper-class circles be regarded as ungentlemanly conduct? The sort of gentleman the lesser ranks were supposed to aspire to emulate liked to be seen as an effortless sort, one to whom everything came by birthright, privilege and entitlement rather than sweat or toil. Indeed, to be called "enthusiastic" in the 18th century was to be insulted, implying, as Katharine Whitehorn averred in *The Observer*, "a reckless lack of sober judgement".

Trying too hard simply wasn't done. Being seen to be doing so was far graver. Not if you were a *proper* Englishman – or even the sort that would come to be characterised by Hollywood as either a well-bred cad (Cary Grant, George Sanders, David Niven) or a well-bred secret agent/spy (James Bond may have been played *by* a Welshman, an Irishman, a Scot and even an Australian model but he has never been played *as* anything but a pukka Englishman). Perhaps that's why it took an Irishman, George Bernard Shaw, to inject a tone of reality. If the reasonable man adapts to the world and the unreasonable man expects the world to adapt to him, "it follows that progress depends on unreasonable men".

Amateurism is not really about keeping honest sporting endeavour out of the treacherous clutches of money, but ideology: let's keep this to ourselves, our own social strata, our own sort. Once a sport was popular enough to enable its producers to charge spectators admission, what could be more natural than the advent of professionalism? As King Canute discovered, anyone attempting to hold back the tide might just as well try to hold back the night. Sport's administrators, nevertheless, made the Dane's quest to defy the unstoppable look half-hearted. Amateurism, after all, stemmed from a pair of premises: a) sport should be played in one's leisure time and out of love, hence the early popularity of that most leisurely of games, cricket, the playing of which allowed the wealthy and privileged to flaunt their time-richness; and b) paying people to play it would only encourage those awful working-class oiks.

Now, in the 21st century, we find Matthew Syed revealing in *The Times* that the most burning issue among his readers is "outrage" at the money now swilling around sport. Let's suppose, he proposes, that we brought communist principles to bear, an implicit if unstated urge detectable in many: play games for love and stage them for free. Would vice cease? "Of course not," scoffed Syed, and justly so. "It would blossom. Black markets would flourish. Gambling would be driven underground. These things ran riot in the age of amateurism. Think back to the 5th century where money didn't even exist. Historians agree about very little, but they are unanimous in asserting that pre-money societies were riddled with corruption and duplicity, and even more than today."[11]

For decades, indeed, the waters were muddied still further by an uneasy combination of amateur management and professional performers. If across-the-board professionalism has had considerable drawbacks – led by those intrepid partners in crime, greed and short-termism – the benefits have not been inconspicuous. For all the class and economic barriers that remain in sports such as motor racing and tennis, the unprivileged can climb the ladder to unimagined (and far from unwarranted) riches with greater alacrity than in any other sphere. Look at the boons to safety and comfort at stadiums; at the way television coverage has invited us into front rows from Africa to the Ukraine, at relatively meagre cost; at the way expensive technological developments have seen the small screen, in turn, help make sport fairer, its rewards dispensed with greater justice. Return to amateurism? In the complex world of spectator sport, a world with eyes on the future but feet planted firmly in the past, that's one clock that never needs turning back.

The overriding problem with vilifying money, as Syed affirmed, is the way it obscures far more pressing matters. "Gambling scandals? Blame money. Match-fixing? Blame money. Doping? Blame money. Oafish behaviour? Blame money. All too easy, isn't it? Money has become the universal, catch-all scapegoat. But the real problem is values."[12]

Being an Olympian

The identities of the sports that did most to foster professionalism should not surprise. Bare-knuckle boxing and horse racing, the first two prominent, year-round spectatorial games, relied on elemental appeal – the race to be, respectively, the strongest and the fastest. Then came cricket, baseball, association football and, amid internecine warfare, rugby. Profoundly amateur as it kicked off in the public schools before being invaded by northerners who had the nerve to demand recompense for taking time off factory duties, the sport suffered a split that, even with nearly 120 years on the clock and open professionalism finally entrenched in both codes, remains as unmendable as ever.

Athletics, meanwhile, was openly professional in the early 19th century before the toffs and snobs took control. As Steven Downes and Duncan Mackay assert in *Running Scared: How Athletics Lost Its Innocence*, when Baron De Coubertin founded the modern Olympics, he wanted competitors to be amateurs, because this would be the likeliest guarantee of fair play yet, in effect, what he really wanted to do was "keep the riff-raff out".

> *When the rules on amateurism were being drafted by the eminent Victorians who founded the Amateur Athletic Association, they did so deliberately to exclude artisans and labourers. Such working men could not afford to train and compete for nothing, so by making their sport strictly amateur, the governing bodies reinforced class divisions. There was no historical basis for amateurism, since the ancient Greek Games on which de Coubertin modelled his Olympics were very much professional. But this amateur ethos became ingrained into the concept of the modern Olympics. The leisured rich did not want to compete with working-class athletes, whose muscles had been hardened and toned by manual labour. As the Establishment reinforced the idea that accepting money for competing was beneath the dignity of a true Olympian, the amateur rules were applied to ensure that competitors were banned from receiving their regular job's salary while they were training, and that they never received a penny profit off the track for the fame that they had won on the track.*[13]

The contrast with the ancient Olympics could hardly have been starker. "The whole of Greek life, it could be said, was geared towards the production of Olympic athletes," wrote Tony Perrottet. "For some, the path to Olympia had begun even before they were born. It was known that if a pregnant woman dreamed she was giving birth to an eagle, then her son was surely destined to become a successful athlete. If a father dreamed he was eating his son's shoulder, then he would profit from his son's wrestling career. If he was devouring his son's feet, logically, the family would make a fortune from his running."[14]

Fast forward a couple of millennia. Shortly before the London 2012 Games, Dwayne Wade, one of the NBA's leading lights, caused a right old stink, asserting that he should be "compensated" for taking part. Not because he needed the money (anything but, given that he had a contract with Miami Heat worth a cool $100m-plus). In fact, he later tweeted that representing his country "motivates me more than any $$$ amount". His argument was that he deserved some form of recompense for playing over the summer and fulfilling the demands of being an Olympian.

> *It's a lot of things you do for the Olympics, a lot of jerseys you sell. We play the whole summer. I do think guys should be compensated. Just like I think college players should be compensated as well. Unfortunately, it's not there. But I think it should be something, you know, there for it.*
>
> *The biggest thing is now you get no rest. So you go to the end of the season, [Team USA] training camp is two weeks later. You're giving up a lot to do it. It's something you want to do. But it's taxing on your body. You're not playing for the dollar. But it would be nice if you would get compensated.*[15]

Can you imagine Tom Cruise making a press statement of that ilk? Or Bob Dylan? Or Chris Rock? Sure, they all do the occasional gig for charity, but provide their services for nothing at a big, money-spinning, absolutely-for-profit show? The International Olympic Committee likes to think it is more fortunate in its performing seals. Yes, funding may be available, and in some instances there are considerable rewards to be had, but for the 10,000-odd sportsfolk who qualify for the Olympics, what matters, so far as the IOC sees it, is the getting there and the being there: the honour. What, though, of those who are already champions in a major spectator sport, whose bank accounts are already overflowing, whose schedules are already crammed? Where is the motivation? Wade's sentiments sum up the folly in making the Games so bloated.

By way of reinforcing Wade's point, Mark Cuban, the owner of the Dallas Mavericks, the reigning NBA champions, called on either the IOC or USA Basketball to pay players to go to the Games for one incontrovertible reason: these organisations benefited materially from their presence. This prompted a column in *The Times* by Michael Johnson, the only man up to that point to win the Olympic 200m-400m double, one of the most resplendent athletes of all. "As much as we'd all like to believe that every athlete participating at the Games is doing it purely for the opportunity to achieve Olympic glory and to represent their country, I can tell you that there's much more to it than that."[16] If it was a surprise that he should bother stating the blindingly obvious, the fact that he felt obliged to do so spoke volumes for the idealism some still attached, unrealistically and unfairly, to the Olympics.

Johnson said he would have "welcomed" being paid to participate in his three Olympics, especially the 1996 Games in Atlanta, where he had elevated sprinting to an unprecedented peak of attainment. The Games were promoted using his image, he reasoned, but not a cent did he ever receive from the IOC. The economic benefits that did come his way stemmed from the companies whose products he endorsed. "The Olympic system," he said, "is atypical of most business or professional arrangements whereby the organisation that benefits most pays the talent providing the spectacle."

Johnson's concern lay less with the millionaire footballers and basketballers and golfers and tennis players, to whom the Games did not constitute the foremost measure of achievement, than with those competing in "traditional" Olympic sports such as "wrestling, synchronised swimming, diving and even athletics". Quite how he decided that the second of these was "traditional" is a complete mystery – "water ballet" had only been introduced as an official event at the Games in 1984 – but the point remained. Given that the IOC has so often been guilty of rampant hypocrisy – as we have seen – why should participants be obliged to struggle financially, to borrow off family and friends? "I believe more should be done to support these athletes," Johnson continued, "but I also understand that somehow the Olympic system works with its ambiguous mixture of professionalism and amateurism."

To call the Olympics' particular mixture of amateurist doctrine and professional intent "ambiguous" is to be diplomatic in the extreme. Government-backed athletes, masquerading as members of the armed forces, had long been ten-a-penny. As long ago as the 1960 Games, moreover, the German 100m gold medallist Armin Hary had the nerve to accept sponsorship money from both Adi and Rudolph Dassler, the rival fraternal owners of Adidas and Puma (no less controversial in retirement, Hary was convicted for fraud, though the two-year jail term was reduced to a fine and by 2010, aged 72, he had completed his return to credibility, running a foundation promoting youth sport). Nearly 30 years earlier, Paavo Nurmi, whose nine Olympic golds did so much to cement Finnish nationalism following independence from Russia, had been banned from the Los Angeles Games after being paid for running in the US.

Along the "standard career path" for those Greek Olympians, warranted Perrottet, all the roads above hyper-local level were paved with money and gifts, culminating in the Games of Zeus. "The crème de la crème would step forward around the Greek world to face off in the Peloponnesus; no matter how many lesser victories an athlete had racked up, the Olympic Games were the ultimate challenge. And although the top prize was theoretically just an olive wreath, it brought many earthly rewards. Every city in Greece promised generous cash prizes to an athlete who brought home an Olympic crown; fringe benefits might include triumphant parades, lifetime seats at the ampitheater, generous pensions, civic positions, free meals – not to mention the undying respect of one's peers." Their lifestyles, indeed, would have been "as far removed from those of average citizens as NFL players' today". In his essay "On Choosing a Profession", the physician Galen regretted that his more talented countrymen were spurning law and medicine in favour of athletics.[17]

One-eyed and clear-sighted

To an Englishman, the notion of leisure, attested Derek Birley, evolved during the 19th century, particularly the 1840s. Lord Shaftesbury, to whom socialism and chartism were "the two great demons in morals and politics", sponsored the Ten Hour

Act, passed in 1847, reducing working hours for women and children; three years later, mills were shut on Saturdays from 2pm. To Birley, these constituted "the first small steps towards freeing the workers to join in the new leisure activities which the emerging new health-conscious and moralistic middle classes of the public schools were shaping". Cricket, though, was not among them. Reasoned Birley: "It was already, at its highest, most influential levels, freezing, if not frozen, into the patterns of a pre-industrial age, of the privileged besporting themselves with their retainers."[18] By the end of the century, English cricket would make its most symbolic statement, formally classifying the highest form of the game as… well, first-class, naturally.

If cricket was the first professional team game, the growing pains would prove chronic. The first county club was Sussex. Formally constituted in 1839, it was originally referred to, in deference to its regal patronage, as the *Royal* Sussex County Cricket Club. The mainstays were the Lillywhite family, who over the club's first six decades supplied no fewer than five leading players, one of whom, Fred, became the game's first eminent statistician and compiler of the multi-volume *Cricket Scores and Biographies* – an invaluable source for all subsequent historians and number-crunchers. Cousin James, meanwhile, would become England's first Test captain. Another early contributor to the club's growth was John Wisden, a fine bowler who took part in the trip by an All England party to North America in 1859-60 that constituted the competitive arts' first overseas expedition, but is far better remembered as the founder, three years later, of *Wisden Cricketers' Almanack*.[19]

The next decade brought three more county clubs: Nottinghamshire (1841), Kent (1842) and Surrey (1845). The Nottinghamshire mainspring was William Clarke, a brick-layer turned innkeeper with one functioning eye. Not that that hampered his vision unduly: here, after all, was the entrepreneur who pioneered cricket as a spectator sport.

Establishing a ground next to the Trent Bridge Inn, he invited Sussex to play the first match there and later convened a meeting of what Birley called "interested local worthies" to form Nottinghamshire CCC. Experiencing difficulty attracting spectators, Clarke decided to seek his fortune in London, where, nearing 50, he joined the MCC groundstaff, not a remunerative calling but one that provided opportunities aplenty to play at Lord's and impress selectors. In good part because he had cottoned on to the profitability of bowling for catches (not until 1836 had bowlers been credited for such dismissals), he became one of the stars of the 1845 season. Not short of psychological ploys, one amateur described by Birley as being "of the next, purer-minded generation" accused Clarke of "preying on the terrors of his victims by making caustic and cocksure remarks".[20]

In 1846, Clarke assembled his first itinerant All-England XI for a three-match tour of the prosperous but unfashionable north. So marked was their superiority, they were happy to be outnumbered by the opposition: sides of 18 took them on in Manchester and Yorkshire; in Sheffield they confronted 22. Many teams had previously taken the field as "England", but here, for almost certainly the first time, was one worthy of such a billing, numbering as it did most if not all of the very best cricketers available. Besides their generous hospitality, the host clubs paid plenty for the honour, including "part or all of the money at the field-gate", according to that expert mythologist James Pycroft in his 1851 book *The Cricket Field*, one of the game's first forays into hardback. Thus could Clarke pay his players a fee (£4 to £6 per game, the same rates as MCC, which "with masterly timing", noted Birley, had only just been reduced) plus expenses, and still pocket a tidy sum.

Two years later, the All-England XI was a full-time venture for Clarke, challenging MCC's dominance with 25 to 30 matches a season; come 1851 the fixture list ran to 34 three-day games. As Peter Wynne-Thomas assured me in early 2013 while he was beginning the final draft of his biography of Clarke, this "completely transformed the watching of the game and just as important all over the British Isles, not just as we have today a handful of centres that get large crowds three or four days a year".[21] Even the Oxford-educated Pycroft approved. Characterised by Birley as "southern Tory to the gills", he doubtless deemed Clarke's county-trotters a tad vulgar yet conceded that they "tend[ed] to a healthy circulation of the life's blood of cricket, vaccinating and inoculating every wondering rustic with the principles of the national game".[22]

"Establishment mythology has usually represented Old Clarke's initiative as an assault upon a citadel, an attempt to overthrow authority," argued Birley. "In fact it was an attempt to fill a vacuum: on the one hand bringing first-class cricket to places that had never known it; on the other hand providing regular employment for professionals throughout the summer months. Neither of these objectives would have been recognised by MCC as any of their business. What they did do, apart from running their own teams, having ceremonial dinners and pontificating about the laws, was arrange a few prestigious matches such as North v South and Gentlemen v Players, and for these the All-England players were still available. MCC was dying from self-indulgence without any help from Old Clarke."[23]

Gents v Plebs

"The urge to form county clubs," explained Birley, "was part of the latest phase in the battle between town and country. There was an element of nostalgia in this, for already cricket was an emblem of Britain's blissful rural past." There was also more than a hint of snobbery. After all, "the first thing socially aspirant industrialists did when they could afford it was to buy a 'place' in the countryside, not to live in but to use for leisure and prestige."[24] Social divisions underpinned the showpiece fixtures. From 1806, the Gentlemen and the Players crossed swords every season, often twice. By the time they stopped in 1962, the latter had prevailed almost twice as often – 125 wins to 68.

Here was a microcosm of the English class system, a world where leading cricketers were either gentlemen, who were ostensibly amateurs with family money or proper jobs, or players – professionals. Yet so long as they weren't too creative with their "expenses", the gents almost invariably went home more handsomely rewarded. They also did the captaining, occupied the prime batting berths and left most of the bowling to their social inferiors, especially the tiresome variety that necessitated actually running to the stumps. The post of "assistant secretary" would be specifically devised for such folk, allowing them to have their cake, eat it and demand another slice (not to mention guaranteeing invites to dinner parties from which the commoners were firmly excluded). As this practice continued into the next century, an alternative name for them would enter the lexicon: "shamateurs".

On the scorecard, these shamateurs would be prefixed by "Mr" while the openly professional were listed with surnames first, a priority inspired by those rigidly hierarchical public schools. Not that the distinctions ended there. A Pathé newsreel estimated to date from between 1910 and 1920 – but almost certainly a Gentlemen v Players fixture – shows the fielding side descending the pavilion steps while the batsmen make their way out from their less salubrious dressing room via the front row of benches.[25] At Old Trafford, home to Lancashire CCC, the professionals were not even permitted to change in the pavilion, being confined to a room elsewhere; even when the ground's new pavilion was finished in 1895, they were equipped with one lavatory to the amateurs' three.

The segregation did not stop there. Amateurs travelled to away fixtures by first-class rail; the pros were confined to third-class. They also stayed at different hotels or lodging houses. If they were accommodated in the dining room at lunchtime, they sat at separate tables and even pondered different menus. "The players in the 1880s and 1890s may have been some of the first popular sports stars within the cricket world but they remained second-class citizens," observed Ric Sissons. "Their subordinate position was perpetuated by a combination of paternalism, dependence, deference and strict discipline. Again in this respect they were no different to any other Victorian workers."[26]

* * *

One of the first men brave enough to challenge this segregation was the last fielder seen descending the steps in that Pathé newsreel. Percy Fender was Surrey's enterprising amateur captain, a wine merchant whose incaution and refusal to be stifled almost certainly cost him the Test captaincy – and quite probably a seat in Parliament (he declined Conservative entreaties to stand three times); it also enabled him to set a record for the fastest first-class hundred – in 35 minutes against Northamptonshire in 1920 – which would endure for more than six decades. By 1923, noted his biographer, Dick Streeton, reporters from London's 19 morning and five evening papers "were just starting to comment on Fender's habit of coming on to the field through the same gate as his professionals. Several linked this with comments on the anomaly of having a father and son with different status in the same side."[27]

Lord Harris, MCC president as long ago as 1875, may have been in his eighth decade but he was still club treasurer and the most influential force in English cricket – "an autocratic figure", attested Streeton, "serving cricket and cricketers faithfully by the dictums of his time, and a man of rigid principles throughout his long life".[28] The scion of a landed Conservative family, he had attended Eton and Oxford and served in the Boer War, captained Kent for 18 years and been just the second cricketer to toss a coin on his country's behalf. He respected Fender, and vice-versa, but the latter's mischievous nature and disinclination to tug forelock led to a feud.

Inevitably, His Lordship did not think much of Fender's efforts to blur the line between amateurs and professionals. "We do not want that sort of thing at Lord's" is the succinct summation of the "wigging" Harris duly administered. When Fender incurred his wrath again with a published letter tactlessly suggesting that Harris may have been guilty of double-dealing, he was summoned to the committee room again. The rough translation of the ensuing scolding runs along the lines of "Don't you ever write about me, my views or MCC in print again, young man."[29]

The power of Grace

The number of county clubs swelled. Cambridgeshire, Hampshire, Lancashire, Middlesex and Yorkshire had all joined the ranks by the mid-1860s, whereupon the following decade saw the press begin to clamour for a formal championship in preference to the prevalent ad-hoc-ness. One critical phase began in 1873 with the inception of a registration process, obliging players to state before the start of the season whether they intended to play for their county of residence or birth. Finally, at Lord's in December 1889, representatives of the eight leading counties agreed on the format for an official County Championship. Touring teams nonetheless continued to be popular until the early 1880s, but by then the only remaining alternative for entrepreneurs lay in sending sides abroad, most alluringly to Australia. The man they all wanted aboard was Dr William Gilbert Grace – "WG".

Heavily bearded, bulky of frame and even weightier of all-round achievement, Grace was not only the finest cricketer in England; only Queen Victoria and her prime minister, William Gladstone, rivalled him as a public figure. He was also widely billed – and not exclusively by the English press – as the most famous sportsman on Earth. Only a tiny proportion of the planet were privileged to watch him play, granted, but newspapers were the prime means of communication, and according to Fleet Street, home to the most influential, he was the first sporting superstar. His status was confirmed in 1871, when he not only became the first batsman to tally 2,000 runs in a county season but, in a summer that saw the next-most prolific scorer, Harry Jupp, aggregate 1,068, ploughed on to amass 2,739, a record that would stand for a quarter of a century. Of the 17 first-class centuries hit that year, WG accounted for 10. (Note to baffled Americans: think Babe Ruth, The Prequel.)

For once, that lyrical *Manchester Guardian* cricketer-fancier Neville Cardus had no need to tax his fertile imagination nor draw on fanciful exaggeration. "He was King of Cricket by born right, and he looked it every inch, every ounce, never incongruous on the sward even in his last years of benignly accumulating flesh and greying beard. But it must never be forgotten that at his high noon he was a superb example of manhood, every muscle quick in him, no superfluity, his brow classical and his eyes keen and fine. He was a boy when the round-arm bowling changed to overarm; which means he had to counter a species of attack different from that by which so far his skill had been practised. Apparently he noticed no difference, for the solemn truth is that in a few seasons he smashed fast bowling, discredited it, or to use the stronger and more appropriate word from Charles Dickens, he 'spifflicated' it."[30]

In the only widely available film of Grace, he can be seen practising at Lord's in 1899 alongside the Maharajah of Nawanagar, more commonly known as Kumar Shri Ranjitsinhji, or, for far greater convenience, Ranji. The Indian was assuredly no slouch with the bat himself.[31] Grace "revolutionised cricket", Ranji observed (albeit quite possibly with the aid of one of his many ghostwriters). "He turned it from an accomplishment into a science; he united in his mighty self all the good points of all the good players and made utility the criterion of style… he turned the old one-stringed instrument into a many chorded lyre."[32] The public concurred. "Admission 3d," proclaimed notices outside grounds. "If Dr W.G. plays, Admission 6d."

Officially, WG, then qualifying to become a doctor, was an amateur; otherwise, he would not, could not, have been chosen, year after year, to captain the Gentlemen. Keith Booth deftly summed up the conundrum: financially, he couldn't afford to play as an amateur; socially he couldn't afford to play as a professional.[33] So he became a shrewd and prosperous shamateur. "One well-known cricketer," as *Lillywhite's Cricketers' Companion* observed discreetly in 1878, declining to cite Grace, "has made larger profits by playing cricket than any professional ever made."[34]

Simon Rae, Grace's most recent biographer, made no bones about his subject's significance – or his double standards:

*The timing of Grace's emergence onto the scene in the mid-1860s
happened to give him an enormous say in the future of the game,
which hung in the balance between, on the one hand, a demor-
alised MCC and the few amateur-controlled counties and, on
the other, the northern professionals who, with their touring
teams, had the makings of an alternative power structure
wholly independent of Lord's. Grace was the pivotal figure in
this power-struggle. With his explosive talent, he was the man
the crowds wanted to see, and they would have followed him
into either camp. In throwing in his lot with the MCC he effectively headed off a schism which could have seen the amateur
and professional elements drift apart, and handed the control
of the game back to the Lord's establishment. He demanded
nothing in return except to be allowed to flout that establishment's most sacred tenet, amateurism.*[35]

Grace made substantially more money from cricket than those
naïve enough or simply unfortunate enough to be openly
professional. Early in 1872, the Melbourne Cricket Club, the
Australian MCC, wrote to Grace in the hope of persuading
him to bring his talents Down Under. The reply staggered his
suitors: he wanted £1,500 – equivalent to more than £50,000
today. By illuminating comparison, the *entire* gate receipts
for Lord's that summer would amount to barely double that
sum. Unsurprisingly, that audacious demand alienated both
Melbournites and the similarly enthusiastic South Australian
Cricket Association, but WG would get his way. He knew he
was the game's beesiest knees. He knew his worth. On one
occasion during a minor fixture, or so the hoary old story goes,
he refused to vacate the crease after being bowled, replaced
the bails and, dripping with disdain, informed the umpire:
"They've come to watch me bat, not you umpire."

Later in 1872, a syndicate of MCC members agreed not only
to meet Grace's stipulations but to fund the Australian voyage
(first-class berths, naturally), and even proffer expenses, for WG
as well as his future bride, Agnes. By contrast, the genuinely

professional members of the touring party for the 14-match expedition, recruited by Grace, would be paid £150 per head, plus £20 spending money. Naturally, they travelled second-class.[36] When the All-England XI met South Australia at Adelaide in March 1874, Grace insisted on taking half the gate money, plus £110.

He also attracted opprobrium for breaching, or so it seemed, his contract with another promoter. "We scarcely know how to characterise the mean and sordid character of this business," fumed the *Wallaroo Times*. "For the sake of pursuing a few pounds in Adelaide, Mr Grace or his agents... have forfeited any claim they had to the character of men of their word, or gentlemen; and they may be assured they will leave the colony with that stigma attached to them."[37] A century later, Benny Green would bemoan WG's refusal to come clean and renounce his amateur status, which would have brought an already belated end to "the hypocrisy of a two-tiered social structure".[38]

* * *

Yet as canny as many Englishmen were when it came to profiting from cricket's burgeoning box-office appeal, the Australians made them seem, well, amateurish. Which was ironic, given that, theoretically at least, their players played the game for the life rather than a living. The fuse was lit by the first fully representative tour of England in 1878, led by Dave Gregory, a venture that saw the tourists succeed Clarke's All-England XI as the game's elite troupe. Forming a joint stock company, they contributed £50 per head towards expenses and returned home having pocketed around £750 apiece – ample for a couple of houses, maybe three, in an acceptable Sydney suburb. Not until the advent of the Indian Premier League 130 years later, calculated Malcolm Knox, would a cricketer reap so much from a single season's batting and/or bowling.[39]

For the next three decades, warranted Knox, the Australian players kept the "fabulous" takings from their expeditions to Blighty on a short leash. The English professionals, not unsurprisingly, were more than a tad peeved: not only did these shrewd blighters corner the gate receipts; they also enjoyed a goodly number of the social privileges hitherto reserved strictly for the amateurs. Before the century was out, as we shall see, the backlash would generate international cricket's first outbreak of industrial action.

Rucks and mauls

No sport has endured a schism to match the one that tore rugby apart. The inception of the Yorkshire Cup in 1877 marked the culmination of the first chapter in a north v south potboiler that continues to this day, even though the essential differences between union and league extend, in playing terms, to 15 players v 13 and, in the case of the latter, no lineouts. In spirit, they run fathoms deep.

The furniture-shifting was triggered by the working-class invasion of middle-class territory. On 4 December 1870 *The Times* published a letter jointly signed by the secretaries of London's pre-eminent clubs, Richmond's Edwin Ash and Blackheath's B. H. Burns, seeking a way through the chaos imposed by varying codes of rugby: "Those who play the rugby-type game should meet to form a code of practice as various clubs play to rules which differ from others, which makes the game difficult to play." On January 26 the following year, at the Pall Mall restaurant, close to Trafalgar Square, representatives of 21 clubs, the vast majority London-based, attended a meeting that led to the birth of the Rugby Football Union. "Legend has it that there would have been 22," notes Huw Richards in *A Game For Hooligans*, "but the Wasps delegate had gone to the wrong place and liked it so much he wanted to stay."[40]

The resulting committee invited three Old Rugbeians, lawyers all, to compose a set of laws, approved that June. The responsibility fell largely on the shoulders of L. J. Maton, conveniently housebound by a broken leg. His reward, notes Richards, "was a supply of tobacco from his fellow drafters" and, in 1875 and 1876, the RFU presidency. "By a fine irony", significantly, the committee outlawed hacking once and for all, though this was mourned by some: another Old Rugbeian, Edward Guillemard, "reminisced warmly" about games where one might see "a couple of players vigorously engaged in kicking each other's shins long after the scrimmage had broken up".[41]

As the century faded, the challenges facing British rugby, relates Richards, emanated from a wrangle between north and south, the latter represented by the RFU. "In the north, rugby spread beyond the exclusivity of pioneer clubs like Liverpool and Manchester. Stuart Barlow's research on Rochdale shows the middle classes – which, like those of Wales and New Zealand, were smaller and more locally rooted than in London and its suburbs – encouraging working-class participation and rapidly being overtaken by it. Church-based clubs were succeeded by those 'independent of middle-class patronage, based on street, district or public house'."[42] Players competed on behalf of their communities, added Barlow, "rather than to enshrine the ethics" of muscular Christianity. "The ethic of 'fair play' was subsumed by the desire to enhance local pride through securing victories against rivals."[43]

"No sport sets out to be professional," reasons Richards. "It becomes, though, not only possible but likely when large numbers of people are prepared to watch it and there are skilled players for whom extra income is important. Neither condition applied in London. Both did in Yorkshire."[44] Lancashire, too, for all that football was preferred and the county RFU was dead-set against cup competition. Formed in 1867, Rochdale RFC were usurped by a so-called "open" club, Rochdale Hornets, whose derby disputes with St Clements were soon pulling in 5,000-6,000, out-drawing internationals.

In 1878, Wakefield Trinity's Harry Hayley signalled Yorkshire's social diversification when he was picked as its first onfield working-class representative. Being on low incomes, the likes of Hayley could patently ill-afford to take unpaid leave from their jobs, necessitating compensation. In 1874, Hull had started stumping up for half its players' train fares; five years later, they were paying the entire sum. The club accounts for the 1883-84 season encompassed £18 for "loss of time"; Trinity had already been making such payments openly since 1881.[45] Two years earlier, in response to the players' expectations of remuneration for participating in the Yorkshire Cup, the county committee adopted MCC's strictures on cricketing amateurism, thus allowing those who found themselves out of pocket to claim suitable expenses.

By 1886, relates that passionate and fantastically energetic rugby historian Tony Collins in *Rugby's Great Split*, the "tattered" state of the amateur flag and the rising influence of working-class players and spectators in the north, Yorkshire especially, were causing consternation. "In January, press reports spoke of 'the appearance on the scene of the much dreaded and detested professional footballer – the man who plays not for love and honour but for gain' and disclosed that it had 'an array of convincing evidence' of at least two examples of such players."[46] In a move perceived as pre-meditated, Pudsey appealed against their defeat in the first round of the Yorkshire Cup by Manningham, claiming that two of the opposition players, J. Birmingham and W. Pulleyn, were receiving more than out-of-pocket expenses. "Interestingly," points out Collins, "both Pulleyn and Manningham's captain admitted that the club had promised to find him a job, something that was illegal by the end of the year but over which the committee took no action." Manningham presented six sworn statements that the pair had not been paid, whereupon the tournament committee rejected Pudsey's claim.

The start of the following season found the *Bradford Observer* wondering whether rugby was too popular while the *Yorkshire Post* expressed grave concern over the "grave dimensions" attained by the debate over professionalism: "It is scarcely possible for matters to continue in the present unsatisfactory condition...The RFU is determined to purify the game in these parts by the legislative action of its members after careful consideration."[47] The theme of resistance was maintained in the 1886 *Football Annual* by Arthur Budd, a member of the RFU committee, who objected to the fact that, just six months after "the legitimisation of the bastard" – i.e. professionalism – the FA Cup final had been contested by two professional clubs. "The Rugby Union committee finding themselves face to face with the hydra," he warned, "have determined to throttle it before he is big enough to throttle them."[48]

"Why are so few public school men and clergymen found in our leading fifteens?" was the *Yorkshire Post* correspondent's strictly rhetorical question. "It is because the associations of the game are now becoming thoroughly distasteful to any gentleman of sportsmanlike feeling. They do not care to be hooted and yelled at as part of a sixpenny show or to meet and associate with men who care nothing for the game other than as a means to an end."[49] Collins' perception is that those hooters and yellers regarded themselves "as participants in the match ritual, rather than mere observers".

> *And, just as working-class players sought money for their efforts, working-class spectators saw the match as a spectacle and demanded value for their monetary outlay. Although not articulated as such, rugby football had become a site of conflict between the expression of working-class cultural practices and the dominant cultural codes of the public-school ethos.*[50]

That October, an RFU general meeting decreed that any payment for playing or training would henceforth be illegal, as would the employment of any player by the club or by any of its members. The impact did not manifest itself in Yorkshire until March 1888, when two entrepreneurial cricketers, Alfred Shaw and Arthur Shrewsbury, enlisted 15 northern and half a dozen southern players for a paid 30-week tour of Australia and New Zealand, where they would play matches conducted according to the strictures of both rugby and the local football variant. Halifax's Jack Clowes confessed all to the Yorkshire committee and offered to return his £15 fee, but when the RFU declared him professional he was already sailing south with the party, preventing him from participating in the matches.

The RFU ducked the bouncer. Andrew Stoddart, England captain at both rugby and cricket – who assumed the tour leadership after Broughton Rangers' Bob Seddon had drowned while sculling up the Hunter River in New South Wales – had pocketed an initial fee of £50; his final reward is unknown, but two lesser amateurs – on what was retrospectively classed as the first British Lions tour – were offered £200 to cover expenses. That the RFU took no action, reckons Collins, can be attributed to the simple reason that any investigation would have implicated Stoddart and his fellow gentleman amateurs. "If the charges of professionalism had been pursued, the RFU would have had to ban one of England's leading sportsmen and declare illegal the generous advantages of the gentleman amateur's expenses. And to have maintained the ban on Clowes but taken no action against Stoddart would have been to admit openly that different, unwritten, rules applied to different classes of players. Nevertheless, by ignoring both their own regulations and the overwhelming evidence of payments, the RFU had laid bare the underlying class bias of the amateur ethos – a middle-class gentleman was by definition an amateur, whether he was paid or not, and was not to be judged by the standards of other, working-class, men."[51]

* * *

The culmination of this microcosm of the wider class struggle was the historic meeting on 29 August 1895 in Huddersfield, which took place, wrote the late Geoffrey Moorhouse in his vivid (and pointedly named) history of rugby league, *A People's Game*, amid "the splendid Corinthian architecture of the town's principal hostelry", the George Hotel; this "spoke eloquently of Huddersfield's textile prosperity". The railway station was next door; The George had recently been redecorated and refurnished from top to toe, "and its billiards and other facilities were presided over cordially but firmly by Mrs M. A. Botting, Manageress".[52] At 6.30 "sharp", 21 northern clubs voted unanimously to form a Northern Rugby Football Union, pledging themselves "to push forward, without delay, its establishment on the principle of payment for *bona-fide* broken-time only".[53]

All bar the Dewsbury representative then tendered their resignations to the RFU. "Mr Holdsworth stated that he had not yet had a chance to consult his committee on the subject; nervously adding that although they had no doubt they would agree with the course adopted by the others, he did not feel he could accept the responsibility of forwarding the resignation off his own bat. Which was just as well, because Mr Holdsworth had misjudged the temperature back at Crown Flatt (or perhaps had privately estimated it all too accurately)."[54] A few days later, a large majority of the Dewsbury Football and Cricket Club Committee decided to withdraw from the new concord. Still, Stockport would expand the army of defectors, leaving the game, as Collins concludes, "utterly and irrevocably split".

Within 15 years, the exodus had amounted to more than 200 clubs. This would prove an unmixed blessing for rugby union, "amputating England's most fertile regions", as Richards puts it, and hence thwarting the dominance anticipated at the RFU by dint of the nation's population and wealth, which in turn bred a competitive and vibrant Home (later Five, still later Six) Nations Championship. And although the union code on the other side of the Bristol Channel was also depleted, the absence of a fully tooled England XV helped Wales emerge as the strongest force in European rugby in the 20th century. "What Marxist-Leninism was to the Soviet Union and papal infallibility to the Roman Catholic Church," noted Richards, "amateurism would be to rugby union for the next century."[55]

* * *

In 1896, 56 clubs entered the inaugural Challenge Cup; a year after that, the lineout was abolished. In 1906 came the key rule changes: manned in many competitions by 12 players, teams were formally fixed at 13; "play the ball" replaced rucks, allowing the tackled player to backheel the ball to a colleague. The following year came Australia's turn when the New South

Wales Rugby Football League was founded at a Sydney hotel – situated, spookily enough, in George Street. Thereafter, the game became the dominant code in that state as well as Queensland. Then, in 1910, came what Collins describes as "the final piece in the jigsaw": the Northern Union's first tour of Australasia.

"Symbolically, the tourists' departure marked the end of the odyssey that working-class rugby had made since the miners and millworkers of the north of England first ran with an oval ball in their hands. From now on, the northern working-classes' relationship to rugby was based entirely on a different sport and a different culture to that which the rugby union had provided… the fear of working-class domination saw the development of an amateur ideology that was ultimately incompatible with either mass working-class participation or the growth of a commercial, mass-based leisure industry. This was the rock that split asunder the consensus of rugby's leaders."[56]

In 1922, the Northern Union morphed into the Northern Rugby Football League. In 1929 the Challenge Cup final was savoured by more than 41,000 at Wembley Stadium. A quarter of a century later, in the same year France hosted the inaugural Rugby League World Cup (only a four-nation affair, admittedly), the Cup final replay between Warrington and Halifax at Bradford's Odsal Stadium drew 102,000, a record for either code; anecdotal evidence suggested 120,000 were present. In terms of fulfilling public desires, domestic rugby union had long been a distant speck in the rear-view mirror. Not until the 20th century's final decade would that iron-clad class curtain display any inclination to part.

Fores and foursomes

At the time of writing, the lone golfing "Grand Slam" had been the GB and US Amateur and Professional foursome nailed by Bobby Jones in 1930. Though there was no record of exactly when the change took effect, experts contend that it took until 1960, when Arnold Palmer proclaimed his intention to match Jones by landing the US Open, Masters and PGA in addition to the British Open. Yet there are still all too many days – as we will discuss in a later chapter – when we relive the sport's exclusivity of the early 1960s, a time when a plummy English advertising executive could bemoan the loss of a vaunted colleague to a severed foot (as in an episode from *Mad Men*) on the ground that "he'll never play golf again".

A letter dispatched by Prestwick Golf Club to seven other leading clubs on 6 April 1857, contends Robert Browning, is where "the history of championship golf really begins". Each recipient, it proposed, should send four members to play "double Matches, or Foursomes", whereupon the final pair would split and tackle each other. They were also asked to state a preference for the venue: St Andrews or Prestwick. Such was the resultant enthusiasm, the Honourable Company and four other clubs also declared their interest (in the event, two of the entrants failed to muster a team). At St Andrews on the last three days of July, 11 clubs competed in a series of 18-hole contests for a silver claret jug, won by George Glennie and Lieutenant J.C. Stewart, two notable St Andrews players whose success won them life membership of Royal Blackheath.[57] Three years later, on Wednesday 17 October 1860, eight professionals assembled at Prestwick for three rounds over the 12-hole links, with "Old Tom" Morris, the local pro, emerging as victor; the following September, on the eve of the second tussle for the Championship Belt, the Prestwick committee signed the Open Championship Charter: from then on, the competition would be "open to all the world".[58]

In the view of Peter Lewis, the first director of the award-winning British Golf Museum and author of the acclaimed book *The Dawn of Professional Golf*, 1894 was the pivotal year in the evolution of professional chipping and putting. For one thing, it marked the first time the British Open had been staged outside Scotland, in England; more significantly, the tournament yielded its first English professional winner, J.H. Taylor: along with James Braid and Harry Vardon (whose six Open titles remain unchallenged), Taylor would "dominate and symbolise" the professional game up to the outbreak of the First World War. "Their heyday coincides with an unprecedented growth of the game both in Britain and abroad, a growth which they helped to fuel."[59]

At the outset of 1894 the four home nations (plus the Isle of Man and Channel Islands) boasted 716 clubs – 356 in England, 301 in Scotland – compared with 147 a decade previously; courses were attached to nearly 70% of them. City golfing societies, primarily a Scottish development, enjoyed huge growth, soaring from 33 (all north of the border) in 1889 to 516 in 1914 – 417 in Scotland, with 271 in Edinburgh alone compared with London's 53. In 1890, furthermore, there were 30 clubs and 18 courses for women, almost invariably attached to men's clubs; come 1914, the respective figures were 479 and 51.[60] The introduction in the 1850s of the comparatively cheap and durable gutta-percha ball – made from the juice of a South-East Asian tree, the Palaquium, and simple to mass-produce – was credited for this explosion; Lewis saw it as "a tool that enabled the expansion to take place when other conditions were ripe".[61]

In 1900, the *Blackpool Herald* summed up the game's impact in the popular Lancastrian seaside town as well as neighbouring Lytham St Annes: "Golf has not only built hotels or enabled them to be built, but it has built boarding houses and club houses and made them into paying concerns. We have people taking furnished houses or buying or building houses that they may live near to good links. Golf has made St Annes; it is now making Fairhaven."[62]

Joining a club and playing the game, nevertheless, were considered expensive everywhere bar Scotland, persuading Saxon Browne to point out, in 1906, that "in no country as yet, except Scotland, have the lower classes shown any enthusiasm or aptitude… the reason, of course, being that facilities for the game have not yet been afforded them, nor has the prevailing opinion that golf is an expensive game suitable only for the moneyed or leisured classes yet been exploded."[63] It was the club professional who tended to the needs of these fortunate folk. "In common with the other major sports, and cricket in particular, there was a great gap between gentlemen and players," asserted Lewis. "Even the most successful professional golfers relied on the patronage of amateur players."[64]

It is telling, nonetheless, that not until 1897 did the formation of the R & A Rules of Golf Committee see a body take responsibility for the rules. Not until 1909, moreover, was the form and make of clubs prescribed; and not until 1920 was the size and weight of the ball even regulated.[65] By then, the "gutty" had been usurped by the rubber-cored ball, an American innovation that flew, on average, 30 to 50 yards further. It was patented in 1898 by employees of the Goodrich Rubber Company, the Ohio firm also responsible for the invention, in 1900, of the automatic golf-ball winding machine, enhancing the production process.[66]

The lot of the leading professional at the end of the 19th century was not modest. Having played a match, unusually, in January, Vardon formally began his 1899 campaign in Eastbourne on April 1. From then until October 27 he wended his way, in turn, to engagements in Leicestershire, Scotland, London, Surrey, Hertfordshire, Porthcawl, London, Sandwich (for the Open), Scotland, northern England, Derbyshire, Scotland, Ireland, Cornwall, Sheffield, Nottingham and London before finally calling a halt after a date in Norfolk. By the end of July, affirming the increasingly gruelling nature of his trade in 1914, George Duncan had played 43 matches at 27 venues, never mind seven tournaments.[67] Rumours of stinted efforts circulated; most notoriously, Baird, Taylor and Varndon were accused of agreeing to pool their prizemoney for the 1908 *News of the World* tournament, an unthinkable notion duly quashed by *Golf Illustrated*.

Rounding the bases

The end of the American Civil War in 1865 marked the start of the baseball boom, supported, as George Vecsey writes, "by the relative prosperity and hopefulness of a postwar nation", particularly in the northern states. "With trains running, factories smoking, cities growing, there was space and time and money for green enclosures, for entertainment, and inevitably for sport."[68] Professional team sport began four years later with the formation of the Cincinnati Red Stockings, who won 65 and tied one of the 66 games they played around the country, winning an invitation to the White House from that prolific Confederate-basher, President Ulysses S. Grant.

The Red Stockings were managed by Harry Wright, who kitted them out in uniforms, introduced diets and banned smoking and drinking (the last two strictures were not, needless to add, observed religiously). It was an early sign of cosmopolitanism that Wright's team contained just one player from Cincinnati; the other eight were imported and, as Vecsey attests, "paid for their baseball skills while allegedly making hats, selling insurance, keeping books, and building pianos to live up to the vestigial amateur pretensions of the day". Even so, as Keith Booth observes, the notion of playing games for money sat rather easier with "a less class-conscious society" than it did in England.[69]

In 1871, the Red Stockings, now based in Boston, were among the founder members of the National Association of Professional Base Ball Players; five years later, it was renamed the National League. In a far more momentous development, 1879 brought the reserve clause, without which the management-labour disputes that would bedevil the game a century later might not have been quite so necessary. In secret, the National League clubs each agreed to "reserve" up to five players who would become bound to their current employer for the duration of their career, an agreement soon extended to include all players in their league. In 1890 the Sherman Act was passed, prohibiting business activities that reduced competition – unless the activity was baseball. Indeed, in 1903, as part of the Cincinnati Peace Compact between the National and American Leagues that ushered in major league baseball as we now know it, the owners broadened the clause's remit yet again, to encompass the junior league. Later, another clause was added to the standard player contract, giving employers the "option" to renew contracts for an additional season under the same terms. The repercussions of this American brand of feudalism would reverberate long and wide.

* * *

Progress was rapid on the gridiron, too. In 1892, William "Pudge" Heffelfinger, an All-American guard who had prospered under Walter Camp's revered tutelage at Yale, was paid $500 (worth nearly $13,000 in 2013) to turn out for the Allegheny Athletic Association against the Pittsburgh Athletic Club; a quarterback from Indiana College, John Brailler, then just 16, is generally acknowledged as the first player to openly turn pro, accepting $10 from the Latrobe YMCA in Pennsylvania to appear in a game in 1895. The following season every Allegheny Athletic Association player was paid – for the club's entire two-game schedule.

It was inevitable that Pennsylvanians should figure so prominently. "As the first collegiate players moved beyond the ivied halls of the academy," note Jeff Silverman and Charles Hardy III in their history of football in the state, "the game graduated with them to the athletic clubs and associations they joined." There it captured imaginations in the western and northeastern coal towns, in the steel towns around Pittsburgh and in Bethlehem. "Football's appeal among blue-collar workers and immigrants was magnetic; the game called for the same kind of grit they had to muster just to get by every day."[70]

After fielding a footballing incarnation in 1902 (coached by that consummate multi-tasker, Connie Mack), baseball's Philadelphia Athletics, in consort with the Pittsburgh Stars and the Philadelphia Phillies, formed the first professional league; by 1904, there were seven teams in Ohio, increasingly the game's stronghold. During the First World War, however, surging salaries, unchecked freedom of movement in search of the optimum deal and the signing of pre-graduation students combined to create a sporting wild west. Unanimity, of outlook and rules, was imperative.

Conceived in a car dealership in Canton, Ohio – future home to the NFL Hall of Fame – the first organised national league, the American Professional Football Association, was born in 1920. Its constituents were a far cry from today's gridiron giants, with no fewer than five hailing from Ohio alone: the Canton Bulldogs, the Cleveland Tigers, the Dayton Triangles, the Akron Professionals, the Rochester (N.Y.) Jeffersons, the Rock Island Independents, the Muncie Flyers, the Decatur Staleys, the Chicago Cardinals, the Buffalo All-Americans, the Chicago Tigers, the Columbus Panhandles, the Detroit Heralds and the Hammond Pros. The list makes intriguing reading, both for the preponderance of minor cities represented and the mostly mild-mannered names – Jeffersons? Heralds? *Triangles*? The first star to dazzle was Canton's most bullish Bulldog, Jim Thorpe, a Native American. Two years later, the APFA was rebranded in the rather more familiar guise of the National Football League.[71] Comprising 18 teams, the NFL included another Ohioan entrant, the Oorang Indians of Marion, an all-Native American team featuring Thorpe, sponsored by the Oorang dog kennels.[72]

Propelled by George Halas, founder, owner and head coach of the Chicago Bears, the NFL grew with alacrity: by 1925, there were 23 teams, up five from the previous year. Then came Harold Edward Grange, the "Galloping Ghost" and pride of Pennsylvania, "Red" to one and all for ever more. That year, the half-back graduated from the University of Illinois and signed for the Bears in a deal that netted $100,000 apiece for him and his manager/agent, C.C. "Cash and Carry" Pyle. Grange played 18 games in three months, pulling in 75,000 spectators at New York's Polo Grounds, 73,000 in LA.

"More importantly for the NFL," stresses Evan Weiner in *America's Passion: How a Coal Miner's Game Became the NFL in the 20th century*, "the Galloping Ghost brought the pro league much-needed publicity." Pyle informed Halas that Grange was seeking a five-figure contract and one-third ownership in the Bears for the following season; Halas refused. Pyle then leased Yankee Stadium in New York and petitioned the NFL for a franchise; feeling threatened, Tim Mara, the owner of the New York Giants, gathered the support he required and Pyle's request was turned down.[73] Cue the upstart American Football League, which attracted nine teams (including Rock Island, who defected from the NFL) but dissolved after a single season. Meanwhile, Halas pushed through a measure to ensure college players could not be signed before graduation – a stroke he himself had pulled with Grange.

The march of soccer

It may surprise some to learn that the first professional manager in Italian football was an Englishman, William Garbutt, who joined Genoa in 1912, a prelude to stints with AS Roma, Napoli and Athletic Bilbao in Spain. His players referred to him as "Mister" and the term stuck: "The Mister" is still the name by which Italian managers are referred. "Garbutt is historically important," attested Matthew Barker in *When Saturday Comes*, "not least because it seems he moved abroad for purely sporting reasons; other British football pioneers across the globe tended to be overseas for business purposes."[74] Garbutt, of course, hailed from the home of professional football. Europe was slow to catch on: not for almost 40 years did Austria (1924) follow suit, followed by Czechoslovakia (1925), Italy (1926), Spain (1928), France (1932) and the USSR (1936).

Teams representing the Royal Engineers and the Civil Service were among the 15 entrants for the inaugural FA Cup, all but one, Glasgow's Queens Park, hailing from within a short crow's flight of London (for all that their entire income that year had been £6, the Glaswegians contributed more than one-sixth of that sum, a guinea, to the purchase of the original trophy, then put a few noses out of joint by reaching the semi-finals). Within a dozen years, the field had expanded to 100, stretching (Queens Park aside) from Redcar and Coatham on England's north-east coast via Southport and Birmingham to Rochester in Kent. "It is difficult to be exact," conceded Tony Mason in *Association Football And English Society 1863-1915*, about when footballers became professionals. In 1876, two Scots, Peter Andrews and James J Lang, joined a Sheffield club, Heeley FC, but, despite various claims, "no satisfactory evidence" of them being paid has been uncovered. Three years later, Darwen played Turton "for the benefit of two Scotch gentlemen" who had played for the former – Love and Suter. "There is not much doubt," wrote Mason, "that Suter was paid for playing and Love was probably giving his services for a consideration. Even before that, Suter had played for Turton in the final of their own challenge cup in 1878 and 'the Second Prize money, £3 won by the Turton First Team, be handed over to C. Tootill, that he pay Suter out of it'."[75]

Not for nothing, notes Russell, were the 1880s among the most critical decades in football history. Rumours of professionalism were rife from the outset, giving birth to the popular and long-running euphemism "boot money" – at the end of a game, a player might find half a crown in his footwear. In 1881, the *Midland Athlete* observed that, while it knew of no "glaring" instance, "we do know of cases where men have received more than their legitimate expenses… it is no uncommon thing for influential members of a club to obtain situations for good players as an inducement"; nor for club funds to be used "to find a small business for popular players who pose as 'mine host' before their admiring clubmates".[76]

"None was more alive to the situation than Charles Alcock," says Booth of the formidable administrative all-rounder who had a foot in each of the two main sporting camps and whose "dual background of the industrial revolution and public school served him well".[77] In the middle of the 19th century, what was not yet referred to as first-class cricket had appeared destined to comprise touring XIs making a living for themselves (or trying to) by playing local clubs, but the outlook changed with the formation of the county clubs, who ran the game together with MCC, "both acmes", as Mason put it, "of aristocratic patronage and middle-class exclusiveness" who "kept the professionals firmly in their place". Cricket, therefore, "was a model for the football administrator faced with the issue of professionalism".[78]

It was a prolonged 1879 FA Cup tie, claims Booth, that brought "the first stirrings of professionalism – or, at least, the first perceived". This came about as a consequence of the inclusion of Love and Suter in the unheralded Darwen side that, despite trailing Old Etonians 5-1 with 15 minutes remaining, forced not just one replay but two. This was the season that saw Darwen, along with Nottingham Forest, become the first clubs from north of Watford to challenge the competition's southern monopolists. Inhabitants of the mill town had financed the first trip to The Oval; Old Etonians, the FA and the public co-funded the second before the outsiders ran out of steam and support, losing 6-2 in a second replay. Old Etonians took the Cup, and regained it in 1882 when, or so legend has it, Arthur Kinnaird, the captain, celebrated by standing on his head in front of the pavilion. "If the rumour is true," theorises Booth, "it was a gesture of symbolic significance, for from that point the whole ethos of amateur football was turned on its head. Never again would the Association Cup be won by another amateur side."[79] Emboldened by the Lancastrians of Darwen, two clubs from nearby Blackburn prospered: in 1883, Blackburn Olympic defeated Old Etonians to become the first winners from outside London, only to fold in 1889; the very next season saw the start of a hat-trick of triumphs by the considerably more durable Blackburn Rovers, formed after a meeting convened by John Lewis and Arthur Constantine, both Shrewsbury School old boys.

* * *

When it came to professionalism, Alcock refused to turn ostrich. In the 1881 *Football Annual*, he had commented that it would "be well for those who have the interest of the game at heart to recognise the existence of a problem that will in all likelihood have to be mastered before long".[80] Not long afterwards, the Amateur Athletic Association ruled that a professional cricketer could not compete as an amateur; in contemplating whether football should go down the same path, Alcock – with considerable understatement – called it a "knotty" dilemma. He believed that professionalism, properly managed, was both inevitable and desirable, but such sentiments were suffocated by demands for more punitive measures against what many perceived as an evil.

One especially prickly issue was the movement of players from one town or district to another, particularly for cup ties. Many officials took exception, deeming this to be against the spirit of the game. In 1883, according to a letter published in the magazine *Football*, Nottingham Forest nailed up a number of placards in Sheffield offering a £20 reward to anyone supplying evidence that would establish that three Sheffield Wednesday players who had recently played against Forest had only joined the club shortly beforehand.[81] Come the following season, according to *Athletic News*, the game had "developed into a vast business institution".[82] Bolton Wanderers, it reported, had spent £1,082 the previous campaign and, despite playing most of their matches at home, emerged with a profit of just £11. Few doubted the prime source of expenditure.

Yet as Russell argues, the distinction between amateur and professional football was always blurry. "There was never a 'pure' amateur game in which the extrinsic pleasures of 'playing the game' overrode financial considerations; public school old boy sides expected and received substantial 'expenses' on their provincial tours. However, if amateurism was an aspiration sometimes muddied in practice, its supporters unfailingly recognised challenges to the ideal. Hostility toward emergent professionalism (not actually illegal until 1882) took many forms, with practical concerns that wealthier clubs might upset the game's competitive balance mixing with fears about the example set by the existence of men paid only to play and the status anxieties experienced as 'gentlemen' saw mere 'players' encroach upon their exclusive social space."[83]

If the acquisition of players and use of financial and other inducements were "probably reasonably widespread", deduced Russell, the centre of innovation for professionalism was east and central Lancashire. "Coming to the game at the very moment of its emergence as a popular, competitive sport, the towns and villages of the region embraced the practices of nascent professionalism far more readily than was possible in earlier amateur-dominated centres such as Sheffield and Birmingham. When, in 1884, the vehemently anti-professional Scottish FA named over fifty emigré players requiring special dispensation to play in Scotland, a clear accusation of professionalism, all but Aston Villa's Archie Hunter were playing with Lancashire clubs."[84]

In October 1884, the FA introduced an array of draconian regulations, including a ban on clubs playing any other club, whether affiliated to the governing body or not, that paid or imported players. Lancashire led the response, supplying the entire membership of the British Football Association, a pressure group that received legal advice that the ban was unenforceable – a major factor, believes Russell, in the FA's decision to rescind it just a month after imposing it.

"Lancashire FA representatives," records Russell, "were key advocates for professionalism at the three General Meetings called to debate the issue in 1885. At the last of these, on 20 July, professionalism with strict controls over players' residence qualifications, movement between clubs and the wider role within administration of the game was finally conceded. That outcome resulted from, at first sight, an unlikely alliance between the industrial and commercial middle-class of Lancashire and the largely public-school-educated upper and upper-middle classes of London and district. For a brief moment the extra-sporting tensions that so clearly existed between these different fractions of the propertied classes and between north and south and province and metropolis, did not operate according to type. Lancashire had passed too far in the direction of professionalism to consider a change of direction, but in much of provincial England a strong investment in amateur ideology and a considerable mistrust of upstart Lancashire (a magnet for players from other regions) led to strong resistance. The leaders of London football had neither direct experience of professionalism nor expected to have any, making their acceptance of compromise much easier. Tired by the impasse and realising how little progress had been made by repression, some of the most unlikely individuals now accepted the inevitable."[85]

"Association football had made remarkable progress in Britain between about 1870 and 1885," concluded Russell.

> *In many ways, its growth and structures mirrored larger shifts in British society. The urban working class was trusted (mainly) to gather in large numbers to watch sport just as, since 1867, it could be trusted with the vote. The middle class's recreational life widened just as its larger economic, civic and political role had done from the 1830s, while, as ever, the upper class made concessions when necessary and often on its own terms. The game was also, however, developing an autonomous dynamic, providing a new and powerful mechanism, at least within male life, for the expression of collective and personal identities rooted in place, class and gender. Although the "footballisation" of society, the penetration of its every level by discourses from and about the game, was still a hundred years away, a sport that had a formal existence of barely twenty years was playing a far greater role in daily life than its founders can have ever imagined.*[86]

"Moneybags United"

In 1884-85, the last Football League season before professionalism was legalised, the Bolton Wanderers balance sheet, noted Mason, highlighted the "growing complexity" of football club finance and administration. That it excluded player wages in no way undermines the evidence that they were paid (according to *Athletic News*, Aston Villa paid their playing staff £479, six shillings and sixpence over the course of the same season). The biggest outgoing, at £698, three shillings and fivepence, was the visiting teams' share of gate receipts; next came travel and "entertainment" for opposing clubs – £481, 13 shillings and threepence; next, at £278, two shillings and ninepence ha'penny, came "rent, rates, ground and gate keeping, police, accounts etc".[87]

In early 1888, a few months before Jack the Ripper began his murderous spree in east London, William McGregor, an Aston

Villa director, sat down to write a letter that may or may not have been inspired by a news item the previous year about an American college football league with a fixture list and a symmetrical schedule. Proposing a similar venture, he posted his idea to his own club as well as to Blackburn Rovers, Bolton Wanderers, Preston North End, Stoke City and West Bromwich Albion. The initial conflab took place at Anderton's Hotel in London on 23 March 1888, on the eve of the FA Cup final. McGregor's own suggestion, "Association Football Union", was deemed to be too, well, rugbyish. Thus it was that the Football League was formally created in Manchester on 17 April at the Royal Hotel. Drawn from the Midlands and the North-West, 10 of the 12 founder members, points out Dick Holt, came from towns boasting populations in excess of 80,000, the exceptions being Accrington Stanley and Burnley.

As the league expanded, the diverse backgrounds of the players' paymasters became ever more illuminating. Mason examined the occupations of 740 directors of 46 clubs between 1888 and 1915 and revealed, among other gems, that more than a fifth were wholesale or retail employers, a category that included "gentleman's outfitter, tobacconist, coal merchant, grocer, butcher, pawnbroker, furniture dealer, china and glass merchant, baker and confectioner, and wholesale fruit merchant"; the next most populous sector, at 12.1%, was the professions (lawyers, surveyors, accountants), followed by the drink trade (12%) and manufacturing (10.7%). Compare that with the members of the FA Council in 1903: 15.2% were schoolmasters, 10.9% accountants and journalists.[88]

Not that all that many would have been in it for the money, reckoned Mason, who pointed out that the Aston Villa directors opposed running their club for profit "because that would be against 'true sport'"; even when it became a limited company in 1896, the chairman expressed his aversion to seeing it "become purely a money-making machine"; he wanted "the truest exposition of football to be found and the finest development of athletes to be seen". There was no question "of any private individual making a profit" commented the *Athletic News* of the 30,000 spectators who attended the Sheffield derby in December 1896 – the proceeds went "to the advancement of football in Sheffield".[89]

Some, on the other hand, made a pretty penny. H. A. Mears, a London builder and contractor, purchased the London Athletic Club's premises at Stamford Bridge in 1896, but after failing to sell it on to the Great Western Railway and St George's Hospital he resolved to make it home to a new football club: Chelsea, whom the Mears family would control for the best part of a century. He charged more than £2000 per year in rent and profited further via his catering company. Across London, meanwhile, Sir Henry Norris, a property developer and estate agent who had bought Arsenal when the club fell upon hard times, emulated the owners of the Cincinnati Red Stockings: in search of bigger crowds, he relocated it from Woolwich across the Thames to Highbury.[90]

Then there was John Houlding, the Everton president. A brewer, hotelier and leading local Tory, he owned part of the land on which the club's original ground had been built, acted as agent for the remainder, loaned the club money at a fruitful interest rate and held the sole concession rights to matchday refreshments. Acrimony ensued when he sought to raise both rent and interest and the dispute was only solved when the club moved to Goodison Park in 1892; thwarted by the FA in his plans to use the "Everton" name, Houlding built his own club from scratch: Liverpool FC.[91]

Concern for bottom lines manifested itself in a bizarre court case surrounding a First Division match in October 1893 involving Newton Heath, still nine years from being reborn as Manchester United. Although comfortable 4-1 winners against West Bromwich Albion, Newton Heath were castigated for their approach by William Jephcott in his report the following Monday for the *Birmingham Gazette*: "It was not a football match, it was simple brutality, and if these are to be the tactics Newton Heath are compelled to adopt to win their matches, the sooner the Football Association deal severely with them the better it will be for the game generally… I notice that next week Newton Heath have to play Burnley, and if they both play in their ordinary style it will perhaps create an extra run of business for the undertakers."[92]

The Newton Heath directors were livid, the upshot a libel action that began the following March at Manchester Assizes. "We don't say that it is a company to make profits," said the club's counsel, "but we have to pay expenses, and pay our officers and players. And if we were to be struck out of the Football Association and the Football League, then our matches would not be so important… so many people would not come to see our play."[93] Witnesses included the club secretary, Alfred Albutt, the match referee (who strenuously disputed Jephcott's account), a clutch of reporters and the Reverend B. Reid, who expressed dismay for what he had seen as a tepid game. For the defence, Mr Gully QC said he had never previously heard of a company being formed for sporting purposes presenting itself as a trading company and suing for damages because of an unflattering report.

Jephcott refused to recant. The jury was vetted to guard against infiltration by Newton Heath supporters – and perhaps even those of neighbouring Ardwick, forerunners of Manchester City – but still found for the plaintiffs. The judge ensured celebrations were decidedly muted, denying "The Heathens" costs and awarding damages amounting to an unprincely farthing, then the lowest coin denomination. "The *Birmingham Gazette*," applauded one weekly publication, "has rendered a service to the football world and to newspaper reporters by its defence of the action… as a result it is improbable that any football club will venture to imitate Newton Heath."[94] Today, of course, they pursue another tack, banning unsupportive reporters from the pressbox. Or refusing, like Sir Alex Ferguson, to talk to specific media organisations that have the audacity not to be obsequious or dare to paint a club or official in a less than saintly light.

* * *

Come the First World War, concluded Mason, professional football clubs were "mostly limited liability companies with a largely middle-class body of shareholders and a directorate whose occupational composition would almost certainly reflect the economic structure of the town". So long as nothing went horribly wrong, the directors, in effect, exerted complete control. The "consensus" view within the FA and the Football League was against "the dominating individual capitalist, the money-bags United".

"Before the 1901-02 season there was no maximum wage," points out Mason, "and, although it is impossible to document it is certain that some clubs paid more than they could realistically afford. The suggestion is obvious that many football directors did not always run the clubs on the strict business lines which they were wont to apply to their commercial activities. Had they done so, many more clubs would have gone out of business."[95] *Athletic News* endorsed this stance in September 1909: "We look in vain in the financial papers for quotations in shares of football companies… No one who is out for a business return would look at football shares. Directors have to do all the work freely. Not one club in fifty has paid interest on shares, year in and year out."[96]

Luckless Jim

It depends on your criteria, of course. In terms of consistent superiority over a prolonged span, the names form a disorderly queue, each jostling for our devotion. Among those dependent on neither machine nor horse, Don Bradman, Rod Laver, Michael Jordan, Diego Maradona, Martina Navratilova, Pelé and Muhammad Ali all compel consideration. This young century, indeed, has already blessed us with a generous helping of towering figures: Usain Bolt, Roger Federer, Lionel Messi, Muttiah Muralitharan, Rafa Nadal, Shane Warne and Zinedine Zidane. In terms of their impact on the development and popularity of their sport, W. G. Grace and Babe Ruth remain untouchable. For skill and temperament alone? Across a range of disciplines, it is hard to imagine anyone outjuggling the other "Babe", the divine Ms Didrikson (of whom more anon). So long, that is, as you discount Jim Thorpe. That this pair represented two of spectator sport's less populous enclaves – those occupied by women and Native Americans – is far from the least of their feats. Thorpe's other misfortune was to strut his barely credible stuff in an age when, thanks to Avery Brundage, the long-time president of the American Olympic Association and later IOC emperor, professionalism, even in the US, remained an unpardonable sin.

Versatile is too slight an adjective and too shallow a catch-all to encompass Thorpe's brimming bag of tricks and talents. Running, throwing, jumping, hitting, catching, skating, swimming or snookering: they all came naturally to this consummate competitive artist. At the 1912 Stockholm Olympics, he struck gold in both the pentathlon (broad – i.e. long jump, javelin, discus, 200m, 1500m) *and* decathlon. Only one other man has played football *and* baseball for the New York Giants. He also played professional basketball, excelled at lacrosse and more than held his own in the ring and on the rink, with cue in hand or racquet. So deft and nimble was his footwork, he even took the 1912 inter-collegiate ballroom dancing title. In the 1980s and 1990s, Bo Jackson and Deion Sanders, too, would send jaws crashing to floors – and be fabulously rewarded – for excelling on gridiron and diamond; the riches that might have flowed today from a portfolio like Thorpe's are inconceivable. And he did it all, he said, "for the fun of the thing".[97]

* * *

Born in 1887 into the Sac and Fox tribe on an Oklahoman reservation (his original name, Wa-Tho-Huck, meant "Bright Path"), Jacobus Franciscus "Jim" Thorpe attended the Carlisle Indian Industrial School in Pennsylvania (at those Stockholm Games, another Carlisle scholar, Lewis Tewanima, would take silver in the 10,000 metres). In one game between Carlisle and West Point, the cry went out for Dwight Eisenhower to "Stop that Indian!" only for the future general and White House tenant to be promptly and comprehensively bypassed.

Tragedy and triumph reigned hand in glove. By his teens Thorpe had suffered the premature deaths of his twin brother and both parents yet, as the First World War approached, he was at once the nation's leading gridiron player *and* its most complete athlete, as testified by those twin Olympic golds. The ensuing tidal wave of congratulatory letters and telegrams included messages from, among others, the Secretary of the Interior, the Commissioner of Indian Affairs and his President. On his return to New York he was greeted by a tickertape parade and an estimated 25,000-strong welcoming committee: "I couldn't realise," he responded, "how one fellow could have so many friends." The clamour was repeated in Philadelphia, where 10,000 people took part in the parade, reported *The Red Man*, a Carlisle School publication. "*The Red Man* is proud of these two young men, and the Indian race is to be felicitated on their achievement. It should mean much in awakening among Indians a desire for greater physical and mental perfection, and for more care in guarding the health and increasing the strength of Indians everywhere."[98]

Precious few of those friendships lasted. The following year, the forces ranged against him struck with irresistible force: as a college student living hand to mouth, it emerged that he had accepted a few dollars for playing semi-professional baseball – alongside fellow members of his tribe – in 1909 and 1910. Exposed by a Massachusetts newspaper, this was a contravention of the sacred tenets of amateurism, as propounded by the Amateur Athletic Union. "I hope I will be partly excused by the fact that I was an Indian schoolboy and did not know about such things," he wrote to the AAU, seeking compassion. "I did not know that I was doing wrong, because I was doing what several other college men had done, except they did not use their names." His pleas fell on predictably deaf ears. "Ignorance," Brundage, whom Thorpe had twice trounced to win his Olympic medals, would later repeatedly declare, "is no excuse." In fact, Thorpe had been betrayed by his coach: claiming ignorance of Jim's semi-professional dalliance, it was his minder-cum-chaperone, Glen "Pop" Warner, who had prepared the letter.

A year after his Stockholm triumphs, Thorpe was ordered to return his medals to the AAU, who erased his records; when the American Olympic Committee apologised to the IOC, the latter demanded its medals back. "Not for the first or last time," recalled one contemporary report, "a sports organisation stuck to the letter not the spirit of the law."[99]

The second half of Thorpe's life could scarcely have been more bathetic. He spent several seasons with the New York Giants before being fired by John McGraw, a racist tartar of a manager who once called him "a dumb Indian" for missing a sign on the basepaths and costing the team a run.[100] He became the first president of the American Professional Football Association and was still a potent running back at 41, but age is no respecter of even superhuman bodies. Nothing could replace sport. He appeared in more than 50 movies but divorced twice; alcohol became a constant companion and he died at 64 in a California trailer park, in poverty. "To this sad generality we must add Thorpe's additional burden of an Indian heritage in a largely racist nation, a burden that destroyed him in both a general and specific way," added Stephen Jay Gould, the world-renowned palaeontologist who subtitled the book he most enjoyed writing *A Lifelong Passion for Baseball*. This, for Gould, ranked "among the saddest incidents" in American history. "I cannot begin to measure, or even understand, the generality, but a man of Thorpe's intense pride must have railed inwardly – with a galling bitterness that may have propelled him to self-destruction – against the stereotype of his people (gross enough as an abstraction) constantly applied to his own being."[101]

Thorpe's death in 1953, a year after Burt Lancaster brought him to the silver screen in *Man of Steel*, spurred renewed moves to reinstate his medals. Not until 1973, the year after Brundage finally vacated his IOC throne, did the US Olympic Committee restore Thorpe's amateur status; even then it took the best part of another decade for the medals to be returned to his family. In fact, they were replicas: the originals, it was said, had been stolen from a museum.

"The act that barred Thorpe could never be justified," Grantland Rice, one of the era's leading sportswriters, insisted in his memoir, *The Tumult and the Shouting*, published shortly after Thorpe's death.

> *Thorpe was truthful when he maintained that all he got from summer baseball…was barely enough to pay expenses. In those days – in fact until recently – college ball players from all over the map and particularly the Ivy schools, played on summer teams, including various hotel teams for far more cash than accrued to Thorpe and were still held as clean, pure amateurs and passed for football, track and other college sports. What right did the AAU have to Thorpe's private gifts, fairly won in those 1912 Olympics? They merely robbed the Indian in cold-blooded fashion.*[102]

According to Abel Kiviat, one of his futile pursuers in Stockholm, Thorpe was "the greatest athlete who ever lived… All he had to see is someone doin' something and he tried it… and he'd do it better." On 17 April 1999 came a banquet organised by the Jim Thorpe Sports Hall of Fame, with resolutions by Philadelphia state house and senate representatives supporting the campaign to recognise Jim as the "Greatest Athlete of the Twentieth century". Also in attendance were Senator Rick Santorum and staff from the House of Representatives, all lending support to Jim's daughter, Grace. In Oklahoma two years later, at the Sac and Fox Community Building five miles south of Stroud on Route 99, four days after what would have been Thorpe's 114th birthday, family, friends, tribal members and supporters assembled for the Jim Thorpe Honour Day.

He was also voted the "Best Athlete of the First Half of the 20th century" by the Associated Press and, in an unabashedly biased 2001 poll run by ABC's venerable *Wide World of Sports* TV show (Pelé was alone among the 15 nominees in not having acquired fame and fortune in North America). Even members of Congress were of a like mind, though they did at least have the modesty to hail him "America's" greatest all-rounder. The qualification was unnecessary.

The Babe

If cricket owed its initial mass popularity to WG, baseball owes every milligram as much to The Babe – Babe Ruth. It is one of those quirks of history that 5 January 1920, the day the Volstead Act was passed, ushering in Prohibition, the Roaring Twenties and the Jazz Age, was also the day that the New York Yankees announced that they had bought the redoubtable Boston Red Sox pitcher, George Herman Ruth – the man who, more than any other cultural figure, symbolised the possibilities of postwar America. "Probably at no other time," declared Harold Seymour of the period from 1903 to 1930, "did baseball enjoy a stronger emotional grip upon Americans."[103] That Ruth materialised into the game's greatest hitter and most flamboyant personality just as the Black Sox saga was persuading long-time lovers to jilt the national pastime remains one of the most fortuitous and happiest of sporting coincidences.

In baseball terms, in attaining greatness as both hitter and pitcher, Ruth remains unique. In playing him as a full-time batter, the Yankees unleashed both a tormentor and a necromancer. When he arrived, noted Miro Weinberger in *The Yankees Reader*, the Yankees were "a debtor, tenant team"; by the time he left in 1934, they were not only the most powerful and successful force in the major leagues but the wealthiest and most famous club on Planet Sport – and on their way to being demonised as the Evil Empire. And not simply because the "Sultan of Swat" could hit a small ball a hellishly long way. Perpetually overweight, he was an outsized character in more ways than one. An avid burner of both ends of the candle, not to mention an industrious philanderer, he was larger than life and a hedonist supreme: a walking advert for the irresistibility of glory and temptation. At the time of writing, no sporting artefact had fetched more than the £2.7m paid in 2012 by the memorabilia auction house Leland.com for one of his early Yankee jerseys.

"The phrase is that he revolutionised the game," noted John Mosedale in 1974. "It has been said so many times that it slides easily on the tongue, and its truth is forgotten. Until Babe Ruth came along, the home run was eschewed as almost vulgar."[104] Despite being a pitcher, he tied for the home run lead with 11 in 1918; the previous year, Gavvy Cravath led all major league hitters with 12, and there were just 339 home runs. Come 1921, just his third season as a full-time outfielder, Ruth set the record for career home runs with 132, breaking a mark set the previous century. Until the Babe boomed into view, the man usually associated most closely with the round-tripper was J. Franklin Baker of the Philadelphia Athletics, whose best season brought a dozen. His nickname, "Home Run" Baker, commemorated his feat in the 1911 World Series, when he had the audacity to hit two in successive games. In the 1919 season, Ruth ripped up the record books with 29. And that was merely the hors d'oeuvres.

At the heart of Ruth's rebellion lay his free spiritedness, his refusal to be cowed by anything so piffling as custom and precedent. Born in Baltimore in 1895, he saw little of his father, who ran a saloon at what is now Oriole Park at Camden Yards, the Baltimore Orioles' innovative retro-styled stadium; in 2007, the club erected a statue to the Babe two blocks from where he was born. With his mother in poor health, he quickly developed a taste for freedom and wilfulness, acquiring such a reputation for theft, vandalism and general incorrigibility that he was sent to St. Mary's Industrial School, where he lived until he was 19; parental visits were infrequent.

It was there that he evinced a rare aptitude, and appetite, for baseball. "When they let him out," recalled one teammate, "it was like turning a wild animal out of a cage."[105] Five months later he was pitching for the Red Sox. On his first day in Boston, he met a 16-year-old waitress, Helen Woodford, and soon married her. Teammates called him "Baby", then just "Babe".

"Lord, he ate too much," recalled Harry Hooper, an experienced and highly literate colleague with a fondness, uncommon among professional baseballers even then, for maintaining a diary:

*He'd stop along the road when we were traveling and order half
a dozen hot dogs and as many bottles of soda pop, stuff them in,
one after another, give a few big belches and then roar, 'OK boys,
let's go'. George was six foot two, and weighed 198 pounds, all
of it muscle. He had a slim waist, huge biceps, no self-discipline
and not much education – not so very different from a lot of
other nineteen-year-olds. Except for two things: he could eat
more than anyone else, and he could hit a baseball further.[106]*

Teammates and opponents alike teased him about his appetite
and much more besides. "They mocked him, jeered him, made
pointed insults about his round, flat-nosed, heavily tanned
face," wrote Robert Creamer, Ruth's principal biographer. "They
called him monkey, baboon, ape, gorilla. The terms were not
used with rough affection; they were insults, harsh comments
on his homeliness, his ignorance, his crudity."[107] When he was
still relatively new on the professional scene, someone noticed
how, after taking a shower, he always put back on "the same
sweaty underwear" he had taken off after a game then kept
it on for days on end. He reacted to the jibes "by abandoning
underwear completely and for years thereafter wore nothing at
all beneath his expensive suits and silk shirts".

Even so, he was already sufficiently aware, of both his ability
and the potential rewards, to have acquired what we would
now term an agent, a Boston friend named Johnny Igoe; he also
demanded that Harry Frazee, the Red Sox owner, double his
salary, from $7,000 to $15,000 – guaranteed for two years. Only
the veteran Ty Cobb was being paid more. This at a time when
renting a six-room house cost $60 and, as Creamer discreetly put
it, "a full-time 'hired girl' received room and board and a few
dollars a month".[108]

With attendance declining and the previous autumn's World
Series receipts having been diminished by the war, Frazee
insisted he was in no position to pay such a sum. Negotiations
were protracted. The counter-offer was $8,500 per season; Ruth
made it clear that this was not enough, that he wanted to stop

doubling as a pitcher and regular outfielder, and even that he was contemplating becoming a professional boxer (a Boston promoter, or so he claimed, had offered him $5,000 to fight Gunboat Smith, a leading heavyweight). At length, Frazee, who also needed money to finance a Broadway play, sold him to the Yankees and their owner Colonel Jacob Ruppert, a prosperous brewer, for $125,000 and a guaranteed loan, when required, for $300,000. In his first year in New York, he hit 54 home runs – nearly twice the record he had set in Boston the previous year and more than 14 of the 15 major league franchises managed *in total*; as a direct consequence, the Yankees became the first baseball club to draw one million spectators in a season. The next year Ruth clubbed 59 homers. With the Red Sox fans being obliged to wait until 2004 before celebrating another World Series triumph, the near-misses in between – most notably in 1975 and 1986 – were blamed on the "Curse of the Bambino".

Ruth's reinvention, moreover, could not have been timelier – not only because of the Black Sox but the death of Ray Chapman, who in August 1920 had become the major leagues' first fatality. After that astounding first season as a Yankee, Ruth's salary flew all the way from $10,000 to $70,000. A new source of income, endorsements, was also tapped to considerable effect. Wrote Mosedale: "The club owners publicly, and perhaps in their heart of their hearts (for who knows what is in a club owner's heart?), deplored the financial element of Ruth's climb to fame – he and Charlie Chaplin were called the best-known men in America, not excepting President Coolidge – but every ball park in the major leagues had been enlarged since Ruth's debut."[109]

When Yankee Stadium, "The House That Ruth Built", was opened on 18 April 1923, The Babe, reported Fred J. Lieb in the *New York Evening Telegram*, "appeared several minutes after the rest of the team and the crowd gave the Big Boy a great hand".[110] Presented with a large box containing a gilded bat and other mementoes, he was "snapped with several urchins, one about five years old, in a baseball uniform. The kids are all for the Babe, and he is for the kids."[111]

A measure of the affection he commanded was the way his vast earnings were accepted by the public as his due. In 1933, with the Depression still biting deep and hard, everyone in baseball was taking a wage cut, including Ruth's teammate and rival Lou Gehrig ($27,500 to $22,500) and even Commissioner Landis ($50,000 to $40,000). What, though, of the Babe? Shouldn't he suffer too? In a poll conducted at a shelter run by the Salvation Army in Manhattan, home, wrote another of Ruth's biographers, Leigh Montville, "to more than 2000 home-less, jobless, destitute men", the residents were asked if anyone should be able to earn $80,000 for a year's labour, which Ruth had in 1931. Of the 572 who answered in the affirmative (only a few more, remarkably, were revulsed by the idea), 185 voted for "any" US president; next, with 140 votes, came the Babe, five ahead of the actual president, Franklin Roosevelt. Among the extensive group accorded two votes or one were Albert Einstein and Thomas Edison.[112]

In 1927, Ruth whacked, biffed and clobbered 60 home runs, a professional pea-sheller at play, powering the Yankees' so-called "Invincibles" to another World Series crown. Other glories followed but his career ended in sad anti-climax: the Yankees traded him to the Boston Braves, where Ruth hoped a managerial post would come his way but never did; nor, to his chagrin, did any others. Still, he did bid adieu to the game with a home run, the 714th of a matchless career; better yet, it was the first one ever hit at Pittsburgh's Forbes Field to vacate the premises: has any sporting giant ever said to have left the stage so thunderously?

Felled by cancer at 53, Ruth had been in his grave for more than a decade when, in 1961, Roger Maris, a man so different he might have been from another cosmos, supplanted him at the top of American sport's most hallowed chart. One of those avidly monitoring Maris's progress was a budding comedian, Billy Crystal, a lifelong Yankees fan whose absorbing and heartfelt 2001 film *61** would underscore the extent to which Maris's feat was substantially longer on the bitter than the sweet. So fraught and agonising was the chase, the record-breaker's hair fell out by the clump and the commissioner himself, who just happened to be Ruth's trusty chum Ford Frick, did his utmost to preserve the extant mark. A decidedly unlucky 13 years later, while Hank Aaron was en route to outstripping Ruth's career haul of 714 home runs, he was besieged by poison-pen letters and death threats from those who believed no American had the right to usurp the untouchable Babe, let alone an African-American.

* * *

It is possible, just about, to exaggerate Ruth's importance. There are those, for instance, who contend that, but for him, cricket might have overcome the innumerable obstacles strewn in its path and carved itself a much bigger slice of American sporting affections. By way of justification for such an outlandish theory, Bart King is ritually cited.

John Barton King was North America's first and, to date, last great cricketer. Putting his wares on display for the Philadelphians on three tours of England, he was a punishing batsman good enough to hit 344 in an innings, still a record for a North American, and an even better fast bowler, good enough to top the first-class averages and bowl the great Ranjitsinhji first ball. Drawing on his experience as a pitcher, he was one of the first successful exponents of swing bowling and was acclaimed, indeed, by no less an authority than Plum Warner, the former England captain, as "at least the equal of the greatest of them all".[113] At The Oval, he more or less beat Surrey on his own, taking six wickets in addition to scoring 98 and 113 not out. Another day, or so it was claimed, came an even more vivid demonstration of his self-belief: playing for Belmont against Trenton in the Halifax Cup at Elmwood Cricket Ground in Philadelphia, he was said to have emulated Rube Waddell, a great if highly eccentric pitcher, by banishing the fielders from the field so he could finish the innings on his own. While the tale is almost certainly apocryphal, even the possibility of someone spinning such an improbable yarn speaks volumes for his reputation.

When King died in 1965, even *The Times* ran an obituary: had he been an Englishman or an Australian, theorised Warner, "he would have been even more famous than he was".[114] Yet for all his undoubted talents, the last of those tours was in 1908. Had someone of comparable gifts stepped immediately into his boots, who knows, but by the time Ruth became a Yankee, there were no discernible signs of a legacy, much less a sustainable one.

The reality, of course, is that cricket didn't stand an earthly, even in a land whose adoration of its national pastime had received such a battering in the aftermath of the Black Sox scandal. Resistance was far too entrenched. The diamond's debt to its towering standard-bearer is nonetheless incalculable. Does any spectator sport owe more to a single practitioner than baseball owes George Herman Ruth? Some might make a plausible case for Michael Jordan, who elevated basketball to such unforeseen heights of popularity, but Kobe Bryant and LeBron James have eased the longing for the man who built the Nike Empire. The Babe, on the other hand, is irreplaceable, deathless.

Hollywood has honoured him, after a fashion, with two movies: William Bendix took on the rich but unenviable role in 1948, succeeded 44 years later by John Goodman. "Terrible movie. Ran out all the myths and extended them to their illogical conclusions and then invented a dozen new ones," fumed Creamer after seeing the Bendix version; he would have detested the 1992 model even more, featuring as it did, in the gargantuan Goodman, an even grosser caricature of Ruth's less than svelte physique. "For thousands of people, maybe millions," Creamer continued, "William Bendix in a baseball suit is what Babe Ruth looked like. Which is a terrible shame, because lots of men look like William Bendix, but nobody else ever looked like Babe Ruth. Or behaved like him. Or did all the things he did in his repressed, explosive, truncated life."[115]

II. Pride and Prejudice

The oik who roared

The sports that resisted professionalism's troublesome and allegedly sordid clutches with the greatest obstinacy were athletics, tennis and, as we have already elaborated to a degree, rugby union. It says much for its global growth – and the narrow early constituency of the first and third – that the second of these capitulated first, in 1968, two decades before the runners and three before the scrummers.

The so-called "Open Era" came three decades too late for Fred Perry. Britain's greatest on-court champion by a street or three, notwithstanding the recent rise of Andy Murray, here was a prophet persistently denied honour in his own land. Born at the far end of the wrong side of the tennis tracks, Perry was profoundly and proudly un-middle-class, the son of a cotton-spinner in North-West England who became a Labour MP. In Sam Perry's drive for office, as Fred's biographer Jon Henderson wrote, "can be discerned the absolute single-mindedness that would make his son an irresistible force in tennis".[1] Perry's working-class heroism, though, stirred few at the time, primarily because of his chosen vehicle for advancement and the era in which he chose it. Not by any means did his relentless quest for self-improvement meet approval from all his countrymen. Reporting for *Esquire* on the defeat of Australia's Jack Crawford that brought Perry his maiden Wimbledon singles triumph in 1934, John Tunis detected resentment that "a poor boy without a varsity education should have yanked himself up to the front".[2]

Drawing on skills he had accumulated as an untutored world table-tennis champion, Perry enjoyed the purplest of patches from 1933 to 1936, winning eight grand slam titles: one Australian and French Open, three US Opens and, uniquely for a Briton, three on the trot at Wimbledon. He also spearheaded four consecutive Davis Cup final triumphs; not since the last of these, in 1936, have British hands hoisted that trophy. Yet as much as he respected him, Bill Tilden, the American who had dominated the men's game in the first half of the previous decade, couldn't quite decide whether the Englishman's unorthodoxy made him the game's best worst player or its worst best. "Had Perry played an instrument, he would have loved the improvisation of jazz musicians," proposed Henderson. "His sporting and social lives were played to the rhythms of those who relished doing things differently. They were underpinned by discipline but distinguished by originality. His famous running forehand – with the ball taken impossibly early – was the product of a conflation of these controlled, yet innovative, sides."

Perry was still basking in victory's first glorious flush in July 1934 when he was reminded, as Henderson put it, "that the son of a Labour MP had to do more than win Wimbledon to be accepted by the panjandrums of the All England Club". Perry was honest enough to admit that his own account of what happened, told half a century later in his autobiography, "was almost certainly closer to the truth in essence than detail".

As he wallowed in the victor's bath, he claimed, he had overheard a plummy-toned committee member informing Crawford that he would have been a more deserving winner. The runner-up received a bottle of champagne; the winner's token of appreciation amounted to an honorary All England Club member's tie slung over the back of a chair. "All my paranoia about the old-school-tie brigade," Perry would readily confess, "surfaced with a vengeance."[3] Since "we've got to have the bloody upstart", one insider grudgingly conceded after he first won selection for the Davis Cup, "we might as well knock him into shape and try and get the best out of him".[4]

An ambitious grand slam winner of that era had two choices: turn professional (from the late 1940s, joining Jack Kramer's burgeoning tour would become an attractive option) or, as Richard Evans deftly put it in *Open Tennis: The First Twenty Years*, "put bread on their table by receiving money under it".[5] Wonderful days, he asserted, "for racists, snobs and blinkered buffoons".

The initial breach in the amateur wall had been achieved, unsurprisingly, by the French marvel, Suzanne Lenglen, who earned $100,000 (half from her 50% share of the net gate receipts)[6] for a North American tour in 1926 with Mary Browne and Howard Kinsey and the reigning Olympic champion, Vincent Richards; despite its success, though, there was no second tour. In 1930, Bill Tilden turned professional after winning Wimbledon, and, as Perry remembered, "he really started the pro circuit as it is known today".[7]

In the wake of his third successive Wimbledon crown in 1936 Perry, too, turned professional, plying his trade in exhibition halls and wood-clad skating rinks in the US, a nation with whose inhabitants and ethos he had already come to forge bonds; bonds strong enough to persuade him to take citizenship. It was there, wrote Henderson, that "he encountered more evidence of the spirit of inclusiveness that distinguished the New World from the snobbery and class divisions of England"[8] – so long, of course, as your face was the right complexion.

Not that Perry's face ever fitted in his homeland. Nor did leaving it on the verge of the Second World War do much for his image: the sniping about fleeing a ship under fire is countered by the evidence, including the insistence, after that first Wimbledon triumph in 1934, that if he turned pro he would not return to England. When he did leave, he quickly suspected, once war was declared, that he should return; but doing so, he believed, would jeopardise his change of citizenship. Assuredly no shrinking violet, he had already crossed swords several times with the blazer brigade; ever since he had disavowed amateurism, a decision that barred him from the game's showpieces and cost him his honorary membership, the All England Club, he claimed, had treated him like a leper. "I'm not sure," he quipped darkly, "but I believe they dipped the door of my locker in an antiseptic."[9]

The mutual hostility softened once the "Open" era began, but it still took until 1984 for Wimbledon to erect a statue in his honour. The knighthood predicted for Murray was never remotely a consideration, even though Perry had other strong strings to his bow. Countless thousands who care nothing for tennis are familiar with the name of the trailblazing sportswear company he set up in the early 1950s, whose short-sleeved, angular-collared t-shirts would be adopted by numerous subcultures, beginning with Pete Townshend's original followers, London's mid-Sixties Mods. In 1957, furthermore, with the USSR eager to find outside assistance to produce players capable of competing successfully in the international arena, a Soviet delegation approached Perry, leading to three trips to the Soviet Union. During the first, in 1958, he urged his hosts to make a grand gesture and finally send a competitor to Wimbledon; how he smiled when Anna Dmitrieva reached the junior final.[10]

Perry, as Henderson trumpeted, "helped define an age that pointed towards a more meritocratic future" while anticipating another wherein "the manufacturing and marketing of celebrity were to become a huge international industry generating fortunes and idolatry on a scale that in the 1930s would have seemed incredible".[11]

David and the Philistines

Pancho Gonzales was a tremendous player with a short fuse who rocked Wimbledon to its rafters. That his name is not on the honours board as a singles champion is supremely emblematic of the bumbling nature of tennis administration as the Sixties broke. In February 1960, at a meeting of the International Lawn Tennis Federation in Paris, three delegates known to favour the motion on the table – to introduce professionalism – failed to vote, ensuring the proposal was defeated by the slenderest of margins: one of them had been busy arranging the evening's entertainment, one was in the gents and the last had nodded off. That night, "while amateur delegates sipped champagne on the Seine", wrote Evans, "the game of tennis found itself anchored to the hypocrisy of amateurism for another eight years".[12]

Evans credits three Americans and a Frenchman with introducing the game to plain dealing:

- Jack Kramer, the son of a Las Vegas railroad worker who grew up to be the 1947 Wimbledon champion, organiser of the first fully-fledged professional tennis tour and the first executive director of the Association of Tennis Professionals;

- Lamar Hunt, the son of a Texas oil tycoon who became a sporting entrepreneur and, together with a New Orleans sports promoter, David Dixon, instigated, bankrolled and marshalled World Championship Tennis (having already promoted American football, basketball and ice hockey, Hunt would also do more than anyone bar Phil Woosnam to inject soccer into the American consciousness);

- Donald Dell, a Washington lawyer and former Davis Cup player who founded ProServ – whose clients included his close friend Arthur Ashe, who in 1968 had become the first black man to win the US Open and, seven years later, the Wimbledon singles title; Dell did everything in his considerable power to control the game via the ATP;

- Philippe Chatrier, who as president of the International Tennis Federation from 1977 to 1991 dropped the "Lawn" from the governing body's original title (grass was, after all, becoming an increasingly lesser-spotted stage for top-flight tennis) while fighting tooth-and-nail to preserve a semblance of tradition – in Evans's eyes a "thin-skinned, moody... strange, complex man with the mentality of a dreamer", who, "unlike most dream merchants... possessed the drive and the organisational skills to market his vision and make it viable".

The man who shook tennis to its senses, though, was an English member of the old order, Herman David, the chairman of the All England Club who in 1967 had the *cojones* to denounce the game as "a living lie" and, in Evans's admiring words, kicked professional tennis "out of the womb".[13]

Born in Birmingham in 1905, educated at Stonyhurst and Oxford University, David represented Britain in the 1932 Davis Cup and, after spending the Second World War with the RAF, served as non-playing captain from 1953 to 1958. An authority on industrial diamonds and chairman of the Diamond Development Company, his motive in rejecting the absurd pretence that saw players billed as "amateurs" despite making their living from the game was, according to his anonymous obituarist in the *Catholic Herald*, "based on moral grounds".[14]

Within a week of his allegations about the game's flagrant duplicitousness, the *Sunday Times* published a two-page spread backing David to the hilt. The players' tea-room during Wimbledon fortnight, wrote Evans, was depicted "as an open market with tournament directors from around the world bartering for the services of 'amateur' players".[15] Top of the wanted list was Manolo Santana, the 1966 champion, at $1,000 per week – under the table, naturally. Two decades later, Santana told Evans he and Australia's Roy Emerson, who had won the previous two All England singles titles, were raking in "15 hundred a week".

> We had come to an agreement between ourselves to ask for that and most of the tournaments could easily afford it. Some just wouldn't pay, of course. When I went to Australia in '65 to play the Davis Cup final, the Australian LTA wanted me to play in their Championships. But when I told them the price they refused. So I didn't play. When Emmo played in Spain he got paid. For a couple of years it was simply better for us to remain amateur because all the other top players had turned pro... I stayed with the "shamateur" system, embarrassing as it was. I was relieved when Open Tennis came in. It ended all the hypocrisy.[16]

David dealt a double body-blow to the old order: not only would Centre Court play host – in August 1967 – to a professional tournament featuring Rod Laver, Ken Rosewall and other erstwhile Wimbledon favourites; the following summer's strawberries-and-smashes fiesta would be open to all. And if the ILTF objected, who cared. Preceding Wimbledon by a month, the French Open of 1968 was actually the first "Open" grand slam but as soon as David mapped out the immediate future, warranted Evans, everything changed.

With the immediate influx of money came knotty and perplexing new issues that shook an ancient sport to its core. The relationship forged that year between Mark McCormack's International Management Group and The All England Club proved to be the opening shot in a war few if any had foreseen. Initially, the new era saw players finally receiving suitable and ethical remuneration, but what it ultimately signalled, corroborated the tennis writer Stephen Tignor, was the sport's "transfer from the British Empire to the American Empire".[17] Control shifted from "the ILTF's grey-haired volunteers to a motley, contentious cast of US-based agents, lawyers, Barnum-style promoters and dilettante millionaires, all of whom had been barred from the lawns for nearly a century". One such agent was David Falk, who went on to manage NBA luminaries such as Michael Jordan and be accused of marketing team players as if they were tennis players – i.e. one-man brands.[18] Evans nonetheless argues that, "despite the overnight arrival of so many get-rich-quick merchants, those who soldiered on through the early upheavals and lived to tell the tale were almost exclusively people who cared as much for the game itself as for the dollar it was earning them."

Laver would become the toast of Hunt's WCT tour as well as of its early rival, the National Tennis League, bought out by the Texan in 1970. "No one was really high on 'I've got to win this tournament for my career'. There was no career, because you're playing amateur tennis," Laver reflected in 2012[19], recalling the reality of official tennis 50 years earlier, when he became just the second man – after Donald Budge in 1938 – to win all four of the game's major crowns in the same calendar year. Turning professional immediately, he had been barred from the grand slams for six years before finally earning a seemly living from his talents, winning five US Professional Opens in seven starts and 65 events in toto: no one who saw him could doubt that they were watching the game's premier practitioner. In 1968, his status no longer subject to disparagement by the game's gin-swilling establishment, he became the first "Open" Wimbledon champion. The following year, uniquely, yielded a second Grand Slam, and he was soon reaping the far from insubstantial fruits of a more organised and rewarding schedule via WCT and the NTL.

Reminisced Laver: "[Lamar Hunt] said, 'Hey, I got $1 million. I want to get a promoter. You could play 50 tournaments, $20,000 in total purse. Find the tournaments, find your best 32 players that you can sign up'. It was a different world. To play for $10,000 in those WCT matches, that was big money in our world."[20] Launched in 1968 with a troupe of just eight players – the so-called "Handsome Eight" – WCT lasted until the formation of the ATP Tour in 1990.

* * *

In 1978, now covering the game for *World Tennis* magazine, Gordon Forbes, who had represented South Africa in the Davis Cup during the shamateur era, turned his diaries into a fascinating, lid-lifting book, *A Handful of Summers*, in which he compared now and then with authority, wit, frankness and benevolence – and barely a shred of envy for the riches then possible. At the Centenary Wimbledon in 1977, he witnessed a new game. "Tennis has changed. Come into money and gone absolutely public. One walks about in the players' enclosure, trying to get tea, and hearing things like 'contracts', 'franchises', 'legal representatives' and 'twelve point five million by May'. It's the day of the superstar. The superstar, the supercoach, the how-to-books, the tennis universities and the tracksuits with the stripes down the side. And a whole new set of people who follow the game. At Queens Club on Sunday they had a sort of combination backgammon – pro-celebrity tennis day, seething with the jet set, glamorous people carelessly strolling and emitting expensive smells."[21]

The real Supermac

Mark McCormack was not the first sports agent-cum-manager, not by any means. He was, though, the first to truly recognise the economic possibilities for modern professional sportsfolk in the televisual age. Aside from an expansive portfolio of sporting heroes ranging from Bjorn Borg, Seb Coe and Michael Schumacher to golf's mightiest, Tiger Woods and Jack Nicklaus, his company, International Management Group, also counted among its clients the Nobel Foundation, the Smithsonian Museum and the Royal & Ancient, not to mention Margaret Thatcher, Mikhail Gorbachev and a pope.

Such was the diversity of McCormack's passions, he conceived the World Matchplay Championships and launched the Hampton Court Music Festival. In 1990, *Sports Illustrated* anointed him "the most powerful man in sport", confirming what everyone in the know knew; a dozen years later, not long before his death, *The Sporting News* could still feel justified in nominating him as one of the 10 most powerful players in the competitive art business. When he died, IMG boasted 80 offices in 32 countries; when his shares were sold, his family reaped $750 million. And all because McCormack had cottoned on to the inescapable fact that sports-folk were not paid what they were worth.

It was as a lawyer that McCormack, a keen golfer himself who had qualified for the US Open as an amateur, signed a rising star by the name of Arnold Palmer, whose zestful, attacking approach earned him a devoted, vocal following hitherto unseen within the restrained world of golf – Arnie's Army. McCormack built an empire out of it. "He made golf a business," said Nicklaus. "Then, you look at all the other areas and arenas he entered, and you see that he made managing people a business – a viable business. He truly was an inno-vator."[22] "Managing people" was a hands-on matter. In 1976, he got wind of a promising English amateur and hotfooted it from Houston to Sunningdale to play a round with him. His swing, McCormack told him, had shades of the rising professional Jerry Heard: the youngster was most chuffed, having modelled it on the young American's.[23] Thus did McCormack make the acquaintance of one of his most productive clients, Nick Faldo, who would land six majors as well as a knighthood.

"You have to have the best available professional advice," mused Faldo, Britain's most successful golfer of modern times, "and when it comes to it you really can't get past McCormack's. I know, the empire's enormous and people wonder, 'How am I going to be treated?' but they have different departments. IMG also organise golf tournaments. It all helps. People think that McCormack's got a monopoly on golf and they say that must be wrong. But if you get in there and you're part of it then you can get into these tournaments. Whether that is right or wrong, you're making money which is what you're employing them for. They do your income tax and all that sort of thing. You know that whatever problems you have you're not the first client to have had them... They're doing Bjorn Borg's taxes. Imagine his and Arnold Palmer's tax problems."[24]

Kerry Packer's Flying Circus

Because it demonstrated the shift in power brought about by advances in technology and, in particular, broadcasting, the most important intrusion into cricket's cosy ruling combination of brandy, cigars and omnipotent old-boy network came in 1977. The timing could not have been more ironic. In March, generations of Ashes heroes gathered in Melbourne to celebrate Test cricket's 100th birthday, the centrepiece a non-Ashes Centenary Test; eerily, Australia won by 45 runs, precisely the same result as in 1877. While the matey festivities were in full flow, however, the majority of the combatants were resolutely keeping a secret that would survive into May. It was a secret that would lead to the most far-reaching uprising yet mounted by a group of cricketers. Nor does the irony stop there. Quake the earth it may well have done, but it was a rebellion that gave a game in thrall to yesterday a vibrant tomorrow. Of course, it had everything to do with the fact that, for the majority, playing elite cricket remained a strictly part-time occupation.

The fearless, garrulous outsider who shook it all up was Kerry Packer, an imposing, sweary Australian media tycoon who personified just about everything that was un-English, even un-cricket. That ruthless former captain of the Mongolian first XI, Genghis Khan, "wasn't very loveable", Packer once averred, "but he was bloody efficient". The puppet Packer on *Spitting Image*, the brilliantly satirical British TV show that would portray Thatcher and her cabinet with even profounder irreverence, was a grinning clone of one of history's most proficient mass murderers, an impeccable illustration of the hysterical over-reaction to the Sydneysider's coup.

Howzat! Kerry Packer's Cricket War, the 2012 Australian dramatisation of the birth and growth of Packer's venture, captures two key moments particularly well, both focusing on John Cornell, who would go on to wider fame as co-writer of the box-office-busting *Crocodile Dundee* with his partner, the actor and comic Paul Hogan. Aghast to learn how much more handsomely he and Hogan were being paid for their show than Dennis Lillee was for being the planet's pre-eminent fast bowler – not to mention a focal point for national pride – Cornell proposes an exhibition match and sets about finding someone with "deep pockets and big balls". Packer not only had both, he went several steps further, signing up the world's best to star in a completely different new show that some would chortlingly bracket with *Monty Python's Flying Circus* – a deadly serious hybrid of sport and razzmatazz called World Series Cricket. Prevented from billing his shows as Tests, Packer went one better: they would be Supertests.

In episode two of *Howzat!*, with the second WSC season beckoning, Cornell, despairing of a way to persuade followers of the official product to turn up or tune in, hits upon the idea of a promotional song. Visiting a Sydney advertising agency, he consults a couple of creatives and informs them that since Packer's project was "up against 100 years of history", what was needed was "a new history... a war cry". The shudderingly catchy upshot, *C'mon Aussie C'mon*, aired ad nauseam on

Packer's Channel 9 network accompanied by jolly footage of the players, topped the Australian pop charts after its release in early 1979. Seizing national awareness, it can be seen as the turning point in what was portrayed as a war for cricket's soul but was actually about something far more tangible: the quest for a fair day's pay for a fair day's work.

* * *

The new order was triggered by a skirmish that bottled the very essence of the old. Packer believed in the magnetism of sport in general and cricket in particular. As Gideon Haigh, author of the definitive account he felt no compunction whatsoever about calling *The Cricket War*, underlined in the History Council of Victoria's 2012 Annual Lecture, "the football codes were still obstinately, ostentatiously parochial; not even the Olympics rivaled the atavistic pleasure of beating the Poms."[25] This persuaded Packer to make an audacious bid to cover the national team on Channel 9, a much livelier broadcaster – its critics would say crasser – than the Australian Broadcasting Corporation. For decades, however, the ABC had enjoyed a mutually agreeable relationship with the Australian Cricket Board, a non-profit concern with no reserves, premises or even full-time employees – but still a monopoly. "The players are not professional," affirmed Alan Barnes, the secretary of the New South Wales Cricket Association who doubled up in the same role for the ACB from his Sydney office, where, as Haigh writes, "he kept the files on the floor and his scotch and cigarettes in the filing cabinets". If the players had issues with their conditions of employment, added Barnes, "there are 500,000 other cricketers in Australia who would love to take their place."[26]

Packer offered $A1.5m for exclusive TV rights; a few months earlier, the ABC had secured the extant three-year deal by offering $A210,000. He was still turned down flat; the consolation prize of commercial rights – still some years from even hinting at the vast riches generated now – was a slap in the face. When he emerged from the meeting with Bob Parish and

Ray Steele, respectively the board's chairman and treasurer, Packer was livid. As he saw it, not unreasonably, he was far too loud for these buttoned-up stuffed shirts, not to mention too much of a philistine. Although a heavy smoker, he was also teetotal. It was hard to think of anyone being further from the right sort.

"Packer had expected rather a lot of the ACB," allows Haigh. "But the meeting confirmed his prejudgment of the ACB and ABC as clubmates. His father had once advised him to join any club he wanted to join before he was thirty-five: after that too many people wouldn't like him. Now he was thirty-eight, he might have to think about founding his own."[27]

* * *

Although it was Lillee's dissatisfaction that encouraged the Australian rebels, the key to Packer's takeover bid was the towering and more problematic figure of Tony Greig. A 6ft 7in South African who had migrated to Sussex in 1967 to seek his cricketing fortune while his Apartheid-riven country was isolated, he had achieved the not inconsiderable feats – for an epileptic outsider – of not only becoming his adopted country's best all-rounder but climbing all the way to England captain. His Scottish father, Sandy, had performed heroic service as an RAF fighter pilot during the Second World War; Tony was cut from the same intrepid cloth.

Not by any means, though, did the rewards match his labours. At the time, his Test fee was £210 – less than the cost of flying out his family for the Centenary Test, an overhead he bore himself. Five years earlier, his fee for spending five months representing England in India, Pakistan and Sri Lanka had been a faintly insulting £2,000. Ladling insult upon injury, the contract contained a footnote stating that MCC would be happy to pay the unprincely sum into a Jersey bank. As his tour captain Tony Lewis would pointedly remark shortly after Greig's death in 2013: "What did they expect our families at home to live on?"[28] In a letter to Packer shortly before Greig agreed to become his chief recruiter (a communiqué the latter did not make public until 2012), he encapsulated the professional sportsman's insecurity:

> *Kerry, money is not my major concern. I'm nearly 31 and probably two or three Test failures from being dropped by England. Ian Botham is going to be a great player and there won't be room in the side for both of us. England captains such as Brian Close, Ray Illingworth and Colin Cowdrey lost the captaincy before they expected. I don't want to finish up in a mundane job when they drop me. I'm not trained to do anything. I went straight from school to playing for Sussex. My family's future is more important than anything else. If you guarantee me a job for life working for your organisation, I will sign.*[29]

The impetus for the players' revolt, however, stemmed from far beyond Sussex. At the time, virtually the only way to earn even a quasi-decent living as a cricketer if you weren't English was to join a first-class county, an option that had opened up in 1968 with the introduction of the Immediate Registration Rule: no longer would overseas players be obliged to spend years serving a period of residential qualification. The cream of the crop flocked to Heathrow Airport, from the Caribbean especially. That so few Australians were signed was less a reflection of a dip in traditional quality than that they invariably had proper jobs.

Here were teachers, estate agents, bankers, salesmen: part-timers dependent on the school holidays or the extent of their employer's patriotic largesse. It was by no means unusual for county players to stay in the saddle into their 40s; in Australia, 30 was pushing it. Between 1954 and 1969, records Haigh, the national average weekly wage doubled from $80 to $190, but the base Test fee went up by just 19%; in the mid-1950s, the likes of Keith Miller, the game's best player and most charismatic presence, were earning four times that national mean; come the end of the next decade the gap had been halved. Meanwhile, those who kept the Ashes, figuratively if not literally, in Australian hands from 1959 to 1971 were confined to less than 3% of the board's total broadcasting and gate income.[30]

* * *

In mid-May 1977, the secret was no more, courtesy of a 97-year-old Australian newspaper, *The Bulletin*, chairman K. Packer Esq. In plotting the game's biggest entrepreneurial venture since William Clarke launched his All-England XI in 1848, one scheduled to start the following Australian summer, Packer had secured the signatures of the *crème de la crème* – 18 Australians, four West Indians, four Pakistanis, three of Greig's England confreres and five of his Test-starved countrymen. In time, that original crew would all but double. In England, official sanctions were more immediate. Greig was instantly stripped of the England captaincy yet remained in the team – well, the Australians were in town. In due course, others followed. At Lord's in July, the ICC banned the defectors from official international cricket; some were excommunicated from domestic duties. Unsurprisingly, Australia surrendered the Ashes in a one-sided series that saw captain Greg Chappell and his equally distracted comrades lose 3-0, their biggest loss in England since 1886.

The vendetta ran deep. A t-shirt sported by my good friend Mark Ray, who would play for New South Wales and captain Tasmania before heading for an illustrious career with laptop and camera, encapsulated the popular view: "Death to the Circus". Ian Davis, a young New South Wales opener who had made 68 for Australia in that Centenary Test, had long felt blessed to have found a job at the Commonwealth Bank, thankful that Alan Davidson, the former Test all-rounder, had smoothed his path. "The bank even sent me to England in 1977 on full pay. They'd always been very generous and accommodating, but on our return the mood change was palpable. They questioned me about signing with Packer and basically said I had to pick one or the other. Suddenly I was out of work. Packer heard about it and immediately took all his money out of the bank. 'Stuff you,' he said. The boss of the bank even rang and asked if I could talk to him. 'No way,' I said. 'What do you reckon Kerry would have said to me!'"[31] The depth of the antipathy Packer had aroused astonished many. "None of the WSC players knew they were going to be outlawed and ostracised the way we were, unable to play nor even practise with our grade clubs. At the time we felt they were signing for three months of TV cricket."

* * *

Nearly a score of the pirates came from the Caribbean; nowhere did Packer's money find a more receptive home. "While WSC money provided a decent upper-middle class income in Australia," recorded Haigh, "in the West Indies it conferred tycoonhood. At Caribbean rates of exchange, a $A20,000 a year contract was up to forty times the average per capita income."[32] As that noble Caribbean commentator and journalist Tony Cozier calculated, in the space of a few seasons they could earn as much as they would have in a 15-year Test career. After he had led the West Indies to victory at the inaugural World Cup in 1975, Clive Lloyd reminded me many moons later with an enduring blend of disbelief and derision, neither he nor his charges received a penny by way of a bonus.

> In fact, we received nothing extra for winning the 1979 tournament either. Bar a walking stick, a gold medal and a gold chain that my wife now wears with pride, we got our fee and that was it. The board never said, 'Let's give these guys something to remember these marvelous occasions by'. I had to fight to get the fee up in 1979. The board were about to pay us £100 again but I kicked up a fuss. So did Mike Brearley and eventually we got £200. People don't understand how bad it was in county cricket either. When I first went to Lancashire in 1968 I got £2,500 for five months. Money was never a factor with me but then you start to see sports people doing various things for themselves in a financial sense and you want your kids to be in a better position. So we decided to better our situation,

not just for ourselves but also for the young players coming
through. Because of Packer we got a minimum wage in county
cricket. Kerry Packer was the greatest thing that happened to
all sportsmen, not just cricketers.[33]

Arletha Haynes, single mother to the young Barbadian batsman
Desmond Haynes, who would be snapped up by Packer in 1978,
grew tearful when she told me how the oldest of her three sons
did all he could for her and the rest of the 14-strong "family
circle" incorporating aunts, uncles and cousins. Home was
ramshackle Holders Hill, where even swinging a rat in the
pinched passages separating the houses was out of the question.
Desi had started life crammed into a two-room dwelling with 11
others, deprived of electricity and illuminated by an oil lamp.
There was no streetlight outside. "And no water," as Arletha
emphasised. "Desi had a big head and we used to send him up
the hill with a bucket on it." Thanks to him, by the time we met,
in 1992, she was comfortably ensconced in a smart modern brick
home half a mile further up the hill.

"We was real poor, moving from rent house to rent house.
I was worn out from looking after his brothers. But he looked
after me. He was all I had to depend on when I got the sack. He
helped all the members of the family circle. I took sick, got told
it was cancer, so he bought me a home, furnished it too. Then he
[set me up with] a shop." But even though, like their Australian
counterparts, the Caribbean public at large was in no way
unsympathetic to the players, there were still plenty prepared
to tar her boy as a traitor: "What he had to put up with, all those
nasty words, was terrible."[34]

At first, the cash-strapped West Indies board – who would
gratefully host WSC games in due course – continued to sanction the selection of Lloyd and company; it didn't last. In March
1978, Haynes and the militant Deryck Murray were dropped
for the third Test of an official tour by a drastically weakened
Australian party; the raging Lloyd resigned as captain. The
five remaining WSC players duly withdrew their labour just as

Packer was flying out to Guyana, whereupon the West Indies board announced that the quintet would play no further part in the series.

The outcry across the Caribbean was ferocious. Jamaica's *Daily News* charged the administrators with "bungling, slitting their own throats, being guilty of asinine statements and lacking the courage of their own convictions".[35] On 4 April, the Pan African Secretariat, a radical Jamaican group, claimed to have mobilised 100,000 people to boycott the fifth Test while calling for the removal of "autocratic, oligarchic planter-class representatives" from the board. A week later, the Committee in Defence of West Indies Cricket was launched in Trinidad, calling on Packer to bring WSC to the Caribbean, on Trinidadians to boycott the fourth Test and on the board to resign en masse. The committee also expressed the view that the board had "acted in a high-handed and arrogant manner with no regard for the interest of the cricketers and cricket-loving people of the Caribbean" and, "acting as lords and barons, have continued to administer West Indies Cricket in their selfish interest, adopting at all times a Massa [ownership] policy in dealing with the West Indies cricketers".[36]

When Packer fetched up in Barbados at the ritzy Sandy Lane golf club, having dispatched planes to transport his Caribbean employees there too, Haynes took to him. "He was a big man in every sense of the word and I liked him. He seemed like someone who meant well. He wanted to make money, sure, but he also had a great feeling for the game and he knew that the players deserved to be better rewarded. He also made sure you realised that it was serious cricket you'd signed up for, not some knockabout fare."[37]

* * *

Next stop, London's High Court, where, backed by Packer's capacious pockets, three of the players banned from Test and county cricket sued the Test and County Cricket Board for restraint of trade – Greig, Mike Procter (who was not eligible for the former anyway, being South African) and Greig's Sussex and England colleague, the maverick fast bowler John Snow, tormentor of Australian batsmen and vicar's son. After 31 days, Lord Justice Slade delivered his verdict: running to 221 pages, it took him five and a half hours. The bans, he concluded, "would preclude the players concerned from entry into important fields of professional livelihood", "subject them to the hardships and injustice of essentially retrospective legislation" and "deprive the public of any opportunity of seeing the players concerned playing in conventional cricket… for at least a number of years". Furthermore, the defendants had "acted without adequate regard to the fact that WSC had contractual rights with the players concerned which were entitled to the protection of law". The players won the day, plus costs it was estimated would amount to £200,000.[38] In *Wisden*, Gordon Ross's report was head-lined – with all the snobbery that governed English reactions at the time – "The Packer Circus".

At first, nonetheless, the venture seemed doomed. World Series Cricket may have attracted the game's best and brightest – only a handful, mostly Englishmen who could afford to do so, resisted Greig's overtures and Packer's cheques – but the Australian board was hardly about to hand over its prime stages to a piratical whippersnapper: dwarfed by those for the offi-cial Tests against India, crowds for the inaugural 1977-78 WSC campaign, played out at football grounds and secondary cricket venues, were barely worthy of the name.

The answer was innovation. Experiments ranged from field-placing restrictions to counter negativity and hot-housed pitches that could only be dropped into place by helicopter; from white balls and black sightscreens to day-glo pastel uniforms. All would form part of the game's future furniture. Most pres-cient of all was Packer's own dazzlingly bright idea: day-night matches. Better for visibility under lights, the white ball proved so hard to pick up against the players' white pads that one umpire failed to spot a clear lbw. The answer was something still more radical – coloured kit. Animated by "the yellow and strawberry colours", approval came from the watching England captain, Brearley, who was eager to witness the first techni-colour contest in Sydney. It was more "dramatic", he enthused, "because one could see who was on which side".[39]

For Haigh, "the most profound and revolutionary" aspect of Packer's new packaging was "perhaps the simplest". The vision emanated from David Hill, his endlessly creative and influential producer, who liked nothing better than multiplying the number of cameras at his disposal, in good part because he was mightily fed up with obliging viewers to watch proceedings from behind the batsman's behind. Now the game was screened from both ends of the pitch, enabling every delivery to be watched, far more revealingly, from behind the bowler's arm. "Until that stage," as Haigh warrants, "television coverage of sports events had been about replicating as close as possible the experience of being at the ground, which, of course, involved sitting in one seat. All of a sudden, thanks to Kerry Packer, the home viewer enjoyed *for free* a luxury unavailable to the most privileged live spectator."[40]

* * *

With help from *C'mon Aussie C'mon*, the marketing began to bite. While the official Australia team were being crushed 5-1 in the Ashes series that clashed with its second season, WSC crowds soared, ignited by night games. In a BBC radio interview with Tony Lewis, Greig submitted a pithy summation of the need for insurrection: "I know everyone in England is disappointed with me, mate, but they needed a shock. We've shaken them up now."[41]

The initial tremors had been felt on 14 December 1977. The stage was Melbourne's VFL Park, where spectators turned up for a fresh twist on an ancient tale: a night match. When Bertrand Russell made that observation about the notion of a leisure-rich lower class being shocking to the wealthy he surely had cricket uppermost in mind. Other sports less encumbered by climactic conditions and conventional colour codes (white kit, red ball) were well ahead of the game; no other major spectator sport clung so long to the principle of staging games at unsociable hours. At

VFL Park, the lights were switched on at 6.30, after which a white ball was used, yellow and orange having been deemed unsuitable. English reactions ranged from distaste to prescience. John Woodcock observed that Australians, "being always early with their evening meal", were "well-suited by night-time sport". David Frith attributed his nausea to fatigue: "If I'm prejudiced at all perhaps it is in favour of cricket in God's sunshine." Alan Lee's conclusion was unarguable. Packer had "struck gold" and would "arouse the envy of the traditional authorities".

That envy took root on 28 November 1978. The first 5,000 arrivals at the Sydney Cricket Ground found themselves under a hail of giveaway white balls dispensed by Chappell and his Australian team, who took the field to the chorus of *C'mon Aussie C'mon*. Of the eventual 50,000 witnesses, more than 5,000 were admitted free after Packer assented to a police request to open the gates to those still queuing. That the match was played at the SCG was indicative of the sea-change. After the members of the all-powerful ground trust had employed their learned friends to keep out WSC, Packer's friend, the New South Wales premier Neville Wran, not only sacked them but had pylons installed. Here, contends Haigh, was the tipping point: "Packer, his retinue and 50,000 fans storming the establishment's sanctum sanctorum."

The incongruity of it all," marveled Adrian McGregor, then reporting for the *National Times* and later Greg Chappell's biographer. "That Packer at that moment, so absolutely removed from the hoi polloi, should have... achieved the proletarianisation of cricket. He had enticed sports fans out of the pubs... transforming the subtleties of international cricket into the spectacular that is night cricket."[42]

Not long afterwards, the ACB sheepishly announced that the official tour by England had generated a loss of $445,000. Thus it was that peace broke out in Melbourne on 30 May 1979, cited somewhat mischievously by Haigh as official cricket's answer to Munich on 30 September 1938 – with Parish in the Neville Chamberlain role. In exchange for disbanding WSC and returning the players to the fold, PBL Pty Ltd, a subsidiary of Consolidated Press, would receive the "marketing rights" to Australian cricket for 10 years, which meant being responsible for the televising, promotion, merchandising and sponsorship of international cricket. As Haigh puts it, this left the board with nothing to do save "pick the teams and man the turnstiles".[43]

News of the deal drew jeers from the other national boards, the loudest from a cluster of whingeing Poms: the way they saw it, the ACB had dived into bed with the enemy. "While Packer enjoyed World Series Cricket," reasons Haigh, "he never lost sight of his original purpose, which was not after all to build a cricket attraction, but to obtain exclusive broadcast rights for cricket in Australia; he had always been prepared to sell the players back to the game as part of a quid pro quo. Now that his quid was flourishing, he could demand a mighty quo. It was called the 'peace agreement', but it wasn't so much an armistice as an unconditional surrender."[44]

Snapped on that pivotal November night in 1978, Patrick Eagar's photo of Sydney's illuminated sky, set off against the grass and the pale lime roof of the pavilion, has lost none of its artistry or symbolism. Here was the riposte to that orgastic green light at the end of Daisy Buchanan's dock, the one that so tantalised Jay Gatsby: instead of encouraging cricketkind to beat on, boats against that incessant current, borne back ceaselessly into a delusory past, it lit the way forward, to a future few even realised it needed.

The Free Enterprise Games

Montreal staged the Olympics in 1976; its taxpayers were still footing the bill well into the next century. Come the following decade, the Games were in peril: the soaring costs of the infrastructure required to put on a three-week show for the planet was becoming cripplingly expensive, the risks prohibitive. "It seemed that only massive state investment, as in Moscow, or everlasting debt could allow a city to stage the Olympics," declared Steven Downes and Duncan Mackay in their biting study of the end of shamateur athletics, *Running Scared*. "Thus it was that, when the IOC met in Athens in 1978 to decide on the venue for the 1984 Games, there was only one candidate: Los Angeles. For the IOC it was very much a case of 'take it or leave it'."[45]

For the first time since 1896, a bid to stage the Games went unaided by central government funding. The bid, which saw the IOC offered a $225m TV deal for US rights, was tendered not by the state of California, then making swingeing cuts in public expenditure under the governorship of Ronald Reagan, but by a group of local enthusiasts buoyed by the near-$1m surplus LA had enjoyed from hosting the 1932 Games. "They were sure that this success could be achieved again," write Downes and Mackay, "provided the IOC allowed a degree of leeway over the manner in which they arranged the Games. Faced with no alternatives, the IOC agreed."[46] The upshot, a profit of $200m, made staging the Olympics more desirable than ever, hence the mountainous sums increasingly lavished on subsequent bids; it also kicked professional athletics out from under the table.

Professionalism had begun impinging on the Olympics following the exit as IOC president after the 1972 Munich Games of Avery Brundage, who died three years later. Having won the decathlon in Montreal, Bruce Jenner set the ball rolling, raking in $3m from endorsements and TV roles. The tide was not for turning. From 1982, albeit tentatively, athletics' governing body, the Federation of International Amateur Athletics Associations, founded in Stockholm by 17 nations in 1912, began permitting competitors to be formally compensated for participating in international events. In 1987, the IOC finally excised the word "amateur" from its charter, freeing the individual governing bodies to set their own rules.

Come 1992, when Linford Christie took the men's 100m gold in Barcelona, "almost anything" went, insist Downes and Mackay. Instead of commanding maybe £15,000 per race in appearance fees from European meeting promoters, Christie could demand £25,000. As an Olympic champion the Londoner also received a £50,000 bonus from Puma, his kit sponsor; when he renegotiated his contract, he upped his annual retainer to £120,000. Call it the Olympic Factor. As an indication of the chasm in caché separating it from other athletics meetings, witness Canada's Donovan Bailey. Not unnaturally, having won the 100m title at the 1995 World Championships in Gothenburg, he anticipated a hero's homecoming. However, in a bathetic scene, he took some friends to a night-club in Toronto and tried to persuade the chap at the door to waive the $5 admission by informing him of his identity. The bouncer was clearly none the wiser. "But I'm Donovan Bailey," he proclaimed. "Who?" wondered the bouncer. "The world 100 metres champion," replied Bailey. Whereupon his unimpressed obstructor advised him that the charge was still $5.[47]

What ensued over the next two decades was not always ethical or pretty, by any means, yet who could doubt that it was progress? If nothing else, those LA Games had paved the way for the penultimate link in the chain fence of shamateurism to be severed, terminating once and for all the stigma attached to running and jumping and throwing for financial reward (though not until 2001 did the IAAAF relinquish its first A). Nevertheless, notes Downes, the growth in British government funding in the quest for shiny medals has done little either for those beneath the elite or for the long-term future. After *Running Scared* was published in 1996, a lack of sponsors and TV deals saw the British Athletics Federation go bankrupt. "Like rabbits from a hat, commercial agents then produced a long-term BBC TV contract and sponsorship deals, still running after a decade – largely thanks to the London Olympics. The collapse of the British Athletics Federation, and the business connections between the sport, the sponsorship agencies and the Olympic bid has always been worthy of a second volume of *Running Scared*." The collapse of the BAF begat a new governing body, UK Athletics, one that, by 2006, was "entirely unaccountable to the clubs" and served only 200 "funded, elite athletes". A relationship, Downes warranted, "somewhat like the Premier League and a Sunday morning football club – or a dog and a lamppost".[48]

If Downes conveyed those sentiments to me with relish, he seemed utterly justified. In 1992, British athletics, to all intents and purposes, was run by its chief promotions officer, Andy Norman, a former policeman with fingers in quite a few pies and a fondness for thrusting brown paper packages under tables. He also acted as an agent for leading track and field exponents, among them Fatima Whitbread, the Olympic javelin medallist for whom he had left his wife, which did nothing to dissuade those inclined to believe he was abusing his position. The allegations mounted, among the most persistent that he had been guilty of perverting samples in a doping inquiry involving one of his clients. Yet his status as a one-time law enforcer meant that, so far as officialdom was concerned, he should always be taken at his word. Which is why, as Downes puts it, "he thought he was invulnerable".[49]

When Cliff Temple wrote a damning article about him for the *Sunday Times*, following up a TV documentary, Norman rang Temple and threatened to put it around that he was sexually harassing the female athletes he coached, among them the Olympic medallist Shireen Bailey. Unbeknown to Norman, Temple recorded the entire half-hour conversation, then lodged a copy of the tape with his sports editor, Chris Nawrat, for safekeeping. The following February, Temple threw himself under a train. In the coroner's view, Norman's threats would have been enough to push him over the edge. Norman was sacked from his job the next day. The Channel 4 News investigation won Downes a Royal Television Society award.

Eventually thrown out of the family home by the long-suffering Whitbread, whose horrific childhood ill-deserved such a charmless and ugly prince, Norman died in a council flat in 2007, an enduring symbol of the sins of shamateurism and the crimes of professionalism.

The last fortress

Contrary to popular belief our players are not paid cash for playing as such, but are given cars and numerous perks which, as far as I'm concerned, is professionalism, so who are we fooling here?

Those refreshingly frank sentiments were expressed in 1995 by Louis Luyt, president of the South African Rugby Board and a chap likened by Derek Wyatt, the England winger turned Labour MP, to a cross between the media magnate Robert Maxwell and Marlon Brando's Don Corleone. By then, rugby union's amateur principle had been eviscerated, says Huw Richards with some understatement, "to the point where it looked hypocritical". That was the year the 15-a-side code became the last major adult spectator sport to bite the professional bullet. That its rulers were able to keep above-the-table trade at bay for so long can be traced to the fact that, for more than a century, theirs had been a game played in the main by the professional classes, bankers and lawyers and doctors, to whom all that rucking and mauling provided an opportunity to blow off some steam at the end of the working week. It was also because, unlike football, cricket and tennis, rugby was not a truly global sport. And, like athletics and tennis, it was unashamedly shamateur. Instead of appearance fees, the illicit backhanders were known as "boot money", an epithet dating back to those shady pre-professional days of English football.

All the same, as early as 1962, the internationalist-turned-journalist Vivian Jenkins had calculated that, between August 1961 and April 1964, the England players who had toured South Africa (with the Lions) and New Zealand would have but one rugby-free month. According to Bert Godwin, the Coventry hooker, said trips had cost him £400 in lost income, not to mention a further £8 per trial or international.[50] The next decade, which brought domestic Merit Tables and sponsored cup competitions, saw the demands pile ever higher. Another England international, John Watkins, claimed in 1979 that he was losing three months' work each year. Six years earlier, invited to deputise for South Africa and tour New Zealand, the Scottish RFU had felt no option but to decline: key players could not wangle the time off. Needless to add, defecting to rugby league, to full-time professionalism and lesser status, remained anathema to all bar the few considered good enough. At the time standards in rugby league were arguably higher, especially the brand showcased in the 1980s by Australians such as Wally "The King" Lewis.

"Players were becoming what athlete Chris Brasher had termed 'timed professionals'," attests Richards. "Stories proliferated of 'blindside remuneration' and cash payments for after-dinner speaking or opening new clubhouses." Demand for professionalism, nonetheless, was anything but loud, hence the denunciation of J. J. Williams, the flying Wales and Lions wing, who argued in 1974: "We're virtually full-time players. The only difference between us and the soccer professionals is that we don't have to hang around the club all day…They'll have to pay us in the end, you know. Scrap all this nonsense and let us earn a bit from something we can do well."[51]

There were some concessions. In 1973, the regulations ditched all specific references to rugby league; amendments were made for rugby journalists and teachers, though as Richards relates, the case of the former 13-a-side player R. M. Reid, then Aberdeen University's assistant director of physical education, "prompted debate of almost Talmudic complexity over precisely what the phrase 'accepted educational duties' meant in terms of coaching and selecting university teams".[52]

"Every major union in the world let down its players in some respect in rugby's central bargain," Stephen Jones would bemoan in 1989: if the players were to be asked for more and more and still not be paid, "they must be treated wonderfully well".[53] That they were not may readily be gleaned from the autobiographical reflections of Gareth Edwards, the brilliant scrum-half and teacher anointed in a 2003 *Rugby World* magazine poll of international players as the greatest rugby player of all. Published shortly after he retired in 1978, it is even more sobering to be reminded that the book resulted in a ban from coaching or any other involvement in the game.

I would ask for one change, and that is for a more generous atti-tude to the international player. I do not mean that he should be paid, but I do believe a more realistic slice should be taken out of big-match expenses so that he can stay in the best hotels, eat and enjoy himself without too much restriction and involve his wife too. When you play in a match which has attracted a gate worth over £150,000 you do not want to stay in a second- or third-rate hotel. Nor do you wish to be told that only one bottle of wine is allowed between four, that telephone calls to your home are to be paid by you and so on. For special duties, which have required years of effort (as well as of pleasure), you need special treatment when it can be afforded. Advertising and television income surely make it possible.[54]

Scottish and Irish players, he added sympathetically, had until only recently been given a solitary jersey to last the interna-tional season; trade it sportingly with an opponent and you had to buy the replacement – and every replacement thereafter. Even in the brave new world of kit sponsorship, "a Scotsman told me that their Union still makes them pay a nominal price for it".[55]

The demands had escalated, off the field as well as on. "Apart from the actual rugby, which involves matches, travel, squad practices, sports forums, dinners, dances, raffles, auctions, opening shops and stores, there is the interference with your private life. There is no way that my wife and I can have a night in complete privacy in a restaurant near home. Television, or rather the result of it, has no mercy."[56] To aggravate matters, at club level, a professional outlook was expected. Accused by Cardiff colleagues and supporters of not training hard enough after returning from a short tour of South Africa in 1977, Edwards hit back hard. "I said I believed that rugby was still an amateur sport, and that I liked to think, when I woke up in the morning, that I could have a game or go back to sleep. That exaggerates the situation, because I would not want to let down any side, but it emphasises the amateur approach, that my life is mine and that it was my choice at the end of the day. Looking back now

I can see that my attitude was a natural reaction to the life that had been very much imposed on me."[57]

The boundaries were being skirted most audaciously in France, where the dominance of the props and backs of Béziers was being fuelled by a dietician, medical testing and monthly earnings of around 3000 francs, plus bonuses. Apparently, according to the club's chief coach, Raoul Barrière, Narbonne and Perpignan paid even more. "We were not pros; we had a pro approach, which is different," he stated, splitting hairs impressively. "Remuneration was the means to obtaining performance, never a goal in itself. Money allowed players to train better, more often and for longer."[58]

Edwards was more prescient than he can have imagined. "The mood is ripe among players," he mused in 1978, "as it was for Kerry Packer with the cricketers, for a privateer to step in." Indeed, Packer himself would prove to be one of them. A leak in August 1983 publicised plans by David Lord, an Australian entrepreneur, who claimed to have signed 203 leading players for an international circus on £100,000-a-year contracts. Which to Jean-Pierre Rives, France's magnificent flanker and captain, sounded a lot like Senator McCarthy's extravagant and wildly fluctuating claims about Communist infiltration. The venture did indeed come to naught, but the threat prompted an emergency conflab of the International Rugby Board, which had one happy consequence: the launch, four years later, of a World Cup, held in New Zealand.

The end, when it came, was sudden. In 1995 came Packer's own World Rugby Corporation, promising 30 franchises and a 352-match season, which by early August had secured 407 signatures on contracts provisionally agreed by the majority of the squads playing in the World Cup – barring, that is, those from England and Ireland. A fortnight later, on the eve of the World Cup final, Rupert Murdoch's News Corporation announced it had paid an bewildering £370m to broadcast provincial and international fixtures in Australasia and South Africa, now united as SANZAR, the formation of which effectively marked the end of amateurism.

Such riches also did plenty to dissuade rugby league clubs in Murdoch's own Super League from pursuing union's brightest. The New Zealand RFU counter-offered the All Blacks more than £100,000 per year per head but this was rebuffed by their flinty captain, Sean Fitzpatrick. Mike Brewer, the flanker, gave one dismayed official, Rob Fisher, the benefit of his clairvoyance: "I hope you enjoy the last meeting of the IRB."[59] But whereas nobody was in the slightest doubt that the NZRFU, bolstered by the Murdoch windfall, had the guaranteed resources, the Packer venture, denuded by the mogul's current commitments to horse racing and rugby league, did not. Soon enough, the southern hemisphere players, of whom the most sought-after signature belonged to the tournament's freakishly unstoppable star, Jonah Lomu, accepted an official deal. Packer's reported response was in no way atypical: it was "a stupid game played by a bunch of fucking poofters".[60]

Come the week before the final the WRC project was more or less dead in the water. "The established game also had the advantages of heritage and shared memory," reasoned Richards. As Peter Fitzsimons, author of *The Rugby War*, wrote in an open letter to Phil Kearns, the Wallabies captain, the choice was little of the sort, resting as his options did between "honour, glory, the Wallaby jersey and enormous riches guaranteed" and "dissension, civil war, enormous bitterness, pissing on the Wallaby jersey and only the possibility of slightly more riches".

A week after the All Blacks had unexpectedly lost a World Cup final best known for the hitherto inconceivable sight of Nelson Mandela in a Springbok jersey, the IRB met in Paris, where the day was carried by the logic of chairman Vernon Pugh: "Whether or not we promote it, the game will be openly professional within a very short space of time. If we do not participate in, and direct and control, that change, the IRB and the unions as we know them may no longer be running the game." According to Nick Farr-Jones, a lawyer as well as Australia's captain, the Paris delegates resembled men emerging from "their own funeral". As Richards observed, it had been a century, "less only three days", since the Huddersfield show-down that created two codes.[61]

The southern hemisphere unions had been planning for the revolution, as Michael Lynagh, the fly-half who served Australia so adroitly as World Cup-winning playmaker in 1991 and, from 1993 to 1995, captain, recollected nearly two decades later. Here, instead of resisting the inevitable, the unions "welcomed it, embraced it, and had a ready-made product to satisfy the tele-vision channels that would back this transformation financially",[62] hence the inception in 1996 of both the Super Rugby tournament for clubs and the Tri-Nations Championship. Up north, however, the apparent belief in some quarters that the code should remain amateur bred the impression "that they were not prepared". As a consequence, argued Lynagh, the players were snapped up by the entrepreneurs now running the leading southern hemisphere clubs, who thus controlled them, kicking off a replica of the club-v-country arm-wrestling that had long dogged English football, subsequently aggravated in Europe by the French and showing no signs, as I write, of slackening in intensity.

Unsurprisingly, with all the money beginning to swill around in union, it was the league clubs that suffered, espe-cially in England. In the so-called "Clash of the Codes" between Bath RFC and Wigan RLFC in 1996, an intriguing and primarily commercial experiment, the latter prevailed comfortably on aggregate, walloping the westcountry side 82-6 under league rules at Maine Road – aided by three tries from Martin "Chariots" Offiah – before going down 44-19 at Twickenham under union rules. That same year, the RFL Championship was replaced by the 14-team Super League, the chosen few augmented by a French representative, the ultimate goal success against the champions of the Australasian National Rugby League in the annual World Club Challenge. Union professionalism, though, also prompted a sea-change: lured by higher salaries, league stars began flourishing in the English Courage League; before long, Wigan's Henry Paul and Jason Robinson were lining up for Bath.

When the cross-code debate was fleetingly revived in 2003, with each half played according to different regulations, a modest gathering at St Helens' Knowsley Road saw Sale Sharks, armed with a fair few league converts, take the first period 41-0 against the Saints and edge home by two points overall. Enhanced by a card-sharp's sleight of hand and a tap dancer's toes, Robinson's attacking brio would do much to win the World Cup for England in 2003. Genius 2 Snobbery 0.

Globalisation and child labour

Emboldened by the advent of free agency, American cultural imperialism gathered pace in the final quarter of the 20th century. By the late 1980s, the likes of Croatia's Drazen Petrovic, Lithuania's Arvydas Sarbonis and Sarunas Marciulionis, a member of Russia's 1988 Olympic gold-winning basketball team, had begun to infiltrate the NBA; two decades later, the league's leading lights included a Spaniard, Pau Gasol, a German, Dirk Nowitzki, and a Frenchman by the exceedingly English name of Tony Parker. In recent seasons the NFL has boasted players from American Samoa, Haiti, Nigeria, Poland, Tonga and even Scotland, though most of the intruders were brought up in the US. The first European to cut ice in the NHL was Borje Salming, a Swede who debuted for the Toronto Maple Leafs in 1973; the Eastern European incursion, unavoidably delayed by the Cold War, began, suitably enough, the year the Berlin Wall fell, 1989, when Russia's Sergei Priakhin debuted for the Calgary Flames. Like its predecessor the North American Soccer League, Major League Soccer could not have got off the ground without the likes of David Beckham.

Having opened its doors to African-Americans in 1947, Major League Baseball began attracting Latin Americans, who would become even more fixated on the diamond as an alternative means of advancement to soccer and boxing; not until 2009, by acute contrast, did the Cleveland Indians become the first franchise to sign a continental European – Martin Cervenka from the Czech Republic.

By 2010, 28% of major leaguers were from overseas[63], the most celebrated Ichiro Suzuki. MLB's first Japanese superstar, "Ichiro" (as he is known from Tokyo to Topanga Canyon) was an instant hit in 2001 when, after nearly a decade of prosperity in his native league – the most competitive outside the US – he traded in the Orix Blue Wave for Seattle's Mariners. In 2004, he broke the single-season record for base hits, a milestone that had withstood all challenges for 84 years, swelling his fame in Japan to such proportions that, if you sent him a postcard addressed, simply, to "Ichiro" – or so they say – it will reach him. Yet he has nevertheless resisted, suggested Leonard Cassuto, professor of English at New York's Fordham University and editor of *The Cambridge Companion to Baseball*, "assimilation into the star-making apparatus of American sports". He seldom speaks English and, indeed, "has limited need for American celebrity except on his own terms". Concludes Cassuto: "More global ambassador than humanitarian, Ichiro has done more than anyone else to consolidate Japanese interest in the American major leagues. He has also made the Japanese game much more familiar to observers in the United States."[64]

By now, though, baseball's dominant sector hailed from closer to home: between 1996 and 2007, eight of the American League MVPs were Hispanic. In the latter year, Alex Rodriguez, having become the first MVP with a bottom-placed club during his days with the Texas Rangers, re-signed for the New York Yankees in a record-scuppering 10-year deal worth $275m, making him the best-paid sportsman in America if not the world. In 2011, Albert Pujols, National League MVP in 2005, 2008 and 2009, by common consent the best baseballer of the age, left the St Louis Cardinals and signed a 10-year contract with the Los Angeles Angels of Anaheim for $240m in addition to extras such as a hotel suite on all road trips and a luxury suite at Angels Stadium for the Pujols Foundation. Such towering deals had quite a bit to do, of course, with the economic possibilities opened up by the advent of free agency, which will be discussed in the next chapter. That, though, does not account for the Latino-isation of Major League Baseball.

In his foreword to *The New Face of Baseball*, Tim Wendel's 2003 fine account of the rise of Latino baseballers, the respected sportscaster Bob Costas expressed considerable pride in this redistribution of sporting privilege: "Since the United States' inception, we've prided ourselves on being a melting pot – a place where talent, not connections or family linkage, has been the bottom line. While that may be difficult to argue in some fields, it still rings true for baseball."[65] There remained, nevertheless, plenty of cause for disquiet, even disgust, not least in commissioner Bud Selig's decision to hold the 2011 All-Star Game in Arizona, a state notorious for racial profiling and punitive anti-immigration measures.

* * *

MLB could have spent the past few decades funding talent development within its own inner cities; instead, it opted to invest billions of dollars in talent from Latin America, especially Venezuela and the Dominican Republic, which in 2010 supplied 62% of foreign major leaguers and 80% of those on the next rung down.[66] There, after all, 15-year-olds could be signed on the cheap and groomed in major league academies, the first of which was developed in the Dominican Republic by the LA Dodgers in 1987. "It's globalisation," observed Dave Zirin, "but instead of bats and gloves being cheaply stitched together for Major League use, it's human beings."

All of which, reckoned Zirin, caused MLB franchises to join the White House in heaving a sigh of relief at the death in 2013 of Hugo Chávez, the socialist Venezuelan president who refused to kow-tow to Washington.

> *He told the clubs that they would have to institute employee and player benefits and job protections. He wanted education and job training, subsidized by MLB, to be a part of the academies. He also insisted that teams pay out 10 percent of players' signing bonuses to the government. Chávez effectively wanted to tax MLB for the human capital they blithely take from the*

country… Sure enough over the last decade, the number of teams
with "academies" in Venezuela has dwindled from twenty-
one to five. The threats of kidnapping and violence are often
cited by teams as the primary reason for this move, but the facts
say otherwise. As one major league executive said anonymously
to the LA Times, "Teams have left Venezuela because of issues
with the government and security that have made it more diffi-
cult to do business there. Absent those problems, there would be
a lot more teams here using academies."[67]

MLB's recruitment targets in Venezuela and the Dominican
Republic are under 18 and hence, as defined by international
human rights law, children. By comparison with their American
peers, moreover, these children come from impoverished
backgrounds, are less well-educated, less experienced and, as
Arturo J. Marcano, a lawyer who has advised the Venezuelan
players' union, and David P. Fidler, a law professor at Indiana
University, aptly sum up, "more vulnerable". The dynamics of
the Latin American free-agency system "thus propel MLB teams
to go after children, whereas the approaches taken in the United
States, Canada, Puerto Rico, Mexico and Asia generally result in
MLB teams signing a smaller number of adults with more education, experience and economic means. Controversies involving
age falsification by older Latin American players and their
buscones… confirm that, to MLB teams, younger Latin American
players have more potential than older ones."[68] *Buscones* train
and then sell on youngsters to MLB teams in exchange for a
share of the often substantial signing-on fee.

According to Marcano and Fidler, three factors contributed
to the emergence of Venezuela and the Dominican Republic as
dominant suppliers: exposure to baseball via military, political, economic, and cultural interactions with the US; attempts
by MLB franchises in the early 20th century to search for Latin
American talent, and the new baseball economics – a combination of rising union strength, leaping salaries and, above
all, free agency, which allows access to players "younger, less

educated, and less experienced than players subject to the MLB amateur draft", who are obliged to finish high school, "or those obtained from the Mexican, Japanese, or South Korean systems".[69] Inevitably, this led to controversies over age falsification by older players. In 2000, long after MLB had introduced the "17-year-old rule" prohibiting players of lesser age being signed, the Associated Press reported that scouts were believed to be guilty, on an annual basis, of clandestinely signing "hundreds" of underage Latin American boys.[70]

"A lot of us have pulled off tricks so we can sign," confessed one teenager in the 2012 documentary *Pelotero* ("Ballplayer"). "People change their ages and all that. But that's what you have to do." This was all facilitated by the *buscones*. It was they who sought out the most talented youths then housed, fed and clothed them in exchange for up to 35% of their signing bonus. Not that this bothered MLB clubs in the slightest. They were happy not to be dealing with the faster-talking agents who were proving the bane of their lives, happy to keep those bonuses down. In 2009, the *Pittsburgh Tribune-Review* reported a transaction between Rene Gayo, the Pirates' Cuban-born Latin American scout, and a *buscon*:

> *When Gayo quietly asked how much cash it would take to sign the shortstop, Olivo replied $200,000. Gayo quickly countered with an offer of $80,000. Grinning, Olivo offered his hand… The deal between Gayo and the buscon is not binding, as no player may officially be signed until July 2. But Gayo is confident it will stick, as his and Olivo's reputations are on the line…*[71]

Those bonuses, however, would not stay low for long. In 2010, the Yankees fired Carlos Rios, their director of Latin American scouting, and Ramon Valdivia, the club's Dominican Republic scouting director, for feathering their own nests.[72] In 2011, as part of a plea deal with the US government, David Wilder, director of player personnel for the Chicago White Sox, admitted that he and two club scouts, Jorge Oquendo and Victor Mateo, had profited from a scheme to inflate the cost of signing 23 teenage

Latinos and divvy up the mark-up: the scouts would identify desirable players then recommend to Wilder both the size of the signing bonus and their own slices. Between 2005 and 2008, the average such bonus rocketed by more than $100,000 from the 2004 mean of $29,000, heightening the starkness of the contrast with Latino starlets of the 1990s such as David Ortiz ($10,000) and Pedro Martinez ($6000).[73] Wilder benefited to the tune of at least $402,000. The sting might have continued but for the customs official who searched his baggage on a return trip to the US and found nearly $40,000 in cash. All three plotters were fired. After Wilder pleaded guilty to one count of mail fraud, the judge recommend he serve between 41 and 51 months in prison.

"MLB made a Faustian bargain with the Dominican Republic that it can neither clean up nor break, the fraud too deeply rooted in the system and the player pipeline too important to its daily operations," concluded Yahoo.com's justly angry young columnist Jeff Passan in 2012. "And because it happens in a place of immense poverty, where little English is spoken and less attention paid, baseball skates by with the overwhelming majority of its fan base unaware that the foreign country producing the largest number of major league players does so with a factory-farm mentality, its waste and run-off polluting all that surrounds it."[74]

In 2009, with performance-enhancing drugs now adding further danger and disrepute to the mix, MLB sought to do something about this noxious situation. A committee chaired by Sandy Alderson, a vastly experienced club executive, was deputed to investigate the leagues' interests and conduct in the Dominican Republic. Alderson raised the possibility of increasing the minimum age for eligibility to 18 and expanding the draft to encompass Latin America. In 2011, he joined a joint MLB-Players' Association committee set up to study the international market because the latest collective bargaining agreement, argued Andy McCullough in New Jersey's *Star-Ledger*, "penalises clubs for what the league deems excessive spending in Latin America".[75] Between times, though, he had accepted an offer from the New York Mets to be their general manager, a decision Marcano and Fidler regretted, fearing for the reforms he had championed. "Without effective implementation and sustained oversight of the new governance regime, the reforms will turn into wasted opportunities to transform a system that has not adequately protected and promoted the best interests of Latin American children into one that reflects the responsibilities MLB must shoulder as the centre of gravity for the globalisation of baseball."[76]

When cases of identity fraud began to emerge it was illuminating to read the simultaneous proportionality and heartlessness of Yahoo.com's David Brown: "Nobody here cares that players in a poor country lie for what they think is a better chance to play in the majors. And we surely don't care if some of these players are exploited. We barely care about exploitation of Americans. Finding the next Jose Reyes — no matter what it says on his birth certificate — that's Alderson's job."[77]

In 2009, Yewri Guillén, an uneducated 16-year-old from the Dominican Republic, signed for the Washington Nationals and received a $30,000 signing bonus. However, with vigilance over identity fraud growing, he was soon suspended for a year following allegations that he'd lied about his date of birth. While his family hired a lawyer to fight the suspension, he lived and trained without pay at the Nationals' academy in his homeland. "I didn't think he had any teeth because he never smiled," said Johnny DiPuglia, the Nationals' international scouting director. "And he always had watery eyes – there was always sadness in his eyes."[78]

At the start of 2011, everything had been smoothed out. Guillén was bound for the US, for his shot at glory. He returned home to get his travel documents in order, but the headaches that had been pounding away were increasing in intensity, prompting his family to take him to a clinic. He returned to duty but the condition had not alleviated, and on April 7 his aunt and uncle rushed him to the best private hospital available. However, since his contract had still not been finalised he had no health insurance, and was refused treatment when his family were unable to stump up the $1300 admission fee. He was moved to a more affordable Cuban-Dominican clinic nearby, where doctors diagnosed bacterial meningitis. On April 15, the day he was due to leave for the US, he died.

MLB claimed that the Nationals had followed protocol and had done all they could; the club promised to vaccinate all academy players forthwith; everyone dutifully expressed their sorrow. On motherjones.com, Ian Gordon painted a fuller picture:

> *There wasn't a certified athletic trainer, let alone a doctor, to evaluate Guillén at the Nationals' academy, a spartan training camp with cinder-block dorms. No one from the team accompanied him to Santo Domingo or intervened when he couldn't get into the Clínica Abreu. (The club didn't cover the costs of his treatment until after he was admitted to the Cuban-Dominican clinic.) And following Guillén's death, the club required his parents to sign a release before handing over his signing bonus and life insurance money – a document also stating that they would never sue the team or its employees. Guillén's death is the worst-case scenario in a recruiting system that treats young Dominicans as second-class prospects, paying them far less than young Americans and sometimes denying them benefits that are standard in the US minor leagues.[79]*

"We ain't come to play SCHOOL"

In theory, college sport should have no place in this book. To make an exception in the case of the American student athlete is an unhappy obligation. Indeed, college football, dominated as it is by states where there are no NFL teams, draws vast crowds and even huge TV audiences. According to Kevin O'Malley, a bigger college sports media consultant, television contracts for individual college sports conferences had soared by an average of nearly 350% since 2008. The latest television deal for the Southeastern Conference (SEC) swelled the league's annual pot from $69m to $205m. Come the end of the decade, thanks to the inception of the SEC's own television network and the addition of two universities, O'Malley forecast that the SEC would produce more than $300m in annual television earnings.[80]

Even in the early 21st century, there remained one sporting arena that appeared to adhere strictly, even religiously, to the essential tenets of shamateurism: the sports run under the auspices of the US National Collegiate Athletic Association – especially, and most brazenly, American football. As was underlined in October 2012 when Cardale Jones, Ohio State's freshman quarterback, traumatised the nation – or, rather, those who continued to kid themselves that, despite all the evidence, collegiate sports were somehow purer than the major leagues – with the following tweet: "Why should we have to go to class if we came here to play FOOTBALL, we ain't come to play SCHOOL, classes are POINTLESS." The tweeter was promptly benched for the next game. The resulting furore was all the more surprising when you consider that Jones was merely his university's *third-string* quarterback.

These days, according to a 2011 article in *The Atlantic* magazine by Taylor Branch, much of the NCAA's moral authority ("indeed much of the justification for its existence") lies in its claim to protect what it calls the student-athlete. "The term is meant to conjure the nobility of amateurism, and the precedence of scholarship over athletic endeavour. But the origins of the 'student-athlete' lie not in a disinterested ideal but in a sophistic formulation designed, as the sports economist Andrew Zimbalist has written, to help the NCAA in its 'fight against workmen's compensation insurance claims for injured football players'."[81]

The term "student-athlete" entered the lexicon in the 1950s, when the widow of Ray Dennison, who had died from a head injury sustained while playing football for Colorado's Fort Lewis A&M Aggies, filed for compensation death benefits. "Did his football scholarship make the fatal collision a 'work-related' accident?" wondered Branch. "Was he a school employee, like his peers who worked part-time as teaching assistants and bookstore cashiers? Or was he a fluke victim of extracurricular pursuits?" The Colorado Supreme Court ultimately agreed with the school's contention that he was not eligible for benefits, since the college was "not in the football business".

"The term student-athlete was deliberately ambiguous," continued Branch. "College players were not students at play (which might understate their athletic obligations), nor were they just athletes in college (which might imply they were professionals). That they were high-performance athletes meant they could be forgiven for not meeting the academic standards of their peers; that they were students meant they did not have to be compensated, ever, for anything more than the cost of their studies. Student-athlete became the NCAA's signature term, repeated constantly in and out of courtrooms."[82]

In March 2013, amusingly, came a plea for help. Lawyers for the NCAA filed a claim in federal court stating that, should the rules on amateurism be lifted, as proposed in an ongoing lawsuit surrounding the use of college athletes' names, likeness and images, some colleges might be forced to shut down Division I or Bowl Subdivision football because of the financial and legal burden that would result from the need to share revenue with other sports.[83] "Their supporting evidence," reported Patrick Hruby on sportsearth.com, "included a series of teeth-gnashing written statements from college sports administrators, including a joint declaration from University of Texas athletics director DeLoss Dodds and women's athletics director Christine Plonsky that reads a bit like a ransom note."

If amateurism is the big lie of college athletics, a hokey philosophical fig leaf for a tax-evading, labour price-fixing cartel, then the notion that college sports will collapse if revenue-producing athletes receive more money is a subsidiary strain of uncut malarkey. Mohammed Saeed al-Sahhaf was more honest. Pollyanna was less of a drama queen. Because while Dodds and others assert that paying football and men's basketball players less than their market rate keeps overall costs down – thereby allowing athletic departments to fund feel-good charity projects like women's lacrosse – it's arguably the case that the distorted

amateur sports economy actually drives costs up. To under-
stand why, start with a single number. $1,107,391.00. That's the
amount of money that Texas reportedly paid Dodds in 2012.[84]

* * *

Founded more than a century ago, the initial premise of the
NCAA, claims its website, was to protect young footballers
"from the dangerous and exploitive athletics practices of the
time"[85], a time when students were increasingly being alienated
by the frequency and extent of injuries. Theodore Roosevelt, one
of the nation's more sportily-inclined presidents, summoned
the powers-that-be to the White House and soon afterwards
the rules were modified. In December 1905, no fewer than 62
higher-education institutions became charter members of the
Intercollegiate Athletic Association of the United States.

Before and after the inception of the Super Bowl, all manner
of Cotton and Rose and Orange Bowls were beloved by millions,
enticed by loyalty to the colleges they had attended – and in the
20th century at least, student numbers in the US were the envy
of the world – but also the promise of a more fluent, free-flowing
game than that offered by the professionals. The ethical grey
areas were happily ignored for decades as college football, courtesy of broadcasting fees, became ever more prosperous.

That said, not everybody in academia found the allure of
football irresistible. In 1939, Robert Maynard Hutchins, president
of the University of Chicago, despairing at what he saw as the
sport's destructive influence, announced that the college team,
then one of the so-called "Big 10", would cease to exist. William
Fulbright, his counterpart at the University of Arkansas and a
future senator, hailed Hutchins for his "courageous defence of
the university and its true function" and for defying "the worst
excrescences of our educational system". Such rare but welcome
concern for educational principles was recalled by Alexander
Wolff at the start of an open letter, published by *Sports Illustrated*
on 12 June 1995, to Edward "Tad" Foote, president of the
University of Miami, calling on him to follow Hitchins' example.

The previous year, the *Miami Herald* had published the results of a two-month investigation, reporting that NFL players and Luther Campbell, a member of the controversial rap band 2 Live Crew, had offered financial incentives to players at the University of Miami between 1986 and 1992. A touchdown, apparently, could fetch up to $500. A so-called "big hit" could also command a pretty penny, a foretaste of "Bountygate", the scandal that saw the New Orleans Saints fined $500,000 and a string of players suspended for operating a bounty system between 2009 and 2011 that incentivised the extreme physical targeting – and even maiming – of opponents. The only people who did not express disgust were those who were labouring under the apparent illusion that they were already paid for doing just that.

In the past, it bears emphasising, the NCAA had occasionally had cause to come down hard, even to the extent of invoking the so-called "death penalty". In 1951, the Manhattan Jaspers basketball team, a popular attraction who represented City College of New York and played their home games at Madison Square Garden, were suspended for two seasons following revelations about point-shaving (in effect, match-fixing). After Junius Kellogg, a leading player and the first African-American to play for Manhattan College, told authorities he had been approached by a former player and offered $1000 to throw a game (he politely declined), an investigation unearthed widespread gambling and corruption within college basketball: 86 games between 1947 and 1950 were reportedly affected; seven schools and more than 30 players were implicated, though many more were believed to have eluded detection. Four decades later, the NCAA cancelled the Southern Methodist University Mustangs' 1987 schedule following a string of violations, including a slush fund set up to distribute under-the-table payments to players from the mid-1970s until 1986.

That 1995 *SI* cover, most atypically, was not the usual action image or arty portrait but a statement whose shock value could hardly have been designed for more shuddering impact: "Why the University of Miami should drop football". In addition to the traditional crimes and misdemeanours – arsons, burglaries, assault and sexual battery – Wolff cited a financial aid scandal that saw 57 students implicated in what federal agents described as "perhaps the largest centralised fraud upon the federal Pell Grant program ever committed". The litany of improper payments made by agents prompted one student, angered by the non-delivery of an instalment, to storm into an agent's office and hold a gun to his head. Wolff concluded his impassioned plea by quoting Foote's own words from 1982: "Universities exist for teaching and research, not winning games."[86] Foote, needless to add, declined to heed Wolff's advice.

Meanwhile, the evidence piled up. Later that same year, the NCAA ruled that the football, baseball, women's golf and men's tennis programmes at the university had despoiled "bylaws governing extra benefits, financial aid, amateurism, institutional drug policy, ethical conduct and institutional control".[87] The university, it decided, had permitted or supplied more than $412,000 in "excessive aid" to student athletes between 1990 and 1994. From February 2003 to February 2005, the same university served a probationary sentence for further infractions. In 2011, Nevin Shapiro, a distinctly shady Hurricanes fan then serving a 20-year jail sentence for his role in a $930 million Ponzi scheme, claimed he had provided thousands of outlawed benefits to seven coaches and 72 athletes – at the very least – between 2002 and 2010.[88] These ranged from cash, gifts and prostitution to parties at his mansion and yacht cruises. When one of the recipients of his largesse impregnated a woman, asserted Shapiro, he offered to pay for an abortion. *SI*'s Stewart Mandel described Shapiro as a "jocksniffing, 5-foot-5 sleazebucket with one hell of a Napoleon complex" but still elected to cast Paul Dee, the former Miami athletic director whose sacking Wolff had advocated 16 years earlier, as the villain:

> *Dee, you may recall, was the Committee on Infractions chairman for [the University of South Carolina's] much-publicised case last summer involving former stars Reggie Bush and O.J. Mayo.*

It was Dee who, in announcing some of the stiffest penalties of the last 20 years (a two-year bowl ban and 30 docked scholarships), closed with the preachy reminder that "high-profile athletes demand high-profile compliance".

Dee, Miami's AD during most of the period covering Shapiro's allegations, is retired and no longer under NCAA jurisdiction. Still, it seems only fair he should spend a day at USC's Heritage Hall wearing a sandwich board with the word "Hypocrite". See if this sounds familiar: "We didn't have any suspicion that he was doing anything like this. He didn't do anything to cause concern." I'm fairly certain I heard Pete Carroll say something to that effect, repeatedly, about Bush's time at USC. He insisted there's no way he or anyone else at the school could have known that Bush's parents were living the high life in San Diego – a defense Dee and his committee sharply rebuked.

But no, those were the words of Dee himself, Tuesday, to the Palm Beach Post, *in regards to Shapiro's allegations. Seriously. The same guy whose committee lamented the access outsiders had to the Trojans' locker room and sidelines also told the Post that, "[Shapiro] would come by, ask to go out to practice and we would send one of our staffers to accompany him." You can't make this stuff up.*[89]

This stirred Wolff to write another open letter, this time to the president of the University of Miami, Donna Shalala; not that his conclusion had changed. "'If something is broken, we will fix it,' Foote said in '95. 'I believe and predict that the difficulties that have plagued the team in the past are history.' Because they're clearly not, you should do what President Foote didn't and drop football, at least temporarily."[90]

In the end, it took a shocking scandal at Penn State University, the true extent of which did not begin to emerge until 2011, to inflame the nation. For closing ranks to protect Joe Sandusky, the former assistant coach convicted of sexually abusing ten young male students in cases dating back to the 1990s, the college was banished from major games for four years and fined $60m; even more shamefully for many, a decade's worth of victories accrued by Joe Paterno, the most successful head coach in NCAA annals and perceived as a saintly figure until he was found to have covered up Sandusky's crimes, were annulled.

Paterno was 85 when he died in January 2012; nine months later, by when three more ex-students had claimed to have been abused by him two decades earlier, Sandusky was 68 when he was sentenced to a minimum of 30 years' imprisonment after one of his victims recounted, explicitly, at least 40 acts of inappropriate sexual contact in the showers, including wrestling matches, soap battles that led to Sandusky attempting oral and anal sex.[91] The defendant denied all charges. "About the only thing that didn't come out of his mouth was an apology," reported the Associated Press. "Mental health professionals say it's not unusual for sex offenders to avoid taking responsibility, either in a bid to get out of legal trouble or because they're in psychological denial. Prosecutor Joe McGettigan dismissed Sandusky's comments as 'a masterpiece of banal self-delusion, completely untethered from reality'."[92]

As Pete Thamel reported in the *New York Times*: "The language of the NCAA bosses who handed down the sanctions... was unrelievedly grim: the sexual abuse scandal... was the worst chapter in the history of intercollegiate athletics and a cause for universities across the country to take stock of whether their athletic [programmes] had become 'too big to fail', and thus 'a grave danger' to the values and integrity of their institutions."[93] Yet as Thamel underlined, the rise in revenue resulting from the boom in college sports "stands in contrast to the dismal financial climate in the United States and is a huge factor in considering the degree to which the Penn State scandal may or may not resonate at universities".

* * *

Addressing Jones's tweet, Dave Zirin offered his customary compassion. "'We ain't come to school to play classes' will most likely be a quote of mockery that rings through the ages. But Cardale Jones has also hit on something factual. Ohio State football, like a select sampling of the sport's aristocracy, has morphed over the last thirty years into a multi-billion dollar business. Even in the shadow of sanction and scandal, according to *Forbes Magazine*, the Buckeyes program creates $63 million in revenue every year and accounts for 73% of all the athletic department's profits."[94] Forbes also calculated that, for every game it hosts, Ohio State benefits to the tune of a sum not unadjacent to $3m.[95]

How can a supposedly amateur sport, run by educationalists, possibly be a multi-billion-dollar going concern? How, in short, can "university sport" occupy the same sentence as the p-word? To a degree, this is a cultural issue. Given that what Zirin calls "this moral cesspool" has been allowed to persist for so long, flying barefacedly in the face of every scrap of evidence, it may be concluded that Americans are not all that bothered by this seemingly blatant contradiction. Delve a bit deeper and it gets murkier still.

In 1978, Woody Hayes, the legendary Buckeyes coach, was paid $40,000; in 2012, the same post was earning Urban Meyer a *base* salary worth 100 times that; and that was before the six-figure bonuses, not forgetting handy extras such as membership to a snooty golf club and use of a private plane. Most gallingly of all, he was the highest-paid public employee in Ohio, pulling down three times the annual remuneration commanded by the state president. Nor was he alone in his conspicuous wealth: in 2012, three of his peers were on even loftier salaries. All told, at least 64 coaches were paid more than $1m that year, half of them more than double that and nine of those in excess of $3m.

Zirin, though, argued that the contradictions and confusion stem from the players ("18-22-year-olds treated like a hybrid of campus Gods and campus chattel") being "given nothing but the opportunity for an education they often have neither the time nor desire to pursue". The way he sees it, the nation is effectively telling them "to do exactly what Cardale Jones said, and 'play school'".

Sport "has gotten so disproportionate to the rest of the economy, and to the academic community, that it is unbelievable", contended an incredulous Julian Spallholz, a professor in the food and nutrition department at Texas Tech, where in 2011 the football coach Tommy Tuberville received a $550,000 raise. "This kind of disproportion in the country is why people are occupying Wall Street."[96]

6 Well-Paid Slaves: Sport and Players' Rights

Fame is a great place to visit but a lousy place to live
Peter Gabriel, musician[1]

Have we really marched this far down Cynical Street? You know when proportion has gone AWOL when a leading sportsman vows to donate every last penny of his salary to charity and is accused of perpetrating a "brilliant PR stunt". Such was the sarcastic, desultory response by Des Kelly of the *Daily Mail* in 2013 after David Beckham announced his intention to give away the £3m he was due to earn with Paris St Germain. In her deliciously wicked weekly turn as "Celebrity Watch" in *The Times*, Caitlin Moran aimed her barbs at Kelly and his grudging breed:

> *"For a global brand like that, it's peanuts," he went on – a sentiment then repeated on Twitter by a battalion of the professionally negative. Although generally averse to handing out admonishments or advice, CW hopes all those gleefully manhandling massive cynicism boners are equally vocal when someone famous does something that's actually unpleasant and/or dumb, rather than giving millions of pounds to some orphans.*[2]

Such cynicism, of course, is underpinned by envy. Not only do successful sportsfolk now pull down six-, seven- and eight-figure salaries, they achieve such riches doing something generally considered, unfairly, to be child's play. Worse, they do something most of us would kill to do – prolong youth. They do so, moreover, not only by "playing" but playing something they have played since childhood, something swishing around in their blood, something they love. Or so the theory goes. The truth, of course, is at once vastly different and appreciably more admirable.

"Yes sir." That, for a century or more, was the default reply of the professional team sportsman to orders, whether issued by coach, manager, chairman or owner. Historically, the idea of employers fixing wages or prices has rarely been a cause of public debate, but woe betide the employee who dares challenge them. It also goes without saying that, but for the hookers, the stoppers, the wicketkeepers and the point guards, spectator sport would be about as fertile a venture as tackling consommé with chopsticks. It is they who perform on stage day after day, night after night, teasing and pleasing, uplifting and downcasting, and all despite the perpetual threat of injury, even death. And all without a safety net, a second take, a stroke of Tippex, an editor or producer who knows all the knobs to press, and when, to keep one's shortcomings from wider exposure. Nothing is as live, or as alive, as spectator sport. And the players, of course, are the reason. Who pays to watch a manager or a chairman? Yet so controlling and autocratic have the administrators and owners habitually been – even the most high-handed film producer would blanch at some of the scams – this colossal debt has never been acknowledged remotely as it should. *A Well-Paid Slave*, the pitch-perfect title of Brad Snyder's biography of Curt Flood, the man who did most to change the player's lot, might well be the most accurate characterisation of the equivocal standing of the sporting hero up to the final laps of the 20th century.

Flood himself supplied the self-description. Interviewing him on ABC's *Wide World of Sports* in 1970, four days after the St Louis Cardinal outfielder had announced his decision to sue Major League Baseball for his freedom, Howard Cosell, a garrulous, self-promoting yet pin-sharp and probing broadcaster, asked him how someone earning $90,000 a year, among the game's highest salaries at the turn of that decade, could feel like a slave. The response was characteristically eloquent and thoughtful yet profoundly blunt: "A well-paid slave is nonetheless a slave."[3]

* * *

For millions upon millions sport is the passion of our youth and the enchantment of our maturity. When we watched the athletes parade in the Olympic Stadium on Friday evening, we were watching role models in the truest meaning of the term; the kind of people we might have become had we only possessed the drive, determination, and God-given talent. In the course of the next few weeks, we shall be made aware of their shortcomings. Cheats will be exposed, drug-takers will be revealed and the usual quota of scandals will become fodder for public debate. But, by and large, the good guys will win, the rascals will fade and fail and a kind of nobility will prevail. Because, stripped of its cynicism, such is the way of sport.[4]

Patrick Collins, 2012

In 1912, the world's most famous professional sportsman was a boxer, Jack Johnson. Despite losing his world heavyweight title to Gene Tunney in 1926, Jack Dempsey made $717,000[5] from the fight – more than Babe Ruth earned in his entire career; the Sultan of Swat may have earned the wrath of many of his countrymen when he signed a deal worth $80,000 for a season's work, but that still paled beside Tunney's cut. To read the top two entries on the 2012 *Forbes* list of the 100 highest-earning sportsfolk (spanning the period 1 June 2011 to 1 June 2012, encompassing prizemoney, salaries, bonuses, appearance fees, licensing and endorsements)[6] would have been to imagine that, for the lords of sport, nothing much had changed. Both were boxers, Floyd Mayweather Jr and Manny Pacquaio. From Jack Johnson to Wladimir Klitschko, the most elemental of spectator sports has always paid well for those who scale the loftiest peaks. Scan the names beneath, however, and the theme is less familiar.

Mayweather earned his entire $85m – $8m more than Leonardo Di Caprio, Hollywood's No.1 – in the ring. Contrast that with the chap in eighth place, Beckham, the highest-paid footballer, $37m of whose $46m stemmed from commercial spin-offs, let alone the one in third, Tiger Woods, only $19.4m of whose £59.4m came directly from on-course income – and that was after losing major sponsors such as Tag Heuer and Gillette in the fallout from his marital infidelities. As a further measure of the income streams now on tap, LeBron James, No.4 on the chart, gleaned a proportion of his $53m from a marketing deal with the Fenway Group, giving him a stake in Liverpool FC.

The division of spoils also made intriguing reading. Sixty-eight per cent of the top 50 hailed from five team sports (American and association football, baseball, basketball and cricket), including 14 from the NFL, eight from MLB and seven from the NBA; of the 16 top earners in individual pursuits, seven came from motorsport and three each from boxing, golf and tennis. The lone woman in the top 50 was the tennis player Maria Sharapova, whose $27.5m trailed the highest-earning actress, Kristen Stewart, by just $7m, a sum that flowed primarily from endorsements (her only female companion in the top 100 was Li Na, the Chinese tennis player whose triumph at the 2011 French Open made her the first Asian-born player ever to win a Grand Slam singles title; the upshot was no fewer than seven multi-million-dollar endorsement deals, no mean feat in a sluggish sponsorship market). That 76% of those 50 plied their trade in the US will doubtless quell any lingering doubts about the most fruitful stage in town. The presence of Sharapova, Li Na, Mahendra Singh Dhoni and Sachin Tendulkar, however, highlighted the strides made by, and potential of, Eastern Europeans and Asians.

Yet while value brings power, the gamekeepers are still bent on keeping the poachers in line. In their current bubble-world of free agency and no-trade clauses, mansions and baby Bentleys, whopping endorsement deals and stage-managed interviews, it is staggering to think how the tables have turned over the past half-century. Heartening, too. Nothing, arguably, proclaims this louder than that, in the winter of 2012-13, for the first time since Major League Baseball owners consented to salary and contract arbitration in 1974, not one of the 133 players took his claim as far as a hearing, the upshot of the clubs' increasing willingness to sign their younger players to multi-year deals.[7] Some, though, might consider the price excessively high. Lockouts and strikes have disfigured, even ended, recent seasons in all the main American team sports and more besides.

Resistance is spreading. In 2011, the basketballers of the Israeli Women's Premier League went on strike after the number of imports permitted on court was raised from three to four. Yet professional sportsfolk, it is clear, still have much to accomplish in the battle for equality, as was born out the following year, when the Federation of International Cricketers Associations (FICA) instituted legal proceedings against the Bangladesh Cricket Board, which had still to pay in full those invited to participate in their spanking new all-star T20 league. Payment was eventually made but matters had not improved overmuch by the time the Bangladesh Premier League reopened for business in January 2013. Three weeks after the agreed deadline for players to receive the first instalment (ie. 25%) of any sums due, the English batsman Owais Shah revealed that he had yet to receive a penny of his $75,000 fee. "Amateurish" was how Tim May, FICA's Texas-based Australian chief executive, characterised the BCB. "The players are very seriously considering some sort of boycott simply because there is little else they can do. They were promised 25% of their fees as soon as they arrived in Bangladesh, another 25% before the last game and the final 50% within 150 days of the end of the event. In most cases, those first payments have not been made. As for the rest of the fees the players are owed, well, good [luck] seeing that."[8] A year later, with the league's credibility further undermined by match-fixing, overseas players hired by the Chittagong Kings, such as Ravi Bopara and Ryan ten Doeschate, were still waiting.

Rebels and a clause

A week before the 1896 Ashes Test at The Oval, five home professionals, Bobby Abel, Billy Gunn, Tom Hayward, George Lohmann and Tom Richardson, understandably envious of the higher rewards commanded by the tourists, demanded £20, double the set fee; when inevitably rebuffed, they withdrew their labour. They were also motivated by the growing consternation and anger over W. G. Grace's status. "The ultimatum to the Surrey Club," observed Benny Green, "was inspired in part by a genuine sense of grievance at being underpaid, but partly also by a well-founded suspicion which could not be proven that Grace, although an amateur, was receiving payment in excess of anything the professionals were receiving."[9] A *Punch* cartoonist toasted "Fair Play, Fair Pay, and Friendliness".

The counter-offer from the Surrey committee, records Ric Sissons, was "ten pounds and expenses or they will be out of the match". Gunn's terms were simply "not accepted". The four Surrey men were summoned to a special committee meeting hours before the match was due to start, whereupon all bar Lohmann backed down, signing a statement that read, in part: "The Australians have made and are making large sums by these fixtures and it seemed to us only reasonable that we should beneficiate in a small way out of the large amount of money received...but after further consideration we wish to withdraw our refusal to play."[10]

Lohmann refused to sign the letter until he had communicated with Gunn; both were omitted from the final XI. On the third and final day of the match, 12 August, Lohmann, having been informed that Surrey would not pick him again until the issue was resolved, attended another committee meeting, where his apology was accepted and he consented to a press statement expressing his "sincere apologies" at the use of the word "demand" in the original letter of 3 August. Charles Alcock, the Surrey secretary, felt likewise, taken aback as he had been by "a peremptory demand and not a request for consideration". The players, adjudged *Wisden* the following spring, had been "right in principle" but their action had been "ill-judged and inopportune".[11]

As the Australians prepared to sail home a few weeks later, *Athletic News* published a cartoon entitled "The Motherland's Farewell", a farewell, observed James Bradley, with a "barbed edge". While it "ostensibly expressed the imperial sentiment of cultural cohesion symbolised by cricket... several of the Australians were pictured in a boat called the 'Golden Fleece' which was weighed down to the gunwales with four large sacks of gold."[12]

There was a precedent for industrial action. In 1880, bridling at the sums the touring Australians were said to be raking in from gate receipts, a practice felt by many to be beyond the pale, seven Nottinghamshire professionals, including Arthur Shrewsbury, demanded £20, double the usual fee, to play in a hastily-arranged match against the tourists at Trent Bridge, organised with typical opportunism by one of their own number, Shrewsbury's business partner Alfred Shaw. Henry Holden, the club secretary, agreed but regretted such speedy acquiescence; in a letter to each member of the professional staff, he insisted they sign a contract making themselves available for all the county's fixtures: Shaw, Shrewsbury, William Barnes, Wilfred Flowers, Fred Morley, William Scotton and John Selby demurred. In return, they demanded, among other things, that an official early-season fixture against Yorkshire the following year, organised by Shaw, be allowed to proceed. The club refused, setting in train a strike by the septet, one that would be briefly truncated by an intervention from MCC yet still linger on deep into the 1882 season. To James Lillywhite, editor of the eponymous and popular *Cricketers Annual*, it marked "a distinct and material alteration in the relations between paid cricketers and their employers which vitally affected the interests of every club of any importance".[13]

In 1896, Abel, Hayward and Richardson backed down under pressure but Gunn and Lohmann, who still holds the Test record for the lowest bowling average and strike-rate, were never picked again. Lohmann was certainly ahead of his time. "He was an atypical professional cricketer coming as he did from a middle-class background," noted the sports historian Wray Vamplew. "He was also fierce in his defence of the rights of the player in a game constrained by amateur ideals. This led to him becoming the first professional cricketer to obtain a contract which guaranteed him an income irrespective of how well he played, or indeed whether he played at all."[14]

In *Wisden*, editor Sydney Pardon published the statement released by the Surrey committee on the eve of The Oval Test, wherein the allegations against Grace received an "unqualified contradiction", and touched on the matter himself but lightly, more or less stating that "The Great Man" could do as he wished:

> *No doubt there are some abuses, but as a famous cricketer – a county captain and quite behind the scenes – has assured me that he does not know more than half-a-dozen men, playing as amateurs, who make anything out of the game, the evil would not seem to be very widespread. Mr W.G. Grace's position has for years, as everyone knows, been an anomalous one, but 'nice customs curtsey to great kings' and the work he has done in popularising cricket outweighs a hundredfold every other consideration.*[15]

Transatlantic parallels

As befits North America's first major professional sport, the battle for players' rights has been fought most persistently and strenuously in baseball. That it became the most militant of spectator sports was inevitable and just. Those who stood up to be counted, from John Montgomery Ward to Curt Flood, were all driven to do so by what some consider the least admirable example of American sporting exceptionalism: the so-called "reserve clause" which bound players to employers in a manner that could be characterised as feudal were that not too weak a word.

Imagine if your employer was not only empowered to slash your salary but they could prevent you seeking another job in the same field. Imagine if alternative employers would not approach you either, regardless of how highly you were regarded. Imagine that the only route to a new job was an involuntary overnight relocation to an office 2,000 miles away. Welcome to the wild and wacky but highly unamusing world of baseball industrial relations, and in particular the scruple-free world of the reserve clause.

* * *

John Montgomery Ward was not your common or garden professional sportsman. A graduate of Columbia Law School who wed a Broadway actress, he co-founded the Brotherhood of Professional Base Ball Players to fight against the endlessly insidious reserve clause, which kept salaries low and made each player his club's exclusive property, forever subject to an owner's whims and liable to be traded without consultation. It was Ward, too, who penned its manifesto. "There was a time when the National League stood for integrity and fair dealing. Today it stands for dollars and cents… Players have been bought, sold and exchanged as though they were sheep instead of American citizens… Like a fugitive slave law, the reserve clause denies him a harbour or a livelihood, and carries him back, bound and shackled, to the club from which he attempted to escape."[16]

When Albert Spalding and the other major league owners exhibited their contempt by fixing a maximum salary ($2,500) and renting uniforms to players, 56 major leaguers joined the Players' League under the aegis of Ward and other like-minded players. "I am for war without quarter," vowed Spalding, who was prepared to fight "until one of us drops dead" and imposed a blacklist while simultaneously striving to lure back leading lights such as King Kelly with bribes. With three leagues now to choose from – the National, the Players' and the American Association – attendances fell. The Players' League and the Brotherhood died a swift death, the National League devoured the American Association and both the monopoly and the reserve clause remained. "Like every other form of business enterprise," declaimed Spalding, "Base Ball depends for results on two interdependent divisions, the one to have absolute control of the system, and the other to engage in… the actual work of production."[17]

* * *

A parallel can be drawn between the reserve clause and the retain-and-transfer system favoured in English football since 1893. At the turn of the century, League players comprised the filling in a sandwich squeezed by the prejudiced patricians of the FA, who detested the very idea of professionalism, and the Football League, run primarily by businessmen and industrialists who abhorred sharing gate receipts. The League's first two decades had seen the clubs paying players as much or as little as they wished, but in 1900 a maximum weekly wage of £4 was imposed (worth £322 in 2012).

"What is more reasonable than our plea that the footballer, with his uncertain career, should have the best money he can earn?" wondered Manchester City's peerless Billy Meredith, the "Welsh Wizard", who also happened to be a pioneer of the sporting endorsement ("Grand Central Railway posters before the 1904 FA Cup final," writes Huw Richards in the *Cambridge Companion to Football*, "carried a marketing message purportedly from Meredith, plus a picture of him firing the winning goal into the top left-hand corner of Bolton's net. Matching life to art, he scored the only goal at Crystal Palace by doing precisely that."[18]). "If I can earn £7 per week," added Meredith, "should I be debarred from receiving it?" Absolutely, according to the League.

Inevitably, despite the wage ceiling, irregularities proliferated. More than half a dozen clubs were fined, including Manchester City and Middlesbrough, whose 1905 purchase of Alf Common from their north-east neighbours Sunderland for an unheard-of £1,000 – at a time when transfer fees ranged between £300 and £500 – prompted sceptical shareholders to investigate the accounts and report the club to the FA.[19] Meredith conceded not only that he had been paid £6 by City in 1902, but that after that FA Cup triumph two years later he had received bonuses amounting to £53.[20] In 1905, anonymous allegations led to him being found guilty of attempting to bribe an Aston Villa player; in implicating his employers during a further FA investigation in 1906, he turned the spotlight on City, 17 of whose players, past and present, were fined and banned for life from playing for the club. According to his biographer John Harding, whose research into early football has been invaluable, the unproven accusations transformed "a taciturn but essentially contented man into a bitterly aggressive critic"[21] bent on improving the players' lot.

At Manchester's Imperial Hotel on 2 December 1908, soon after he had completed his 18-month ban and transplanted his considerable wares to the red half of the city, Meredith convened the first meeting of the Association of Football Players' and Trainers' Union, whose title was commonly abridged to exclude its less prominent members. A few months later, while the AFPU was seeking membership of the General Federation of Trade Unions, the FA withdrew recognition, then responded to the ensuing strike threat by banning its members from the start of the following season, whereupon membership withered precipitously. Widely referred to as "Outcasts FC", the most vocal loyalists came from Manchester United, Meredith among them; when insufficient amateur replacements were found, the club's opening fixture was at severe risk. The deadlock ended when Tim Coleman, the Everton forward, pledged his support, emboldening his peers. The union was re-recognised and agreement was reached whereby players could be paid bonuses to supplement the maximum wage.

The first, ill-fated challenge to retain-and-transfer came in 1912, when the AFPU backed an attempt by Herbert Kingaby, formerly of Aston Villa, to have the standard contract declared a restraint of trade, but the case was lost and the union almost went bankrupt.

* * *

In the spring of 1911 baseball's finest were roused once more when Addie Joss, a formidable and popular 31-year-old pitcher with the Cleveland Naps, collapsed after an exhibition game and died 11 days later from the illness he had tried so hard to disguise – meningitis. Grieving teammates voted unanimously to miss the next day's game in Detroit and pay their respects. The Naps owner persuaded Ban Johnson that it would do the game's image few favours were the American League president to order them to play, so the game was postponed, but the episode underscored the players' insecurity and resentment, most notably for the reserve clause. One extreme consequence, as we have seen, was the inability of certain players to resist the lure of gamblers in the interests of an easy extra buck. "The employer tries to starve out the labourer, and the labourer tries to ruin the employer's business," reasoned the pre-eminent pitcher, Walter Johnson. "They quarrel over a bone and rend each other like coyotes… our business philosophy is that of the wolf pack."[22]

In 1912, the players formed the Fraternity of Professional Base Ball Players of America, their goals twofold: terminate the reserve clause with extreme prejudice and secure a larger – i.e. more appropriate – share of the profits. Not unexpectedly, the owners ignored them. The result was the Federal League.

When Clem met Peter

We want to see tough, formidable characters – the guys you love to hate… As soon as someone gets a bit of fire in the belly – not argy-bargy, but a bit of sledging or lip, a bit of aggro in the game – it gets stamped out so quickly. People then judge those guys, who get nailed. So what ends up happening is that people go into their shell and are too afraid to express themselves.

Shane Warne[23]

I like a bit of mongrel myself, whether it's a man or a dog.

George Bernard Shaw

On the whole, successful Australian sportsmen don't do mild, much less meek. Hence that great Australian leg-spinner Shane Warne's bristling lament shortly before the 2013 Ashes series. The local preference is for another m-word: mongrel. As in "he's got a bit of mongrel". Clem Hill had his fair share.

In 1905, in the wake of the country's federation, the Australian Board of Control was founded, triggering not one but two bitter cricketing power struggles: one of the inter-state variety, one pitting players against boards. In 1912, the antipathy between Hill, Australia's captain, and Peter McAlister, a fellow selector, culminated in a fistfight that resulted in Hill, Warwick Armstrong and four more of the nation's leading players, the "Big Six", missing the impending tour of England.[24]

The players were adamant: they had the right to choose the tour manager, and nominated Frank Laver, in his forties but still a prolific bowler. They also accused the Board of Control of being unjust and malign, a stance supported by the South Australian Cricket Association but opposed by the mighty Melbourne Cricket Club. Amid talk of an independent tour of England – a financial and logistical nightmare and hence a non-starter – a boycott by the "Big Six" gathered weighty public support. Thus it was that the 1911-12 Ashes tour by England was plagued by an undercurrent of hostility in the home camp. Small wonder England won each of the last four Tests.

Before the fourth Test, Hill sent a telegram to McAlister asserting that the team should include Charlie Macartney, injured freakishly after a net pole fell on his head, and suggesting that two teammates, Amstrong and the ageing batting maestro Victor Trumper, help him make his decision. McAlister cabled back, suggesting Hill himself be dropped. "Quoted in isolation, as it invariably is," wrote Armstrong's biographer, Gideon Haigh, "McAlister's wire seems the utmost provocation: one who'd never made a Test fifty advising a captain with eight hundreds to stand aside. In context it is more comprehensible: the response of someone already affronted. Yet it was McAlister's high-handed resistance to the co-option of Armstrong and Trumper in the selection process that irked Hill as much as, if not more than, the final tactlessness."[25] At a team meeting convened by Hill, it was determined that the half-dozen players deemed certain-ties to tour England – himself, Armstrong, Trumper, Hanson Carter, Albert "Tibby" Cotter and Vernon Rainsford – should lead any protest. "In a nod, perhaps, to Ambrose Pratt's popular 1911 adventure novel *The Big Five*," wrote Haigh, "they would be known to posterity as the 'Big Six'."[26]

Two weeks later, George Crouch was appointed tour manager instead of Laver. The tension was heightened by Jim Kyle, a highly thought of Victorian fast bowler who had been quoted by a newspaper reporter complaining that he had been dropped for the state's game against the tourists for being loyal to his rebellious captain, Armstrong: never would Kyle represent his state again.

Unsurprisingly, the board were not about to allow the players to dictate who should manage the Ashes tour, not least given that the post drew 70 applications. Laver, moreover, was felt to have been disloyal to his employer during the 1909 tour, questions having been raised as to whether the players under his charge were playing for themselves or the board – and by extension, or so the mandarins liked to think, their country.

The selection meeting convened at Sydney's Bull's Chambers in the first week of February, bringing together the antagonists in that telegram tiff. Heated words were exchanged by McAlister, who had had no compunction in voting himself on to that 1909 Ashes tour, and Hill, whose brazen refusal to sign his tour contract had diminished Laver in the board's eyes; Clem struck his fellow selector in the face, then resigned from the committee. One of the telegrams that poured in to Hill offered him $600 to fight Jack Johnson, the world heavyweight champion. "Hip Hip," began another, "Only regret blighter still living."[27] He and the rest of the Big Six also withdrew their services for the remaining two Tests. "They must be patriotic and fight for their country when called upon to do so," commended "Plum" Warner, the convalescing England captain, diplomatically disguising his delight at the prospect of another facile victory. In the event, all the rebels played in that fourth Test. Each was accorded a sympathetic ovation; Hill, according to the umpire Bob Crockett, arrived at the crease with tears in his eyes. All bar Cotter participated in the final Test, too, but none sailed to England.

That several eminent books of cricketing scholarship have ignored this episode altogether – including the thickest and purportedly most comprehensive of them all, *Barclays World of Cricket* – offers more than sufficient evidence of the distaste of sport's chroniclers for players' rights. To be fair, even Hill barely touched on the affair, contenting himself to a quote from Warner's tour book: "Men cannot show their best form amid an atmosphere of trouble, uncertainty and misunderstanding."[28]

A Tale of Two Jimmys (And a George)

By the 1950s the boot money game in England had grown more sophisticated: four parts Hush Puppies to six parts Cuban heels. Football League gate takings were understated and the players benefited – as, conveniently, did the club's tax liability. Not until 1974 would the game emulate cricket and abolish the distinction between amateurs and professionals; before that unacclaimed day, a more meaningful battle had to be won.

At the turn of 1958, the Football League management committee reneged on a promised new pay deal under which players would be guaranteed £20 per week all-year round, adjusting the figure to £17 plus £3 per first-team appearance. "It was smack-in-the-eye day," reported the *Daily Mirror.*[29] Instead of receiving 2.5% of any transfer fee paid for their services, moreover, players would be entitled to a maximum of £300. "Some players will undoubtedly think they would be better off in a lower division, where they would be certain of a first-team place at £3 a time," reasoned Jimmy Hill, the charismatic, loquacious and media-savvy chairman of the Professional Footballers' Association – the new name for the AFPU. "Surely this kills incentive to get to the top."[30]

At the heart of the ruckus lay television. Although matches had been brought to British hearths in 1936, followed two years later by the game's first live broadcast, and despite the FA's continued willingness to authorise the broadcasting of international fixtures, the Football League resisted granting its assent to the screening of highlights, much less live coverage, fearing the impact on attendances. Two developments in that decade had made the game more attractive to viewers: the launch of BBC's *Sportsview* in 1954 and the arrival of floodlights – Southampton were the first to erect permanent pylons in 1950. It was the growth of evening games that first occupied the union, focusing minds as it did on the question of extra payments.

* * *

In 1945, with professional football in England due to resume action after the Second World War, the Football League had rejected the AFPU's demand for a minimum wage of £8; a strike was only averted when the union accepted a £1 increase on 1939 pay levels while securing the introduction of bonuses: £2 for a win, £1 for a draw.

This, then, was the climate in which Jimmy Guthrie, a fiery Scottish socialist, became chairman of the AFPU. In 1943, as Portsmouth captain, he had written a plaintive letter to the union secretary, Jimmy Fay, summarising the growing resentment: "The football player has been hard hit and I am sure no one will deny that 30 [shillings] is a very meagre sum. Many players are having a very hard time making ends meet... All we ask for is a square deal. I don't think we are getting one."[31] The maximum wage had nothing whatsoever in common with a square deal, not least since players stood to gain nothing from transfers unless they were both good enough and fortunate enough to attract interest from continental Europe. And even though the wage ceiling had risen to £15 a week by the mid-1950s, the average wage was only around half that.[32]

That this ancient and flagrantly unfair imposition was finally consigned to history in 1961 was due in no small measure to Guthrie. From 1946 to 1957, he toiled long and hard as chairman of the AFPU to transform the players' association into a fully-fledged, respected trade union with a London base, bringing it to the Trades Union Congress in 1955 – for the first time since 1909. It was there that he characterised his members as "the last bonded men in Britain".

FIX THESE FACES IN YOUR MEMORY

EIGHT MEN CHARGED WITH SELLING OUT BASEBALL

Early doors: Spectators at the Eton v Harrow match (*top*) take the afternoon air at Lord's, 1895; W. G. Grace (*left*), the first sporting superstar, a professional masquerading as a gentleman; the Chicago White Sox (*above*), aka the 'Black Sox', the best team in baseball in 1919, driven to throw the World Series by their Scrooge-like owner Charlie Comiskey

Ringmasters: Charles Alcock (*above*), the man behind the FA Cup, the Ashes and international football; Henri Delaunay (*right*), footballing trailblazer, a leading figure in France's immense contribution to the evolution of international sport; "Slavery" Avery Brundage (*below*), a staunch proponent of amateurism whose prejudices and intransigence sullied the Olympic Games

Race men (1): Jack Johnson (*right*), the first African-American world heavyweight boxing champion, demonised and hounded by white America; Learie Constantine (*below, second from right*), the great Trinidadian cricketer who would be made a Lord in recognition of his work in British race relations, leads out a Commonwealth XI against England at Lord's in 1944

Race men (2): Jesse Owens (*above*) after receiving one of his four Olympic gold medals at the 1936 'Propaganda Games' in Berlin, confounding Adolf Hitler's claims of Aryan supremacy (note Nazi salutes), but soon fell on hard times; Tommie Smith and John Carlos (*left*) make their Black Power salute at the 1968 Olympics, sport's most reverberant political statement, and suffered grievously for it

Prophets with honour and without: Don Bradman (*right*), the greatest sportsman of all and an enduring symbol of Australian nationhood; Fred Perry (*below*), Britain's only Wimbledon men's singles champion between 1936 and 2013 but ostracised for turning professional

Race men (3): Jackie Robinson (*above*, with Brooklyn Dodgers' owner Branch Rickey) endured the racism of opponents and even teammates when he became the 20th century's first black major league baseball player; Basil D'Oliveira (*left*) brought the iniquities of apartheid to the world's attention, earning the love of millions of Englishmen as well as Nelson Mandela's gratitude

Dark days: Emily Davison (*above*), a courageous suffragette, was killed trying to stop the King's horse at the 1913 Derby; Jim Clark (*right*), widely regarded as one of the greatest F1 drivers, fell victim to the callous regard for safety at Hockenheim in 1968; the 1989 Hillsborough disaster (*below*) saw 96 Liverpool FC supporters die – not until 2012 was the official cause confirmed

Sexual liberation: Mildred 'Babe' Didrikson (*left*), all-rounder supreme, multiple Olympic medallist and the first woman to compete on the men's PGA Tour; Martina Navratilova (*above*, with her rival and friend, Chris Evert), the queen of tennis, advanced the cause of lesbians in sport; Justin Fashanu (*below*) came out in 1990 but suffered cruelly for his bravery

Guthrie had been further stirred by the sudden exit from League football of Frank Brennan, an imposing central defender celebrated by Newcastle United fans as the "Rock of Gibraltar". In 1955, Brennan won an FA Cup-winner's medal only to plummet speedily into non-league obscurity at North Shields: having the gall to reject a pay cut was the lesser crime; he had opened a sports shop in direct competition with Stan Seymour, a powerful Newcastle director. More than 2,000 fans packed the City Hall to pass a vote of no-confidence in the board.

"We seek your help to smash a system under which now, in this year of 1955, human beings are bought and sold like cattle," continued Guthrie in his address to the TUC, "a system which, as in feudal times, ties men to one master or, if he rebels, stops him from getting another job. The conditions of the professional footballer's employment are akin to slavery. They smirch the name of English democracy."[33] Having had no option but to accept this inequitable system or quit, Brennan, he stressed, had had the courage to take the latter course.

During his tenure, Guthrie achieved no end of small miracles, from regular maximum wage increases, a provident fund and a players' charter of rights right down to a union magazine; his ultimate ambition was to devise a membership package incorporating insurance, healthcare, legal advice and pensions.[34] Adamant that his members should be paid an additional sum for playing at night, he brokered a deal worth £2 to £3 per televised outing. "It was this," the website of the AFPU's successor, the Professional Footballers' Association, would record, "that would lead, unwittingly, to the union receiving a bonanza from TV rights some decades later."[35]

Guthrie's methods, though, "were often slapdash", while a "tendency to commit scarce union funds to schemes that sometimes flopped" troubled senior figures. After a disagreement over an insurance scheme, Guthrie was voted off the management committee, ostensibly because, unlike secretary Fay, he could not be paid. Jimmy Hill succeeded him, and was soon embroiled in the so-called Sunderland Affair, which saw several

Roker Park regulars being permanently suspended for refusing to answer questions about under-the-counter payments. Hill and his committee demanded a major inquiry and organised a petition: those who had accepted illegal fees were especially urged to sign. The Football League relented, reducing the bans to fines. Nonetheless, the days of the maximum wage were plainly numbered.

Under-the-table payments were also in vogue to dissuade English players from joining the small but budding exodus to Europe, led by John Charles, the so-called "Gentle Giant", who joined Juventus from Leeds United for a then record British record fee of £50,000, and was adored in Italy. The abolition of the maximum wage, states Anthony King in *End of the Terraces: The Transformation of English Football*, stemmed from its palpable incompatibility with progress in wider society, particularly "in the context of the increasing affluence of Keynesian society". Hill's central argument, cannily spelled out in the press, was threefold: 1) Players had fallen *behind* average working-class earnings, leaving them being paid less than those who watched them; 2) The maximum wage was illegitimate because, rather than be regarded as working-class, they really ought to be treated as professionals in the entertainment business; 3) They should have complete freedom of contract.[36]

Harvesting rock-solid support from players and press, Hill knew he could bring the League to an unprecedented stand-still. It also helped the cause appreciably that, being an active player of some repute with Fulham, not to mention far more at ease around journalists, he offered such a refreshing antidote to the homburg-wearing, cigar-chomping grumps who ran English football while indulging themselves in circumspect, riddle-ridden language. His pronounced chin, decorated by a jaunty beard, didn't hurt either: how the cartoonists adored him. Few were surprised when he went on to ground-breaking success after joining lowly Coventry City as manager later in 1961. In taking the unfashionable Midlands club from Third Division to First he coined a new nickname, The Sky Blues, and spearheaded the so-called "Sky Blue Revolution", pioneering pre-match entertainment and matchday magazines, and even composing the club song (tune courtesy, probably sardonically, of The Eton Boating Song).

"In all fairness, just think a moment and work out how much your football costs you on a Saturday afternoon," Hill suggested to readers of *Striking For Soccer*, his account of the events of 1961. "I know how much you might pay on London Transport or Corporation transport going to the ground. If you call in at the local on the way to the match and you've got two or three pals with you, it's going to cost you a few shillings… if you are honest you will admit that the three shillings which you pay to stand on the terracing represents only a small part of the amount of money you spend in connection with attending a football match."[37]

* * *

At the time, amid the acres of newsprint devoted to the £100-a-week contract Fulham teammate Johnny Haynes achieved thanks to Hill, it was quickly forgotten that the PFA's list of demands to the League in 1961 was actually headed by the even more ancient retain-and-transfer system: abolish it or, at the very least, perform rapid and radical surgery. But what on earth would happen, the clubs wondered fearfully, should the transfer system they regarded as their economic lifejacket be drowned? "It was this fear of the unknown," relates the PFA's own account, "that led the League to pull off a shamefully audacious coup."

> *Like the players' representatives, the Football League management committee gave the impression that they were free to negotiate and any agreement between the two parties would be binding. So when League president Joe Richards finally shook hands with Jimmy Hill in full view of the nation's press as a last-minute "historic agreement" was reached, Hill thought he was shaking hands on the deal there and then, which included radical changes to the contract system as well as the lifting of the ceiling on wages.*

> *It was the latter item that hit the headlines the following day.*
> *Fulham chairman Tommy Trinder had made the extravagant*
> *claim that he would pay Haynes £100 a week if the maximum*
> *was scrapped. This is what the press chose to concentrate on,*
> *while the rest of the deal seemed to have been forgotten. When,*
> *some months later, a full meeting of League clubs simply threw*
> *out the key aspects of the 'agreement' relating to contracts – in*
> *effect reneging on what Richards had brokered – the publicity*
> *caravan had moved on.*[38]

With clubs now at full stretch to pay wages that came remotely close to capturing the players' commercial value, retain-and-transfer came under renewed and unreturnable fire in 1963 when George Eastham, supported by Hill and Cliff Lloyd, the PFA secretary, took Newcastle United to the High Court. Eastham's contract had expired, and he had wanted to move to Arsenal, but although Newcastle had finally granted the necessary approval by the time the case reached court, he persisted, convinced that a principle was at stake.

The omens were inauspicious: after all, this was the first challenge to the system since 1912. Coolly and crucially, Lloyd was persuasiveness personified as he countered claims that terminating retain-and-transfer would impact disastrously on competition and the professional game as a whole; Newcastle's initial decision to deny Eastham his desired transfer was adjudged an unreasonable restraint of trade. From now on, the club holding a player's registration could only retain it by offering him a new contract that was at the very least equally rewarding and definitely of no shorter duration (almost invariably one or two years). Yet not until the introduction of the Players Standard Contract in 1981 would players be permitted to request a transfer when their contracts expired.

Sports Law, an authoritative and oft-updated compendium first published in Britain in 1998, cites the Eastham case as the first to demonstrate "the susceptibility of sports governing bodies to attack on the basis of restraint of trade".[39] Judge Wilberforce's ruling certainly carried a potentially chilling message for every unenlightened sporting authority – i.e. the vast majority:

> *The system is an employers' system, set up in an industry where the employers have succeeded in establishing a united monolithic front all over the world, and where it is clear that for the purpose of negotiation the employers are vastly more strongly organised than the employees. No doubt the employers … consider [it] a good system, but this does not prevent the court from considering whether it goes further than is reasonably necessary to protect their legitimate interests.*[40]

The Pilic Affair

If Jan Kodes is Czechoslovakia's second best known male tennis player after Ivan Lendl, this has less to do with the fact that he won the Wimbledon men's singles title in 1973 than that he did so after 79 fellow competitors withdrew in support of another child of an Iron Curtain state, Yugoslavia's Nikki Pilic. Unlike them, Kodes wasn't a union man. The Association of Tennis Professionals, he would reflect in his 2010 memoir, was still "in diapers". Even today, "they are still able to pull out [the] Pilic scandal with a threatening tone. It became a precedent for dealing with player frictions."[41]

According to Richard Evans, the "funniest thing" about the formation of the ATP, "which signalled the beginning of the end for the amateur officials who liked to think they ran the game, was that it was those very same officials who instigated it".[42] So long did tennis take to dignify professionalism, as soon as the players started receiving their just desserts over rather than under the table, further ructions with administrators were inevitable. The first attempt to form a players' union was made in the early 1960s by Ken Rosewall, Earl "Butch" Bucholz, an American Davis Cup player and later one of Lamar Hunt's "Handsome Eight", and Tony Trabert, a retired five-time grand slam winner. Rendered redundant by Hunt's World Championship Tennis and the advent of official professionalism, it was followed at the end of the decade by the shortlived International Tennis Players' Association, the brainchild of John Newcombe – who would succeed Rod Laver, his fellow Australian, as world No.1 – and Charlie Pasarell, the volatile American.

They were foiled by the US Lawn Tennis Association, whose indoor championships were then promoted by Bill Riordan. Attending an early ITPA meeting during the 1970 US Open, Riordan blithely informed Newcombe and Pasarell that he "represented all the players who were not represented by Dell or [Mark] McCormack", the leading players' agents. "After a long meeting," remembered Pasarell, "it became obvious we were not on the same wavelength so the whole thing sort of fell apart."[43] Riordan went on to manage the early career of Jimmy Connors, around whom he devised a series of lucrative but misleadingly labelled "winner-take-all" televised matches which – the promoter subsequently confessed while preparing to take Connors to court for breach of contract in 1977 – had involved guaranteed fees rather than prizemoney.

Brokered by Kramer and Dell, peace broke out between the USLTA and WCT in April 1972, vitalising the players. In Caesar's Palace the following month, Dell addressed them, ramming home the sore need for an association and how to accomplish it. The upshot was the ATP. That winter, executive director Jack Kramer and legal adviser Dell flew hither and thither trying to win over the amateur officials, urging unity. Kramer had a close ally in Philippe Chatrier, then president of the French LTA, but Allan Heyman, the ILTF president, was intent on continuing to run the professional game and the brewing explosion erupted in the so-called "Pilic Affair".

In May 1973, Yugoslavia were due to meet New Zealand in a Davis Cup tie; not unnaturally, the head of the national tennis association, General Korac, wanted Pilic, the country's No.1, to participate – not least because he happened to have married his niece. Denying the general's claim that he had "categorically" agreed to play, Pilic declined: as a WCT player, he would have defied his contract had he failed to compete in the doubles playoffs scheduled in Montreal for the same weekend as the New Zealand tie. Korac suspended him for nine months, but although the ILTF was obliged to support this, Chatrier and Dell pressurised Heyman; Pilic was allowed to play in the French Open and presently had his ban slashed to a single month.

Frank Keating captured him with customary brio: "Pilic certainly did not like umpires and was a lean-boned and lissom athlete on court; off it he could be broodily dark and explosive. He thought anyone who even looked like a hippie should be shot, preferably through the heart by him... A few years after the boycott it was snowing outside the Royal Albert Hall for an evening tournament in December and Pilic emerged from the picturesque car-park gloaming in a great long leather coat and carrying his rackets like rifles. For a moment it seemed one was living a Tolstoy novel."[44]

Pilic's fellow players were enraged. During the Italian Open in Rome, more than 40 ATP members signed a statement expressing their willingness to boycott any tournament from which Pilic was barred – even Wimbledon, now just a month away. In Nottingham the following week, a further 20 signed; in Hamburg, a score or more said they would enter Wimbledon but walk out on the opening day. Cliff Drysdale, South African pioneer of the double-fisted backhand and now ATP president, tried in vain to persuade Heyman to appoint an independent arbitrator. Kramer flew into London and fell foul of the local press. "Kramer Should Resign!" roared a headline in the *Daily Express*. "Stupid! The Money-Mad Stars of Tennis!" spluttered another, this time in the *Evening News*. The editorial that apparently justified such an assertion read, in part: "It is time to go home Mr Kramer. Leave us to enjoy the game the way we like it. Clean."[45]

Keating, then "legman" for David Gray, *The Guardian*'s chief tennis correspondent, found himself squirming as he spent those tumultuous days "legging it between Wimbledon, Queen's Club and the Gloucester and Westbury hotels where the warring parties were assembled". In 12 months "just about every regular professional player outside the Iron Curtain (whose national federations paradoxically denied any truck with unions) had signed up with the ATP but the ILTF confidently fancied it could split the union's confraternity at this very first challenge simply because every player wanted to compete in the 'world championship', that is on the strawberry fields of London SW19. How wrong could it get? But it was a close-run thing."[46]

Harassed and exhausted, Pilic volunteered to withdraw from the Wimbledon draw (in which 80 ATP members were due to feature) and flew back to Split, but there was no turning back for his confreres, who knew such a gesture would be pointless and self-defeating. How typical of the chasm separating the warring parties that when Arthur Ashe, the ATP vice-president, had the audacity to spend an extra 15 minutes practising at Queen's Club, an official harangued him in a tone that was some distance from courteous.

On the Wednesday before Wimbledon commenced, the seven-strong ATP council voted for an immediate boycott, a decision that would see Kramer banned from BBC commentary duties *sine die*. "We were so conscious of the momentous decision we had taken," Ashe recalled, "that we all decided to go home and sleep on it and come back and have another vote the following day."[47] It was a blow, Chatrier would inform Evans many years later, from which the ILTF could not recover. "And so it came to pass," proclaimed Keating, "and 79 players made immediate plans to fly home. England's No.1 Roger Taylor, an ATP founder, agonised before putting Queen's and All England first – and his fellow members decently sympathised but fined him £2,000. The Romanian Ilie Nastase claimed he had been ordered personally by his president Ceausescu to play but his compatriot Ion Tiriac sneered that Nastase had forged the letter and could not produce it, so the ATP fined 'Nasty' £2,000, too."[48]

"Although the ATP was to squander the position it had earned for itself, the battle had not... been fought in vain," summed up Evans. "From it grew the idea of a professional council to administer the world-wide sport, which was growing at such a rate and in so many different directions that the idea of [ILTF secretary Basil] Reay and a rotating part-time president trying to run it all from Barons Court was ludicrous."[49]

Crash Test Dummies

Blaming their tools may be a time-honoured custom among inadequate workers but some alibis hold more water than others. At an emotionally charged meeting on the eve of the 2013 German Grand Prix, the Grand Prix Drivers Association threatened to strike: confidence in the durability of their cars' tyres had been punctured. That there had been no fatalities in the previous race at Silverstone, scene of five serious blowouts, had owed more or less everything to sheer luck. How apt that the scene of this rebellion should be the Nurbürgring, where a considerably more neglected generation of drivers had walked out just before the 1970 race. Half a dozen years later, in the wake of Niki Lauda's near-fatal crash, they resolved to have nothing whatsoever to do with the circuit Jackie Stewart dubbed "The Green Hell". Only major reconstruction had restored grands prix to the venue in 1984. "There were six issues with the tyres," Jenson Button, one of the GPDA's three directors, lamented there 29 years later. "Once, you can go, OK, but six – it's a lot."[50] You could only admire his self-restraint.

A few hours earlier, Button and his fellow drivers had stood up as one in a nearby cinema, delivering an ovation. They had just seen *Rush*, Ron Howard's cockle-chilling film about the deep-thinking Lauda and James Hunt, the flamboyant English playboy who when asked by Stirling Moss, another daring British driver of an earlier vintage, to reveal the secret of his success, replied pauselessly: "Big balls." Their duel for the 1976 F1 crown saw the latter prevail at the very last and the former all but surrender his life (he was read the last rites). Here was both rivalry and, having shared a one-bedroom flat in London early in their careers, friendship. With dreadful irony, it was Hunt who lived faster and died far younger, suffering a fatal heart attack at 45.

Now chairman of the Mercedes team, Lauda was at the screening, still scarred by the fireball that engulfed his Ferrari at the Nurbürgring after he had pleaded forlornly with his fellow drivers to pull out of a race requiring competitors to navigate a 14.7-mile rollercoaster of a circuit with more than 170 corners and, as Stewart observed with the last word in ruefulness, "15 takeoffs". As Lauda watched his team practise 37 years later, how he must have envied their good fortune to compete in a more safety-conscious age.

* * *

It is surely a fact to be celebrated, however demurely, that sports-folk had, by the final quarter of the 20th century, managed to develop sufficient resolve, principle and muscle to cause events to be cancelled. No band of sporting rebels, though, has ever had a cause quite as incontrovertible as the speed junkies of Formula 1, whose uprising so emboldened others.

Staking one's life on the efficiency of a machine is also never less than a perilous business. That motorcyclists still choose to tackle the dastardly bends and unsettling hills of the Isle of Man TT, a killing field for more than a century, can nonetheless diminish compassion. Sympathy for their four-wheel brethren comes even harder. In the case of Formula 1, unlike the more blue-collar NASCAR, they are surrounded by the obscenely wealthy. They are also paid a pretty penny (or a dashing dollar). In 2011, Dale Earnhardt Jr., earned $28m, while three other NASCAR luminaries pulled in more than $20m; by the time Michael Schumacher, the seven-time F1 champion, retired for the first time in 2006, he had accumulated an estimated $800m; in 2010-11, by when he had returned to the wheel, salary, bonuses, prize money, appearance fees, licensing and endorsements were allowing him, in the 12 months ending 1 May 2011, to earn $34m; of the top 15 earners in sport at that juncture according to *Forbes*, three were from F1 – Schumacher, Fernando Alonso and Lewis Hamilton.[51]

No other competitors in spectator sport risk their lives so readily or regularly as the four-wheelers, not even those TT death-sniffers. At the time of writing, since the F1 championship began in 1950, 47 drivers had lost their lives, either in grands prix, practice or non-Championship events; the death of Dan Wheldon in October 2011 took NASCAR's casualties to 53. While safety measures have steadily reduced the fatalities – F1 saw 15 in the 1950s, 14 in the 1960s, 12 in the 1970s, four in the 1980s and two in the 1990s, and none since Ayrton Senna in 1994 – the threat remains omnipresent. All of which made it desperately hard to forgive those behind "Crashgate", a despicable scandal at the 2008 Singapore Grand Prix wherein Renault instructed Nelsinho Piquet Jr., the son of a former F1 champion, to help Alonso's title aspirations by causing a crash. Two years later, after team principal Flavio Briatore had vehemently denied the allegations from Piquet père and fils, accusing them of blackmail, the High Court ordered Renault to pay substantial damages for libel.

When he passed away in 2012, obituaries of Dr Sid Watkins, the eminent neurosurgeon who became the official F1 doctor in 1978, listed the lives saved by the Liverpudlian they called "The Prof": Rubens Barrichello, Gerhard Berger, Martin Donnelly, Karl Wendlinger and Mika Hakkinen, whose heart he twice restarted before performing a trackside crycothyrotomy. I am unaware of any other sport, moreover, that has crowned a posthumous world champion, as F1 did in 1970. Jochen Rindt, a gifted and driven German racing, somewhat mysteriously, with an Austrian licence, had already promised his wife he would retire if he won the title that season when, with two races to come, he died after swerving into a crash barrier during practice for the Italian Grand Prix. A court ruled that the barrier had not been properly installed.

Watkins was also centre-stage for an even graver tragedy. During practice for the 1994 San Marino Grand Prix, Roland Ratzenberger died and Barrichello barely survived. The latter's close scrape plainly spooked Senna, Barrichello's fellow Brazilian. This prompted Watkins, a personal friend, to suggest Senna retire there and then and accompany him on a fishing trip. Senna resisted; within a few minutes of the start, in a seemingly preordained outcome captured chillingly in *Senna*, an electrifying if dreadfully sombre 2010 documentary, one of the most recklessly dazzling drivers of all had crashed, fatally. Even if Senna's approach to his trade – though it would be more accurate to call it his calling – was not beyond reproach, the waste was as wanton as it was criminal.

* * *

The dilemma faced by F1 drivers in the 1960s was that the greater speeds facilitated by advances in car manufacturing were not matched by any enthusiasm on the part of those running grand prix circuits to make them safer, much less supply adequate marshalling or medical assistance. Seeking improvements in the wake of a spate of fatal crashes between 1958 and 1960, the GPDA was founded in May 1961; four months later, Wolfgang Von Trips was denied the world title when he was killed at Monza.

Stewart had every reason to emerge as the GDPA's most militant voice. In 1968, his good friend and fellow Scot, Jim Clark, acclaimed as the era's finest F1 driver, left the track and collided fatally with a tree during a Formula 2 race at Hockenheim in Germany. That same day, Stewart had been inspecting a circuit near Madrid, politely requesting the removal of unnecessary hazards at key points and posing questions such as "Does that telegraph pole have to be there, right beside the track at the exit of the corner?" or "Could those trees be removed please?" The response, he recalls, "was sometimes constructive but often obstructive". At Brands Hatch that same year, the authorities were asked to install a crash barrier to protect competitors from an array of trees beside the track. "It's not necessary," came the heartless reply. "They're only small trees."[52]

Two years before Clark's demise, another near-fatal accident in heavy rain at Belgium's notorious Spa Francorchamps circuit had persuaded Stewart to campaign for more humane working conditions:

In similar conditions at a F1 Grand prix today, yellow flags would be waved to indicate the hazards ahead, enabling the drivers to proceed with care. There was no warning system in 1966. I was lying third when I reached the Masta Straight, with only John Surtees and Jochen Rindt ahead of me… I headed towards the Masta Kink, a right-left-right swerve in the middle of the straight. I drove into a river of water at 170mph, immediately lost control… and aquaplaned off the tarmac. My car had effectively become a missile and it proceeded to flatten both a woodcutter's hut and a telegraph pole before careering over an eight-foot drop and finishing on the lower patio of a farmhouse. The chassis of the car was severely bent around me. What had prevented me from smashing into a tree and being instantly killed? Good fortune, that's all.[53]

For 25 minutes Stewart was trapped. With no apparent regard whatsoever for their own safety, he was dragged out by two fellow drivers, England's courtly Graham Hill, a firm friend, and Bob Bondurant, an American who'd been incredibly lucky to escape unscathed himself just a few minutes earlier. Stewart's reflections cast no positive light at all on those who should have been attending to their safety.

Graham and Bob got me out using the spanners from a specta-tor's toolkit. There were no doctors and there was nowhere to put me. They in fact put me in the back of a van. Eventually an ambulance took me to a first aid spot near the control tower and I was left on a stretcher, on the floor, surrounded by cigarette ends. I was put into an ambulance with a police escort and the police escort lost the ambulance, and the ambulance didn't know how to get to Liège. At the time they thought I had a spinal injury. As it turned out, I wasn't seriously injured, but they didn't know that. I realised that if this was the best we had there was something sadly wrong: things wrong with the race track, the cars, the medical side, the fire-fighting, and the emergency crews. There were also grass banks that were launch pads, things you went straight into, trees that were unprotected and so on. It was ridiculous.[54]

From then on, until quick-release steering wheels became a standard, Stewart always taped his own spanner inside the cockpit.

To some, the chief villain was Colin Chapman, the creative brains behind Lotus. The innovative London engine designer built the most competitive cars of the age; from 1963 to 1978, with Clark, Hill, Rindt and Mario Andretti at the wheel, Lotus won seven constructors' and six drivers' titles. It may be concluded, given their choice of profession, that dying at the wheel was a price Clark and Rindt were prepared to pay; that Chapman seemed prepared to allow them to pay it is more troubling. His philosophy was simple and unscrupulous: the lighter the car the better. If this made them more fragile, well, nobody was forcing anyone to drive them. That, though, does not defend the times his cars were not properly tested.

Come the end of a decade aptly characterised in the title of a recent BBC documentary as "The Killing Years", fear had bred fury. "We began to ask every track owner to have these potentially life-saving barriers installed around their circuits," remembers Stewart. "The GPDA also started to demand that every F1 driver should be compelled to don flameproof overalls, thermal underwear, officially certified helmets, six-point safety belts or harnesses, and high-quality thermal socks and gloves to provide effective protection against burns. Through 1968 and 1969, we resembled dogs with a bone. In every interview, at every opportunity, we raised the issue of safety, alternating dire warnings with new demands. At one stage, the team owners said they agreed with everything we were saying but asked if we couldn't give the circuits more time to make the changes. No, we said, because that could be one year too long for some driver, and his widow and his family."[55]

The campaign was identified with Stewart, who copped enormous flak from some of Britain's less empathetic souls. The following letter, signed by one T. C. W. Peacock and published in a motoring magazine, gives a flavour of the grotesque objections:

There is little in motor racing today for which I can thank Stewart. I have enjoyed the motor racing scene less since he arrived rattling his money box and waving his petitions... It is unthinkable for any professional to accept the challenge and then try to change the rules to make it all safe and cosy. This is plain cheating. Perhaps this insecure, driver, diarist and emotional motorist should concern himself with the less dangerous but equally lucrative world of entertainment.[56]

At length, there was no option but to down tools. In 1969, the drivers' concerns about the Francorchamps track led them to boycott the Belgian Grand Prix; the following season, they did the same at the Nürburgring, forcing the German Grand Prix to be switched to Hockenheim. In 1973, they refused to compete at Spa unless safety measures were implemented – along with the Nurbürgring, this was one of the circuit's two most prestigious circuits, so such a move, recollects Stewart, was deemed to be "sacrilege". The race was switched to Zolder, where the tarmac broke up during practice; after the drivers vowed not to proceed until repairs were made, they were done overnight.

Yet still the fatalities mounted. The death at the 1973 US Grand Prix of Francois Cevert, his Tyrell teammate and protégé, seared deep into Stewart's soul; he retired that season. No longer, he said, did he have any desire to see friends and colleagues die. He had decided, nonetheless, to step down months earlier. Helen, his wife, felt the decision was his alone to make, but his choice of work was having a deleterious impact on his young son, Paul. Stewart's friend Jo Bonnier, whose sons attended the same Swiss school as Paul (as did Natasha Rindt, daughter of Jochen), had died following a collision at Le Mans in 1972, whereupon Kim Bonnier told Paul, "Your father's going to be next."

The following season, almost inevitably, had brought a swift reminder that even strong cars with good mechanics can be deadly. During practice for the South African Grand Prix, Stewart braked to no avail while approaching a corner at 176mph. Veering "violently" off the track, he sped towards an eight-foot high concrete wall. "For the first and only time in my racing career, I thought this was going to be the end. In those few milliseconds of crisis, when everything seemed to be happening in slow motion, I had one of the most unusual experiences of my life. I literally seemed to come out of my own body and I distinctly recall feeling as though I was looking down on myself as I fought to get the car under control. Even now, I can still hear the noise of the car going off the track and the noise of the car being torn apart as it ploughed through the three lines of chain-link fencing, which, ironically, in my role as GPDA president, I had asked to be installed to retard the velocity of the car in a situation exactly like this."[57] The car came to rest against the wall. He had been saved by the fencing.

Less fortunate was Roger Williamson, the promising young British driver who crashed fatally during that season's Dutch Grand Prix amid the sand dunes of Zandvoort. As he lay trapped in the fiercely flaming husk of his car, David Purley stopped his own vehicle and attempted the forlorn task of rescuing him. Televised live across the world, the aftermath is even more intensely shocking when viewed today. As Purley struggles fruitlessly to extinguish the fire, an act of selflessness that would win him the George Medal for bravery, a solitary marshal stands by, clueless and useless. As the minutes drag on, there is no sign whatsoever of an ambulance. Meanwhile, as the smoke billows across the track, obscuring visibility, the show goes on.

The GPDA had attained "extraordinary power and influence", claimed Stewart, but 1973 proved to be a high-water mark as the FIA "and other parties" gradually removed the GPDA's teeth.[58] On the plus side, the rising importance of sponsorship eventually left the sport with little option but to clean up its act. This would take time, but whether it was Marlboro, John Player or Durex, who wanted their brand associated with death (or at least any more than was strictly necessary)?

Stewart handed the torch to Watkins. Upon his appointment as F1's chief medical officer the latter insisted on treating the drivers as family. Distrust evaporated when it soon became abundantly clear that he felt trackside facilities were woefully inadequate. He had not long been in the job when Ronnie Peterson died the day after his car burst into flames following a crash on the very first lap of another Italian Grand Prix: not for fully 18 minutes did an ambulance arrive. Watkins immediately demanded that Bernie Ecclestone, chief executive of the F1 Constructors' Association, henceforth provide improved equipment, an anaesthetist, a medical car and a medical helicopter. Other deaths followed before such belated innovations begat a safer environment. At the 1985 British Grand Prix, the drivers presented Watkins, now president of the medical commission appointed by FISA, the governing body, with a silver trophy. "To the Prof," began the inscription, "our thanks for your valuable contribution to Formula 1. Nice to know you're there."[59]

It is a measure of Watkins' impact that the GPDA was disbanded in 1982, only to be revived after that tragic 1994 San Marino Grand Prix. Just hours beforehand, with the most savage of ironies, the drivers had not only proposed reforming the GPDA but had appointed Senna as one of its directors.

Miller time

If 1966 is engraved on the memory of even those English men or women who weren't actually born by then, it was no less memorable, if probably a mite less pleasurable, for baseball-smitten Americans. That was the year the Major League Baseball Players Association, seeking a new leader and, far more important, inspiration, approached two starkly contrasting candidates. One was Richard Nixon, then best-known as a failed Republican presidential candidate. Another was Marvin Miller, a 49-year-old lawyer from New York moulded and hardened by his years working for the United Steelworkers Union. Lovers of counter-factual history would have a field day mapping out the plot had Tricky Dicky not declined, insisting he had bigger fish to fry.

Miller's arrival, as the union's face, voice, cheerleader and all-round mastermind, ushered in a veritable workers revolution, encompassing free agency, spiralling salaries and eight strikes in 30 seasons. When he joined the MLBPA, the average salary was $19,000; by the time he left that relentlessly hot seat in 1982, having incurred the wrath of millions who had yet to comprehend why a young man required a commensurate wage as a reward for entertaining them doing something they would happily have done for nothing, it had soared to $241,000.[60] Public approval, never more than tentative, would wane as the average salary soared into the multi-millions; Miller wasn't in the least bit surprised.

To Jim Bunning, the Philadelphia Phillies pitcher and later US senator who approached Nixon on the union's behalf, Miller was baseball's Moses, the man who led the players "out of the land of bondage".[61] If baseball could erect its own Mount Rushmore, contended the historian Bill James, Miller's craggy likeness would be there. According to Jim Bouton, the former New York Yankees pitcher and author of *Ball Four,* the 1970 book that lifted the lid on jock culture, today's players should thank him every time they accomplish a key hit: "Instead of pointing to the sky [they] should be pointing to Marvin Miller." As should everyone who now plays sport for a living.

"Succeeding generations of players know so much more about trade unionism, solidarity and what it can produce than their predecessors did," said Miller three decades later when asked to cite his foremost source of professional pride. "I'm proudest of the fact that I've been retired for almost 29 years at this point and there are knowledgeable observers who say that this might still be the strongest union in the country. I think that's a great legacy."[62] Miller's death the following year prompted an impassioned tribute on ThanksMarvin.com, a website set up by former major leaguers: "Marvin led us from a history of no rights to parity with the owners. Most of us were very respectful of our opportunity to play a sport for a living, and certainly didn't want to offend our employers. But Marvin pointed out how grossly unjust the situation was. With grace and dignity, he slowly but surely led us into a position of equality."[63]

Raised during the Depression, motivation came early for Miller. "All through the early 1930s, my father, who was a retail store salesman, saw the businesses that employed him go downhill and all through the Depression, my father got more and more anxious and concerned and I was old enough to be aware of all of that... you couldn't help but observe the breadlines, the increase of the number of people begging in the streets, the people selling apples." His parents became active trade unionists. "I have a very early memory of going to a store where [my father] was working and finding him on a picket line. Also my mother... became one of the early members of the city's teachers' union. As the thirties progressed and the [Congress of Industrial Organisations] and industrial unions formed, everybody was aware of the ferment of the [labour] movement."[64]

Not until Miller took the bull by the proverbial horns did major leaguers start to build an effective bulwark against management. In 1946, Robert Murphy, a labour lawyer, announced the inception of a new players' union: its chief targets were salary arbitration and a minimum wage ($6,500 per annum) and, furthermore, that half the proceeds from the sale of a player should go to the owner of the hands and legs concerned. After the owners offered $5,000 and a pension plan the renewed militancy soon subsided. That same season, 18 major leaguers accepted handsome offers to defect to the spanking new Mexican League, the brainchild of Jorge Pasqual, a liquor dealer. However, wrote Ken Burns and Geoffrey Ward, "ceaseless rain, interminable bus rides, spicy food, erratic lighting and odd playing conditions (railway tracks ran through one outfield)" quickly combined to drive the rump of the defectors back home, where they were blacklisted for five years for showing "avowed Communistic tendencies".[65] Four of the suspendees threatened to take the owners to court, and hence test the reserve clause, persuading the owners to settle out of court rather than risk losing their precious antitrust exemption. At length, echoing Spalding in 1891, an amnesty was declared.

Miller came to the job knowing full well the scale of the task before him. In 1966, five years after the maximum wage was abolished in English soccer, the minimum major league salary was $6,000, an advance of just $1,000 on 1947. In the 1950s, Ralph Kiner of the Pittsburgh Pirates headed the home-run hitters one season then accepted a pay cut the next. In the wake of the 1972 work stoppage that would so drastically alter the balance of power, Vida Blue, a formidable young pitcher for the Oakland Athletics and recipient of the previous year's two highest accolades in the American League – the Cy Young and Most Valuable Player awards – walked out of the club and joined a plumbing company. Even when he relented, he failed to secure the salary he was seeking. Close observers insisted he was never the same player again.

Historically speaking, far from backing the Robin Hoods against the Sheriffs of Nottingham, many journalists had happily supported the owners. For decades, after all, the latter had been paying their travel and hotel expenses; the post-match drinks and buffet were almost invariably all a homesick hack could desire. Some decried Miller as that most un-American of beasts – a communist; reporters such as Dick Young seldom stinted in their attacks on his motives and integrity. Nor did the owners roll out the welcome carpet with any perceptible enthusiasm.

"In the airport [after a game]," Miller would recall, "I bumped into American League president Joe Cronin... When my flight was finally announced, he said: 'Young man, I've got some advice for you that I want you to remember.' Young man? I was forty-nine years old. The advice? 'Players come and go, but the owners stay on forever.' I would remember his remark, but not for the reasons he wanted. As much as any single statement I'd hear, it reflected the prevailing attitude of baseball's brass... He had completely misunderstood me, my motivations, and my means of operating. Basically he was saying, 'Watch me and you'll understand what it takes to stick in baseball. If you don't play ball with the owners, you'll be gone.'"

Within a decade, the owners were whistling a less cocky tune. The first players' strike came in 1972, the prize improved pension benefits; Miller's mastery of the law proved decisive. As it did in 1975, the year the words "free" and "agency" entered the dictionary as a combination. There were further strikes in 1976 and 1981, again both successful. Bit by bit, the fans, while disgruntled by the inaction, came to suspect and distrust management even more. Free agency in baseball – which preceded the equivalent in American football by more than a decade and a half – was one of the most critical developments in sporting history. Miller likened working conditions prior to 1976 to "a plantation". Players were chattels. A century after the birth of the reserve clause, they still had no choice as to where or for whom they could play.

Miller's main assets, reflected Howard Bryant in his vital, superbly researched book *Juicing the Game: Drugs, Power, and the Fight for the Soul of Major League Baseball*, was that he was a devotee who, rather than telling the players what they wanted to hear, preferred to educate them. He "fought issues so miniscule it seemed their only purpose was to tip the power balance in the players' direction".[66] Take, for instance, a luncheon held by the Archdiocese of New York. The then Yankees owner George Steinbrenner – the shipping magnate from Cleveland turned erratic omnipresence and enthusiastic sacker of managers satirised affectionately by *Seinfeld* – had insisted his players attend; four refused, so Steinbrenner fined them $500 apiece. Miller wrote Cardinal Cooke a letter explaining his position and filed an official grievance. He did the same after a Houston Astros player was fined for not holding his cap over his heart during the National Anthem.

"Each victory," wrote Bryant "underscored exactly how unjust the system had been for so long; with each defeat, the owners drew more scorn from the public and from the very press that years earlier tended to defend ownership."[67] Murray Chass of the *New York Times* highlighted Miller's willingness to spend time with the media, especially the press, explaining the salient issues and thus engendering greater understanding of, and compassion for, the players. "He took the time to educate," Chass told Bryant. "The owners hated that. They thought he had the players brainwashed. All he did was challenge them to look at the facts...People said I sided with the union. I didn't see it that way. I tended to believe the side that never lied to me. They didn't lie. The owners did."[68]

Flood warning

In 1969, Curt Flood, one of the leading lights of the powerful St Louis Cardinals, the major leagues' most multiracial club, defied a century of subservience by refusing to consent to a proposed trade to the Philadelphia Phillies. Contrary to its jealously guarded self-image, Philadelphia, the "City of Brotherly Love", was in reality a mite short on goodwill to all men. In 1947, when Jackie Robinson embarked on his major league career, nowhere did the racial epithets fly thicker and faster.

For the next few years, as his biographer Snyder, a lawyer by trade, related, Flood battled tirelessly to overturn the decision in America's highest courts of law, seeking the overthrow of the reserve clause. Flood knew, as Miller had warned, that this would probably end his career. It did just that in 1972. Flood lost a 5-2 verdict in the Supreme Court, his cause undermined by the reluctance of his understandably fearful fellow players to testify on his behalf. Yet joyless as those efforts proved, his articulate persistence publicised the outrageous flaws in the system.

In *Curt Flood In The Media*, Abraham Iqbal Khan suggests, with good reason, that his subject was impelled not by the greater good but by his own sense of what was right for him; he also proposes, with less good reason, that his importance has been exaggerated. Flood's stand made free agency inevitable. The creaking reserve clause was riddled with holes by 1975, the year an arbitration panel upheld a player's right to finish the final year of his contract and then sell himself to the highest bidder; free agency followed the next year, the immediate beneficiaries a pair of pitchers, Andy Messersmith and Dave McNally. Not for another 20 years would Jean-Marc Bosman achieve the same for the world's most popular spectator sport.

Flood lived some of his remaining years in exile, in Europe, but was by no means forgotten. The MLBPA paid a hefty share of his medical bills after he revealed that he was dying of throat cancer in 1995, and lacked the funds to pay for treatment. At his funeral, the Reverend Jesse Jackson gave one of the addresses: "Baseball is better. And people are better. America is better... Thank God that Curt Flood came this way. I love you Curt."[69] Another speaker was George Will, whom Flood had remembered writing a glowingly supportive article about him in 1993. The column finished with the following poignant words: "[Flood] once said, 'I am pleased that God made my skin black, but I wish He had made it thicker.' Friends of baseball, and of freedom, are pleased that He didn't."[70]

Not long after his death in January 1997, two days after what would have been his 59th birthday, Flood's name was enshrined in law. For more than a century, thanks to the reserve clause, baseball had been exempt from the laws that govern all other American businesses. The Curt Flood Act of 1998, however, hammered one small nail into the coffin of this anachronism, removing the antitrust exemption as it applied to labour negotiations. That said, the impact of this is felt to have been minimal: even now, the game remains above general antitrust laws. By 2006, Congress had considered the issue no fewer than 60 times since 1950; the Flood Act remains the closest it has come to tangible, meaningful progress. Worryingly, the owners supported it. Most economists concur: Congress should, at the very least, limit this unique privilege.

Yet for all their vast and valiant contributions, at the time of Miller's death in November 2012, neither he nor Flood, scandalously, had been elected to the Baseball Hall of Fame. Then again, in 2008, Miller had taken the unprecedented step of writing to the Hall committee and telling its members where they could jolly well put their nomination:

> *The anti-union bias of the powers who control the Hall has consistently prevented recognition of the historic significance of the changes to baseball brought about by collective bargaining... I find myself unwilling to contemplate one more rigged Veterans Committee whose members are handpicked to reach a particular outcome while offering a pretense of a democratic vote. It is an insult to baseball fans, historians, sports writers, and especially to those baseball players who sacrificed and brought the game into the 21st century. At the age of 91 I can do without a farce.*[71]

Collusion

A scarcely credible ruse that ultimately and justly netted the players a far from insubstantial fortune in back pay, the appalling saga over collusion stemmed from the baseball owners' collective refusal to sign any free agents between 1985 and 1987. The aim, no doubt, was to give the uppity players' union, and Miller especially, a bloody nose; in effect, argued Miller, what the owners actually did was refuse to strengthen their teams, thereby agreeing, in effect, to pre-determine the destiny of the season's spoils. A fix by any other name.

This so disgusted Andre Dawson, a star outfielder with the Montreal Expos whose knee problems had made him desperate to leave the Stade Olympique's unyielding artifical turf, that he told the Chicago Cubs he would play for them in 1987 for whatever they fancied paying: he accepted a one-year salary of $500,000, less than a third of what he would otherwise have been worth as a free agent. Livid, the players' union filed a formal grievance in February 1986, then again in February 1987 and again in January 1988.

Thomas Roberts, the original arbitrator, and George Nicolau, his successor, pored over the mass of evidence culled from 71 days of hearings. As a precedent, the players were reliant on the 1977 Collective Bargaining Agreement, in which they had agreed not to work together to put pressure on an owner, thus averting a repeat of the joint-walkout before the 1966 season by

Sandy Koufax and Don Drysdale, the celebrated Los Angeles Dodgers pitchers; in return, the owners had agreed not to collude among themselves. Roberts and Nicolau both found for the players. When the case was finally settled in 1987, the owners paid a suitably dear price: $280m.

The issue resurfaced after both the 2002 and 2003 seasons, when, according to the authoritative website baseball-reference.com, players alleged that there were "improprieties in the negotiation of certain free agent contracts that pointed to collusion among owners".[72] In 2006, the owners agreed to make a lump-sum payment of $12m, drawn from luxury-tax funds, to settle dozens of claims and pending grievances. Nothing came of subsequent allegations but the damage had been done. In a lengthy examination of collusion in *The Wayne Law Review*, published in 2008, Marc Edelman quoted Fay Vincent, the former MLB commissioner: "The effects from collusion so thoroughly polluted the whole relationship between the union and the owners that the impact is still being felt." Vincent made especial mention of his successor, Bud Selig, and Jerry Reinsdorf, owner of the Chicago White Sox, "two ringleaders of collusion", for being "adamant in saying [baseball] owners need to violate the [Collective Bargaining Agreement] and take away from players what they had fairly bargained to have".[73]

Not that collusion was remotely new. As Miller claimed in his trenchant autobiography, *A Whole New Ball Game*, a book as important as any ever written about the competitive arts, it had long been "an everyday part of baseball". Witness salaries, he suggested. "There had been an unwritten rule for years (a collusive 'understanding') that said no player... would be paid more than $100,000 a year... [and] each club agreed not to talk to any player who belonged to another club; violators were to suffer stiff penalties." Then there was the reserve clause, and, most shameful of all, the owners' unwritten pact not to sign black players, a collusion that spanned almost the entire first half of the 20th century. We will return to this shameless terrain.

The slaves get angry

> *The World Series, the American institution that survived two*
> *world wars, the Great Depression and a Canadian winner,*
> *succumbed to union action yesterday when the moribund*
> *1994 season was officially declared dead. With the players'*
> *strike in its 34th day, the acting baseball commissioner, Bud*
> *Selig, called off the remainder of the season following the*
> *loss of 433 games and almost $300m (£196m) in revenue.*
> *The national pastime, played more than a century ago by the*
> *troops of Robert E Lee and Ulysses S Grant, was halted in*
> *modern fashion – by fax.*[74]

The 2004-05 NHL strike, which erased the entirety of the league's
88th season, did not register all that high on the Richter scale of
hold-the-back-page drama. Partly because ice hockey languishes
a distant fourth among North America's most popular team
sports, and partly because of what began on 12 August 1994.

That day, at the height of one of the most engrossing major
league baseball seasons for years, with longstanding records
being threatened and surprise contenders mocking the form-
book, brought the most infamous outbreak yet of sporting
coitus interruptus: all 700 members of the MLBPA downed tools.
A month later, Selig bowed to the inevitable and cancelled the
World Series. The most significant labour dispute in sporting
history had begun, not in a communist republic or a socialist
state or a Trotskyite cell in Sweden, but in the front garden
of the royal palace of full-blooded, no-holds-barred, surviv-
al-of-the-absolute-fittest capitalism. Following as it did the rise
and entrenchment of the players' association as possibly the
world's best-known, wealthiest and most powerful trade union,
the players' strike of 1994 can be seen as the most un-American
sporting saga of all.

The cause – the owners' unilateral decision to impose a
salary cap, something the union believed, understandably,
would damage its members' freedom to earn their true market
worth – found a nation divided. Given that the negotiations

were widely seen as a trial of strength between management and workers, albeit with the added twist of celebrity, 24-hour media coverage and oodles of money, nobody could quite decide whom they should despise more fervently. In surveys, most fans roasted the players for being plain greedy. The *average* salary – and remember that we are talking about 30 teams here, each with 25-man rosters that might change personnel a dozen times a season – was more than £1m. Even more respondents likened the owners to 13th-century English barons: dictatorial, stubborn, unreasonable and probably even greedier. After all, many of those fellows, among them the men who also owned McDonald's and Blockbuster, were already billionaires.

"For those in baseball who lived through it," wrote Bryant, "1994 represented a demarcating line between the old baseball and the new... If it had always been a business, now it was a game for corporations. The reality was that the strike was much harder to gauge in the long term. If anything, subsequent years proved that it was not so devastating after all." Recalled Rich Levin, baseball's top public relations man: "It was bad, don't get me wrong. It was like a pox on both your houses. The fan's attitude was, 'I don't care who's right and who's wrong. You're both assholes.' But I never thought the game was on life support."[75]

What happened in August 1994 was the culmination of all Miller's victories, large and small. There could be no question, though, that the strike – whose climax saw President Bill Clinton intervene in search of peace, and was only settled when a New York judge found the owners guilty of negotiating in poor faith – remains, to date, sport's most divisive and damaging slice of industrial action. Or should have been.

Yet somehow, unfashionable, unhip and unhinged as it was, baseball made a remarkably swift recovery for a seemingly terminal patient, courtesy of an epidemic of milestones, spiced by the addition of inter-league games and an extra tier of playoffs. This was, however, a rebirth fuelled to a considerable degree by performance-enhancing drugs, as was confirmed by 2007's Mitchell Report, which fingered nearly 100 culprits.

That said, a portion of the blame for baseball's long-running steroid opera can be traced to the union's resistance – thinking the issue was recreational drugs – to dope-testing, for which the repercussions are still being felt. In August 2013, MLB, having already suspended five players for their links to Biogenesis of America, a defunct anti-ageing clinic in South Florida accused of distributing banned PEDs, slapped bans of at least 50 games on a further 13, three of whom had played in the previous month's showpiece All-Star Game. Not since Judge Landis banished the Chicago Eight, or so it was reported, had so many major league miscreants been punished in a single day. The lone appellant was Alex Rodriguez, the second-best-paid player in team sport behind Kobe Bryant but whose reputation had so declined that, since confessing to having used steroids between 2001 and 2003, his nickname had mutated from "A-Rod" to "A-Fraud". On the verge of his first outing of the season after a hip injury had necessitated a four-month layoff, the then 37-year-old New York Yankees third baseman, scheduled to earn $29.5m in 2013 (just shy of $1m less than Bryant), was suspended without pay for the remainder of the season and the entire 2014 campaign (though he was allowed to play on until the appeal had been heard).

Even more culpable was the misguided decision by President Clinton to sign the 1994 Dietary Supplements Health and Education Act (DSHEA). Designed to provide a broader range of legally available remedies, it enabled potential offenders to skirt the 1990 Anabolic Steroids Act by reversing the burden of proof: instead of drug companies being obliged to prove the safety of their products, the responsibility would lie with the Food and Drug Administration to prove they were unsafe.

Miller, meanwhile, hoisted the standard to the last. The public perception of the owners v athletes debate, he added, remained the same as when his mission began.

We know that the players have become wealthy, but no one says that there's $8 billion in revenue. There's no mention of that, no mention of the fact that if you did a simple subtraction,

revenue is $8 billion and players' salaries were something like
$3 billion. You only concentrate on one side of the table and you
give people a false impression. And that's terrible.[76]

The Bosman Ruling

Where America leads, the world so often plods behind. In
December 1995, the European Court of Justice struck a powerful
if belated blow for the continent's professional sportsfolk by
sanctioning free agency. Thwarted in his bid to move from Club
de Liège to Dunkerque, Jean-Marc Bosman, an unprepossessing
Belgian footballer, had decided he wasn't ready to take no for an
answer, and his courage and persistence were duly rewarded.
So, too, his patience – the verdict came fully five years after he
instigated the case.

The ramifications were far greater than even the club owners
feared, though a chat with their baseball counterparts would have
prepared them better. Pre-Bosman, players could only change
employers if the two clubs concerned consented, and agreed a
fee for his services (though free transfers were common); post-
Bosman, footballers and others became free agents once their
contract expired. Pre-Bosman, UEFA regulations limited teams
to fielding three overseas players in European competition;
post-Bosman, the sight of Chelsea, Arsenal or Benfica fielding
entirely foreign-born teams was anything but uncommon.
Pre-Bosman, agents were largely peripheral figures, luxuries
for the leading lights only; post-Bosman, the Ten Percenters ran
the show. Pre-Bosman, salaries, while rising, could be held in
check; post-Bosman, they exploded. And it was the supporters
who did much to finance them, via rocketing admission prices
and TV subscriptions.

For the already lavishly-heeled, this was good news.
Buttressed by the economic boom triggered by the formation of
the Premier League, the import-heavy English clubs enjoyed a
renaissance in the Champions League. But as the stakes rose, so
did the casualties. While the rich got richer, some clubs, notably
Leeds United and Portsmouth, overreached, banking, literally,

on continued success – the one thing not even money can guarantee. Scores of highly-paid players went wage-less. Deprived of transfer income, further depleted by the collapse of deals with ITV Digital and Setanta, and with debts only temporarily eased by "parachute" payments following relegation, even those who had enjoyed the early fruits of the boom plummeted into the nether divisions. As UEFA's chief executive Lars-Christer Olsson apprised the BBC's Tom Fordyce: "Those clubs who had access to all the money started to rob the smaller clubs, not just to get stronger themselves but to weaken the opposition." Yet even the giants did not prove immune. Most shocking of all, in 2012, Glasgow Rangers plunged into administration owing an estimated £134m.

Whichever way you looked at it, the gulf between European and American sport was shrinking fast. The main difference was that European clubs, for whom relegation was a perpetual threat, were not shielded by their protectionist leagues. Whether that makes for better sport is probably a question of taste.

As for the determined agent provocateur himself, football's Curt Flood reaped little. Bosman was 25 when he embarked on his case only to be stranded in limbo while it wound its course. A year after his victory, he was forced to quit his latest club, third division Vise, because, he said, he could no longer make a living from the game. By 2011, he was living on benefits and antidepressants. "I have made the world of football rich and I find myself with nothing," he lamented. "I cried tears of blood because of it, I suffered enormously and I've never had recognition from players."[77] His lawyer, Luc Misson, told Fordyce: "He gave his career to a court case to serve a cause, but he sees that the transfer fees are still there, quotas on home-grown players are making a comeback and the rich clubs are richer and the poor ones are poorer."

Freelancelots

"The Indian Premier League is not about cricket. It is about money." So asserted Richard Gillis, a business journalist and sometime cricket correspondent of the *Irish Times*, shortly after that first, resoundingly successful IPL season. "Its defining moment took place not on the field of play but in a Mumbai hotel where the best players in the world lined up to be bought by India's new business elite, mobile phone magnates and Bollywood actors; the media buzz began to dissipate only when the cricket started."[78] Here was a world utterly alien to cricket: a player auction for a domestic tournament worth far more to a player than a Test series. More than any other team sport, cricket has long been about country first, club second; the IPL relocated the goalposts. It also added considerably to the WICB's in-tray.

The unprecedented size of those contracts – Kevin Pietersen and Andrew Flintoff soon secured six-week deals worth $1.5m – left the most marketable players in unprecedented control over their own destiny. Fixture clashes between the IPL and the international schedule at least gave them a choice: committing to the IPL could mean losing international match fees – or even the "central" contract which tied them to their home board rather than their club, a transformation that had begun in Australia before enveloping the rest of the international circuit. This dilemma posed especial difficulties for those qualified to play for England, where the start of the season coincided with the IPL.

Flintoff and Pietersen compromised, agreeing to participate in the IPL for three weeks and hence not miss any England games; unlike them, however, Kieron Pollard played for the West Indies, an international team that offered nothing like the same rewards, much less financial security. Indeed, poorer national boards, such as those of Sri Lanka and West Indies, accepted the new economic reality, and the shift in the players' priorities. Sri Lanka actually cancelled their tour of England in 2009 because almost their entire first-choice XI had won IPL contracts. The addition of another BCCI brainchild, the T20 Champions League, supplemented by other T20 leagues, left cats and pigeons on even more familiar terms.

Born in Trinidad, Pollard and his two sisters were raised by their poor single mother. "There are a lot of criminal activities, and stuff like that," he recalled. "Being the eldest, I was the one who had to go to school in order to have a better life."[79] On his first-class debut against Barbados he gave notice of the immense power of his strokes with 126 off 71 balls, and was soon called up to the West Indies' one-day side. Failing to impose his talent, he was contemplating the scrapheap by mid-2009: unlike his counterparts in England, India and Australia, he couldn't earn a living playing at the lower professional level in his country of origin. "Yes, I wasn't performing," he told the *Daily Telegraph*'s Jonathan Liew. "But afterwards, nobody called or said anything. If I had given myself until 25 and not made it big, I would have gone back to school and become a law enforcer. So my only way out was to get back into the West Indies team by playing for Trinidad. Luckily enough, they had just qualified for the Champions League."

The final of that tournament, in Hyderabad in October 2009, changed Pollard's life. When he took guard, Trinidad needed 80 from seven overs to beat New South Wales. Less than half an hour later, the game was won with nine balls to spare, Pollard having walloped 54 off a mere 18 balls. "The rewards came after that one innings. It just got out of my imagination. I got a call from the IPL, something I had wanted to join before but couldn't get a sniff. Then a contract in Australia. Then an English contract." He was on his way to becoming the first professional cricketer to become a millionaire without playing a Test match.

By 2011, Pollard had four freelance gigs, with Trinidad, Mumbai, South Australia and Somerset. "I don't think anyone who had those things coming towards them would not take it. With the situation I was in, with my family, it was a decision I had to make. People have said a lot of things: 'T20 freelancer', 'it's only about the money'. But my instinct is to provide and to play cricket. My two sisters are still at school, my mum is still at home, and I provide for every one of them. I told my mum that she doesn't have to work now."

The most controversial freelancer, though, has been the consummately laid-back Jamaican, Chris Gayle, whose boldness at the top of the order was as valuable a commodity as any in the game as the Noughties ended. In 2011, he was a double-barreled shotgun for hire in T20 leagues in Bangladesh, India, Zimbabwe and Australia; in the last, he actually turned out for *two* sides, Sydney Thunder and Western Warriors. Praise was considerably thinner on the ground when he confessed, during the 2009 West Indies tour of England, that he "wouldn't be so sad" if T20 superceded Test matches. Meanwhile, criticism of the coach, Ottis Gibson, saw Gayle, West Indies captain from 2007 to 2010, begin a year-long international exile after the 2011 World Cup; it took an intervention by Baldwin Spencer, Antigua's prime minister and chairman of CARICOM's Prime Ministerial Sub-Committee on Cricket, to end the impasse.

Yet while this meant foregoing his impending county stint with Somerset, Gayle was in a sufficiently powerful position to insist on two conditions: 1) he would not be subject to any victimisation or discrimination by the West Indies Cricket Board or its employees, and 2) be permitted to fulfil his current IPL contract, barring him from participating in the remaining two Tests of the Australian tour of the Caribbean.[80] He eventually returned to the fold in June 2012, joining the West Indies tour of England just in time to see Dinesh Ramdin reach 100 in the Edgbaston Test and celebrate by brandishing a handwritten note directed at one of his sternest critics, Sir Viv Richards: "Yea Viv talk nah." In the Sky Sports commentary box, one of Sir Viv's former teammates, Michael Holding, made his disgust plain; more painfully for Ramdin, the match referee, Roshan Mahanama, fined him a slice of his match fee. It was an incident that suggested the critics wanted to have their cake and not only eat it but demand another slice. On the one hand, Sir Hilary Beckles, one of the Caribbean's most respected academics and a non-executive member of the West Indies board (who in 2014 would work alongside 14 Caribbean heads of state in pursuing reparations from their erstwhile British masters), had railed against Gayle, claiming that cricket in the islands had been "hijacked by an uncaring cabal of mercenary moneyseekers, players without attachment to traditional sources of societal concerns". Yet here was Ramdin being fined for displaying his commitment.

The Bangladesh Premier League's laxity over payments, together with the 11th-hour cancellation of the 2013 Sri Lanka Premier League (not one of whose eight franchises paid the tournament fee or the bank guarantees for player payments), suggest that the T20 bubble is likelier to burst than inflate further. The questions nonetheless remain. Has the pendulum swung too far? Has it swung as far as it needed to? Time alone will tell, though it is a measure of the way this issue splits participants and observers alike to suggest, without wishing to be flippant, that it may well boil down to your notion of fair play.

The next war zone

> *In an industry where the employer is carting money, the players have the lowest salaries in any team sport in America, the lowest pensions, the worst collective bargaining agreement, the shortest careers, and the worst and most serious disability rate. And nobody is explaining that. And even Obama, when he gets asked, goes into cliché mode. "Oh, I think the owners and players are sufficiently capable of dividing up $9 billion." He contributes nothing to what's going on. In fact, he obscures it.*
>
> **Marvin Miller on the NFL, 2011**[81]

At one stage, as the franchise owners locked out the players from training camps, it looked as though the 2011 NFL season would be the first to be disrupted since a 24-day strike in 1987. Asked to consent to an extended 18-game season and various other onerous conditions, the Players' Association dug in its collective heels and, less than 48 hours before the latest final deadline, executive director DeMaurice Smith announced that the two extra games were now off the agenda and then insisted that there would be no significant financial "givebacks" unless the owners opened their books. The latter resisted, claiming that they had already furnished the union with more than enough financial information. Meanwhile, the NFL commissioner, Roger

Goodell, announced that a lockout would see his salary plunge from $10m to $1m, which prompted no sympathy whatsoever.

This was a dispute again characterised by many, including Barack Obama, as a struggle between billionaires and millionaires. This, argued Zirin, "is a ridiculous act of moral equivalency where none exists" – an echo of a previous White House incumbent's disdain for the MLB strike. "Here's the reality. You have thirty-one of the richest people in the United States – people with generational wealth – going against a workforce with careers that last just 3.4 years. It's a workforce that draws almost exclusively from poorer socio-economic backgrounds. It's a workforce that will die more than twenty years earlier than the typical American male."[82]

Peace, after a fashion, broke out a month before the new season. The regular-season schedule remained at 16 games but the players came off worse. Under the old deal, revenues were split roughly 50-50 between owners and players; the new agreement shifted the balance to 53:47. A team salary cap of about £73.6m, including bonuses, was imposed, and something similar for the next two seasons. A new salary system would be introduced to deal with the issue of rookies' pay; players would be granted unrestricted free agency after four seasons with a club, up from three under the old deal. "We didn't get everything that either side wanted… but we did arrive at a deal that we think is fair and balanced," said Smith. "Our guys stood together when nobody thought we would."[83]

But how much does America care about those players and, more specifically, the bodies they put on the line for the nation's entertainment, bodies whose average shelf-life is shorter than the unrestricted NFL free-agent eligibility requirement of four years? Not a lot, judging by California's Assembly Bill 1309. Hence the co-authored op-ed piece in the *San Francisco Chronicle* in June 2013 wherein Tom Brady and Drew Brees voiced their opposition. If passed, the bill would entitle out-of-state workers – from Hollywood stars to migrant farmers – to sue for compensation if hurt in action, yet California lawmakers wanted to deny these rights to NFL players. "This bill would [leave] no room for judges to make fair and reasonable decisions for thousands of pending and legitimate claims by professional athletes," stated the quarterbacks. "There are players – real people with real families – out there who are literally fighting to save their legs and get the medical care they need for the injuries they suffered at work."[84]

Governor Jerry Brown endorsed the bill – and subsequently passed it – for a very practical reason: some 3,500 cases had been brought in California by NFL alumni, suing the league for its role in concealing or underplaying the effects of brain trauma. By summer's end, the league had agreed to a $765m out-of-court settlement with 4,500 ex-players, an estimated third of the historic workforce. The unprecedented ruling stemmed from a neurological study of Andre Walters, a defensive back who had spent most of his dozen NFL seasons with the Philadelphia Eagles, who had committed suicide at 44: his brain tissue was described as resembling that of an 85-year-old Alzheimer's patient, prompting the *New York Times* to urge parents to prevent their children from taking up the sport.

This may well prove to be the start of an extremely painful and costly period for our ringmasters. Anecdotal evidence suggests that the footballers of the 1950s and 1960s, whose livelihood obliged them to head sopping wet leather, could have been at greater risk of early onset Alzheimer's; the death at 59 of the former England centre-forward, Jeff Astle, who had been suffering from a degenerative brain disease, was attributed to "death by industrial injury". More pressingly, the NFL settlement is worrying rugby union, a sport wherein professionalism, inevitably, has raised the stakes and multiplied the serious injuries – and whose combatants have never even been given the option to wear protective helmets. Indeed, Dr Willie Stewart, a Glasgow neuropathologist, has diagnosed one case of brain damage and believes that 1% of Six Nations players could be affected.[85]

For now, there is but one certainty: the long-term future of America's favourite spectator sport has never been less certain.

Animal cruelty

Tastes change. After Michael Norgrove died following a fight in London in April 2013, the first fatality in a British ring since 1995, outraged editorials condemning such contests were conspicuous by their absence, a void that could largely be traced to boxing's decline in popularity. Yet while cock-fighting and bear-baiting have long since faded from fashion and legality – at least in respectable circles – bullfighting is not the only arena in which animals are still suffering for our pleasure.

Some may be surprised to learn that steroids are a permissible treatment for horses in Australia, and that Lasix, a masking drug, is widely used in the US, where medication rules differ from state to state. Life is different in Britain. In Britain, or so the stereotype has long insisted, we like animals far too much to do nasty things to them (bar hunting them down for fun). Yet amid the shock, anger and hand-wringing that followed the revelation in 2013 that 11 mounts trained by Mahmood Al Zarooni for Sheikh Mohammed's Godolphin stable had tested positive for anabolic steroids, any public or media expressions of concern for the impact on the horses were suppressed with consummate expertise.

That summer, 38 trainers were interviewed by the British Horseracing Authority and 43 horses were identified as having been treated over the previous three years with the same banned product (Sungate) from the same Newmarket veterinary practice; vets, however, are not accountable to the BHA, there were no positive results and so, even though a "strict accountability" rule is applied to trainers, all nine of those linked to the steroid-tainted horses – three of whom were understood to have trained Classic winners – escaped censure.[86] Again, for all that Alan Lee's report in *The Times* contained a strong dose of indignation, there was no compassion to be found for the horses. The BHA tried to explain why this differed from the Godolphin case, the consequences of which saw Al Zarooni disqualified for eight years. "A typical intra-muscular injectable anabolic steroid has around ten times the concentration of Sungate," said Jenny Hall, the (interim) chief veterinary officer. A recommended dosage, she elaborated, would normally contain around 50 times the volume of anabolic agent in a single Sungate treatment. In other words, the quantity explains the disparity. Amid it all, the lone, miniscule consolation was that those taking the drugs, for once, did not offer any weak excuses.

If steroids are a relatively new issue in the equine world, fatalities are not. After two horses died at the 2011 Grand National, a safety review led to improvements costing almost £250,000 to the four-and-a-half mile course, including stricter pre-race screenings and changes to three fences that had claimed half the fallers since 1990. In the event, only 15 of the 40 starters finished in 2012 and two more had to be put down. One of them was Synchronised, the gelding so many had been willing to follow his Cheltenham Gold Cup triumph by taking the National, the first such double since 1934; instead, like so many before him, he fell foul of Becher's Brook. Made of spruce trees, this notoriously unforgiving obstacle had long been especially punishing because of the size and angle of the 6ft 9in drop on the landing side – lower than the take-off.

"This place was like a morgue for days afterwards," recalled Synchronised's trainer, Jonjo O'Neill, a former jump jockey. "We brought the poor old lad back and buried him here but it was just bloody awful. It was like losing one of the family." That didn't stop O'Neill taking a pot-shot at the National's critics. "There are people out there stabbing and shooting, killing randomly. Sometimes, it seems we in racing are being put in the same bracket as murderers. Some of the things said about us are a bloody insult – as if we are animals ourselves."[87] Any animal rights activist worth their salt would have had a field day with that last sentiment.

Up to and including the 2012 race, 69 horses had lost their lives as a consequence of the National's perils: 18 in the 19th century; 10 more up to the start of World War II; eight more from 1946 to 1969 (including four in 1954 alone), and 33 since.

From 2000 to 2010 six of the 439 entrants died, more than twice the rate in other steeplechases. Velká pardubická, a Czech cross-country marathon run since 1874, has long been cited as continental Europe's most rigorous examination of equine ability and nerve; it also has more obstacles than the National (31). But while it, too, has had its share of fatalities, safety measures – shallower ditches, shorter jumps – began in earnest as long ago as 1994; three horses had had to be destroyed in 1992; a year later, only one completed the course. The headline in *The Prague Post* the following year was predictably callous: "Horses Gain, Fans Snooze". [88]

Becher's has always been the bête noir-in-chief for Aintree entrants, though the blame for havoc lay elsewhere in 1967, the year the National most resembled an 18th century battlefield yet also the year of its most romantic result. At the 23rd fence, the smallest on the course, Popham Down veered across the track, causing what the BBC commentator called "a right pile-up": of the 28 horses that sought to jump, just one made it at the first attempt, leaving Foinavon, the 100-1 shot, to race away, becoming the longest-priced winner since the very first National in 1839 (not until 2009 would there be another 100-1 victor). That the race suffered only one casualty – and not even at the 23rd – was a small miracle. In 1984, the 23rd was named "The Foinavon".

To the equine-loving Simon Barnes, the contrast between public acclaim for Paralympians and growing unease over the National stemmed from a society less liable to see vulnerability as weakness, one more inclined to be empathetic. "We do not want to see a racehorse die, but we are quite happy to see limbless athletes playing volleyball. A generation back, the opposite was true. So here is a really uncomfortable truth: it's about compassion… We are not happy with the reckless waste of people and horses, but we are more than happy to applaud athletes in wheelchairs. We are indeed going soft. The Grand National requires us to be harder than we wish to be." [89]

"If we were to ban sport on account of it there would not be much left," reasoned the main leader in *The Times* the day before the 2013 National, insistent that the show must go on. "The question is whether enough is done to mitigate the risk."[90] In the event, the changes to the circuit were hailed as an unalloyed success: there were "just" two fallers and no casualties, though two horses did die earlier in the three-day festival, one after collapsing in mid-race, the other after falling. Some were particularly happy that the landing side of Becher's Brook was levelled further, but that cut little ice with the RSPCA, which still argued that it constituted an unfair test.[91]

Not that Aintree has been alone in victimising horses. According to data analysis by an animal rights group, Animal Aid, of the 95,000 mounts saddled up in British racing in 2011, nearly 200 (0.19%) died during or in the immediate aftermath of a race; the ratio, not unnaturally, was even more grievous in National Hunt meetings.[92] Of those ridden by Tony McCoy, by common consent the era's foremost jump jockey, 20 had died – one fatality per 199 rides. Carrying Ruby Walsh (one fatality every 116 rides) was especially fraught with risk. "This kind of attrition rate is typical of all jump racing," lamented Andrew Tyler, a director of Animal Aid, "The sport is inherently lethal to horses."[93]

Now tinker with Tyler's statement, replacing "horses" with "people". Some would argue that that merely drags us into motor racing territory. As a species, we don't appear to have too much trouble with that beyond environmental concerns: the contestants, after all, have the right to withdraw their labour. Yet had the safety measures for drivers been as tardy or paltry as those taken for our four-legged friends, the GPDA would be manning the ramparts. The prospect of an equine players association, sadly, remains as remote as magicians inviting rabbits to form a union.

7 The Us Syndrome: Sport and Internationalism

Economy up, magic weather, Lions win, and now for Andy
Sunday Times front-page lead headline, 7 July 2013

On the first weekend of July 2013 Britain was drunk on sporting success, collectively and lustily cheering the Lions to a series-clinching hammering of Australia's finest (bar a few infirm stars) and then Andy Murray to that oh-so-elusive Wimbledon singles crown. According to early estimates, around a third of the population tuned into the latter. The Lions had last completed a victorious tour in 1997; the last time a Briton had lifted the men's trophy named, to give it its full title, The All England Lawn Tennis Club Single Handed Champion of the World, a swastika was flown on Centre Court, the average house price was £550, a pint of beer was 14p, university graduates had *two* votes in general elections and Fred Perry's triumph over Baron Gottfried von Cramm could only be witnessed if you were within those ivy walls. No Briton under the age of 77 could remember back that far.

But what did those rousing athletic tales signify? A good time for all – or something more? Would the revellers feel inspired? Would they go about their work the following week with greater urgency, efficiency and ambition, even boldness? Thus far at least, possessing considerably more sporting champions per capita than China, India, the US or Russia appears to have done little if anything for Jamaica's economic and social struggles – but then why should it?

What is the true value of art or sport in straitened times? Is the so-called "feelgood factor" reality or illusion? A debate by the Centre for Cultural Policy Studies at the University of Warwick in 2013 sought to tackle these ticklish questions. David Wright quoted the Caribbean-American writer Audre Lorde, the self-styled "black, lesbian, mother, warrior, poet", who asserted that "poetry is not a luxury" but, rather, supplies the "light" that enables us to examine ourselves. "If, in its broadest sense, culture is the symbolic representation of social life," said Wright, "then the 'need' for art/culture – including popular culture – as a forum in which a society can reflect on its broader values is arguably keener at times of crisis."

"The problem," acknowledged Chris Bilton, "is that it's very difficult to articulate 'cultural value' – anybody who went to the Olympic Park last summer, or saw Cheek by Jowl at our own Warwick Arts Centre last month, may have experienced feelings of community, excitement, emotion or uplift. But researchers struggle to convert these sensations into robust evidence. So whilst many people working in the arts remain convinced that the arts are essential to social cohesion and spiritual development, academics are prone to ask awkward questions like 'whose community?' and 'who benefits?' Consequently cultural policy continues to fall back onto the familiar economic arguments – especially in tough economic times."[1]

The impact of sport on society has long been the subject of dissenting views, dating back on these shores, at the very least, to the 1970 General Election. That was when Harold Wilson made the purportedly grave error of putting his prime minister-ship on the line four days after a World Cup quarter-final against West Germany in Mexico had seen England rescue defeat from the throat of victory. When Wilson had announced the election date three weeks beforehand, Labour had held a 7.5-point lead in the polls, but that melted as fast as Alf Ramsey's side had done in the sapping heat of Guadalajara.

To Frank Keating, along with many considerably closer to the action, it was anything but a coincidence: "Wilson categorically pooh-poohed any Mexican connection – 'governance of a country has nothing to do with a study of its football fixtures'

– but years later in his memoirs Denis Healey, then defence minister and later chancellor, let slip that as early as that April the Premier had called a strategy meeting at Chequers 'in which Harold asked us to consider whether the government would suffer if the England footballers were defeated on the eve of polling day?' Even more explicit in his published reflections of the period was serious football fan (Grimsby Town) Tony Crosland, then local government minister and later foreign secretary, who blamed the defeat 'on a mix of party complacency and the disgruntled *Match of the Day* millions'. Nor was Wilson's minister of sport, former League referee Denis Howell, in any doubt. 'The moment goalkeeper [Peter] Bonetti made his third and final hash of it on the Sunday, everything simultaneously began to go wrong for Labour for the following Thursday.'"[2]

On the Monday morning following the Guadalajara calamity, Howell and Roy Jenkins, the home secretary, held "a massed factory-gate meeting" in Birmingham: "Roy was totally bemused that no question concerned either trade figures nor immigration, but solely the football and whether Ramsey or Bonetti was the major culprit. I tried to be good-humoured about my answers, but for the first time I had real doubts and knew the mood was changing fast – and afterwards my wife Brenda came back from canvassing and said: 'I don't like the smell of it at all; it's just like 1959 [a Tory landslide] all over again.'"

It could well be that failure is more influential than success: how much simpler to blame than thank. But surely applying smiles to lips and strumming songs in hearts is the full extent of sport's promise. Chubby face pinkening in the broiling after-noon sun as he sat directly behind David Cameron in the Royal Box, Scotland's First Minister, Alex Salmond, might have begged to differ as he greeted Murray's defeat of Novak Djokovic by jubilantly hoisting a Saltire flag, which had the temerity to scoff at All England Club rules by being more than two foot square. All the better to certify, with a referendum on independence just a year away, that the champion was Scottish first, British second.

* * *

"In the field of popular culture the world was American or it was provincial." Or so declared Eric Hobsbawm, the venerated Marxist historian (who only conceded late in life, admittedly, that his defence of Soviet communism had been misplaced). In *The Age of Extremes 1914-1991*, the fourth volume of his sagacious history of the past 200-odd years, he added a proviso: "With one exception, no other national or regional model established itself globally." That exception was sport.

> *In this branch of popular culture – and who, having seen the Brazilian team in its days of glory will deny it the claim to art? – US influence remained confined to the area of Washington's political domination. As cricket is played as a mass sport only where the Union Jack once flew, so baseball made little impact except where US marines had once landed. The sport the world made its own was association football, the child of Britain's global economic presence, which had introduced teams named after British firms or composed of expatriate Britons… from the polar ice to the Equator.*[3]

In theory, in terms of importance, skill and entertainment, international sport is the apex of the competitive arts. Competing at that level, the highest level, on behalf of one's nation of birthplace/residence/convenient adoptive home, is deemed an honour and, in the main, regarded as such by the honourees. For sportswatchers, it is the one time they can shelve county, state, provincial, city, town or even village loyalties for the greater good. Let's be frank. Nationalism may be a multi-headed beast of burden but it doesn't half give us a good excuse for some damn fine sport.

For a century and more, for Australia's cricketers, the chief objective has been to pummel the Poms. New Zealanders view Australians with similar underdoggish distaste, likewise Argentinians the Brazilians and the Dutch the Germans. For most of the second half of the 20th century, the Cold War was played out as zealously on running tracks and hockey rinks as it was in the Kremlin and the Pentagon. But as the 21st century gathers steam, the old certainties are being challenged, even threatened. International cricket, as we have seen, has lost ground to the IPL; the Davis Cup has declined to near-irrelevance; southern hemisphere tours by the British and Irish Lions run an increasingly distant second to the World Cup and even club rugby.

The difficulties in turning the tide are considerable, particularly in football, where the Champions League and the national domestic leagues rule the roost with a cocky, unaccommodating strut. In the summer of 2013, political pressure grew, not only for FIFA to be more flexible in its scheduling of the World Cup, but, specifically, to switch the 2022 tournament, due to be played in Qatar, from summer to winter. This made complete sense – provided, that is, one agreed that holding football's biggest event in the desert was beneficial to the game's growth rather than merely the latest proof of the governing body's long-running lust for suitors with generous pockets. When Gianni Infantino, general secretary of UEFA, dared to support this radical departure publicly – which of course meant doing the unthinkable and advocating a break in the European league season – he had the gall (or so Englishmen saw it) to question the historical determination of football as a game for windswept days and gloomy skies. "Why," he wondered, "did England, who brought to us this beautiful game, decide that football is for the winter and not for the summer? Cricket."[4]

Not quite every European was aghast at this intrusion into footballing nature. Just a few weeks earlier, in fact, support for summer league fixtures had come from no less powerful a figure than Karl-Heinz Rumenigge, chairman of both Bayern Munich and the European Club Association. By stark and in no way unexpected contrast, the apoplexy in England at such heretical proposals knew few bounds – and not solely among cricket followers, long accustomed as we are in any case to having our season encroached upon by the European Championships.

The irony of all this was not lost on Simon Barnes, who lamented the decline in status of the Lions, the Davis Cup and

Test cricket as well as that of international football. "These sporting vulnerabilities are not driven by public demand. There is nothing inevitable about what is happening. You cannot explain it in monetary or Darwinian terms. In many cases, these vulnerable species are hugely popular; the heart of the sport; what we follow sport for."[5]

* * *

"Australian bowls Sussex to victory in two days." Seldom has one mini-headline been so loaded. A cross-reference buried in Mike Atherton's preview in *The Times* of the second Test between England and New Zealand in May 2013, it should by rights have read "Magoffin bowls Sussex to victory in two days." Steve Magoffin, after all, had been on the county cricket circuit for quite a few summers and would thus have been familiar to most *Times*-reading aficionados of the sport, even if they didn't necessarily know he was Australian. This, though, happened to be an Ashes summer: ahead lay five Tests against the oldest enemy. At the time, moreover, the England camp had been instructed not to mention the A-word, lest focus be distracted. National duty be damned. No newspaper worth its salt was likely to pass up the opportunity to rub their noses in it.

Samuel Johnson, granted, was eminently justified in denouncing patriotism as the last refuge of the scoundrel, yet sport without nationalism would be a fearfully duller spectacle. It would also mean less. As Hywel Bishop and Adam Jworski stressed in their 2003 paper for *Discourse & Society*, "'We Beat 'em': Nationalism and the Hegemony of Homogeneity in the British Press Reportage of Germany versus England during Euro 2000", the international sporting contest is "a rich site" for the study of those "omnirelevant phenomena" – national identity, the nation and nationalism.[6] Fuelled by two distinct surges, post-First World War and after the fall of the Berlin Wall, it has brought out the worst in us, competitors, spectators and observers alike, and sometimes the best. Let's call it The Us Syndrome.

Disunited kingdom

One subject, two perspectives, the first courtesy of George Orwell, whose well-worn take was first aired in 1945, shortly after Moscow Dynamo had finished a brief but unbeaten, rapturously received and handsomely attended trip to Britain, during which they gave Arsenal, in particular, a footballing lesson. Orwell was somewhat less enthralled. Consider the following extract from the newspaper article that yielded his enduring if possibly overstated line about sport being "war minus the shooting":

> *If you wanted to add to the vast fund of ill-will existing in the world at this moment, you could hardly do it better than by a series of football matches between Jews and Arabs, Germans and Czechs, Indians and British, Russians and Poles, and Italians and Jugoslavs, each match to be watched by a mixed audience of 100,000 spectators. I do not, of course, suggest that sport is one of the main causes of international rivalry; big-scale sport is itself, I think, merely another effect of the causes that have produced nationalism. Still, you do make things worse by sending forth a team of eleven men, labelled as national champions, to do battle against some rival team, and allowing it to be felt on all sides that whichever nation is defeated will "lose face".*
>
> *I hope, therefore, that we shan't follow up the visit of the Dynamos by sending a British team to the USSR. If we must do so, then let us send a second-rate team which is sure to be beaten and cannot be claimed to represent Britain as a whole. There are quite enough real causes of trouble already, and we need not add to them by encouraging young men to kick each other on the shins amid the roars of infuriated spectators.*[7]

Fast-forward to August 2011. While riots rip apart the nation's cities, England's cricketers are drubbing India in a four-match Test series, rising to the summit of the world rankings for the first time. The results of a contemporaneous survey conducted by Chance To Shine, the self-styled "single biggest school sport development initiative ever undertaken in Britain"[8], and Brit Insurance, sponsors of the England team, claimed that the success of Andrew Strauss and his colleagues had united "a country that frequently doesn't feel united". Six out of 10 respondents, furthermore, agreed that sporting victories on the international field made them "personally happier".

As was readily apparent, and in a refreshingly broader manner, 12 months later. In a democratic and highly imaginative Olympic opening ceremony, directed by Danny Boyle, the mind and eyes behind such box-office gems as *Trainspotting* and *Slumdog Millionaire*, the focus was not merely the capital city but Britain itself, weakened as it had been by Scottish and Welsh devolution. "Team GB" was a chant few thought they would ever hear at Wembley.

Befitting the cradle of so many spectator sports, living in England means being inordinately spoilt for sources of personal fulfilment, even joy – though this can, of course, be a double-edged sword. Standing tallest in terms of competitive artistry and excellence, much the most alluring attraction of the many sporting attractions on the second weekend of June 2012 – which included diverse and top-class treats such as the European Football Championships, the NBA and NHL playoffs, a Formula 1 grand prix and a rash of rugby union internationals and MLB local derbies – was the men's singles final of the French Open between Novak Djokovic and Rafa Nadal.

On Saturday 10 June, England's rugby unionists were on duty in Durban, going down 22-17 to a markedly superior South African XV; on the same day, having seen the first two-fifths of the match washed out (the first time the elements had wrought such havoc since 1964), the national cricket team finally began the third Test against the West Indies at Edgbaston. The next day brought the continuation of the Test as well as the climaxes of cycling's Critérium du Dauphiné in France (won by Bradley Wiggins and Team Sky), the Curtis Cup (Great Britain and Ireland's amateur golfers beat their American counterparts for the first time since 1996 and only the ninth time in 40 such debates since the biennial event began in 1932) and the Canadian Grand Prix, which saw Lewis Hamilton and Jenson Button take on Formula 1's other bravest and filthy-richest (Hamilton won). Twenty-four hours later, the national football team kicked off against France in their opening assignment of Euro 2012, in Donetsk, industrial powerhouse of Ukraine. This inspired a *Times* sub-editor to compose one of the paper's better headlines in recent memory, albeit one that testified to the more measured expectations that now attended English fortunes following the hubristic hype surrounding previous tournaments: "Donetsk best thing: England draw first match".[9]

Think of yourself as British or even United Kingdomish, moreover, and the emotional tugs grow exponentially. In the 24 hours leading up to England's African adventure, all the other "home" nations had been on a rugby union battlefield somewhere: Ireland in New Zealand (lost heavily), Wales in Australia (lost relatively narrowly) and Scotland in Australia (won, staggeringly, albeit on a mudheap). The last of these was the only one worthy of three patriotic cheers.

Being British over those few days meant being less concerned with aesthetics and improbable heroism than flag-flying. Disturbing evidence of patriotic excesses soon followed, albeit from another quarter. Shortly before their team met Poland in the European Championships, 5,000 Russian football fans were permitted, bewilderingly, to parade through the streets of Warsaw – a somewhat foolhardy gesture given the 92-year-old scars that still festered from the Battle of Warsaw. Nobody was taking this lightly. "*Newsweek*'s Polish edition," reported Rory Smith in *The Times*, "had cast Franciszek Smuda, the coach, as Josef Pilsudski, the hero who orchestrated the Miracle at the Vistula, the decisive conflict… and the moment that ensured Polish freedom."[10] Come the match, Legia Warsaw fans were said to have provoked "sporadic, but intense, outbreaks of violence" around the National Stadium. The same tribe that, just a few months earlier, had unfurled a massive banner (in Arabic-style lettering) before their UEFA Europa League match with FC Hapoel Tel Aviv, calling for a jihad. Footage on YouTube brought back distinctly unpleasant memories of "the English disease". A photograph of five Polish men assaulting a Russian supporter went viral.

Final score: Poland 1 Russia 1, 184 people detained by police, 156 of them Poles. The next day, a Warsaw court fined and issued suspended jail terms of up to 12 months to eight of them. English racists, meanwhile, strove to maintain the nation's less-than proud traditions: after England had lost to Italy in the quarter-finals, around 150 Bedford residents ran at a small section of the town's Italian community, attacking vehicles and committing at least one assault. There were three arrests. Nick Cataldo, co-owner of a third generation Italian café, had to barricade himself in. "It happens every time England play Italy in Bedford. I don't believe this 'In Italia '90 nothing happened' because I remember a gang of England fans lining up along the wall opposite my café waiting for us to come outside. It's terrible – we're all from the same town."[11]

A far more benign side to nationalism could be seen at the London Olympics. Even among those members of the media not paid to cover sport for a living, enthusiasm soared. "We now have Channel 4's Paralympics to look forward to – I wonder how that will fit into its constant gawping at disability," was the typically arresting opening to the verdict proffered by the *Sunday Times'* colourful TV reviewer A. A. Gill, for whom the Games "are now essentially a quadrennial television series", its audience "enormous, the joy, excitement and goodwill universal". Indeed, "Super Saturday" was "possibly the best day I've ever had watching TV, and I'm not that keen on sport. And, just when we thought it couldn't possibly get any more perfect, Great Britain lose a penalty shootout to South Korea. That was a gift from the god of ball games. Nothing has punctured the bloated cynicism of football like the Olympics."[12]

Yet not everyone obeyed the implicit edict about all Britons being obliged to express unbridled enthusiasm. "Former front-man of The Smiths Morrissey has slammed Great Britain fans for their support of the country's athletes in the London Olympics, asking: 'Has England ever been so foul with patriotism?'," seethed the *Daily Mail*. "The rock star, who has come out with controversial remarks in the past, has said that he cannot even bring himself to watch the Olympics, slating the presence of the Royal Family and David and Victoria Beckham in the process. He even likened fans of the country's growing support of their athletes to a mindset held by the populace of Nazi Germany in the late 1930s."[13] For once, the actual words, published as part of a diary entry on Morrissey's True to You fan website, fully bore out the *Mail*'s claim.

A very sporting dilemma
On 24 January 2012, two tales of sporting folk took my eye, both published in *The Times*. The first, on the news pages and enticingly headlined "Spurs manager 'received bungs in bank account named after his dog'", recounted the opening proceedings in the trial for tax evasion of Harry Redknapp, then manager of Tottenham Hotspur and regarded by the majority of English football journalists as the next boss of the national team. Although he would be found innocent, the adverse publicity generated by the court proceedings was widely seen as the reason for the hiring of a less compelling if no less English candidate, Roy Hodgson.

The story was deemed of sufficient importance to the nation for an expansive photo to be published on the front page of the paper, capturing the unusually grim-faced Redknapp leaving Southwark Crown Court. "Mr Redknapp, 64," reported David Brown, "is the most successful English manager in the game today, having led Portsmouth to FA Cup success and Tottenham to the Uefa Champions League quarter-finals last season."[14] That such a lavish claim could be made on the basis of such a minor collection of feats may have beggared belief, but it underscored in indelible ink a contradictory fact of modern sporting life. Namely, that sport and nationality are at once inextricably entwined and mutually oblivious.

The second story saluted Lawrence Tynes, who had kicked the winning field goal in the National Football Conference final, earning the New York Giants a meeting with the New England Patriots in Super Bowl XLVI. English newspapers cover American football because the game is broadcast here and the armchair following is substantial, not out of any sense of national interest. Only very occasionally is there a local angle, and this time it was Tynes, born to a Scottish mother and US Navy Seal father in Greenock, on the south side of the River Clyde. *The Times* described Tynes, who helped the Giants win the 2008 Super Bowl, as "one of only three Britons"[15] to have won North American sport's biggest bauble. But was that claim truly justified? Tynes Sr. was stationed in Florida when his son was 11; aside from a season for the now defunct Scottish Claymores, he had spent his life in the States. Andy Murray watchers will be familiar, moreover, with the way Tynes is generally referred to by English newspapers as a "Briton" rather than a Scot (so long as he's a successful Briton). In the greater scheme of things, such fine distinctions matter not a jot, but whether we like it or not, sport and nationalism feed off each other and sustain each other. It is certainly hard to think of another field of human endeavour – or at least one outside the forging of a family unit – that does so much to persuade a populace that there really is such a thing as "us".

Yet in sporting terms, it feels as if there has never been less excuse to be nationalistic. Starting with the Colombian football revolution in the late 1940s, the Spanish and Italian import drives of the 1950s, the lifting of import restrictions in cricket's Sheffield Shield and County Championship in the 1960s and Major League Baseball's creeping multinationalism over the final quarter of the 20th century, domestic leagues became more inclusive, casting aside protectionist restrictions. Then came the Champions Leagues, first and foremost in football, less conspicuously in cricket, though the latter found more than enough compensation in the Indian Premier League, the most popular and profitable start-from-scratch league in sporting history.

Over the past 20 years, Americans have become accustomed to rooting for Russians and Cubans and Venezuelans, Frenchmen to cheering on Africans, Scots to hailing flash little Sassenachs, little Englanders to toasting Germans. Just about everyone who has heard of them, moreover, has a soft spot for that dynamic tennis duo, Amir Hadad and Aisam-ul-Haq Qureshi, an Israeli-Pakistani doubles act who in 2002 dedicated their improbable 2nd-round upset of the No. 11 Wimbledon seeds to that noblest of causes, peace. "The bloodshed in the Middle East means [Quereshi's] pairing with an Israeli is wrong," was the quoted response in *The Times* of Saeed Haid, a former Pakistani champion. "Although he is playing in his private capacity," stressed Brigadier Saulat Abbas, a prominent sports official, "we officially condemn his playing with an Israeli player and an explanation has been sought from him. Since we have no links with Israel, Qureshi may face a ban."[16] Despite such pressure, the following year, Hadad and Qureshi were not only still in harness but being acclaimed as winners of the Arthur Ashe Humanitarian Award (and runners-up for the Anne Frank Award For Moral Courage by the UK arm of the Anne Frank Trust). In 2010, Qureshi shared the same award after linking up with an even less desirable ally, Rohan Bopanna, an Indian.

The spread of talent, too, is deeply satisfying. In 2012, the world's best-known boxers were a pair of Ukrainian brothers, a Filipino and an American; the most respected batters, in cricket and baseball, respectively, an Indian and a Dominican Republican; the most celebrated footballers Argentinian and Portuguese; the reigning champion on four wheels German, on two wheels Australian; the pre-eminent golfer Irish; the top male tennis players Serbian, Swiss, Spanish and Scottish, their female counterparts Russian, Belarusian, Polish and Czech; the fastest runner Jamaican; the fastest marathon runner Kenyan; the most accomplished freestyle swimmer Chinese. The foremost international collectives were distributed with no greater geographical bias: Spain (football), England (cricket), New Zealand (rugby union), Russia (ice hockey), the US (basketball) and Japan (baseball).

Sport has also shown politicians the way over international co-operation. FIFA, the IOC and the International Cricket Council (in its Imperial guise) all predate by half a century or more the World Bank, the International Monetary Fund, the World Health Organisation, the World Trade Organisation, the International Criminal Court and the International Labour Organisation. "One by one our global institutions are being hollowed out and disregarded. It sometimes seems that only the Olympics survive," bemoaned Matthew Parris in *The Times* during the 2012 Games. "Whatever the self-tanning, self-upholstering and self-serving pomposity of the IOC, some kind of principle, some kind of uplift, still shines through these Games." The Olympics, he concluded, "could end up as the world's last great multilateral institution".[17]

One had only to monitor the growing unrest in Brazil, stage for the 2014 FIFA World Cup and the 2016 Olympics, where concern for economic deprivation has taken a distant back seat to showing the planet how to put on a jolly good bash, to question whether "great", in this instance, should apply strictly in its quantitative sense. Shortly before the 2013 Confederations Cup semi-final between Brazil and Uruguay in Belo Horizonte, an estimated 100,000 protestors massed outside the stadium just as Congress was acceding to two of the movement's chief demands: earmarking oil revenue for public education and health, and ditching legislation that would have stymied investigations into government corruption. That same day, in a further sign of the movement's impact, an MP convicted of corruption became the first legislator in 25 years to be jailed.[18]

Why, then, are politicians so willing to lavish colossal sums on sporting events? Matthew Syed makes a compelling case in calling it "jackpot politics" and blaming "the seductiveness of the grand gesture... a headline-grabbing, consciousness-defining, aggrandising piece of symbolism".[19] In other words, the very opposite of what the vast majority of the planet actually need: an end to poverty, inequality and corruption, a process that, even when it is not being over-optimistic, can take generations, even centuries.

Still, lowering language barriers and burying ancient enmities in the name of bats and balls must surely, on balance, be A Good Thing. *Jeux Sans Frontières*, a sporty twist on the Eurovision Song Contest, drew huge audiences for the BBC in the 1960s and 1970s with the aid of treacherously slippery slides, full-bucket-carrying sprints, copious helpings of slapstick and look-how-silly-we-look national costumes, but where would we be without our *jeux avec frontiers*? More insular, for one thing.

For St George and America

Even the brightest Venusian might be somewhat baffled, upon inspecting an English newspaper in 2012, to read a sports page mentioning "England fly-half Toby Flood", "England-qualified Irish batsman Eoin Morgan" and "English driver Lewis Hamilton". Especially when augmented by mentions of "Indira Gandhi, the former Indian prime minister" and "Sachin Tendulkar, the India batsman". To trace how we got to this surreal juncture, let's start at the very beginning, with the very first international team fixture: a cricket match that drew 10,000 spectators to the St George's Club in New York's Bloomingdale Park, on the south side of Staten Island, on 24 and 25 September 1844. In fact, the sides competing for $1,000 were the touring Toronto club and St George's; not until 1853 would the participants in this now-annual contest be formally known as the USA and Canada. But what's a spot of retroactivity between friends?

As is the way with creation stories, Deb K. Das offers a different account. "The match came about because in 1843, a New York team had landed penniless in Toronto and were fully financed and entertained by their magnanimous hosts. In order to honour this Canadian gesture, the New Yorkers invited the Canadians to play in New York. The US team was drawn from several New York clubs, and also included players from Philadelphia, DC, and Boston (the other centres of US cricket at the time). The Canadians, too, tried to come up with a representative team. All the posters and advertisements of the match from that period, which are available in cricket libraries, refer to a 'Canadian vs. USA' match, not a New York vs. Toronto fixture. There were about 20,000 spectators at the match, and bets of around $120,000 (close to $1.5m in today's currency) were placed on the outcome."[20] The visitors won a close two-innings game by 23 runs when the Americans' No.11 "failed to arrive in time to bat".

The magnanimity of the Toronto club, related Kevin Boller, press officer and historian of the Canadian Cricket Association, emanated from a hoax perpetrated "some four years earlier by a certain 'Mr. Phillpotts'", who had invited St. George's over to play Toronto on the northern shores of Lake Ontario. "On the afternoon of August 28, 1840 eighteen travel-weary members of the St. George's Club turned up in Toronto following an exhausting journey through the state of New York by coach and across Lake Ontario by steamer only to discover that the members of the Toronto Cricket Club had no knowledge of any such cricket match. The sociable 'Mr. Phillpotts' who had originated the whole episode could not be located, which of course, came as no big surprise to everyone involved." Such was the embarrassment of Toronto officials, a hastily convened meeting saw a challenge match organised between the clubs for a stake of £50 (then $250) a side. "Despite the hurried arrangements a sizeable number of spectators turned out and the band of the 34th Regiment entertained the gathering. His Excellency the Governor of Upper Canada, Sir George Arthur added a regal touch to the occasion by putting in an appearance."[21]

Bullocky and Dick-a-Dick

In terms of international competition, the British did most to light the torch, most notably, and inevitably, through cricket. In 1859, George Parr led a party of English professionals to North America on what can fairly be regarded as the inaugural international sporting tour, playing matches in Montreal, Hamilton and, against a combined Canadian-American side, in Rochester – in a blizzard. Such was the apparent chasm in ability, the tourists remained unbeaten and untroubled despite permitting their opponents to field twice as many players. The trip also yielded the first tour book, written by Fred Lillywhite, who accompanied the party with his printing tent, producing the latest score for transmission by electronic telegraph, first used commercially in 1839 for the stretch of the Great Western Railway between Paddington and West Drayton. Cue one of the more intriguing what ifs, courtesy of Rowland Bowen:

> *There can be very little doubt that but for the American Civil War there would have been another tour before nine years passed, and if that unhappy conflict had never broken out, nor lasted as long as it did, it is difficult to see how our natural opponents at cricket would have been not Australia but the USA, and, possibly Canada.*[22]

Australia it was, albeit not, at first, in the guise one might expect. The first formal, full-scale cricket tour, spanning 1867 and 1868, was undertaken by a party of Aboriginals. "Of interest," wrote Colin Tatz, "is what the quaint, sometimes generous, sometimes carping British press made of the 'exploits of an impossible coffee-coloured team'. The black physique fascinated them."[23] The names were nothing if not exotic to English ears – "King Cole", "Bullocky", "Dick-a-Dick" – though one supplied a pertinent reminder of the reality of black-white relations in the 19th century: "Jim Crow".

"It must not be inferred that they are savages," stated *Sporting Life*. The *Rochdale Observer* described the players as "generally stalwart men". To the *Sporting Gazette*, they were "sturdy-limbed too, notwithstanding their slight peculiarity of build, deep in the chest, and with an almost English width across the shoulder". The same paper forecast a surprise for those anticipating the mysterious tourists would be broad of nose, thick of lip and bedecked in the "wool" of the negro: "The Australians were handsome, good-tempered looking fellows... quite the race one would expect Macaulay's New Zealander to spring from." To *The Times*, they were "perfectly civilised, and are quite familiar with the English language". The "public relations men", wrote Tatz, "did a fine job".

Patronising comments were more easily located in the match reports. "Batting, save that of [Johnny] Mullagh, is sadly wanting in power," noted *The Times* of the defeat by Surrey at The Oval, where the running between the wickets was "much at fault". Nevertheless, on their exhausting 47-match trek, Mullagh and his colleagues won as many matches (14) as they lost.[24] After each contest, spectators were treated to displays of "Australian" and "native" sports such as boomerang- and spear-throwing; Dick-a-Dick amazed all present when he threw a ball 107 yards. The tour's centrepiece was a game at Lord's against MCC on 12-13 June 1868. The tourists were led by Charles Lawrence, a Sydney hotelier and coach who had played for Surrey; the host XI included the Earl of Coventry and Viscount Downe. In a letter to *The Times* shortly before the centenary of the match, John Mullaney, Professor of Prehistory at the Australian National University and author of *Cricket Walkabout: the Australian Aboriginal Cricketers on Tour 1867-8*, expressed his dismay that the historic event had bypassed contemporary commentators: "It is regrettable, because treating it as a non-event represents a slight to the dignity of Australian Aborigine people… It is unfortunate that this interesting episode in amicable race relations, in a period not noted for its tolerance, has made so little impact on the game."[25]

Sadly, albeit with much historic inevitability, the players dispersed upon their return home, lamented Tatz, "many dying prematurely and in obscurity". Only Mullagh, the party's "black 'W.G.'", found fame: an all-rounder described by David Frith, the eminent cricket historian, as "a kind of early [Garry] Sobers", he could bat forcefully and elegantly, bowl rapidly and keep wicket. A second tour, planned for the following year, was scrapped. Led by Daniel Christian, only the second cricketer of Aboriginal descent to play for Australia – his paternal roots lay in the Wiradjuri tribe of central New South Wales – a party of indigenous cricketers paid homage in 2009, tracing the original tourists' footsteps on a tour of Britain. Another landmark came in 2012, when the Australian National Indigenous

Team toured India, their ranks bulging with the best players then competing in the Imparja Cup, the annual Aboriginal tournament in Alice Springs.

Looking back at Mullagh and his comrades (two of whom, Dick-a-Dick and Johnny Cuzens, were buried in the same cemetery as members of his family), Geoff Clark, former chairman of the Australian and Torres Strait Islander Commission, warranted how difficult "in all aspects of life" their circumstances were. "White laws stripped them of virtually any control over their own lives. Endemic racism blocked or destroyed their careers. Disease, poverty, dispossession and crime decimated their numbers. For the 1868 team there were no ticker tape parades or lucrative contracts. They returned to obscurity and early deaths."[26]

* * *

Nearly 150 years later, no indigenous cricketer had represented Australia at its favourite sport. Jason Gillespie, whose forbears had been members of the Kamilaroi tribe, preceded Christian in 1997 when he became the first cricketer descended from mankind's oldest continuous culture to pull on the baggy green cap, but by 2012 the most prominent sign of encouragement was the presence of Josh Lawlor, a left-arm fast bowler and captain of the national Indigenous XI, in the New South Wales XI. In a 2005-06 survey of Australian clubs, reported Paul Connolly in *The Global Mail*, indigenous players made up 1.35 per cent of junior players and 1.94 per cent of senior players. "Whether there has been any change to these figures in the intervening years is impossible to say," he wrote, for the simple reason that Cricket Australia, the national governing body, "has no accurate data".

"*The Global Mail* was told, anecdotally, that there is a good proportion of indigenous players playing club cricket today, particularly in urban areas. That said, there is no evidence that this proportion has risen to 2.5 per cent of all participants, let alone the 4.5 per cent (or 25,000 out of a projected 550,000) that Cricket Australia targeted (for 2009) in 2006. Tellingly, Cricket Australia's 2011 census made no mention of indigenous numbers."[27] Paul Stewart, a Melbourne University academic and chairman of the Victorian Indigenous Cricket Advisory Committee, apprised Connolly of his view that the image of cricket as a white man's game had yet to dissolve. "[It's still sometimes seen as] a white, middle-class activity that's not open to embracing indigenous cricketers within the club culture," said Stewart, whose ancestors came from the Taungurong tribe in central Victoria. "From my experience, boys I know tend to drop off the radar because of that. Racism has played a part in some instances."

The contrast with the nation's other favourite team sports is instructive, vivid and damning. The Australian Football League (AFL) noted on its website in 2013 that there were around 70 Aboriginal players at the leading clubs; in a sport not all that dissimilar to a traditional Aboriginal game, Marn Grook – one played by Tom Wills, Australia's first conspicuous cricketer and the man behind the rules of Rules – this amounted to roughly 10% of the workforce. At the same time, 12% of National Rugby League players identified themselves as Aboriginal, doubtless inspired in particular by Wendell Sailor. Named Man of the Match at the 2000 World Cup final, the burly Torres Strait Island winger went on to become not only the country's first rugby leaguer to switch to union but also to appear in that code's global showdown. Granted, union, confined for so long to New South Wales and Queensland and based heavily on the products of private schools, has a far smaller share of indigenous players than league or the AFL, but it has offered for our appreciation Lloyd McDermott, who in 1962 became the first Aboriginal to be picked for the Wallabies, refused to tour South Africa as "an honorary white", defected to rugby league and wound up as the first indigenous barrister. Two decades later came the Ella brothers, above all Mark, a dazzling fly-half who enchanted British audiences on Australia's "Grand Slam" tour of 1984 then promptly retired at 25.

In fairness, as Stuart Wark, a research fellow at the University of New England, pointed out, these figures, as with black British footballers in the Premier League, do not reflect the demographics: people of Aboriginal or Strait Islander heritage comprise around 2-3% of the total population, a share reflected in the proportion of Aboriginals playing grade cricket.[28] The cost of taking cricket up seriously, far heavier than that required to pursue the various football codes, remains a major deterrent to the indigenous population. Has cricket, for so long the premier national sport in a land that quietly pursued a "White Australia" policy up to the 1970s, been a reluctant encourager? It is hard to conclude otherwise.

Birth of the Ashes

> *Belsize Park, North London, July 2000. As the last England captain bar one to bow out with a record worth telling his grandkids about ([Bob] Willis, with seven wins and five defeats, is the only successor to have retired in profit), what did [Mike] Brearley the psychotherapist regard as the source of the national cricket team's ills? Big sigh. "I don't know what it is. Something to do with proper toughness, which comes from leadership, personality-types. Once you get the bit between your teeth, don't give up. The best Aussies have that but we don't seem to. It's parent v child: deposed authority figures can be ambivalent, often resentful."[29]*

Mike Brearley might not have anticipated how far the pendulum would swing a decade later, but nobody was getting too carried away. Yes, England's cricketers have had marginally the better of the most recent episodes in spectator sport's longest-running international soap opera, but the overall score remains a long way from parity.

* * *

As already noted, the early English tours of Australia were not representative – or at least not officially. In 1876, James Lillywhite and John Conway, a fast bowler from Victoria who worked as a journalist, joined forces – at the latter's suggestion

– to organise a tour that saw a dozen professionals set sail for Australia in mid-September aboard the P&O steamship *Poonah*. Criss-crossing Australasia, Lillywhite and his confreres would travel 7000 miles from first match to last.[30]

The expedition climaxed in mid-March at the Melbourne Cricket Ground: Lillywhite's hand-picked heroes versus a combined Victoria and New South Wales XI, primarily for betting purposes. Dubbed "a grand combination match" by Conway but later enshrined as the first Test match, it resulted in a 45-run victory for the Australians, for whom Charles Bannerman scored what would come to be regarded as the first Test century. Remarkably, the Woolwich-born opener's 165 out of 245 in his side's first innings amounted to a 67.35% share, still a record 135 years later.

A fortnight after that prototype encounter, a return match was played for the benefit of the tourists, who repaired some of their reputation by winning what would be honoured as the second official Test match. Conway then linked up with Lillywhite and Dave Gregory, captain of the combined XI, to orchestrate the first tour of England since Dick-a-Dick and his fellow Aborigines. "Why, they ain't black!" a spectator reportedly exclaimed as the tourists took the field against Nottinghamshire the following summer, a comment that did not go down terribly well with Gregory and Co. "The president of Cambridge University CC, the eccentric heavyweight Revd. Arthur Ward, apparently persisted in this misapprehension, giving rise to similar stories,"[31] noted Derek Birley. When Ward's boys came to Lord's for the Oxford-Cambridge Varsity Match, the president found himself in the company of A.G. Steel and Fred "The Demon" Spofforth, the vaunted Australian fast bowler who had played in the second Test of 1877: Steel introduced Spofforth as "the demon nigger bowler". If Spofforth, as Birley deduced, really was "less amused before the MCC match by members' casually racist enquiries about the tourists' form", his revenge was mighty: 10 wickets for a piffling 20 runs as the Australians romped to victory in a contest done and dusted inside five hours.

At The Oval four summers later, having been described by one reporter as "hardly quite as good as he was two years ago",[32] "The Demon" captured 14 English wickets for just 90 runs, inspiring the best-known and most important obituary in the annals of the competitive arts. After Australia had secured an astonishing seven-run victory despite setting the home team a mere 85 to win, Reginald Shirley Brooks, editor of the *Sporting Times* and an accomplished satirist, published a mock notice:

In Affectionate Remembrance

OF

ENGLISH CRICKET,

WHICH DIED AT THE OVAL

ON

29th AUGUST, 1882,

Deeply lamented by a large circle of sorrowing

Friends and acquaintances.

R.I.P

N.B. – The body will be cremated and the
ashes taken to Australia

That footnote carried a serious message ignored for 130 years. Brooks' late father, Shirley, a novelist, playwright and journalist whose own mastery of satire had hoisted him to the editorship of *Punch*, had been one of the pioneer campaigners for human cremation; unfortunately, he died in 1874, 11 years before it was legalised. Mike Selvey, a former England fast bowler and even better *Guardian* cricket correspondent since 1986, offered a different take on the legend in 2013: in that mock obituary, Brooks Jr "was suggesting that the body of English cricket should be treated in a manner that he was not able to accord his own father".[33]

The next chapter, contends David Frith, remains the most "enchanting story in cricket".[34] A few months later, at a Christmas party during the next English tour of Australia, a damsel from the backwoods named Florence Morphy presented the touring captain, Ivo Bligh, the 9th Earl of Darnley, with a modestly-proportioned terracotta urn, a token of her considerable esteem. "The mystique has been preserved: no removal of the fragile cork and no forensic examination has been permitted," acknowledged Frith, for once happy to sheath his historian's instincts and bow to uncertainty. "Does it house the ashes of a stump (unlikely), a bail (possibly), a cricket ball (who knows?), or even a lady's veil (a distinct possibility if the recollection of an elderly relative of Ivo Bligh's is to be accepted)? The intrigue intensifies if one accepts the account discreetly uttered some years ago by the butler at Cobham Hall, the Bligh/Darnley family seat. Evidently a trustworthy man, he disclosed that one morning a maid who was dusting the mantelpiece accidentally sent the urn toppling to the floor. Somehow it survived the impact, apart from a small chip, but the original contents escaped and were hastily swept up. The butler saw to it that the urn was refilled immediately with cold ash from the fireplace. Or so the story goes."

Whatever its contents, that tiny urn, 110 millimetres high, would endure as the trophy, known as The Ashes, for which the two nations would henceforth compete. In theory, it should have spent most of the past 130 years or so in Australian hands, but such is its fragility, it has only ever left Lord's twice since it was bequeathed to MCC by Bligh's widow in 1927: for Australia's bicentenary in 1988 and in 2006, when Adam Chadwick, the MCC curator, booked it a business-class seat from London and took it on a 14-week tour of the nation's museums. It had been insured for a seven-figure sum; the box it was transported in took 18 months to design. Perceptions of two nations can seldom have been constructed from such slight foundations.

The Tartan hordes

In June 2012, the FA announced that England would play Scotland the following year, as part of its 150th anniversary celebrations. The Scottish FA had been clamouring for a reunion, all the more so with the 2014 independence referendum looming. The

previous such encounter had been in 1999, during the qualification campaign for the European Championships – just the third
time the nations had met since 1989, the year the 118-year-old
annual fixture was abandoned as a consequence of scenes of
street rampages and violence in Glasgow, still available for
your de-edification by dint of the small-but-beautifully-formed
miracle that is YouTube.[35] By then, in any event, the fixture had
sagged in significance: five years earlier, just over a century
after its inception, the Home International Championship had
been scrapped.

Having a foot in both camps (Glaswegian father, East London
mother), my own view can be relied upon for lack of bias, albeit
not when it comes to living less than an Usain Bolt sprint from
Wembley Way in the early 1980s, by when the biennial invasion
by my tartan-clad half-brethren had become a Groundhog Day,
a perpetual second leg of the Battle of Bannockburn. In 1977, to
cite the most notorious afternoon, Scottish fans celebrating their
team's 38th victory over the "auld enemy" (to just 35 defeats)
ripped down the Wembley goalposts. As if to emphasise the
folly of such hubris, the decline began the very next year, when
Scotland lost at Hampden Park; in 15 encounters between 1977
and 1999, they prevailed just three times to England's 10 (an
illuminating parallel can be drawn with the similarly inflected
rugby union rivalry between England and Wales: by the end of
the 1970s, Wales held a 40-33 advantage, since when economic
reality has held sway, England winning 24 to Wales's 16).

The first official discussion that spawned the inaugural
England-Scotland encounter occurred on 3 October 1872, when,
at the same meeting that gave rise to the first regulation-sized
balls ("not more than 28 in. nor less than 27 in."), half a dozen
FA members made a resolution, recorded by Charles Alcock: "In
order to further the interests of the Association in Scotland, it
was decided during the current season that a team should be
sent to Glasgow to represent England."[36]

The idea had been taking root for a while – 1869 had seen the
first of five games between "England" and "London Scottish",

the latter drawn from clubs such as Harrow Chequers, Old Etonians and the Civil Service. "Let it be clear," insisted that much-travelled football writer Brian James, "at this time the match was not seen as an opportunity to test the standards of the two nations; the Scots who first suggested the game were seeking help in spreading football north of the Border rather than the chance to prove that it already existed in strength."[37]

The FA wrote to its members requesting their assistance in paying their representatives' rail expenses. The initial fixture was originally scheduled for a Monday, but was delayed until the following Saturday after the Scots complained, not unreasonably, that "many of those who would play or who might witness the encounter would be engaged upon their businesses". The English agreed, reluctantly, pointing out that this would injure their cause since some of the team would be forced to travel north by night. The negotiations were significant, wrote James, "as evidence of how differently the game was being developed in the two countries". England "still clung to a vision of football played by the upper classes to which the working public may be admitted on sufferance" whereas in Scotland the game had developed "as a sport of the people".[38]

It says much for cricket's stature, even north of Hadrian's Wall, that the game was played on 30 November, in the Partick area of Glasgow, at the Hamilton Crescent cricket ground. It was watched by a crowd estimated at between 2,000 and 4,000, reportedly generating receipts of £109, and despite failing to produce a single goal, drew a rave review from *Bell's Life in London*: "A splendid display of football in the really scientific sense of the word, and a most determined effort on the part of the two representatives of the two nationalities to overcome each other."[39] The visitors "had all the advantages" in terms of pace and weight (an estimated average of two stones per man), reported the *Glasgow Herald*, but Scottish teamwork nullified this. *The Graphic* opted not to give its readers a blow-by-blow account because "both ourselves and readers would get into a fog among the profusion of technical terms, such as 'crowding up', 'backing', 'banding', 'hindering' and dribbling'".[40] Controversy loomed when Scotland's Robert Leckie drove a shot atop the tape that served as a prototype if flimsy crossbar, only for the home crowd's cheers to be doused by the umpires, who ruled that the ball had not entered the goal.

As a 10-year-old, Walter Arnott set off with his pals after breakfast to walk the five miles to Partick, where they met "as great a congregation as I could imagine being about the place". Having exhausted what few pennies they had, they saw the game only by kind permission of a cabbie, who consented to them viewing proceedings by perching on his cab and peering over the wall. Arnott's subsequent devotion to honing his own ball skills resulted in a record-setting 10 consecutive caps against the "auld enemy". Not that he was alone in being so enthused: 12 Scottish clubs were established in the wake of the match, more than doubling the national tally; the following year, moreover, brought the formation of the Scottish FA.[41]

Two Anglo-Scottish duels stick out for strictly footballing reasons, both mortifying home defeats for England. In March 1928, the tallest of Scotland's five forwards was Alex Jackson, all 5ft 7in of him, yet so uninhibited were they by the sodden surface, and so utterly did they master the England defence, the 5-1 scoreline flattered the hosts: thus were the "Wembley Wizards" born. As *The Times* reported: "Scotland, by over-indulgence in the pleasant pastime of making the English defence look supremely silly, cheated themselves out of a sixth and possibly a seventh goal, and just on time England scored in the only way that looked possible for them – direct from a free kick."[42] In the *Daily Mail*, J. H. Freeman offered equal helpings of praise and embarrassment: "In all the annals of international football I do not think there is a parallel to this match. The inferiority of the England side was so marked that the confusion and bewilderment of the individual players, against the science and skill and pace of Scotland's dazzling team, became positively ludicrous... Scotland's whole team played with a dominant mastery that was made to appear sheer effrontery."[43]

If anything, Scotland's 3-2 triumph at Wembley in 1967 was even more reverberant. In the sides' first meeting since England's World Cup triumph, the most competitive element was the philosophical dispute between two English-based Scots, Jim Baxter and Denis Law. The latter's response to learning – towards the end of an indifferent round of golf – that the Sassenachs had taken the Jules Rimet trophy had been to splutter angrily about it capping his day. To him, the name of the game was goals and a statistical shellacking; to Baxter, the aim was to play keepie-uppie and nutmeg the opposition, to taunt and humiliate. Taking especial pleasure from his interchanges with the opposition's dynamo, he asked Alan Ball, he of the famously high-pitched voice, whether he thought he would be a player once it broke. Recalled Tommy Gemmell, the Celtic full-back: "Denis was shouting, 'Let's give them a doing', while Jim was saying, 'Ach, take the piss' and demanding the ball from everyone."[44] At the final whistle, the visiting hordes, estimated at 40,000, invaded the pitch and began digging up sods of turf with fingers and pocket-knives – the whole of the centre-spot, reported James, wound up in Glasgow.[45] The jubilant scenes from Wembley to Piccadilly Circus were "perhaps the most dramatic" in the history of the fixture. In Portugal six weeks later, Celtic rubbed it in, becoming the first British side to win the European Cup and earning immortality as the "Lisbon Lions".

At length, while their anti-Englishness never abated, the so-called "Tartan Army" were said to have more or less renounced hooliganism in the 1980s, a change of tack rendered considerably simpler by the absence of their annual outlet. "A vital part of the Tartan Army's repertoire," wrote Richard Giulianotti in *Football: A Sociology of the Global Game*, "involves establishing their national identity through a differentiation from England and 'Englishness'. By presenting themselves as 'anti-English', the Scots play upon the national stereotype that 'English fans are hooligans'; hence, the Scottish fans are also 'anti-hooliganism'."[46]

Towards mutual appreciation and goodwill

The Olympics grew, however sputteringly. For the 1900 edition in Paris, 24 participants are officially cited, including Argentina, Cuba and Mexico, but, again, more have been identified – Haiti, Iran, Luxembourg and Peru.[47] In one of the Games' less admirable experiments, live pigeon shooting was introduced for the first and last time.

Necessitating as it did a much bigger trek for the Europeans, the next Games crossed the Atlantic and brought regression: a poorly-organised event in St Louis that ran alongside the World's Fair, it drew just a dozen teams. At first, the American hosts promised to send a boat to pick up the European participants but reneged on this, keeping the opposition numbers down, with the upshot that the US, with 78, won 74 more golds than the next-best rewarded entrant, Germany. Pride of place went to a local hero, George Eyser, a German immigrant who in his youth had lost a leg in a train accident yet achieved gymnastic glory with a prosthetic one: in a single day he scooped up six medals – a bronze, two silvers and three golds.

The launch of the 1908 London Games underlined the Olympics' burgeoning political symbolism. Attended by King Edward VII and other bluebloods such as the Maharajah of Nepal and the Crown Princes and Princesses of Greece and Sweden, the opening ceremony formed part of the Franco-British exhibition at Shepherd's Bush, subsequent home to such fabled local institutions as the BBC and The Who. The first international exhibition co-organised and sponsored by two countries, it was, noted alliancefrançaise.org, "a celebration of British and French industry, business, culture, and empire", the express intention of which was to "promote the entente cordiale between France and Britain" – that "adroit and charming phrase, the general adoption of which among us is a delicate compliment to the French language, suggesting more than it expresses". The phrase stood "for mutual appreciation and good-will, for common aims and interests; it covers sentiment, understanding and material relations; and in all these senses it has been conspicuously promoted by the exhibition."[48]

The official budget for that first London Olympics was £15,000, but while receipts topped £21,000, the cost of constructing the White City Stadium ran to £60,000. Oxo, the official caterer, provided refreshments for marathon competitors by way of Oxo-themed drinks and rice pudding; runners were also furnished with wet sponges and eau de cologne.

This time the field was 22, drawn almost exclusively from the neighbourhood: only Australasia (Australia and New Zealand), Canada, South Africa and the US, all firm friends of Britain, did not belong to what we now know as Europe. *The Times* captured the mood: "We are having our friends to see us in order that we may have a good time together, and may strengthen our mutual good will by comrade-ship."[49] Comradeship and goodwill were less visible in the tug-of-war, where the US team, beaten by the Liverpool Police, accused their opponents of wearing illegal footwear, then withdrew when the appeal was rejected.

Here, by the same token, was arguably the United States' foremost concession to non-insularity. As self-contained as it so willingly was when it came to its most popular spectator sports, the Olympics was different. Its importance as a boost to the collective well-being was summed up in 1928 by Major General Douglas MacArthur:

"Athletic America" is a telling phrase. It is talismanic. It suggests health and happiness. It arouses national pride and kindles anew the national spirit. Nothing is more synonymous of our national success than is our national success in athletics. If I were required to indicate today that element of American life which is most characteristic of our nationality, my finger would unerringly point to our athletics escutcheon.[50]

In 1950, Congress incorporated the United States Olympic Association and awarded it exclusive rights to Olympic symbols. Two years later emerged a seemingly one-man rebellion in the highly unlikely shape of Avery Brundage, the first American

IOC president. A converted isolationist, he conveyed his concerns in his opening address, submitting five proposals to strengthen the Olympic Movement, the last of which suggested keeping "a happy balance between justifiable national pride and the use of sport for national aggrandisement". While declining to define "justifiable pride", "national aggrandisement" or "happy balance", he echoed the suggestion to the US Olympic Association, warning that "if the Olympic Games as a result of unbridled chauvinism degenerate into contests between the hired gladiators", contests seen by the larger nations as "an attempt to build national prestige or to prove that one system of government is better than another", the Games would "lose all their purpose".[51]

Brundage acknowledged that monitoring and combatting political interference at a local level was "difficult, if not impossible" and that change could only be made by close co-operation between the IOC, the international federations and the national Olympic committees. At an IOC meeting in 1960, a few months before the Rome Games, he disputed the view espoused by Philip Noel-Baker, the Labour MP, diplomatic and academic who had carried the British flag (and won a silver medal) at the 1920 Antwerp Games. While the latter contended that "the Victory Ceremonies in the Olympic Games are a supreme example of this marriage of national and international patriotism and pride", Brundage advocated a study of "the desirability of eliminating the use of national flags and hymns". It might be preferable, he said, "to use a fanfare of trumpets instead of national hymns in the victory ceremonies" and that when the Olympic flag was raised at the opening ceremony, "perhaps all national flags should be lowered": contestants "should come simply as sportsmen and not as representatives of a country". In keeping with this, he also attacked subsidised national programmes to produce elite competitors. Needless to add, he harboured further objections to the publication of a medals table, reasoning that the bigger countries were invariably at the top but that, per capita, they were near the bottom.[52]

It is hard to take issue with Brundage on any of this. It is rather harder – as subsequent chapters will relate – to justify his conduct before and during the 1936 Games in Berlin, inarguably the most repellent instance of the Olympics being used as a nationalistic tool, not to say a racial one.

The All Blacks: Punching above their weight

> *We are a people of a thousand faces and gestures. A people fighting to preserve our history against everything and against all the evidence and possibilities. A shrewd, vain and happy people who make good use of our natural wonders with the naturalness of the carefree. A people who love everything around them and who know how to extract the wisdom of a lifetime from every second. And a people who love football.*[53]

Those sentiments could have been expressed by any number of people from countless lands. They belong to the late Sócrates Brasileira, the slender Marxist playmaker who pulled the strings so expertly for the wonderful Brazil side that would surely have won the 1982 World Cup but for a narrow defeat in a fabulous match decided by the lethal finishing of Italy's Paolo Rossi, restored to favour not all that long after being convicted of match-fixing.

Why, for more than half a century, has the world viewed Brazilians, long scarred by poverty and political instability, as the benchmark of not just collective black sporting talent and footballing excellence but footballing sorcery? Brazilians will point you in the direction of the *Malandro*, a figure from national folklore whose ancestors were slaves (not until 1888 was slavery abolished in Brazil). "He is a con-man, a trickster," explained Simon Kuper. "He works alone, and obeys no rules. Though poor, he manages to dress well, to eat in the best places, and to charm beautiful women. The point is that Brazilians see themselves as *Malandros*: he stands for the national character. Or at least, he did."[54]

Brazil have won five World Cups, more than any other nation. The skill of *los Malandros* has plenty to do with it, but it would be the height of political correctness to deny that sheer weight of numbers does not. Kuper and Stefan Szymanski addressed the population factor in their 2009 book *Why England Lose: And other curious phenomena explained* (or, to give it its full, alternative and profoundly American title, *Soccernomics: Why England Loses, Why Germany and Brazil Win, and Why the U.S., Japan, Australia, Turkey – and Even Iraq – Are Destined to Become the Kings of the World's Most Popular Sport*). Brazil, they reason, will almost always have the edge on Chile, just as Italy and Germany, the next most successful World Cup entrants, will almost always have the upper hand against Romania and Sweden.

"How is it that some countries outpunch not only their own weight, but rivals who appear to be better equipped?" wondered Huw Richards. "It can also be asked about clubs, but nations make for a more satisfactory study. They have to play the hands they are given. England cannot sign Cristiano Ronaldo or hope to see their fortunes transformed by the patronage of some oil-rich potentate. And of course the big factor in the international fortunes of football nations is population. Italy and Germany between them thwarted the World Cup ambitions of the very best teams produced by Austria, Hungary and the Netherlands. But there's still a lesson here. Those countries were able to all but close the gap on much bigger neighbours. The Hungarians of 1954 are only that single defeat away from being the serious alternative to 1970 Brazil in what Americans habitually term the GOAT (Greatest of all Time) debate. The Dutch misfortune was running into perhaps the best of all German teams on their own soil – but we still remember them rather than their 1974 conquerors. And what they had in common was a culture of not only playing football but thinking and talking about it. The Danubian style emerges [in the 1920s], amid much else, from the coffee-house ferment of late Hapsburg and early Succession State Vienna and Budapest."[55]

As evidence of the degree to which English football had fallen behind by the 21st century, Richards cited Steve McClaren's discovery that an opponent was planning a tactical change against his Dutch club Twente Enschede, prompting the former England manager to ask a 21-year-old midfielder how he could counter the shift. "He proceeded to talk for 20 minutes on the tactical aspects of our game plan, in terms of how we defended and attacked," McClaren recalled. "After 20 minutes I said, 'Very good, that's exactly what we were going to do – and by the way, where did you learn that?' He said, 'We've been doing this since we were eight or nine'… Could I have that conversation with a 21-year-old in England?"[56] The question was strictly rhetorical.

"The Dutch are a product of the culture epitomised by that lad at Twente," reasons Richards. "That intellectual engagement with the game and its possibilities places their game at the tactical cutting edge, creating football that is memorable both aesthetically and in terms of results. We [British] had our own, earlier, example in Scotland. The game may have been codified further south, but the Scots were the first really to think about it and look for different ways of playing, creating a passing game that crushed England teams still relying on founding fundamentals in the late 1870s and early 1880s. Vestiges of that culture still remain. On the odd occasions I get to football in Scotland I look forward not only to hearing some world-class invective, but a general level of terrace discourse some way ahead of what I am likely to hear in more normal haunts at Barnet or wherever Swansea are playing. And while Scots may bemoan the current state of their game, it is worth asking if there is another European nation of five million that can point to four clubs capable of reaching (and three who won) European finals and a long succession of World Cup qualifications."[57]

Given the fact that Brazil boasts around 195 million more inhabitants than New Zealand, the beguiling question is not why its footballers have been so successful but why the All Blacks are their rugby union counterparts? Or, to fine-tune slightly, why is the constant quality of their play the standard to which all other rugby nations have aspired since 1905, when a London newspaper is said to have reported that the first New Zealand party to tour Britain, immortalised as "The Originals", played as if they were "all backs"; according to Billy "Carbine" Wallace, a magnificent fullback, this resulted in a series of typographic errors describing them as "All Blacks". In *Century in Black: 100 Years of All Black Test Rugby*, Ron Palenski trades myth for something more prosaic, stating that they were first described as such the day after their opening match, a 55-4 thrashing of Devon at Exeter that saw Wallace score three tries, collect 28 points and kick his goals in a sunhat. The line appeared in the county's *Express and Echo*, which referred to "the All Blacks, as they are styled by reason of their sable and unrelieved costume".[58]

Which nations have the greatest cause to elevate sportsfolk to sainthood? Consider, first, the record of Brazil's footballers alongside that of Australia's Test cricketers, both time-honoured brand leaders:

- In 938 internationals up to 26 June 2013, in a sport where the best seldom cross swords, Brazil had won 587 and lost 157; only Holland earned parity (three wins apiece); only Argentina (38 wins to 41 in head-to-heads) bore more than a passing resemblance to a regular threat;
- In 754 Tests up to 30 June 2013, in a far more concentrated and reasonably balanced international sport where draws were the commonest result for more than a century, Australia's cricketers won 1.77 times as often as they lost; they were also the only nation with a winning record against all the others.

Now let's throw in a couple of younger outliers. Only two men have won squash's World Open more than four times: Jansher Khan (eight) and the man he displaced as the game's foremost exponent, Jahangir Khan (six); the latter, indeed, is Pakistan's most celebrated sportsman, having set, from 1981 to 1986, the extant record for a winning streak by a professional athlete: 555 matches; both hail from Nuwai Kelai, a village in Peshawar.

For Kenya's athletes, the 1968 Olympics, held five years after their country had secured independence from Britain, signified the start of an even more remarkable feat of single-nation dominance. Naftali Temu (10,000m) was the first to strike, followed a few days later in the blue-riband 1,500m by Kip Keino, who beat Jim Ryun by 20 metres – an Olympic event record that still stood after the latest London Games – and later said he had been "prepared to die for my country". The third gold was won in the 3000m steeplechase, perhaps the most exacting of all foot races; given that apartheid's tentacles had seen them join their fellow Africans in boycotting the Games of 1976 and 1980, by 2012 Kenya had collected every gold in that event for which they had subsequently competed, a victorious sequence that currently stands at 10. At the 1988 Seoul Olympics, all but one of the men's golds from 800m to marathon went to Kenyans.

Twenty-four years later, David Rudisha became the first runner to dip under 1min 41secs for the 800m; at that moment, the event's best three times all belonged to him, as did six of the fastest eight and ten of the top 17. Most of these arch-competitors, moreover, come from the same area – the altitude-heavy Rift Valley. In time, other nations would set up training camps there, leading in turn to Olympic heroics such as those perpetrated by Mo Farah, who so delighted Britons in 2012 with a 5,000m-10,000m double. In the annals of team selection, securing a place in the Kenyan middle-distance team may well be the stiffest challenge yet.

It would also be remiss to overlook the runners and scrummers who have worn the red jerseys of Wales, drawn from a population that currently stands just over 3m and Europe's most successful rugby union internationalists over the past century. From there have come not only some of the code's most indelible talents (Bleddyn Williams, Barry John, Gareth Edwards, Phil Bennett and Leigh Halfpenny, to name but five) but the bulk of the British and Irish Lions team that achieved that historic series victory in Australia in 2013. All the same, for unstoppability, no sportsmen have done their nation prouder than another band of unionists – the All Blacks.

In 501 internationals up to and including a thumping series-settling victory over France on 22 June 2013, they had won

379, lost 104. More significantly, they had proved themselves against the next best ad nauseam: 215 of those victories had come at the expense of their most testing regular opponents, Australia, England, France and South Africa, against whom their winning percentages, respectively, were 67.81, 77.14, 75.93 and 56.47. Even against the united might of the Lions – albeit always on home soil – it was 76.32. And still complete satisfaction remains elusive. Justin Marshall, their erstwhile captain, captured the extent of ambition and the burden of expectation: "All Blacks are stimulated first and foremost by perfection, by searching for the ultimate game. You'll never achieve that, but they still seek it, and because of the demands of our public they'll keep seeking it."[59]

* * *

Rugby union's most extraordinary factoid is that the All Blacks, often unnerved by expectation, failed to win more than one of the first six World Cups, though amends were made in front of their jubilant countrymen in 2011. But from what otherworldly foundations did their otherwise staggering domination spring?

Step forward Jamie Belich, Oxford University's Professor of Commonwealth History and New Zealand's pre-eminent historian, the academic who redefined his country's founding myth in his PhD thesis, *The New Zealand Wars*. Yes, Maoris were treated better by white New Zealanders than the Aboriginals were by white Australians (as evinced by the early presence in that dusky jersey of Maoris such as George Nepia); not, as had long been propounded, because New Zealanders were kinder people but because, quite simply, the Maoris were less inclined to be pushed around than the Aboriginals.

"Both rugby and New Zealand were sites in which marginal gentility sought to assert and entrench itself," wrote Belich in *Paradise Reforged*. "The aspiring and insecure New Zealand gentry opted for the matching sport."[60] That, though, was insufficient to secure rugby's status as the national game. The surge to dominance, attests Balich, began in the 1890s and climaxed in the mid-1920s, by when rugby club members outnumbered those for tennis, the country's next most important sport, by two to one; their ranks were four times as thick as soccer and rugby league combined.[61] While the "intersections between New Zealand, rugby union and marginal gentility" were crucial, Belich also cites three other factors – "populism, moral evangelism and recolonisation itself", of which the first has been "laundered out of, or glossed over, the official version". This contribution stemmed primarily from lower-class children, "the bridge by which folk sports made their way to New Zealand", and ship crews.

Come the 1930s, *Truth*, the leading newspaper, "had succumbed to rugby with the fanaticism of a convert, discussing it in a 'reverential language which saw rugby as some type of pseudo-religious activity'. The organ of populism had to concede that rugby had become part of the essence of Better Britain, proving both Britishness and superiority with every victory over fellow dominions and mother countries. Rugby continued to be used, certainly to the 1960s and arguably to 1981 [when, as we shall see, the nation was bitterly divided over the maintenance of sporting links with South Africa], to powerfully assert a strong and distinctive New Zealand collective identity."[62]

In essence, then, to adapt the title of a chapter in the government website's "Encyclopaedia of New Zealand",[63] is it all about a quest to be "Better Britons"? Nowhere, for all that New Zealanders have held the world mile record, collected F1 and world showjumping titles and set a Test wicket-taking record, have its denizens been better Britons than on the rugby field. Balich's conclusion is salient and succinct. Cricket may be the most quintessentially English of games, but rugby, "one of the very few things that unite even Ireland", is "the most British".[64]

The Irish Question

The most complex relationship between sport and nationalism could long be found in Northern Ireland. Amid the climate of sectarian hatred between Catholics and the "loyalist" Protestant majority that divided the Irish so bloodily in the 20th century, the impact on sport was sad and profound. In 2012, David Hassan and Philip O'Kane examined "the rationale for the limited use of sport by a range of paramilitary organisations in Northern Ireland to supplement their wider political and ideological aspirations". While it was wrong, they believe, to cite sport as "a consistent or substantial factor in the ethno-sectarian conflict", it was deployed strategically by terrorist organisations and thus "rarely ill-conceived even if the outcomes of their actions were almost always unjustifiable and, ultimately, futile".[65]

The one game to unite north and south was rugby union, but this was attributable to the fact that the players were predominantly middle-class and privately educated: Mike Gibson and Jackie Kyle, probably the finest players ever to don the green shirt, were both Protestant graduates of Queen's University, Belfast. "Home" was Lansdowne Road, Dublin; the players deemed themselves British, and toured with the Lions. Nationalist antagonism was kept at bay, noted Dick Holt and Tony Mason, by "the social solidarity of professional men".[66] Gibson, Kyle and Willie-John McBride, who led the most successful of all Lions tours, to South Africa in 1974, "required a supple and detached view of sport". In 2013, reflecting one of sport's more surprising evolutionary developments, the headquarters of the International Rugby Board, the Six Nations, the British and Irish Lions and the European Rugby Cup were all in Dublin. How far we had progressed since 1972: at the height of The Troubles, the Five Nations title was shared that season because neither the Scots nor Welsh were willing to travel to Dublin.

Boxing, too, had one Irish governing body, the Irish Amateur Boxing Association, obliging Ulster fighters to represent Eire. Inevitably, this generated complications. The youngest member of the 1988 Olympic team at 18, Wayne McCullough, a Protestant from the Shankhill Road, was awarded the honour of carrying the national flag in Seoul. When he and Michael Carruth won silver and gold in the Barcelona Games four years later, a civic reception was thrown in their honour in Dublin, and the greeting from the Taoiseach, Albert Reynolds, was affectionate; in Belfast, by contrast, Carruth's feat was ignored while the welcome accorded McCullough was diffident. He was less a hero than an embarrassment.

Far more readily accepted, to a degree, was Barry McGuigan, the "Clones Cyclone". The grandson of an Irish Republican Army captain, he sensibly pursued an entirely neutral stance, inspiring the cross-border slogan "Leave the Fighting to McGuigan". A Catholic from the south, he wed a Protestant, fought in Britain and won the world featherweight title in 1985, a dove of peace emblazoned on his shorts. "At a dark hour in Ireland Barry McGuigan's spirit shone a light towards peace," avowed the best-known Irishman of the times, Bono. "Barry's not only a champion, he's a hero." Nationalists, however, dubbed him "Barry the Brit" for not fighting under the Irish flag. Indeed, as he would reveal in his 2011 autobiography, published not long after he was honoured with a UN Inspiration Award for Peace, the IRA gave him cause to carry a gun.

"I was told there was a plot to kidnap me... Security forces on both sides of the border were keeping an eye on me. It came at a time when people were disappearing and not long after the kidnapping of the racehorse Shergar. So I was issued with a gun and the police taught me how to shoot it... My suspicion is it was all about ransom – attempting to raise money for terrorist activities. But I think the terrorists then realised that because of my popularity and non-political stance, kidnapping me had the potential to backfire."[67]

McGuigan returned to the front pages in 2013 when the young fighter Carl Frampton, whom he was now managing, challenged the Spaniard, Kiko Martinez, for the European super-bantamweight crown. "If I had the option of boxing at an Olympic Games for Ireland or Great Britain, it would have been Ireland, because I was looked after by Ireland from an early age," said Frampton, who hails from a resolute Unionist stronghold in Tiger's Bay, North Belfast. "I'm a Protestant from a staunch Protestant area, but I was proud to box for Ireland.

But in Commonwealth events, I was proud to box under the Northern Ireland flag."[68]

As an amateur, McGuigan, who came from Clones in County Monaghan, one of the Republic of Ireland's three Ulster counties, won a gold medal for Northern Ireland and represented Ireland at the Olympics, but the dearth of professional fighting in the south pulled him, like so many other aspirants, to the mainland. "Ulster was my provincial title, it was literally 500 metres down the road," he would reflect. "I didn't want to travel away, I was a homebird and all my fans were in Ulster anyway. In order to box for the British title, I had to take out British citizenship." He was entirely justified in stating that this was "a bold and dangerous thing to do in those fraught times".[69]

Three decades later, by when the slow inroads made by the 1998 Good Friday Agreement meant that just 7% of Belfast schools were of mixed religion[70], those fraught times had returned, with Unionists threatening the fragile peace. "It doesn't seem a nice place to live right now," acknowledged Frampton. "People are entitled to their opinions and to [peaceful] protests, but when cars are being burnt out, it's not nice. It is as bad as it has been in the last ten years." Ever the optimist, McGuigan expressed the fond hope that his protégé could unite Belfast. "He's a Protestant kid going out with a Catholic girl, he is the epitome of what Northern Ireland is all about with a shared future. Time has moved on, things have changed. We have now got to the stage where we don't want any flags, we don't want any anthems, he simply goes in and gives people a good time."[71]

In this context, then, the competitive arts could scarcely be described as bridge-builders. Soccer had the potential to assume that role; instead, it aggravated that hatred. Crowd violence marred clashes between the leading Protestant (Linfield) and Catholic (Belfast Celtic) clubs: at the conclusion of the fixture on Boxing Day in 1948, the Linfield crowd assaulted the Belfast Celtic players with brutal intent, breaking the legs of one forward, who never played again. Games between the communities were a no-no; Belfast Celtic pulled out of senior football in Ulster, never to return. "This was a different and darker world," attested Holt and Mason, "where sport and nationalism was neither festive nor ritualised." Rather than represent a national consensus, sport "reflected and exacerbated existing national divisions".[72]

* * *

The Gaelic Athletic Association proved a robust and rugged symbol of resistance. It was founded in 1884 by Michael Cusack and Maurice Davin; the patrons were Michael Davitt, the founder of the Irish Land League recently released from an English jail, Charles Parnell, president of the Land League, and Archbishop Thomas Croke, a leading nationalist. Their purpose was to protect ancient native sports, primarily hurling and Gaelic football, and hence challenge what was regarded as British sporting imperialism.

What dismayed the passionate Croke, venting his spleen in a letter to Cusack published by *The Nation* in 1889, was "the ugly and irritating fact that we are daily importing from England not only her manufactured goods, which we cannot help doing... but together with her fashions, her accents, her vicious literature, her music, her dances and her manifold mannerisms, her games also and her pastimes, to the utter discredit of our own grand national sport and to the sore humiliation, as I believe, of every genuine son and daughter of the old land. Ball-playing, hurling, football kicking according to the Irish rules, 'casting', leaping in various ways, wrestling handygrips, top-pegging, leapfrog, rounders, tip in the hat and all such favourite exercises and amusements amongst men and boys, may now be said not only dead and buried but in several locations to be entirely forgotten and unknown."[73]

The biggest event in the Irish sporting calendar has long been the All-Ireland football final, which drew more than 90,000 to the GAA-owned Croke Park in 1961. Tattooed far more indelibly on Irish memories, albeit for vastly different reasons, was the match there on 21 November 1920, Bloody Sunday. With the war of independence raging, the Royal Irish Constabulary avenged the killing of 14 British undercover agents by the IRA, fatally shooting 14 innocent spectators.

Many militant Ulster Catholics were adamant: they would not, could not, play what they perceived to be "British" sports. To Derek Birley, former Vice-Chancellor of the University of Ulster, the GAA survived its early financial difficulties, and an internal rift engendered by the decision to bar membership to the RIC, "and undoubtedly helped to bring sport to many working-class athletes – at a price. It was an irony that in Ireland professionalism was kept at bay both by rampant nationalism and by the handiness of England for those sportsmen who wanted to earn a pound or two, which Irish clubs and associations could not afford to pay."[74]

GAA members were prohibited from playing other sports until the 1970s, leading to the banishment, among others, of Con Martin. A remarkably versatile ballplayer from County Dublin, he transported his considerable Gaelic football skills to the Football League, kept goal for what was then known as Eire in a surprising win over Spain in 1946, and three years later scored from the spot to set up the first victory by an overseas team on English soil. However, when it came to light that, while helping Leinster take the Gaelic championship in 1941, he had simultaneously been playing association football for Drumcondra, he was banned from the former sport and prevented from collecting his medal until 1971.[75]

Perhaps inevitably, the GAA also served as a fertile recruiting ground for the IRA and hence became a target for the Royal Ulster Constabulary and Protestant paramilitaries alike during the Troubles. The 3,000th killing during those dreadful decades occurred outside a GAA club; in 1988, en route to a GAA fixture, Aiden McAnespie was shot dead by the occupying British Army – whose soldiers were not permitted to join a GAA club, a constraint also imposed on the RUC. "The cycle of retribution was remorseless," warranted Holt and Mason with nary a trace of exaggeration, "and sport was trapped within it."[76]

The one-sided special relationship

At the turn of the 20th century, by when the America's Cup sailing challenge was entering its fourth decade, sporting empires old and new began to meet on a regular basis in other spheres. In 1900, Dwight Filley Davis, a Harvard student from St Louis, offered a large silver punchbowl for a team competition in his favourite sport, lawn tennis, which initially attracted participants solely from the US and the British Isles (as the Limey collective was billed), who contested five of the first six Davis Cup finals. By the outbreak of the First World War, Austria, Australasia, Belgium, Canada, France and Germany had all joined in.

The current century found the ITF all but defining self-delusion, billing the Davis Cup as the "greatest annual competition in team sports"; the truth was far more prosaic. Novak Djokovic attributed his rise to the top of the men's rankings to helping Serbia lift the trophy for the first time, but the nicest way to describe the general attitude of the leading players was ambivalent. Hence the clandestine meeting at Roland Garros during the 2013 French Open, where Pat Rafter, the Australian team captain, exhorted his fellow captains to press for fundamental changes to the format: without such surgery, a relic would become an irredeemable anachronism. Then again, in as profoundly individual a sport as tennis, the allure of collective endeavour was never going to endure too long once professionalism was formalised. Golf was different, possibly because it embraced professionalism so much earlier, but more likely because its major team events pitted Britain against the US. Founded in 1953 by John Jay Hopkins, a Canadian industrialist, the Canada Cup, a two-a-side tourney subsequently reborn as the World Cup, has never achieved remotely the prominence desired.

Peace brought a surge of exclusively Transatlantic tussles. In 1922 came the Walker Cup (amateur men golfers), followed the next year by the Wightman Cup (women's tennis), the Ryder Cup in 1927 (professional men's golf) and, in 1932, the Curtis

Cup (amateur women golfers). The Wightman Cup would live on until 1989, when the chasm in quality finally persuaded the organisers to give up on a long-lost cause. In 1979, a similar fork in the road was reached in the Ryder Cup when, six years after the Irish had joined the sinking ship, and with 10 successive meetings having failed to produce a single British victory, the Americans began confronting a side representing Europe: the first major sporting collective to do so; the women professionals followed suit when the Solheim Cup was inaugurated in 1990. Reflecting the continental revolution started by the flamboyant Seve Ballesteros and accelerated by his fellow Spaniard José-Maria Olazábal and Germany's Bernhard Langer, the men's tide would turn, eventually with a vengeance.

Ad break: American exceptionalism revisited

What's with the obsession of wanting to make baseball into a worldwide sport? Football sure isn't. And you know what, we Americans don't care and those Europeans also don't care. It really doesn't matter because everybody's fine with it.
Comment from Tomo Kurihara, *Bleacher Report*, 2013

The turbulent inter-war years, a period dominated by new political ideologies and an enhanced, spikier nationalism, saw a mushrooming of international championships, hitherto confined in many sports to the Olympics.

1920: *First ice hockey world championships and Prix De L'Arc De Triomphe*

1923: *First Le Mans 24-Hour race*

1927: *First world table tennis, world professional snooker championships*

1930: *First FIFA World Cup and Empire (later Commonwealth) Games*

1934: *First US Masters (golf) and European Athletics Championships (men only)*

1935: *First European basketball championships*

1936: First world speedway championships

1938: First world canoeing championships

Post-1945, this internationalism continued apace, notably among sports no longer quite so keen to accept the Olympics, let alone amateur events, as the pinnacle:

1949: First world volleyball, motor-cycling, water-ski-ing and badminton (team) championships; first Badminton Three-Day Event (equestrianism)

1950: First world motor racing (Formula 1) and basketball championships

1953: First world show jumping championships

1954: First rugby league World Cup

1956: First European Cup final (football)

1959: First World Student Games

1960: First European Championships and World Club Championship (both football)

1962: First world rowing championships

1964: First world matchplay championships (golf)

1965: First European Athletics Cup

1966: First world bowls championships

1967: First world lacrosse championships

1971: First hockey World Cup

1973: First cricket World Cup (women)

1975: First cricket World Cup (men)

1977: First world badminton championships (individual)

1982: First world fencing championships

1983: First world athletics championships

1987: First rugby union World Cup

2006: First baseball World Classic

Note that first entry. That there has been a world championship for ice hockey since 1920 – the Olympic Games served this function until 1968 – constitutes a loud raspberry, one might assume, to those who believe New Yorkers and Californians and Kentuckians have no interest in international sport. However, this can most readily be traced to the fact that the game is hugely popular beyond the Hudson River, notably in Canada, Eastern Europe and Scandinavia. Now note that last entry – both the year and the sport. Not until the first decade of the third post-Old Testament millennium, did baseball, the United States' national pastime for the best part of two centuries, institute a world championship.

As touched on earlier, American exceptionalism is reflected in its long, sterling and at times strident resistance to any football code that does not call a scrum a scrimmage or a match a game. This does much to explain why international sport has always been inconsequential in two of the three of the most popular US professional team games, and more or less so in the third. For a nation seldom shy about flexing its muscles and imposing its beliefs on others, a nation so obsessed with allegiance to the flag – the national anthem is sung before major and minor sporting events alike and players are fined for not properly observing the ritual – this seems most curious. Likewise that none of the United States' three favourite spectator sports – baseball, American football and basketball – belongs to a regular international circuit to match those in soccer, cricket and rugby.

Baseball, basketball and all that grappling on the gridiron are identified almost exclusively with their nation of origin. That said, the wheels are turning, slowly but perceptibly. The Most Valuable Player of the 2011 NBA finals was Germany's Dirk Nowitzki, who four years earlier had become the first European player to win the seasonal award. Baseball's most celebrated exponents of the early 21st century, as measured by deeds in Major League Baseball, the planet's most magnetic league alongside the IPL and the English Premier League, hailed from Cuba, the Dominican Republic, Japan, Panama, Puerto Rico and Venezuela.

* * *

Whether or not you acknowledge a nation's size and population as a contributory factor, the club v country debate in American sport, in contrast to almost everywhere else on Planet Sport, is barely audible. What matters in American sport, in short, is American sport. Throughout the Second World War, while bombing stopped play in cricket and football, for baseball it was World Series business as usual. Texas, Ohio and Pennsylvania may turn out many of the galaxy's finest golfers, runners, fighters and overhead smashers, but – and here lies perhaps the greatest irony – the land that does most to celebrate and encourage the individual prefers team sports.

In many respects, American sport occupies a parallel universe to British sport. Until 2011, TV revenues were shared equally in American football, not according to a team's win-loss record. The draft system, whereby promising young practitioners of the major professional team sports are signed from universities in descending order of quality, allows the prime choices to go to the teams that fared the worst on the field the previous season. There is no relegation or promotion in the NFL, NBA, MLB or NHL. Nor are those leagues elitist: over the past four decades, major league baseball has all but doubled its membership. No less busy in its recruitment drive has been basketball – which in the 1990s, under the canny entrepreneurial guidance of commissioner David Stern, transformed itself into one of the planet's hippest and most profitable sporting attractions. Fifty years ago, there were eight NBA teams in two conferences; in 1976, there were 18 in four divisions; 30 years later there were 30 in six. This should not, though, be mistaken for charity. Joining such clubs means stumping up multi-million-dollar entrance fees, shared gleefully by one's fellow franchise owners.

Nor – not even in Ryder Cup years when the home crowds have been as biased and offensive as any – is there an American national team whose fortunes are chronicled on front pages as well as back, its heroes handed presidential acclaim and tabloid roastings. Not here does a nation's self-esteem and identity stand or fall on the result of a qualifying group match against the might of Andorra. A Pete Sampras or a Tiger Woods – until his recent fall from grace – may do more to boost American self-image than a consistently successful team, but sport there is still more about entertainment, and the entertainment industry, than symbolism.

Which further explains why there is no Pan-American Football Championship to scrap for, let alone a World Cup for the quarterbacks and running backs of the New Orleans Saints and New England Patriots to dominate. Baseball's leading professionals thumbed their noses at the Olympics, where Fidel Castro's Cuba, unconscionably, have been more successful. For that matter, how many Americans have ever competed in Formula 1? Why bother when you have NASCAR and the Indy 500?

Basketball's quadrennial World Championships began in 1950, and it is a measure of the game's spread that the honour of staging its reincarnation as a World Cup fell to Spain. The US victory in 2010 was their first in 16 years, and only the third since 1954. The remainder had been carried off by Argentina, Brazil (two), Soviet Union/Russia (three), Spain and, topping the chart, the former Yugoslavia (five). The event takes place outside the NBA season, but nobody would ever claim that the league's foremost players have regarded it as a career pinnacle in the way that a cricketer, footballer or rugby player of either code regards his or her World Cup. That Michael Jordan, by common consent the greatest basketballer of all, never deemed it worth his while to compete in the sport's biggest international tournament testifies to this comparative lack of enthusiasm. Nor do LeBron James or Kobe Bryant have any time for such non-domestic trifles, though that could conceivably change given the noises made by the NBA about withdrawing players from Olympic duty to bolster negotiations over profit projections when the event returned to its original World Cup status in 2014. For the foreseeable future, being fit for the NBA remains the be-all and end-all.

Even the birth of the World Baseball Classic altered little. While it demonstrated the spread of talent, its impact was diluted by the decision of many leading major leaguers to preserve their bodies and energies for the coming domestic campaign; Albert Pujols and Jose Bautista opted out but, in the main, there was an abiding sense that the sons of the Caribbean and Latin America, let alone the Cubans and Japanese, the last of whom won the first two tournaments, felt rather prouder to be flying their flag than the Americans.

Whether the American public give more than a hoot for all this is doubtful. It said much for the event's low profile in the home of the game, and the relative lack of interest his readers held for international competition, that Thomas Boswell felt obliged to preview the inaugural tournament thus:

> *You probably don't know much about the WBC. But you will soon… Every great player is keenly aware of what's on tap and almost all get a special excitement from representing his country. Like golf's Ryder Cup, the WBC has a chance to emerge as an event that means more to the players than it does, yet, to the public. When fans find out that athletes are passionate, they generally join the enthusiasm. If that proves true, then the WBC may be the surprise event of '06. Just to hint at the level of interest outside the United States for the 16-country event, there have been more than 3,500 requests for media credentials to the WBC – more than for the Winter Olympics.*[77]

American passion proved harder to rouse. The relative lack of teeth-gnashing following a shock defeat by Canada was certainly indicative of a degree of all-round apathy. Nor was there much consternation when the US lost in the semi-finals of the second tournament in 2009. Nothing much had changed four years later, when Mark Teixera, one of the leading lights on duty for the strongest Team USA yet, summed up the consensus view in a manner most observers would have found utterly inconceivable had the event been prefixed by the acronym FIFA, IRB or ICC, calling the competition "an exhibition".

MLB's pre-eminent pitcher, Justin Verlander, its beefiest hitter, Josh Hamilton, and rising stars such as Bryce Harper and Mike Trout were all missing from Team USA. "What are they afraid of?" wondered ESPN's Jayson Stark.

We all know the answer, right? They're afraid of getting hurt, screwing up their season before it starts, letting down their team and ticking off the folks who run their respective teams. Hey, sure they are. But here's another question: Have they checked the facts? MLB has done extensive research about the WBC and the impact it's had on the health of players who took part in it. And you know what that research determined? That the health risks of participating are more myth than reality. Here are the facts:

- *Players who didn't play in the WBC in 2009 were nearly twice as likely to spend time on the disabled list that April as players who played – 17.8 percent of non-WBC participants versus 9.5 percent of those who did participate. Only 11 of the 115 players on a WBC roster made a trip to the DL [disabled list].*[78]

- *There were 73 players on the disabled list when the 2009 season opened. Only two of them were players who were involved in the WBC. Just one (Rick VandenHurk of Team Netherlands) was a pitcher. The other (Ichiro Suzuki) wasn't actually "injured". He was out with an ulcer.*

- *In only two of the past eight seasons has baseball started the season with less than 9 percent of active players on the disabled list. It happened to be the two years in which the WBC took place during spring training – 2006 and 2009.*

"Some believe that for the WBC to gain popularity among American fans, Team USA has to win the tournament," reported Anthony McCarron in the New York *Daily News* shortly before the opening group game in Phoenix against Mexico. "But some fans are solely concerned about their players getting injured while away from their major league teams and are actually relieved when a big name such as Justin Verlander passes on playing. 'We're going to need their support, because the other countries, they have nothing but support, so we need the USA to back us up and we'll feed off them,' said second baseman Brandon Phillips of the Reds."[79]

Mexico won, which at least incited a bit of a rant from Kevin Kernan in the *New York Post*:

> *America's game is turning into America's shame. On a night Team USA was humbled 5-2 by Mexico at Chase Field in the World Baseball Classic… as R. A. Dickey was shelled, Major League Baseball commissioner Bud Selig talked about the importance of the globalization of the game and of one day having a "real World Series". Yes, it is a new baseball world.*[80]

In England, of course, a defeat of that ilk would have had the tabloids sharpening their switchblades. At the nadir of his tenure as the England football manager – a draw with Saudi Arabia – a headline in the *Daily Mirror* sought to sum up the nation's ire towards manager Bobby Robson, who would lead his country to the FIFA World Cup semi-final two years later: "Go! In the name of Allah, Go!" Come the World Baseball Classic, conversely, the *Washington Post* did not even send Boswell, its baseball-adoring chief sportswriter.

"There are two teams out there. One team is trying to play cricket, the other isn't"

Banning weapons "might be a nice idea but it is one that is always doomed", acknowledged Sam Kiley in his review for *The Times* of Robert M. Neer's *Napalm: An American Biography*. "Belligerents use whatever it takes to win. It's good that napalm is now naughty. But, as Neer demonstrates, war just isn't cricket." That cricket should still be a byword for fair play in 2013, given what even those resistant to its charms know of its history, is nothing short of dumbfounding. Two images, both from the 1980s, should suffice: that fearsome Guyanese fast bowler Colin Croft barging into a non-compliant New Zealand umpire and Javed Miandad, the most combative player to wear the green of Pakistan, bat cocked, threatening to biff the equally provocative and confrontational Dennis Lillee. All the same, that most durable of sporting clichés had surely been rubbished once and for all during the Ashes series of 1932-33, the encounter that gave us one of the most controversial and loaded words in the sporting lexicon.

Bodyline. Eight decades have been and gone yet still the term resonates, triggering shudders of English guilt and Australian fury. No other sport but cricket, with its pristine self-image and symbolic clout, could have stirred up such a stink. On one level, the sorry saga with the oddball name (as Bodylinegate, it would sound conspicuously sillier today) embraced politics, imperialism, nationalism and notions of what is, isn't and might or might not be cricket. On another, it stemmed from fear of fast bowling – or, more specifically, of being hit by a very hard ball. Maurice Leyland, a gritty Yorkshire and England batsman of the interwar period who saved his obstinate best for the Australians, expressed it best: "None of us likes it but some of us don't let on."[81]

England v Australia has always been about colonisers and colonised, anxiety and aspiration, old world and new – and never more so than it was in that winter of 1932-33. The arguments that still rage around that tour may seem somewhat disproportionate when set against the more complex issues besieging sport today, but that should not dilute or diminish the debate. In fact, although the superficial trigger was bodyline bowling, the root cause was actually as much politics as ethics.

In 1929, showing scant sympathy for a Depression-riddled dominion, the British, eager to stamp their authority amid a shifting world order, had devalued the Australian dollar and urged banks to be stricter on loans. Payments were defaulted. Dispatched from the Bank of England to sort things out, Sir Otto Niemeyer visited Melbourne and concluded that the populace was living "too luxuriously".[82] So he recommended cuts in wages and pensions. When these were imposed, strikes broke out, the mood stridently anti-Pom. Retaliatory tariffs were slapped on British goods; demand mounted for an Australian, rather than British, governor-general. Empire Day, stipulated a law passed by the New South Wales Labour Party, would no longer be celebrated; nor did the state's schoolchildren have to salute the Union Jack.

From Buckingham Palace came disquiet over the first local governor-general, a chap with the Pythonesque name of Sir Isaac Isaacs. In 1932, Whitehall responded by ordering Sir Philip Game, the governor-general in situ, to sack Jack Lang, the bullish New South Wales premier, who had had the audacity to refuse to meet interest payments due to London owners of government bonds. "It seems the people of New South Wales had democratically elected the wrong person," as the comedian and social historian Mark Steel reasoned with all due sardonicism.[83] The relationship between mother country and troublesome teen was plumbing unimagined depths. The "Bodyline" tour began five months later. For the England team in general, and captain Douglas Jardine in particular, defeat was not an option.

* * *

What fascinates still about this reverberating drama are the three main actors: Jardine, the Bombay-born son of a Scottish lawyer, Harold Larwood, a miner-cum-fast bowler from Nottinghamshire, and their target, Donald Bradman – "our Don Bradman" as the popular song had it – the slightly-built lad from the New South Wales bush who had honed his prodigious batting skills behind the family home, hitting a golf ball against a water tank with a single stump. The 1930 Ashes series had seen him announce his genius. In those five Tests he helped Australia regain the urn by amassing 974 runs, an individual record that seems destined to remain unchallenged. In the third Test at Headingley, seven weeks before his 22nd birthday, he set a new Test record, amassing 334 – 309 in a single day, a feat still unmatched in international annals. "Bradman versus England" proclaimed the *Eastern Daily Press*. "He's Out" rejoiced the late extra edition of *The Star* after he was eventually dismissed (cue a gift of $A1000 from A. E. Whitelaw, a countryman who had prospered as a soap manufacturer after settling in England – a gift worth 50 times as much half a century later).[84]

No sportsman, arguably, has ever meant more to a young nation. From mid-1930 until late 1943 it has been calculated that more than 20% of Australian adults were unemployed. In 1932-33, according to the 1933 census, two-thirds of those who were not earned less than the basic wage. "Susso" – sustenance allowance – amounted to less than half that. Bradman made them forget their plight, however fleetingly. Half a century before *Crocodile Dundee* presented a rather different face, as Bob Hawke, the former Prime Minister, warranted, "the international image of Australia was very much that of Bradman".

By the time he retired in 1948, Bradman's Test average would be a dizzying 99.94: this still makes him *more than half as good again* as any batsman who has ever regularly exercised his talents at the highest level. Aside from a relentless focus and an unquenchable thirst for absolute dominance, the key lay in a highly unorthodox technique, one that enabled him not only to score with extraordinary rapidity but keep the ball on the ground. In *The Art of Cricket*, he offered a priceless pointer: "There should be all possible emphasis on attack, on the aggressive outlook, and if technique is going to prove the master of a player and not his servant, then it will not be doing its job."[85]

There is a case to be made for Bradman as the ultimate sporting phenomenon. When Charlie Davis, the creative Australian statistician, devised a formula to calculate athletic greatness, Bradman topped the chart. Limiting himself to baseball, basketball, cricket, football and golf, Davis used average and standard deviation (σ) to establish that his nearest rivals were Pelé, whose goals-per-game superiority over other professional footballers was 3.7 σ, and Ty Cobb, whose batting average was 3.6 σ above the overall baseball mean; Bradman's average was 4.4 σ above the norm.[86] The miracle is that he achieved what he did over a span of 20 years while being obliged to cope with the daily pressures that went with being a national symbol (even in his 80s he was receiving up to 400 letters each week – and answering the lot). His is a sustained reign of unimaginable excellence that will almost certainly always resist time's claws. Only in that 1932-33 Ashes series did he appear remotely mortal.

* * *

England's sole glimmer of hope sprang from the final Test of that 1930 series. Although Bradman made a magisterial 232 at The Oval, for a few sweet if fleeting moments, he looked vulnerable to Larwood's searing pace. "I've got it," exclaimed Jardine upon seeing the newsreel footage. "He's yellow." Thus, in his mind, was a strategy born.

The son of a barrister and former first-class cricketer, Jardine had been on the 1928-29 Ashes tour but had chosen to focus on his business interests as a solicitor during the summer of 1930. He had fomented a relationship of mutual loathing with the Australian crowds, provoking them by wearing a multi-coloured Harlequin cap and even alleging, at one juncture, that "all Australians are uneducated, and an unruly mob". Appointed to lead England's next tour of Australia, he resolved to attack Bradman with a well-worn strategy known as leg-theory, about which, he asserted in his contemporaneous account of the tour, *In Quest of The Ashes*, "there is nothing new".[87] Executed by Larwood, who was recorded at 93mph, and further abetted by fielders placed expressly to catch any shots he might fend off his body in self-defence, it was transformed from a negative gambit into a terror tactic that nonetheless stayed within the rules if not the spirit of the game. Crucial was Jardine's visit in the summer of 1932 to the Belgravia flat of Frank Foster, the eccentric fast bowler who had combined so lethally with Sydney Barnes to help England wallop Australia in the winter of 1911-12. It was Foster who advised Jardine about the field placings.

Jardine returned from Australia a national hero, his ploy a resounding success for all that it had necessitated starting sport's first significant diplomatic row. Bradman was cut down to size, averaging, by his own revolutionary standards, a comparatively modest 56 in a series England won 4-1.

* * *

"Bodyline", the word by which Jardine's brand of leg-theory would come to be known, was actually a reporter's invention. In filing his report of the Sydney Test, Hugh Buggy of the

Melbourne Herald, having already used the phrase "bowling on the line of the body", tried to cut the costs of the telegram by abbreviating this to "bodyline bowling". Little can Buggy have suspected that his invention would come to symbolise the precariously thin line between fair and unfair play, between sportsmanship and gamesmanship.

National outrage erupted during the second day of the third Test, watched by a new record crowd of 50,000 at the Adelaide Oval on 14 January, a day that left deep if not irreparable scars. The first flashpoint came when Australia's captain and opening batsman, Bill Woodfull, a devout Christian heartily respected by both sides, was struck over the heart by a rearing ball from Larwood. After a painful few minutes Woodfull resumed his innings, but before he could confront the next ball, Jardine – according to Larwood – clapped his hands, stopping the bowler, then motioned his fielders into the so-called "leg trap". Abuse poured from the stands; Bill Johnson, one of the home selectors, declared it "the most unsportsmanlike act ever witnessed on an Australian cricket field". "Cancel the remaining two Tests," demanded the president of the Victorian Cricket Association, Canon Hughes. "Let England take the Ashes for what they're worth."[88]

"I saw some of Adelaide's octogenarians in the members' enclosure rise to their feet, flush scarlet of face and, with their Adam's apples throbbing, count Jardine and his team out," recollected Dick Whitington, then a 20-year-old spectator and later a much-travelled cricket reporter. "Respectable Adelaide men they were, professional and business men, scions of Adelaide's Establishment. I knew some of their daughters. They had not seen Bodyline bowling before... they did not want to sit without protesting while it was being aimed at the heart and head of a badly stricken man, a man who in their opinion stood for all the finest qualities that had come to be associated with cricket."[89]

Later – according to a leak many believed to have been sprung by Bradman – Woodfull was lying on the dressing-room massage table when Sir Pelham Warner, the tour manager, walked in to express his concern. The taciturn Woodfull made no bones about his displeasure, banished the humiliated Warner and delivered the game's most memorable and symbolic soundbite: "There are two teams out there. One is trying to play cricket and the other is not." Those words still represent the very essence of how the game is perceived, and perceives itself.

"Not Cricket!" harrumphed the front page of the *Daily Telegraph*. The headline over Neville Cardus's report in the *Manchester Guardian* (albeit one, he admitted to his readers, that he had filed from England) was "Hooligans".[90] Tempers boiled over again on day three, a Monday. Bert Oldfield, a gritty little wicketkeeper whose injuries in the First World War had left him with a steel plate in his head, resisted at length before Jardine again signalled for a leg-theory field. Oldfield ducked into a rapid delivery from Larwood and deflected the ball into his temple, fracturing his skull. An inch either way and he would almost certainly have been killed.

Oldfield blamed himself for losing sight of the ball ("It wasn't your fault, Harold," he was said to have murmured; indeed, although he later denied calling it "a fair ball", victim and assailant would become close friends). Inevitably, the packed house saw it all a little differently. "The hooting and shouting, the expression of indignation and outrage, rose to a new intensity," wrote David Frith in *Bodyline Autopsy*, his definitive account of that tempestuous tour.

> *Obscenities rang out and men were jumping up and down, waving their fists. "Go home, you Pommie bastards!" was one of the more moderate cries as the groundfire persisted. The policemen in their dark uniforms and white helmets tensed all around the ground and moved into some sort of strategic position, the horses of the mounted section now restive. The SACA [South Australian Cricket Association] office put in a call to Angas Street police headquarters asking for reinforcements to be sent. Some came on motor-cycles. An Adelaide barrister standing by the pickets at the front of the Giffen Stand was*

*actually invited by a mature police inspector to jump the fence
if he wished: "I won't stop you." It was a shameful but almost
understandable reaction.*[91]

On Wednesday 18 January, the final day of the match, the
Australian Board of Control voted to dispatch a cable of
complaint to Lord's:

*Bodyline bowling assumed such proportions as to menace best
interests of game, making protection of body by batsmen the
main consideration. Causing intensely bitter feeling between
players as well as injury. In our opinion is unsportsmanlike.
Unless stopped at once likely to upset friendly relations existing
between Australia and England.*

The aggressive tone – above all the use of the word "unsportsmanlike" – was exacerbated by the fact that journalists
informed the MCC president, Viscount Lewisham, of the cable
by awaking him at 2.30am. Gilbert Mant, covering the tour for
Reuters, claimed it was the agency's first major scoop since the
assassination of Abraham Lincoln. Few Australian journalists backed the board's response. Melbourne's *Age* newspaper
thought the tone was unjustified; *The Sydney Morning Herald* ran
an image of Australian cricket holding a pistol to the head of the
English authorities. On the other hand, while he believed the
cable could have been delayed until the series was over, Walter
Hammond, the tourists' premier batsman, felt it was warranted.
More typical of the English reaction was a damning phrase in
the *Daily Herald* – "undignified snivelling".

The reply arrived on 23 January. "We, Marylebone Cricket
Club, deplore your cable," commenced the cable. "We deprecate
your opinion that there has been unsportsmanlike play." The
final sentence made it abundantly clear that an apology was the
very last thing on their minds: "We hope the situation is not now
as serious as your cable would seem to indicate, but if it is such as
to jeopardise the good relations between English and Australian
cricketers, and you consider it desirable to cancel remainder of
programme, we would consent with great reluctance."

The Australians insisted there was no need for such a drastic step and, after a further flurry of cables, the tour completed its stormy course. The wounds were profound. Notwithstanding his series-swinging 33 wickets, Larwood was cast as the arch-villain, fall guy for Jardine the toff. In 1934, with the next Ashes debate beckoning, he was urged to apologise by Sir Julien Cahn, a prosperous businessman and two-time Nottinghamshire president, who, unbeknownst to the bowler, had been dispatched by J. H. Thomas, Secretary of the Dominions. Knowing refusal would bar him from resuming hostilities, and unlike his more acquiescent 1932–33 co-terrorist, Bill Voce, a county colleague and close friend, he held firm: "I have nothing to apologise for, sir… I'm an Englishman – I will never apologise." In the *Sunday Dispatch*, having been "given the go-by" for the first Test, he proclaimed himself "unrepentant".[92] Needless to add, he never played for his country again. The true architect of bodyline, Arthur Carr, moreover, was sacked as Nottinghamshire captain for defending his fast bowlers. The Empire had carried out "another of its favourite tricks", warranted Mark Steel. "At the point of appearing to overstep the mark, protect the officer and sacrifice the private."[93]

Nor, despite accepting responsibility "for all the trouble that was caused", did Larwood relent. "Was bodyline against the spirit of cricket?" he mused in the penultimate chapter of his autobiography. "I am still not satisfied that it was. I have come to realise that [it] was against the spirit of the game as applied to lower grades of cricket. On rough or uneven ground against batsmen unskilled in the hook, it was palpably dangerous. It probably would have harmed the game if it had continued unabated in junior and social ranks. But you do not expect Test batsmen to have any weaknesses. If they have, the bowler has the right to exploit them." Only upon meeting the opposition many years after the fact did he discover that, convinced they would be caught, they had collectively eschewed the hook, which "explains why we all thought [they] were frightened". While absolving Bradman of criticism, he wished he had "shown more of the traditional spirit".[94]

"Sometimes I stand out in my back garden," begins the final line of *The Larwood Story* (subtitled "a cricketer's autobiography", the lack of capital letters testifies to his innate modesty). "When the wind blows I can hear the mob on the Hill roar..." Had he seen *Apocalypse Now*, he would doubtless have observed that it smelt like victory.

Jardine himself scarcely lacked for critics. Frank Foster, who had counselled him about his field placings in apparent innocence, was among the most vehement, even cutting a gramophone record to express his dismay. "Douglas Jardine, I am ashamed of England's win," he wrote by way of apology in *Smith's Weekly*, an Australian periodical. "I will face you on your return with these words on my lips..."[95] Jardine remained at the helm, leading a successful tour of India in 1933-34, but come the following summer's Ashes, in the interests of a soothing series, he was deposed. A year later, "leg theory" was formally outlawed.

Denounced for decades as a ruthless cad and source of national shame, admiration for Jardine was restored, to a degree, by Christopher Douglas's sympathetic if not uncritical 1984 biography. "Father was an intensely shy and private person, and never complained about his treatment by the cricketing world," recalled Jardine's daughter, the Rev. Fianach Lawry, "although he did say on more than one occasion that Bodyline bowling, and the field set for it, had all been agreed with the MCC before the tour commenced."[96] In his foreword to the 2005 reprint of the unrepentant *In Quest of The Ashes*, Mike Brearley, submitted a valuable insight: "Perhaps part of Jardine's extreme loathing of the Australian public was down to their forcing him to examine (and doubt) the truth of his own supposed 'chivalry'."[97]

Jardine's account supplied proof that cricket's most discordant and contentious chapter still retains a pull on public heartstrings and publishers' purse-strings. It included neither a thimble-full of remorse nor a single mention of the B-word (he sticks resolutely to "leg-theory"). By the same token, some Australians believed their countrymen had over-reacted. In his own engrossing account, *Cricket Crisis* (published in 1946 and reissued after his death), Jack Fingleton, who spent much of the rest of his life writing about the game from the pressbox with an erudition and insight appreciated in England as much as his native country, argued that a "misguided nationalism obtruded itself".[98]

Today's commentators whistle a different tune. "What lingered was psychological," reflected that fine Australian writer Christian Ryan in 2013, "a suspicion of the English gentleman, a sense that, while Australians wish to win, the English will break bones/rules/morality to win… Australia's ride through our current decade's economic travails is something [government] treasurer Wayne Swan attributes partly to 'an enduring determination for our country never again to be at the whim of anyone'. That determination's cause, Mr Treasurer? 'I believe, Bodyline.'"[99]

A family at war

The edgiest of the long-running international rivalries trip off the tongue: Brazil v Argentina, Germany v Holland, USA v USSR, Australia v New Zealand, New Zealand v South Africa, England v South Africa, New Zealand, Australia, India, Pakistan, France, Scotland, Ireland and Wales (and just about any other regular opponent). Many, fundamentally, are about Big Brother v Little Brother. None, though, packs quite as much bitterness, albeit for supporters rather than players, as India v Pakistan. Indeed, the scarcity of such contests since Partition has rendered their unique tension even tauter, and ever more electric.

The early flurry of Test series was notable only for the sheer negativity of the cricket: defeat was unthinkable, and, by dint of their very length, Test matches, more than any other form of athletic endeavour, encourage attack to be eliminated in pursuit of the allegedly honourable draw. Lala Amarnath, who led India at home to Pakistan in 1952-53, described the series as "a war of attrition". His memories betray the sense of unease, accentuated by thoughts of what might have been. "Abdul Kardar [a teammate before Partition] was the [Pakistan] captain and Amir Elahi, who had made his debut in the [1947] Sydney Test in Australia for us, was playing for the opposition. Political reasons had pitted us against each other. We were staring bitter reality in the face. There were Fazal Mahmood and Imtiaz Ahmed in the opposition, players who would have been invaluable in Australia."[100]

Then, for 17 years from 1961, there was no sporting contact whatsoever. When India toured Pakistan in 1978, moreover, conditions were less than ideal. Nor did it soothe Indian breasts that the Pakistanis, in playing terms, had their measure, as they would for the next two decades. By 1996, wrote Ramachandra Guha, "it seemed clear that cricket matches between India and Pakistan stoked rather than subdued national passion. This might have worried the peacemongers but it was greatly to the liking of commercial sponsors."

Yet in Chennai three years later came a scene that encapsulates spectator sport's prowess at bridge-building like few others. India had just been beaten by Pakistan by the excoriatingly tight margin of 12 runs, one of the closest-run things in Test history. "Every once in a while," Cricinfo's editor Sambit Bal will reflect a decade later, "there are moments in sport that transcend the action on the field and yet help establish the very essence of sport by carrying it beyond the confines of nationalism, and indeed victory and defeat."[101] That moment occurred at the end of a match that had seemed destined never to take place.

Away from the pitch, the loathing was entirely mutual. Political negotiations between India and Pakistan had resumed in 1997 yet nobody even dared hint that significant progress was being made. Encouragement was minimal. Eleven months ahead lay the hijacking of Indian Airlines Flight IC 814, bound for Afghanistan – the latest in a succession of episodes to exacerbate tensions. As Pakistan's first tour of India in a dozen years gingerly shifted from nice idea to lift-off, Indian fundamentalists had threatened disruption. One minor incident, one overheated debate, and the whole venture, never more than fragile, would have been abandoned. All that was forgotten when that wily and inventive spinner Saqlain Mushtaq, inventor of the doosra ("the other one"), deceived Javagal Srinath to guide Pakistan over the line. As the armed troops girded their loins and steadied their trigger fingers, something rather wonderful happened, as Bal would recall.

"But just as the security forces were getting into position to tackle any unpleasantness that may have arisen, the crowd in Chennai, stunned at first by the turn of events, rose to their feet and began to clap. It wasn't delirious or frenzied, but measured and sustained. The Pakistan team immediately took their cue and ran a victory lap around the ground. For anyone with any experience of India-Pakistan cricket, this was a deeply moving, even seminal, moment."[102]

The nations continued to meet on neutral turf (Toronto, Sharjah) and in tournaments – notably the 2011 World Cup semi-final, where India won only for success to be shrouded in match-fixing allegations. However, the prospects of either touring the other appeared dim and distant until April 2012, when cricket was reported to have formed at least part of the menu, possibly dessert, when the Indian prime minister Manmohan Singh and Pakistan's president Asif Ali Zardari met for what was described as an "informal" lunch (the latest verbal fisticuffs had revolved around India's refusal to grant visas to Pakistani cricketers, preventing them from playing in the IPL). The following January, Pakistan popped over the border for a batch of 20- and 50-over matches, the prelude, it was hoped, to something more expansive, though the outbreak of border skirmishes that month caused a brace of scheduled hockey tours to be cancelled.

What did emerge from this fleeting reunion was the sense of a profound shift in sensibility. "After many years the recent series was all about cricket," rejoiced Suresh Menon, editor of *Wisden India*. "It might be too early to assert this but we can certainly whisper it: an India-Pakistan series has been elevated to ordinariness – this despite the media and especially television's attempts to whip up jingoism and anger."[103] On one level they succeeded. Much the hottest potato for chat shows and phone-ins was the visa granted to the former Pakistan captain Javed Miandad, whose daughter-in-law's father is Ismail Dawood, India's most wanted terrorist.

No longer, Menon contended, did India and Pakistan play for national honour or religious superiority. "Instead they play to ensure that sponsors and television channels recover the obscene investments they have made and gone on to make unheard-of profits. A worldwide audience of around a billion ensures that the media remain interested... Perhaps laughter and tolerance are beginning to replace the intensity and despair. Or perhaps Indian supporters are in transition too, with the youngsters refusing to carry the baggage of the earlier generations. Or perhaps it was just a glimpse into innocence before the politicians and the media take over the job of influencing the impressionable." His conclusion, for all that, was almost perversely comforting. "If religion has trumped nationalism, commerce has trumped religion and that is as complete a comment on our times as one can get."[104]

African pride

By contrast, as a shining emblem of the positives of nationalism, nothing gleams quite like the Africa Cup of Nations, hailed by Matthew Syed as "perhaps the most important sporting event on the planet". Not because of the football but "the politics of identity".[105] Yes, Syed was fully aware that he could be accused of "intellectual and emotional absurdity" in even mentioning nationhood in the context of post-colonial Africa. In Nigeria, after all, religions abound and hundreds of languages are spoken, defying British attempts at unification.

"But this is where football – dramatically and possibly uniquely – changes everything," argued Syed, who went on to quote from *African Soccerscapes*, Paul Alegi's preconception-smashing book about the social history of African football: "Africans are 90-minute patriots." After all, as Eric Hobsbawm stated, "The imagined community of millions seems more real as a team of 11 named people."[106] Still, as Eric the Proudly Red suggested on another occasion, it remains a matter of personal philosophy as to whether that is an unequivocally good thing.

All of which explains why, as Syed pointed out, "national symbolism, patriotic rhetoric and the entire arsenal of nationalistic propaganda" are constructed around African teams. Many of the qualifiers for the 2012 African Cup of Nations had even traded foreign coaches for local ones, the better "to cement the idea of a national story". It had taken a long time to write.

In *The Cambridge Companion to Football*, Paul Darby relates how, for decades, Africa's efforts to gain admission to the wider football fraternity were consistently thwarted. "Under the stewardship of a succession of European presidents, FIFA regarded Africa largely as an irrelevance and until the late 1950s the world body simply refused to countenance Africa's lobby for democratisation in the international game. For example, attempts to secure a place on FIFA's Executive Committee and organise a continental confederation for the African game in the first half of the 1950s were routinely frustrated by the world body's European constituents. Africa's calls for a more equitable distribution of World Cup places was met with similar intransigence and it took an African boycott of the qualifying rounds of the 1966 competition to secure a guaranteed berth for future tournaments."[107]

That's why the 2010 World Cup finals, the first to be held in Africa, meant so much, especially when Ghana were awarded a penalty with the last kick of their quarter-final against Uruguay; sadly, Asamoah Gyan missed, denying his country the honour of being the first from the continent to reach the last four. Behind the tears and the pride, though, lurked grave concerns about morality and future. In 2003, Sepp Blatter described European clubs who recruit African players as "neo-colonialists who don't give a damn about heritage and culture, but engage in social and economic rape by robbing the developing world of its best players". He also characterised their recruitment of young Africans as "unhealthy if not despicable".[108] As Darby stresses, for all the benefits, both to national teams and economies, "the trade is oriented around talent extraction and this de-skills and impoverishes the domestic game across Africa". Alegi, meanwhile, contends that "economics and historical affiliation will trump the idea of nationhood". For Syed, the jury is still out: "What is certain is that nationalism is central to the future of Africa in its widest sense, and football is central to the future of nationalism."

Flag-wavers of convenience

Do they see me putting my pounds in a South African bank account? And the answer is no. And do they see me buying property outside England? Or planning on a future elsewhere? No. I'm thinking about which school my daughter is going to go to here. It's quite evident when someone is a mercenary. People can sniff it from a mile away... Some spectators go on about it. You should hear the comments when I'm fielding. I guess they're trying to be funny, or clever. [109]

Jonathan Trott, England batsman, 2012

Some sportsfolk have been more flexible than others, and by no means exclusively in modern times, when, as transport shrank the globe, easing mobility of labour, sport, its appeal so long tied to the apron strings of nation state and patriotism, began to ease its restrictions. In 1936, nine of Britain's 12-man Olympic ice hockey team had been raised and trained in Canada. Alfredo Di Stéfano, onfield architect of Real Madrid's early dominance of the European Cup and by common consent one of the greatest of all professional footballers, played for Colombia and Spain in addition to his native Argentina – but still never participated in the World Cup finals.

Postwar realpolitik bit deep. As the Cold War dragged on, Martina Navratilova fled her native Czechoslovakia for the US. Basil D'Oliveira, South Africa's best non-white cricketer, fled apartheid to fulfil himself in England: his inclusion in the party picked to tour his homeland in late 1968 saw the expedition abandoned, doing much to fuel the sporting boycott that helped bring the Republic's minority to its senses. Unable to represent South Africa in official cricket, Kepler Wessels made his debut for Australia in 1982 and won 24 Test caps, flew back home to play for a "rebel" Australian team then captained South Africa when they returned to the Test fold in 1992. Riki Flutey, a Maori, helped New Zealand win the IRB Under-19 world title in 1999 and played stand-off for the All Black Under-21s before relaunching his career in England, winning 14 caps and becoming just the second man (behind Tom Reid more than half a century earlier) ever to play for and against the British and Irish Lions. And, just as Navratilova, citing her disgust with George W. Bush, eventually reclaimed her Czech citizenship, Flutey returned to New Zealand in 2012 after the birth of his fourth child.

One early flexible trailblazer, Sammy Woods, moved from Sydney to England at 16 to complete his education, became a folk hero in Somerset and wound up playing for both sides in Ashes matches during the last dozen years of the 19th century, in addition to representing England at rugby union. Of the 14 men to have represented more than one nation in Test cricket, as of June 2013, all bar two had done so at least six decades earlier.

Few, though, cared quite so little for notions of nationhood as William "Billy" Midwinter, one of five men to play for both protagonists in Ashes encounters, all of whom did so in the 19th century. He was nine when his family emigrated to Australia, and was picked, in 1877, for that inaugural Test in Melbourne, taking five wickets in the first innings. Returning to England that summer to play alongside W. G. Grace for Gloucestershire, he went back again with an Australian party the next year only to be more or less kidnapped by Grace, who ensured he was whisked across London from the tourists' match at Lord's and drafted into the Gloucestershire XI playing Surrey at The Oval. Staying with Gloucestershire for the rest of the tour and the next few seasons, he was chosen in the MCC party for Australia in the winter of 1881-82, playing four Tests, then re-emigrated to Australia the following winter and subsequently played twice against England.

Nobody fussed too much about such things a century ago. For one thing, awareness was limited, in good part because the media's tentacles did not extend remotely as far and wide as they do now. For another, nation statehood was in its infancy. As it matured, so flying multiple flags became a badge of dishonour. In the late 20th century, however, as rewards rocketed and labour mobility grew to unprecedented levels, regulations eased. In 1995, Greg Rusedski, a Quebecois by birth and upbringing who just two years earlier had become the first Canadian tennis player in 20 years to be ranked in the ATP top 50, was permitted to represent Britain, land of his father; within three years he was BBC Sports Personality of the Year, for many the ultimate seal of acceptance. British tennis may have been on its uppers but his duels with Tim Henman – *arriviste* versus establishment, free-market capitalist versus restrained old-school Tory – were always loaded with piquancy.

Supremely unbothered as they tend to be by any inclination to play the world at sport, to North Americans this has never amounted to even a tissue of an issue. With the best hitters in major league baseball now sending chunks of their paycheques back to Latin America, and basketball and ice hockey welcoming increasing numbers of Europeans, perhaps that's why the local football code continues to tickle the greatest number of sporting fancies. Not for nothing is it billed as "America's Game".

Is it in the blood?

Between 1982 and 1994, among Anglo-Caribbean citizens, the share of those born in Britain rose from 54% to 62%; by 1997, 96% of those aged 15 or under were British-born. In 1999, there were 6,000 migrants, down from 8,700 in 1990. Black Britons, who by 2004 accounted for 2% of the overall population, appeared far keener to assimilate than those of Asian descent, by now roughly four times as numerous. According to the *Fourth National Survey of Ethnic Minorities*, published in 1997, 75% of Anglo-Caribbean children born between 1992 and 1996 had at least one British-born parent. Half of all males had a white partner, and 33% of females, compared with 20% of Anglo-Indians.

Holt and Mason offered some illuminating comparisons. In 1986, when Anglo-Caribbeans still accounted for just 2% of Britons, they made up 33% of the Commonwealth Games athletics team – up from just two constituents in 1969. In boxing, which banned black fighters from challenging for a Lonsdale Belt until 1947, they comprised a similar proportion of the 600 professionals in the 1980s. By 1992-93, half of all full-time black British footballers (then accounting for one in four league professionals) were playing in the Premier League. "In spite of the growth in numbers," concluded Holt and Mason, "those black players who did succeed had to be not only good but better than the white competition."

Developments and statistics of this ilk drove me to conduct an investigation spanning much of 2003 and 2004. Why had the numbers of black faces in county cricket more than halved in the space of 20 years? The result, an article initially published in *The Wisden Cricketer* under the title "Whatever happened to the black cricketer?" and reprinted in edited form in both *The Observer* and the London *Evening Standard*, brought me my one and only journalism award – the UK section of the EU Journalism Award "for diversity, against discrimination" (albeit only because I chanced upon a poster and was told that the only way to get nominated was to embrace immodesty and submit it myself). There was no single answer; there never is. My conclusion could only be broad: assimilation, recognition and advancement were all feasible, yes, but cricket was no longer hip (thanks in good part to the sudden decline of the West Indies team, so plain to those who watched them during their sorry tour of England that summer, but also because of the rise in popularity of basketball among Anglo-Caribbean youth); now football, understandably, was seen as the more profitable vehicle. But there was no escaping the sense, derived from the dozens of people I spoke to, black and white alike, that there was a further deterrent: imperialist attitudes and institutional racism remained ingrained.

Two years later, a new cult hero emerged: Mudhsuden Singh Panesar, a spin-bowling Sikh born in the South Asian migrant hotbed of once-sleepy Luton, just north of London. Summoned for his Test debut in 2006, "Monty" (nobody outside his family calls him by his given name) is now one of the most prolific slow bowlers ever to represent England and something of a cult hero, if still almost painfully shy. It helped, admittedly, that his batting and fielding were often laughingly amateurish, tapping so readily as such flaws did into the marginal English preference for underdogs over bulldogs, but he would not have been in a position to melt hearts and prejudices had he not been capable of bewitching and bewildering the best – including Sachin Tendulkar, a supremely apposite maiden Test victim. It says much for these more inclusive times that, when he was persistently excluded at the expense of his former Northamptonshire colleague, Graeme Swann (who was plainly the handier asset, being the better batsman and fielder as well as bowler), I failed to detect even a hint of a glint of a suggestion that this was evidence of that institutional racism.

* * *

What roused the fury of some English cricket followers in the last quarter of the 20th century was the alleged infestation of the national XI by those born in the Caribbean and South Africa. Tony Greig took all manner of verbal blows after trading in the purported honour of captaining England for a more prosperous future, but he once assured me that none hurt or rankled more than the assertion by John Woodcock, a fair and normally kindly cricket correspondent of *The Times*, that he was "not an Englishman through and through".

Local resentment bubbled to a head in 1995, when *Wisden Cricket Monthly* published a provocative tract headlined "Is it in the blood?" The highly articulate spleen-venter was Robert Henderson, a British National Party sympathiser and retired civil servant living on a disability pension in multi-racial Hoxton. In his warped view, the likes of Philip DeFreitas (Dominica), Devon Malcolm (Jamaica) and Gladstone Small (Barbados) were simply not "unequivocal Englishmen". Such comments should be contemplated in the light of an interview in the *Los Angeles Times* published in April 1990, shortly after the two pacemen had bowled England to their first Test win in the Caribbean in 16 years, in which Small and Malcolm had been similarly type-cast by Norman Tebbit, Maggie Thatcher's favourite skinhead. Tebbit's unwitting invention of the so-called "Tebbit Test" would endure as a symbol of unease amid the march to multicultur-alism, one ruthlessly and profitably exploited by that shrill voice of white-middle-Englishness, the *Daily Mail*. "A large propor-tion of Britain's Asian population fail to pass the cricket test," Tebbit declaimed. "Which side do they cheer for? It's an inter-esting test. Are you still harking back to where you came from or where you are?"

Perhaps the utterer of those words had missed his customary copy of *The Times* eight days earlier, when Simon Barnes had acknowledged how far cricket had come from being an (osten-sibly) English game. After all, it had come under the influence of "Islam, Indian politics, Partition, Tamil separatism, Marxist writing, Rastafarianism, the New Zealand Prime Minister, the Bishop of Liverpool, Bob Marley, aboriginal and maori rights", not to mention posing questions about "the importance or other-wise of the rights of mankind to freedom in the face of the forces of oppression". Small wonder a "pleasant, footling pastime" had become "an expression of national, regional and racial pride".[110]

Outrage awaited Tebbit's comments when they made their way to British breakfast tables. Unsurprisingly, the South Asian diaspora bridled, denouncing such views as hurtful, not to say disgraceful. Jeff Rooker, a Labour MP, called for Tebbit to be prosecuted for inciting racial hatred; Paddy Ashdown, the Liberal Democrat leader, suggested Thatcher should condemn the "outrageous and damaging remarks". To some, on the other hand, here was simply an example of Fleet Street's undimmable capacity for transforming molehills into mountains.

I should declare an interest here. The quote Henderson wielded to ram home the point of his rant came from Nasser Hussain. The quote, as it happens, was culled from an interview

I had conducted in the summer of 1989 with Hussain, then 20, shortly before he became the first Asian-born player since the Second World War to represent England on a sporting field (provided, that is, we discount Douglas Jardine, Colin Cowdrey and Bob Woolmer, all born in India while their fathers were working there). Was it, I asked Hussain, a case of head English, heart Indian? Yes, he concurred, that just about summed it up. The *Daily Telegraph* published the interview the next day, whereupon Hussain's mother dashed off a letter to the editor, adamant that her son could never have said such a thing. I knew otherwise. Henderson wrote to me on a number of occasions thereafter, as he did several other reporters, seeking support for his anti-interloper cause; he had assumed that Hussain's admission – which, to Henderson, cast doubt on the extent of his commitment to the national cause – had angered me as it had him. It had not, anything but.

To these ears, it was precisely the sort of pragmatic outlook required; it told me this self-assured young man had the mental attributes not only to overcome the slings and arrows of the little Englanders but to flourish at the highest level. Views were politely exchanged until I realised how pointless it was: why bother arguing once you have come to the conclusion, however belatedly, that your powers of persuasion are not quite as irresistible as imagined and the chances of effecting a change of heart in your opponent are roughly on a par with your prospects of out-thinking Stephen Hawking? As I write, with the Internet now supplying a handy platform, Henderson is still infecting message boards with his xenophobia.

Those darts of his struck oil, if not quite in the way envisaged, or even hoped. With its approving reference to the "Tebbit test" – it was possible, Henderson suggested, "that part of a coloured England-qualified player feels satisfaction...at seeing England humiliated, because of post-imperial *myths* [my italics] of oppression and exploitation"[111] – the publication of that "Is it in the blood?" article led to a rowdy and very public fallout. David Frith, founding editor of *Wisden Cricket Monthly*, was sacked; DeFreitas and Malcolm, then Derbyshire teammates, sued the magazine and settled out of court; Malcolm's just-ly-gotten gains made his dream of establishing a cricket school in Sheffield a reality. "He suggested [we] were interlopers," DeFreitas bemoaned to me in 2004, the perpetrator's name forgotten more efficiently than the fury he provoked. "That was *so* out of order, *so* wrong."

Then Devon met Nelson. In late 1995, as England began their first tour of South Africa for 31 years, the party were greeted by Nelson Mandela, who got on famously with Malcolm. At *last*, thought Devon: respect. Before long, manager/coach Ray Illingworth and his aide Peter Lever were dismantling the bowl-er's action and decrying his attitude. According to Illingworth, Malcolm, who had skittled nine South Africans for 57 at The Oval 15 months earlier, still the best Test return by an English fast bowler, had "no cricketing brain". A. Sivanandan, director of the Institute of Race Relations, jabbed back. "In football, by and large, it's the fans that are racist, but in cricket, it's the estab-lishment. It's institutionalised racism. The smell of imperialism is in your nostrils all the time."[112]

Not that that stopped Hussain. In 1999 he became the first Anglo-Asian to lead his adopted country into sporting battle. Over the next five years, in partnership with another outsider, the Zimbabwean coach Duncan Fletcher, he would emerge as a national hero, dragging English cricket from the bottom of the heap to very near the top, his secret a combination of fiery competitiveness and adroit man-management. Towards the end of his tenure, moreover, he would even feel secure enough – as we shall see – to take a political stand.

Champions without portfolio

In Carson City, Nevada on St Patrick's Day 1897, Irish-born "Gentleman" James J. Corbett was counted out, the world's first feature film was completed and a new world heavyweight champion was crowned: Bob Fitzsimmons. A flamboyant black-smith-turned-prizefighter, he had been born in Cornwall but left with his family at the age of nine for New Zealand, where he made his name as a fighter, before moving on to Australia and then the US, the pugilist's promised land. Owing to the exigencies of the day, he had been obliged to take out US citizenship to fulfil his ambitions and returned to the land of his birth only fleetingly, though thousands thronged the streets of London that March evening for news of his tussle with Corbett, which was soon being seen in theatres in the form of Enoch J. Rector's 100-minute documentary, *The Corbett-Fitzsimmons Fight*.

An all-round entertainer and sure-footed self-promoter who acted on stage and film and was fond of titilating audiences by clambering into a cage to grapple with Nero, his pet lion, Fitzsimmons would make New York his home, count among his pals Teddy Roosevelt, the US president, and be commemorated in marble by Gutzon Borglum, the man behind those presidential busts on Mount Rushmore. According to the enthusiastic sculptor, he was "one of the best specimens of manhood in the world".[113]

We Britons may feel entitled to acclaim him as our first undisputed world heavyweight champion, but he came of age and began his professional career in Australia and New Zealand, and never once fought in the land of his father. The Fitzsimmons Arms, a Grade 2 listed pub in Coinagehall Street, in his birthplace of Helston, stands as the most enduring monument to this slice of *fin de siècle* sporting heroism: the sign above the door depicts a painting of Fitzsimmons from the rear – broad back rippling, sinewy forearms cocked for battle.

* * *

More than a century later, in 1999, Lennox Lewis was hailed as the first Briton to emulate Fitzsimmons when – in one of the more bizarre demonstrations even this controversy-addicted branch of showbiz has ever witnessed – Riddick Bowe renounced the heavyweight crown by dumping his championship belt in a dustbin. Yet the precise nature of Lewis's geographical allegiance was even cloudier than Fitzsimmons'.

Born in East London to Jamaican-born parents, he left for Toronto at 12 and won an Olympic medal for Canada; not until 1992, when he knocked out "Razor" Ruddock inside four minutes at Earl's Court, did Fleet Street truly begin claiming him as one of their own. This was attributable in good part to the connection with the public forged by Frank Bruno, a boxer of Jamaican-Dominican parentage whose self-deprecating, often comical image was more calculated than most gave him credit for. It certainly fitted rather more neatly and cosily into contemporary stereotypes and expectations of a black British hero (and immeasurably more so than that uncompromising maverick Daley Thompson, the only sportsman BBC viewers voted among their 100 "Great Black Britons"). Lewis, by contrast, gave the impression that, while he, too, was politeness personified, he had no intention of being pigeonholed.

The three-way relationship between Lewis, Bruno and the British public proffered a revealing snapshot of the ambiguities and convolutions of national and racial identity in a multi-cultural society. When the pair, both West Ham United fans, crossed gloves at Cardiff Arms Park in 1993, the night air was thick with a thoroughly modern sort of symbolism: Bruno entered the arena in a pair of trunks stitched with the words "The True Brit", accompanied – his camp seemingly oblivious to the Welshness of the venue – by the exclusively English strains of *Land of Hope and Glory*; Lewis opted for the more militant, less nationalistic rhythms of reggae, wrapping himself in both a Union Jack and the flag of St David. Only the Welsh national anthem, *Land of My Fathers*, was sung: Lord Brooks, a Welsh senior steward of the British Boxing Board of Control, had ordered that *God Save the Queen* should not be played. "The crowd will only boo," he reasoned. "It would not be fitting."

If the animosity between the protagonists appeared manufactured to some, to others Bruno's seemed both genuine and well-founded. "It's no secret that I haven't always got on well with Lennox Lewis," was how he began the chapter "Lennox And Me" in his autobiography, ghostwritten by the estimable

Kevin Mitchell. "It's about self-respect. It's about identity and pride. It's about my place as a black Briton, a representative of my community. And it's about how he disrespected me."[114]

Inevitably, that Cardiff encounter, billed as the century's first all-British world heavyweight title bout, found the hype cranked to the max. The final blow of the phony war was struck by Lewis, who mocked Bruno for "dressing up in girls' clothing" for his stint as a pantomime dame, a role – or so ran the clear inference – to which the champion could never have even contemplated stooping. "To be fair, I played my part," conceded Bruno.

> It was all about our roots. He went on about being a Londoner, which I found hard to take. I was born and bred here after all. But when the papers said he'd called me an Uncle Tom I blew my top. He denied it but I got my lawyer, Henri Brandman, to issue him with a writ for libel. Things calmed down later, and we withdrew it; but I had to let him know he couldn't take liberties. The papers thought it was a stunt – but I was deadly serious. To be accused of sucking up to the white man – I can't tell you what an insult that is. It goes to the heart of who I am… I'd heard some of this crap before… People said – but never to my face – that I had sold out to a group of white guys, that I was lording it up in a big mansion in Essex with my white wife. They said I wasn't "street" enough. Ask anyone I grew up with. I was very connected with my roots. I know my culture…What made it twice as bitter for me was I'd never thought of Lennox as British…To me he is a Canadian… I think it was Lennox who had the identity problem. I was comfortable being a black Briton.[115]

Lewis knocked Bruno out that night, but for all that he was the most successful heavyweight to box under the capacious umbrella of the Union Jack, and for all that he was voted BBC Sports Personality of the Year in 1999, it was a salient fact that, in 2008, four years after his retirement, he was inducted into Canada's Sports Hall of Fame. In the *Oxford Companion to Black British History*, Bruno rates a nod but not Lewis. Of all Britain's black boxing champions, of which there have been a vastly disproportionate number in demographic terms, "none expressed their Britishness more than Bruno".[116]

Lewis would be considered British enough to inspire 6,000 Britons to fly to Las Vegas in 1999 to see him take on Evander Holyfield. Yet notwithstanding the fact that he was much the better boxer, he still failed to replace Bruno in British hearts, let alone command the global reverence customarily reserved for that most conspicuous rarity of the Alphabet Soup Age – the undisputed heavyweight champion. In 2003, Robert Weintraub found himself puzzled enough by the public reaction to Lewis's sluggish defence of his title against Vitali Klitschko in Los Angeles to compose an incisive, sympathetic piece for slate.com headlined "No Love for Lennox":

> *Much as Larry Holmes was castigated for Not Being Ali, Lennox gets static for Not Being Tyson. As both men discovered, demolishing their respective bêtes noirs in the ring did little to change that notion. Boxing is a sport where misanthropy is more necessity than vice, and introspective types are seldom embraced by fans. Floyd Patterson and Archie Moore valued intelligence in and out of the ring but wound up being pitied as much as lauded. In an era when only hard-edged athletes cut through the media haze, Lewis sips tea and plays chess. Without plentiful tattoos or a penitentiary stare, he doesn't have a prayer.*[117]

Lewis, believed Weintraub, also "had two strikes against him, one for being British and one for being a good guy". Only the previous week, George Foreman had told the *Los Angeles Times* that the trouble with the champion acclaimed as the best since Holmes was "the fact that he's not from anywhere". That Lewis's "Britishness is crossed with a Jamaican dreadlocked vibe", added Weintraub, "makes him seem more like the comic villain in a Guy Ritchie movie than the heavyweight champ".[118]

Plastic Olympians

As the financial rewards for Olympic glory grew following the relaxing of the amateur doctrine, so nationality proved an increasingly flexible and convenient friend. Qatar and Bahrain have led the way over the past decade in recruiting African runners by offering cash incentives to take up citizenship, so much so that the International Association of Athletics Federations was obliged to tighten its rules on transferring allegiance. Russia got in on the act for the 2012 Winter Olympics, granting citizenship to South Korea's short-track skater Ahn Hyun-soo, winner of three Olympic golds in 2006.

During the build-up to the 2012 Olympics, the *Daily Mail's* anti-"Plastic Brits" campaign was fatally undermined by the memory of the 1984 Games in Los Angeles and the furore over Zola Budd. A frail but talented white South African long-distance runner who competed in bare feet, she had been denied an international platform by the indefensible iniquities of apartheid (rather than, as others portrayed it, by the anti-apartheid movement), yet competed for Britain following a concerted, costly and shameless campaign by the same paper. When Ian Wooldridge reported that her father, Frank, was planning to apply for a British passport – Zola's paternal grandfather was a Londoner – in the hope of participating in the 1988 Olympics, Sir David English, the *Mail* editor, seized upon the story as a potential circulation-booster.

For most mortals then in Budd's position, it would have taken between 13 months and two years to process and issue a passport; English boasted that it would take him a couple of days. He wasn't that far off – despite objections from leading members of the Thatcher government, it took just 10. English's largesse knew few bounds: he offered the Budds a house, £100,000 in cash, a job for Frank and a handsome deal for Zola to write an Olympic diary; he even promised to fly over her coach, Pieter Labuschagne. The family were flown to Amsterdam, and then by private jet to Southampton, then held by the *Mail* in Guildford under virtual house arrest until she left for Los Angeles.

Writing in *Sports Illustrated* following Budd's failure to break the world 3,000m record at an event held near Cape Town (since South Africa was excommunicated it wouldn't have stood), Kenny Moore captured a youngster caught up in something wildly beyond her control: "As photographers paced and growled outside, Zola sat hunched in a corner of the stadium offices, like a frightened fawn."[119] When she eventually showed her face in England she was greeted by demonstrations and boos. "To the world," the *New York Times* reflected nearly a quarter of a century later, "Budd was a remorseless symbol of South Africa's segregationist policies. To the *Daily Mail*, she was a circulation windfall."[120]

Budd herself would claim ignorance, though some might question her purported naivety. "Until I got to London in 1984, I never knew Nelson Mandela existed," she told a reporter in 2002. "I was brought up ignorant of what was going on. All I knew was the white side expressed in South African newspapers – that if we had no apartheid, our whole economy would collapse. Only much later did I realise I'd been lied to by the state."

The story could hardly have been more pregnant with Shakespearian tragedy. In the Olympic 3,000m final, Mary Decker, America's sweetheart, pushed Budd then complained Budd had tripped her. When Budd tried to apologise, Decker was livid. "Get out of here!" she hissed. "I won't talk to you." Budd was disqualified, and although she recovered, setting world records at 3,000m and 5,000m and winning the world cross-country title in 1985 and 1986, her parents' divorce hit her badly, not least because her father, a repressed homosexual, cut off contact.

Urged to denounce apartheid, obstinacy got in the way. "My attitude is that, as a sportswoman, I should have the right to pursue my chosen discipline in peace," she wrote in her autobiography, published in 1989. "Seb Coe does not get asked to denounce Soviet expansionism; and Carl Lewis is not required to express his view on the Contra arms scandal. But I was not afforded that courtesy and it became a matter of principle for me not to give those who were intent on discrediting me the satisfaction of hearing me say what they most wanted to hear." Later in the same volume, however, she spoke her piece: "The

Bible says men are born equal before God. I can't reconcile segregation along racial lines with the words of the Bible. As a Christian, I find apartheid intolerable."[121]

Upon examining her, a London doctor declared her "a pitiful sight, prone to bouts of crying and deep depressions… [with] all the clinical signs of anxiety". After flying back to South Africa, she blurted out to the press: "I have been made to feel like a criminal. I have been continuously hounded, and I can't take it anymore."

When South Africa returned to the fold for the 1992 Games, Zola ran for her native country but failed to qualify for the final. There was to be no fairytale ending, but then nobody ever expected otherwise.

"Yoo-rop"

It teased and tormented but, at the last, the putt slid wide, short-circuiting Jim Furyk's premature celebration and sucking the crowd's energy clean out of the Chicago afternoon air. Furyk bent slowly forward and sank his hands heavily into his haunches. Anyone dropping into the extensive acres of the Medinah Golf Club from Mars or Venus unaware of the significance of his red-white-and-blue-striped shirt need only have seen the bowed peak of his cap, shielding his anguish from view, to realise that the plot had gone horribly awry.

Furyk stayed like that for what seemed at least half an eternity, frozen in disbelief while searching, straining, yearning for the physical and mental strength to emerge from what must have felt like a bottomless pit of endless despair. Not only had he let himself down; he'd let his teammates down, his country down. At length he gathered himself, regained his outward poise, the stern, unemotional poise that distinguishes golfers from all other beasts in the sporting jungle, and shook hands with Sergio Garcìa, the Spaniard who had profited from his miss.

About half an hour later, Germany's Martin Kaymer sank a putt on the 18th, pumped his fists, hoisted his arms in triumph and leapt into Garcìa's arms. A Scottish flag fluttered behind him. "Yoo-rop, yoo-rop" chanted a heavily outnumbered knot of unAmerican spectators, then "Olé, olé, olé". Defying all predictions, Team Europe had roared back, unprecedentedly, from a 10-4 deficit, retaining the Ryder Cup. As Kaymer related his feelings to a TV interviewer, more flags could be seen: an English one, a Spanish one, another cross of St Andrew. Nor did you have to be Spanish to have a lump in your throat at the sight of José-Maria Olazábal's welled-up eyes as he drank in the momentousness of it all. The tears were primarily for the late Seve Ballesteros, his former foursomes partner, spiritual elder brother, Spain's first golfing giant and the man who did most to inject the Ryder Cup with an untested new potion called Europeness.

The spirit, mind and money behind it all belonged to Samuel Ryder, a highly successful seed merchant from Preston whose enthusiasm for fairways and greens led him to become the principal sponsor of British golf in the 1920s. In 1927, he inaugurated the Ryder Cup, which he would hardly recognise today: half a century later it had grown so one-sided that Great Britain and Ireland had been obliged to summon reinforcements from continental Europe. As Spanish, Italian, Swedish and German golfers rose in prominence and rankings, and the number of municipal courses in the region multiplied, so an increasingly competitive European PGA Tour spurred the British and Irish to reassert themselves. Dominant for so long and now further challenged by Australasians, South Africans and even contenders from Japan and Fiji, the Americans declined. Only once in the new century had they won Samuel Ryder's pot.

By 2012, however, not only were most of Europe's best regulars on the US PGA Tour but the signs of a Stateside revival were unmistakeable, hence the lack of surprise when Davis Love III's team, supported by the whoop-whoops of a robustly patriotic gallery, led by six points on the second evening with two fourballs still in progress. The astonishing final-day comeback was the collective handiwork of a European collective comprising four Englishmen (one born in South Africa), two Scots, two Northern Irishmen, a Belgian, a German, an Italian, a Spaniard and a Swede. Eight nations – and once upon a time there would have been eight national anthems; now it's just *Ode to Joy*. Mind you, just as the West Indies cricketers readying to play New Zealand in Sri Lanka the following day would show themselves to be almost uniformly familiar with the unofficial Caribbean anthem, *Rally Round West Indies*, it was hard to recall anyone but Herr Kaymer singing along in Chicago.

Patrick Kidd, writing in *The Times*, was wryly sceptical. "We cheer for a united Europe not just because we want them to win but because we want the Yanks, with all their OTT patriotism and vocal gratitude to God, to lose. The Ryder Cup is our biennial reminder of the Old World's restraint. The people of this continent may have spent 1,000 years trying to kill each other, but at least none of us shout 'get in the hole' every time one of our players hits his drive."[122] The headline was impeccable: "Say it loud, I'm European and I'm proud(ish)". Kidd's point is a valid one. The most enduring international sporting event involving the US remains the America's Cup, 162 years young as I write: now all but absent from the radar of sports editors, it was only ever perceived as worthy of editorial inches when the Americans were in danger of being toppled, especially if the toppler was an Australian.

Post-Medinah press reactions on either side of the Atlantic were illuminating indeed. On the FOX Sports website, Greg Couch asked the now perennial questions: "Do Americans just not care about the Ryder Cup as much as the Europeans do? Is there something about our culture that keeps us from understanding how to play golf as a team, rather than a bunch of uptight individuals?"[123]

On the front page of the website edition of the *Washington Post*, one of the most sober and even-handed American newspapers, a narrow win for the local NFL team took precedence over the humbling in Chicago. The perceived importance of the event, mind, was such that the paper's report was bylined "Associated Press" – shorthand for "we didn't bother asking our own man to attend to such trifles" (Thomas Boswell, the

Post's longstanding golf correspondent, was busy covering the local baseball teams). Yet even the *Daily Mail*, whose attitude to Brussels, the Euro, political unity, immigrants and foreigners in general has seldom been characterised by warmth, could scarce forbear to cheer the "Miracle at Medinah". That said, it was probably no coincidence that the headline over the front-page snap of a joyous Rory McIlroy did not actually contain the dreaded E-word.

The latest riveting and emotional conclusion to spectator sport's most philosophically complex and fascinating international event confirmed once and for all that, to those for whom golf is duller to watch than drying ditchwater, matchplay is vastly superior to strokeplay. Indeed, such are the multi-lensed, multi-screened, drama-heightening capacities of television, viewers see far more – and hence feel far more – than spectators, prompting the thought that the day may not be far away when multinational matchplay leagues replace the individualism of strokeplay in the affections of the global audience. As a combination of team and individual sport, Ryder's brainchild followed the lead of the Davis Cup; as a symbol of the possibilities for a post-nationalist era it is both incomparable and distinctly heartening.

* * *

But now imagine what this sporting life would be like without flags and anthems. Imagine, in other words, a world for which an entire new history has to be created. Mike Marqusee for one is not averse to the idea at all.

> *If I had my way, I'd ban nations from sporting competitions. I'd like to see cricket's big matches contested by city-based clubs, as in football (Bombay v Manchester, Bangalore v Melbourne, Lahore v Cape Town). And, as in football, I'd like to see these city-based clubs incorporating players from all over the world. Critics of big-time Premier League football will throw up their hands in horror, but remember that it is the unbridled power*

of commerce that has poisoned the Premier League, not the admixture of nationalities. In cricket, as we have seen, that power inflates the importance of national success or failure. Wouldn't it be nice if we could undercut it by choosing other types of identities?[124]

Since meeting at Lord's in 1993, Mike and I have been good friends. His books on Muhammad Ali and cricket are as incisive and insightful as any I have read on those subjects. There is nobody I respect more for their views on the sport-politics nexus – not to mention Bob Dylan. Here, though, we diverge. That said, since writing those words he has conceded to me, as the Indian Premier League has waxed and waned, that he may have been mistaken.

"The specific problem with the IPL is the privatisation of cricket. And we've seen all the consequences. I think it's this particular combination of private ownership, a new (to me very limited) format (Twenty20), and the attempt to magic identities or loyalties out of thin air that makes IPL so unattractive as a package. Sporting identities and loyalties are produced by historical experience, so IPL could never hope to emulate the English Premier League. And that's a good thing in our postmodern society of contrived, instant (opportunistic) identities and allegiances. Still, when teams called India and Pakistan play against each other, the context ensures that there's some pretty poisonous politics injected into the occasion. National identities in sport can be doubled-edged and dangerous, so we always have to keep a critical eye on how they play out, who is included, who is excluded, celebrated or vilified."[125]

A world without The Ashes? A world without the Barmy Army or the occasionally satisfying complexities of the Ryder Cup? A world without New Zealand v South Africa or anyone v England? It might well prove to be a less divisive world, though as new histories evolve, whatever replaces national teams could become every bit as poisonous; given that those nations are most unlikely to disband anytime soon, it would also be less adept at connecting disparate peoples and setting an example to the politicians. It would also be less fascinating and bewitching. Putting up with the rough, I would hazard, is just about justified by the warm buzz of the smooth.

8 Reluctant Partners: Sport and Politics

Of course, what those who say they want "politics out of sport" really mean is that they want other people's politics out of sport; they want no politics but their own (i.e. corporate and state sponsored messages about competition and identity).

Mike Marqusee[1]

SPORTING David Cameron hit 'em for six in India yesterday — playing cricket with a "slumdog" team in a city park. The PM, who has a reputation for chillaxing, joined young players from Mumbai's shanty towns. After four furious fast balls his middle stump went flying and he joked: "I'm not expecting a call-up from England soon."

The Sun[2]

SPORT AND POLITICS: two words, according to some, that should never exist in the same sentence unless followed immediately by the words "should never mix". Anyone who tries to segregate these two worlds, as Dave Zirin warrants, is "trafficking in myth".

They want us to believe that sports and politics together are as painful a mash-up as Mitt Romney getting cornrows or Hillary Clinton cutting a salsa album. It is certainly easy to understand why this is so readily accepted. Many of us watch ESPN to forget at all costs what they are doing on [the cable TV political channel] C-SPAN.[3]

Some, though, are more on the ball. On a trip to India in early 2013 that saw *The Times* hail him as "batting for Britain" in pursuit of a brand new "special relationship", David Cameron had enough savvy to realise that he needed to deflect attention from crimes present and past, alleged and proven (corruption in the sale of helicopters to the Indian Air Force, the 1919 Amritsar massacre that cost at least 379 lives). What better than a spot of cricket on a grassless expanse in Mumbai? Photo-ops galore, a chance for the planet's declining ranks of sub-editors to exercise their punnybones on some patriotic headlines, and for the PM to woo a few million Indians. He may be a toff from Eton but he can't be all bad: after all, he does like cricket.

As we have seen, ancient rivalries, such as the one that keeps Celtic and Rangers supporters at daggers drawn, have often taken us to the dark side, yet the overlap between sport and the purported "real" world has produced more than its fair share of illuminating improbabilities. On one level we could point to the delightful irony in North America's major sports – they may operate in the citadel of capitalism but they do so along all-for-one lines, sharing the wealth (albeit not all) and keeping the have-nots in business: free enterprise with a socialist twist. The same principles apply to cricket's County Championship, most of whose 18 current combatants make an annual loss and are sustained by income from international fixtures, events that would not generate the profits they do without the players the clubs have nursed and groomed. After a fashion, the philosophy in English football was of the sharing, caring persuasion too until 1992, when the haves broke away to form the Premier League.

Many of those upful moments, though, stem from sport's capacity to defy the politicians. No story, arguably, has been more heartening for longer than the one dating back to a fabled Christmas during the First World War, when British and German troops vacated trenches and dispensed with weapons to play a football match in no-man's land. Then there were those two days in 1967 when Pelé, the world's reigning champion ball artist, took his boots and genius to the Nigerian capital, Lagos, for an exhibition match; the country may have been mired in a brutal and terrifying civil war, but for the 48 hours the Brazilian was there, hostilities ceased. Examples of sport's helplessness in the face of political reality, sadly, are appreciably easier to come by. For that humane Uruguayan writer Eduardo Galeano, the entry for November 21 in his book *Children of the Days: A Calendar of Human History* commemorates "The Saddest Match In History": the Soviet Union's refusal to play their scheduled 1973 World Cup qualifier against Chile because the National Stadium in Santiago was being used for torture by General Pinochet's dictatorship. That FIFA refused to relocate the game tells you everything you need to know about the efficiency of the blinkers habitually donned by our ringmasters.

Sport is about people, which makes it inherently political. It is also, or so we fondly believe, the one true meritocracy; the one arena in modern life where the only qualification for success, regardless of race, class or gender, is ability. Trouble is, professional athletes have long been so wary of expressing anything that even hints at a political view – primarily, in recent times, because they fear the commercial consequences – that precious few dare poke their head above the parapet. Which is why, now more than ever, anyone perceived as embodying the struggle to establish or preserve equality of opportunity and treatment, and hence setting a wider example, attains heroic status.

Thus it was that Dave Zirin dedicated his book, *A People's History of Sport in the United States*, to "the rebel athletes": besides Muhammad Ali, the boxer who, more than any other sportsman, can be said to have emboldened an entire race, this particular roll of honour is headed by Jackie Robinson, the first black baseballer admitted to the major leagues in the 20th century; Billie Jean King, the tennis champion who publicised and advanced the cause of women's rights; Martina Navratilova, the Czech émigré who did the same for both women and homosexuals; and Tommie Smith and John Carlos, defiant authors of the "Black Power" salute. We will return to them.

Of course, the irony is that, for all those perpetually misguided and often knowingly hypocritical calls to keep politics out of sport, the competitive arts have long been the ultimate political football. Indeed, an enduring symbol of this is that trusty metaphorical standby beloved by journalists, "political football". At local, national and international level, sport has been a tool – for advancement in other spheres, as a distraction from more pressing issues, as a barometer of superiority, whether class, regional, national, ideological, religious or racial. Think of the shamateurism that allowed the middle-classes to keep out the riff-raff and rabble and thus maintain their control of athletics and tennis; of the five decades Major League Baseball maintained its bar on African-Americans; of the 1936 Berlin Olympics, the "Propaganda Games" designed to promote the might and right of Nazism; of the tussle for Cold War supremacy that produced state-sponsored steroid programmes on both sides of the Berlin Wall, grievously damaging hundreds of athletes and even children; of the way, at the 2012 Olympics, table tennis served as a public arena for North and South Korea to channel their considerable differences.

Matters certainly did not kick off promisingly at Hampden Park, when South Korea's flag was erroneously displayed beside the faces of the North Korea women's football team. The latter left the field in protest, delaying the start by half an hour. Reporting on the all-Korean ping-pong ding-dong ("a game pretty much hyped as 'winner takes peninsula'"), Marina Hyde's effervescent blend of verve, insight and sly wit were all present and correct in the following passage for *The Observer*:

> *As you'll be aware, the Bumper Book of Olympic Cliché dictates that we must classify international sport as war by other means. It's why British sporting commentators always refer to Germany as "the Germans". It's why ice hockey is often held to have been a significantly more successful cold war weapon than several intercontinental ballistic missiles. Yet so frenetically, dementedly aggressive is elite table tennis that the question with the Koreas match seemed not so much whether it was war by any other means, but whether the entire war between the two nations – technically still going on after six decades without*

a peace treaty – had not in fact been table tennis by any other means. Nuclear tests, ship sinkings, incursions into the demilitarised zone – all these seemed faintly tame compared with the extreme whiff-whaff, the stony-faced speed drives and the North Korean team's insistence on applauding points they'd won for just a couple of unsettling seconds too long.[4]

One chapter cannot possibly cover such expansive, complex, treacherous and sometimes surreal terrain, so while this one focuses on the relationship between sport and governments, the next two deal, respectively, with race and sexual politics. Given that a number of stories have feet in a couple of those camps, there will be a modicum of blurring.

"More able for warre"

The relationship between sport and the political elite goes back a mighty long way. According to Egyptian royal dogma, warranted the historian Donald Kyle, pharaohs competed in races to assert their supremacy. Rules were discarded; they couldn't lose because their people "could not contemplate infirmity of will or loss of power".[5]

"The only thing I am afraid of is the activity of the athletes, in case it deceives any one of our young men into preferring it to a genuine art, through offering, as it does, bodily strength and popular fame and daily public payments from the elders of our cities, and honours equal to those given to our outstanding citizens." So, the best part of 2000 years ago, charged Galen, a Roman doctor whose work would influence practitioners for centuries; in damning sport, interpreted Jason König, his intention was to "advertise his vision of medicine as a profoundly philosophical activity".[6]

Then there was James I of England, whose "Kings Majesties Declaration to His Subjects concerning lawfull Sports to bee used" (aka *Book of Sports*) was published in 1618. In it, he claimed that discouraging sport "cannot but breed a great discontentment in Our people's hearts", a mood that could only lead to increased consumption of alcohol in public houses, where drinkers would be targets for all manner of "idle and discontented speeches". They would be susceptible, in other words, to those who would foment resistance to the Crown, even revolution.

King James also had an even less admirable motive: sport, archery above all, was worth protecting and encouraging because it served to make his people "more able for warre".[7] Twentieth-century dictators such as Benito Mussolini, Adolf Hitler and Josef Stalin regarded sport's function in the same light. Fascism, Nazism and Communism, the three political ideologies that muscled in on Capitalism's sacred territory in the 20th century, all utilised sport to their advantage, for propaganda and war itself, and never more unscrupulously than the East German authorities whose enforced steroid programme ensured a wholly disproportionate share of Olympic and World Championship medals in the 1980s, leaving the winners with irretrievably damaged bodies and lives. It remains to be seen whether the more recent revelations about their fellow Germans shove us down a similarly black hole.

"German sport," Joseph Goebbels, the Nazi propaganda minister, declaimed in 1933, "has only one task: to strengthen the character of the German people, imbuing it with the fighting spirit and steadfast camaraderie necessary in the struggle for its existence." Then again, capitalists have been no different. Dwight Eisenhower, US president in the 1950s, affirmed the breadth and durability of King James's dubious philosophy: "The true mission of American sports is to prepare young men for war."

Some may deem such stances to be justly, necessarily patriotic; those cognisant of the cause of most if not quite all wars would note the mercenary purpose. Either way, sport is indivisible from time, place and context – and hence politics. Sport, in short, is dictated by politics.

The Olympian shadow
Of all the stages for the competitive arts, none, unsurprisingly, has been a handier platform to espouse political causes than the Olympics, as successive USSR leaders demonstrated. "From

their origins as war games, we can surmise that athletics and the competitive spirit were bound up with the formation of the Greek state," argue the sociologists Alan Tomlinson and Gary Whannel. "Among the Greeks, state societies based on slavery and patriarchy were established in prehistoric times. By the time of *The Iliad*, Greek communities were dominated by small elites of aristocratic males who took their higher standard of living from the labour of the slaves they had captured, exchanged, or raised, as well as from the tribute from vassal states and the booty from fresh expeditions... Throughout the Olympic period, while economic growth, urbanisation, and further conquest led to the development of a more complex class-structure, the Greek (and Roman) citizenry was highly dependent on slave-labour. Even in democratic Athens, 40-50 per cent of the population were slaves. Even women who were not slaves enjoyed little freedom. They had no political rights, their property was controlled by their male relatives, and they were officially confined to the household. Most city-states practised female infanticide to regulate the population, so males outnumbered females by as much as two to one... The Olympics strengthened and celebrated this system of power."[8]

Scepticism about Baron De Coubertin's motivation, moreover, does not seem totally unfounded. "It is arguable," observed Tomlinson and Whannel, "that de Coubertin and his supporters in the French government of 1889 were less motivated by educational altruism than by fear that young male Germans and Czechs (Czechoslovakia was then part of Austria) were in better physical and military shape than their French counterparts – a matter not to be ignored in war-torn Europe."[9] For the Stockholm Games, just two years before the outbreak of the First World War, de Coubertin himself strongly advocated the introduction of the modern pentathlon, a military-sports discipline; George Patton, the future Second World War alumnus who dubbed it the "Military Pentathlon", came fifth.

In Beijing in 2008 there were more than 10,000 competitors representing 205 nations (86 of whom won at least one medal).

At some time or other, according to the Nielsen Ratings, 4.7bn people watched the TV coverage (according to FIFA, the 2010 World Cup attracted 2.2bn viewers). If you have a political point to make, where better to make it? That's why Sacha Baron Cohen chose the Olympics as a ripe target for satire in his 2012 film, *The Dictator*. Hailed by Peter Bradshaw in *The Guardian* for its "weapons-grade offensiveness", the movie was banned in Tajikistan (one of the planet's least prosperous nations, presided over by a president, Emomali Rahmon, with reportedly no interest in his subjects' well-being whatsoever): it was, or so went the highly dubious reasoning, incompatible with the Central Asian nation's "mentality".[10] Even Rahmon, nevertheless, might have chuckled at the opening scene. As Admiral General Aladeen, tyrannical ruler of Wadiya, an imaginary rogue state in North Africa, Cohen wins 16 gold medals, aided by his insistence on firing the starter pistol himself while already halfway down the track and shooting all his rivals.

Better yet, you don't even have to wait until the opening ceremony. In May 2012, an Olympic commercial aired on Argentine TV featuring the hooded figure of Fernando Zylberberg, the national hockey captain. The 90-second film showed him training, running past a number of British landmarks and winding up at a memorial to the Falklands War, the savage if mercifully brief conflict between Britain and Argentina in 1982 that may yet go to a replay. At a time when the future of the Falkland Islands was once more the subject of fierce debate, the payoff line was nothing if not pleasing to Argentine ears: "To compete on English soil, we train on Argentine soil."[11]

This proved acutely embarrassing to Sir Martin Sorrell, chief executive of the planet's biggest marketing group, WPP: the advertising agency responsible. Young & Rubicam, was, after all, part of his not inconsiderable empire (though Y&R claimed it had been unaware that the project had involved its Argentine subsidiary, which you may or may not choose to believe). "It is totally unacceptable," he said. "We are appalled and embarrassed." Claudio Morresi, Argentina's sports secretary, insisted his country would not be using the Games as a political tool, which seemed disingenuous at best. Zylberberg was reported as saying he had had no idea that the contract he had signed was with his government. To William Hague, the British foreign secretary, it was plainly a propaganda stunt: "But I don't think trying to misuse the Olympics for political purposes will go down well with other countries."

Il Duce

In Italy, perhaps more than any other nation, sport and politics have long been indivisible. "It is simply no coincidence," asserted Paddy Agnew, the long-serving Rome correspondent for the *Irish Times* and author of an acclaimed history of Italian football, "that two of the most powerful figures of the last 100 years of Italian public life, namely Fascist dictator Benito Mussolini and media tycoon-cum-prime minister Silvio Berlusconi, made no bones about attaching themselves to the bandwagon of football. In their different ways and, albeit, with links to very different teams – Mussolini to the Italian national team of the 1930s, Berlusconi to the modern outstanding club side, AC Milan – both men had an intuitive understanding of the ground-breaking role that football could and does play in modern Italy."[12] Berlusconi sought to promote himself by constructing a vast media empire in which AC Milan was at first, observed Agnew, "merely an addendum"; Mussolini wanted to promote "an organic, patriotic, nationalist and united nation through football". Sport, he insisted in a private conversation just three months after his March on Rome in 1923, a de facto coup, "represents the exaltation of the moral and physical force of youth and enhances a country's prestige... [it] will become the trademark of fascist Italy."[13] True, he did use other sports to help achieve this but it soon became abundantly clear to him that no sport could shine a candle to football in the Italian consciousness. Arguably, claims Agnew, he was the man who invented the "stadio comunale", the local authority-run stadium intended for football and often other sports such as athletics. State funds financed the erection of stadiums from

Milan (the original San Siro), Bologna, Florence and Genoa to Pisa, Palermo, Rome and Turin.

Mussolini loved sport. Whether swimming, hitting forehands or the chins of fellow boxers, he needed no convincing of its pleasures or value. One day, a thought struck him: the human body would make a splendid metaphor for the Fascist state. *Risorgimento* was the overriding aim: national unity. At first, he advocated the virtues of non-competitive sport as a means of accustoming young people to discipline, racial affirmation and training for military ends, but the 1930s brought a change of tack: not only could sport improve international relations and offer plentiful opportunities to glorify the state, it could be handy, wrote Angela Teja, when it came to "concealing the economic and political problems".[14]

Mussolini headed the first anti-Capitalist regime to see sport as integral to effective government; a goodly portion of his techniques, moreover, would be imitated by Hitler, of whom more, inevitably, anon. Football, in fact, can be interpreted as the catalyst for the repressive measures instigated by Mussolini in the mid-1920s. In October 1926 he journeyed by train to Bologna for the fourth anniversary of his rise to power, to preside over the opening of the city's new "Littoriale" stadium, brainchild of Leandro Arpinati, the local Fascist leader. When Il Duce entered the ground on a white horse the reception was suitably ecstatic. Reported the Fascist newspaper, *L'Assalto*:

> *When… we saw the mighty Duce enter like a conductor of people, bathed in the light of the sun that had finally driven away the clouds, greeted by a mass that only Eternal Rome will have seen paying tribute to a "triumph" and to a victorious consul, we truly thought the hearts of all Italians must have been beating with his.*[15]

As he was being driven back to the station, shots were fired at Mussolini. "In the ensuing chaos," as Agnew portrayed the scene, "a 13-year-old boy, Anteo Zamboni, son of a well-known local anarchist, was brutally beaten to death by the crowd, which had identified him as the would-be assassin. The dynamics of this ugly incident remain unclear. What is sure, however, is that the alleged assassination attempt gave the green light for a whole range of highly repressive measures. By the end of 1926, new legislation had re-introduced the death penalty, had banned all political parties other than the Fascist party and had set up a special Fascist police service. Clearly, the Fascist dictator was always going to ride roughshod over free speech and fundamental democratic principles, but the Bologna stadium incident provided a perfect excuse."[16] "Il Duce", more-over, would come to be regarded, in the words of the respected scholar John Hoberman, as Fascism's "great political athlete".[17]

The 1926 crisis, related Agnew, prompted the Viareggio Charter, which oversaw a radical reorganisation of Italian foot-ball: the leagues were realigned and, in effect, this established both professionalism and the transfer market. More impor-tantly, the Charter placed Italian football's governing body, the Fascist-controlled FIGC (Federazione Italiana Giuoco Calcio), under the wing of the Italian Olympic Committee, regarded as an appendage of the Fascist party. It was, therefore, the FIGC which in the 1929 season instigated the first truly national Italian league championship (until then, there had been Northern and Southern leagues). There is good reason, then, to hail Mussolini for inventing Serie A.

The apogee of his growing appreciation of the value of inter-national contact was Italy's hosting of the FIFA World Cup of 1934, for which he lobbied strenuously. Though keener on phys-ical education as a path to national self-improvement, General Franco, Mussolini's Spanish fascist counterpart, was sufficiently clued-up on the political usefulness of sport to throw his regime behind a football club, Real Madrid – who would repay him by dominating the early years of pan-European club competition – but was otherwise unwilling to throw money at it; Mussolini was. "In addition to draining marshes and building roads, the stock in trade of dictatorial regimes," testified Bill Murray, "the Fascists built modern soccer stadiums as monuments to their glory."[18] Helpfully, Italian arms lifted the trophy. Presided over by their venerable tubby coach, Vittorio Pozzo – who had managed his country to Olympic gold as long ago as 1912 and whose teams lost only seven times in the whole decade – the triumph was not greeted with universal gratitude.

Many pointed to a timely reversal of the ban on foreign players in Serie A, allowing as it did three former Argentine internationals, Raimundo Orsi, Luis Monti and Enrique Guaita, all of whom had played in the 1930 final, to make a conspicuous and vital contribution. ("If they can die for Italy," reasoned Pozzo, "they can play football for Italy.") Others would insist that the referees had been complicit. Handpicked by Mussolini himself, the appointments for the quarter-final replay against Spain and the semi-final against Austria's *Wunderteam* (vanquishers of Italy at the 1932 Olympics) proved especially inspired. After the first, *Basler Nationalzeitung*, a suitably neutral Swiss newspaper, charged that Rene Mercet had "favoured the Italians in a most shameful manner"; the second was settled when Ivan Eklind saw no earthly reason, even though the Austrian goalkeeper had been bundled over the line, to disallow Enrique Guiata's "goal". Rewarded with the gig for the final (one of his linesmen, just happened to be Louis Blaert, whose officiating during the original quarter-final had been keenly questioned), Eklind spent a fair chunk of the preceding evening in conversation with Il Duce, presumably to share their admiration for Prince Machiavelli.

At the World Cup in France four years later, as Pozzo's side filed out to meet Norway for their opening assignment, an estimated 10,000 political exiles on the terraces fuelled a furious greeting. Police had to be summoned to restrain the anti-Fascist protestors but Pozzo was anything but cowed, ordering his players to give the customary salute with his usual war cry, "Team, Be Ready, Salute". This was the cue, Pozzo recollected, for "a solemn and deafening barrage of whistles and insults". Cue another exhortation from Pozzo: "Team, Be Ready, Salute". The players raised their arms once more, "to confirm we had no fear". For the quarter-final against the hosts, they were clad in all black – party colours. A couple of weeks later they became the first nation to retain the FIFA title (as I write, only Brazil have emulated them). Pozzo was long touted as a major tool of the state apparatus, yet he aided not only the anti-Fascist resistance but the flight of Allied prisoners of war. As John Foot argued in another meritorious history of Italian football: "Much of the fascist influence on sport – as in Italian everyday life – was symbolic."[19]

Not that Mussolini was content with boasting of his world champion footballers. Having chosen his brother to head the national boxing commission, he interceded in 1930 when Primo Carnera, "The Ambling Alp", was threatened with deportation from the US. Later that year, a *New York Times* reporter claimed Il Duce was "now running boxing in this country".[20]

When Mussolini invaded Abyssinia (now Ethiopia) in 1934, the promoter Mike Jacobs demonstrated his opportunism by arranging a bout between Carnera, around whom swirled rumours of gangland backers and profoundly dodgy dealings, and Joe Louis, an up-and-coming black fighter. "Blacks wanted to see Louis destroy the representative of an aggressive Italy," wrote Jeffrey T. Sammons, professor of history at the University of North Carolina. To John Hope Franklin, conversely, the conquest of Abyssinia symbolised "the final victory of the white man over the Negro".[21] Some in the northern press portrayed Louis as Abyssinia and Carnera as Italy; the southern press "all but ignored the fight's racial and international implications", declining to make the link between the modestly proportioned African nation and the country's own black populace, and ignoring reports of voluble complaints about the threat to the Abyssinian president, Haile Selassie, a black icon.[22]

In June 1935, Louis knocked out Carnera in six rounds. "What had started out as an Alp," related one contemporary report, "looked about the altitude of a chicken croquet by the time Joe got through with him."[23] Black youths reportedly scampered through Harlem yelling "Let's get Mussolini next".

Louis, warranted Anthony Edmonds, one of Muhammad Ali's many biographers, had achieved "symbolically what black Americans vehemently hoped Haile Selassie would do in fact". Louis, concluded Sammons, also represented "black pride and a nascent Pan-Africanism".[24] We shall return to him.

Football and appeasement

After Hitler had wrested power in Germany in 1933, his radical restructuring of the country led to the foundation of the *Deutsche Reichsbund für Leibesübungen*, under the direction and steward-ship of the *Reichsports-führer*, Hans von Tschammer und Osten. "In December 1935 Sir Eric Phipps, the British ambassador in Berlin, noted the 'tightening' of Nazi control over German sport as well as the political 'exploitation' of sporting victories," wrote Peter Beck in *History Today*. "The close of 1935 also saw the appearance of a manual for political education in German, *Deutschland über Volk, Staat, Leibesübungen*, which left its reader with little doubt as to the political role of sport. For example, it asserted that 'gymnastics and sport are thus an institution for the education of the body and a school of the political will in the service of the State. Unpolitical, so-called neutral gymnasts and sportsmen are unthinkable in Hitler's state'."[25]

By then, moreover, the systematic exclusion of Jews from sport and recreation had begun. In 1933, Eric Seelig, an amateur champion, was expelled by the German Boxing Association, and Daniel Prenn ditched from the Davis Cup team. Gypsies suffered too: in the same year, Johann "Rukelie" Trollman, the middleweight boxing champion, was banned.

To Hitler, contended Jean-Marie Brohm, sport was a "char-acter school", churning out "authoritarian, aggressive, narcistic and obedient character types".[26] Just the ticket for the nation's budding stormtroopers. Germany, though, had been a sporting pariah since the First World War. There was no invitation to the 1920 or the 1924 Olympics; the four British home nations refused to compete with its teams at club or national level. Entry to the League of Nations in 1926, however, led to a thaw: two years later came a return to the Olympics; come decade's end, the national football team were playing Scotland; England relented in 1930.

Cognisant of the deteriorating and increasingly brutal treatment of their counterparts in Berlin, Bonn and Munich, trade unionists and Jews protested long and loud when it was announced that England and Germany would meet again at White Hart Lane in 1935, but Sir John Simon, the home secretary, refused to intervene. Portraying the FA as "a quite independent body", he advocated the need "to keep up in our country a tradition that (this) sporting fixture is carried through without any regard to politics at all". More to the point, asserted Beck, the Foreign Office felt that abandoning the match would have been "likely to prompt a hostile German reaction, thereby conflicting with the basic foreign policy objective of conciliating Germany". [27] Although England won 3-0, the *Börsen Zeitung* greeted the game glowingly: for Germany, it insisted, it had been "an unqualified political, psychological and sporting success".

Three years later, with the teams scheduled to meet once more, this time in Berlin, Sir Robert Vansittart, chief diplomatic adviser at the Foreign Office, stressed to Stanley Rous, the FA secretary, how important it was "for our prestige that the British team should put up a really first-class performance. I hope that every possible effort will be made to ensure this". Rous assured him that every player "will do his utmost to uphold the prestige of his country" and pressured clubs to release players. By the day of the match it had been agreed: the England team would give the Nazi salute – a decision based on the experience and advice of both Nevile Henderson, the British ambassador to Berlin who believed in soliciting German sympathy, and Rous, who had attended the Berlin Olympics and was wary of German sensitivity to such ceremonies as well as allegations that Hitler had been agitated by the apparent failure of the British team to adequately acknowledge his presence.

Although the instruction aroused much heart-searching among the players and indignation aplenty in Fleet Street, explained Beck, FA officials "justified the gesture on the grounds that it would ensure a friendly reception by not only the huge swastika-waving crowd present in the Berlin stadium but also the larger audience tuned in to the radio commentary throughout Germany and beyond. The political significance of the gesture was obvious." In giving the salute the players faced Der Führer's box, which in addition to Henderson was brimming with dignitaries such as Goebbels, Goering, Hess, Ribbentrop and the country's leading sports administrator, Hans von Tschammer und Osten. Having only just returned from Italy, Hitler himself was absent: hindsight, points out Beck, suggests he was engaged in preparations for action against Czechoslovakia.[28]

In an incident-free contest, England won 6-3. Sport, concluded Beck, "was a contributory factor at both the official and popular level to the policy of appeasement": the Berlin match was "part of the English government's strategy of cultural propaganda, and as a means of scoring points as well as goals at Germany's expense".[29]

The Alternative Olympics

In July 1992, the five-ring circus reopened for business at Barcelona's Montjuic Stadium, whose foundation stone had been laid more than six decades earlier by Comte Henri de Ballet-Latour, then IOC president. It was constructed as part of the city's ambitions to host the Olympics, ambitions that were scheduled to be resolved, one way or another, at the 1931 IOC general meeting. A marquis and five counts were present at the Ritz Hotel in the Catalan capital but attendance was otherwise sparse: a postal vote would decide the host city for the 1936 Olympics.

As socialism spread across Europe in the early 20th century, so the continent became the scene for an alternative Olympics – the Workers' Olympiad. Active throughout Europe since the 1850s, workers' sports organisations held little truck with the aristocrats and industrialists who ran the real McCoy. The first alternative Games were organised by the Socialist Workers' Sport International (SASI) and staged in Frankfurt from 24-28 July 1925; in light of events a decade later, when the Nazis shook perceptions of socialism to the core, how curiously apt it seems that the host city should have been German.

The left-wing sporting roost was ruled by two mutually exclusive workers' clubs. In one corner stood SASI, backed by the social democratic parties and the International Federation of Trade Unions; in the other stood Red Sport International (RSI), aka Sportintern, founded by revolutionary Communists. Inevitably, these clubs mirrored the seemingly irreversible split between the reformist and revolutionary wings of the socialist movement. As the political gulf widened to unbridgeable proportions, all imprecations to unify were resisted. [30]

Less concerned with winning and losing than mass exercise, the inaugural Workers' Olympiad was the largest gathering of sportsfolk yet: 2,954 men and 135 women had participated in the 1924 Paris Olympics, yet more than 100,000 – children included – were in Frankfurt. In 2012, London's Tate Modern screened a 60-minute documentary, *The New Great Power* (*Die Neue Grossmacht*), "an early masterpiece of social cinema" directed by William Prager, whose assistant, Leni Riefenstahl, would leave a far heavier imprint on Olympic history in Berlin 11 years later. Prager's film, enthused the Tate website, stands testimony "to the original power of international political ideals, expressed through sport".[31]

In all, SASI ran three summer Workers' Olympiads, plus a winter model. In Vienna in 1931, both versions were larger than their "official" counterparts. National flags were conspicuous by their absence, displaced by the Red Flag. There was no Olympic Village, no fabricated temporary community created from tarted-up neighbourhoods: working-class competitors stayed with working-class families. On one poster in Frankfurt a socialist worker flailing a vast red flag was depicted standing over broken rifles and a battered swastika flag. The motto of those games was unequivocal: "No More War".

Fate, though, took a mocking hand in July 1936 when the "People's Olympiad" opened in Barcelona, which had vied with Berlin to host that year's summer Olympics. The counter-attraction

had been swiftly organised by the socialist Spanish government elected five months earlier; back in 1931, 10 days before
that IOC general meeting at the Ritz, Spain had been declared
a republic, leading many to suspect that this was the reason so
few members had turned up, swinging the fateful postal vote.

The mayor of the Catalan capital welcomed 5,000 competitors
and 20,000 spectators to the feistily entitled "Popular Olympics",
whereupon the next day saw the onset of the military uprising
that ignited the Spanish Civil War. Abetting the republican
forces were many of those who had turned up at the Montjuic
Stadium. The city bitterly opposed General Franco; thousands
paid with their lives. His vengeance was complete in December
1965, when his beloved Madrid went toe-to-toe with Barcelona,
at stake the honour of being the nation's candidate to stage the
1972 Olympics. Three days before Christmas Eve, the date of
the vote, deception entered the fray when Barcelona's leader
received a phone call telling him it wasn't worth turning up: "It's
not important," he was told, "It's just to settle the accounts."[32]
Madrid, unsurprisingly, got the nod. There was some poetic
justice in the comical conclusion: the Madrid bid failed, apparently because the wrong official signed the application form.

Not until 1992 would Barcelona finally beat Madrid to
become the Olympics' first Spanish host. It didn't hurt that that
nation, mercifully free of Franco, was now a democracy. Nor,
for that matter, that the IOC president was one of the city's own
sons, Juan Antonio Samaranch. Mind you, stresses Andrew
Jennings, Samaranch was "a 37-year Nazi" and "discussion at
the IOC of his Francoist history was taboo".[33]

Slavery Avery and the Propaganda Games

For years they restricted the number of Jews in schools, medical
schools. In America, as much as they hated blacks, they hate
Jews even more. Blacks they were scared had too big a penis.
Jews they hated, even with little penises.
Boris Yellnikoff in Woody Allen's *Whatever Works*, 2009

Before he became Hitler's propaganda minister, Dr Paul Joseph Goebbels had already given due notice of his cunning. In 1930, he orchestrated a protest against *All Quiet On The Western Front*, a Hollywood film depicting the suffering of German soldiers during the First World War. Standing up during the screening in Berlin, he screamed "*Judenfilm!*" (Jewish film), whereupon his brownshirts unleashed stink bombs, sneezing powder and white mice on the auditorium, provoking panic. "Within ten minutes the cinema was a madhouse," claimed Goebbels. "The police are powerless. The embittered masses are violently against the Jews." Other orchestrated episodes ensued and the movie was banned: an era of non-stop state censorship had begun. In a precursor to wider American complicity, Joseph Breen of the Production Code Administration refused scripts that cast Germany in an unflattering light until 1939, when the accumulated evidence of cinema newsreels persuaded him to permit the release of *Confessions of a Nazi Spy*.[34]

Hitler was initially dead-set against bringing the 1936 Olympics to Berlin – primarily on economic grounds – but Goebbels was in no doubt about their potential worth to the Third Reich. Hailing it as "a splendid opportunity to demonstrate German vitality and organisational expertise", he duly secured funding to the tune of 20 million reichsmarks (approximately $US8m).[35] Jesse Owens subverted the marketing strategy by snapping up an unprecedented four golds and, according to hardy and almost wholly baseless myth, sending Hitler scurrying from the stadium to avoid having to hand a gold medal to a black man, but the Games were still a shameless showcase for Aryan supremacy: the hosts topped the medal table, evincing the nation's renewed greatness and the power of the Third Reich. As emphasised by Sarah J. Bloomfield, the curator of the Holocaust Museum in Washington D.C, even Owens's astonishing one-man show failed to mask the overwhelming success of the Games as propaganda (most artfully and chillingly expressed in Riefenstahl's documentary, *Olympia*), creating "an illusion of a peaceful and tolerant nation". And the world acquiesced, wanting "to believe this illusion, allowing itself to be completely deceived".[36]

"On virtually every other banner we saw there was a swastika," remembered the Jewish-American sprinter Marty Glickman, who claimed he lost a relay gold medal because Avery Brundage, the president of the American Athletics Union, the most powerful governing body in US sport, was so willing to appease the hosts. Brundage, in fact, was said to be quite a fan of Herr Hitler. Or, to be more exact, of his beliefs. Bent on insulating the Games from the meddlesome tentacles of societal norms, on building an impenetrable bubble, he would preside as IOC president from 1952 to 1972, earning an unmatched reputation both for his zealous guarding of De Coubertin's legacy and his distaste for the equality of the species. The Propaganda Games was the first time the world saw his hand.

Spectator sport has had its fair share of rotten apples; from match-fixers, cheats and thugs to corrupt mandarins and heartless managers, from the bottom of privilege's ladder (Mike Tyson) to the very top (Lord Frederick Beauclerk). It is exceedingly hard, though, to think of any who have brought the competitive arts into quite such disrepute for quite so long as Brundage – or so subtly. As Carolyn Marvin of the University of Pennsylvania summed up,

> *Although the Iron Chancellor of amateur sport regarded himself as the last true defender of the strict separation of sport and politics, he also frequently insisted that more than the future of amateur sport was at stake in shielding sport from political manipulation. Upon sport for sport's sake depended the healthy psychological valuation of individual effort and excellence that was at the very heart of a democratic way of life. Moreover, fit bodies and competitive spirits were in Brundage's view essential for the continued success of American capitalism at home and abroad. Though he never acknowledged the political colouring of his vision of the Olympics, he regarded them as a kind of international mission for spreading democratic values in*

the continuing ideological battle between Communism and the American way of life.[37]

The son of a Detroit stonemason, "Slavery Avery" competed in the 1912 Stockholm Games, finishing sixth and 16th in the pentathlon and decathlon behind that consummate all-rounder Jim Thorpe. A firm endorser of the prejudice nurtured by his Chicago golf club – one that, like so many, barred Jews – he made his fortune in construction, the fruits of which included an Asian art collection that now comprises the bulk of a San Francisco museum. The Olympics, though, were his passion. In 1930 he was elected president of the US Olympic Committee, a post he would hold for the best part of a quarter of a century; three years later he learned that that his goal was within reach – election to the IOC. Ensuring that the American team not only turned up in Berlin but triumphed would erase any lingering obstacles, hence the rapid erosion of his apparent initial support for a boycott. "Several people criticised Brundage for being somewhat intransigent in his positions and in his way of leading," notes the official IOC archive. "However, everyone agrees that he was always faithful to his convictions and to defending the two major Olympic ideals, i.e. amateurism and the non-politicisation of sport."[38] Not everyone saw this as an entirely admirable trait.

Arnd Krüger had access to Brundage's papers. As a sports historian at the University of Göttingen, and a former Olympic middle-distance runner who had studied in the US, he approached him from two perspectives. In the 1930s, the Olympics marked the only time the US sporting public as a whole was stirred by international competition. In 1936, furthermore, the dish was spiced by politics, "keenly felt in a nation with an influential Jewish minority and whose major athletes included a small but significant number of blacks".[39] As disquiet spread, the options, interpreted Krüger, were threefold: the Games could be cancelled (as in 1916, when the First World War intervened), transferred (Rome and Tokyo had previously expressed an interest in playing host) or held in Berlin; the last of these would risk a boycott so depleting – Germany, after all, could hardly be said to have been showing undying respect for the purported Olympic "spirit" of racial, religious and political tolerance – that it "would have no propaganda value for the organiser".[40]

Talk of a boycott intensified as news emerged of German Jews and Catholics being subjected to sporting apartheid. Brundage was apoplectic – albeit only about the latter. The Games, he reasoned, belonged "to the athletes and not to the politicians". Cue a letter to the IOC president, Count Henri Baillet-Latour, on behalf of the Amateur Athletic Union:

> *I am not personally fond of Jews and of the Jewish influence but will not have them molested in one way or another. In 1933…
> [the] AAU resolved that it would not certify any Olympic athletes for the Games in Nazi Germany until and unless the position of the German Olympic committee… is so changed in fact as well as in theory as to permit German athletes of Jewish faith or heritage to train, prepare for or participate in the Olympic Games of 1936.*[41]

Among those supporting a boycott were Judge Jeremiah Mahoney, who rotated nine terms with Brundage as president of the AAU between 1928 and 1937. Like Al Smith and James Curley, governors, respectively, of New York and Massachusetts, Mahoney was among a number of Catholic leaders so disposed. The Catholic journal *The Commonweal* advised boycotting an Olympics that would "set the seal of approval upon the radically anti-Christian Nazi doctrine of youth."[42] At the same time, it should be noted, US businessmen, defence contractors and bankers were happy doing business with Nazi Germany, many of whom would later be accused of collaboration.

In 1933, as part of a general economic boycott, the American Jewish Congress and the Jewish Labour Committee had begun staging mass rallies in consort with the non-sectarian Anti-Nazi League, protesting against Nazi persecution. Those Jewish groups that declined to lend formal support, such as the American Jewish Committee and B'nai B'rith, did so in part because they feared that such a posture might trigger an anti-Semitic backlash. Individual athletes also took a stand. Milton Green, the Harvard captain who took first place in the 110 metres hurdles in the regional trials, qualified for the national eliminators alongside his fellow Norman Cahners, a fellow semite: both boycotted the final hurdle.

According to a 1935 Gallup poll, 43% of respondents favoured an American boycott, yet although Brundage clung stubbornly to his perception of a conspiracy between Communists and Jews, reasoned Guttmann, this was not *because* of his anti-Semitism but the *cause* of it.[43] And behind that, argued Guttmann, lay the heated debate over whether to attend the Berlin Games: the way Brundage saw it, boycotting the Olympics would be political, and the Olympics should always be above considerations of "politics, race, colour, or creed".[44] Gustavus Kirby, a staunch defender of the principles of equality who believed sport to be "the only true democracy",[45] wrote an angry letter to Brundage, the protégé who had pipped him to IOC big-wiggery: "I take it that the fundamental difference between you and me is that you are a Jew hater and Jew baiter and I am neither."

In November 1935, the American IOC representative, Ernest Lee Jahncke, a former assistant secretary of the Navy and a decent man of German Protestant descent, wrote an impassioned letter to Baillet-Latour: "Neither Americans nor the representatives of other countries can take part in the Games in Nazi Germany without at least acquiescing in the contempt of the Nazis for fair play and their sordid exploitation of the Games." Refusing to soften his stance, Jahncke paid an unprecedented price the following July, becoming the first man expelled by the IOC. Not until 2004 would Indonesia's Bob Hasan swell the ranks of that particular club; as with the third member, Bulgaria's Ivan Slakov, Hasan was thrown out for being corrupt; João Havelange would have joined them had he not resigned before being pushed.

On behalf of the USOC, Brundage went on a fact-finding mission to Germany, where he met Hitler and shared smiles and handshakes for the cameras. IOC pressure had persuaded the authorities to organise training courses in Ettlingen, where one attendee was the Jewish athlete Paul Yogi Mayer. Later a coach, teacher and sportswriter, he would be present at the Berlin Games but subsequently fled to England, serving in the Second World War, teaching art and sport in London's East End and helping the children of holocaust victims. Those courses, he charged, "were ultimately deceitful examples of the inclusiveness that Germany was now compelled to demonstrate".[46]

Brundage came home and wrote a pamphlet, "Fair Play for American Athletes", urging his subjects not to become involved in the "Jew-Nazi altercation" and alleging that a "Jewish-Communist conspiracy" was trying to keep his country out of the Games. "The fact that no Jews have been named so far to compete for Germany," he reasoned in July 1935, "doesn't necessarily mean that they have been discriminated against on that score. In forty years of Olympic history, I doubt if the number of Jewish athletes competing from all nations totalled one percent of those in the Games. In fact, I believe one-half of one percent would be a high percentage."[47] A good memory, clearly, was not one of Brundage's assets: at the 1932 winter and summer Games alone, 23 Jewish athletes had won medals.

A month after Jahncke's letter, the anti-boycott lobby in the AAU prevailed by just two and a half votes, giving a green light to other undecided nations.[48] Before long, posters began to appear over Europe, reported Shirley Povich, the Jewish sportswriter who would cover the Games for the *Washington Post*, depicting Hitler "in full Nazi regalia and full Nazi stature", declaiming "I summon the youth of the world to the Olympics." This notwithstanding the fact, noted Povich, "that the Olympics are supposed to be an invitation affair with a natural anathema to the word 'summons'. Thus the Nazis were not long in prostituting their role as Olympic hosts."[49]

Now the Nazis boxed clever. For the Winter Games at Garmisch-Partenkirchen in the Bavarian Alps, signs outside the toilets read "Dogs and Jews are not allowed". When Baillet-Latour objected, Hitler spoke plainly: "Mr President, when you are invited to a friend's house, you don't tell him now to run it, do you?" The Frenchman pointed out that, once the five-ring flag was raised over the stadium, "it is Olympia and we are masters there", whereupon the signs vanished. Two popular "half Jews" were selected for Garmisch, including Rudi Ball, a past Olympic medallist who took gold with the ice hockey team. Fourth in the same event were Hungary, featuring the Jewish trio of Sandor Miklos and brothers Andras and Laslo Gergely.[50]

There were some refuseniks. Among the prominent athletes who refused to attend were Ivan Osiier, who'd won a fencing gold for Denmark in 1912 and would win another at 59, and the former discus champion Lilian Copeland; the Australian boxer Harry Cohen registered as a professional and thus avoided being invited to fight. Frank Fisher was not the only Jew in the Czech water polo team but he was alone in being unwilling to participate. Some were simply bypassed by anti-Semitic selectors: three leading Austrian swimmers, Judith Deutsch, Lucie Goldner and Ruth Langer, were banned for two years. Others, such as the members of the Maccabi World Union, were instructed not to take part. Even non-Jews excluded themselves, including a number of US basketballers and the entire Dutch wrestling team. On the other hand, wrote Mayer: "The majority of Jews… who wanted to demonstrate by their achievements the invalidity of Hitler's pronouncements, took part – and won some medals."[51]

Then there was Gretel Bergmann. A Jewish high-jumper, she was chosen only to be dropped at the last – an enormous, shameless U-turn. Denied admission to Berlin's High School for Physical Education, Bergmann was completing her studies in London when her father, much to her delight, came over to see her win the British high jump title in 1934, then revealed his true purpose: he was taking her home because she was wanted for the German Olympic team. Failure to return, Mayer attested in *Jews And The Olympic Games*, "would have [had] 'severe consequences', not only for her family but also for the Jewish sports organisations".

Bergmann and her family subsequently moved to the US, where she became the national champion at shot put as well as high jump, and married Bruno Lambert, another German émigré whom she had met on that Ettlingen course. Interviewed more than 70 years after she had been deprived of her moment in the sun, for a film made for the Washington DC Holocaust Museum, she said she had felt trapped between the proverbial rock and an extremely hard place: had she competed in Berlin, she would have been "a loser, either way", she explained. "Because, had I won, there would have been such an insult against the German psyche (how can a Jew be good enough to win the Olympics?) that I would have had to be afraid for my life, I am sure. And had I lost, I would have been made as a... joke."[52] Things change. In 1996, she was guest of honour of the German National Olympic Committee at the Atlanta Games.

Mayer attended the opening ceremony in Berlin:

We watched Adolf Hitler and his entourage descend the steps from the Langemark Chapel into the arena. By visiting this memorial to the young students who had given their lives in an attack whilst singing the "Deutschlandlied" in the First World War, Hitler tried to bridge the gap between a heroic past and his new nationalism... In the parade were, of course, the black American competitors – whom Goebbels attacked in his daily newspaper Der Angriff as the "black auxiliaries of the American team"...[53]

There were two Jews in the US team, Glickman and Sam Stoller. They were scheduled to run in the 4 x 100m relay but Brundage and his fellow selectors replaced them with Owens and Frank Metcalfe. Brundage claimed that the team needed to be strengthened and that the inclusion of two star black runners would be another kick in the teeth for Hitler. Few accepted this at face value. "Of course, the general public would not have noticed that Glickman and Stoller were circumcised Jews!"

remarked Mayer with a sizeable dash of sarcasm. "However, the Americans must have been of the opinion that for Hitler, from his balcony, it would have been even more offensive to face two Jewish sprinters on the podium than two blacks, in which case their actual reasons were to minimise the potential humiliation felt by Hitler."[54] Blacks before Jews, then, for all that Brundage was scarcely fond of Owens, who confided to colleagues that he felt awful for the excluded runners and had been deeply distressed at being thrust into the controversy. Much to the watching Mayer's pleasure, the US quartet won the relay by 15 metres; Slavery Avery still banned Owens when he returned home.

For his part, Glickman believed he and Stoller were jettisoned partly because of anti-Semitism and partly because Brundage didn't want to cause offence. When he heard, many years later, that Stoller had rejected the former as a factor, Glickman was astonished. "So why would Sam then leave the team and go right back home and say he would never compete again? It had to be that. What other reason could there be?"[55]

But if Glickman and Stoller were withdrawn to satisfy Hitler, why did Glickman think that Owens and other African-Americans were permitted to compete? "There were six to seven gold medal winners who were black athletes. Sam Stoller and I would have been gold medal winners but we were two relatively obscure athletes, two Jewish athletes. It was relatively unimportant to take the Jewish athletes off the relay team and replace them with black athletes, whereas there would be no American Olympic track team without the black athletes because they won the 100, 200, long jump, 400, 800, high jump and medals in every track event in addition to those. There was no way they could remove all the black athletes from the Olympics, whereas this was just dropping two guys from the relay team."[56] Goebbels' department, it should be stressed, had decreed that "special care should be exercised not to offend Negro athletes".[57]

Povich summed up the fiasco with typical adroitness:

> As America's triumphant track and field athletes head home-
> ward from Berlin, olive-crowned and basking in a slew of new
> records, a diffident voice that is beginning to boom in a crescendo
> is asking: What price Olympic glory? And the little group that
> for two years strenuously opposed American participation… is
> beginning to find vindication. They are the folks who refused to
> believe that the leopard would or could change his spots; who
> distrusted the Nazis when the Nazis said – as the American
> threat to withdraw from the games began to develop – that there
> would be no discrimination against non-Aryans… To which
> echo is now flinging back a rasping "Oh yeah?"[58]

As evidence of the narrowness and prejudices of Brundage's
one-track vision, the Glickman-Stoller episode could not
have been more revealing. He was far from his country's only
prominent Nazi sympathiser but, unlike Henry Ford and Joe
Kennedy, he never recanted or apologised. At an "America
First" rally in 1941 at Madison Square Garden he praised the
Third Reich; eventually, the distinctly right-wing America First
Committee expelled him for expressing his love of Hitler a little
too enthusiastically.[59]

Max and Joe

No sporting story from the Nazi era was quite as bewildering,
or ultimately uplifting, as that of Max Schmeling, the boxer
otherwise known as the "Black Ulhan", who achieved more
as an ex-champion than he ever did inside the square circle.
Handsomely-constructed and possessed of what was considered, admiringly, as a scientific approach, he found an audience
in the US as a Jack Dempsey doppelganger and became the first
German to win the world heavyweight title in 1930. However,
having done so after Jack Sharkey had struck him below the belt,
he returned home derided as the "Low blow champ" and soon
faded from view, whereupon a controversial loss to Sharkey in
the rematch found him resurrected as a hero. One notably humiliating defeat (albeit mostly for Herr Hitler) came at the hands of

Max Baer, who had a Star of David stitched into his trunks and boasted of his Jewish ancestry. Whether this was made up or exaggerated by way of provocation/intimidation, nobody was quite sure, but the clowning Baer played the part to the hilt. "Every punch in the eye I give Schmeling," he goaded, "is one for Adolf Hitler."[60] He even offered to fight Schmeling in Hamburg but Hitler demurred. Not that anyone was left doubting the Führer's fondness for boxers. A revolution of "fancy-men, deserters and similar riffraff" would have been impossible, he insisted, had the "intellectual upper class... all learned to box".[61]

Sporting failure could incur a heavy price in Nazi Germany. After suffering a succession of defeats by the American Donald Budge, Baron Gottfried von Cramm, the country's leading tennis player, was arrested on morals charges and never heard from again.[62] Yet Schmeling recovered, and mapped out a path back to the throne. Then, at Yankee Stadium in June 1936, the subtext of the Louis-Carnera duel returned with a vengeance as Hitler's Aryan Superman met the "Brown Bomber" at Yankee Stadium. Initially, Schmeling had hesitated, prompting the North American press to argue that the Nazis opposed inter-racial contests; after all, Julius Streicher, a Nazi official, had recently expelled a black wrestler from a Nuremburg event because a representative of the master race could not possibly be permitted to be beaten by non-Aryans.[63]

When terms for the Louis-Schmeling were agreed, the National Association for the Advancement of Coloured People (NAACP), the Anti-Nazi League and the German press rose up in unison; there were rumours, moreover, that victory would see Hitler appoint Schmeling as his minister of physical education – even though Goebbels, anticipating a heavy defeat, had insisted that newspapers play down the fight. In the event, Schmeling knocked Louis down early and, eventually, out. The press turned on the loser, writes Sammons, "like a lover scorned, questioning his will, his intelligence and his ability; some suggested that he was no more than a media creation, having built his reputation on has-beens. The northern press quickly jettisoned him as a symbol of America and let him sink alone. Its harshly critical treatment seemed to be a face-saving gesture to protect its own credibility as well as the national image. The southern press only had its own reputation to protect and expressed a sense of betrayal and crushed pride. With few exceptions, racial or international concerns were absent."[64] The delighted Goebbels, meanwhile, authorised the making of a movie, *Max Schmeling's Victory – A German Victory*. As for Hitler, he was happy whenever Schmeling fought in the US, knowing he would serve as a reliable mouthpiece, reassuring one and all that they shouldn't believe what they read, that everything in Germany was both hunky and gloriously dory.

Writing with familiar bile in the *New Orleans Times-Picayune*, William McG. Keefe, one of Louis's most fervent critics, proclaimed Schmeling's victory as proof of white supremacy: "The big bad wolf had been chased from the door. It took the Black Ulhan to prove that the black terror is just another fragile human being."[65] Such views may have been simply old-style Southern racism, but the fact remained that, according to an opinion poll conducted as late as June 1940, less than 5% of Americans favoured declaring war on Germany.

Plans proceeded apace for Schmeling to meet the world champion, James J. Braddock, the improbable conqueror of Baer and a genuine Depression-Era hero, played seven decades later by Russell Crowe in *Cinderella Man* – the nickname bestowed on the Irish-American by Damon Runyon. That Braddock's chances were perceived as slim fuelled a backlash: promoters, a chunky proportion of whom were Jewish, resolved not to let Schmeling, as the *Charlotte Observer* put it, "take the title back to Germany and present it to Adolf Hitler for the German museum".[66] Whereupon a suspicious hand injury to Braddock forced the proposed Madison Square Garden encounter to be postponed from September 1936 to the following June. "When circumstances indicated that the Braddock-Schmeling bout would not take place in America," recounts Sammons, "Frank Hague, mayoral boss of Jersey City and a friend of Braddock's, undertook to 'help' the champion by rescheduling the fight in Europe. Although the ever-scheming, entrepreneurial Hague, a man of considerable wealth with little visible means of income, had ulterior motives – he planned to use the heavyweight championship as an entrée into the lucrative optical supplies market via a Dutch firm – the episode demonstrates what was a clear link between sport, greed and diplomacy."[67]

Much to German fury, Mike Jacobs persuaded Braddock to put his crown on the line against Louis, who duly became the first African-American to contest the title since Jack Johnson. He seized the opportunity with both terrifying fists, defeating the courageous but outgunned Braddock in front of 50,000 at Chicago's Comiskey Park. "For one night, in all the darktowns of America," rejoiced that erudite English observer of American mores, Alastair Cooke, "the black man was king."[68] Louis, though, was far from satisfied: he was bent on avenging that humbling loss to the German.

So it was that Louis and Schmeling resumed their debate at Yankee Stadium in June 1938, accompanied by boycott threats from Anti-Nazi groups and heaps more hype. Women protestors outside Jacobs' office on West 49th Street distributed photos of Schmeling shaking hands with Hitler, chanting "Schmeling is a Nazi". Meanwhile, the Nazi newspapers, under order from Goebbels, quoted Schmeling as declaring that "the black man will always be afraid of me. He is inferior."[69] Schmeling denied this absolutely – he was "not a superman in any way" – but the damage, in American eyes, had been done.

As the showdown neared, Schmeling took the loyal but daring step of refusing Goebbels' request to sack his manager, the scion of an orthodox Jewish-Hungarian tailor and now known as Joe Jacobs (no relation to Mike); his namesake offered to contribute 10% of the profits to aid Jewish refugees.[70] President Roosevelt invited Louis to the White House, felt his biceps and remarked, "Joe, we need biceps like yours to fight Germany." Louis greatly appreciated this. "Let me tell you, that was a thrill," he would recollect. "Now, even more, I knew

I had to get Schmeling good."[71] In the *Durham Morning Herald*, Art Buchwald would recall the youngsters in his hometown believing in three certainties: "Franklin Roosevelt was going to save the economy… Joe DiMaggio was going to beat Babe Ruth's record" and, most important of all, "Joe Louis was going to save us from the Germans."[72]

A record audience of 70 million radio listeners, a nation for once truly united, however fleetingly, did not tune in for long. Pelted with banana peel and other refuse as he made his way to the ring, Schmeling was lucky to last two minutes. To watch the YouTube footage is to see a cowering figure, afraid to throw a blow; one crunching shot to the ribs from Louis, as Budd Schulberg so memorably described it in *Esquire*, made him "scream like a frightened girl or a stuck pig".[73] The American press, even a few reporters from below the Mason-Dixon line, were exultant. "The Aryan idol, the unconquerable one, had been beaten," declaimed the *Charlotte Observer*, "the bright, shining symbol of race glory has been thumped in the dust. That noise you hear is Goebbels making for the storm cellar."[74]

In *History Today*, Robert Weisbord and Norbert Hedderich recreated the elated response across the land:

> *In Harlem the reaction was ecstatic and, at first, non-violent. However, by early morning missiles of all description were being flung from roof-tops and out of windows. In Chicago crowds celebrated by firing shots in the air and by setting off firecrackers. Blacks of all ages celebrated in the streets. Years later, Jersey Joe Walcott remembered that in his hometown of Camden people came "pouring out of their houses. They were so happy. It was like New Year's Eve". In Detroit, meanwhile, the city most closely associated with Joe Louis, 10,000 blacks in the "Paradise Valley" section joyously sang and danced.*[75]

* * *

Later that year, the story took a profoundly unexpected turn. Helpfully, Schmeling's wife was Anny Ondra, a popular actress who had starred in a couple of early Alfred Hitchcock classics (and, less memorably, with her husband in the less-than-imaginatively entitled 1935 film *The Knockout*). The Schmelings' circle was wide, numbering prominent Nazis such as Heinrich Hoffmann, Hitler's photographer, as well as Jewish artists and performers, yet while Max never denounced his leader, and was drawn to him as he was to all powerful figures, he was assuredly no advocate of anti-Semitism. So closely did he hug cards to chest, a chance meeting with Goebbels prompted a bemused broadside from the propaganda minister: "What do you really think, Herr Schmeling? You do what you wish. You don't bother about the law. You come to the Führer, you come to me and still you constantly associate with Jews."[76] Yet not until 1989 did the full extent of Schmeling's defiance come to light. Amid the carnage of Kristallnacht, that dreadful night of 9 November 1938 when paramilitaries and civilians attacked the Jews of Nazi Germany and Austria, scores of whom were killed and tens of thousands taken to concentration camps, he had sheltered Henri and Werner Lewin, a pair of Jewish brothers in their early teens.

Confounding rumours that the pair had fallen out, Schmeling sought out Louis in Chicago when he was permitted to visit the US in 1954. Sealed with a handshake, the reunion was emotional. Schmeling subsequently stated that the experience was more meaningful to him than a third bout would have been.

How deeply ironic, then, that the hero of these Disunited States, where the Ku Klux Klan roamed and black men were lynched, was a second-class citizen with no right to vote, to urinate in a whites-only public toilet or sit at the back of a bus. Being Joe Louis, as we shall see, was arguably even more complex than being Max Schmeling.

When the Cold War boiled over

Russian communism failed, ultimately, because its economic model created an ever-widening gap in living standards between East Europe and West, one that became ever harder to conceal. The foremost tragedy of Russian communism, which found more believers than any other brand, is that between 7m and 10m Russians had to die for it, though it must be stressed that not until 1957 did the Soviet people learn even a grain of truth about the innumerable horrors perpetrated at the behest of Joseph Vissarionovich Dzhughashvili. The second foremost tragedy of Russian communism is that it gave all other strains of communism, not to mention Marxism and socialism, an irreparably bad name. Unlike its British and American counterparts, however, the Russian empire was not by any means enamoured of the competitive arts.

Unlike his sometime pal Hitler, Josef Stalin had virtually no interest in sport as propaganda – save, that is, for those occasions, such as the discus ring or the gymnastics hall or the weightlifting stage, where victory was, if not assured, then pretty damned likely. Never mind those despicable capitalist institutions baseball, cricket, golf and tennis: topping the Olympic charts was the goal of successive Cold War Communist leaders, a task eased by administrative hypocrisy. When the USSR joined the Olympic movement in 1948, the IOC acquiesced to the professionalism of Soviet athletes, having concluded that it was better to have the USSR inside the tent than out.

No powerful country or region has placed such a premium on the pommel horse, the high beam, the asymetric bars and the somersault as a measure of athletic excellence and all-round national goodness. The Olympics mattered most because they made it possible for the accursed capitalist pigs of the USA to be outwitted, beaten and embarrassed in front of an awful lot of people. By the same token, as Brohm seldom tired of reiterating, no popular political creed of the 20th century saw less point in professional sport, much less ballgames. "As the centre of the world communist conspiracy, the Soviet Union has not forgotten that sports can prove to be of great use as a weapon in the class struggle," observed John N. Washburn, a diplomatic specialist, in a 1956 edition of the influential quarterly *Foreign Affairs*. It would nonetheless be difficult "to find a spirit more alien to de Coubertin's ideals of moral purity and nobility than the Soviet concept of sport ... as a weapon of class warfare for international Communism".

Not that the USSR could resist capitalism's favourite sporting tipple. In 1936, the year Stalin embarked on his Great Purge, a process of subjugation by mass execution that brought death to dissident Red Army plotters and hundreds of thousands of innocent citizens, the USSR witnessed the birth of its own professional football league, whose leading lights were paid on a par with leading writers, academics, film stars and ballet dancers. Its architect was Nikolai Starostin, who together with his brother Andrei had defied the customary link between football clubs and state ministries to found Spartak Moscow expressly for food workers. To support Spartak would soon come to be perceived as a sign of disaffection and disloyalty. As Robert Edelman related in his history of the so-called "People's Team", this was part of the process Nicholas Timasheff would dub the "Great Retreat" – from the values of the revolutionary state into the treacherous arms of Westernised ritual.[77]

The trigger for the league was a proposal in 1935 from Jean-Bernard Levy, a French businessman and arch-proponent of professional football. Aware that Spartak and Dynamo, Moscow's leading clubs, were planning tours to play French workers' teams, he invited a combined Spartak-Dynamo selection to help ring in the new year by coming to Paris and take on an all-star, multi-national team assembled under the banner of his own pride and joy, Racing Club. Racing won 2-1, but such was the fight put up by the Soviet combination, and so much interest did the match arouse, Starostin's plans for a professional league, backed by his patron Alexander Kosarev, the head of the Komsomol youth organisation, gained fresh impetus. Less fortuitously, Starostin also made a dangerous enemy in Lavrentii Beria, the head of Stalin's secret police, the NKVD, whom he recollected as "a crude and dirty left half" from a Georgian side he had played against in the 1920s. This engendered a ferocious rivalry between Spartak and Dynamo; unhelpfully for Starostin, the latter were an offshoot of the Dynamo Society affiliated to the Interior Ministry, and thus perpetually a subject of Beria's affections and strategies.

Nor was Starostin's cause aided by the USSR's leading athletes, Serafim and Georgii Znamenskii. As Spartak members they had joined that Parisian jaunt, but in his report the former complained that Starostin had been far too amiable towards his bourgeois hosts and acted like "the owner of a private sports club". Again and again in the press, Starostin was accused of prioritising elite sport over mass physical culture. "And of course," acknowledges Edelman, "it was true that the Starostins found organising high-level spectacles more compelling than teaching grenade-throwing to factory workers."[78]

Kosarev was arrested and shot when the Komsomol was purged in 1938, as the BBC Scotland reporter Stevie Miller recalled before Celtic played Spartak in the 2012-13 Champions League:

Without his powerful patron Starostin was isolated, and Beria soon showed his power. After Spartak defeated Dinamo Tbilisi in the semi-final of the 1939 Soviet Cup, Spartak beat Stalinets Leningrad 3-1 in the final. Beria was not going to let the defeat of his favourite team go unpunished, and a replay of the semi-final was ordered – after the trophy had been presented. The original referee was arrested, but Spartak still triumphed, beating Tbilisi 3-2, much to Beria's chagrin. "When I glanced up at the dignitaries' box, I saw Beria get up, furiously kick over his chair and storm out of the stadium," recalled Starostin. One night in 1942, Starostin states, he awoke to a pistol being held to his head; Beria was to take his revenge.[79]

Starostin and his three brothers were incarcerated for two years in Moscow's feared Lubyanka prison before being sentenced to 10 years' hard labour for the crime, claimed Nikolai, of "praising bourgeois sport". However, notes Miller, "there is evidence that he was actually convicted on charges of fraud – a not uncommon practice in Soviet times". Nikolai found himself in demand in the labour camp as a coach, earning himself better rations and sleeping quarters. In 1948, he was summoned to coach the Red Air Force team by Stalin's son, Vasilii. When Beria made his objections plain, he was forced to take shelter at the general's home, but after being exiled to another coaching post in Kazakhstan, the death of Stalin Sr. in 1953 saw him granted an amnesty. A year later he returned to Moscow, where he presided as Spartak president until four years before his death in 1996.

* * *

War brought the German invasion, aka Operation Barbarossa, and, in its slipstream, the so-called "Death Match". Played in the summer of 1942 in occupied Kiev, the antagonists were a powerful, well-fed German army team and the immensely skilled but supposedly famished and sickly stars of Dynamo and Lokomotiv Kiev, who were said to have been given jobs in a bakery by a supporter, shelter too. Billed as "Start, City of Kiev All-Stars", the benighted representatives of that beleaguered city – which had around 400,000 inhabitants before the war but was subsequently left with just 80,000 – scorched to a 5-1 victory: not what Goebbels had in mind at all. After seeing Hitler groan and fume as Norway beat Germany 2-0 at the Berlin Games, the propaganda minister had written a disbelieving entry in his diary: "100,000 left the stadium in a depressed state. Winning a match is of more importance to some people than the capture of a town in the East."[80]

Start strung together a succession of handsome and rousing wins, including a 5-1 thrashing of the Luftwaffe – no mean feat in a game refereed by an SS officer. Was this why, in the autumn of 1942, Goebbels banned international fixtures in both Germany and the occupied territories? "How much a part the Star games played in this decision we do not know," acknowledged Andy Dougan, author of *Dynamo: Defending the Honour of Kiev*, "but it seems reasonable to assume they had a hand in it."[81]

After whipping Rukh 8-0, a number of players were carted off by the Gestapo. Nikolai Korotkykh, a member of the NKVD, died under torture; for three solid weeks, teammates were interrogated daily; in exchange for his freedom, Pavel Komarov turned informant. Others were hauled off to a labour camp where, the following year, three more were killed: Ivan Kuzmenko, Oleksey Klimenko and goalkeeper Nikolai Trusevich, the last of whom had been accused, without apparent foundation, of working for the NKVD (though there is no consensus, even now, over whether this was a Nazi plan or a result of reprisals). Fortunate to be labouring in a work squad in the city that day, three more, Makar Goncharenko, Fyodor Tyutchev and Mikhail Sviridovsky, escaped; the story goes that they hid until Kiev was liberated.

"There have been persistent attempts to discredit the Start players," writes Dougan. "Some insist that they were not shot for beating the Germans, but for stealing bread from the bakery. From time to time, witnesses are presented to support this view, but since the most credible of them was only five years old at the time of these alleged thefts, the arguments do not really stand up. One intriguing theory suggests that the prime movers of the team – Trusevich, Klimenko and Kuzmenko – were among a number of partisan volunteers who agreed to stay in Kiev to organise resistance against the Germans. This version makes them doubly heroic, since they would know that by staying in the city they were almost certainly going to their deaths."[82]

Four years before his own death in 1996, the last survivor, Goncharenko, the winger who had escaped the labour camp, gave a radio interview; given his advancing years, his shakiness on one key issue was forgiveable. On the one hand he stated that the escape plan came about after Tyutchev had apprised him of the deaths of their three teammates, but later contradicted himself. "A desperate fight for survival which ended badly for four players," he called it. "Unfortunately they did not die because they were great football players, or great Dynamo players, and not even because Korotkykh was working for the NKVD. They died like many other Soviet people because the two totalitarian systems were fighting each other and they were destined to become victims of that grand scale massacre.

The death of the Dynamo players is not so very different from many others."[83]

In 1971, at the behest of Leonid Brezhnev, the Soviet premier, a monument was erected in honour of Goncharenko and his colleagues at Dynamo Stadium. The full facts remain elusive but that didn't dissuade Hollywood from making *Escape To Victory* – one of three celluloid recreations. Its heroes, inevitably, were Allied prisoners: soon to play John Rambo, a Vietcong-slaughtering avenger, Sylvester Stallone would not have convinced anyone as a pinko Commie footballer.

In the 1970s, the Soviet national team and the army-based Dynamo Kiev were more or less one and the same. The marriage, though, was not as fruitful as wished. Kiev were dashingly impressive in the 1975 European Cup-Winners Cup final but never won the European Cup; in European Championships (one win in four finals, in 1960, when only four teams competed and Spain refused to play their quarter-final against the USSR on political grounds) and World Cups (where they finished fourth in 1966), the returns were decent, no more. Then again, attempts to build national teams around a single club rarely work. For his first match as England manager in 1977, Ron Greenwood picked seven Liverpool men and saw unmighty Switzerland secure a goalless draw. Turning the routine into the special is tricky when you kick off with the same teammates every time. More significantly perhaps, Kiev were a predominantly Ukrainian team; their joy at representing the Russian empire can hardly have been unconfined.

Ironically, given that it will present the former Soviet Union with its best chance yet to win sport's biggest bauble, staging the 2018 FIFA World Cup will come too late for Georgians and Ukrainians to cheer for Mother Russia.

When Teeside turned Korean

North Korea, argue Jung Woo Lee and Alan Bairner, "is argu-ably the least understood and the most reclusive country in the world".[84] Bafflement, therefore, was rife in 2010 when

Middlesbrough Ladies FC were invited to become the first British football team to visit the secretive communist state, a venture billed as a "friendship" tour. Here, though, was simply a renewal of one of sport's unlikelier alliances.

In 1966, just 13 years after British soldiers – including many from the Middlesbrough area – had fought and died fighting for South against North in the Korean War, Whitehall threatened to refuse visas to the North Korean footballers who were due to play their World Cup fixtures at Ayresome Park. The threat subsided, but the *Chollima* were still expected to endure a hostile reception. Instead, Teesside embraced them, encouraged, no doubt, by the fact that, at an average height of 5ft 5ins, they truly were the little guys.

A goal by Pak-Doo-Ik gave the Koreans victory over Italy (whose players were greeted on their return home by a hail of rotten tomatoes) and an exceedingly special relationship was secured when the Koreans swept into a three-goal lead before losing to Portugal in the quarter-finals. The surviving players returned to Teesside in 2002, shortly after the release of *Game of Their Lives*, a documentary about that World Cup campaign, and again on its 40th anniversary. Even though Ayresome Park had been demolished to make way for a housing estate, the development incorporated a bronze sculpture purportedly marking the very spot where Pak had kicked himself into folklore.

Things had grown sinister by the time North Korea next qualified for the FIFA showpiece, in 2010, when their eccentric leader Kim Jong-Il decided to lend a hand. As befitted someone who had benefited appreciably from North Korean weapons in his demolition of the Matabele tribe, Robert Mugabe, Zimbabwe's similarly despised dictator, had greeted that qualification by dispatching a celebratory gift: an ark populated with pairs of giraffes, baby elephants, warthogs, zebras and, according to cultfootball.com's Rob Kirby, "other animals the Bible considers essential to post-diluvian life".

Then, the North Korean national coach spilled the beans on the secret behind the team's success. North Korean manager Kim Jong-hun reportedly got his coaching mandates straight from the man himself by means of an invisible headset that the Dear Leader had invented. According to Radio Free Asia, the coach received "regular tactical advice during matches" from Kim Jong-Il "using mobile phones that are not visible to the naked eye". Now that's innovation. Of course, it's not like he hadn't invented impressive things before. North Korean history books proclaim that Kim Jong-Il invented the hamburger in 2000. He named it Double Bread with Meat.[85]

By now, football was supplying a lonely bridge between North Korea and Japan, however rickety. As they had been for some time, diplomatic relations were non-existent: North Korea had been demanding compensation for Japan's savage colonialism from 1910 to 1945; Japan had imposed economic sanctions in the wake of missile tests in its airspace and abductions of its citizens in the 1970s and 1980s. The Japanese media reported that when the national team, Samurai Blue, arrived in Pyongyang in November 2011 for their first match there in 22 years (the nations had often played on neutral soil), they were delayed from entering the country for four hours, their food confiscated, their mobile phones and laptops banned. In a distinctly unfunny echo of Griff Rhys-Jones's Constable Savage in *Not the Nine O'Clock News*, guards allegedly scolded players for laughing and leaning against a wall.

"The sportsmanship on the pitch was just as welcoming," reported *The Economist*. "The Japanese anthem could barely be heard over the boos of about 50,000 North Koreans in the stadium. Only 150 tickets were reserved for Japanese fans, who sat in a corner, under the eyes of North Korean soldiers. The Japanese team played politely, receiving no penalties. Its host took a more rugged approach, earning seven yellow cards; one player was sent off by the referee (a Bahraini). 'It was a war zone itself,' Japan's *Asahi* newspaper wrote about the stadium, which shook with the roar of frenzied fans. 'If a Japanese supporter tried to stand up to cheer, a guard quickly noticed and pantomimed him to sit down.'"[86]

The Age of the Boycott

That close squeak over Berlin meant that the modern game of boycotting, the upshot of Cold War hostilities, did not kick off for another 20 years. In 1956, several Western European governments shunned the Melbourne Games in the wake of the Soviet invasion of Hungary (in a less well-remembered withdrawal, the Chinese backed out over the decision to allow Taiwan to send a delegation). Twenty years later, racism stirred consciences when 28 nations, the vast majority from sub-Saharan Africa, stayed away from Montreal after the IOC refused to expel New Zealand for its sporting links with apartheid South Africa (the People's Republic of China and the Chinese Republic also pulled out: neither recognised the other).

Full attendance was becoming a pipedream. In 1980, the US led a mass withdrawal from the Moscow Games, all protesting the Soviet invasion of Afghanistan; four years later, the Soviet bloc (including Cuba) repaid the insult by declining to go to Los Angeles. It was difficult, moreover, not to interpret the prime purpose of the 2008 Games in Beijing as an attempt to bury memories of the 1989 Tiananmen Square massacre, where a democratic protest culminated in several hundred civilians being slaughtered by the Chinese army.

Another boycott had been strongly mooted before the 1968 Olympics, when African-American athletes, encouraged and supported by Dr Martin Luther King, formed the Olympic Project for Human Rights, which aimed to orchestrate a withdrawal, partly in protest over Vietnam and global disadvantage but mostly the abhorrent treatment of America's black population. Its demands were fourfold: the restoration of Muhammad Ali's heavyweight title, taken from him after stating he had "no quarrel with them Vietcong" and refusing to fight in Vietnam; the banishment of South Africa and Rhodesia from the IOC; the hiring of black coaches (those in place were older white men, judgement and behaviour governed by racist assumptions); and the removal of the reviled Brundage. While unsure (or unwilling to say) whether he would have joined them, that arch-competitor Bob Gibson, the St Louis pitcher, told the *Los Angeles Times* that he admired the activists, not to mention both medium and message: "They're taking a terrific chance – risking an awful lot. I don't know what their goals are. But if they feel that the country has been kicking them in the rears for fifty years, then I agree with them."[87]

King's assassination a few months before the Games may have sapped the OPHR of its impetus, but what followed was the most iconic of all sporting protests, exposing Brundage as the toxic tyrant his critics had long known him to be. It also highlighted one of the indisputable benefits of the Sixties. The death of deference had long been overdue, especially the unearned variety.

John and Tommie[88]

Since October 1968, to be John Carlos has been to unite and divide. Even as he approaches 70, he still has the same knack for polarising as Brian Wilson retains for harmonising. For many, his partnership with Tommie Smith remains the most admirable and daring act in sporting history. Respectively bronze and gold medallist in the fastest 200 metres race yet run, the American sprinters were responsible for the most iconic image of the umbilical link between the competitive arts and political reality, the so-called "Black Power Salute" that shot through the Mexico City Olympics like a 1000-volt current, electroshocking the multi-millions watching the first Games to be broadcast live from Nantwich to Nantucket.

To talk to Carlos four-and-a-half decades after the fact, as I was privileged to do in May 2012, was to reappraise the single most memorable intersection yet between sport and politics. For one thing, he was quick to stress, his and Smith's protest was not exclusively about black power – represented by Smith's upraised right fist – or even black unity, as proclaimed by his own clenched left hand. He also left his tracksuit open – "a major breach of Olympic etiquette" – as a salute to Harlem's underclass, "to black *and* white". Which is why his story belongs in this chapter rather than the next: black may have been the colour, but equality for all was the aim.

The initial spur was that abortive OPHR boycott, in which Carlos had been heavily involved. When the pair met in a heat, Carlos told Smith he was "stewing" at the failure of the planned action to attract more than 50% support. As he wrote in *The John Carlos Story*, published in 2011, "I wanted to make some sort of statement."

He "didn't care a lick" what precious metal dangled round his neck: his ambition was to win a place on that podium. "I wasn't there for the race. I was there for the after-race. I made it clear to Tommie that we would both be on that medal stand. Tommie nodded his head with a dead-serious look on his face and then we started talking about the symbols we would use. We had no guide, no blueprint. No one had ever turned the medal stand into a festival of visual symbols to represent our feelings. We decided that we would wear black gloves to represent strength and unity. We would have beads hanging from our neck, which would represent the history of lynching. We wouldn't wear shoes to symbolise the poverty that still plagued so much of black America... all we would wear on our feet would be black socks."[89]

As the day approached, his mind swirled. "I thought about how humiliating and difficult it was for a black man to get a decent job... about the way drugs were as easy to find as a bottle of soda pop in any ghetto in America... about Harlem when I was growing up and how people overnight would become junkies, shells of people, zombies before my young eyes... about the greatness that black people had brought to the table for America, how we built this country from the sweat of our brows and arches of our backs, and then, in turn, we were always second-class citizens... we could be heroes as long as we stayed in between the lines."[90]

He also thought about Jesse Owens. When Brundage got wind that something was brewing in Mexico City, remembers Carlos, he sent Owens into the locker room "to calm us down and prevent us from making any kind of statement...and said, 'If you wear those black socks you're not going to be able to race as fast', and people looked at him like, 'You don't even understand why we are wearing these socks'."[91] Which struck many as more than a little ironic. After all, as Carlos reflected, Brundage and the IOC "had scorned and shunned Jesse for decades for the crime of being a black superstar. They didn't even let him back in the stadiums or put him in front of a microphone until we started talking smack about our boycott in 1966. Then the IOC took Jesse, put a suit on him, stuffed some money in his pocket, and told him, 'We want you to be the voice of the good black American.' The next thing you knew, Jesse was in our locker room saying to us, 'Hey, the greatest thing is to represent the United States in the Olympic Games'."[92]

To Harry Edwards, lynchpin of the OPHR – which Carlos helped launch and whose badge he and Smith wore on that Mexican podium – their protest was "inspirational". At the opposite end of the spectrum came Brent Musberger, an uncommonly ambitious young journalist reporting for the *Chicago American*, who denounced them as "black-skinned stormtroopers" and grew up to be one of America's best-paid, most sponsor-friendly and, sadly, influential broadcasters.

In a *Daily Mirror* column headlined "Will Mankind Ever Grow Up?", Peter Wilson, "The Man They Can't Gag"[93], drew a comparison with those Propaganda Games: "To anyone who was in Berlin in 1936, the demonstration which Tommie Smith and John Carlos put on in Mexico City in 1968 meant a multitude of different things. An optimist would have sighed, a pessimist laughed, a philosopher shrugged. It was, according to how you are constituted, ironic, tragic, farcical, or inevitable... Both were an expression of arrogant disassociation with the 99% white majority of the crowd... The irony was that their salute, had they but known it, was a parody of the one the Nazis used to express their solidarity. And as they left the rostrum so, like Owens, they were booed by a section of the crowd. Have we – we, the human race – then not progressed at all in thirty-two years?

"Owens's gesture proved the puerility of racialism, and his flying spikes pierced its very heart in Berlin. I rose to the supreme athlete. Two years later, in his own country, I squirmed as he took part in gimmick, carnival-style races against horses and baseball players. Now Owens is an honoured citizen of the great country of his birth. But the lot of the ordinary Negro has not marched apace with the acceptance of the outstanding black man… That I think – and as a white man I can never go further than 'thinking' on this subject – is the reason why Tommie Smith and John Carlos put on their little charade." He closed with a heartfelt wish: "That, as the world gets more leisure and more facilities for its enjoyment, we shall all of us accept those whom we meet in an ever-widening field of sport for what they are and not what they look like. If that can be achieved, then the Olympic Games will not have been a complete waste of time."

For the crime of incurring Brundage's wrath, Carlos and Smith were immediately sent home. "It's childish," said Jim Alder, the British marathon runner, disgust writ large. "The American Negroes are right to protest. They may be Americans here, but they are niggers back home."[94] "Signs on a third-storey window told of support for the US Olympic Committee, plus racial implications: 'Wallace for President. Win the war in Vietnam'," reported Shirley Povich. "Interestingly enough, a probe proved that these third-storey rooms were occupied by members of the US Olympic rifle team, members of the National Rifle Association, which is not famous for its advocacy of the Negroes' progress in America." There was reason, concluded Povich, "for thinking the Olympic panjandrums blundered in dealing out the ultimate punishment to Smith and Carlos". This, after all, "trebled the impact of the entire episode and also the martyrdom of those two militants, who now are better able to carry their cause to more places".[95]

Twenty-four hours after Carlos and Smith thrust their fists into the floodlit Mexico City air, Lee Evans, a fellow OPHR activist, obliterated the world record in taking the 400m gold. In emulation of the Black Panthers, he and his fellow American medallists, Ron Freeman and Larry James, received their prizes wearing black berets. "I am certain Evans was not thinking of anything like a gold medal," divined Wilson. "He was running to prove that Black Power has to be reckoned with."[96] Sadly, Evans would see Carlos and Smith as having stolen his thunder.

Back to the context of that "stormtroopers" jibe, published under the headline "Bizarre Protest By Smith, Carlos Tarnishes Medals". Typed Musberger (as Jack Kerouac was once advised by a snooty publisher, there's a world of difference between writing and typing): "One gets a little tired of having the United States run down by athletes who are enjoying themselves at the expense of their country." As Dave Zirin points out, having dug out the offending article on microfilm in order to demand an apology from Musberger:

Musburger doesn't once address why Smith and Carlos did what they did or quote them directly. He does, however, find time to mock them repeatedly. He describes Smith and Carlos as "juvenile", "ignoble" and – this actually is bizarre –"unimaginative". Musburger calls Tommie Smith "the militant black". In describing a scene of Carlos trying to defend their actions, Musburger writes, "Perhaps it's time 20-year-old athletes quit passing themselves off as social philosophers."… As for the actual stormtrooper-sympathiser, Musburger refers to Brundage as a kindly old grandfather and with great affection and addresses him as "Avery". No mention of course that many of the athletes called him "Slavery Avery".[97]

Decades later, to be fair, Musberger did admit he'd been "a bit harsh", which represents a climbdown, albeit of millimetric proportions: "Smith and Carlos aside, I object to using the Olympic awards stand to make a political statement."[98]

To the Reverend Jesse Jackson Sr, conversely, Carlos and Smith had delivered "a statement for the ages", an "act of righteous defiance" that "lifted us all to a new level of dignity and shared responsibility to improve the conditions of the poor the world over". The US establishment let rip with both barrels. "Angrier, Nastier, Uglier" sneered the cover of *Time*. Years later, Brundage could still see only "warped mentalities and cracked personalities".

Even fellow African-Americans jumped on the bandwagon of derision. George Foreman, who began his climb to fame, glory and grilling machine fortune by winning the heavyweight boxing gold that October, celebrated pointedly, waving a miniature Star Spangled Banner. Carlos remembers Foreman's anti-solidarity well, but while he is forgiving, the thought of Brundage's anti-humanity still enrages. No wonder he denounces him as "sport's J. Edgar Hoover". To Andrew Jennings, Brundage was sport's Dr Evil: "[João] Havelange was a charismatic thief. [Sepp] Blatter is a shabby one desperately frightened that his criminal world will come unglued in his lifetime. In some ways the loathsome Samaranch was the cleanest because he never knew decent values. Brundage was thoroughly evil and still needs a bigger slating than he's had so far. I'm sure there's more digging to be done."[99]

Back home, Smith and Carlos met death threats and dead ends. Work came grudgingly, albeit less so for Smith, who spent three seasons playing American football for the Cincinnati Bengals before becoming assistant professor of physical education at Oberlin College in Ohio; not that this prevented him from putting his gold medal up for auction (to his shock, the $250,000 reserve price was not met). Shadowed by the FBI, Carlos also had a stint in the NFL but otherwise worked as a gardener, in a grocery store and an aluminium factory; resisting an invitation to become a drug dealer, he found renewal as a high-school guidance councillor. Then, on the 37th anniversary of that historic night, a statue of the salute was unveiled at San Jose University, propelling him from his shell.

The legacy is complex. If Carlos and Smith hadn't flung open the doors for those looking to better society from an Olympic platform, would 11 Israelis have lost their lives in Munich four years later? Would snipers have been assigned to occupy London's roofs throughout the 2012 Games? Perhaps some prices are worth paying, however steep. Besides, if Elvis Presley hadn't ignited rock 'n' roll, somebody else would.

* * *

Even the supporting cast paid dearly for their temerity. For wearing the OPHR badge on the podium, Peter Norman, the 200m silver medallist, was ostracised in his native Australia, where the long-entrenched, anti-immigration "white Australia" policy had only begun to wane in 1966 and where Aboriginals continued to be treated much as blacks were under apartheid. Carlos and Smith attended Norman's 2006 funeral as pallbearers.

Two years later, Matt Norman, Peter's nephew, made an award-winning documentary about his uncle's support for Carlos and Smith, *Salute*, the success of which doubtless contributed to the parliamentary debate in 2012 that brought the first hint of a governmental apology to his uncle. Dr Fraser Leigh urged acknowledgement of Norman's bravery, insisting he deserved a posthumous apology "for the wrong done by Australia in failing to send him to the 1972 Munich Olympics, despite repeatedly qualifying". He also proposed belated recognition of Norman's "powerful" role in "furthering racial equality".[100]

Munich

In 1972, when the Olympics returned to Germany, the Federal Republic, as Michael F. Krüger, Stefan Nielsen and Christian Becker attest in their 2012 contribution to the journal *Sport in History*, "was keen to present itself as especially progressive, creative and innovative, precisely the opposite of what the world still remembered from the pre-war games in Berlin". The organisers "wanted to demonstrate in particular that sport in West Germany was free and independent of politics and not exploited politically".[101] If only.

Some might say Brundage received his come-uppance in Munich, his final Games – and twice over. They featured a record-sinking performance by the Jewish swimmer Mark Spitz, winner of seven gold medals, and the most tragic chapter in modern Olympic history. As 7,000 athletes slept in the Olympic Village early on the morning of 5 September, eight Palestinians from the terrorist group Black September scaled a chain-link fence and burst into Connollystrasse 31, the apartment complex where the Israeli team was lodging. Carrying gym bags full of grenades, Kalashnikov rifles and submachine guns, they killed the Israeli wrestling coach and a weightlifter while taking nine others hostage. One was the fencing coach, Andrei Spitzer, whose wife Ankie watched the saga unfold on television while staying in her native Holland with her parents, nursing their newborn child.

In the afternoon, she received a phonecall from Golda Meir, the Israeli prime minister: there would be, could be, no negotiations with terrorists. "Spitzer saw her husband on-screen, clad in an undershirt, getting struck in the head with a rifle," related Jon Wertheim after interviewing Ankie for *Sports Illustrated*. "When a government spokesman declared that the terrorists had been killed and the Israelis were OK, Spitzer's father opened a bottle of champagne. But Spitzer wasn't going to celebrate until her husband called. He, of course, never did. It was 3:20am when she heard Jim McKay's now famous declaration: 'They're all gone.'"[102]

* * *

Not that Brundage was going to let anyone rain on his parade. In consort with the likes of Walther Troger, the man in charge of the Olympic village, and Israeli officials who were in regular contact with Meir, he declared that to halt proceedings would hand victory to the terrorists. The leader of the depleted Israeli team, Shmuel Lalkin, felt likewise, but he and his countrymen could hardly carry on. Nor did the representatives of Norway, the Netherlands, the Philippines and the German Democratic Republic, the last convinced that to continue might be seen as a victory for the West. Others cried off as individuals. After his unparalleled gold rush, Spitz left hurriedly, under police protection: at that juncture, nobody was clear whether the attack had been anti-Israeli or anti-Semitic. Fortunately, Spitz was handsome, and he soon turned from his chosen profession, dentistry, to modelling.

In 2012, a petition boasting 110,000 signatories from 155 countries called for a minute's silence in memory of the massacred at the opening ceremony in London. Presented to Jacques Rogge, the IOC president, it fell, as ever, upon stony ears. In a campaign she had waged before every Olympics since 1976, now supported by both candidates for that November's presidential election, Barack Obama and Mitt Romney, Ankie Spitzer had once again been rebuffed by the IOC. She was once told that it would offend protocol, even though there have been formal acknowledgements of atrocities ranging from the Bosnian conflict to 9/11.

Public pressure mounted. The NBC presenter Bob Costas announced he would stay silent for one minute while on air. Two nights before the ceremony, Rogge agreed to dine with Spitzer and Ilana Romano, widow of the murdered weightlifter. "For 45 minutes she sat across a table from Rogge at his makeshift office at the Park Lane Hilton and laid out her case again," wrote Wertheim. "She recalls asking Rogge to acknowledge the political winds. 'What do you think, I'm blind?' he asked Spitzer. 'Yes, I do think you're blind,' she shot back. 'Because every normal thinking person would say, "It's not about the little poor widow banging on my door every four years." It's about the morally right thing to do.' Finally Rogge leaned across the table, Spitzer says. 'I'm not going to do it.' As he leaned in to hug them, they turned away, vowing to return."[103]

Spitzer branded officials "chickens and cowards", accusing them of bowing to the threat of a terrorism attack. "I have told Rogge to make a stand, make history," she said. "He told me his hands were tied. I said, 'My husband's hands and feet were tied when he was taken hostage and murdered at the Olympics'.

He does not have the balls to make a stand." She also claimed that the IOC had been resisting such requests for four decades because it feared an Arab boycott.

The German dope trick

Blame it on the Greeks. The origin of the word "doping", relates Larry Bowers, the United States Anti-Doping Agency's chief science officer, has been attributed to the Dutch word "doop", a viscous opium juice, "the drug of choice" of the ancient sons and daughters of Athens and Salonika.[104] For some, this vexatious topic has had no more dispiriting case study than Lasse Viren, the reedy bearded Finn who achieved one of the most awesome feats in athletics history, not only winning both the Olympic 5,000m and 10,000m but doing so at successive Games, in 1972 and 1976. In one race he fell over, losing dozens of yards and several seconds, and still prevailed. Only later did the allegations begin. Even now it cannot be said with any certainty that he was an early beneficiary of blood doping, not outlawed by the IOC until 1986, but the mud has buried a legend.

Infinitely sadder than Viren, though, were the victims of state-sponsored doping in the former German Democratic Republic during the Cold War, under the guise of State Plan 14.25, the scruple-free programme run by the Stasi, the state's notoriously efficient national security police and intelligence organisation. Worse, many of those who benefited from such performance enhancement – strictly in the short term – were not only underage but, as they asserted in criminal trials following German unification, entirely unwitting.

It would nevertheless be fallacious, contend Thomas M. Hunt, Paul Dimeo, Matthew T. Bowers and Scott R. Jedlicka in *The International Journal of the History of Sport*, to surmise that this was entirely attributable to Cold War rivalry. After all, the political tension between the constituents of the Eastern bloc was almost pluckable, its sporting symbol that bloody 1956 Olympic water polo squabble between Hungary and the USSR. East German sport, and especially its doping programme, "demonstrates that the relationship of the GDR to the Soviet Union was no exception".[105]

Soviet political motives, reasoned Richard Nixon during a meeting in 1971 with Willy Brandt, the West German chancellor, should always be judged in terms of their assessment of Germany as "the key to Europe".[106] It would not, however, be wholly accurate to call East Germany a puppet state, argues Mary Elise Sarotte, a historian at the University of Southern California: "The East German tail did not wag the Soviet dog. However, the Soviets feared East Germany's potential to start wagging."[107]

Indeed, note Hunt et al, "the attention given by Moscow to East German sporting initiatives reflected a more general concern that one or more members of the Soviet satellite system might use sport in a way that expressed symbolic opposition to their authority."[108]

In the build-up to the 1968 Olympics, noted a Stasi memorandum, a Soviet sports physician (referred to only by his surname, Korolkow) turned down an invitation to work with his GDR counterparts "on specific training challenges presented by the upcoming Olympics". Instead, Korolkow was said to have gone to West Germany in search of pharmacology that had yet to reach his side of the Iron Curtain.

"The West Germans are taking advantage of a specific situation," concluded the memorandum. In contrast with other European states, the Soviets could not treat their athletes with "mass-produced medications" and, at international events, relied on the generous co-operation of doctors from other nations. Such practices, in fact, "may create serious difficulties in our collaboration with Soviet physicians".[109] Shortly after the inception of the Stasi programme, moreover, the GDR's leaders resolved to conceal it from Moscow. According to Hunt et al, "They believed that the accomplishments of East German athletes provided them a unique (if limited) opportunity to shed the GDR's standing as a subservient actor that conceded Soviet authority at every turn."[110]

Before steroids became a cause célèbre, much conjecture surrounded the gender of athletes, particularly those from the

USSR. These had risen to such a pitch that, in 1966, the IOC introduced verification tests. Fortunately for her, felt many in the West, Tamara Press, the Soviet shot-putter and discus thrower who in 1960 and 1964 had struck Olympic gold three times and silver once, had retired by then, as had her sister Irina. At that stage, the link between sport and state had mostly been the subject of rumour, and arguably western propaganda. State Plan 14.25 took that relationship to another level altogether.

The first fruits were apparent in Munich, where the East Germans had the audacity to claim more Olympic gold medals than the hosts. In September 1973, the Parisian newspaper *France-Soir* published a prescient warning by Jean Pierre LaCour of sorcery to come, particularly from female athletes, hitherto neglected as contributors to the concept of sport as national panacea.

> *There is talk of a sort of "vaccine against fatigue". It consists of an injection of toxic substances which allows the body to combat fatigue more efficiently. It is believed that male hormones are given to the girls, who, in addition to an increase in vigour, develop a superiority complex with respect to other females from foreign countries. Another device is the use of a doping substance, not currently detectable, which virtually guarantees maximum performance with 98 percent chance of success, as compared to classic training which is about 68 percent successful. These accusations are terrible. The only way for East Germans to answer these accusations is to open their training camps. A simple denial will not be sufficient.*[111]

Success in the pool in Montreal four years later – including victories in 10 of the 11 individual women's races – was accompanied by scepticism from several rivals, notably Shirley Babashoff, the American swimmer who had been favoured to win a clutch of golds but wound up with just one. Pointing out that her vanquishers had remarkably deep voices earned her the condemnation of the American press, who accused her of sour grapes and nicknamed her "Surly Shirley". Responded one GDR official: "We are here to swim not sing."

When Olympic testing for testosterone improved towards the end of the decade, the GDR upped its game, too. In 1977, the shot-putter Ilona Slupianek tested positive for anabolic steroids: at such an early juncture in testing history, detection was almost always foiled by halting steroid use shortly before a major event. Around the same time, notes Daniel M. Rosen in *Dope: A History of Performance-Enhancement in Sports from the Nineteenth Century to Today*, the Kreischa testing laboratory near Dresden was cannily taken over by the GDR government, enabling access to IOC testing protocols and procedures. "The institution could not only test for whether an athlete had taken banned substances," he wrote, "they could also use data gathered from their own experiments, and from anti-doping research they were privy to, in order to further their Olympic ambitions."[112] This and subsequent fine-tuning saw tens of thousands of tests come up negative.

Prince Alexandre de Merode, the head of the IOC medical committee, hailed the 1980 Games in Moscow as the "purest" Olympics yet. The reality, in the shape of unofficial test results, was somewhat less utopian. The general belief, nevertheless, is that Soviet and East German leaders had by no means adopted the same approach to doping regulation. Two years later, at the European Athletics Championships, came the latest sign of shifting fortunes as the GDR, a nation of just 17m inhabitants already buoyed by second place in the 1976 and 1980 Olympic medals tables, netted 13 golds to the USSR's six: just one symptom of a wider sporting decline that led to a mass purge of Soviet officials and coaches in 1983.[113] Order was restored the next time both nations competed in the summer Games, in 1988, with the USSR topping the medals table after pocketing 55 golds and 132 medals all told. The GDR's feat in again finishing second ahead of the USA – with 37 golds and 102 medals – nonetheless proffered further evidence of Communist domination, however much this masked the prevailing disunity. In track and field, indeed, dog and tail were evenly matched, collecting 27 medals apiece.

As the decade drew to a close, related Barbara Cole in *The East German Sports System: Image And Reality*, the GDR's Olympians continued to "return home as heroes from competition abroad and enjoy a higher standard of living than afforded most East German citizens", stoking popular resentment towards the government and even the athletes. On 9 November 1989, the privilege of foreign travel, hitherto confined almost exclusively to athletes, was extended to all East German citizens. Finally, the Berlin Wall had fallen.

* * *

"They are the forgotten victims. For three decades, East Germans ran, swam and shot-putted their way to glory, winning Olympic gold medals, setting world records and – so it seemed at the time – demonstrating the superiority of communism. But this month the human cost of East Germany's extraordinary sporting success will be laid bare in a courtroom in Hamburg."[114]

Thus reported that resourceful *Guardian* correspondent Luke Harding in November 2005 as nearly 200 East German competitors launched a case against the German pharmaceutical giant Jenapharm: the erstwhile GDR firm, they claimed, had knowingly, from the 1960s until East Germany's demise in 1989, supplied the steroids distributed to them by trainers and coaches. To cite merely the first of several outrageous cases, Catherine Menschner, a former swimmer who had endured seven miscarriages, discovered – after researching Stasi files – that she had been part of a secret class for steroid trials, hence her constant need for painkillers.

Not unexpectedly, Jenapharm had blamed "the heads of the Socialist Party and the government who wanted to demonstrate the abilities of the GDR by achieving success in sporting events, and on the other hand the sports physicians and trainers who used the doping substances on the athletes". In 2013, *Der Spiegel* would report that pharmaceutical companies had paid millions of pounds to the former GDR to employ more than 50,000 patients in state-run hospitals as unwitting guinea pigs for drug tests in which several lives were lost. "According to a Stasi report, in 1981 alone, the companies sent East German researchers about 250 invitations for what were usually lavishly funded trips to the West. 'To promote their commercial interests,' the Stasi files read, the companies took advantage of 'opportunities involving corruption and bribery'." These international conglomerates included Schering, now the owners of Jenapharm.[115]

By now the chickens were queuing up to roost. The previous month, the unified German athletics federation had announced that it was checking 22 national records set by GDR athletes, this after Ines Geipel, a member of the record-holding women's 4x100 metres relay team, had set the ball rolling by admitting to having used PEDs and requesting that her 1984 record be struck off. Meanwhile, Karin König, a swimmer, also confessed to doping (between 1982 and 1987) and was preparing to sue the German Olympic Committee for damages, a test case that could open the floodgates for more than 100 such suits.

At the outset of the new millennium, German officials took the highly unusual step of volunteering to scrap some of the records broken by their athletes (as of July 2013, Marita Koch's 400m mark of 47.60secs was still 1.10secs ahead of the fastest time this century). By then, more than 300 coaches and officials had been fined or sentenced to (admittedly brief) jail terms for their role in the steroid explosion. In July 2000, a Berlin court ordered the former East German sports minister Manfred Ewald and its erstwhile medical director Manfred Höppner to pay small fines and serve suspended sentences of one to two years after being convicted of causing bodily harm to 142 former East German sportswomen, who claimed that their daily training regime included taking up to 30 vitamin pills and shots. While Höeppner apologised, Ewald, once a member of the Hitler Youth, maintained his innocence until his death in 2002.

In December 2006, 167 former athletes learned that they would be compensated, albeit by a modest £6,000 apiece, the costs jointly borne by the German federal government and the German Olympic Sports Federation. "We accept the moral responsibility," said Thomas Bach, the latter's president and a future IOC president. "Money alone cannot offset their suffering," proclaimed the plaintiffs' lawyer, Michael Lehner.[116]

Oral-Turinabol, the so-called "blue bean", was the anabolic steroid de jour, its testosterone direct from Jenapharm. It could do all kinds of wondrously useful things, such as enhancing the speed of both recovery and muscle build-up; the side-effects included female infertility, heart disease, breast and testicular cancer. Others took due note of the benefits. According to the *New York Daily News*, some of the designer steroids at the centre of the infamous BALCO doping ring in the early years of that decade "were concocted by Patrick Arnold, a 'rogue chemist' who testified that he cooked up his creations after researching the East German documents".[117]

The number of athletes who had developed serious ailments ran to around 800, headed, in the public consciousness, by Andreas Krieger, who as a champion shot-putter named Heidi had absorbed so many male hormones she had felt compelled to change her sex. Then there was Rica Reinisch, a swimmer who at 15 had won three gold medals at the Moscow Olympics. "The worst thing was that I didn't know I was being doped," she told Harding. "I was lied to and deceived. Whenever I asked my coach what the tablets were I was told they were vitamins and preparations."[118]

"We were a large experiment, a big chemical field test," Geipel, now president of the group Help for Victims of Doping, told the BBC's Mike Costello in 2013. "The old men in the regime used these young girls for their sick ambition. They knew the mini-country absolutely had to be the greatest in the world. That's sick. It's a stolen childhood." Thanks to a pair of indefatigable campaigners, Professor Werner Franke, a microbiologist at the University of Heidelberg, and his wife Brigitte Berendonk, a former child athlete whom he had met after she defected to West Germany, a great number of damning hospital documents were saved from the shredder after the Wall came down. Around 2,000 athletes, says Franke, were added to the programme every year:

"We know this very exactly because there have been many court cases with all the details. The youngest athletes were around 12 or 13. And it was not just pills, injections also." Krieger was bluntness personified: "I still say today that they killed Heidi."[119]

At a Mexican training camp in 1984, Geipel fell for a local athlete. Bent on leaving her homeland to study and "start a whole new life" in the US, she returned home to reveal her plans to her boyfriend, whereupon he informed her that he was actually a member of Stasi. Now a writer, she recounted for Costello a plot that subsequently featured in a not entirely fictitious novel, *The Fifty-Fifty Feeling*:

> *Firstly, they wanted to find a man in the GDR who looked like the Mexican I'd fallen in love with. They thought if I met a man who looked like the Mexican, then everything would be good again. There wasn't such a man. Then they tried to force me to commit to the Stasi. But I didn't do it. The last stage was that they didn't see any other option than to operate on me and cut through my stomach. It's all in the files… they cut the stomach in such a way, through all the muscles and everything, so that I couldn't run any more and didn't have a way of getting to the rest of the world any more. The plan started with the sentence: "She is to be strategically extinguished." That's Stasi speak. It means she's to be thrown out of the sport.*[120]

But do we yet know the whole truth, even now? Has our perspective been coloured by western propaganda, by the timeless tendency of history to be (re)written by the winners? The most remarkable aspect of the criminal trials, to Cole, "is not how many testified, but how few". Of the relatively small proportion of 1,000 athletes invited to testify by ZERV, the Central Investigation Office for Government and Unification Criminality, just 300 responded. Nor, she insists, do the inconsistencies stop there.

"The testimonies of these athletes were decidedly mixed in terms of damning or praising the system, or of accusing or absolving their former coaches of doping. Three hundred is a remarkably low figure, given that there were an estimated 89,440 athletes at all tiers of the sports system hierarchy from the 1980s alone. This does not even take into account the hundreds of thousands of participants involved in elite sports during the other three decades of the GDR's existence. Also remarkable about the trials is the fact that evidence used to support accusations against GDR coaches and sports physicians was based on Stasi files. The Stasi files not only lack credibility among East German citizens, athletes, and many prominent West German intellectuals and other FRG citizens, but they are also considered to be a highly inaccurate source by the trial's own court-appointed physicians... Dr. Norbert Rietbrock even states that he disagrees with the conviction rulings of numerous coaches by the presiding judge in the trials, Hansgeorg Brautigam. Rietbrock asserts that, while it is possible that the ingestion of steroids in conjunction with birth control pills by the female swimmers during their training years might have led either to birth defects of the women's children or to other health injuries, these assertions are not medically proven. Rietbrock expresses dismay that the verdicts of the trials were based on medical speculation as well as the dubious Stasi files."[121]

Having interviewed a number of athletes, Cole concluded that, while "only a few genuinely believed in the superiority of socialism over capitalism", most claimed they were no different to other competitors, that their spur was glory. "Yet the vilification of the GDR sports system after the Wall by the media, the courts, and a few historians, stands in stark contrast to the views of the athletes themselves. The stunning post-Wall successes of East German athletes debunk critique of the system, as the legacy lives on." Her "most compelling finding" was that the image of sport in the GDR has never reflected reality: "One illusion has merely replaced another."[122]

This may or may not be the case. It does not require that big a leap, after all, to accept the implicit contention that many athletes, whether or not they were aware of having taken steroids, might have been eminently prepared to pay a price for their moment in the sun, ignorant as they were of quite how hefty it would prove. At bottom, however, those who pressed those blue pills into their hands betrayed their trust.

For all one's suspicions about perennial American anti-Communist rhetoric, therefore, it was difficult not to be appalled by a *New York Daily News* investigation into Red Bull's Diagnostics and Training Centre, a facility near the company HQ in Austria. In 2013, sponsored athletes and coaches, it transpired, were working there under the supervision of one Bernd Pansold: formerly in charge of the Dynamo Berlin FC medical centre in East Berlin, he had been convicted of administering hormones to underage female athletes from 1975 to 1984. One of Pansold's recent visitors, indeed, had been Lindsey Vonn, a US Olympic skier who happened to be dating Tiger Woods at the time, though her publicist originally denied that she had gone to the centre.

"It's surprising to me that any corporate entity would hire a convicted doctor," said Steven Ungerleider, a visiting scholar and psychologist at the University of Texas, who entitled his 2001 book on the subject *Faust's Gold*. "One has to wonder why with all the sports medicine people out there you would hire a person effectively banned from sports to work with your elite athletes."[123]

* * *

In 2013 came a coda that might have made a few former East Germans feel a little better. According to "Doping in Germany from 1950 to today", an 800-page study conducted on behalf of the German Olympic Sports Federation at Berlin's Humboldt University, West Germany, too, funneled sizeable chunks of taxpayers' money into secret doping research. The foundation of the Federal Institute of Sport Science (BISp) in 1970, under the auspices of the interior ministry, set in train a programme of "systemic doping" that lasted decades, spanning a wide range of sports and even drawing children as young as 11 into its sticky web.[124]

The various potions included anabolic steroids, testosterone, amphetamines and the hormone erythropoietin, more commonly referred to as EPO. Many of the supposed revelations substantiated longstanding allegations. Footballers, the researchers affirmed, began using drugs shortly after the Second World War, during which amphetamines had been popular. The supposed vitamin C shots given to members of West Germany's 1954 World Cup-winning team contained pervitin, aka speed; three players in the side that lost the final 12 years later tested positive for ephedrine, a banned stimulant (though in all fairness, it might well have been one of the ingredients in a cold decongestant). Two German newspapers, the *Main-Post* and *Maerkische Oderzeitung*, reported that the BISp had funded experiments with anabolic steroids before the Munich Games. At the 1976 Olympics, there were more than 1,200 instances of German athletes benefiting from Berolase and thioctacid, a cocktail of PEDs as yet unbanned. "There's a systemic connection between research and forbidden substances and in using them for athletes," Giselher Spitzer, the research leader, had told the Associated Press in 2012. "That's why we call it systemic doping."[125]

The programme was not a reaction to developments in the east, insisted the newspaper responsible for leaking the results of the study, *Süddeutsche Zeitung*, but ran "parallel" to it. A spokesman for the interior ministry, which still runs sport in Germany, said it had a "great interest in completely clearing up and evaluating the doping past in both parts of Germany".[126] The shadow cast over one of the most successful sporting nations of the postwar era could well be lengthy.

Martina – Part 1

Defection from East to West was a recurring theme of the Cold War. As the 20th century drew to a close, the cream of Cuba's baseball players began arriving in the home of capitalism, lured, not unnaturally, by the vast sums on offer; each migrant was greeted as affirmation of The American Way. The most celebrated defector, though, was Czech – Martina Navratilova.

Born Martina Šubertová, tennis ran through her family's female veins. Agnes Semanska, her maternal grandmother, had been a more than handy player, likewise her daughter, Jana. The latter, however, suffered grievously at the hands of her father – "a nasty little man", as her own daughter would remember; a parent-coach, his approach to child-rearing and motivation left something to be desired. Martina needed no greater incentive to succeed. "He would torture her, not let her drink any water if she played badly, or else he'd sprinkle cold water on her in the morning to wake her up. He was so nasty that she finally just quit. Wouldn't play."[127]

Martina was bent on making amends, but to do so, she soon realised, would almost certainly mean leaving her troubled homeland. She had been 11 when Moscow's tanks rumbled into Prague, 16 when, in 1973, she first set foot on American soil, for a tournament in Florida. "For the first time in my life I was able to see America without the filter of a Communist education, Communist propaganda. And it felt right."

That the Czech tennis federation insisted on holding on to her early professional winnings did little to instil loyalty. "The federation claimed that I was too young to keep that kind of money – but as far as I could see I wasn't too young to earn it on a tennis court. They also said they'd control my endorsements; imagine these bureaucrats making deals with equipment manufacturers in the West – what a mismatch." Someday, she decided, "you're not taking all the money I earn".[128]

Returning home after the US Open in 1974, she decided to defect. "I wanted to be a world-class tennis player, I wanted to live in America, maybe I even wanted to become an American citizen sometime in the future... I was still debating the issue with myself when the bureaucrats made up my mind for me." The upshot was a succession of road-bumps that made her fear her dreams would come to naught.

The problems began in earnest after she had helped win the Federation Cup, the female equivalent to the Davis Cup, when she detected jealousy among the Czech officials. "They started saying I was becoming 'too Americanised', that I had better start behaving myself or I'd be in trouble." Nobody threatened

Martina. "We already had plenty of those from the Russians. Who needed threats from a fellow countryman?" Vera Sukova, a Wimbledon finalist in 1962 and now the women's national coach, repeatedly urged her to practise the pragmatic art of pride-swallowing. "You've got to cool it," she would say. "You'll get yourself in trouble and everybody else in trouble. Just play the game. Do whatever it takes. Be smart."[129]

Navratilova was exceedingly smart, but not in the way Sukova meant. In August 1975, while playing in a tournament in New York, she resolved that now was the time. Counseled and assisted by Fred Barman, a lawyer hitherto known only for his work with showbiz figures, a press conference was arranged. "It was a zoo," she would remember. "'I want my freedom', I kept saying. The American sports reporters kept harping on whether I had a boyfriend in America or whether I wanted to make more money, but I don't think they were getting the point. Maybe unless you've lived in Eastern Europe, it's hard to know the difference between East and West. I wasn't defecting for political reasons, I emphasised, but I couldn't help adding: 'Anybody that complains about life here should go to Europe and they would understand. Go to a Communist country, go to a Socialist country. They would understand then'."[130]

A fortnight later, Navratilova would recall, the Czech tennis federation issued a statement: "Martina Navratilova has suffered a defeat in the face of the Czechoslovak society. Navratilova had all possibilities in Czechoslovakia to develop her talent, but she preferred a professional career and a fat bank account. She did not realise that she also needed an education."[131] Sukova tried to dissuade her from migrating. When they met in a Denver coffee shop, Navratilova was accompanied by Barman and a Czech-speaking FBI agent, Sukova by a chap from the Czech embassy who did his level best to work on the teenager's "paranoia and fear of authority". If she tried to return home after her visa expired on 30 October, she was told, she would be jailed for two years. "That told me a lot. That they could even think about jail meant I would be in big trouble if I ever set foot in my country again. I remember my father telling me: 'Don't ever come back, no matter what I tell you. They might put us up to it or we would be so emotional we would beg you to return, but don't. The years will pass, we'll come and see you, but don't come back.'"

The advice did not fall on deaf ears. Among Martina's 19th birthday presents was a green card. Yet her inspirational story, as we shall see, was far from done. Age and experience, for all that, would broaden her perspective. "The most absurd part of my escape from the unjust system is that I have exchanged one system that suppresses free opinion for another," she told CNN's Connie Chung in 2007. "The Republicans in the US manipulate public opinion and sweep controversial issues under the table. It's depressing. Decisions in America are based solely on the question of how much money will come out of it and not on the questions of how much health, morals or environment suffer as a result."

Chung was stung. "Can I be honest with you?" she asked. "I can tell you that when I read this, I have to tell you that I thought it was un-American, unpatriotic. I wanted to say, go back to Czechoslovakia. You know, if you don't like it here, this a country that gave you so much, gave you the freedom to do what you want." As ever, Navratilova refused to back down. "And I'm giving it back. This is why I speak out. When I see something that I don't like, I'm going to speak out because you can do that here. And again, I feel there are too many things happening that are taking our rights away."[132] A year later, she reclaimed Czech citizenship, having previously revealed the shame she felt about George W. Bush to the daily newspaper *Lidove Noviny*: "The thing is that we elected Bush. That is worse! Against that, nobody chose a Communist government in Czechoslovakia."[133]

* * *

Other Communists were not for turning. Teofilo Stevenson was one of the sporting titans of the second half of the last century. Olympic heavyweight boxing champion in 1972, 1976 and 1980, he was denied a fourth gold when Cuba joined the USSR's boycott of the Los Angeles Games. "Amateur", though, remained a flexible and strictly relative term: Fidel Castro ensured Stevenson had a handsome home and a better-than-average job. At the height of his renown, Bob Arum, the American promoter, offered him $8m to turn professional and fight Muhammad Ali, then the reigning professional monarch, a contest to smack lips the world over. Stevenson resisted. "I don't believe in professionalism," he was quoted as replying, sparking cynicism over whether his lines had been prepared by Castro's press advisers. "I prefer the affection of eight million Cubans."[134]

Pakistan and terrorism

The ghosts of Munich re-emerged in January 2010. In an effort to demonstrate that normalcy had returned there following a protracted and bitter civil war, the African Cup of Nations was being staged in Angola. As it crossed from the Republic of Congo into the oil-rich independent state of Cabinda, the bus carrying the Togo national football team was attacked by the Front for the Liberation of the Enclave of Cabinda (or so the pro-independence terrorist group claimed); three passengers were killed, including the side's assistant coach. This, though, was merely the latest sorry chapter in the burgeoning history of terrorism in sport, the vast majority, almost inevitably, involving cricketers.

The Sri Lankan civil war was a major factor. In April 1987, the New Zealand cricket team cut short a tour there after a car bomb killed 100 people at a bus station in Colombo. In November 1992, in the same city, a suicide bomber detonated a bomb outside a hotel where the New Zealand team were having breakfast, killing four people; five players and the coach were allowed to return home on compassionate grounds. In February 1996, Australia and the West Indies refused to play their World Cup warm-up matches in Sri Lanka after a huge bomb blast killed 80 people and injured 1,200 in Colombo.

Then came 9/11. In 2001, the New Zealand cricket board cancelled a scheduled tour of Pakistan in the aftermath of the attack on the Twin Towers. The following year, a suicide bomb blast outside the Karachi hotel the New Zealand team were staying in for the second Test led to the abandonment of match and tour. The explosion, in which 11 French navy experts as well as two Pakistanis lost their lives, also injured the team physiotherapist. In March 2008, the Australian cricket team withdrew from a tour of Pakistan after a spate of suicide bombings. Later that year, in November, a terrorist attack in Mumbai left more than 160 dead, persuading the Indian cricket board to cancel a tour of Pakistan, whose militants were widely blamed for the atrocity. In January 2009, a dozen gunmen opened fire on a convoy of buses in Lahore, including one carrying the Sri Lankan cricket team. Six policemen and a driver were killed, seven members of the touring party injured.

Pakistan's national team now embarked on a non-stop road trip, playing "home" fixtures in the United Arab Emirates (and two Tests on neutral turf in England). In April 2012, Bangladesh agreed to become the first international side to resume visiting that distressed land, playing a one-day international and a T20 fixture. Many believed this to have been attributable, primarily, to Bangladesh's sense of indebtedness: the nation's elevation to ICC full member status at the turn of the millennium had owed everything to the patronage of the Asian bloc. The ICC's decision not to send its elite umpires to Pakistan reflected the governing body's security concerns; to many, leaving the decision to arrange tours to the nations concerned while clearly not wanting to risk the lives of its own employees constituted a clear abrogation of responsibility.

Writing in the Pakistani newspaper *The Dawn*, Hassan Cheema expressed grave reservations. "Surely, the proposals for international teams and players to tour Pakistan should come when we have reached a semblance of normalcy and peace. Instead we have decided to assume our existing state as normalcy. What do we have to gain from a tour? An improvement in the image of the country? For the sake of what? A probable attack and the loss of lives for guests of this country? We are told that they'll be provided maximum security: this, a country which couldn't protect its most popular leader and the governor of the largest province (in addition to many other parliamentarians and mere plebs whose lives apparently count for less) in the past five years alone. The reluctance of many to visit Pakistan may have something to do with how much they value their lives – rather than a vast conspiracy by the BCCI."[135]

In the event, the itinerary was squeezed down to two matches over three days, then cancelled altogether. On the same day the Pakistan board belatedly delivered its security plan to the ICC, a petition was filed in the Dhaka high court by a university teacher and a Supreme Court lawyer challenging the Bangladesh board's decision to send the team to Pakistan. Justices Farid Ahmed and Sheikh Hasan Arifa decreed that the tour should be postponed by four weeks, killing it stone-dead. "The actions and words of [Mustafa] Kamal certainly give the impression of confirming rumours that there has been a deal reached between the PCB and Kamal," said Tim May, the chief executive of FICA. "What has resulted since has been a series of actions and comments that rather than reassure everyone of the safety of such a tour... have created heightened apprehensions and doubts amongst players re the safety of the tour and the motives of those involved in the decision."

Support 1 Interference 2

As if it didn't have enough on its plate, the ICC had finally got around to tackling political influence and interference – a century or more too late, of course, to undo the damage done by, among others, the English ruling classes. In 2011 came the Woolf Report, a long-time-coming independent review of the game's governance chaired by Lord Woolf of Barnes, formerly Chief Justice of England and Wales.[136] Acceding to one of the recommendations, it was decreed from Dubai that, within two years, all full members "must have changed or adopted their constitution to comply with the provisions of free elections and non-interference from government bodies" or else face sanctions, and possibly suspension.[137] At the time the deadline was set, the board chairman and president in Pakistan and Bangladesh respectively were appointed by government decree, while the Sri Lankan board effectively answered to the sports ministry, which had twice in the space of two years appointed ad-hoc interim committees to run the game on the island, a period that encompassed arguably the most infamous instance since apartheid South Africa of the connection between cricket and state.

Within a year of becoming an MP in 2010, Sanath Jayasuriya, a hero of Sri Lanka's 1996 World Cup triumph but now a fading 41 and utterly match-unfit, had been recalled to play for his country against England, a decision reportedly ordered by the government – a government accused of war crimes. Not, of course, that cricketing politicians are a rarity. For some years, indeed, the Oxford-educated former Pakistan captain Imran Khan had had designs on his nation's premiership. Yet at the same time, the ICC itself was headed by Sharad Pawar, the former BCCI president and merely the latest government minister in India to insist on influencing the course of cricket there.

All of which made the comments of Zaka Ashraf, the first elected chairman of the Pakistan Cricket Board, both illuminating and somewhat discouraging. "Ashraf isn't a full-fledged politician but is a member of the Pakistan People Party's Central Executive Committee," reported Umar Farooq, who noted that the PCB needed to amend its constitution, introducing a formal election process, in order to meet that ICC deadline. "I am a big follower of the democratic system but in any case there is always one man behind the gun," said Ashraf, the accompanying smile indicative of a man unaccustomed to serious contradiction. "I don't see any flaw in the system or in the constitution, the fault actually lies in the people who are at helm of the affairs... I'm not involved directly nor do I take any direct decisions but I seek explanations before giving an approval."[138]

Ashraf had been appointed in 2011 for an indefinite period by the PCB patron, the incumbent President Asif Ali Zardari, a pal from their days at Cadet College Petaro, from where the former leader had been expelled.[139] Knowing sighs were duly exchanged when, in May 2013, the Islamabad High Court ordered Ashraf's suspension over what it called the "dubious" process to elect him. The "entire process", declared Justice Shaukat Siddiqui, "appeared to be motivated and polluted".[140]

The Bangladesh Cricket Board made a move in the desired direction, amending its constitution to allow elections for president, though the National Sports Council stipulated that there should be three government-appointed directors. In the event, in November 2012, the ICC began backtracking. The Woolf Report had acknowledged that "governments taking an interest in the development of cricket and providing support and patronage to Member Boards may be acceptable or even desirable". The aim was to achieve "an appropriate balance between support and interference".[141] Explained Alan Isaacs, the ICC president: "In this part of the world and lots of other countries, quite honestly, cricket and other sports depend on the government. We are having a little bit of post-change review. I am not making any comment about what those changes might result to, but I think we are having a period of reflection."[142] Sadly, inevitably, the Woolf Report was rejected.

New world disorder

"International sport today has a reach that rivals that of governments,"[143] proclaimed a *Times* leader column in 2012. This can, of course, be interpreted in two opposing ways. First, the good way. Those living in the Ivory Coast have a life expectancy of just 54, so when, in 2007, Didier Drogba, the Chelsea striker, announced plans to fund the building of a £3m hospital in Abidjan, it represented something rather more than another charitable donation by another allegedly overpaid sporting icon. Inside a year, Drogba had helped his country reach the FIFA World Cup finals for the first time, whereupon the pleas of the Ivorian football federation, sensing it could unite another nation riven by civil war, suddenly found a willing listener: President Laurent Gbagbo finally acquiesced and resumed peace talks. Again, the respite proved all too temporary: the casualties mounted and the hospital project remained on hold. However, during a more durable ceasefire, Drogba redoubled his efforts. "I'm blessed," he readily admitted. "I'm lucky because my voice can be heard a little bit more than other voices. I can ring the president if I need something but I prefer not to do that. I prefer to fight and do things by myself."[144]

Now the bad way. In 1996, Nigeria's football team, the Super Eagles, were the pride of Africa and the talk of the game. Here, ran the confident prediction, were the continent's first footballing power. Then, a few days before they were due to begin the defence of their African Cup of Nations title, the nation's dictator, General Sani Abacha, ordered their withdrawal, saying he feared for their safety. It was widely assumed that he did so to snub the South African president Nelson Mandela, who had repeatedly called for an oil boycott of Nigeria for executing Ken Saro-Wiwa and eight other dissidents. The Confederation of African Football (CAF) banned Nigeria from the 1998 tournament, instigating the precipitous decline that, by 2012, would find the country at No.45 in the FIFA rankings – lower than five African neighbours.[145]

It is worth pausing, therefore, to recall the first Nigerian football tour of Britain, in 1949. Before setting off, the players were given strict instructions: their brief, wrote Phil Vasili, author of *The History of Black Footballers in Britain 1886-1962*, "was to watch, listen and learn – not only about the way football was played in Britain but, more importantly, about how superior the British political and economic system was to the alternatives on offer to Africans".[146] In Algeria a few years later, noted Allen Guttman, the FLN regarded soccer as "an instrument for sedition", providing a means of meeting, planning, mobilising and advancing the organisation of the movement's quest for national liberation.

* * *

Few sporting events in recent memory have turned the spotlight on opposing political factions quite so efficiently as the Bahrain

F1 Grand Prix, notably in 2012 and 2013. Reported Kevin Eason in *The Times*:

> *The apparent success of yesterday's Bahrain Grand Prix is a success not for King Hamad al-Khalifa of Bahrain, nor for Bernie Ecclestone, nor even for Sebastien Vettel, who took the chequered flag for Red Bull. It was a success for tear-gas, attack dogs and brutality. This was a sporting event that should not have happened. That it did is to the shame of Bahrain and Formula One alike.*[147]

In the aftermath of the so-called "Arab Spring" of 2011, Bahrain saw dozens of protesters killed, doctors and paramedics sentenced to jail for treating casualties, and the state's leading human rights activist resort to a hunger strike. The Bahrain Grand Prix was first postponed then cancelled, yet despite the violence of the ongoing clashes between the kingdom's Sunni authorities and its Shia majority, and threats of disruption by demonstrators, Jean Todt, the FIA chief, decreed that the petrol-heads should not be deprived in 2012.

The benefits of staging a grand prix are plain. In addition to the £25m race fee, according to the ruling government, revenues for the first eight staged in Bahrain (from 2004 onwards) ran to more than £850m. But with Iain Lindsay, the British ambassador, declaring in 2013 that £1bn worth of business awaited UK companies there, the priority was clear. "There is no point in pretending," insisted Eason, "that the Bahrain Grand Prix was not designed as a political tool by the government here to send a message to the world that all was well and the Arab uprising has been quelled in this isolated kingdom."[148]

John Yates, formerly the Metropolitan Police's assistant commissioner and now a security consultant, claimed that Bahrain could feel safer than London – which rather begged the question as to why, in 2012, the drivers were transported to the track in bulletproof cars. Moreover, Todt and Ecclestone, the F1 chief executive, restricted their public utterances on the issue to safety concerns, missing (no doubt intentionally) the bigger picture: the ethical and moral dimension. Not that sponsors such as Santander and Vodafone were terribly vocal on that score.

Four days before the 2012 race, as protesters marched peacefully, a firebomb narrowly missed a car carrying four Force India mechanics, prompting the team to pull out of a practice session – they wanted to return to their hotels in daylight. Twenty-four hours later, police broke up a demonstration with stun grenades and a dozen Sauber mechanics avoided a road fire set by demonstrators. On the eve of the race the body of a protester was found, but come the big day, the threatened disruption never materialised. "Perhaps pro-democracy protesters, though determined and resourceful, are not strategically strong," wondered Paul Weaver in *The Guardian*. When one of the leaders was telephoned two hours before the race, she asked whether it had started. "As the chequered flag fell on the race that should never have been, the drivers were aiming towards a vast cloud of dense black smoke. The cloud hung in the air briefly before wind and darkness removed the stain from the sky."[149]

Predictably, the show also went ahead the following year. As tickets were made available and the £200m circuit staged a driving day for women, Amnesty International warned that the grand prix could trigger a public release of pent-up frustration and fury. To Dr Ala'a Shebabi, a British-born campaigner whose husband had been jailed during the uprising, to stage the race at such a juncture was unconscionable: "The people in Bahrain are struggling. There is a containment policy that means they cannot move. Demonstrations were banned and more than 30 protest leaders were stripped of their citizenship, which means they are trapped. Formula One is only a sport, but it is a sport of the ruling regime in the eyes of the people. It will come to Bahrain but the people will be waiting with their frustrations and anger."[150] And so they were. Following clashes with security forces, tens of thousands of anti-government protesters blocked a major road before the start, many carrying banners with the slogan: "Don't race on our blood".[151]

Calling it "a cowardly tale", *The Times* quoted Mark Twain: "It is curious that physical courage should be so common in the world, and moral courage so rare."[152]

Argentina's glory and the "Dirty War"

For this chapter's final tale we must turn to what may one day be regarded as the last word on the sport-politics non-divide. As their country prepared to host the 1978 World Cup finals, Argentinians were not a happy breed. Driven to the brink of bankruptcy by austerity measures imposed by the International Monetary Fund, public protests, strikes and revolts so shook the nation that Marxist ideologues became convinced all was set fair for a revolution. There was, though, no left-wing unity – the Communists, it was said, merely did Moscow's bidding, and the Kremlin was never going to permit such a trifling matter to detonate their precious if shaky détente with Washington. Meanwhile, the military junta led by General Jorge Videla was being held responsible for the disappearance of 30,000 citizens in the so-called "Dirty War" (as if war could ever be characterised as clean). The World Cup was Videla's pet project, the immaculate distraction. Estimates have it that the final cost ran to $700,000 – three times as expensive as the next tournament in Spain and easily the dearest to that point; "25 Million Argentinians Will Play in the World Cup" trumpeted the junta's slogan, prompting a public remix – "25 Million Argentinians Will Pay for the World Cup".[153]

* * *

Indebted as it was to a Glaswegian schoolteacher, Alexander Watson Hutton, Argentina's contribution to the spread of football is considerable: it was home to the first club, first national association and first league in South America, not to mention, in 1867, the first recorded game outside Europe, between teams of English workers. That such trailblazing has been perennially downplayed is the price, one supposes, of being constantly compared to Brazil, an arch-rivalry perhaps best summed up by the fact that, in Alex Bellos's excellent history of the Brazilian game, *Futebol: A Brazilian Way of Life*, there are but two references to Argentina. While Brazilian football has largely been characterised as a celebration of *futebol-arte* (art-football), the approach on the other side of Paraguay is often, and most flatteringly, described as pragmatic, the contrast symbolised by the dispute over which of the two nations was responsible for siring the game's grandest exponent, Diego Maradona or Pelé. In 2000, Maradona was voted "Player of the Century" in a FIFA poll, securing almost three times as many votes as the Brazilian. FIFA then decided to add a second award, which went to Pelé. Many, and not solely Argentinians, contended that he was rewarded for his public image and constant support of the governing body (not to say Viagra), whereas Maradona was not only being punished for his criticism of FIFA, but also for his drug addiction and psychiatric problems.

The links between game and government came to the fore in Argentina during the turbulent 1970s and 1980s. In 1982, when General Galtieri's military dictatorship launched its campaign to reclaim the Falkland Islands from Britain, war and football, attested *Sports Illustrated*, "were deliberately blurred". Galtieri was ruthlessly imaginative and efficient in disguising the political reality. Along the roads connecting airports to venues his soldiers erected makeshift walls, concealing slums from visiting teams, journalists and officials; political prisoners were sent to distant military bases. As a consequence, several journalists returned to Europe praising the human rights record of the same regime responsible for "disappearing" dozens of inhabitants on a daily basis, then dumping them into the River Plate. "To the generals, creating a nationalist frenzy was a policy,"[154] wrote Simon Kuper. The World Cup song, *Vamos Argentina, Vamos a Ganar* (Go on Argentina, go and win), was "cranked out again" for the Falklands.

The 1982 World Cup prompted a renewed rush of overt nationalism and patriotic slogans; dismay at the national team's early exit was held to have helped hasten the junta's removal. At the next World Cup, Argentina met England in one of the more politically-charged ties in the tournament's history: Maradona, having blatantly punched home the opening goal, claimed that "The Hand of God" was responsible. "A country very accustomed to flouting the law fell in love with such mischievousness," warranted Ezequiel Fernandez Moores.[155] In the late 1990s, Etcétera, a troupe of politically-inspired Argentinian performance artists, began staging theatrical events in front of the houses of former murderers and torturers. During the 1998 World Cup match between England and Argentina, Etcétera staged a satirical soccer match, "Argentina vs. Argentina", in front of Galtieri's former residence, culminating in a ball filled with red paint being kicked into the house.

* * *

If the junta hoped to benefit from the surge in nationalist fervour in 1978, seldom can one team's progress in a sporting event have supplied such balm. With Mario Kempes's golden boots to the fore, Argentina swept through the first group phase with style, panache and passion, every performance greeted with rapture on the terraces and delirious dancing in the streets. Nevertheless, the size of the task confronting Kempes and company as they kicked off the final game of the second phase was as clear as it was daunting: to qualify for the final ahead of Brazil, 3-0 winners over Poland earlier that day, only victory by at least a four-goal margin would suffice. That their opponents in Rosario were Peru, moreover, served as a pertinent reminder of the political backdrop.

A few weeks before the tournament, in the early hours of 25 May, 13 Peruvians were detained on subversion charges in Lima and Arequipa, among them two admirals, a journalist and 10 leftist leaders. Flown to Argentina's Jujuy Airport and assigned to the 20th Infantry Regiment as prisoners of war, they were transferred to the basement of the Federal Police Central Department in Buenos Aires and coerced into signing a request for political asylum. According to one of the detainees, Ricardo

Napurí Shapiro, the original plan was to apply "the escape law" and throw their bodies into the sea from a helicopter. That they escaped, narrowly, was thanks to a journalist, who, smelling something fishy, snapped photos of the aircraft and its passengers at the Jujuy Airport. These were published in a local periodical, the news spread across the world via the thousands of reporters covering the World Cup. Videla's lone option was to send the prisoners to Europe.[156]

With nothing to gain bar South American bragging rights, the talented Peruvians twice hit a post early on but then the roof fell in: they lost 6-0. Ramón "El Loco" Quiroga, their eccentric goalkeeper, had been born in Rosario, provoking all manner of speculation. Brian Glanville thought the losers "lay down abjectly"; Claudio Coutinho, Brazil's dismayed and incredulous coach, forecast that, when they next heard their national anthem at a World Cup, they would feel no pride; local newspapers reported that the Brazilians had tried to coax a defiant display by the Peruvians by way of a bribe. "Some thought they were bribed [to lose], some thought they were simply frightened by the torrid atmosphere," wrote Glanville in his justly and oft-reprinted history of the tournament. "Whatever, it was a shabby way for Argentina to reach the [final]."[157] That they went on to beat Holland 3-1, Kempes netting twice, did nothing whatsoever to quell the conspiracy theorists.

In a 1998 interview with *La Nación*, a Buenos Aires daily paper, Quiroga denounced the Peruvian lineup as inadequate; yes, he had suspected certain teammates of complicity. Of those who benefited from the deal, he alleged, "some were to die and others were to become dead to football".[158] In July 2010, Videla, now 84, went on trial – with 19 other defendants – for the alleged murders in 1976 of 31 left-wing activists, dragged from their jail cells in Cordoba and shot. A 1990 presidential pardon having recently been overturned, he was already serving a life sentence for abuses committed during military rule. He also faced charges abroad, for the murder of expatriates from Italy, Spain, France and Germany. "Argentina's victory [in 1978]," reported the BBC at the start of the new trial, "was used to try to clean the international reputation of the military government at a time when reports of massive human rights violations had been seeping out."[159] Five months later, Videla was sentenced to life imprisonment in a civilian jail.

March 2012 yielded another piece in the puzzle. During an extradition hearing in Buenos Aires, the former Peruvian senator Genaro Ledesma claimed that Argentina's victory in Rosario had resulted from a deal struck between Videla and General Francisco Morales Bermúdez, then Peru's military ruler. Ledesma alleged that the latter had agreed to throw the match as part of "Operation Condor", a clandestine plan cooked up by himself and Videla to help each other dispose of meddlesome activists. A report in the *Moscow News* began, aptly, with a quote from Arthur Conan Doyle: "Once you eliminate the impossible, whatever remains, no matter how improbable, must be the truth."[160]

Norberto Oyarbide, Argentina's federal judge, ordered Videla and Albano Harguindeguy, the junta's interior minister, to explain the kidnapping and torture of the 13 kidnapped Peruvians; he also ordered the detention and then extradition of Bermúdez, now 90. Could it yet be that a World Cup triumph will be declared null and void?

9 No Normal Sport in an Abnormal Society: Sport and Race

I. Disunited States

The title of this chapter comes from the rallying-cry of Sam Ramsamy, the London-based chairman of the South African Non-Racial Olympic Committee (SAN-ROC) from 1976 to 1990. During those years, in the words of E. S. Reddy, the former director of the United Nations Centre against Apartheid, he was "the principal strategist of the struggle against apartheid sports". It is hard to think of another maxim that so perfectly encapsulates why sport and politics, above all sport and racial politics, have always been entwined.

Reflecting the outer world all too vividly, of all the battles fought in the sporting arena, none has been quite so ubiquitous, even now, as that over race. And nowhere has this struggle been more bitterly fought than in the United States. Nowhere, by the same token, have black sportsfolk done more to light a torch for their brothers and sisters to follow than in the ring. From 1937, when Joe Louis ascended what was then the throne of thrones, until 1991, when the warring acronyms (WBA, WBC, IBF, WBO, Uncle Tom Cobbleigh and his cat) made unanimity impossible, just two of the undisputed world heavyweight champions were not black – Rocky Marciano, an Italian-American, and Ingemar Johanson, a Swede, and both were done and dusted by the end of the Fifties.

Now consider the rest of the sporting kaleidoscope, notably the games with the inescapable middle-class ring. Think global.

African-Americans began dominating the Olympic sprints when Eddie Toland took the 100m-200m double in 1932; sub-Saharan Africans the long-distance medals when Ethiopia's Abebe Bikila won the 1960 marathon in bare feet. The first African-American medallist was the hurdler George Poage, collector of a brace of bronzes in 1904, though not until William DeHart Hubbard won the long jump in 1924 did individual gold arrive. The first non-white tennis player to win a grand slam title was Althea Gibson in 1956, six years after she became the first member of her race to compete at the US Open, five after she repeated the breakthrough at Wimbledon; more than 40 years passed before Tiger Woods became the first of his to claim a golfing major in 1997; not for another 11 years would Woods' English counterpart, Lewis Hamilton (he, too, hailed from a mixed-race, middle-class background), become the first black driver to win a Formula 1 grand prix, then claimed the world title the following season. (William "Willy" Theodore Ribbs, Jr., a Californian, had been the first to make inroads: moving to Europe after university, he won the 1976 Formula Ford title but never progressed further than an F1 test drive; in three NASCAR races in 1986 his best finish was 65th.) Yellow jerseys, meanwhile, remained as distant as ever, never mind show-jumping laurels. This century, on the other hand, barriers in Olympic cycling, gymnastics and swimming as well as bobsled and speed-skating have all been broken.

Team-wise, the contenders disqualify themselves for one reason or another. While stirring symbols of multiracialism, neither the Brazilian nor the French FIFA World Cup winners boasted uniformly black personnel; the Harlem Globetrotters have been bewildering opponents since 1929, but laughter rather than competition has been their main aim and while they won the World Professional Basketball Championship in 1940, the "world" bit meant the United States. Nigeria (1996) and Cameroon (2000) may have struck Olympic gold, but long gone are the days when that tournament was the ultimate signifier of footballing ability. Which leaves a succession of West Indies cricket teams, particularly from 1963-66 and 1976-95. We shall return to them.

Given the contribution of race to modern discourse, one section is insufficient to cover the requisite ground. This one, therefore, dissects the American experience while the next focuses on the British Empire and its aftermath. What unites them is their message: at the very least, in affording opportunities denied in other spheres, and making heroes of the oppressed and the disadvantaged, sport has made the planet more aware of the abominations of racism.

* * *

Life is all right in America
If you're all white in America

Given life and texture by Puerto Rican immigrants, Stephen Sondheim's lines from *West Side Story* were all too true when he wrote them in the mid-1950s. As the son of well-to-do Jewish New Yorkers, he was acutely aware that there really were two United States: one for the whites, one for every other hue. Change would come, albeit, as yet, nothing like as thoroughly as it might. In 2013, the major league baseball teams from Atlanta and Cleveland were still known, respectively, as the Braves and the Indians, while the capital's NFL representatives were still the Washington Redskins. As Jackson B. Miller from Eastern Oregon University noted in the *Quarterly Journal of Speech*: "Letting go of Native American symbols in our sports arenas, for some fans, means letting go of precious myths about how the West was won."[1]

To several members of the House of Congress, this went a long way beyond the pale. "The use of the 'R' word is especially harmful to native American youth, tending to lower their sense of dignity and self-esteem," Eni Falaomagaeva, American Samoa's delegate, declaimed on the House floor. He and nine fellow congressmen had recently written a letter to Daniel Snyder, the Redskins' owner, urging him to change the club's 80-year-old name (not that the franchise's original name, the Boston Braves, was any better); similar letters had been sent to the NFL commissioner, Roger Goodell, and the owners of the NFL's 31 other franchises. "It also diminishes feelings of community worth among native American tribes and dampens the aspirations of their people," continued Falaomagaeva. "Whether good intentioned or not, the 'R' word is a racial slur akin to the 'N' word among African-Americans, or the 'W' word among Latin Americans."[2]

When it comes to discussions of a racial nature, no competitive artist (an epithet more apt in this case than any) springs more readily or inspirationally to mind than Muhammad Ali, whose first step upon winning the world heavyweight title was to renounce his slave name, Cassius Clay. Lionised as he now is by the white liberals whose fathers had once despised him, it may surprise some to know that he never joined the Civil Rights movement but instead, as a Black Muslim, demanded a separate black state. Given that enough Amazonian rainforests have already been plundered to chronicle this fistic ballerina's impact on boxing, sport and the planet at large (the most insightful fruits being Mike Marqusee's rousing *Redemption Song: Muhammad Ali and the Spirit of the Sixties* and Thomas Hauser's brilliant brick-thick biography, *Muhammad Ali: His Life and Times*), the focus of this section is those whose example emboldened him.

If the civil rights struggle is often seen as the most important recurring theme of the 20th century, sport was far from alone in offering a means by which prejudice could be defeated (if not demolished), rights asserted and identity forged. During the Depression, four decades before Ali made his indelible mark amid the Sixties' breathless swirl, blues and jazz, music born of slavery and resistance – and founded on the thirst for freedom – had played their part. Singers such as Billie Holliday and Bessie Smith, together with daring innovators such as Duke Ellington and Louis Armstrong, won American hearts and many more besides.

As a purveyor of role models and rebels, sport was more potent, though some were adamant that the pursuit of success on the field distracted from the bigger picture – none more vehemently than John Hoberman, a white university professor who contended that sport was detrimental to black Americans. "Sports fixation damages black children by discouraging academic achievement in favour of physical self-expression, which is widely considered a racial trait," he wrote in his controversial 1997 book *Darwin's Athletes: How Sport Has Damaged Black America and Preserved the Myth of Race*. "Some educators understand that the self-absorbed style promoted by glamorous black athletes subverts intellectual development." One Chicago school for black boys, he pointed out approvingly, had adopted "a policy of stylistic abstinence". Out went gum-chewing, saggy tracksuit bottoms, sunglasses, earrings and fancy hair designs – "in short, a complete repudiation of the showy male style flaunted by many black athletes". Such policies "confront an intense peer pressure that equates academic excellence with effeminacy and racial disloyalty and identifies 'blackness' with physical prowess. Educators who think about solutions to this crisis see themselves in direct competition with the sports world."[3]

Inevitably, the flak flew thick and fast for *Darwin's Athletes*, primarily for what was perceived to be Hoberman's racist slant, though close inspection of the text suggests this may have been a knee-jerk reaction. Reviewing the book, Jeffrey Sammons portrayed it as "insidious", "shameless" and "offensive";[4] not unnaturally, this prompted a riposte from the author, who conceded that his work was "one-sided" but took strenuous issue with other criticisms, such as Sammons' assertion that Hoberman had formed "an ideological alliance with a despised caste of black 'conservatives'" and accused students of prejudice.

Yet even if you appreciate Hoberman's reasoning, it is tremendously difficult to make a case that black society would have been worse off without its sporting icons. In his review, Sammons had aligned with the author to a degree, quoting an article he had written some years earlier for the *Journal of the American Medical Association*, urging the abolition of boxing: "The physicians who argue that boxing keeps young men off the street, out of crime, and away from drugs – a questionable argument at best – are not praising a sport but signaling a dismal failure of the American Dream for many. For there is little difference between what boxing supposedly helps them to avoid and the tragic option the sport represents."[5] On many occasions, nonetheless, he had had to ask himself a key question: "Do I wish that Muhammad Ali had never existed?" The answer was unhesitating: "Of course not. I might wish that he did not have to be a boxer to gain the kind of attention and take on the kind of symbolism that he did, but that would be to wish for an entirely different America. Moreover, without Muhammad Ali I would not be writing this piece, for it is because of his inspiration that I chose to become a scholar of sport."[6] Sportswriters the world over would echo that sentiment.

More than half a century before Ali, it was another boxer, Jack Johnson, the first world-renowned black athlete, who personified the possibilities for his race while shouldering a heavier burden than any of his successors. Before we examine his stormy life, though, let us pick over the argument that has plagued and undermined full appreciation of black achievement, in the ring and on pitch, court and track, for far too long.

The slave gene

"Is it a coincidence," David Walsh, chief sportswriter of the *Sunday Times*, wondered in 2012, "that Britain's most recent winner of the men's 100m, Linford Christie, was born in Jamaica, that Canada's last winner, Donovan Bailey, was also born in Jamaica? It is inconceivable that this summer's Olympic 100m won't be won by a Jamaican or an American."[7]

Such certainty proved well-founded: Christophe Lemaitre, the medium-sized white hope, opted out of the 100m and finished sixth in the 200m. The odds had always been forbidding: as of May 2013, the 100m had been run in under 10 seconds 600 times, of which just seven had been the work of a Caucasian; one Caucasian, to be precise: Lemaitre, dubbed "Le Premier Blanc" by his fellow Frenchmen. His dismay at the racial subtext was clear when he recalled a letter sent to his father by the Ku Klux Klan, asking permission to appropriate him as a totem. "People used to think that no white sprinter could run under ten seconds. Now I am the first and I hope that will help others to unlock this mentality. I hope it will make people think that you can run faster whatever you look like."[8]

In a 1995 address to the British Association for the Advancement of Science, Sir Roger Bannister, according to many, undermined his legendary status as the first athlete to run a mile in under four minutes by entering this endlessly prickly debate. "I am prepared to risk political incorrectness," he declared, "drawing attention to the seemingly obvious but under-stressed fact that black sprinters and black athletes in general all seem to have certain anatomical advantages."[9]

As rancorous as the reaction was, there was nothing Bannister said that hadn't already been aired more extensively. The previous year, *The Bell Curve*, by Richard Herrstein, a Harvard psychologist, and Charles Murray, a political scientist, had sparked a ferocious outcry by claiming that white people were intellectually superior to African-Americans. As Walsh reflected: "Black people and in particular black athletes were vulnerable to the false logic that physical prowess and intelligence were inversely proportional. It was a pernicious argument but it suited many white people to embrace it. There was also a less sinister but devaluing tendency to assign the success of black athletes solely to their 'natural athleticism' with the unspoken assumption that they didn't have to work so hard."[10]

They are accustomed to such slights in Kenya's Rift Valley. Adhararandan Finn, a journalist and cross-country runner, spent time there trying to discover the source and turned his experiences into a winning memoir, *Running With The Kenyans*. For years he had been telling friends the story of Annemari Sandell, a promising junior athlete in Finland who at 16 had spent six weeks training in the Valley before the 1995 world cross-country championships in chilly, sodden Durham, where the author saw her romp home. "What had happened to her out in Kenya?" he wondered. "What did she find that turned her into a world champion? Could I find it too?"[11] Finn found out enough to run the New York marathon in under three hours; in broader terms, he made a more important discovery. The advent of prize and appearance money in the 1980s had had a sizeable impact, of course, with the road usurping the track as the main springboard for Kenyans. "Now that running is firmly established as the way out, as football is in Brazil or cricket is in India," attests Finn, "all over the Rift Valley people… are taking it up in their thousands, and the result is that Kenya is now dominating long-distance running more than ever."[12]

In 2000, Rift Valley was the focus of *The Difference*, a Channel 4 TV documentary[13] about the findings of researchers from the Danish Sports Science Institute who had spent 18 months in Eldoret, the capital of the north-western province and home to the Kalenjin tribe – supplier, at the time, of no fewer than a dozen of the world's top 20 distance runners, all living on a plateau 7000ft above sea level. High altitude increases the number of red blood cells available to ferry oxygen around the body and is thought to explain their conspicuously low heart rate. These sports scientists had found that Kalenjin from the district of Nandi Hills outperformed other Kenyans. "To test whether Nandi Hills runners were 'born with talent'," reported John Arlidge in *The Observer*, "the scientists chose three groups of schoolboys at random – one from Denmark, one from the Nandi Hills and one from Eldoret – who had never had athletic training. After three months of instruction, the groups competed against each other over 10,000 metres. The Nandi Hills group outper-formed not only the Danish boys, but also those from Eldoret. To confirm the findings were no fluke, the scientists pitted two of the Nandi Hills boys against one of Denmark's top-ranked distance runners, Thomas Nolan. The schoolboys won."[14]

Experts interviewed for the documentary observed that the Africans had "bird-like legs, very long levers which are very, very thin", allowing them to "bounce and skip" over the ground, in turn enabling them to take off after each footfall far faster than the Europeans. While the Danes were "pullers", landing heavily, sinking into the ground and almost having to pull themselves forward, the Nandi Hills boys, who "flowed through the running motion", were "bouncers". Bengt Saltin of the Danish Sports Institute concluded that this demonstrated that the Nandi Hills Kalenjin hold a genetic advantage over other athletes: "There are definitely some genes that are special here." Mike Boit, one of Kenya's first middle-distance icons, concurred: "The genetic inheritance is there."

* * *

In *Taboo: Why Black Athletes Dominate Sports and Why We're Afraid to Talk About It*, published in 2000, Jon Entine, a white American, achieved similar notoriety to Herrstein and Murray, arguing that African-Americans dominated the most "democratic" US sports – running, basketball and football – because of evolutionary migration, a plethora of fast-twitch muscle fibre and other biological and cultural factors. "Entine asserts, wrongly, that resistance to his thesis is rooted in 'political correctness'," countered Jon Morgan in the *Baltimore Sun*. "Actually, there is good reason to be sceptical of broad-brush racial grouping. It has been used to justify everything from the Holocaust and slavery to separate whites-only water fountains."[15]

Of late, an alternative view has begun to gather steam. In another Channel 4 documentary broadcast shortly before the 2012 Olympics, Michael Johnson, perhaps the greatest of all male sprinters, submitted his take. "All my life I believed I became an athlete through my own determination, but it's impossible to think that being descended from slaves hasn't left an imprint through the generations." Through a visit to a Texas library he had discovered that he, too, was descended from slaves. "Difficult as it was to hear, slavery has benefited descendants like me. I believe there is a serious gene within me." Reinforcement came from Bill Amos, professor of evolutionary genetics at Cambridge University: "I wouldn't be surprised if the survivors of the slave trade weren't cleaner in some sense.

I don't mean anything in particular by that other than that they've many potential harmful mutations that everyone else has a bit more of."[16]

All of which begged the question: why weren't Ethiopians and Kenyans emulating their prowess in endurance races over shorter distances? Science thought it had an answer – ACTN3, the so-called speed gene. In 2003 a team of seven scientists published a study in *The American Journal of Human Genetics* in which 429 elite Australian athletes were tested for ACTN3. We all have two copies of the gene, each of which comes in one of two variants: R or X. The former instructs the body to produce alpha-actinin-3, a protein found only in fast-twitch muscle fibres, which contract rapidly and violently, enabling explosive movement; the latter prevents creation of the protein. None of the 32 Olympic sprinters analysed possessed two X variants. "In fact," stated David Epstein in *Sports Illustrated*, "it seems that all an ACTN3 test can do consistently is tell someone he *isn't* going to make the Olympic 4×100 relay team. But even that sweeping conclusion leaves room for exceptions, such as the Jamaican sprinter who was recently found to have the 'wrong' copies of the explosiveness gene, or the Spanish long jumper who also has them yet sailed more than 27 feet and twice made the Olympics."[17]

Another vociferous riposte to Entine came from Albert Mosley, a professor of philosophy at Smith College in Maine and co-author of *Affirmative Action: Social Justice or Unfair Preference?* "The usual argument has been that European and Asian achievements outstrip African achievements in the sciences and mathematics because Europeans and Asians are naturally smarter than Africans, that is, have a higher IQ. Entine has merely turned this argument around: African achievements outstrip European and Asian achievements in athletics because they are naturally faster and stronger... If this were the case, then it would seem to make sense for parents of African descent to encourage their children to cultivate athletic skills, rather than intellectual and mathematical skills. This line of argument has appealed to many blacks, and even more whites. It is a view that I believe is damaging. It promotes stereotypes that have been developed to justify the exclusion of whole groups of people from opportunities they are not considered naturally endowed for. The fact that such stereotypes might contain a grain of truth is no redeeming feature."[18]

The Galveston Giant

"The problem of the twentieth-century is the problem of the colour line." Regarded by many as the heart and soul of the Civil Rights movement, William Edward Burghardt Du Bois was prophetic indeed when he penned those words in 1903 in *The Souls of Black Folk*. Unlike Booker T. Washington, his fellow black leader (who was less concerned with the collective than the individual), Du Bois believed in the power of sport for good: "I have long noted with silent apprehension a distinct tendency among us, to depreciate and belittle and sneer at means of recreation, to consider amusement as the peculiar property of the devil, and to look upon even its legitimate pursuit as time wasted and energy misspent."[19] It is hard to think of a sporting champion who has been belittled and sneered at quite as much as Johnson. Martin Peters, the clever England midfielder of 1966, was hailed by his manager, Alf Ramsey, as being 10 years ahead of his time; "The Galveston Giant" had the misfortune to be decades ahead of his.

* * *

The silver screen was made for the ring, as Thomas Edison himself demonstrated – the subjects of the great inventor's experiments with moving images at the end of the previous century had included boxers. The elemental appeal of "show-business with blood", as Frank Bruno astutely put it, is almost indivisible from cinema's visceral approach; both tap into our least admirable instincts. "Movies," as Kevin Mitchell has winced disapprovingly, "glamourise violence in a way that works as drama."

That the most successful of ring movies to date has been the interminable *Rocky* franchise (more than three decades and counting) remains one of Hollywood's less credible contributions to sporting lore: Sylvester Stallone's passport to fortune, after all, told the long-running, and mostly triumphant, tale of a *white* heavyweight, based on the improbable march to a 1975 world title shot, against Ali, of one Chuck Wepner, the so-called "Bayonne Bleeder", who had initially been granted his chance by a black champion (Apollo Creed, a smooth-talking, loud-mouthed, utterly blatant double for "The Greatest").

The first African-American to claim the heavyweight crown was Johnson. Indeed, a century before Barack Obama moved his family into a capacious old mansion in Washington D.C., this former Texas dockworker owned the planet's best-known black face. While he was by no means the first black cultural achiever, nor even the first black sporting achiever (the previous 100 years had seen Tom Molineaux become a leading boxer, Isaac Murphy win three Kentucky Derbys and Major Taylor the American cycling championship), he was certainly the first to set the ancient order quaking in their jodhpurs.

It was the dawn of popular culture; cinema and radio were in their infancy. Ken Burns, director of the documentary *Unforgiveable Blackness – The Rise And Fall of Jack Johnson*, based on Geoffrey C. Ward's award-winning book of the same name, saw his subject as "the first African-American pop culture icon".[20] That he should achieve this status through boxing was not in the least surprising. Black servants had a long if not proud tradition of fighting each other on plantations to entertain their masters. As boxing gravitated to something faintly resembling respectability and became one of the few sports amenable to inter-racial contests, John L. Sullivan became the first world heavyweight champion in 1882 then refused to defend his crown against any non-whites. When James J. Corbett beat him in 1892, he maintained the exclusion zone. Between 1903 and 1932, the likes of Harry Wills and Sam Langford would be acclaimed "Coloured Heavyweight Champion of the World", and buckled on the belt with honour, but, like Peter Jackson before them, were denied the opportunity to unite the titles.

Johnson did not so much break as smash the mould. Pursuing his man wherever he pulled on his gloves in public – and buying ringside tickets for every bout – he eventually followed the globetrotting Tommy Burns (real name Noah Brusso) all the way to Australia in a bid to capture the Canadian's world title. On Boxing Day 1908, the pair traded punches before a bumper crowd of 20,000 – the country's biggest sporting gate to date. The stage was the newly completed Sydney Stadium, an outdoor venue in the seemingly hospitable surrounds of Rushcutters Bay. The Australian government has posted footage of Johnson's preparations on the web, with a good-sized throng watching him grinning and gurning his way through a series of exercises – a natural extrovert if ever there was. Judging by the look on their faces, the experience, for many, had much in common with a trip to the zoo.

Commercial films of major fights had become an extremely profitable business indeed. On this occasion, however, the politicians were petrified – what mayhem might ensue should the footage show black whupping white? As Johnson delivered the knockout blow, police intervened, stopping the fight and shutting down the cameras.

Johnson's menace and omnipotence were such that he inspired the term "Great White Hope", a label slapped on whichever representative of the dominant race happened to be in the opposing corner (it was said that he overlooked black opponents for the first five years of his reign because white fighters meant bigger purses). Exuberant celebrations across the US followed his 1910 defeat of Jim Jeffries, the inaugural "Great White Hope"; these were reported in the press, misleadingly, as "riots". Angry whites lashed out; police had to prevent lynchings: of the 25 people killed, 23 were black. A documentary of the fight, costing $250,000, was exhibited internationally; inevitably, it was banned in many US states.

Sudden bursts of outrage about boxing's brutality drew a sceptical response from Du Bois. "The cause is clear: Jack Johnson... has out-sparred an Irishman. He did it with little brutality, the utmost fairness and great good nature. He did not 'knock' his opponent senseless. Apparently he did not even try. Neither he nor his race invented prize-fighting nor particularly like it. Why then this thrill of national disgust? Because Johnson is black... we have yet to hear, in the case of white America, that marital troubles have disqualified prize fighters or ball players or even statesmen. It comes down then, after all, to this unforgiveable blackness."[21]

Johnson's triumph inspired a popular ditty, sung to the tune of a spiritual:

The Yankees hold the play,
The white man pulls the trigger;
But it make no difference what the white man say,
The world champion is still a nigger

Johnson was the white supremacist's nightmare. Intelligent, articulate and charming, an early star of radio for whom endorsements flowed (he even patented a medicine), he dressed swankily and lapped up opera. He was black, proud and extremely loud. Pulled over for a $50 speeding ticket, he gave the officer a $100 bill; when the latter protested that he didn't have anything like enough change for that much, Johnson insisted he keep it: the return trip, he reasoned, would be made with no less disrespect for the speed limit. He also thought nothing of consorting with white women, wedding no fewer than three. Emphasised Burns: "He was scandal, he was gossip, he was a public menace for many, a public hero for some, admired and demonised, feared, misunderstood, and ridiculed."[22]

His enemies (of whom there was never the vaguest shortage) strove to bring him down, finding an accomplice in the Mann Act, passed in 1910: twice he was tried for "transporting" women across a state line "for immoral purposes". The first case, in October 1912, collapsed: before the year was out, he had married Lucille Cameron, the 18-year-old prostitute in question, prompting a couple of peace-loving and spiritually enlightened Southern ministers to call for him to be lynched. In 1913, after being convicted (by an all-white jury), he fled for Montreal, then France and, after the outbreak of the First World War had deflated the European boxing market, South America. In 1915, now 37, he defended his title against a mountainous cowboy, Jess Willard, watched by a crowd of 25,000 at the Vedado Racetrack in hot and humid Havana. "Throughout the fight," reported the *Sioux City Journal*, "the Cubans kept shouting words of encouragement to Willard, such as 'Kill the black bear!' and 'Knock him out!'"[23] Under-trained and over-confident, Johnson lost in round 26. Thus did white America wrest back this most symbolic of sporting crowns. Not for another 15 years would a black boxer be allowed to try and reclaim it.

Denied a passport back to his homeland, Johnson found refuge in Spain and Mexico before finally giving himself up in 1920. He served his sentence, and in 1932, accompanied by his third wife, Irene Pireau, sailed to Europe, where he fought a number of exhibition bouts in Paris; plans to open a boxing school in Berlin were scuppered by the untimely ascent of Hitler. In 1946 he was killed in a car accident. Not until 2013, a century after his conviction, did the US Senate vote to press President Obama to pardon him. At her husband's funeral, Irene revealed the source of her love to a reporter: "I loved him because of his courage. He faced the world unafraid."[24]

"That's *my* story." Thus, during his own exile from the ring, did Muhammad Ali tell James Earl Jones when he went backstage after seeing the actor play Johnson in *The Great White Hope* on Broadway, a role he would replicate in the screen version. Swap white women for religion and indeed it was.

Born to please

But was boxing the right arena to promote equality? "Boxing is only possible if there is an endless supply of young men hungry to leave their impoverished ghetto neighbourhoods, more than willing to substitute the putative dangers of the ring for the more evident, possibly daily, dangers of the street," theorised Joyce Carol Oates, a celebrated novelist and essayist with a weakness for pugilism. Black boxers "have been acutely conscious of themselves as racially *other* from the majority of their audiences, whom they must please in one way or another, as black villains, or honorary whites".[25]

> To see race as a predominant factor in American boxing is inevitable, but the moral issues, as always in this paradoxical sport, are ambiguous. Is there a moral distinction between the spectacle of black slaves in the Old South being forced by their white owners to fight, for purposes of gambling, and the spectacle of contemporary blacks fighting for multimillion-dollar paydays, for TV coverage from Las Vegas and Atlantic City?[26]

Murphy and Taylor also paid for their success. The jockey was hounded from the track in the 1890s by false allegations; the cyclist was forced to flee to Europe, as Gerald Gems and Gertrud Pfister relate in *Understanding American Sports*, after white rivals "banded together to obstruct and endanger him".[27] Another trailblazer to suffer the consequences was Frederick Douglass "Fritz" Pollard. One of the first black professional American footballers – a running back with the Akron Pros – he was told after one game: "You're a nigger, but you're the best goddamned football player I ever saw."[28] In 1921, while still playing, he was appointed the sport's first African-American head coach. Five years later, the NFL banned all black players and coaches. Pollard set up his own black team and issued challenges to NFL members by way of exhibition matches, but none had the gumption to accept. The Fritz Pollard Alliance Foundation now works to "promote diversity and equality of job opportunity" in the NFL.[29]

Post-Johnson, boxing, too, enforced an informal but rigid colour bar. Jack Dempsey, who reigned supreme for most of the 1920s, repeatedly assured his fans that he would never defend his crown against a black man. "Few observers doubted," wrote

Sammons, "that exclusionary racial policies provided a short-term boon to boxing, as the neutralisation of 'black menaces' brought with it legalisation and commercialisation. While baseball, which took similar steps at the same time, could hide within its team structure the effects of a diluted talent pool, the one-on-one nature of boxing clearly revealed them."[30]

Then, in the mid-1930s, came a beacon of light, in the shape of an immensely powerful puncher by the name of Joe Louis Barrow, the anti-Johnson. The son of an Alabama sharecropper, great grandson of a slave and great-great grandson of a white slave owner, he was born in 1914, lost his father to a mental asylum when he was two and in the next decade moved with his mother and siblings to Detroit, where his early ring sorties saw him fight under the name Joe Louis – the better to shield his activities from the woman who bore him. Fifty victories in 54 amateur bouts brought him to the notice of a notorious numbers racketeer, John Roxborough, who, abetted by his partner, Julian Black, advised him that a black boxer required black management, not to mention friends. Crucially, Roxborough urged Louis, whose taciturn public image was partly an attempt to disguise a stammer, to court white America, the better to outflank the prejudice fanned so recklessly by Johnson. Roxborough even laid down a behavioural code, containing items such as:

- *Never have your photo taken with a white woman*
- *Never enter a nightclub alone*
- *No soft fights*
- *No fixed fights*
- *No gloating over a fallen opponent*
- *Don't let anyone know what you're thinking, especially not the cameras*[31]

At first Louis accepted the slender pickings on offer and fought as frequently as possible: between July 1934 and the following June he fought no fewer than 22 times, winning the lot, 18 by knockout. Small wonder Mike Jacobs began courting Roxborough and Black, offering his considerable services as a promoter. Having set up the Twentieth Century Sporting Club in consort with three leading sportswriters from the Randolph Hearst empire, Jacobs could also guarantee assistance from the media. At last, a bonafide "race contender" (the *Charlotte Observer* dubbed Louis "the negro clouter") had arrived. We have already traced his path to national and racial glory, so, for now, let us leave the summation to his son, Joe Louis Jr: "What my father did was enable white America to think of him as an American, not as a black. By winning, he became white America's first black hero."[32]

Bigotry is bigotry

In 1982, when Arthur Ashe called time on his brilliant, trail-blazing tennis career, he turned down an offer to teach at Yale University and plumped for Florida Memorial College. In preparing his course syllabus, he soon discovered, to his "surprise and chagrin", that next to nothing had been written about the African-American contribution to sports history. The only books he located that in any way fitted the bill, Edwin B. Henderson's *The Negro in Sports* and A.S "Doc" Young's *Negro Firsts in Sport*, had been published in 1938 and 1963 respectively. "I was baffled by this poverty of information," he would recall. "After all, in major sports such as boxing, baseball, football, basketball and track, African-Americans comprised a disproportionately high percentage of the leading athletes."[33] In talking to historians about the reasons for this, he came to an unsurprising conclusion (unsurprising, that is, to those familiar with the way newspaper editors and especially historians had long peered down their noses at sport, the "toy department"): namely, "snobbery and timidity".

"Burning with a sense of obligation", Ashe set about making amends. By 1988 he and his team of researchers had completed *A Hard Road to Glory: A History of the African-American Athlete*, a three-volume labour of love covering the subject from 1619 to the mid-1980s. It was "an emotional experience", Ashe remembered, "because it dealt so intimately, at almost every stage, with both the triumph and the tragedy, the elation and suffering, of blacks as they met not only the physical challenge of their sport but also the gratuitous challenges of racism. No sport was exempt from this painful double history, so that compiling the record was fairly relentless exposure to disappointment."[34] Nobody personified that elation and suffering more profoundly than Jesse Owens.

* * *

Owens and Louis were bound together by history and circumstance. "Jesse and Joe had been born within eight months of each other in Alabama," writes Donald McRae in *In Black & White: The Untold Story of Joe Louis and Jesse Owens*, the 2002 William Hill Sports Book of the Year. Grandsons of slaves, sons of sharecroppers, both were impaired by a speech defect. "Their families moved north in the 1920s and then they discovered themselves in sport – Jesse as a runner on the sidewalks of Cleveland and Joe as a fighter in a Detroit gym. They soon realised how much they also loved pretty girls and swanky clothes." Yet the differences gaped. "Joe never smiled in public; Jesse rarely stopped grinning. Jesse looked as if he had found paradise as he ran 'smooth as the west wind', and for free, on the amateur track; Joe marched silently into the obscenely-moneyed and gangster-ridden world of professional boxing. Joe was surrounded by an all-black entourage; Jesse's mentors and coaches were white. Jesse had made it to college; Joe was dismissed as a virtual illiterate."[35]

As the 1936 Olympic Games neared, the *Amsterdam News* called upon black athletes to withdraw. "Preserve the Olympic Ideal" the paper urged. Walter White, the NAACP president, wrote an open letter to Owens, a gold medal contender in several events, urging him to "help strike a blow at intolerance".

I realise… how hypocritical it is for certain Americans to point the finger of scorn at any other country for racial or any other kind of bigotry… [but] the issue of participation in the 1936

Olympics, if held in Germany under the present regime, tran-
scends all other issues. Participation by American athletes, and
especially those of our own race, which has suffered more than
any other from American race hatred, would, I firmly believe,
do irreplaceable harm.[36]

Although Owens spoke out against the Nazis, Avery Brundage's silvery forked tongue persuaded him and other black athletes that to withdraw would waste all those years of training and dreaming, and that representing their country was paramount. Besides, it could scarcely be argued that African-Americans back then were treated vastly better than German Jews. Eighteen of the former would compete in Berlin, three times the quorum at the previous Olympics; almost all hailed from white universities, underscoring how inferior sporting facilities were at the few black ones.

It was on a "warm spring day" at Ferry Field in Ann Arbor, Michigan on 25 May 1935, recalled Grantland Rice, that Owens left his first indelible imprint on sportingkind. In "little more than an hour" he showcased his speed as a runner and jumper, not to mention his "uncanny stamina".[37] First he won the Western Conference 100 yards, equalling the world record; half an hour later, he ran the fastest 220 yards yet witnessed, then repeated the feat in the 220-yard low hurdles. Competitive hunger plainly unsated, he proceeded to not only become the first American to stretch to 26 feet in the long jump but, in supplanting the extant world record, go nearly threequarters of the way to 27; not until the Sixties would anyone leap further.

On 19 June the following year, Schmeling outsmarted Louis. The way *De Werkampf*, a monthly publication, saw it, America and her allies "cannot thank Schmeling enough for this victory for he checked the arrogance of the Negroes and clearly demonstrated the superiority of white intelligence"; he had "saved the prestige of the white race" exulted the weekly official newspaper of Hitler's SS, *Das Schwarze Korps* – translated, somewhat ironically in this context, as The Black Guards.[38] In Berlin, during the first week of August, Owens put the prestige of the white race firmly back at risk.

The weather, recollected Rice, was cold and wet, "hardly the weather that Owens would have chosen, for Negroes generally function best in intense heat".[39] Within the space of four days, nevertheless, he ran eight sprints and soared off the long-jump board half a dozen times, setting nine Olympic records and equalling two. He matched or beat the world 100m record three times and set a new mark for the 200m; in five of his legal jumps he beat the Olympic peak. A haul of three individual gold medals was supplemented in the 4x100m relay. Not for nearly five decades would Carl Lewis match that unprecedented collection. "Watching Jesse run and jump that day," remembered Rice, "I began wondering if there was a set of limitations to any human's speed."[40] The Jesse Owens Award remains American track and field's highest annual accolade.

The most heartening part of this fairytale was the helping hand proffered in the long jump final by Lutz Long, the very blond and decidedly blue-eyed champion of Germany. In each of his first two leaps Owens overstepped, whereupon Long, with Hitler looking on, told his opponent he was good enough to take off from six inches behind the board. Advice gratefully and smilingly received, Owens atoned in style, sealing the gold before demolishing the world record with his final jump. To Rice it seemed he had "jumped clear out of Germany".

Stepping into the pit to hug Owens, Long was the first to offer congratulations. "They walked past Hitler, arm-in-arm," as McRae paints the scene, "talking and smiling as the applause rolled down from the grandstands."[41] As they awaited the medal ceremony, they relaxed on the grass, stretched out on their stomachs, and talked about Hitler. According to Owens' own account, Long "didn't believe in Aryan supremacy any more than he believed the moon was made of green cheese, and he was disturbed at the direction in which Hitler was going".[42] The bond between them, observes McRae, was clear: "Jesse visited Lutz in the Olympic Village that evening. Despite

Lutz's fractured English, and Jesse's non-existent German, they communicated over the next few hours. Two apolitical young men had much in common. They had both been born to poor rural families who had moved to the city in search of work. They were also married, with a child each. They agreed to remain in touch after the Games. They were, said Jesse, two uncertain young men in an uncertain world."[43]

As for the man who was making that world ever more uncertain, Hitler had reportedly left the building during the early stages of the long jump final, sparing him from presenting a medal to one of the competitors he had so gracelessly dubbed America's "African Auxiliaries". After doing the honours on the opening day of competition, he had been instructed by Count Baillet-Latour to hang a medal around the necks of all the winners or none; he opted for the latter course. It therefore cannot be said, as many have, that he had flounced off expressly because of Owens, though few resisted the temptation to put two and two together and construct any amount of symbolism. "'Adolf' snubs U.S. Lads" roared the *Afro American*.[44]

"This story is not just a fairy tale," countered the German relay runner Waither Tripps in a letter written to the director of the West German TV station ZDF on 14 March 1984 following the latest reiteration of the snub story. The letter was subsequently printed in *The Journal of Historical Review*, a somewhat dubious organ published by a pseudo-scholarly body based in California, The Institute for Historical Review. "It is a wretched lie. Today the truth is suppressed for presumably political reasons. But it will not die. There are too many contemporary witnesses. I am one of them."[45] According to the author of the article, Mark Weber, Tripps later stated that Hitler had invited all the Olympic medallists to a post-Games reception at the Reich Chancellory, where he shook Owens's hand. The journal to which Weber made that radical contribution, it seems worth pointing out, is deemed to be the chief mouthpiece for Holocaust denial.

Besides, as Owens would subsequently point out, his own president, the purportedly saintly Franklin D. Roosevelt, had hardly shown him much, if any, respect, and would forever keep his distance.

Towards desegregation

On Monday 15 April 2013, wherever you went to watch major league baseball, telling the participants apart was a strenuous task. Each of the 300-odd players on view wore the same number on the back of his shirt, 42, a ritual since 2009. That year, even the umpires wore "42" patches. Forty-two was Jackie Robinson's number, the one he wore on his major league debut on 15 April 1947, when he became the first black major league baseball player of modern times, a feat whose symbolism cannot be overstated. And this was Jackie Robinson Day. The most revered of all competitive artists deserved nothing less. "It's always meaningful when this day comes around," said Bo Porter, the manager of the Houston Astros. "For me, though, it's every day. I was able to play, coach and manage baseball because of him. He means a lot to this country, and for me, I honour him every day."[46]

Born on the last day of January 1919, in Cairo, south of Albany, Robinson grew up at the epicentre of Georgia's so-called "black belt". No other state, asserted Du Bois, "can count a million negroes among its citizens – a population as large as the slave population of the whole Union in 1800".[47] Robinson was actually preceded into sporting lore by his elder brother Mack, second to Owens in the 1936 Olympic 200m final. The shoes Mack ran in that day were the same as the ones he had worn in junior high school. "When he got home, only three people met him at the station," recalled his wife, Delano. "There was no celebration."[48] The first public display of the younger Robinson's refusal to kow-tow came while he was serving in the 761st Tank Battalion in 1944, at Camp Hood in Texas, shortly before D-Day. By then, the abominable hypocrisy of battling racism overseas while fostering it at home was becoming unmissable: black and white could fight together but not play ball together.

The brewing disquiet over segregated transport on military bases was coming to a boil following the killing of a black GI by a bus driver in North Carolina. Around the same time, one up-and-coming boxer, Sugar Ray Robinson, and one already great one, Robinson's pal Joe Louis, had been involved in a heavily publicised incident near a military base in Alabama – Louis had had the temerity to use a telephone in the white area of a bus station and found himself jostled by military police. From the Pentagon, meanwhile, reports had emerged of an impending new directive outlawing segregation on military buses.

Whether he was aware of all of this was never clear, but on 6 July, Robinson boarded a bus and sat down next to – by his own testimony to the authorities later that night – "a coloured girl sitting in the middle of the bus".[49] The girl in question was actually the wife of Lt. Gordon Jones of the 761st. "The young woman was light-skinned and may initially have been mistaken for a white woman," wrote David Falkner in *Great Time Coming – The Life of Jackie Robinson, from Baseball to Birmingham*. "A black man seated alongside a white woman on a bus in the South, no matter how innocent their relationship, would have touched off battle-station alarms from Baltimore to Biloxi."[50] The driver asked Robinson to retreat to his appointed place at the back but he declined, then assailed all with his feelings on the matter. It earned him a court martial. The legendary and catalytic resistance of Rosa Parks, subsequently hailed by Congress as "the first lady of civil rights" and "the mother of the freedom movement" for refusing to give up her seat to a white passenger in Alabama, was still 11 years distant.

The court martial was swiftly rescinded, yet even stiffer obstacles remained. A multi-talented athlete – as a running-back and on the track in addition to the diamond – Robinson chose baseball for a career. In this he was helped, initially, by the death, soon after his trial, of Judge Kenesaw Mountain Landis, the man responsible for prolonging the informal "colour bar" that had now polluted the game for six decades.

Landis's replacement, Albert "Happy" Chandler, was more enlightened. While Robinson was making his name with the Kansas City Monarchs in the Negro Leagues, Wendell Smith, his erstwhile roommate and confidant, now a campaigning and resourceful black reporter with the *Pittsburgh Courier*, discovered that Isadore Muchnik, a liberal councillor in Boston, was pressurising the city's major league teams, the Red Sox and the Braves, to integrate. Smith secured Robinson and two other leading black players a trial with the former, but it was never more than window-dressing, and they all left empty-handed. It was no coincidence that, while the Red Sox could have become the first major league team to integrate, they ultimately became the last.

Smith broke his homeward journey in New York to speak to Branch Rickey, president of the Brooklyn Dodgers and the visionary who had invented the farm system as a means of nurturing talent, suspecting he might be the likeliest executive to integrate baseball. Unbeknown to most, Rickey, a conservative lawyer, had been concocting his own plan to do precisely that. His role in Robinson's advancement can never be overstated. His revulsion at the colour bar (strictly unofficial and repeatedly and vigouously denied by Landis) stemmed, he told the broadcaster Red Barber, from an incident at an Indiana hotel in 1904 when he was coaching the Ohio Wesleyan University baseball team. The black catcher, Charley Thomas, was refused a room, whereupon, or so Rickey claimed, the coach found a way round the problem by offering to share his own room with Thomas, who would otherwise have been ejected. Later that night, he found his roommate weeping and tearing at his hands: "Damned skin!" he cried, "damned skin!"[51]

Although Thomas would dismiss this as exaggeration, one of Rickey's daughters, Jane Jones, told Falkner a story from her teenage years that demonstrated, she hoped, just how sensitive her father was to discrimination. She had been summoned to court over a traffic ticket and Branch was lending his support when his attention was diverted by police interrogating a black murder suspect. "Dad walked right over and busted the guy in the grilling. He just didn't want the guy mistreated; he was a lawyer and he knew people had rights and he wanted to see to it that this guy had someone there for him. He wound up giving the guy his card and then, after that, hired him as a chauffeur!"[52]

Without Rickey's support, Robinson would never have penetrated that glass ceiling. That he prospered as he did, as one of the game's most dynamic exponents, owed even more to bravery, persistence and forbearance than skill: the distaste and displeasure of spectators, opponents and even teammates were seldom disguised. Yet Rickey knew him to be a fiery, feisty character, which was why he proposed a deal: your chance will come provided you swear to spend the next three years turning the other cheek.

Robinson was true to his word, maintaining the stiffest of upper lips in the face of fearful abuse, though when the Philadelphia Phillies came to Brooklyn, the invective hurled at him from the visitors' dugout – notably from Ben Chapman, their Alabama-born manager, whom one Dodgers player, Howie Schultz, suggested was "still fighting the Civil War" – roused him to contemplate terminating his pact with Rickey. "For one wild and rage-crazed minute I thought, 'To hell with Mr Rickey's noble experiment.' I thought what a glorious, cleansing thing it would be to let go. To hell with the image of the patient black freak I was supposed to create. I would throw down my bat, stride over to the Phillies dugout, grab one of those white sons of bitches and smash his teeth in with my despised black fist. Then I could walk away from it all."[53]

The mail brought death threats. St Louis Cardinals players had no desire to share the field with him, and threatened to boycott games with the Dodgers. Herb Pinnock, the former Yankees pitcher now running the Phillies, told Rickey he couldn't bring "the nigger" to the so-called City of Brotherly Love. "Very well, Herbert," responded Rickey. "And if we must claim the game nine to nothing, we will do just that, I assure you." The game was forfeited by that very score. "He was under such pressure and stress," Ralph Branca, the Dodgers pitcher, would recall. To the New York sportswriter Jimmy Cannon, Robinson was "the loneliest man I have ever seen in sports".

At times he buckled. "I can't take it anymore, I'm quitting," he told his sister, Willa Mae, during one especially dark early night. At times he even withdrew from Rachel, his devoted wife, who had just given birth to their first child. "He was the kind of person who if he had things bothering him, he'd be unusually quiet," she would recollect. "You had a feeling he was figuring it out, so just let him figure it out."[54]

So ferocious was the hail of hate from the stands, Rachel could only stomach watching him because she felt, somehow, as if her body was shielding him. Helpfully, her husband was also supported forcefully by Leo Durocher, the Dodgers manager then serving a one-year suspension. Durocher recognised his sporting talents and knew there was plenty more where that came from (in two-thirds of the games between white major leaguers and their Negro League counterparts, the latter had prevailed). The rest of the Dodgers players were left in no doubt where "Leo the Lip" was coming from. "I do not care if the guy is yellow or black, or if he has stripes like a fuckin' zebra," he told them. "I'm the manager of this team, and I say he plays. What's more, I say he can make us all rich. And if any of you cannot use the money, I will see that you are all traded."

A more unexpected but no less invaluable ally was Pee Wee Reese. One of a number of white Southerners on the roster, the shortstop from Kentucky was the only one not to sign a statement saying they would rather leave the club than share a dressing room with a black man. During one match on the road, while Robinson was receiving death threats and heckling and all manner of taunts from the crowd, Reese walked over to him either before or during the game and offered, in the words of Ira Berkow of the *New York Times*, "a quiet but significant gesture of friendship and comradeship". Asked by the same paper half a century later why he had acted thus, Reese remained unclear: "Something in my gut reacted at the moment. The unfairness of it? The injustice of it? I don't know."[55]

In 2005, at Brooklyn's KeySpan Park, home to the New York Mets farm team, the Cyclones, a statue of Robinson and Reese was unveiled: the latter's arm draped around the former's shoulders. In attendance were their widows and family. "When Pee Wee Reese threw his arm around Jackie Robinson's shoulder in this legendary gesture of support and friendship," claimed Marty Markowitz, the Brooklyn borough president, "they showed America and the world that racial discrimination is unacceptable and un-American."[56]

Reese and Rickey and Durocher could only protect him so much, of course, yet so stoically did Robinson confront the endless array of obstacles littering his path, so inspiring did he find the personal attacks, even the physical assaults, he was named Rookie of the Year in his first season, helping the Dodgers win the National League. In his slipstream, as proof of a new age of enlightenment – in baseball if not America as a whole – came two more telling transactions: on 5 July 1947, the American League drawbridge was lowered as the Cleveland Indians signed Larry Doby; on 27 August, the Dodgers promoted another black player, Dan Bankhead, a pitcher spotted by the ever-vigilant Rickey.

To many, Robinson was as important to black America, and as effective a consciousness-raiser, as Martin Luther King Jr. His influence extended far beyond his own race. In Brooklyn's Borough Park section shortly after his first outing for the Dodgers, his name was invoked during the Passover meal in the Foner household. As the youngest present, it fell to Henry Foner to ask the traditional question, "Why is this night different from all other nights?" He answered it himself. "This night was different," related Jonathan Eig, author of *Opening Day: The Story of Jackie Robinson's First Season*, "because Jackie Robinson had ascended to the major leagues, to baseball's promised land."[57]

"When Robinson came among us," Pete Hamill would reflect, "you saw what he meant in the stands of Ebbets Field... In 1946, the crowds were almost all white. A year later, the African-Americans, after too long a time, finally joined the other

Brooklyn tribes in the stands. Jews and Irishmen and Italians and blacks all roared together for the team." *Brown v Board of Education*, the 1954 landmark case that reversed a 19th century diktat and ended segregation in public schools, was still seven years away; another 10 would pass before King became a household name in New York. "Robinson's arrival," continued Hamill, "added another dimension to being a Dodger fan, although as kids we could not name it. That dimension was moral. It was about right and wrong. 'This is America, godammit,' my father said. We became the most American place in the whole country."[58]

In his third season, Robinson was voted the National League's Most Valuable Player. Thereafter, having kept his promise to Rickey, he no longer held his emotions in resolute check; the accumulated fury oozed from every pore, but who could possibly blame him? He had already initiated a revolution, empowering dozens of other migrants from the Negro Leagues. From 1949 to 1979, 21 of the National League's MVPs were coloured. His impact also spread far beyond his own land. In the early 1990s, George M. Hauser – author half a century earlier of *Erasing the Color Line*, a white founding member of the Congress of Racial Equality and executive director of the American Committee on Africa – wrote a letter to the *New York Times* listing the Americans he believed had been the most influential supporters of South Africa's Anti-Apartheid Movement: King, Robert F. Kennedy, Eleanor Roosevelt, Hubert Humphrey – and Robinson.[59] "It did not matter if it was South Africa, South Carolina, or the south Bronx, the issue was always the same, and Robinson, in his way, was eternally, universally committed," wrote Falkner. "The world he saw, from the moment he understood that he had a chance to make an impact on it, was one where walls of race and caste might come down and be replaced by new relationships, even, in the case of Africa, new nations."[60]

Along with Jack Johnson and Muhammad Ali, Robinson was one of the three sportsmen who did most to inspire the belief that the colour of your skin need not be a barrier to progress or fulfilment. Unlike Johnson and Ali, however, Robinson had no outlet in the ring, no safe ground – at least for those first three seasons in Brooklyn – to unleash his rage. At all times during those early springs and summers in Flatbush, playing day-in, day-out, he had to restrain every impulse to strike back. For the good, not just of his race, but for every sufferer of prejudice. To have been merely a good professional baseball player would have been ample; that he is still remembered as one of the finest of his generation was the final measure of his greatness.

The inscription on Robinson's grave is his own measure of a man: "A Life Is Not Important Except In The Impact It Has On Other Lives." No sporting life has better lived up to that noble aspiration.

The Road to Jordan

> *The Black aesthetic has not only changed basketball but, after a rough period in the seventies, has been the catalytic force behind the sport's extraordinary growth in popularity and profitability ever since.*
>
> **Nelson George**, *Elevating the Game:*
> *Black Men and Basketball*, **1999**

The official annals of the National Basketball Association state that it was born on 6 June 1946, the day the Basketball Association of America was founded, though not until 3 August 1949 did the BAA merge with the National Basketball League, which had been going in one form or another since 1898. Unsurprisingly, those running the NBA took rather less time than their baseball counterparts to welcome their first African-American contender: however, while Howard Hunter signed for the Washington Capitols in the league's second season, he never saw meaningful action, purportedly because of his relatively modest height, 5ft 9in. Nine inches taller, his teammate Earl Lloyd was rather better placed to become, that same year, the first to step on a court in earnest. But why did it even take that long? Robert Peterson suggests two reasons: the NBA was suffering growing pains and the owners were concerned that they could lose white patronage; more significant was the league's relationship with Abe Saperstein and his Harlem Globetrotters: "Whenever the Trotters appeared on a double bill with NBA teams, gate receipts soared, and so the owners were reluctant to challenge Saperstein for the rights to black players."[61] In 1949, remembered Carl Bennett, the late Fort Wayne Zollner Pistons player and coach in whose living room the NBA had been conceived, the owners' fears had been reinforced by a straw poll conducted by the league's board of governors, the majority of whom were against signing blacks.

Bennett also called a momentous exchange the following year, when Ned Irish, founder of the New York Knickerbockers and, in Peterson's words, an "imperious magnate", requested his fellow governors' approval to sign the Globetrotters' Sweetwater Clifton. "If I don't get it," he warned, "I'm going to walk out of this room and we're going to withdraw from the NBA. We're not going to continue to lose ball games just because you fellows won't approve it." Irish had issued such threats before, but this, as Peterson attests, was different:

> *The other owners paid attention because the NBA needed New York more than Irish needed professional basketball in Madison Square Garden. So, in another straw vote, the governors voted 6-5 in favour of signing black players, Bennett said. "When we walked out of the room, one of the other governors asked how I felt about it," Bennett recalled. "I said, 'Hey, if they're good ball-players and can help win games, what's wrong with it?'. And he said, 'Bennett, you dumb sonovabitch, do you know what's going to happen? In five years we'll be 75 percent black – if we survive. We won't draw any people, and we've just ruined the game of basketball."[62]*

Irish duly signed Clifton: although he could still pay more, Saperstein's monopolist grip on black talent was expiring. Taking a leaf out of baseball's scruffy book, however, the NBA originally enforced an unofficial quota system – no team could have more than two African Americans on the books at any given time.

Brown v Board of Education, happily, was just four years away, and white universities saw athletic African-Americans as a fresh source of income; before the decade was out, the NBA was being graced by colossi such as Oscar Robertson, Elgin Baylor, Bill Russell and Wilt "The Stilt" Chamberlain.

* * *

Saperstein had been well ahead of the pack. In 1926, the Savoy Big Five, an all-black team, were all the rage at Chicago's Savoy Ballroom. A stocky London-born entrepreneur who had grown up on the north side of the city and possessed a smart business brain unpolluted by racist inclinations, Saperstein started booking the Big Five on their nights off. The next year found him arranging his first "barnstorming" game in Hinckley, a village just west of the city, where his own team, Saperstein's New York, underpinned by the leading constituents of the Big Five, won a purse of $75.[63] Come 1929 they were pounding the boards on an exhibition tour of Illinois and Iowa as the New York Harlem Globe Trotters. Saperstein lengthened the name for shrewd commercial reasons – Harlem was then the centre of African-American culture. Not until 1968 would they actually play a "home" fixture in the borough. No matter. The game's greatest salesmen were up and running.

Alerted to the talents of Reece "Goose" Tatum, Saperstein did arguably his best day's work in 1941 when he signed the endlessly skilful Arkansas native, depicted in *Goose*, a 2012 ESPN documentary, as combining the skill of Michael Jordan, the presence of Denzel Washington and the wit of Chris Rock. Saperstein billed him as the "clown prince" of basketball; to Ben Green, author of *Spinning the World: The Rise, Fall, and Return to Greatness of the Harlem Globetrotters*, he was the game's first "crossover" athlete; the comedian Bill Cosby, a basketball aficionado who wrote the foreword to Green's book and thrilled to Tatum as a boy, called him "our Jackie Robinson".

Tatum needed no education in the dark craft of segregation. When a plucky uncle told his employer he would sue him if he refused to grant a pay rise, the latter not only informed the police but threw in a couple of time-dishonoured, utterly false titbits: the rebellious cotton-picker had threatened to kill him and raped his daughter.

The derivation of Tatum's nickname is uncertain: John Willie Banks, his best childhood friend, is said to have given it to him because of his habit, when playing baseball, his first sporting love, of "strutting around like an old goose"; Tatum himself would link it to a leap he once made to catch a football.[64] Alerted to Tatum when he joined the Negro Leagues' Birmingham Black Barons in 1941, Saperstein signed him for the Globetrotters. Green declared it a "marriage of two geniuses". He also described Tatum as the Globetrotters' very own fusion of Charlie Parker and Dizzy Gillespie, then busy forging a brave new word for jazz lovers, bebop. "He had a standard repertoire of gags for every game, but he was brilliant at tailoring those gags – or 'reams', the players called them – to a particular audience, improvising new twists and sudden nuances on the fly. He was like a great jazz soloist."[65]

It was the self-assured, militant Tatum who, in his first outing for the Globetrotters, urged Saperstein to allow black and white to sit together. Wowing them in venues ranging from swimming pools to sold-out arenas, Goose and the Globetrotters found themselves challenged by Max Winter, general manager of the Minneapolis Lakers. In an exhibition game played at Chicago Stadium in February 1948, Saperstein's underdogs won 61-59, easing up, prompting Winter to fling down another gauntlet. In the Windy City a year later, 20,000 saw the Globetrotters win again, 49-45; again, only their free-form larking kept it close. "They didn't just beat Whitey," avowed Green in that ESPN film, "but danced on his grave."

Unfortunately for Goose, the NBA started too late for him to transfer his show-stopping act there. Instead, he went to Hollywood and made two movies, one commemorating Saperstein and the birth of the Globetrotters. The next decade would see Goose, Abe and the Globetrotters undertake a worldwide tour that took in Berlin, Africa, Tokyo and Argentina, where they electrified the Perons. Not for four decades would Jordan gain such brand recognition.

In *Goose*, Ernie Banks, a member of baseball's first wave of African-American major leaguers, recalled Lou Brock, another future Hall of Famer, asking him what it took to succeed. "I said, 'You gotta learn to relax.' He said: 'Relax! You can relax, I can't relax. I don't want to go back to Louisiana picking no cotton. I gotta make it here, I *got* to make it.' That's what we learned from Goose Tatum – we *got* to make it."

Roberto or Bobby?

Baseball's World Series is often and widely disparaged for its doubtful and rather pompous interpretation of globalism. By the 2000s, though, it was beginning to live up to its conflated/inflated name, having featured players born not only in the wider Americas but in Australia, the Caribbean, Japan and even England. Increasingly, though, it was Hispania that ruled the waves, accounting for nearly half the players on the 2012 Series rosters for the San Francisco Giants and the Detroit Tigers – two from Puerto Rico and nine apiece from the Dominican Republic and Venezuela. To a man, they were indebted to Roberto Clemente.

In 1960, almost exactly a year before the film version of *West Side Story* would introduce New York's growing Puerto Rican populace to Londoners, Melburnians and Tokyoans, Roberto Clemente Walker, a Puerto Rican brought up near the metropolis of San Juan, did as much as anyone to help the Pittsburgh Pirates stun the New York Yankees – and pretty much the entire baseball world – by winning the club's first World Series title since 1925. He was not the first Latino major leaguer: as far back as 1871, the Cuban Estaban Bellan, whose Catholic parents had been wealthy enough to send him to New York's Fordham University, had played for the Troy Haymakers of the National Association, a forerunner of the National League.[66] Nor was he the first to claim a batting title: Bobby Avila, a leading light from the ill-fated Mexican League who had debuted for the Cleveland Indians in 1947, achieved that breakthrough in 1954, the year Al Campanis signed Clemente for the Brooklyn Dodgers. Yet to characterise Clemente as the Hispanic Jackie Robinson would not be all that much of an exaggeration; nor would it be unreasonably reductive.

In 2012, a state Senate committee unanimously approved a measure sponsored by the New Jersey senator M. Teresa Ruiz to formally request that Major League Baseball retire the number 21 in Clemente's honour, an accolade hitherto bestowed only on Robinson. "Roberto Clemente was a hero in life and death," said Ruiz. "Not only was he a gifted and talented athlete who was respected and loved by his teammates and his fans, he was a man who was recognised outside of the game for his compassion, generosity and humanitarian concern for people around the world."[67] According to the final words of his obituary in *The Black Panther*, the newspaper run by the eponymous American civil rights activists, Clemente was "a man who strove to achieve his dream of peace and justice for oppressed people throughout the world".[68]

Here, like Robinson, was assuredly no mono-dimensional, apolitical sportsman fearful of offending sponsors. Clemente had supported the Panthers' health clinics and other programmes in Philadelphia, helped younger players come to terms with the function of, and need for, unionism and collective responsibility. He had also set up the Roberto Clemente Committee for Nicaragua in mid-Cold War, at a time when President Nixon and his advisers were telling anyone who would listen that that nation was susceptible to a communist takeover. Its military leader was one Anastasio Somoza, characterised by Zirin as "an anti-communist zealot whose family had stolen 25% of Nicaragua's wealth, murdering and torturing anyone who got in their way" – all for decades and all with the White House's full fiscal and moral support; legend has it that Franklin Roosevelt was referring to Somoza's father when he uttered the unforgettable line, "Somoza may be a son of a bitch, but he's our son of a bitch." And it was to earthquake-stricken Nicaragua that Clemente, fresh from becoming just the 11th major leaguer to amass 3,000 hits, set off on New Year's Eve 1972. Furious that relief supplies were not getting through, bent on making amends in person, he overloaded a cargo plane unfit for purpose and it went down at sea, killing every last passenger; his body was never recovered. The thought of what he might have accomplished in the political arena makes his premature exit all the harder to stomach.

* * *

In sporting terms, Clemente's foremost value lay in the way he inspired Latin Americans to overcome prejudice, leading the gradual and gentle invasion of major league ballparks from those parts of the Caribbean with closer links to the US and baseball than to Britain and cricket. What awaited these pathfinders was an often torrid experience for men doubly disadvantaged, being foreigners as well as unaccustomed to segregation.

MLB demographics have altered dramatically since 1947, primarily in terms of Hispanic representation. Going into the 2012 season the thirty 25-man rosters were 61.2% white, 27.3% Latino, 8.8% African-American, 1.9% Asian, 0.1% Native American or Native Alaskan, and 0.1% Native Hawaiian or Pacific Islander. These figures prompted the Institute for Diversity and Ethics in Sport – whose director, Richard Lapchick, had declared two years earlier that baseball was "light years" ahead of when he commenced the annual study in 1987 – to trim MLB's "grade" for its handling of racial issues from 91.6 to 90.6. Its chief concern was the proportion of African-American players, up slightly year-on-year but long in overall decline. Come 2013 that share was 7.7%, the lowest since the Boston Red Sox became the last major league team to integrate 54 years earlier. Not before time, MLB set up a task force to investigate the causes.

More encouragingly, Lapchick and his colleagues noted a small increase in the percentage of "people of colour" as coaches, team vice-presidents and senior professional staff, albeit one offset by a decrease in the number of managers, general managers and league officials. In all, non-white players accounted for 38.2% of the 750-strong workforce; of that 38.2%, Latinos made up more than 71%.[69] This was by no means unreflective of the changing complexion of the US itself: by 2011, the Hispanic share of the population stood at 16%, having surged past 50m.[70]

Prior to 1947, most Latino baseballers had been subject to the same colour bar as African-Americans; the exceptions were those with lighter complexions. By the end of the 1970s, their darker brethren comprised 10% of major leaguers and 40% of minor leaguers: by 2012, the first figure had more than doubled. Initially, the majority of Latino major leaguers hailed from Cuba, where a professional league had commenced in 1878 and from where the game spread to the wider Caribbean and Latin America, but after Fidel Castro assumed the presidency and outlawed professional sport in 1959, he not only banned his subjects from playing baseball in the despised US but the talent scouts who had been scouring the island, whom he regarded as exploiters of a particularly capitalistic hue. This widened the path for what David Quentin Voight describes in his highly-praised three-volume history of the game, *American Baseball*, as "the new wave", which would see Dominican Republicans, Panamanians and Venezuelans as well as Puerto Ricans prosper in a way undreamed-of before Clemente became a Pirate. "Mostly poor boys, Hispanic prospects learned the game well by playing year round. Once scouted and signed for small bonuses, they came to America seeking gold and glory. Some found this dream, but only after confronting enough cultural shocks, caused by language differences, strange foods, and social isolation."[71] The most disturbing of the shocks to strike Clemente's generation was probably "the racial caste system" – Voight's elegant variation on "segregation":

> *For these outsiders, it was an excruciating psychological experience to engage in a highly competitive sport in a land where*

one was judged inferior because of his skin colour and was
downgraded for Hispanic origins. Caught between cultures, no
one was needed to tell these Hispanic players that they were
marginal men.[72]

Clemente, whose English was extremely limited, was no exception. When he signed that $10,000 contract to play for the Dodgers, the advice offered by his father Melchor, a sugar plantation foreman, was short and sharp: buy a decent car "and don't depend on anyone". The final 48 hours of 1954, by contrast, were heartbreaking for the Clementes. Driving the new blue Pontiac he had bought with his $5,000 signing bonus, Roberto crashed into another car that had run a red light, wrenching his neck and spine. He had been on his way to hospital, to see his elder brother Luis, who had just undergone an operation on a brain tumour; Luis died on New Year's Eve.

A year later, American baseball's complex and often disreputable machinations saw Clemente drafted by the Pirates. The reception he received from the local press, he would tell a trusted Pittsburgh broadcaster years later, was not entirely welcoming. "Every time I used to read something... about the black players, [the writers] have to say something sarcastic about it. For example, when I got to [training camp in] Fort Myers, there was a newspaper down there and the newspaper said PUERTO RICAN HOT DOG arrives in town."[73] The stereotyping angered him. He was also mindful of a recent conflagration involving Vince Power, the fellow Puerto Rican whom he had befriended when the latter came to train in Fort Myers with the Kansas City Athletics: the team bus was pulled over by police, who hauled Power off for taking a Coca-Cola from a whites-only service station. To Clemente, the message was plain: "They say, 'Roberto, you better keep your mouth shut because they will ship you back'." Shy and wary as he was, the quest for justice overrode pragmatism. "This is something that from the first day, I said to myself: 'I am the minority group. I am from the poor people. I represent the poor people. I represent the common people of

America. So I am going to be treated as a human being. I don't want to be treated like a Puerto Rican, or a black, or nothing like that. I want to be treated like any person that comes for a job.' Every person who comes for a job, no matter what type of race or colour he is, if he does the job he should be treated like whites."[74]

Clemente idolised Martin Luther King Jr, noted his biographer, David Maraniss, but in some ways he was closer, in terms of sensibility, to Malcolm X. For one thing, he was far too proud to beg. Whenever the team bus stopped at a restaurant during his early years of spring training with the Pirates, the black players would wait on the bus for their more acceptable teammates to bring back the fries and burgers: it was Clemente who ended the practice, telling his coloured colleagues that they would have to fight him first. To an extent, management buckled, providing them with a separate station wagon.[75]

The outset of the Sixties brought that national coming-out party against the Yankees, who suffered at the hands of Clemente's speed, athleticism and consistent hitting. The first Latino to start a World Series game, he would become the first to win a Most Valuable Player award for both a season (1966) and a Series (1971). Soon after his death (the normal five-year hiatus between retirement and eligibility was waived), he would also become the first to be elected to the Hall of Fame. The legacy of that car crash, however, continued to dog him: spine and neck problems persisted, though sympathy was tempered among those who pigeonholed him as a hypochondriac. "In the long run," contended Maraniss, "this perception was utterly contradicted by his enduring statistics."

Indeed, Clemente played more games for the Pirates than anyone in the club's lengthy history; he also excelled on the big occasion, most notably that 1971 World Series, which his critics spent guiltily gulping back their sniping words. Dr Roberto Buso, his physician in San Juan, told Maraniss that one manifestation of Clemente's sensitive nature was a low pain threshold. "He probably didn't help his own cause by talking so much about his ailments, but that reflected his desire to be perfect more than the need for excuses," deduced Maraniss. "Hypochondriacs cannot produce," Clemente once declaimed. "I fucking produce!"[76]

Mocked by the media for his heavy Spanish accent, an even more understandable source of ire was the disrespect displayed by sportswriters and even bubblegum card manufacturers, who insisted on Americanising his name to "Bob" or "Bobby". The Pirates' Game 7 defeat of the Baltimore Orioles to secure victory in that 1971 Series prompted Roger Angell to hail his overall performance as "something close to the level of absolute perfection, playing to win but also playing the game almost as if it were a form of punishment for everyone else on the field".[77] The most richly symbolic moment of Clemente's career came while sweat and glow were still fresh, when he was asked to say a few words for the TV millions by Bob Prince – who insisted, naturally, on calling him "Bobby". Begging leave to speak Spanish, he addressed his parents. "It was one of the most memorable acts of his life, a simple moment that touched the souls of millions of people in the Spanish-speaking world," attested Maraniss. "For the first time," said Clemente once the cameras had departed, "I have no regrets."[78]

After piloting his club to the 2005 World Series title, Ozzie Guillen, Venezuelan manager of the Chicago White Sox, revealed with no little pride that his study at home contained a shrine to Clemente. Whenever they played in Pittsburgh after his death, Tony Taylor, a Cuban infielder who earned his corn in the National League from 1958 to 1976, would escort his younger Latino colleagues out to the right-field wall once patrolled with such flair and distinction by Clemente. Wrote Maraniss: "He is your heritage, Taylor would tell them, but more than that he is what you can become."[79]

Contemporary reminders are many, including more than 200 public structures in Puerto Rico. San Juan's biggest indoor venue is the Roberto Clemente Coliseum. Roberto Clemente Bridge spans the Allegheny River in downtown Pittsburgh. Humanitarian actions by major leaguers are rewarded with the annual Roberto Clemente Award. A Clemente statue looms large at PNC Park, the Pirates' current home, where, in recognition of his shirt number, the right-field wall is 21 foot high. In the Bronx stands Roberto Clemente Park; Chicago children attend Roberto Clemente High School. There is a Roberto Clemente Stadium in Nicaragua, and another in Clemente's hometown of Carolina, where he is commemorated by street names but most prominently by a cenotaph. "The centre panel is the most telling," warranted Maraniss. "There, between the scenes of Clemente batting, running, fielding, throwing, visiting hospitals, and consoling the sick and the poor, he is depicted standing regal and alone, holding a lamb."[80]

Lacking the "necessities"

The next battleground was the athletic afterlife. Twenty-five years after his own breakthrough, a few weeks before Clemente's fatal mercy mission and just nine days before his own unfairly early death, Jackie Robinson used an invitation to address the Cincinnati crowd before the opening game of the 1972 World Series as a platform to reiterate his heartfelt desire to see a major league club hire a black manager. His namesake, Frank Robinson, soon fulfilled that wish but, 40 years later, the high proportion of African-American and especially Hispanic players (who together comprised more than 36% of the workforce) was in no way reflected in managerial ranks, let alone among administrators and owners. American football, too, had suffered from a similar inequity. Nobody articulated the disparity in outlook more damningly than the general manager of the Los Angeles Dodgers, Al Campanis: the man who had not only signed Clemente but been Robinson's teammate and friend.

On 6 April 1987, Campanis, then in his seventies, was interviewed on the ABC programme *Nightline* by Ted Koppel. Rick Kaplan, the executive producer, was assembling a panel of experts to celebrate the 40th anniversary of Robinson's debut for the Dodgers: who better to elicit memories from than his old roommate and buddy? "Al Campanis embraced Jackie Robinson when it wasn't popular to do it and he was a good guy," Kaplan would recall, "and we thought, 'Who better to help us celebrate than a white baseball player who had celebrated this extraordinary black athlete?'"[81] At one juncture, Koppel asked Campanis to explain why African-American managers and general managers were virtually nonexistent in baseball. The unscripted reply was arresting to say the least, not to say damning: "It's just that they may not have some of the necessities to be, let's say, a field manager, or, perhaps, a general manager."[82] The *necessities*? To Kaplan, it was as if a lightning bolt had struck the studio. An ad break interceded, and Koppel tried to console Campanis, who knew he had dropped the most fearful and offensive clanger.

In the 25 years following the furore, major league clubs appointed just five African-American general managers, only two of whom, Kenny Williams of the Chicago White Sox and Michael Hill of the Miami Marlins, held on to their job longer than a single season. True, there had been several prominent African-American field managers, such as Cito Gaston, who piloted the Toronto Bluejays to World Series crowns in 1992 and 1993, and Ron Washington, who guided the Texas Rangers to the Fall Classic in 2010 and 2011, but the number of appointments have been few and far between. Come the start of the 2012 season, Washington and Dusty Baker were MLB's only African-American managers. "The most lasting change," wrote Zirin, "is that people in Campanis's executive position are now far more polished, far more careful, and have become, like a 21st century politician, experts on being interviewed and saying absolutely nothing of substance. The Campanis lesson for Major League Baseball hasn't been to take on racism in the sport, but find executives who can smile for the camera and talk a cat out of a tree."

The NFL sought to even its playing field in 2003 when it introduced the "Rooney Rule", obliging franchises to interview at least one minority candidate for every managerial vacancy. It was a welcome step, though the benefits were far from immediately apparent. Ten years later, there were four head coaches of colour, including Ron Rivera, a Latino. All told, only 9% of coaches were African-American in a league where 70% of the players were African-American: the greatest disparity in a decade.[83] "In an era in which American society seems to be getting increasingly progressive when it comes to social issues, from acceptance of gay marriage to the re-election of a black president," lamented Yahoo.com's Mike Silver, "the NFL seems to be going backward."

By 2012, the more pressing problem facing MLB lay in the waning number of African-American players, which had plummeted from a high of 27% in 1975 to 8.8%. In 1959, when the Boston Red Sox completed the integration process, the proportion had been more than 17%. Half a century later, no fewer than 10 clubs had, at best, one such representative, drastically reducing the number of potential managers, as Zirin affirmed. "This coupled with the collapse in urban infrastructure, the shuttering of Boys and Girls Clubs, as well as the increasing costs of Little League baseball (and the chirping, unsubstantiated 'conventional wisdom' that inner-city kids just don't like the game because of changing cultural norms) means that African-Americans in positions of actual power will only become more scarce."[84]

The extraordinary talents of Michael Jordan, nonetheless, had certainly amplified the counter-attractions of basketball, a cheaper and far more accessible escape route for the underclass. By 2013, a teenager from the projects was immeasurably less likely to regard Prince Fielder as a role model than Kobe Bryant. In a 2007 article for *Time*, Gerald Early cut to the heart of the matter:

> *The real reason black Americans don't play baseball is that they don't want to. They are not attracted to the game. Baseball has little hold on the black imagination, even though it existed as an institution in black life for many years. Among blacks, baseball is not passed down from father to son or father to daughter. As the sports historian Michael McCambridge points out, baseball sells itself through nostalgia – the memory of being taken to a game by your father when you were a child. But for blacks, going back into baseball's past means recalling something called*

white baseball and something else called black baseball, which was meant to exist under conditions that were inferior to the white version. Even the integration of baseball, symbolised by Robinson, reminds blacks that their institutions were weak and eventually had to be abandoned. As the controversies over reparations for slavery and the Confederate flag have shown, it is difficult to sell African Americans the American past as most Americans have come to know it.[85]

Barry the Bogeyman

Come the 21st century, while black athletes now occupied some of the loftiest plinths in American society, the times had not a-changed that much. Witness the crucifixion of Barry Bonds.

When the spectre of performance-enhancing drugs began to move towards centre stage in the late 1990s, Bonds, a black baseballer and by common consent the most complete player in the game (and already deemed one of the best-ever), was pursued a good deal more virulently than his rival white slugger, Mark McGwire. In April 2011, after more than seven years of legal toing and froing, and millions of dollars in court costs, the perjury counts against Bonds were dropped but he was found guilty of obstruction of justice.

"This wasn't supposed to happen in Barack Obama's America," argued Zirin. "We were told that these sorts of prosecutions wouldn't be the priority of an Eric Holder Justice Department. But just as Guantanamo Bay detention centres and military tribunals have remained in place, the perjury witch-hunt trial of Major League Baseball's home run king, Barry Lamar Bonds, continued unabated and has now reached an ugly conclusion. What did Bonds do to 'obstruct justice'? According to one juror, 'Steve', the obstruction of justice charged was reached because, 'The whole grand jury testimony was a series of evasive answers. There were pointed questions that were asked three or four different ways that never got clearly answered. That's how we came to that.' Wow. Apparently, a 'series of evasive answers' lines you up for a 10-year sentence behind bars.

By that standard, Dick Cheney, Karl Rove, and Scooter Libby should be breaking rocks in Leavenworth for their performance at the Valerie Plame[86] trial."[87] Further support came from Victor Conte, the founder of the Bay Area Laboratory Collective that had supplied Bonds's trainer, Greg Anderson, with the PEDs he denied having knowingly used; Conte had already accepted the consequences and gone to prison. Assuredly no friend of Bonds, he nevertheless railed against the verdict: this, he assured *USA Today*, "is all about the selected persecution of Barry Bonds".[88]

In the event, Bonds was sentenced to two years' probation, 250 hours of community service, a $4,000 fine and 30 days' home confinement, none of which he had served or coughed up by the time the 9th Circuit Court of Appeals judges began hearing his appeal in February 2013. "Federal appellate judges in San Francisco challenged a prosecutor's assertion ex-big league slugger Barry Bonds misled the BALCO grand jury," reported the venerable news agency, United Press International. "Two of the three judges who heard argument in Bonds' effort to void his obstruction-of-justice conviction asked Assistant U.S. Attorney Merry Chan how Bonds' initial rambling answers before the grand jury were misleading if they ultimately were followed by short, direct responses to questions," the *San Francisco Chronicle* reported. "Judge Michael Hawkins noted at one point prosecutors asked Bonds the same question and he flatly denied, three times, that his trainer, Greg Anderson, had ever given him self-injectable drugs... Hawkins said regardless of the truth of Bonds' answers, 'it is no longer evasive'."[89]

Never one to kow-tow to the media, Bonds had caused a furore in 2004 when he spoke with characteristic frankness of his ambition to break every last one of Babe Ruth's records while admitting that he wouldn't mind overmuch if he fell short of Hank Aaron, his fellow African-American, who had so dismayed white America by beating The Babe's collection of 714 home runs (in the event, Bonds would overhaul both). When Bonds was attacked for expressing views that some construed as racist, he was quick to remind his critics that his first wife was white. Racism, he claimed, "is something we, as African-American athletes, live with every day. I don't need a headline that says, 'Bonds says there's racism in the game of baseball'. We all know it. It's just some people don't want to admit it. They're going to play dumb like they don't know what the hell is going on."[90]

"Why are we even here?" his attorney, Cristina Arguedas, had wondered at one juncture during his perjury trial. Zirin's response was pithy and priceless: "We're here because Major League Baseball and the US government [have] long decided that Barry Bonds would shoulder the burden for the steroid era. We're here because a surly black athlete who thinks that the press is just a step above vermin was easy pickings for an industry rife with systemic corruption… this is the story of the black athlete today: die a hero or live long enough to be a villain."[91]

II. For the Common Wealth

I do not agree that the dog in a manger has the final right to the manger even though he may have lain there for a very long time. I do not admit that right. I do not admit for instance, that a great wrong has been done to the Red Indians of America or the black people of Australia. I do not admit that a wrong has been done to these people by the fact that a stronger race, a higher-grade race, a more worldly wise race to put it that way, has come in and taken their place.

Winston Churchill[1]

It is a measure of how we have progressed that Winston Churchill's comments to the Peel Commission on Palestine are exceedingly likely to strike you, more than three-quarters of a century on, as just a tad reprehensible, not to say faintly shocking. That they should have emanated from the mouth of the man voted the greatest Briton of all, in a nationwide BBC poll conducted as recently as 2002 (ahead, some would say perversely, of Messrs Shakespeare, Dickens, Lennon, McCartney, Connery, Shankly and Berners-Lee), only serves to emphasise, yet again, that history is not written by the losers. Mind you, the old cigar-chomping devil was not all that choosy about whom he insulted. After all, he did describe Mahatma Gandhi as "a fakir", railed against the "Jewish conspiracy" and advocated poisonous gas as a means of silencing the "uncivilised tribes" of Iraq. He also wanted to sterilise the mentally ill.[2]

All the same, however far we have come, it remains distinctly sobering to note the racial composition of the crowds when South Africa stages international sport: for football matches, the vast majority are black; when the ball is oval or made of cork, you might well suspect you've jumped into The Tardis and landed 50 years ago. In the former British Empire, this sporting life has never been straightforward.

Cricket and colonialism

The talented and elongated tentacles of that empire meant that no sport has pitted whites against non-whites quite like cricket. In the late 1870s and early 1880s, as Boria Majumdar put it, the cricket field in Bombay became "a site for indigenous assertion".[3] As Ramachandra Guha noted, European polo players were "the agents of disruption", playing on the maidan where the natives customarily played cricket. "Their struggle to evict polo from the maidan provides a fascinating window on the cultural life of the Empire, and demonstrates how quickly and how energetically Indians had made cricket their game."[4]

The first widely celebrated non-white sportsman was Ranjitsinhji Vibhaji, who enchanted cricket-watchers while playing for England and Sussex at the tail-end of the 19th century. While his origins and outward appearance should have made him a rank outsider in late Victorian England, he had overcome those inherent disadvantages by studying at Cambridge University, his chief seat of cricket learning. Not that acceptance was immediate. In his early outings for Trinity College in 1892, recounted Ronald Wild, his first biographer, he "was ignored by other members of the team, and sometimes sat alone and friendless in the pavilion".[5] "It is important to keep in mind," wrote Satadru Sen in the *Journal of Colonialism and Colonial History*, "that had Ranjitsinhji not played English games, he would never have become an Indian prince. He would, in all likelihood, have languished as a minor casualty of the politics of a minor Indian state."[6]

Before Ranji went to Cambridge, professional cricket had been a rather austere game, its unwritten code so entrenched that any shots not played to the offside were regarded as poor form, ungentlemanly and surefire evidence of low breeding. "Ranji" bequeathed it both the leg-cut and leg-glance, technical innovations whose delicacy and hazardous lateness of execution were utterly alien. As was his appearance – and not simply because of his complexion. "The shirt, always of silk, always fully large, was his most distinctive feature," observed one contemporary writer. "It bellied and flapped round his body like a sail at every moment of the breeze. And there he stood at the wicket, the very embodiment of grace and elegance, almost careless and lazy in attitude, so perfect and relaxed was the whole poise of the slight delicate figure."[7]

Ranji is habitually painted as an Anglophile with scant concern for his countrymen, but as Majumdar points out, a speech he delivered to the League of Nations in 1922, wherein he spoke out against restrictions on Indian immigration and the empire's policy towards South Africa, suggests otherwise.

> *I should feel false to my fellow countrymen in India, and also to my fellow countrymen in South Africa, were I to neglect this unique opportunity of summoning to their assistance of their aspirations the spiritual power and the spiritual blessing of your sympathy... What is our ideal? What is our purpose? What is the very reason of our being? Let us have catholic justice and we shall have catholic peace.*[8]

Climbing ev'ry mountain

If the illustrious members of the selection panel for Saturn, Jupiter and Earth were to nominate an All-Time XI to take on any combination of cricketers any other solar system might have up its sleeve, they could go for the safe option: hand the captaincy to Don Bradman and let him do the picking. Or else they could make a wider point and plump for the following: Gordon Greenidge, George Headley, Viv Richards, Brian Lara, Everton Weekes, Frank Worrell, Garry Sobers, Jeffrey Dujon (wicketkeeper), Malcolm Marshall, Curtly Ambrose and Lance Gibbs. Bradman's nominees might conceivably win by a greater distance, but the bravura, joy and sheer affirmation of the human spirit on show would do a great deal more for intergalactic relations.

In the annals of post-slavery civilisation, has any act of mountaineering been more inspirational than the rise through cricket's craggy crevasses of the representatives of a group of far-flung sectors within the segment of the Caribbean once presided over by Whitehall and Buckingham Palace; a collection of superficially idyllic islands known collectively – albeit *exclusively* on the fields of play – as the West Indies. *Sports Illustrated*, the in-house magazine for the American sector of Planet Sport, more or less agreed when, alongside the San Francisco 49ers of Joe Montana and Jerry Rice (well, it is an American publication), it anointed the teams captained by Clive Lloyd and Viv Richards as the joint-best collective of the 1980s. Their foremost contribution, though, lay in alerting the world that the calypsos penned in their honour masked a determination to subvert the traditional world order. If this book could tell just one story of sporting heroism, it would be the journey to their destination.

Cricket clubs were a known presence in the Caribbean in 1806, attested Rowland Bowen, "and probably very much earlier".[9] Economic resources aside, the biggest barrier to inter-island fixtures was the distance between them. In 1900, Demerara, Barbados and Trinidad competed in a triangular series, but not until after the Second World War, when air transport became readily available, did Jamaica commence even semi-regular matches against the other islands. In 1956, British Guiana hosted a four-team knock-out event, repeated five years later with the addition of the Combined Islands team representing the Windward Isles and their Leeward neighbours. Continued travel problems nevertheless rendered an annual competition impractical until the advent of cheaper and more reliable flights. Not until the 1965-66 season did the Shell Shield come into being.

It says much for the hold the game had long exerted that a regional representative team had ventured to foreign fields 80 years earlier. "It took the considerable sum of £1,000, local currency, to launch the first global West Indian missile – fourteen amateur cricketers sent into Canadian and American space during the summer of 1886,"[10] wrote Hilary Beckles. Sailing in three separate boats from Barbados, Demerara and Jamaica, the tourists were "economic members of the inward-looking, decaying sugar world, (who) chose to break with the past and swim against the tide". Of their 13 fixtures against sides in territories growing ever more enamoured of baseball and increasingly antipathetic towards cricket, six were won, five lost and two drawn. "For the post-slavery Caribbean," asserts Beckles, "it was the first giant step into Western modernity, an intensely competitive imperial world quickly learning how to turn its back upon small places which were once of greater value than continental spaces."[11] A reciprocal visit followed the next year; 1887 also brought an account of that pathfinding expedition, *The Memory*, credited to "One of Them", aka Laurence Fyfe, the Jamaican captain. According to Bowen, this was the region's first sporting hardback: it was published in Georgetown, in what was then the sugar-rich island of Demerara, part of British Guiana. These days it is the only venue in South America to stage Test matches.

Another party sailed to England in 1900. The schedule was not afforded first-class status, and although this was remedied for the second such tour in 1906, as Beckles avers, "there remained racial attitudes within the English cricket establishment that viewed West Indian players as inferior and inadequate". In our old pal Plum Warner, fortunately, they had a useful friend and advocate. Born in the Trinidadian capital of Port of Spain in 1873, Pelham Francis Warner was the latest of 18 children sired from two marriages by the son of the island's Old Etonian attorney general, Charles B. Warner, a leading member of the Caribbean white elite, then a spry 68. "In him," writes Beckles, "we see the colourfully textured ways in which colonialism struggled to embrace and promote organised cricket as popular culture." Most significantly, it was Warner who launched "an ideological campaign, in the calm and subtle manner expected of the late Victorian scholar-cricketer, to throw open the gates of West Indian cricket to all men of talent and social quality regardless of their race, colour or class. He was hailed in the West Indies as a supporter of cricket's democratic impulse… and an advocate of its finest, humanitarian values."[12]

The composition of the island XIs at the time offered a twist on the Gentlemen-Players class divide in England. In 1926, as Warner's efforts to secure Test status for the region gathered pace, MCC sent a party to the Caribbean and found the skills of the opposition being apportioned along racial lines: white batsmen, black bowlers. "The ideological assumption," explained Beckles, "was the climactic theory of plantation development which held that white men could not labour at high productivity levels under a tropical sun, and that black men could – hence the slave trade and African populations in the colonial worlds of the Americas. Fast bowling was… considered a process of brutish hard labour while batsmanship was an art – or science – that emerged from the workings of the intellect."[13]

Learie Constantine clouded the waters. Here was both deadly fast bowler and swashbuckling batsman, not to mention one of the most athletic and prehensile fielders the game had ever seen. Cricket coursed through the family veins. A foreman on a Trinidadian sugar estate, his father, Lebrun, had been a member of those first tour parties to England, becoming the first player from the region to score a century there; an uncle, Victor Pascall, had bowled for Trinidad; family practice also featured his mother, who kept wicket. While Learie was "not a pauper", acknowledged his fellow Trinidadian, the writer, political activist and cricket-besotted C.L.R James, "he was not a prince".[14]

Encouraged to train as a lawyer, Constantine gravitated to professional cricket out of economic necessity. "There were big firms who subscribed to all sorts of sporting events and causes," observed James, a dedicated Marxist. "Anyone of a dozen of them could have given him a job at a desk. He could have earned his keep. But the Constantine they recognised bowled, batted and fielded. He had no existence otherwise. There was the Government. He got an acting post in the Education Office. An acting man does not wish to imperil his chances by asking for leave. So that when Constantine was invited to British Guiana to play for All West Indies against MCC [in 1926] he did not ask for leave."[15] Into the breach stepped H. B. G. Austin. The son of a bishop, it was this senior Barbados MP and business tycoon, who also happened to be an immensely influential West Indies captain, who engineered the young man leave on full pay. So much, recalled James, for the sway of the Trinidad elite: "We looked and noted and swore impotently." Indeed, instead of a full-time post in the Education Office, Constantine, like so many black Caribbean athletes of the time, found "refuge in the oilfields", where staff were either white or extremely light of complexion, or black, and "beyond a certain limit dark could not aspire".[16]

Constantine's most important benefactor proved, nonetheless, to be H. C. W. Johnson of Trinidad Leaseholds, "who gave me a fairly good job, took the greatest interest in my cricket, gave me leave whenever I wanted on half-pay, and when I finally left for England [in 1928] told me that my job would be left open for me whenever I came back." It seemed far from coincidental that Johnson was "a stranger to Trinidad and a South African besides".[17]

In James's memorable phrase, Constantine revolted "against the revolting contrast between his first-class status as a cricketer and his third-class status as a man"[18]. His ambition when he arrived in England, where he began his law studies, was to cover himself in such glory with his feats that he would be invited to stay. And so he did, and was: in 1929, he signed as a professional for Nelson, the Lancashire League club, the precursor to a new life in which he and the newly migrated James would share a roof. In many of the towns he played the local children had never seen a coloured face, spurring him to give speeches and distribute pamphlets, the better to foster understanding of what it was like to own one.

There was a rude reminder of the prejudice at work in England when, in 1943, for all the repute he had acquired in his playing days, despite having paid a deposit and despite having been assured that there was no objection to their colour, he and his family were barred from staying at London's Imperial Hotel. He duly instituted proceedings for breach of contract ("for failing to receive and lodge him") but despite winning the suit, the damages awarded amounted to a paltry £5. Not that he laboured under any illusions. "Almost the entire population in Britain really expect the coloured man to live in an inferior area... devoted to coloured people," he claimed in *The Colour Bar*, published in 1954 and one of two tomes he co-wrote with James. "Most British people would be quite unwilling for a black man to enter their homes, nor would they wish to work with one as a colleague, nor stand shoulder to shoulder with one at a factory bench."

"In 1950, when our team was comprised of stars such as the three Ws, Ramadhin and Valentine, it was the rule rather than the exception to find young autograph hunters on the railway platforms asking, 'Is Mr. Constantine with you?'"[19] Thus recalled another member of that white Trinidadian elite, Jeffrey Stollmeyer, who for six decades served the game nobly as Test opener, captain, selector, manager and board president, referring to his second tour of Britain. Called to the Bar, Constantine's tireless work on behalf of Britain's struggling immigrants yielded a place on the Race Relations Board and the BBC board of governors; there was also a trail of honours: an MBE, a knighthood, a life peerage as Baron Constantine of Maraval and Nelson. He returned to Trinidad briefly in the early 1960s, becoming an MP and Minister of Works, but soon grew disillusioned with politics and returned to his adopted home as High Commissioner in London. He was awarded the Trinity Cross, Trinidad's highest honour, but England, nonetheless, had the best of him. In James's view, "if Constantine had had not only honour but a little profit in his own country he never would have settled abroad... had his skin been white, or even light, he would have been able to choose a life at home."[20]

Yet despite the presence of Headley and Constantine, "the components of the team were not welded together to frame a sturdy structure", lamented Beckles. "The team remained riddled with racism and class arrogance, and players from different social backgrounds did not feel each other's needs because no natural channels of communication existed between them. In general, whites did not socialise with non-whites off the field, and blacks were divided among themselves by attitudes derived from their reading of how privilege operated within colonial society." The progress made by Constantine and Headley "effectively highlighted the peculiar legacies of a home-grown apartheid system that seemed on the retreat and therefore not as crude as its counterpart in South Africa".[21]

The next breakthrough came in 1948 when the MCC party arrived for the first postwar tour of the islands: the home board finally bowed to 20 years of "persistent pressure" by the likes of Constantine and political figures such as James and Marcus Garvey: Headley was appointed captain – albeit for only half the scheduled four Tests, in Barbados and Jamaica. That said, by threatening to boycott their match (for which Headley, in the event, was injured), the Jamaican public was felt by many to have forced the selectors' hands. "That a black man from the lower orders of colonial society could lead a prestigious public institution, and direct the cultural activities of white men of property," marvelled Beckles, "seemed more than ordinary."[22]

The Headley genes also proved extraordinary: both his son, Ron, and grandson, Dean, played Test cricket, the latter for England. Never has there been a cricketing dynasty to match George and his worthy heirs.

The final frontier[23]

Nor should James's own role in the development of Caribbean cricket be underestimated. A man of many parts – author, historian, journalist, poet, playwright, lecturer and Anglophile – he spent much of his life in London and McCarthyite America; forced to leave the latter because of his political convictions and actions, he spent the last phase of his rich, driven but far from prosperous life in a modest flat in Brixton, south London. An east London library was named in his honour. In 1987, he was awarded the Trinity Cross.

James's most important work was *The Black Jacobins*, an account of the Haitian Revolution acclaimed as a key study of the black diaspora, which was banned in South Africa until the death of apartheid. Not that that stopped it reaching appreciative hands there, sometimes in the shape of copied chunks, sometimes in clusters of pages. Even so, the best-known of his copious outpourings remains *Beyond a Boundary*. Published in 1963, it has often been acclaimed as the best book ever written about the competitive arts, though to describe it as a sports book is to diminish its breadth as well as to ignore its most famous line: "What do they know who only cricket know?"

While in part a love letter to cricket, *Beyond a Boundary* was first, last and pretty much everything about racial struggle. With clamour for independence from Britain growing, the racial mix of West Indies XIs gradually shifting and the shortlived Federation of the West Indies forming in 1958, the back end of that decade found James, now editing the independence movement's newspaper, *The Nation*, "waging an all-out campaign", as he put it, to install a full-time black captain. Happily, the man whose credentials he tirelessly promoted was Frank Worrell, long admired by James for "the dignity which radiates from [his] every motion".[24] In Constantine's words, he was "a great cricketer and a greater man".[25]

If James was destined to chronicle the rise of his fellow Trinidadian, Worrell was his cause célèbre. "Once in a lifetime," he would rejoice, "a writer is handed on a plate a gift from heaven." Worrell was that gift. In furthering his cause as West Indies captain, James was obliged to surrender a conviction he had once held dear: "According to the colonial version of the game, you were to show yourself a 'true sport' by not making a fuss about the most barefaced discrimination because it wasn't cricket. Not me any longer. To that I had said, was saying, my final good-bye."[26]

One of the most prolific batsmen of the immediate postwar era, Worrell was merely one of three world-class batsmen who had grown up within a short radius of each other in Bridgetown, the capital of Barbados: along with Clyde Walcott and Everton Weekes, he formed a formidable middle-order triumvirate known as the "Three Ws". Together, they laid the foundations for the West Indies' historic first Test series victory in England. That red-letter feat came in 1950, two summers after the first postwar wave of Caribbean immigration; lured by job offers in the needy ranks of London Transport and the new National Health Service, many of those whose relatives had fought alongside Britain in the Second World War had shipped into Southampton aboard *The Empire Windrush*, a social shift that would prove problematic but rewarding for all parties. How they flocked to Lord's and The Oval that mid-century summer. Their reward was a triumph hailed four decades later by John Figueroa, the Jamaican writer and educator, as the start of a crucial contribution to a noble cause, demonstrating to "people ever so sure of themselves, and of their right to win, that the mighty can fall – even in their own territory".[27] A toweringly symbolic Test success at Lord's even sired a popular song, *Victory Calypso, Lord's 1950* by Egbert Moore, aka Lord Beginner, the hook an enduring couplet toasting the matchwinning spinners: *Those little pals o' mine/Ramadhin and Valentine.*

Seven years later, after a collectively calamitous tour of England, Worrell was offered the captaincy, but his studies at Manchester University obliged him to decline. "That offer didn't matter very much to some of us," wrote James.

> *Worrell as captain at home or in India was bad enough, but that could be swallowed by the manipulators. What was at stake was the captaincy in Australia and still more in England. [The board's] whole point was to continue to send to populations of white people, black or brown men under a white captain. The more brilliantly the black men played, the more it would emphasise to millions of English people: "Yes, they are fine players, but, funny, isn't it, they cannot be responsible for themselves – they must always have a white man to lead them."[28]*

Worrell was at the centre of a fraught and complex issue in 1959, when South Africa's non-white communities proposed an informal tour by a West Indies party, which he was projected to lead. James and Constantine took opposing stances. To the latter, acceptance of the conditions laid down by the Pretoria regime was, in effect, an endorsement of apartheid. "Do the Africans who live under apartheid thereby accept it?" countered James. "Surely that is absurd. Do our boys accept it? I cannot see that at all. I once spent six months in the USA organising a strike of sharecroppers. I was kicked around as usual, eating in kitchens when I travelled, sitting in the rear seats of buses, etc. Did I 'accept' segregation? Did I help strengthen it? The facts are that I did exactly the opposite. The sharecroppers whom I worked with had a larger objective."[29]

To James, this landmark expedition was a necessity. Delighted by the stir already created ("the whole world is talking about it"), he touted it as "a brilliant political step". He even wanted to see "an African make a century in the first Test, bowl Sobers and Kanhai for 0 in the same over". It would all be in a good cause, inspiring headlines outside Africa and, more importantly, within. "Think of what it will mean to the African masses, their pride, their joy, their contact with the world outside, and their anger at this first proof, before the whole world, of the shameful suppression to which they are subjected. Will this strengthen apartheid? To believe that is to substitute laws for human emotions."[30] Even before the idea was abandoned, James felt the tour was already "a political bombshell". Now he wanted it to "go on exploding and exploding". The only people who could be hurt were white South Africans: "I want them hurt and plenty."

Scrutinised from a distance of half a century, this perspective may be surprising, knowing as we now do the benefits of sticking to the Sam Ramsamy line about the impossibility of playing normal sport in an abnormal society, as would be reinforced by Nelson Mandela's oft-stated gratitude to the sporting boycotters in general and Basil D'Oliveira in particular for helping bring down apartheid. Indeed, one of sporting history's great what-ifs can be traced to the abortive tour James so enthusiastically supported: had it taken place, D'Oliveira, then South Africa's finest coloured player, might never have written a pleading letter to John Arlott, a vehement denouncer of apartheid, a letter that resulted in him migrating to England and, through his feats, bringing that indefensible regime – and the complicity of the English political and cricket establishment – into focus as never before (in 2003, fittingly, Mandela thanked D'Oliveira in person). On the other hand, when James stated his seemingly uncharacteristic position, the merits and de-merits of isolating South Africa were only just gestating. A few months later, on 21 March 1960, 69 black demonstrators would be massacred outside Sharpeville police station. From then on, resistance would harden, organise and spread, in and out of Africa.

James, and justice, finally had their way when Worrell was appointed to lead the 1960-61 tour of Australia, where his team enchanted crowds with a brand of adventurous and effervescent cricket utterly at odds with the philosophy of the day; in doing so, they envigorated a game dying on its cautious feet.

Almost incredibly, the first Test in Brisbane was tied – the first such outcome international cricket had produced; as I write, there has been just one since. In their previous 13 Tests against the brand leaders, West Indies had won twice and lost 11. Although the hosts would take this series 2-1, the thrills and nerve-gnawing closeness of three of the subsequent four contests confirmed that the West Indies were a force to be reckoned with. The crowd for the opening day of the final Test in Melbourne was 90,800, a record only beaten since by the 100,000 who saw the 1999 India-Pakistan Test in Kolkata. At the end of that gripping match at the MCG, Worrell was feted by a quarter of a million Melbournians, who thronged the city's streets to bid farewell to the man accorded the lion's share of the credit for what is still widely considered to be the most memorable Test series of all. "It was as though," wrote Worrell's first biographer, Ernest Eytle, "they had been delegated by the whole of Australia to express its congratulations and thanks…"[31]: no mean accolade given the deplorable treatment of the Aboriginals and the imposition of a "white Australia" policy. James hailed it as "a gesture spontaneous and in cricket without precedent, one

people speaking to another".[32] From that day on, the protagonists would compete for the Frank Worrell Trophy.

Confirming the abundant class evident under Worrell on
the victorious 1963 tour of England, the next time Australia
met the West Indies, in the spring of 1965, the latter prevailed.
Sobers, the incomparable all-rounder and new captain, was in
his virtuosic pomp; batsmen Rohan Kanhai and Conrad Hunte,
and bowlers Wes Hall, Charlie Griffith and Gibbs were all firmly
in the groove. For the first time in the game's history, neither
England nor Australia ruled the roost.

Apartheid

> *It was only possible for sports to play the role they did in the
> struggle against apartheid because on sport's level playing field
> poor and black nations enjoyed a clout they did not have in the
> military or economic field. West Indies in cricket or the African
> nations in athletics had something the West wanted, and with-
> holding it was a real (if minor) punishment and therefore a lever
> for change. So the sports sanctions preceded and, along with an
> irrepressible mass internal movement, helped pave the way for
> the banking, investment and trade sanctions that ultimately did
> for apartheid.*

Mike Marqusee[33]

The notion of players and teams not being selected on merit
cuts against the grain of everything for which sport stands. In
reality, the examples, of course, are too numerous to mention
individually. Nowhere, though, has this betrayal – for good as
well as ill – been more prominent than in the case of South Africa
before the most important second coming of modern times, the
release of Nelson Mandela. In 1995, now President Mandela, his
approving presence as South Africa's "16th Man" during their
Rugby World Cup final triumph over New Zealand was hailed
as a corner turned, though the team he so visibly supported –
numbering as it did just one black constituent – represented the
Rainbow Nation more in symbolic than demographic terms. As

Simon Barnes recalled shortly after Mandela's death in 2013: "Mandela pulled off the biggest photo-op political stunt of all time by turning up for the final wearing a Springbok shirt – a hated symbol of apartheid – bearing the number of the SA captain, Francois Pienaar...Where Hitler refused to shake hands with Jesse Owens, Mandela shook hands with the hearty blond Afrikaner rugger bugger Pienaar – while wearing his shirt, just like an autograph-seeking fan. Mandela was able to show his nation and the world the greatness of his vision because sport is what it is. Sport was vital in winning the war against apartheid and was perhaps more significant when it came to winning the peace."[34]

D'Oliveira was merely the latest in a long line of non-white cricketers denied the opportunity to represent South Africa. Missing from the party chosen for the nation's first representative cricket tour of England in 1894 was "Krom" Hendricks, a fast bowler of Malay extraction and the pre-eminent black player. Those who were selected had no desire whatsoever to play with or against anyone who wasn't white. The chaps helping the English run the country were no less keen to ensure their flag would be flown solely by their own kind. Two years later, Charlie "Buck" Llewellyn, the son of an English father and a black mother, became the first non-white player to represent South Africa, but suffered from the taunts of teammates as well as erratic selection, driving him to England to live. "The English understood and accepted their policy," reasoned Beckles, "as consistent with their own thinking and sense of imperial order."[35]

For almost the whole of the second half of the next century, the topic of South Africa would cause soul-searching among scores of ringmasters, hundreds of players and millions of sports aficionados. All the same, without wishing in any way to defend the indefensible abhorrence that is apartheid, in whatever guise and under whatever flag, it is worth reminding ourselves, before we examine South Africa's weighty contribution to sporting infamy, of a salient if often overlooked fact: not only were others strongly complicit, but South Africa was not alone in operating a mono-racial sporting system. Even though that first Australian party to England, as we have already seen, was purely Aboriginal, Ian Chappell, one of that purportedly lucky country's greatest captains, was still pushing for full and proper recognition of the tour nearly a century and a half later. In his 2013 film *Utopia*, John Pilger, that formidable Australian documentarian and activist, wonders whether his country has inherited South African apartheid. So far as he was concerned, it was time to share the shame.

* * *

No racial struggle has united the world quite so effectively as the battle to overcome apartheid (for once, the military metaphor seems absolutely appropriate). Introduced in 1948 by South Africa's prime minister, Henrik Verwoerd, this system of enforced segregation and two-tier rights would endure for the best part of half a century, subjugating millions and depriving them of their human rights with a chilling proficiency to which even American segregation could only aspire. Sport contributed weightily to its eventual demise. After all, the apartheid laws corrupted the competitive arts every bit as efficiently as they did everyday existence.

In 1998, Enuga Sreensivasulu Reddy wrote an essay commemorating the 60th birthday of Sam Ramsamy. Entitled "Sports and the liberation struggle", the following extract[36] sketches the background to the institutional forces and mindset that inflamed and united so many.

> *International action against apartheid sport began in earnest in 1963… when Sewsunker "Papwa" Sewgolum, an Indian golf caddie, won the Natal Open Golf Championship. He was not allowed inside the clubhouse where whites were celebrating. The photograph of "Papwa" receiving his trophy in heavy rain outside appeared in many newspapers around the world and greatly helped the boycott of apartheid sport. (He was banned from all major tournaments in South Africa after 1963.)*

Since SAN-ROC [the South African Non-Racial Olympic Committee] was prevented from sending representatives abroad, the British Anti-Apartheid Movement sent appeals to Olympic Committees and other national sports bodies to exclude apartheid sport from international competition. The IOC adopted a proposal by India which led to the exclusion of South Africa from the Tokyo Olympics in 1964. It was formally expelled from the IOC in 1970.

The response of the authorities was repression against the non-racial sports movement. Dennis Brutus, secretary of SASA and later President of SAN-ROC, was refused a passport and served with stringent "banning orders". He managed to escape to Mozambique in 1963 and tried to go to the IOC meeting, but the Portuguese authorities handed him over to South Africa. He was incarcerated on Robben Island and left for Britain on release. John Harris, Chairman of SAN-ROC, was also refused a passport, restricted and then detained. Utterly frustrated, he joined a white armed resistance movement and was executed in 1965. SAN-ROC was paralysed, until it was revived in London in 1966.

The Vorster regime also began openly to interfere in sports. It issued a Proclamation in February 1965, under the "Group Areas Act", prohibiting any mixed sports or even mixed audiences, except by permit. (Until then, segregation in sport was by "custom", not law). In the few cases when permits were granted, the organisers were required to separate spectators by race, with six-foot wire fences, and provide separate entrances, toilets, canteens etc. In some events, only Coloured people and Indians were allowed.

"They'll never let you play"

Fighting American racism was not enough for Arthur Ashe. "I am an African-American, one born in the grip of legal segregation. Aside from my feelings about religion and family, my innermost strivings inevitably have to do with trying to overcome racism and other forms of social injustice, with the search for dignity and power for blacks in a world so often hostile to us. Not the tennis court but the arena of protest and politics would be the most significant testing ground for me in the middle years of my life." He would die at 49, and wrote those words knowing the end was nigh.

That search for dignity extended to South Africa's benighted majority. In 1985, Ashe resigned as non-playing captain of the US Davis Cup team. In truth, as he soon confessed to the sports editor of *Jet*, an African-American magazine, he was "forced out" by the United States Tennis Association. Around the turn of the year, he had been arrested in Washington DC while participating in a demonstration against the South African government's barbaric laws. "I believe that my role in publicly protesting against apartheid probably had something [to do with losing the job]." No, nobody from the USTA had actually said this to his face, but he'd heard it from "other sources". While he had no doubt that apartheid was "abhorrent to some of these people", this implied that he believed some were considerably less perturbed. To such people, "demonstrating in the streets against [apartheid] might be even more abhorrent... but I hate injustice more than I love decorum."[37] He was "no radical", he insisted, but many in sport, he felt, were "terrified of taking a stand on political affairs, or on controversial questions of social justice".

South Africa came "quietly, innocently" into Ashe's life one June afternoon in 1968, at London's Queens Club, perennial stage for the main pre-Wimbledon tournament. Cliff Drysdale, South Africa's leading serve-and-volleyer, mentioned that his national tournament, the first of the brave new world of "Open" tennis, had been scheduled for Johannesburg in the autumn. "They'll never let you play," he assured Ashe. "Why, is it *that* bad?" replied the startled American. "Oh, the Lawn Tennis Association would let you play," explained Drysdale. "I'm pretty sure of that. In fact, they would love to have you come. But you would need a visa to enter South Africa, and the government would never let you have one."[38] Ashe mailed his application; it was rejected. As it would be in each of the following three years.

He was finally granted a visa in 1973, and went back the next year, and the one after that; on each occasion, his insistence that there be no segregated seating was honoured. "I looked apartheid directly in the face, saw the appalling WHITES ONLY and NONWHITES ONLY signs, the separate and drastically unequal facilities very much like those of my childhood in Virginia. I saw the sneer of superiority on the faces of many whites, and the look of obsequiousness, fatalism, cynicism, and despair on the faces of many blacks."[39] One day, while walking round Ellis Park, South Africa's rugby union shrine and sporting citadel-in-chief, he found himself being pursued by a teenaged black boy. Upon being asked why he was following him, the bemused boy offered a plausible alibi: "You are the first truly free black man I have ever seen."[40]

Not that Ashe's visits to the Republic were regarded with universal appreciation. Winnie Mandela, wife of the then-imprisoned Nelson, sent him a note thanking him for coming while warning him, and any similarly inclined Americans, not to imagine they could think for black South Africans. "The best thing you can do," she commended, "is ask the South Africans what you can do to help in their struggle." During one speech at the largely black Howard University in Washington DC, two African students tried to drown the honoured guest out with cries of "Uncle Tom!", "Shame on you!" and "Traitor!" In their estimation, he had betrayed his "black brothers". Shocked, the normally composed Ashe stopped in mid-flow. He was livid. Uncharacteristically, he turned on his assailants: "Why don't you tell everybody in this hall tonight why, if you are so brave and militant, you are hiding away in the United States and not confronting apartheid in South Africa? And also tell us how you as radicals expect to win international support for your cause when you give vent to your anger and rage as you have done here tonight... What do you expect to achieve when you give in to passion and invective and surrender the high moral ground that alone can bring you victory?" Response there was none, but Ashe recalled immediately resuming his speech and completing it in silence.[41]

In 1980, shortly after Ashe's appointment as Davis Cup captain, by when the United Nations had imposed a cultural boycott of South Africa, his countryman John McEnroe signed up for a one-off exhibition match against his arch-rival, Sweden's Bjorn Borg, to be played in Bophuthatswana – in Ashe's words one of the Republic's "phony 'independent' states". The carrots were certainly juicy: $750,000 to the winner and even $600,000 to the loser (reportedly bankrolled, for the most part, by US broadcaster NBC). Tightly controlled by Pretoria, and hence unrecognised by most other nations, the American heavy-weight boxer, Mike Weaver, had recently fought the South African Gerrie Coetzee there. Not wanting McEnroe "to appear to collude with apartheid", Ashe approached his father, John McEnroe Sr., a lawyer as well as his son's chief adviser, warning him of the inevitable outcry. Soon afterwards, McEnroe Sr. announced that the deal was off.[42]

Yet compared with the members of the Commonwealth, Ashe and his countrymen remained largely untouched by the sporting repercussions of apartheid, primarily because of their distant relationship with international team competition. By the outset of the 1970s, sport's role in isolating South Africa, amplified by the D'Oliveira Affair, was in full swing. Though business links with the outside world continued to buoy the National Party, the republic's representatives were no longer participating in either the Olympic Games or football's World Cup. It was not so much that those in command at the IOC and FIFA were given to public tirades about apartheid (anything but), more that the threat of boycotts by other nations would have ruined their showpieces.

A Davis Cup tie between South Africa and the US in 1977 was halted when anti-apartheid protestors ran on to the court in Newport Beach, California and poured a carton of motor oil over the surface, whereupon the home captain, Tony Trabert, leapt from his chair and struck two of the invaders with a racquet; when demonstrators tried to display a banner, they suffered likewise. South Africa's continued inclusion in the

American Zone qualifiers had put several noses out of joint – Canada, Mexico, Venezuela and the Commonwealth Caribbean withdrew, while the wary Colombians gave up home advantage against the Republic and played the tie in Johannesburg – but this attracted comparatively little attention. Only two sports really mattered to white South Africans: rugby union and, to a lesser extent, cricket. It was these sports, both dominated by white nations, that were the last to give succour to apartheid.

How Robert Muldoon ruined The Olympics

In July 1969, HART (Halt All Racist Tours) was founded by University of Auckland students determined to oppose sporting contact with South Africa, whose ruckers and maulers were scheduled to tour in 1973. For New Zealanders, this was the biggest sporting event of all: even beating Australia came second to spanking the Springboks. Proof of the stake the 15-a-side game holds there would come in 1972, in the run-up to a General Election. Norman Kirk, the Labour opposition leader, promised not to interfere with the tour, yet after taking office, he attempted, unsuccessfully, to persuade the NZRFU to withdraw its invitation to the Springboks while at the same time attempting to negotiate with a number of anti-tour activists and groups. According to the police advising him, the tour, should it proceed, would "engender the greatest eruption of violence this country has ever known". Looming, meanwhile, was the shadow of the 1974 Commonwealth Games in Christchurch: if New Zealand was seen to be accommodating South African sport, a boycott of the Games by African nations would be inevitable. Public support for the tour, nonetheless, was strong.

By way of alerting Kirk to the possibilities, the grandstand at Papakura was set alight on 9 April 1973. The PM, though, had already written to the NZRFU days earlier, saying that the government saw "no alternative, pending selection on a genuine merit basis, to a postponement of the tour". Aware of the likely fall-out, Kirk conceded that he would be "failing in his duty" if he didn't "accept the criticism and do what [he] believed to be right… the Government was elected to govern".[43] Kirk paid the price, losing the 1975 election in a landslide. During his campaign, Robert Muldoon, the National Party leader, described the cancellation of the 1973 tour as "one issue on which people will change their vote", and insisted that his government would welcome a Springbok team to New Zealand, "even if there were threats of violence and civil strife".[44]

The Commonwealth Games went ahead, as did sundry tours by international multi-racial cricket parties under the aegis of Derrick Robins, a millionaire businessman and chairman of Coventry City FC, but isolation stepped up a gear after the All Blacks toured South Africa in 1976, just as the world was reeling from the shock of the riots in the black township of Soweto, where hundreds were killed. As a direct consequence of that All Black venture, 25 African nations withdrew from that year's Montreal Olympics. In 1977, aware that a similar boycott might undermine and ruin the next Commonwealth Games, the Commonwealth heads of state unanimously adopted the Gleneagles Agreement, promising to "discourage" contact and competition with sporting organisations, teams or individuals from South Africa.

Muldoon, though, was adamant: sport and politics should not mix. Besides, went his reasoning, how could he legitimately stop his citizens from going where and mixing with whom they wished? And by making it clear that his government would not interfere with sport, Muldoon effectively gave the NZRFU the green light to play ball with the Springboks. Kirk, though, would be vindicated.

It would not be the last time Muldoon brandished a Springbok tour as a political weapon. By the time of the proposed 1981 visit, another election was imminent and, according to opinion polls, support for the tour was high in provincial New Zealand, home to six key marginal constituencies. HART committed itself to non-violent disruption; Muldoon condemned it for spreading lies about the nation overseas. Joining the battle were CARE (Citizens Association for Racial Equality) and NAAC (National Anti-Apartheid Council). These and other anti-tour activists were characterised as stirrers and troublemakers. The tussle between old and new New Zealand was reaching crisis point.

So it was, in July, August and September, that attempts to disrupt the tour, and disrupt the disrupters, found New Zealander divided against New Zealander in the largest civil disturbance the country had seen in more than a generation. More than 150,000 people took part in over 200 demonstrations in 28 centres; between 1,500 and 2,000 protestors were arrested (accounts vary), one-third of them women. "Police," related Huw Richards, "appeared on New Zealand city streets equipped with what David Lange, prime minister from 1984, called 'all regalia of certain fascist countries'."[45] The division of national opinion was symbolised most poignantly by Alan Hewson, the All Black fullback, whose wife, Pauline, was firmly and openly against the tour. Another leading All Black, Graham Mourie, refused to play against the tourists.

What made all this especially ironic was that New Zealand, where attitudes to native Maoris had contrasted so starkly with Australia's treatment of its own native population, had long prided itself on having the best race relations in the world. That said, the Maori were by no means treated as unquestioned equals. When the protesters attacked racism, they participated in increasing numbers, yet were eager, among other things, to learn why their countrymen could campaign about race in South Africa but not at home. As a government-authorised website states: "Some commentators have described this event as the moment when New Zealand lost its innocence as a country and as being a watershed in our view of ourselves as a country and people."[46] Geoff Fougere, a sociologist, argued that rugby union, so long "a mirror to our society", had now smashed that mirror. Chris Laidlaw, the former All Black, believed his countrymen had discovered that "there were issues that loomed larger than the God-given right to go and play rugby on Saturday and to play rugby with whomever you choose".[47] Six years later, visitors to New Zealand universities were still being advised not to mention the r-word.

In cricket and rugby union, nevertheless, the watersheds of 1970 and 1981 did not bring an end to games with South Africa, where meaningful and tangible progress, however insufficient, would be more easily discernible in sport than politics. There were conventional if unpopular tours by representative rugby union parties from England and Ireland, the last in 1984, but by then so-called "rebel" tours had become fashionable, their organisers preying nakedly on the players' often inadequate income (or complete lack thereof in rugby's case – officially speaking).

Confessions of a refusenik

Fast, clever, bushy of beard and wild of hair, John Taylor was known to teammates as "Basil Brush", a nod to the glove-puppet TV fox who cheered up Britons of all ages as the optimistic Sixties dissolved into the bleak 1970s. An open-side flanker best known for the last-ditch touchline conversion that beat Scotland 19-18 at Murrayfield in 1971, he was a weighty if comparatively unsung contributor to one of the unlikeliest of all sporting empires: the Wales XVs that presided over rugby union's Five Nations Championship in the 1970s with bodies of steel, wills of iron and imaginations aflame. Many were schoolteachers, a traditional career route for working-class Welshmen reluctant to spend weekdays in the mines. Theirs, according to Richards, was "the triumph of the welfare state player".

Taylor, though, was not your average rugger bugger. His forbears had been miners and farm labourers, but he attended Loughborough University and was teaching at a large multiracial school in London when he decided that he didn't wish to play games with people whose outlook contrasted so starkly with his own: white South Africans. In a 2012 interview[48] with Duncan Hewitt, one of my former students, he explained his rationale:

> *I just happened to speak with an English accent – except when I had been back to Wales – because I was born and brought up in Hertfordshire, so that undoubtedly influenced my thinking. Rugby was not the be-all and end-all – I had a great belief in*

human rights, was fairly left-wing, supported CND, loved Bob Dylan – that was the mix that underpinned everything. I had always been interested in politics and could never subscribe to the "don't mix sport and politics" cliché – to me history had proved it was impossible for them not to be intertwined. The British government could have done far more but gave tacit approval. It did not want to fall out with the ultra-conservative rugby lobby so was not prepared to make a judgement. I have no doubts that sport is a very powerful medium – apartheid laws were being strengthened until South Africa was totally isolated in world sport. Key figures such as Danie Craven were desperately trying, laughably, to persuade the rest of the world there was no apartheid in sport and they were driven totally by trying to keep South Africa involved in international sport.

When the South Africans undertook their turbulent tour of Britain in the winter of 1969-70, Taylor made himself unavailable for Wales. In fact, he says, his political stance cost him "several" caps.

The Welsh Rugby Union said they would treat it as a matter of "conscience" but still left me out until the last match of the season – fortunately, Wales had a very poor Championship. There was a campaign from the National Union of Miners in Wales, led by the communist, Dai Francis, the father of Hywel Francis MP, to get me reinstated – I'm not sure what influence that had. I was told by several senior RFU figures that I did not deserve to play for my country again. Peter Hain [the South African émigré who led the successful campaign to halt the 1970 South African cricket tour of England and rose to political office] used me quite cleverly – they knew they could not expect me to run on to pitches but I appeared with Peter on news programmes and debates.

In 1968, Taylor had accepted an invitation to tour South Africa with the Lions. He regretted it almost as soon as the plane touched down. "The night before we left," he remembered, "the high commissioner or the ambassador said something to the effect of, 'Don't get involved in our politics; you won't understand them. But our rugby and our girls are great so go and enjoy them.' And then, when we got out there and had our first night in a hotel in Stilfontein, a group of real Afrikaners came to our hotel and, without any prompting from us, launched into an aggressive defence of the apartheid system and how this was the only way to treat the blacks and so on and so forth. I thought, 'Bloody hell! What have I come into?'"[49]

He made a vow to himself: come the next scheduled visit to the Republic six years hence, he would not make himself available. Nor did he disguise his intentions: he was invited to go but, as he recalls, it was a case of motions being gone through. On the day the 1974 Lions were due to depart, 100 anti-apartheid demonstrators invaded the Britannia Hotel at Heathrow Airport. In vain, Hain appealed to Willie-John McBride, the Lions captain, to abort the trip.

Taylor is adamant that, while he urged them to speak out against apartheid, there is no truth in the story that he sought to dissuade his Welsh teammates from going to the Republic.

The rugby world was so entrenched in its relationship with SA it would have been a totally pointless exercise. I did explain in various programmes, articles and discussions why I thought the tour should not go ahead – why a sporting boycott would be an effective tool against apartheid and why it was now imperative because apartheid laws were getting more draconian instead of South Africa becoming more liberal – the well-rehearsed rugby argument at the time was that building bridges would do more good than isolation but I had realised that was nonsense in 1968. As long as white South Africa had international rugby and cricket they were perfectly happy to reject world opinion. I was a little ashamed that rugby seemed to have this attitude that the brotherhood of rugby was more important than the brotherhood of man.[50]

The price of betrayal

The sporting boycott seemed easier to justify than the UN cultural boycott – hence the more or less universal condemnation for the unofficial cricket tours of the 1980s. These sad escapades are more commonly referred to as "rebel" tours, but this is terribly misleading: "rebel" implies some sort of social value, or at least a fight that needed to be won for the general good. Those who joined these ventures rebelled against those who sought to determine whether or not they should be allowed to earn enough money to pay off the mortgage in a land that not only practised even greater prejudice than their own, but had enshrined it in law. Indirectly, they were financed by the South African government. "The idea," summed up Cricinfo's Martin Williamson, "was to bring sport to an entertainment-starved (white) public and to give the impression to the world that things weren't so bad after all. Cricket, a predominantly white sport in the country and one in which the South Africans probably had, for much of that time, a world-class XI, was at the forefront of the PR offensive."[51]

In February 1983, a party of leading if not quite top-rank cricketers from the Caribbean flew out to South Africa. Reaction in the region could in no way be characterised as supportive. They were not the first non-white team to take such a step – a Sri Lankan party had flown there the previous year, the decade's second unofficial tour of the Republic; the first had come a few months before that: the South African Breweries-sponsored visit by Graham Gooch and his band of Englishmen. Again, how singularly inappropriate that word "rebel" now seems: these trips, after all, reinforced rather than challenged the notion that normal sport was possible in an abnormal society.

At the time, the Caribbean's finest, as have seen, were dominant, a galvanising force for racial empowerment. Such was the islands' depth of talent that, over the course of two tours, a second-string squad would get the better of a very strong South African side. These expeditions, though, were regarded in most quarters as the ultimate betrayal. Viv Richards, then the most racially aware and vocal West Indies player, was the organisers' chief target; holding fast to his scruples, he turned down a reported £250,000. So did the other regular wearers of that maroon cap. Those waiting for them to lose form or retire, many of them disillusioned and scraping a relatively modest living from the game, proved more malleable. The sense of grievance grew as the criticism rained: why should we be prevented from plying our trade in South Africa while those bankers and diamond merchants and salesmen were still doing business there? In any other circumstance it would be an open-and-shut case of restraint of trade.

"Only those who have lived in the West Indies will be able to understand the extent to which emotions are aroused in this part of the world by apartheid," affirmed Jeffrey Stollmeyer in his autobiography, completed a few months before the 1983 tour was announced. That said, he also believed that Caribbean governments were not united in their approach to the issue. While urging governments in general to compromise on the "third-party principle" (individuals should be permitted to do what they wished), he was convinced that, if tours to South Africa were sanctioned, international cricket would in all likelihood "become polarised on racial lines", with "disastrous" consequences.[52] Few others were inclined to erect any sort of defence for those bound for the Republic. Apartheid, in the view of Michael Manley, the former Jamaican prime minister, "points like a dagger at the throat of black self-worth in every corner occupied by the descendants of Africa".[53] So far as Michael Holding, the great Jamaican fast bowler, felt the touring party were "selling themselves"; offer them enough money, he suggested, and they would "probably agree to wear chains".[54]

* * *

Clive Lloyd had sought to head off such an eventuality the previous year, submitting a paper to the Caribbean governments proposing that the West Indies board dissuade the leading players by paying them an off-season retainer of \$20,000-\$30,000, anticipating the advent of central contracts. Having been on the receiving end himself, he knew all too well how tempting the South African overtures would be to those outside the first-choice XI.

> *We were always being offered money to go to South Africa. I mean huge amounts, massive amounts, hundreds of thousands of dollars. The sort of money that would have made me comfortable for the rest of my life, but money is not all. I was so disappointed when [the tourists] went. When people arrived in the West Indies, did they have to sign a piece of paper making them an honorary black man? No, of course not. But that's what these boys had to do in South Africa; they were made "honorary whites" for the duration. It was demeaning. Think of all the black guys going back to the days of Jesse Owens – those guys fought for a lot. Think about the things we experienced in England in the '50s, '60s and '70s: "No dogs, no blacks, no Irish" on the guesthouse doors. We experienced bad things in America, prejudices that we had to overcome. The worst thing is for someone to tell you that you are a lesser person because of your colour. I can't accept that.[55]*

While denying he had ever promised to visit South Africa, Lloyd did concede that, while in Sharjah, he had spoken to Dr Ali Bacher, the redoubtable and initially unapologetic engine behind the rebel tours, a former Test captain and an administrator whose determination to "regenerate" cricket in South Africa may fairly be said to have blurred his judgement. The South African Council of Sport warned Lloyd that the Pretoria government would use him for propaganda and that his presence on such a venture would embarrass the very people he sought to help.

Soon after the party left for the Republic under the leadership of Lawrence Rowe, Lloyd found himself in a club in London, where he was approached by the venue's manager, who offered to share a bottle of champagne. The way Lloyd tells it, the manager left him in no doubt what it meant to people that he, Clive Lloyd, had rejected all attempts to lure him to South Africa; even to those way beyond the Caribbean. "Clive," he said, "I respect you tremendously for what you did by not going to South Africa... if you had gone there, I would have put arsenic in that bubbly." Lloyd knew he wasn't joking. "It was by *not* going," he believed, "that people began to question the regime. Sportsmen, whether they like it or not, do have a lot of influence, and we should recognise that. If people respect you, when you speak, they will listen."[56]

South Africa, a calypso composed by Tobago Crusoe, saluted those who resisted temptation:

> *But today although I am rejected By the West Indian Cricket Board of Control I can raise meh hand high and be respected Ah doh see now why I have to sell meh soul I know that I'm broke but I eh scrunting And I eh begging anybody so far So then why should I betray my race For one hundred thousand dollars? Ah say "to hell with South Africa."*[57]

For Rowe and Co, reality soon dawned. David Murray, Everton Weekes's son, was unable to take his white wife with him for fear of disobeying the Mixed Marriages Act; big bad Colin Croft was ejected from a first-class railway carriage and redirected to third-class; little Alvin Kallicharran went to a Wimpy Bar with some white pals and was thrown out. In the opening match against Western Province, Rowe posted a nine-man slip cordon: nobody wanted to field anywhere near the boundary. "We were petrified at first," remembered Franklyn Stephenson, the rangy Bajan who had given plenty of encouraging hints that he might well be the answer to the millions of Caribbean churchgoers praying for a new Sobers. "But chatting to the crowd, I realised that white people wanted to talk to us. They spoke about the things that were going on. Peter Kirsten, their captain, later complained to the press that his team had no support from South African crowds."[58]

The wrath that poured down on the heads of Stephenson et al bordered on the biblical. All too typical was one tirade in the *Trinidad Chronicle*: "The actions of the West Indian cricketers in South Africa show them as being illiterate, greedy, unprincipled, treacherous, easily bought and lacking in foresight and understanding of world affairs. To raise the excuse of financial hardship and want is to be dishonest and deceitful. I say to every decent West Indian: disown them, ban them, subjugate them, deport them."[59]

The West Indies board imposed a blanket lifetime ban on the tourists. Many fled, or never even returned to, their native soil. Left-handed batsman Herbert Chang, reported Jonathan Liew 30 years later, "is destitute and delusional" and can sometimes be seen "wandering back alleys of Kingston, asking which end he is bowling from tomorrow".[60] Richard Austin, billed in some quarters as another new Sobers, never subsequently played competitive cricket and returned to Jamaica; suffering from drug addiction and living on the streets under the name of Danny Germs, he died penniless in 2014. Murray moved to Australia then back to Barbados, where he trod much the same sorry path.

Stephenson sounded a defiant note. Overlooked by the West Indies selectors even after those lifetime bans were revoked in 1989, when last seen he was running his own cricket and golf academy in Barbados; he harbours no regrets. "I felt we started a change of thinking that we were a lower form of animal. We gave people who wanted change a voice. Within a year and a half some of the central tenets of apartheid would come down and that is not a coincidence. If we had not gone, the dismantling of apartheid would have taken 25 years more. We achieved it in about nine years.

"People called me a mercenary, but what do mercenaries do? They fight somebody else's cause. Well, I was a mercenary for the black people's cause, because wherever I've been I've been an ambassador for my country, my race and cricket. If that's being a mercenary, then yes I was."[61]

Sport and race: it never was an exclusively black-and-white matter.

To quota or not to quota

Within the republic and without, post-apartheid South Africa threw up endless problems, some inevitable, some surprising. Some brought joyous solutions. The quota system designed to make sporting teams more accurately reflect the republic's racial mix threw up Makhaya Ntini, the shoeless young shepherd who in 1988 became the first black African to play Test cricket and went on to claim more than 650 wickets for his country. Others emphasised the strides that had still to be taken. In Johannesburg in 2008, during the half-time interval of a Tri-Nations rugby union international that saw South Africa record a memorable victory over Australia, three white men racially abused and assaulted a black female fan in the corridors of the Coca-Cola stadium; as they did so, fellow spectators walked on by.

Affirmative action (or, as we Britons refer to it, positive discrimination) is one of the most controversial issues of our time, most vexingly so when it revolves around race. To some it has plenty of pros, to others, copious cons. To some it provides redress for past and even current prejudice; to others it either ignores other socio-economic factors or simply incites another form of prejudice, often against those unfortunate enough to be paying for the sins of their forbears.

In *Fisher v University of Texas*, which emerged as a potential landmark case in 2012, the US Supreme Court had to decide, bearing in mind the Equal Protection Clause of the Fourteenth Amendment, whether the university was entitled to use race as a criteria for undergraduate admissions. "With an eerie sense of déjà vu commentators are suggesting – as they did a decade ago, when the court considered the use of race in the admissions process at the University of Michigan Law School – that admissions officials should substitute consideration of an applicant's socioeconomic background for his or her race," observed Kevin Brown, Richard S. Melvin Professor at the Indiana University

Maurer School of Law and author of a forthcoming book on affirmative action.

"That would be a massive mistake. First, we must recognise that it's faulty to suggest that this is an either-or choice, because there's nothing that currently prohibits admissions officers from considering socio-economic factors when making admissions decisions. When I was involved in admissions decisions for both Indiana University Maurer School of Law and for scholarship programs at Indiana University, we always took an applicant's socio-economic background into account. We understood, as Obama understands, that disadvantaged kids of all races who grow up in poverty have to overcome obstacles that others in our society do not. Doing that and taking race into account aren't mutually exclusive notions, and shouldn't be thought of that way. Second, we seem to be forgetting why affirmative action was created in the first place. Yes, of course it's true that individuals from poor backgrounds, regardless of skin colour, face obstacles in obtaining the kind of academic success valued by higher education institutions. But blacks and Latinos are disadvantaged in American society, even when adjusting for socio-economic factors."[62]

Affirmative action in sport is no less divisive. It will plainly take decades, perhaps more, to atone for the sins of Verwoerd, Vorster and the Bothas, much less create a society where black and white can exist in genuine and lasting harmony. South African sport has sought to redress matters with its own brand of positive discrimination – namely, selection quotas, known officially as the "target transformation" policy, a step also taken to equally justified and divisive effect in Zimbabwe.

To many, the imposition of quotas destroys the innate meritocracy of sport; to just as many, correcting injustice matters more. "Some sort of compensation or attempt at rectification is due to those non-white sportspeople who were directly or indirectly disadvantaged by apartheid," acknowledged Carl Thomen in his 2008 book *Is it Cricket? An Ethical Evaluation of Race Quotas in Sport*. These "compensatory efforts", he nonetheless concluded, "must not come via the same principles which got us into the mess of apartheid in the first place".[63] In writing the book, he stated, his aim was "to show that the negative consequences of such policies far outweigh any good they may realistically claim to do, and that, in the end, there are better ways to go about fixing the post-apartheid problems".[64] We will return to this debate.

*   *   *

Quotas were introduced, after a fashion, in the 1970s, when the International Wanderers, a private touring party comprising several leading English and Australian players, found themselves facing multi-racial XIs. In Cape Town in 1975, Edward Habane and Sedick Conrad became the first black Africans to play first-class cricket against a touring team since a side of South African Malays had played an English XI eight decades earlier. Such ventures came to an end after the Soweto Uprising of June 1976, where hundreds of schoolchildren were killed while protesting the government's education policies.

Happily, when South Africa returned to the international brotherhood, the Springbok on their chests and caps, by order of the ANC, had been replaced by a Protea – the flowering plant that also lent its name to the non-white teams for whom D'Oliveira won his domestic reputation. That the national rugby union team cling stubbornly to their identity as "The Springboks" says much for the tolerance of the new South Africa while suggesting that creating a sense of true nationhood has been considerably less straightforward in the game clung to with such fervour by Afrikaners as a symbol of strength and independence.

"The heroes of our nation, dedicated to building the foundation of cricket for generations to come," is how Cricket South Africa hails its most important employees. "PURE PROTEA. 100% SOUTH AFRICAN."[65] Its website also states: "We can't undo the past, but we can shape the future." Come the current decade, it was heartening to report that Ntini stood second only to Shaun Pollock – whose father, Peter, and uncle, Graeme, had been robbed of their prime – on the list of South Africa's most prolific Test wicket-takers. Even after Ntini's retirement in 2010 the national XI regularly boasted D'Oliveira's racial heirs (Jean-Paul Duminy, Robin Peterson, Alviro Petersen and Vernon Philander) alongside new-age South Africans of South Asian origin (the Pakistani émigré Imran Tahir and Hashim Amla, a devout Muslim now widely considered the most graceful batsman in the game) and even the very occasional black African such as Lonwabo Tsotsobe. This was held in some quarters to be a direct consequence of a quota system at provincial level, the same quota system that Kevin Peter Pietersen from Pietermaritzburg, the son of an Englishwoman, claimed, unconvincingly, had obliged him to seek his fortune in England. Mind you, he was scarcely the first or last to realise that even playing county cricket was more financially rewarding than representing South Africa.

It was illuminating to dip into Luke Alfred's *The Art of Losing*, published in 2012, and learn that only three members of the South African team at the World Cup 20 years previously had voted in the whites-only referendum that approved the continuation of President F.W. De Klerk's reforms (had the decision gone the other way, warrants Alfred, they would have had to return mid-tournament). In sporting terms, that 68% "Yes" vote marked the beginning of compromise and redress. Ahead lay the tribulations of that quota system.

In 1998, encouraged by the ruling ANC, the United Cricket Board of South Africa laid down the law: the starting XI for each international match should include a minimum four players of "colour". Quotas were also introduced at provincial level. Adherence, though, was never strict. The prickliest row erupted in 2002 when the selectors chose Jacques Rudolph, a white batsman, ahead of Justin Ontong, a coloured all-rounder, for the Sydney Test against Australia, only to be overruled by Percy Sonn, the board president. As a consequence, Ontong, who counted Rudolph as a friend, endured one of the most unappetising of baptisms. A controversial figure whose administrative career would bring him to the heights of the ICC presidency and the depths of fraud allegations and alcohol-fuelled public disgrace, Sonn was roundly criticised by the cricketing fraternity; yet even those who believed he should have been focusing his efforts on improving coaching facilities for black schoolchildren understood where he was coming from. "No doubt Sonn," noted a *Guardian* leader, "has seen too many examples of lipservice being paid to a quota system while, behind the scenes, not much is being done to attack the roots of an historic injustice."[66]

Reflecting the elitism of a sport that had yet to gain traction in a black community vastly more enamoured of football, South Africa's 2007 Rugby World Cup-winning XV numbered only a couple of non-white faces. In cricket, another sport dominated by the elite white schools, politicians and administrators believed reformation should be a top-down process, billed as "targeted transformation". "As long as we have an abnormal society," Norman Arendse, the president of the national board, reiterated in 2007, "quotas and targets are not only desirable but also a constitutional imperative." This had prompted some problematic arguments. When Graeme Smith, South Africa's captain, wanted to leave Ntini out of a critical match in that year's World Cup against England in Barbados, he was obliged to justify himself in a lengthy one-on-one meeting with Gerald Majola, then chief executive of Cricket South Africa. Many argued that the morale of the dressing room was being undermined. By 2010, according to Tony Irish, chief executive of the South African Cricketers' Cricket Association, matters had become intolerable: "The players feel that as soon as a racial number is set for selection of the team (whether or not one calls this a quota or a target) it leads to a divisive dynamic within the team, and it is also degrading to the players of colour who should be there on merit yet are labelled a quota/target player."[67]

Yet Ntini was a rare model for black Africans. Not unnaturally, players bridled at the suggestion that they owed their places to anything other than ability, leading to a letter sent in 2007 to Arendse and his fellow board members by a group of senior players led by Ashwell Prince, who would become the national team's first coloured captain. In it, they demanded an end to "artificial" selection at the highest level. Later that year, Makhenkesi Stofile, the sports minister, scoffed at the quotas as "window dressing", signifying a shift towards the notion that victory on the field would be a better form of inspiration.

In May 2013 I emailed Carl Thomen, expressing my conviction that the quota system had been a necessary evil and wondering whether he had had cause to reconsider his stance. He was not for turning. "I'm not sure that you can infer from the fact that Makhaya and Hashim got their chances when there happened to be a quota selection policy in place, that that policy was *responsible* for their selection. Both those players had domestic averages way above other white cricketers, and most probably would have been selected purely on merit. Perhaps they were thrown in a bit earlier than otherwise (in Hashim's case particularly), but I'm not sure you can credit the quota policies of the time with their success. The problem with quotas is that they are ethically indefensible (for all the reasons I describe in the book), and they actively do damage. 'Necessity' doesn't come into it; they are *evil*, plain and simple."[68] The counter-argument was summed up with typical succinctness by my friend John Young, a sportswriter, author and former schoolteacher from the Western Cape who until recently coached the Pinelands High School cricket team: "Quotas were necessary precisely so that merit could be acknowledged. Good black players would never have been picked without them."[69]

Black and White United – The Ballad of Andy and Henry

It was a sign of the times when, in 2003, two cricketers joined forces to protest against Robert Mugabe's rapacious, ruinous reign as president of Zimbabwe. Hailed at the outset of the 1980s as the revolutionary leader who brought an end to white minority rule in the land formerly known as Rhodesia, Mugabe was already slithering from hero to villain by the time I visited the country in early 1990; come 2003, when Zimbabwe co-hosted the biggest sporting event in its young history, the ICC World

Cup, he had almost – but not quite – reached the bottom of that treacherous hill. Mugabe's land reform had led to the seizure of white-owned farms, ensuring extensive coverage in the British media in particular. Before the tournament began, Henry Huff, a friend of Zimbabwe's leading player, Andy Flower, took the batsman to see the devastation now afflicting his own farm and told him that victory should come second to the team's "moral obligation" to inform the world what was going on. Flower in turn approached Henry Olonga, the fast bowler who had been the first black player to represent Zimbabwe on an international cricket field, convinced that Olonga had "the courage of his convictions" and that a black-and-white protest would strike "the most eloquent balance" and hence have more impact.

Encouraged and abetted by David Coltart, a human rights lawyer who would become the country's minister of sports, education, arts and culture, the pair hit upon a plan to wear black armbands bemoaning the "the death of democracy". According to Olonga, mind, their union had slightly different origins:

> It all started with a phone call. About a month before the World Cup – sometime in January – Andy Flower rang me and said he had a proposal. We went to the News Cafe in Harare and he said he'd been reading the paper and there was a story of an MP, Job Sikhala, who had been tortured. Not only did Andy think it was disgusting that, in a democratic country, Sikhala had been tortured, he was also appalled that it only made the inside story of a national paper. He said someone needed to take a stand. Then he said: "I think that person is you."
>
> He thought we needed to make some sort of protest, like pulling out of the World Cup. I thought that was drastic, but we mulled it over for a couple of weeks. A third party thought it would be better for us to make a peaceful protest — to wear a black armband. We felt it needed to be accompanied with a statement — with "We mourn the death of democracy" as the punchline.
>
> My motivation was that, two years ago, I had been handed a dossier of human rights abuses that have occurred in

Zimbabwe, notably the early 1980s Matabeleland massacres. Up to that point, I'd thought Robert Mugabe was a very fair, true, honest president.[70]

With their teammates oblivious to their intentions, Olonga and Flower issued their statement before the match against Namibia:

Although we are just professional cricketers, we do have a conscience and feelings. We believe that if we remain silent that will be taken as a sign that either we do not care or we condone what is happening in Zimbabwe. We believe that it is important to stand up for what is right. In doing so we are making a silent plea to those responsible to stop the abuse of human rights in Zimbabwe.

Less celebrated was the firm stance of the England team in boycotting their World Cup match against the co-hosts in Harare, on a point of principle that ultimately cost them any chance of qualifying for the final stages. "This," proclaimed their fiery and plain-speaking captain, Nasser Hussain, who had roused his players to action, "has become more than just a game of cricket." The way Hussain spelled out the players' responsibilities in Cape Town's Cullinan Hotel still buoys the spirits.

Look, I know sometimes when we are discussing cricket and tactics, some of you fall asleep at the back during my team talks, but that doesn't concern me now. Some of you are going to have to take some serious growing-up pills and take the issue very seriously indeed. I know a lot of you are young and I apologise for putting this on you, but it's looking as though everyone is going to leave us to make some pretty big decisions here.[71]

And so they were. The buck had been passed down with shamelessly clinical expertise, from Tony Blair to the ICC to the England and Wales Cricket Board. A plea to switch the venue to South Africa fell upon deaf ears. What clinched the boycott was a secret meeting with an exiled member of the opposition to Mugabe's ruling Zanu-PF. One tiny caveat nags. As churlish and uncharitable as it might seem to find even the smallest fault with Hussain's ability to appreciate the world beyond the boundary, would such a laudable protest have been countenanced had the English press not been reporting Mugabe's annexation of white-owned farms with such fury? Means and ends, means and ends…

* * *

A decade later, when the BBC's Alison Mitchell interviewed Flower, by now a highly successful England coach with an OBE tucked away somewhere safe, she found a framed copy of the statement on a wall in his study, a study far from his homeland, a homeland he and Olonga were forced to flee as a consequence of their show of black-and-white harmony. Of the two, Olonga, understandably, had been more naïve. "I thought I could carry on in Zimbabwe – maybe my career would come to an end but I could still live there. But that all changed when I got death threats two or three weeks after the World Cup. I realised the game was up." He, too, found refuge in England, working as a singer and public speaker. While he still wanted to return to Zimbabwe with his wife and two daughters he would "need some guarantees that people who wanted to harm me a few years ago do not still want to harm me".[72]

Flower told Mitchell he was wont to re-read their statement from time to time: "I love the way it was written – the meaning in some of those sentences is very sad because it is a reminder of what was happening in that country at that time and some of the people who went through agony and lost their lives." When she asked him to read it aloud, warranted Mitchell, he "struggled to keep his voice from cracking"; the emotion was "evident in his eyes".

10 The Grass Ceiling: Sport and Sexuality

A racist remark is a sackable offence in politics; a misogynist insult is lighthearted banter. A portion of the left cannot see anything wrong with allying with misogynist Islamists. A portion of the right cannot see anything wrong with wanting women to stay in the kitchen. To use the available clichés, sexism is neither a "red line" nor a "deal-breaker". All kinds of people can indulge in it without fear of the consequences. The wonder of our day is not that Britain is experiencing a feminist revival but that it has taken so long to stir.

Nick Cohen, *The Observer*, 2013[1]

In 1960, Sirimavo Bandaranaike succeeded her husband Solomon as prime minister of Sri Lanka. The first woman of any nationality to scale such a forbiddingly treacherous ladder, she went on to serve three terms. It should therefore have come as little surprise – though it undoubtedly did – when the Barmy Army troops entering Colombo's intimate P Saravanamuttu Oval for a Test match in April 2012 discovered that, rather than the strapping chaps customarily seen elsewhere, the pitch was being tended by a pair of grandmothers. "During a break in play," reported John Westerby in *The Times*, "the sisters emerged barefooted from behind the scoreboard, unmistakeable in brightly coloured saris to sweep up dust and repair the bowlers' footholds."[2] Had the subject been anything other than sport, the letters and emails from countless Disgusteds from Tunbridge Wells would have been winging their way to Wapping. But while the idea of women sweeping up after their menfolk sticks in the craw like a splintered leg of lamb, Amravati Vellai and her sister Saroja, both in their 60s, take enormous pride in their labours and deserve nothing but admiration.

Originally, I never had the vaguest intention of ghetto-ising women's sport in this book. Then, midway through, having reflected on several sporting prejudices while acknowledging the signal contributions of Suzanne Lenglen, "Babe" Didrikson, Fanny Blankers-Koen, Věra Čáslavská, Nadia Elena Comăneci, Ludmila Tourischeva, Billie Jean King, Martina Navratilova, Cathy Freeman and so many others, it became abundantly clear that sidestepping the most obvious and durable prejudice of all, namely sexism, would be akin to writing a history of modern popular music and going straight to One Direction, 50 Cent and the boy Bieber without so much as a wave to Billie Holliday, Ella Fitzgerald, Patsy Cline, Carole King, Joni Mitchell, Laura Nyro and Rickie Lee Jones.

Nick Cohen's point is reinforced rather than undermined by Joan Smith, whose 1989 book *Misogynies* is regarded as a seminal feminist tract. "There's never been a better moment in western history to be born female," she declared in a collection of essays published nearly a quarter of a century later, then decided she was utterly unable to resist a contrary question: "Why doesn't it feel like that?" There was, she regretted, "a chasm between what we expect and actual experience".[3] In spectator sport, that chasm appears unbridgeable, albeit for largely unavoidable reasons.

It is worth drawing a comparison with cinema, the first branch of mass culture to bring women to the forefront in the 20th century. Either side of the Second World War, the Hollywood studio system pumped out movie after movie starring strong, assertive and often complicated female leads played by the likes of Joan Crawford, Bette Davis and Barbara Stanwyck; yet in the 500 top-grossing movies of 2012, just 28.4% of celluloid speaking roles went to women; of these, or so it seemed, the chunkiest always seemed to go to the ubiquitous if magnificent Meryl Streep. Despite Kathryn Bigelow's muscular skills and sensibility, moreover, of those directing, producing or screenwriting the 100 top-grossing pictures, just

16% were women, who accounted for a mere 4% of the directors.[4] We're ready for you to start shooting your own close-ups, Ms Streep. Eagerly.

The ambitious sportswoman's cause is scarcely aided, of course, by the stark and seemingly insurmountable difference in opportunity and rewards, reflecting as they do spectator interest. Of the 10 most bountiful sporting events listed by *Forbes* in 2012[5], only two did not actively exclude women participants – horseracing's Dubai World Cup and the World Series of Poker, the second of which, for the purposes of this book at least, does not qualify. In the same magazine's list of the 100 highest sporting earners in 2013, the loftiest woman, for the eighth consecutive year, was Maria Sharapova (22nd), less than 25% of whose estimated $29m income came from on-court winnings. The only other women in the chart were tennis players too: Serena Williams (68th) and Li Na (85th). That said, the top 10 women athletes all earned in excess of $6m.

So, yes, sportswomen have an even more daunting mountain to conquer than Hollywood actresses (and perhaps even more forbidding than the one now confronting West Indian cricketers). But consider how much worse it might be without one of the precious few acceptable instances of segregation. And at least it can be said with some assurance that the graph is on a distinct upward curve.

Second-class citizens

Sexual segregation is more endemic in spectator sport than most walks of life. Even public toilets are unisexual these days. Still, as Brett D. Mills pointed out in the abstract for his paper *Women of Ancient Greece: Participating in Sport?*, women and sport were a far from unknown combination in Ancient Greece: "Homer's *Odyssey* describes women playing ball and driving chariots; vases dating back to 700-675 BC portray women driving light chariots in a procession; a girl juggling 12 hoops appears on an Attic cup dated around 475-450 BC; feminine acrobatic performance was portrayed in Xenophon's 'Symposium';

aquatic activities were not only recreational but a necessity of everyday life – the earliest known evidence of women involved in swimming was found once again in Homer's *Odyssey*; the only known artefact depicting women in the act of swimming is a red figured vase, dated around 500 BC; accounts of women hunting are found in mythological Greek writings; there is some evidence for women being involved in horseback riding; wrestling for women was introduced by Lycurgus in the ninth century BC; and mythology and art indicate running was the most popular physical activity for women in ancient Greece."[6]

They were barred, nonetheless, from the ancient Olympics in any capacity – those contemplating stealing into the stadium to spectate knew the price of detection by heart: they would be hurled to their death from Mount Typaion.[7] True, they were allowed to compete in a so-called "footrace for maidens" but only so long as they wore a tunic that exposed a breast.

Even the first modern Games, in 1896, found the doors firmly closed. The following table illustrates the inherent sexism of the Olympic "spirit":

Event	Olympic debut for men	Olympic debut for women
100m	1896	1928
200m	1900	1948
400m	1896	1964
800m	1896	1928
1500m	1896	1972
5000m	1912	1996
10,000m	1912	1988
Marathon	1896	1984
400m hurdles	1900	1984
3000m steeplechase	1920	2008
4x100m relay	1912	1928

4x400m relay	1912	1972
Long jump	1896	1948
High jump	1900	1928
Triple jump	1896	1996
Pole vault	1896	2000
Shot	1896	1948
Discus	1896	1928
Javelin	1896	1932

To 21st century eyes, other distinctions might appear even more chauvinistic – or nonsensical. The first men's 110m hurdles final was in 1896; not until 1932 were women permitted their own equivalent – and just as golf clubs still allow women to tee off closer to the fairway, so the race is still run over 10 metres fewer. The closest equivalent to the men's decathlon, first staged at the 1904 Games, is the heptathlon, which debuted in 1984: an improvement on the pentathlon, granted, but still comprising two fewer disciplines.

Nor were other sports immune to such prejudice. In the second running of the Modern Olympics, croquet and tennis opened their grudging doors: the former vanished from the schedule in 1904, never to return; the latter dropped women in the same year, readmitted them in 1908 then found itself ditched as a sport altogether from 1928 to 1988. In 1904, the only sport to include women was archery, though there was an exhibition of women's boxing. Additions were slow. Figure skating entered the lists in 1908, then diving and swimming (1912), fencing (1924) and equestrianism (1952). All of which persuaded Alice Milliat to pioneer the Women's World Games, staged between 1921 and 1936. Not until 1976 did basketball, handball and rowing beckon; hockey finally did so in 1980, 72 years after the men first bullied off. By 1988, sailing and track cycling were on the bill, followed by judo (1992), football (1996), weightlifting (2000), wrestling (2004) and boxing (2012). The opening of that last door, in particular, was hailed as a major breakthrough, which might well be seen as one of the smaller accomplishments in the feminist struggle.

For sport, sexuality is the final frontier, the last hurdle to true modernism. Yes, progress of a very marginal kind has been made in the battle against homophobia (a subject we will move on to), but football remains utterly resistant to a 21st-century mindset: one of the more reprehensible instances of sport lagging furlongs behind society. As Jean Williams related in 2013: "Any sense of irony was completely absent, however, when a newly appointed equality and diversity officer at the FA recently assured me that football had one of the best track records on this issue in sport. Another new equality and diversity appointment at the Professional Footballers Association, which for many years excluded women from its annual gentlemen's dinners, told me much the same thing."[8]

As I write, if we discount mixed doubles in badminton and tennis, the only spectator sports, major or minor, that pit the sexes in direct competition are those where something has to be ridden or driven. Yet even here, unisexual competition is anything but uniform. Although there had been a Tour Feminin in the 1980s, for instance, it was hardly before time that, in 2013, a petition signed by tens of thousands was presented to the director of the Tour de France, Christian Prudhomme, by the race organisers, the Amaury Sport Organisation, calling for the inclusion of women. Not that the portcullis has yet shown many signs of rising.

That said, even Serena Williams wasn't exactly rushing to the ramparts. "I'd be up for it, why not?" chirped Andy Murray during Wimbledon 2013, responding to a fan's tweeted suggestion that he should take on the best female smasher and lobber since Martina. "How about Las Vegas as a venue?"[9] Williams responded with a mix of whimsy and modesty, expressing doubt that she would win a point. Just as Navratilova had done before her match against Jimmy Connors in 1992, she said she should decide both the surface – clay, the Scot's least favourite –

and rules. Then it got a bit silly: "I get alleys (tramlines). He gets no serves. I get alleys on my serves, too. He gets no legs, yeah."[10]

* * *

To a degree, the sexism that pervades sport, has always pervaded sport and will probably continue to do so for a good while yet, can be traced to male identity, an identity never more confused than it is right now. In the post-industrial, post-manufacturing world, claimed Hanna Rosin in *The End of Men – And The Rise Of Women*, "thinking and communicating have come to eclipse physical strength and stamina as the keys to economic success", leaving men uncertain of their role and immeasurably less dominant than at any time since mankind's dawn. "The attributes that are most valuable today – social intelligence, open communication, the ability to sit still and focus – are, at a minimum, not predominantly male. In fact, the opposite may be true."[11] It would be naïve in the extreme to deny that, amid this pursuit of equality, sport, the one highly and expressly profitable arena where physical strength and stamina remain paramount, remains out of step, inevitably and profoundly.

Forget all that twaddle about hunting and providing. The main function of men now is to justify defence budgets and, rather more importantly, to entertain, to supply relief from the angst of survival, and, in the process, enhance our understanding of that angst. Sport is arguably the one remaining arena where, thanks to physical superiority but also to that inherent urge to delay adulthood, men can still strive for excellence without fear of being matched, surpassed or belittled by the sex they have expended so much time and energy suppressing.

In 1975, our philosophical sportophobe Jean-Marie Brohm proffered another perspective:

> *The fact that women are tending to practise sports hitherto restricted to men does not open up any perspective for their liberation, in that it identifies liberation with the emulation of men and hence perpetuates the patriarchal system.*[12]

"The Suffragette Derby"

Historically, the name most readily associated with women's rights and sport is Emily Wilding Davison, though her cause was appreciably wider. A long-time member of the Women's Social and Political Union, already imprisoned nine times for what might now be called terrorist offences, this middle-class governess and activist had been increasingly willing to suffer for the cause of women's suffrage, a protest movement defied for three decades by the wholly unsympathetic and entirely male British ruling class. In prison she had gone on hunger strike; on no fewer than 49 occasions she had been the victim of barbaric force-feeding. Following one such instance of force-feeding, warders drenched her with freezing water after she barricaded herself in her cell; she sued, but damages amounted to a cursory £2. Strapped for money, and with her health ailing, in desperation she targeted the biggest British sporting event of 1913, The Derby, which drew hundreds of thousands to Epsom, from commoners to kings. Historians have suggested that Davison and other suffragettes were seen practising to grab horses in the park near her mother's house, and later drew lots to determine who should disrupt the race.

Carrying a "Votes for Women" scarf she was intending to fling on it, Davison fell at the hooves of the King's horse, Anmer, as the field rounded Tattenham Corner. It was widely asserted that Herbert Jones, the champion jockey whose mount trampled her – and dragged him for a few strides, leaving him badly injured – never forgave himself; he claimed to have been left "haunted by that woman's face". In a Channel 4 documentary[13] commemorating the centenary of Davison's ill-fated dip under the rails, digitalised footage showed the victim ignoring a number of hurtling horses to approach Anmer, contradicting journalist Michael Tanner's assertion in *The Suffragette Derby* that her collision with the monarch's horse was sheer coincidence (Tanner showed his colours by calling her "a bit of a battleaxe" and reporting that lesbianism was "rife among the suffragette sisterhood"[14]). The scarf now hangs in the Houses of

Parliament, an enduring reminder of both needless tragedy and the infinite illogic of prejudice.

Davison had bought a return train ticket (now kept at the Women's Library in London) and was due to attend the Suffragette ball that night. This prompted the widely held conclusion that she had not intended to commit suicide. Whether or not she was an accidental martyr does nothing to diminish the anger behind her protest. The centenary of her death testified to the footprint she left: an opera, *Emily*, received its premiere in Todmorden, Yorkshire; a play about her, *To Freedom's Cause*, came to the London stage; Epsom Downs Racecourse unveiled a memorial at Tattenham Corner (though officials resisted calls for a minute's silence on Derby Day).

Scrutinised through a contemporary lens, the reaction at the time was staggering. In the *Devon and Exeter Gazette*,[15] no fewer than three headlines ("The Derby", "Disappointing Race" and "Disqualification of The Favourite") preceded the first vague hint that something horrendous had happened ("Sensational Incidents"). Nor was there any mention of Ms Davison until the bottom of the column. The *Derby Daily Telegraph*, meanwhile, published one of the most nakedly opportunistic – not to say distasteful – adverts imaginable: "A woman may stop a racehorse, but you can't stop a woman having Grundy's Bacon."[16] The less we say about Grundy's the better.

Not unexpectedly, *The Times* was adamant that sport should never be used as a stage for political statements:

> *Where women are concerned, the natural gallantry of the public always inclines them to take a favourable view, and accordingly they are gradually coming to the conclusion that many of the militant suffragists are not entirely responsible for their acts. The growth of that belief will not improve the prospects of woman suffrage.*[17]

Others saw Davison in a far more heroic light. "Emily Davison paid with her life for making the whole world understand that women were in earnest for the vote," wrote Christabel Pankhurst, who co-founded the Women's Social and Political Union in 1903 with her mother, Emmeline, the leader of the women's suffrage movement (at the latter's funeral in 1928, Herbert Jones laid a wreath "to do honour to the memory of Mrs Pankhurst and Miss Emily Davison"). Emmeline Pankhurst was no less admiring: "Emily Davison clung to her conviction that one great tragedy, the deliberate throwing into the breach of a human life, would put an end to the intolerable torture of women."[18]

Symbolising male leisure, and hence male privilege, sport was among the most prominent targets of the arson campaign carried out in 1913–14 by the WSPU. At Hurst Park racecourse shortly after the 1913 Derby, reported *The Times*, two stands, the stewards' box, press box, kitchen and luncheon rooms were all destroyed. After Olive Hockin was arrested for an attack on Roehampton Golf Club, police raided her flat and found a copy of *The Suffragette*, the WPSU newspaper, alongside wire cutters, a new hammer, a gallon of paraffin, bottles of corrosive liquid and a false car number plate. Other golf courses were targets for acid attacks; the president of the Oxford University Boat Club was warned that militants would disrupt the 1913 Boat Race, though nothing came of it. In December 1913, it took an alert policeman to avert a fire in the County Grandstand at Aintree racecourse: smelling paraffin, he inspected the stand and not only discovered inflammable material on the staircase but, on the floor of the steward's room, a flaming candle atop a can of paraffin as the contents of its perch trickled into a basket of wadding. It had burned down to the last inch.[19]

Progress was accelerated by the First World War, during which women filled jobs vacated by soldiers. By the time it ended, British women had won the vote, following the lead set by their sisters in New Zealand (1893), South Australia (1895) and what was then the Grand Duchy of Finland, which in 1907 became the first to permit women MPs; by 1920, their sisters in the US, too, had the right to vote. It is impossible to quantify how much, if anything, Davison's sacrifice contributed to these steps along the road to emancipation, but when it comes to enduring images of the most radical political development of modern times, there can be little doubting that her fatal demonstration at Epsom promoted the idea of sport as a site for protest.

* * *

Had Emily Davison been alive now, she would hardly have been surprised at the comparatively sluggish progress made by women's sport. To elaborate on an earlier point, while it would be nonsensical to ghetto-ise sport as a celebration of masculinity, it is the one area of modern life where true equality remains unrealistic, at least for the foreseeable future. To cite two of the more inevitable disparities, nearly 30 seconds separate the fastest mile run by a man (Hicham El Guerrouj, 3mins 43.13secs) and the fastest by a woman, and while more than 80 men have run the 100 metres in under 10 seconds, no woman has run it quicker than the 10.49secs Florence Griffith-Joyner managed in 1988; and talk of her use of performance-enhancing drugs, heightened by her early death, has always maintained a question mark over that landmark. Athletics statisticians project, moreover, that it will be another half-century or more before, without the aid of an additional leg or lung, the new Cathy Freeman who follows the next new Cathy Freeman can consider racing the new Michael Johnson who comes in the wake of the next pretender. In golf and tennis, the gap is closing faster. Reliance on biceps and yobbery render the various football and rugby codes safer than most, at least in terms of mixed teams or boys v girls; with two people moving fairly slowly around a very small pitch, which in turn makes low blows/bites/head-butts that much easier to detect, boxing may actually be a lot more vulnerable. Cricket seems even less immune. However tricky it is to picture Katherine Blunt putting the wind up the opposition with quite the same velocity and ferocity as Dale Steyn, how much easier to imagine Mithari Raj giving Monty Panesar a better scrap than Mike Gatting ever gave Shane Warne. And what price a Shanette emerging from Sydney?

Overcoming physical disadvantages, however, has been but a fraction of the problem. For all the conspicuous strides made in sports such as football, cricket, rugby union and boxing, a 2012 survey by the Women's Sports And Fitness Foundation, a British charity campaigning to make physical activity an everyday part of life for women and girls, offered dispiriting evidence that the chasm between the sexes remains.

Loughborough University researchers found that, at the age of eight, around 60% of boys and girls did at least an hour's exercise five times per week; however, while 50% of 14-year-old boys were having regular exercise, the proportion of girls all but halved. The majority of 14-year-old girls surveyed wanted more exercise, but more than half said they had been alienated by the nature and content of PE lessons, which many found too competitive. Also cited was a perceived lack of female sporting role models (43 per cent said they simply did not have enough of them) and a reluctance to exercise in front of boys.[20]

Nor does it help, of course, when a trustworthy and influential newspaper reports, as the *New York Times* did in March 2007, the resignation of a women's basketball coach, Rene Portland of Penn State, ending as it did "a 27-year tenure that included 606 wins and allegations she discriminated *against* lesbian players". A month earlier, Portland and Penn State had settled a lawsuit by a former player, Jennifer Harris, who claimed Portland operated a "no-lesbian" policy.[21]

All the same, there has been no shortage of determined and successful odds-conquerors lately, especially in motor racing and equestrianism. In 2000, Julie Krone became the first woman to be inducted into the American horse racing Hall of Fame; in 2004, Beezie Madden became the first to reach the top three of the show jumping world rankings, and later the first to earn over $1m in prize money; in 2008, Danica Patrick became the first to win a race in the IndyCar Series, fully half a century after Maria Teresa de Filippis had become the first to start an F1 grand prix (Lella Lombardi followed De Filippis in 1974, becoming the first to win a point, but, as of February 2015, only three had emulated her, none of whom collected a point). The extent of the persisting inequality, nonetheless, was perhaps best summed up in 2012, when Sauber appointed Monisha Kaltenborn as F1's first female team principal, elevating her to the ranks of what Martin Whitmarsh, her counterpart at McLaren, described as "the most sexist, machismo bunch of managers you could ever hope to meet".[22]

The following year, propelling her vehicle at 196mph in practice for the Daytona 500, NASCAR's most prestigious event, Patrick outpaced 44 male rivals to become the first woman to win pole position in a major American motor race; not since 1995 had any NASCAR driver taken pole at such a lick. All well and good, but according to one of those quizzing her at the ensuing male-swamped press conference, the sniggeringly big question remained: would she be willing, in the event of victory, to uphold a near-ancient ritual and kiss Miss Sprint Cup? The reply was brisk and dressed in a wink: "There is only one mister I will be kissing, and I don't think they're going to be wearing a Sprint Cup suit."[23] The mister in question was a fellow rookie on the Sprint Cup circuit, Ricky Stenhouse Jr.

Others accused Patrick, then 30, of gaining pole position by unfair means: after all, she did weigh half as much as many of the other contenders. Come the race, as a consequence, she was carrying 40lb of ballast. "Victory will shatter the myth that motor racing is a man's game only," predicted Kevin Eason somewhat recklessly in *The Times*, forgetting to employ the conditional "would" required of all journalists who dare stick their neck, chin and/or nose out. Patrick finished eighth, but you knew what he meant. Niki Lauda, one of the most focused and courageous of four-wheel manipulators, needed no convincing of her promotional potential in Europe. "For ten years I have told Bernie [Ecclestone] he is dopey for not getting a woman into Formula One. If we could get a woman into the top six, you would have twice as many fans in front of the television."[24] To no one's surprise, a famous old hand scoffed. "I think they have the strength, but I don't know if they've got the mental aptitude to race hard, wheel-to-wheel," said Stirling Moss, once the person-ification of the fast-driving, posh-talking F1 macho man. "The mental stress would be pretty difficult for a lady to deal with in a practical fashion."[25]

There is "no biopsychological evidence that female athletes lack resilience", according to Jeff Breckon, a sports psychologist at Sheffield Hallam University. "There is no way of knowing in F1 because we haven't got a sample to test."[26] Still, it was esti-mated that, for every woman entering the sport, there were about 100 times as many men. "The reasons for that are probably as complex as for many other gender inequalities in society and probably not the subject of a sports page," acknowledged Mark Hughes in the *Sunday Times*, citing Susie Wolff, the third-string driver for Williams, as the only woman driver on the F1 horizon. On the other hand, in the longer term, the global economic down-turn, he suggested, was actually improving matters, prompting the smaller F1 teams to hire pay drivers – professionals who bring sponsorship rather than being employed by a team.[27]

Nor, given the long history of women's golf and the inroads into male tournaments made by the likes of Babe Didrikson, Jan Stephenson and Anneka Sorenstam, does it seem exces-sively optimistic to suggest that a woman could win a major this century. The history of women's cricket, too, is lengthy and illustrious: legend has it that the first person to bowl overarm was Christina Willes, who was purportedly unable to deliver the ball in the then-orthodox underarm manner of the early 19th century because of her voluminous dress; English and Australian women have been competing for their own Ashes since the mid-1930s; England's captain, Betty Archdale, later settled Down Under and was voted one of Australia's 100 Living Treasures; the first women's cricket World Cup actually predated the male version by two years. So while envisaging mixed teams in professional cricket is more far-fetched, the fact that a woman, Belinda Clark, was appointed manager of the Australian Cricket Academy in 2005 suggests it may well be within the bounds of possibility.

It is plainly ludicrous, moreover, that sports where performance is related to skill rather than physiological differences – such as archery, diving and shooting – are not already unisexual. Nor is it any less shameful that while Australia's basketballers and Japan's footballers (male branch) flew to London for the 2012 Olympics in business class, their female counterparts were lumbered with economy. Having just won Britain's first medal of the Games, the cyclist Lizzie Armitstead felt compelled to speak up. The sexism she had endured had at times, she said, been "overwhelming and frustrating".

The 2012 Olympics, nonetheless, represented a watershed of sorts: for the first time, every nation selected at least one female entrant, even Saudi Arabia, where fears that exercise promoted immodesty meant that girls have no PE classes or swimming lessons. Brunei and Qatar also lifted their bans on women participants. The lone non-male in the Afghanistan team, Tahmina Kohistani, found herself insulted on a daily basis as she trained for London, the target of countrymen still clinging to the conviction that sport and women must remain mutually exclusive. "Just as sporting boycotts were used to challenge apartheid in South Africa," noted Rachel Sylvester in *The Times*, "so the Olympics may help to break down the sexual apartheid that still exists in some countries."[28]

Yet even the most ardent feminist, male or female, would think twice before proposing that, when it comes to athletics, fights and ballgames, individual contests, elite or national teams should be mixed. There has always been far more to this, though, than being slower, weaker or meeker.

* * *

I think men are losing their way. I think they're losing what they're supposed to be as a man, what their role is, and who they are […]. For men, football is the culture isn't it?… I think there's certainly a lack of things that blokes can do together as blokes, because women push into everything and want to be included and take part. But I'm happy for blokes to do football, as I think it's important that they retain something that they can do together as men.[29]

Thus opined one of the 85 female fans of football and rugby union in England interviewed between 2006 and 2008 by Stacey Pope, a lecturer in sports sociology at the University of Bedfordshire. Their responses are examined in her article on "the meaning and importance" of sport for women, published in the May 2013 edition of the *Journal of Sport and Social Issues*, with particular emphasis being placed on how they answered the question "'Is being a City/Tigers fan an important part of who you are?" – the "City" and "Tigers" being Leicester City FC and Leicester Tigers RFC.

In doing so, Pope draws "tentatively" on Richard Giulianotti's distinction between "hot" and "cool" fandom[30], reflecting the degree and intensity of identification (he describes the latter as "followers and flâneurs"), but takes issue with the distinction he draws between "supporters" and "fans". Whereas the former, he reasons, have a longtime, deeply entrenched emotional investment in their club and support it financially, the latter are latecomers attracted chiefly by the club's success and simply enjoy associating themselves with the attendant celebrity (cf. overseas supporters of Manchester United, Barcelona et al). In collecting her data, Pope found there was "a considerable overlap" between the two sub-categories, and hence found them less than useful.

"Unlike 'flâneurs', my 'cool' fans did not typically switch allegiances between teams or players, and unlike 'followers' all had a clear commitment to one sports club only. In my work, 'cool' fans are defined as those for whom the club is not a central life interest but they still attend matches – occasionally or regularly – though this is usually viewed as one of many leisure activities." She also found "variations" between football and rugby union fans, with the former more likely to be "hot" and the latter "cool", a predictable outcome. "Crudely speaking, rugby union fans were more likely to fit middle-class identifiers than their football counterparts, so these social class differences, along with cultural differences between the two sports, probably played a key role in the different levels of commitment apparent."[31]

One Leicester City fan – who like the respondent quoted above was aged between 45 and 55 – had been involved in fan violence with young men during the 1970s and 1980s, and said she strongly identified both with men in general and, specifically, with archetypically aggressive male fans:

> *I've always been one of the lads, cos I've always done what they've done. Apart from having to use the ladies toilets (laughs)... Because I talk about football so much, men are more entertaining for me than women are. They [women] talk about shopping and the latest clothes from wherever, all this designer stuff. I just haven't got a clue. Whereas you can go anywhere in the world and with your knowledge of football, you can have a conversation with anyone. Well any man anyway. So I've always been in men's company.*[32]

By contrast, notes Pope, "those fans who performed more 'feminine' femininities did not tend to self-identify as tomboys or to play contact team sports. Playing football was often perceived as something that 'girls did not do' [by] these women, and playing rugby was simply out of reach for most rugby fans. Of the 34 rugby fans interviewed only one respondent spoke about playing rugby – she played casually with brothers in the back garden when younger – in contrast to the 22 (out of 51) football fans who discussed how they would often have an informal 'kick-about' usually with 'lads' or male relatives, despite the lack of encouragement and barriers for girls to play organised football at school."[33]

All this, I trust, underlines the difficulties inherent in assessing the degree to which the stereotype remains true: that sport, for participants and especially spectators, is a "male" thing.

Football's "secret" history

Egregious is perhaps the most temperate way to describe the treatment long meted out to women wanting to pursue the world's most popular sport. The second decade of the 20th century saw a number of clubs emerge, headed by the Dick, Kerr Ladies of Lancashire and Fémina, who in 1921 represented England and France respectively in the first women's football international. Prominent on page eight of *The Daily Mirror* were two photographs of Lily Parr, scorer of all five of the "England" goals.[34] An eminent French football figure, Jules Rimet, did his bit, helping organise two matches played by women's teams in 1920 before a crowd of 10,000.[35] Yet in the same year of that inaugural international, even though (or perhaps because) Dick, Kerr had grown accustomed to attracting four- and even five-figure crowds, the FA banned women from Football League grounds, claiming that players' "expenses" absorbed too much from the money being raised for charity but also as a consequence of the widespread view, as Jean Williams put it, that women playing football for money was "unsuitable".[36]

After the war, women played football in Austria, Germany and, so evidence suggests, Russia. They played at colleges in Canada, Hong Kong and the US. In France, they not only began playing at a similar time to their British counterparts but promoted the sport internationally, most notably via the Women's World Games. "By 1925," writes Williams, "there were debates in *Sport und Sonne* about the essentially masculine nature of football, as one article headline indicated, 'Das Fussbalspielist Männerspiel', but notions of the body and permissiveness were changing: the elegant 'sport girl' exemplified by the willowy tennis player in whites and the 'new woman' of boxing and athletics in the Weimar Republic graced the covers of *Sport und Sonne* in the 1930s. In contrast, pioneers of women's football, such as 19-year-old Lotte Specht, were making the Frankfurt weekly press look very much like they had just played a hard match."[37]

FIFA has admitted that it only recently began researching the formative years of women's football. As the 1970s wore on, so more countries lifted bans on the women's game – England in 1971, Brazil in 1975. Rome staged a women's world championship in 1970; Mexico followed suit the next year. All the same, FIFA's claims that the first official international was played between France and the Netherlands in April 1971 remain unfettered by verification.

The first idol

In *Women in European Culture and Society: Gender, Skill and Identity from 1700*, an academic survey published in 2011, Deborah Simonton traces the rise of the female global sports star back to the first appearance at Wimbledon in 1919 of Suzanne Lenglen, a Parisian who paraded her skills before the great, the good and the royal in what Alan Little, the Wimbledon Museum's kindly and devoted honorary librarian, described as "a flimsy, white, calf-length short-sleeved tennis frock with the shirt pleated, whiter stockings and a soft linen hat… 'the Lenglen bandeau'".[38] Rare as it was, such daring chimed perfectly with the times. After all, Lenglen's mother, as Dick Holt has observed, "was worried in case her daughter became too involved in competitive sport and forgot the real purpose of the ladies' game: to stay fit, feminine and to find a man". Lenglen, indeed, grew up "in the new world of jolly middle-class adventure, in which young men experimented with cameras, motor-cars and aeroplanes while their sisters practised forehand and backhand returns of serve."[39]

In Lenglen, declared Larry Englemann in *The Goddess and the American Girl: The Story of Suzanne Lenglen and Helen Wills*, "journalists had at last stumbled upon a subject commensurate with their capacity for hyperbole". Indeed, such was the awe she aroused, her countrymen nicknamed her "La Divine". The focus of those who opposed her rise to prominence "was her sexuality", deduced Jennifer Hargreaves, the leading British chronicler and analyst of women's sport, to whom she "embodied a popular male-defined image of femininity". Put simply, her choice of garb, donned to enhance mobility and flexibility, revealed – or at least hinted at – more of what lay beneath than was deemed acceptable in purportedly polite circles. Some spectators were "excited by her radical image"; others were spurred to walk out on account of her "indecency".[40]

To confine Lenglen's importance to her clothing and general flamboyance, though, would be a gross distortion of her giddy accomplishments. A versatile athlete who had excelled at boating, swimming, golf and cycling, and first flexed a tennis racket at 11, she went on to claim six singles titles at both Wimbledon and the French Open as well as a brace of Olympic golds. Her pre-eminence between the tramlines was absolute. On no fewer than nine occasions she won a singles event without dropping a single game; in 10 seasons she captured 250 titles – 83 singles, 74 doubles and 93 mixed doubles; from 1919 to 1926 she lost just one singles match, winning 179 in succession up to her retirement as an amateur. Her decision to become the game's first professional, though, was presaged by an episode that saw her insult a queen, however inadvertently.

At Wimbledon in 1926, upon discovering she had a doubles tie scheduled immediately after a singles contest, Lenglen asked her mixed partner, Jacques Brugnon, to telephone the organisers and inform them that, because she had already booked a doctor's appointment, she would not arrive in time for the singles. Unfortunately, the message did not reach the referee. As a consequence, when Queen Mary took her seat at 3pm, expecting to see Lenglen in action, she was sorely disappointed. When Lenglen arrived half an hour later she found herself plunged into an argument with members of the All England committee; fleeing to the sanctuary of the dressing room, she was said to have sobbed hysterically. Both her matches were postponed. For one thing, the committee knew that scratching the champion would be exceedingly unpopular with the public; besides, while they could have claimed a walkover, her opponents declined.[41] In the event, "La Divine" withdrew.

"One thing that can be said with reasonable certainty," concluded Steve Wagg, "is that the first female sport celebrity would be drawn from the upper echelons of society." No less likely was that she would be French. "For one thing, influential elements in French society and the French state regarded sport as important in the maintaining of national morale and international profile."[42] In fact, in what Bruce Kidd has characterised as a "breakthrough obscured by time"[43], the first Women's Olympic Games were staged in Paris in 1922 – in flagrant defiance of the IOC.

"She altered the whole aspect of women's tennis," asserted Kitty Godfree, the Englishwoman who relieved Lenglen of her Wimbledon singles crown when the latter withdrew in 1924 and 1926. "Few women before her played the all-court game; but Suzanne volleyed like a man and continually played with the best men of her country in practice in doubles."[44] Others have countered such a warm tribute, asserting that Lenglen did not achieve change singlehandedly but defined a movement already in progress. It would be wrong, furthermore, to neglect the contribution of the burgeoning popular press in Britain, for whom sport and celebrity now served as trusty weapons in the tussle for hearts, minds and, above all, pockets.

The Other Babe

Even before she reached her teens, Mildred "Babe" Didrikson, by any standard the greatest of all professional sportswomen, knew her goal precisely: she wanted to be "the greatest athlete who ever lived". An "odd ambition", warranted Arthur Daley. After all, he reasoned, "the best woman athlete in almost any sport is about on a par with a schoolboy champion".[45]

One of seven children born to Norwegian immigrants, Didrikson won her nickname the day she hit 13 home runs in a softball game. At 16 she was selected for the All-America basketball team. Two years later, in 1932, the Employers Casualty Company of Dallas took the NAAU team title through its lone competitor: Didrikson had done her bit and then some, winning five events and tying for a sixth. Later that year, at the first and immensely more modest LA Olympics, she struck gold in the javelin and 80m hurdles and only missed the high jump title because the judges took exception during the jump-off when she dived over the bar – just as she had been doing throughout the competition. In each case she broke the world record. Then she got serious.

Forfeiting her amateur status after allowing her name to be used in a car advert, she turned to golf, winning the first tournament she entered (she even correctly predicted her first-round score, 77). Marrying a wrestler, George Zaharias, she reigned supreme through the first four years of the Ladies Professional Golf Association tour (1948-51), heading the moneywinners each season. In 1945 she played in three men's PGA Tour events, making all three cuts at the Los Angeles, Phoenix and Tucson Opens. Famously, in a charity event, came an aside from that famously enthusiastic shanker Bob Hope: "I hit the ball like a girl and she hits it like a man."

Arthur Daley, predictably, felt obliged to add the rejoinder his readers demanded: "Behind that steel-sinewed, square-jawed façade was feminine softness and gushy sentimentality."[46] Yet even this snooty male supremacist was awestruck: "The Babe practised sixteen hours a day each weekend. On weekdays, she was on the course at 5.30 am for a three-hour session. Then she went to her regular job." She put in the hard yards in every sense: "I hit golf balls until my hands were bloody and sore. Then I'd have tape all over my hands and blood all over the tape."[47] In 1954, a year after contracting colon cancer, she won the US Open, but died the following year. Already voted the greatest sportswoman of the first half of the century, the Associated Press duly anointed her the century's sporting empress.[48] Now for a counter-argument.

Housewife superstar

It is a measure of the ingrained sexism of sport that, as late as 2012, John Goodbody began his entry for No.5 in the *Sunday Times*' 100 Greatest Olympic Moments with the words "Dutch housewife and mother…" To be fair, he was referring to Fanny Blankers-Koen and, more specifically, her four gold medals at the 1948 Olympics, a record haul for a female athlete that could have been half as much again had she competed in the high jump and long jump, wherein she held the extant world records. The rules, however, restricted her to three individual events. Half a century did nothing to dim her achievements. In 1999 she was voted the dying century's foremost female athlete by the IAAF, a legacy of the way the so-called "Flying Housewife" subverted expectations of her sex.

The daughter of a government inspector and brought up in Hoofdorp, Amsterdam, Francina Elsje Koen was blessed by the encouragement of a sporting family and the challenge of four brothers, quickly learning to swim, skate and play tennis. At 17 she joined the Amsterdam Dames' Athletic Club, cycling 18 miles each way to the gym. With no outdoor track available, it was there that she trained. The following year she competed at the 1936 Berlin Games, finishing sixth in the high jump, then returned home to face, and survive, the Nazi occupation. Training in secret, she was a mother of two when she came over for the second and least showy London Games. She had set half a dozen world records by then but her prospects were scorned. Such disdain, she would reflect, "was just the thing to rouse me". Cue a golden four-gun riposte in the 100m, 200m, 80m hurdles and sprint relay. Four decades later she met Jesse Owens and began to introduce herself. "You don't have to tell me that," interrupted Owens. "I know all about you."

She returned home to a parade, riding with her husband in an open coach pulled by four white horses. "All I did," she kept repeating, dizzy with amazement, "was win some foot races." The media "played up her role as wife and mother", wrote Janet Woolum in *Outstanding Women Athletes: Who They Are and How They Influenced Sports in America,* but "the image they created of her as housewife/mother/athlete helped to dispel the myth that women would lose their femininity while competing in world class track and field races."[49] Like so many, the Second World War robbed her of further opportunity; how well she might have fared in the cancelled Olympics of 1940 and 1944 can readily be gauged by the world records she set during that period for high jump, long jump, 100 yards and 80m. A biography written by Kees Kooman, a Dutch journalist, was published in 2003, entitled *Een koningin met mannenbenen* – "A queen with men's legs". A statue in Rotterdam stands further testimony to the trail she blazed in conjunction with The Other Babe.

Twists and shouts

In 1953, the IOC decided to reassess the suitability of women's track and field. Caring, sharing Avery Brundage referred to "the well-grounded protest against events which are not truly feminine", such as long-distance running and the throwing disciplines. His Slaveriness also contended that the Olympic movement favoured only those events "appropriate to the feminine sex". Even though it was decided to leave things as they were, Brundage still felt obliged to add that around one-third of the national Olympic associations – or so he claimed – "would be happier if there were not events for the opposite sex".[50]

The media was nothing if not complicit in this reactionary movement. That same year, in a column headlined "More Deadly than Male", Babe Didrikson's on-off supporter, Arthur Daley, railed against the "grotesque contortions" of female runners, jumpers and throwers, warranting that "it does something to a guy. And it ain't love, Buster."[51] In a 1960 column entitled "Venus Wasn't A Shot Putter", William Barry Furlong ploughed a similar furrow, likening "patriotic assertions to having the best muscled girls to claiming the best-looking automobile wreck". Women, interpreted Susan Cahn in *Coming On Strong – Gender and Sexuality in Twentieth-Century Women's Sport*, were "a consumer item 'wrecked' for male pleasure by athletic training".[52]

"Ironically," noted Cahn, "the source of the problem – Soviet women's Olympic dominance – provided a partial solution for those officials and journalists who urged support for US women. The American team could shed damning images of unsexed, mannish women by displacing them onto Soviet athletes. Descriptions of 'ponderous, peasant-type Russian athletes' and

'Amazons from the Russian steppes' created a contrasting 'other' whose very presence lent some legitimacy to the less talented US team."[53] Of course, come the Olympics, the Irenas had it.

Title IX

The 1970s were a turning point for women in American culture, symbolised for the masses by *The Mary Tyler Moore Show*, the first TV series to revolve around a relatively new species called the "career woman", which premiered in the first year of that decade. In sporting terms, the key development came two years later, when Congress passed a raft of educational amendments, among them Title IX, a measure that would have revolutionary repercussions for women's sport in the US and, by inexorable if slow extension, the rest of the world. No resident, it ruled, "shall, on the basis of sex be excluded from participation in, or denied the benefits of, or be subjected to discrimination under any educational program or activity receiving federal aid." Athletics may have aroused the most fervent controversy, but a broad range of advances were achieved. Prior to Title IX, many schools refused to admit women or enforced strict limits. Statistical evidence cited as evidence of the strides taken by American women between 1972 and 1994 included collecting:

- 38% of medical degrees, up from 9%
- 43% of law degrees, up from 7%
- 44% of doctoral degrees to U.S. citizens, up from 25%[54]

Between 1972 and 2004 the number of female athletes taking part in high school sports multiplied seven times, from 290,000 to 2 million.[55]

After Serena Williams won her fifth Wimbledon singles title in 2012, she was asked a familiar question, "a question that seems to be posited to every female athlete at every level of competition" as Dave Zirin put it: "Was it difficult for you to control your emotions?" For Zirin it was "a window into why so many women and men celebrated the recent 40th anniversary of the passage of Title IX". There was, he argued, "arguably no piece of progressive legislation that's touched more people's lives", pointing out that, according to the Women's Sports Foundation, while one in 35 high-school girls played a sport in 1972, a third did so in 2012. Before Title IX, fewer than 16,000 women participated in sport at university, compared with more than a dozen times that number now. "All stereotypes about women being too 'emotional' to handle sports," attested Zirin, "were answered when the gyms were unlocked."[56]

In Playing With the Boys: Why Separate is Not Equal, Eileen McDonagh and Laura Pappano contend that "coercive sex segregation does not reflect actual sex differences in athletic ability, but instead constructs and enforces a flawed premise that females are inherently athletically inferior to males."[57] In *Stolen Bases: Why American Girls Don't Play Baseball*, Jennifer Ring tackled, among other revealing issues, the long-held male view that American girls should be confined to softball, even though the roots of baseball lie in rounders – a unisexual if fervently amateur game. After all, not until baseball was professionalised and commercialised at the end of the 19th century were the womenfolk hurried off the diamond. Albert Spalding, notes Zirin, worked to establish a culture that "would mythologise baseball as a manly American game"; like President Theodore Roosevelt and others, he regarded sports and masculinity as being tied closely to US imperialism. "They gave us a primordial ooze where sexism, homophobia, militarism and sports all simmered in the same stew. Straining out what's healthy in this stew has been a slow, arduous, century-long task."

Courting triumph

As has already been hinted at, no sport has seen women move further from that intimidating male shadow than tennis. Indeed, so effective has been the sea-change, they are paid the same prize money as the menfolk at major events. When the Frenchman Gilles Simon complained about this during the 2012 Wimbledon tournament, airing the complaint that his sex had to accept this despite playing up to five sets rather than three,

Maria Sharapova delivered a stinging retort: "I'm sure there are a few more people that watch my matches than him."

That black market tickets for the men's final were expected to be worth five times as much as for the women's equivalent put such a claim into perspective. Hannah Wilks was scornful. "When the only meaningful rivalries are between [Federer, Djokovic, Murray and Nadal], why invest in lesser players battling each other for the dubious honour of being crushed by the top seeds? Watching a predictable demolition in place of a match may be a pleasant way to spend an afternoon, but it hardly gets the pulse racing. Women's tennis is a different story. The top ten boasts legends of the game bumping shoulders with a young generation, all of whom believe they can bust their way into the top echelons...It can be rejoiced in as no-holds-barred competition at its best. Some people call this chaos; I call it must-watch drama."[58]

Hugh McIlvanney begged to disagree. "The Grand Slam events of tennis are immeasurably enhanced by the contribution of the women's game and the generous rewarding of its star performers shouldn't be resented. But there is no virtue in denying that the establishment of equality in prize money...was a clear-cut example of affirmative action, a reflection of gender politics rather than of the market forces that usually govern payment structures in the profoundly commercialised world of professional sport... And, as Andy Murray has emphasised, the shorter matches played by women make it easier for them than for highly ranked men to go for the substantial pots of extra cash in the doubles championship." Sometimes, he concluded, "equality isn't fair".[59] As with all forms of affirmative action, however, it was a case of compensation for the sins of the past. One satisfactory compromise could be to reward all players according to the number of sets won.

* * *

"Show me a young lady who travels the tour and wins matches and I'll show you a tough lady. Regardless of the sadness and loneliness, they come through. Dad may watch from the side-lines and think she wins because she's a bloody good tennis player. But she wins because she's tough." So opined Don Candy, an Australian doubles specialist in the pre-Open era, in *Ladies of the Court – Grace And Disgrace On The Women's Tennis Tour*, a book by the oft-garlanded American novelist and jour-nalist Michael Mewshaw. Having done the same with the men a decade earlier, he spent 1992 rummaging around the courts and locker rooms for insights, tantrums and titbits. "And yet," he wrote, "in contrast to the men, female competitors are expected to fall back into more demure roles as soon as they come off court. Tenacious and hard-nosed as they may be during matches, they have to be charming, good-humoured, modest, soft spoken, and ingratiating afterward. The mark of a male champion can be a Sequoia-sized chip on the shoulder. But women champions are judged not just on their results but on their ability to strike a series of traditional ladylike poses."[60]

The first to defy that unwritten obligation was Billie Jean King. To Chris Evert, one of those who prospered most from her fellow American's ceaseless efforts to promote and improve the fledgling women's professional tennis circuit in the late Sixties and 1970s, she was "a missionary", before adding: "No frontier is too wide, no challenge too intimidating." Billie Jean was "the leader of the pack, the queen of the hill and so proud of women's tennis that she turned the sport into a big-time event", remem-bered Martina Navratilova, who studied her idol so carefully "that I even began arguing with officials at times", reasoning that, "if Billie Jean King didn't mind looking like a competitor on court, why should I?" King "set the standard... made us feel we were all in this together".[61]

"In a world where feminism, or post-feminism, is so often reassessed and derided, tennis is a rare oasis of incontroverti-bility," Alessandra Stanley asserted in the *New York Times* after seeing the TV documentary *Billie Jean: Portrait of a Pioneer*, which first aired on HBO in 2006. "That battle for equality was narrow and hard won, but its gains are lasting. Women's tennis is now as popular as men's, its stars are just about as well rewarded in prize money and product endorsements, and the prestige of the game was enhanced, not weakened, by the incursion. It might not have happened without Billie Jean King."[62]

It was her future husband, the former Billie Jean Moffitt insisted, who had opened her eyes to feminism: while studying together at college, Larry King had pointed out that the sole reason he had won a tennis scholarship and she hadn't was the fact that he was a man and she wasn't. Few tipped her for stardom. Recalling her first doubles victory as a 17-year-old at Wimbledon in 1961, Frank Deford described her as a "chubby little thing with the hideous, tacky glasses". The sense of injustice, though, was acute and innate, likewise the resolve to overcome: to win. King spent the next decade hoovering up titles, benefiting from the yawning dawning of the Open era.

Gaining the respect of her male counterparts was the first phase. In the previous decade, remembered Gordon Forbes: "We watched them, were amused by them, and annoyed when their matches went on too long and held up the starts of our own. We laughed at their funny service actions, and the mighty female swings they made at overheads. 'All arms and grunts and open mouths,' said Lew Hoad once, 'and then a bloody great swing and instead of a smash, out pops a mouse.'" One afternoon at Wimbledon, Forbes was in the changing room and found himself unable to avoid the running commentary being provided by Roy Emerson, the Australian who would wind up with 14 Grand Slam titles and was watching a televised match: "Here's a lob, and here's a lob, and here's a lob off a lob. And here's a smash that turns into a lob. And here's the lob with the wind, that will lob into the Royal Box." Another player interrupted: "What's going on, Emmo?" Cue the damning reply: "Ladies' doubles."[63]

"Billie Jean and her colleagues soon changed *that*," asserted Forbes. "Billie Jean is the modern American female through and through and a great tennis player. More than great," he enthused after King had won an event in Corfu in 1968. "I find, in this book, that I have used up all my adjectives on the men players – I suppose because they are much easier for me to understand. But the girls were as much a part of this section of tennis history as were the men."[64]

King had already confirmed herself as one of the game's all-time titans when, in 1973, a year that had begun with the conclusion of *Roe v Wade*, which legalised abortion in the US, she picked up the gauntlet hurled down by her fellow-American Bobby Riggs, a 55-year-old member of the burgeoning men's senior circuit, and flung it back into his crinkly, sneering face.

That June, three months before she confronted Riggs across a net in Texas in the so-called "Battle of the Sexes", the then-world No.1 had spearheaded the formation of the Women's Tennis Association. The economic plight of the women's professional game at the time was such that, at a tournament in Los Angeles, King had been dumbstruck to learn that the winner of the men's event would earn six times as much as his female counter-part. On 20 June, she coaxed and chivvied 63 female players to cram into a room at London's Gloucester Hotel. "I got everyone in there and told [Dutch player] Betty Stove to lock the door," she recalled 40 summers later. "I said, 'Don't let anybody out because I can't spend one more ounce of my life on this. If we can't make this happen today I'm finished.'"[65]

King was little more than half Riggs' age. Earlier that year, she had initially rebuffed this provocatively sexist challenge, whereupon Riggs, eager to generate publicity and ballyhoo and thus make a few much-needed bucks, had taken on Margaret Court, then world No.1, in California and thrashed her 6-2, 6-1. On Mother's Day. What a card. At one juncture the Australian actually curtsied to him. For King, news of the surrender by Court, who would retire with a still-unmatched 24 grand slam singles titles on her CV, stirred a change of heart. "I was on a long-haul flight when I heard the result and thought 'you've got to be kidding me'," she recollected shortly before the 2013 release of James Erskine's documentary *The Battle of the Sexes*. "I knew I had to play this guy."

The build-up to the King-Riggs match was showbiz at its purest and kitschest and vilest. "It was promoted like an Ali-Frazier fight,"[66] remembered King. Without the self-restraint, that is. Riggs did the TV rounds, baiting her, playing the role of the male chauvinist pig to the hilt. It was all part of the act, of course, to boost box-office takings, but Riggs' misogyny seeped through. "I want to prove that women are lousy, they stink, they don't belong on the same court as a man," he scoffed before delivering the ultimate insult, disdaining any form of preparation.[67] Not that the game lacked sexist pigs. "A women should stay at home and have babies," Stan Smith, the 1972 Wimbledon champion and a US military man down to his best-selling footwear. "That's what she's for. I mean, this women's lib thing could go too far."[68] King "prepared like crazy". The way she saw it, she had no option: "I had to win, I simply had to win."[69] At the time, as she noted, American women weren't even allowed to have their own credit cards.

Intrigue duly stoked, come the big day, more than 30,000 spectators turned up at the Houston Astrodome, the biggest crowd yet for a tennis match in the US. As an 80-piece brass band blared out *Jesus Christ Superstar*, King was carried aloft into the Houston Astrodome in a chair held by four bare-chested muscle men dressed as ancient slaves; Riggs followed in a rickshaw drawn by barely-clad models. He gave her a giant lollipop; she gave him a piglet named Larimore Hustle. But it wasn't all sly winks and jovial nudges. Before the match commenced, King delivered an ultimatum: either ABC dropped Jack Kramer from its commentary team or she wouldn't play. "He doesn't believe in women's tennis," she reasoned. "Why should he be part of this match? He doesn't believe in half of the match. Either he goes or I go."[70] Kramer did, reportedly of his own accord.

The match, watched by a record 100m TV viewers, was a triumph for King and womankind: she swept to victory in three straight sets to take home $250,000: the handsomest sum yet won on a court that wasn't presided over by someone in a silly wig. It was also two and a half times her landmark earnings in

31 tournaments in 1971, the season she'd become the first woman to net $100,000 in tour prize money. The post-match buzz was that Riggs had bet against himself and taken a dive: according to some reports, he took a lie-detector test to quash such patently squalid slander. Even nasty ol' Jack Kramer didn't buy it. "Billie Jean beat him fair and square. A lot of men — especially around our age — were so stunned when he lost that they figured he must have tanked... But what motive would Riggs have for that? Bobby Riggs, the biggest ham in the world, gets his greatest audience — and purposefully looks bad? There's no way. If he had beaten Billie Jean, he could have kept the act going indefinitely. Next they would have had him play Chrissie [Evert] on clay."[71]

The repercussions of her victory were not lost on King.

I got letters from women saying that before, they were afraid to challenge their male bosses at work but when I beat Bobby that day, their lives changed. They demanded raises, demanded better working conditions and do you know what? They got them. In 1973 we had the courage to stand up for what we thought was right and we showed what was possible for women in sport.[72]

* * *

Any lingering doubts about what remained an inconvenient truth for many had all but vanished by 2007, the year women achieved parity of prize money at all four Grand Slam events. Wimbledon was the last to fall into line, and it was a measure of the more rapid progress made by American women in all walks of life that the US Open organisers had taken this step in 1973, fully three decades before the other three majors. "Women's tennis is the leader in women's sports," avowed Billie Jean King when, not unnaturally, reporters made a beeline for her. "Equal prize money is a no-brainer." Granted, the French Open was still offering parity exclusively to the winners, but that soon changed. Even more encouraging was the objection that quickly dawned on the menfolk, who in the words of the player-turned-commentator Peter Fleming would "grow up at some point".[73] In how many other jobs, the oldest profession aside, could a woman earn as much as a man yet put in fewer hours?[74]

All the same, some vices die harder than others. Shortly after the unfairly photogenic Sharapova had won her French Open quarter-final in 2012, she was interviewed courtside by Cedric Pioline, a broadcaster who had been one of the host nation's foremost male players before retiring from singles duty in 2002. Obligingly, in discussing her plans between now and the semi-final, he proffered, gigglingly: "You can go shopping here."

The Bitter Tears of Caster Semenya

Sport first confronted (or, rather, ran away from) transgender politics in 1976, when, a year after what we now call sexual reassignment surgery, the tennis player Renée Richards refused to submit to chromosomal testing and was barred from competing in the US Open, purportedly because of a policy restricting entry to women *born* as women. Suing the US Tennis Association, her immense persistence – an asset easily envisaged of someone born to one of the nation's first female psychiatrists – began to pay off the following year. That was when the New York Supreme Court ruled in her favour, permitting her to step on court against Virginia Wade 17 years after making her debut as Richard Raskin.

Playing until 1981, Renée scaled the heights of world No.20 and later coached Martina Navratilova to two Wimbledon titles. It was a natural fit: two outsiders, one team. What "really moved" Navratilova was Renée/Richard's attempt to reduce a somewhat obstructive Adam's apple "and how the drill cut right through into the trachea", nearly choking the patient. "All I can say is that Renée must have wanted to become a woman very badly."[75]

In July 2009, the next major sexual hurdle reared its head. At the Africa Junior Championships, Caster Semenya ran the year's fastest 800m by a woman to date. A week later, she was subjected to secret gender tests by Athletics South Africa (ASA).

In Berlin 12 days after that, she plunged into the goldfish bowl by winning the World Championship final and almost drowned.

After the race, it emerged that the IAAF had requested gender tests, drawing accusations from South African bodies, including the ANC, that her treatment had been racist. "We condemn the motives of those who have made it their business to question her gender due to her physique and running style. Such comments can only serve to portray women as being weak. Caster is not the only woman athlete with a masculine build and the [IAAF] should know better."[76] In those pre-Berlin tests, it was soon reported, Semenya had had three times the normal female level of testosterone in her body. Meanwhile, Leonard Chuene, president of ASA, was absolutely emphatic: there had been no tests. Repeat: no tests. It was, he insisted, a case of "racism, pure and simple".

Roll on another fortnight and lo and behold, Wilfred Daniels, the head ASA coach, resigns. Cue claims in the *Sydney Morning Herald* that Semenya has male and female sexual organs and is thus, technically, a hermaphrodite. With no job to lose, Daniels claims that Semenya had been subjected to two hours of tests before the Berlin race, and Chuene finally concedes the same while pointing out that Semenya knew nothing of their purpose. On 5 November, Chuene is suspended and ASA apologise publicly to Semenya. Not until July 2010 would the IAAF – which kept the gender tests private – clear her to return to the track.[77]

"What resonates most from the whole Semenya saga are the complexities involved," summed up the Sunderland University quartet of Neil Farrington, Daniel Kilvington, John Price and Amir Saeed in their wide-ranging and valuable 2012 study *Race, Racism And Sports Journalism*. The difficulties perceived ranged from defining gender to "the complexities of dealing with this in public and political arenas, the complexities created when issues of gender and 'race' combine, and the complexities of trying to report it all". From a scientific perspective, since there are wide variations within traditional categories of gender, black-and-white classifications are impossible, not to say divisive; as a partial consequence of this, "the IAAF struggled to deal with this case in a clear and coherent manner". ASA, felt Price et al, also "handled the situation very badly", costing a number of people their livelihoods.[78]

To the dismay, no doubt, of many other academics – and notwithstanding the flourishing by British tabloid newspapers of expressions such as "sex-riddle runner", "gender row runner", "manly athlete", "butch 800m runner" and "drag racer", and even seaside-postcard-type headings such as "BET SHE'S GOT ONE" – Price and his team credited the media, on balance, with a proportionate and sensitive approach. "A world champion… being investigated, and potentially stripped of their gold medal, is a genuine news story. It is true that events were complex and nuanced, which always poses a problem for the space, time constraints and culture of journalism. But most of the reporting of the case was considered and sensitive, and sought to high-light and grapple with these complexities. Sources were drawn from a wide range of ethnic and social backgrounds, while the descriptions of Semenya tended to be neutral in nature. In short, most journalists and publications dealt with a tricky matter pretty well."[79]

There were exceptions, inevitably, most notably in the mass-market tabloids, *The Sun* and *Daily Star*, where certain descriptions of Semenya "can be viewed as part of a tradition which undermines the credentials of black female athletes by taking a narrow ethnic perspective on what it means to be a woman". At best, they concluded, "this was some tabloids being their indiscriminating, crude but largely harmless selves", at worst "another chapter in a long story of racist discourse".

The IOC had dealt with such matters previously, albeit inconsistently, stressed Jane Caudwell, a leading authority on "queer" politics and sport, who cited cases such as that of Stanisława Walasiewicz (aka Stella Walsh). The daughter of Polish parents who migrated to Cleveland when she was three months old, she was wearing her native vest when she took gold in the 100m at the 1932 Games, then returned to her adoptive home to take up American citizenship, marry a boxer and win national titles before being induced into the US Track and Field Hall of Fame in 1975. In 1980, aged 69, she was a bystander in an armed robbery in Cleveland and was killed, whereupon an autopsy revealed her to have possessed male genitalia. "Polish research also indicates that she displayed some female characteristics," emphasised Don Salt, a science writer, and Zoe Brain, a computer scientist, in the magazine *Cosmos*. "Detailed investigation more recently has also revealed that she had the male XY pair of chromosomes. Controversy over her gender remains unresolved, although official documents and history record her as female."[80]

The treatment of Semenya, suggested Caudwell, echoed that of Santhio Soundarajan, another 800m runner publicly shamed three years earlier by the IAAF's decision to reclaim her medal (a silver at the Asian Games in Doha). These cases comprised "our most contemporary exemplars of how sport governing bodies regard women's ambiguous athletic bodies". As of 2011, Soundarajan, unlike Semenya, remained "disqualified". Men, reasoned Caudwell, "have escaped surveillance of their sexed and general bodies. Women have not, and this has left a legacy of suspicion and shame which besieges women's participation in the Olympics. For women athletes, such as Semenya, there are certain ironies that surround their successes."[81]

Caudwell cites a paper entitled "The unforgiveable transgression of being Caster Semenya" by Tavia Nyong'o:

> ... *instead of insisting upon the naturalness of her gender, how about turning the question around and denaturalizing the world of gender segregated, performance-obsessed, commercially-driven sports, a world that can neither seem to do with or without excessive bodies like Semenya's and their virtuosic bodies?*[82]

What pretty much everyone tiptoed around, though, was the elephant on the track. "Just look at her," said Russia's Mariya Savinova in the immediate aftermath of Semenya's Berlin run. "For me she is not a woman," charged Italy's Elisa Cusma

Piccione. "I am also sorry for the other competitors… It is useless to compete with this and it is not fair." Even before the race, the British 800m runner Jenny Meadows told *The Guardian* a year later, shortly after Semenya's return to the starting line, the mood was uncomfortable, with rivals "staring and laughing" at the South African.

> *I would expect the situation to arise again, if I'm honest. I always treat everyone the same but to be honest, even the year previously with Pamela Jelimo [the 800m Olympic champion], all the rest of the girls were obviously looking at Jelimo, just wanting to weigh her up and thinking: "Why can this girl be so far ahead of us?" That's what happens when you're a little bit of a freak of nature just because you are so much further ahead of the rest of your opponents.*[83]

The waters grew greyer still in 2013 when the ghost of Stella Walsh drifted back. Four unnamed elite female athletes aged between 18 and 21 were found to possess XY chromosomes: the genetic definition of a man and a disorder which affects an estimated one in 4,500 people. After tests during the 2012 Olympics showed them to have abnormal testosterone levels, the athletes were referred to scientists at university hospitals in Nice and Montpellier. While each had internal male testes, they were allowed to compete after undergoing surgery to have them removed, in addition to hormone replacement therapy to reduce their testosterone levels to below those found in men – the IAAF's extant test of eligibility.[84]

"The surgeons have neutered these individuals," bemoaned Dr Gedis Grudzinskas, an eminent gynaecologist based at the private London Bridge hospital, who criticised the IAAF for "opening the door to abuse" if such athletes were permitted to compete in women's events. "These women are born with female genitals," said Professor Charles Sultan, head of hormonology at Montpellier University Hospital, "but they assume male char-acteristics at puberty with considerable muscular development, a man's frame and a testosterone level similar to that of a man.

They have the chromosome Y synonymous with masculinity. They can have 25% more muscular mass than their competitors."

In the *International Journal for the History of Sport*, Lindsay Parks Pieper, a doctoral student at Ohio State University and graduate of the International Olympic Academy, likened Renee Richards to Semenya, whose "muscular stature, deep voice and athletic successes all challenged feminine norms and threatened the long-standing gender divide".

> To Richards, being recognised as a "lady" signified societal acceptance. In [a] 2009 interview she explained, "with me it was primarily that I wanted to be acknowledged that I was indeed female". To earn and then maintain this recognition, she consequently embraced the tenets of traditional femininity, from dresses to domesticity. Richards also bowed to the gender stereotypes in sports by emphasising her post-operative, hormone-treated female build as physically inferior to her former male stature. Richards donned pink nail polish for public confirmation, described her depleted strength for athletic inclusion and learned the graciousness of losing to exemplify her womanhood.[85]

Yet however unenviable their experiences, however much Semenya and Soundarajan warrant our compassion, and whatever the perceived rights and wrongs of the cases involving Richards/Raskin and Walasiewicz/Walsh (few of which can be stated with absolute conviction), to regard Jenny Meadows' view as unconscionable does not seem entirely fair either.

The Golf Wars

That golf remains a game, as Nick Pitt put it, "for upper-class, middle-aged, white Protestant men"[86] is beyond dispute, especially the last characteristic. Exhibit A: Scotland's Royal Muirfield Golf Club. After Leith (where this hardy institution began life in 1744) and Musselburgh, it has been home to the Honourable Company of Edinburgh Golfers since 1891; the "Honourable" bit begs more than a few questions.

When the journalist Melanie Reid attended the British Open there in 2013 she entered a time tunnel and emerged in Bloke World. "There is nowhere else in the world, I am fairly confident, where you would find an array of temporary cash machines with the large, jolly exhortation above them: 'Time to take out your wedge.' That's a sand wedge, geddit? It's a resolutely blokey joke. That artless mixture of golf, money, unconscious sexism, bad puns and peculiar insularity can only mean one thing: the Open Championship... What's inescapable at this event is that one starts to think bloke. For Himself, a short-sleeved waterproof jacket by Ralph Lauren, £205... And don't forget Her Indoors – a diamond necklace (£8,000), perhaps? Or a nice pink visor (£20)."

The rest of the upper echelons of the British game were scarcely a beacon of inspiration. Other eminent members of the Open roster – the Royal & Ancient, Ayrshire's Royal Troon and Kent's Royal St George – also clung fast to their lads-only membership policy, facilitated by the 2010 Equality Act, which did not compel change. In 2003, Glenda Jackson, the Oscar-winning actress and long-serving Labour MP, described such sexist attitudes as nothing less than "gender apartheid". Yes, said Vivien Saunders, the former British Open champion and founder of both the women's PGA and the European Tour, she would dearly love to become the first woman member of the R&A, the sport's governing body outside the US and Mexico, but the mountain was inconceivably high. "It would just be so hopeless. No one would ever bother. You'd never get a man to propose and second you. And then another 20 people have to be supporters." In response, to no surprise whatsoever, Peter Dawson, secretary of the resolutely blinkered R&A, made it abundantly clear that his club was assuredly not for turning. "We don't see the Open championship being used for social engineering. We don't see that as valid. We have no problem with women-only clubs, or men-only clubs or mixed clubs. Therefore, we don't actually think there's a problem in that sense."[87]

This continued inequality could be seen in the long-running rumblings over an even more vaunted golfing institution,

Augusta National, home since the tournament's inception in 1934 to the US Masters (all right, *The* Masters). In 2002, Martha Burks, chairwoman of the National Council of Women's Organisations, wrote a private letter to Hootie Johnson, all-powerful chairman of the Georgia club, urging him to admit the club's first woman member. Johnson resisted this entreaty and instead issued a public statement defending the right of private clubs to admit whomever they chose. He also attacked women's groups for taking on such a "trivial" issue. Burk then lobbied The Masters' TV sponsors – Coca-Cola, General Motors and Citigroup – to withdraw their support, prompting Johnson to announce that the 2003 Masters would be advert-free. Burk called on CBS TV to halt coverage, to no avail.

And so the matter rumbled on and off until 2012, when the appointment of IBM's first female chief executive, Ginny Rometty, left Billy Payne, Johnson's successor, in a quandary. IBM was one of the tournament's three main sponsors; its previous four chief executives, moreover, had become members of Augusta National. "If Rometty doesn't become a member, she will have to be accompanied by a green-jacketed member at all times while watching the tournament, which is both annoying and embarrassing," predicted Julie Bort in *Business Insider*. "Either way, the sexist club will have to break one of its ridiculous rules. Augusta will either ditch its infamous anti-women policy and invite Rometty to become a member or it will break its tradition of making corporate sponsor CEOs members."[88] Payne's response to the media clamour was nothing if not typical of Augusta National: "We don't talk about our private deliberations."

This oh-so-superior air kindled memories of that notorious declamation by the club's most famous/notorious former chairman, Clifford Roberts: "As long as I'm alive, all the golfers will be white and all the caddies will be black."[89] Not until 1975 did Lee Elder become the first black golfer to compete at The Masters; it took another 15 years for a member of his race to be granted membership. Some saw it as entirely fitting that Roberts, who co-founded the club during the segregation era, should take his own life on the course. "Exclusion of women is dubious enough when it is practised by clubs with a purely social basis," concluded Hugh McIlvanney. "In the case of Augusta National, which has made itself an influential institution in a global sport, the policy is indefensible."

Meanwhile, President Obama took time out from wrestling with the American economy to offer his support for a petition launched on Change.org, a political activism website, demanding that Rometty be invited to join the club. Mind you, as critics of the Commander-in-chief were not slow to point out, the president did prefer his own golf partners to be men. Just once, reportedly, had he made an exception – a heavily publicised round in 2009 with Melody Barnes, his chief domestic policy adviser.[90] "The gentlemen of Augusta National don't like being told what to do, especially if they were thinking of doing it anyway," wrote Patricia Davies in *The Times*, "but they'll see sense soon enough and it won't be surrendering, it'll be growing up."[91]

Less than a week after Bort's article was published, The Masters was due to tee off once more. Recovering form if not favour following his fall from grace, Tiger Woods suddenly had a heaven-sent opportunity to restore his image. He could have threatened to withdraw in solidarity with Rometty, something an iconic multimillionaire could hardly claim would seriously impair either his marketability or standard of living. Given that taking a stand would almost certainly have regained him some credibility among women, who had inevitably railed loudest about his infidelities, this would surely have permitted his public rehabilitation to be altogether quicker and smoother. True, this might have been greeted as blatant opportunism, but the potential impact of such a protest would have rendered reservations irrelevant. Instead, it was an opportunity spurned and squandered.

A few months later, the walls finally caved in, not just once but twice: Darla Moore, a South Carolina billionaire banking executive, and Condoleeza Rice, who as the US Secretary of State had presided over the invasion of Iraq, were both invited to join Augusta National. "Today, one of the last bastions of male supremacy is no more," rejoiced Christine Brennan in *USA Today*. "Today, Augusta National has made a crucial statement to every girl and woman who has thought about picking up a golf club. The message is simple: You are welcome."[92] Dave Zirin was far less impressed. "I'm sure it's tempting to look at today as an advance for women in sports. But it's very difficult to think that today's national celebration of a multi-billionaire and a war criminal has anything to do with women's liberation... The only way this club could be any kind of symbol of progress and justice is if the people of Augusta, Georgia, a whopping 32 percent of whom live below the US poverty line, took to the eighteenth green and occupied the Masters. Let's see whose side Condi Rice and Darla Moore would be on then."[93]

In the lead-up to the 2013 Open at Muirfield there had been strident objections from two of Britain's leading professionals, Catriona Matthew and Laura Davies, and a further broadside from Saunders. "How clubs who don't admit women are allowed to keep the 'Royal' staggers me. Our current Queen has reigned for 60 years and Queen Victoria was on the throne for 64, so female monarchs have reigned during much of these clubs' existence."[94] Saunders proposed the removal of male-only clubs from the Open rota. Pointedly, Alex Salmond, Scotland's First Minister, turned down his invitation to attend, as did Maria Miller and Hugh Robertson, respectively England's Culture Secretary and Sports Minister. Dawson, noted a duly derisive *Times* leader, had declared that there are times when, to be quite frank, the boys need to be with the boys. "No doubt there are, but that is a flimsy pretext for not allowing women to play one of the world's best courses. Perhaps those golfing men who are such sensitive flowers that the presence of women is so difficult could hire a room in a local pub to enjoy a drink on their own. It is inconceivable that Mr Dawson would justify not allowing Jewish or Muslim members on the grounds that there are times when Christians need to be with Christians. Or times when white people need to be with other white people."[95]

The Love That (Still) Dares Not Speak Its Name

A policeman or a judge or a lawyer can openly be something other than heterosexual. A doctor or teacher or carpenter can be, along with, of course, an actor or a musician or a writer. Even executives on Wall Street now can. But a male athlete in a major sport? Not one has ever emerged, not while he was still playing. Odd – isn't it? – because what sports does best is break down barriers and bring people of all colours and creeds together. Odd that no bat or ball or fist or foot could smash through this wall.[96]

The estimable and forthright Gary Smith expressed those sentiments in *Sports Illustrated* in 2005. Ignorance, though, betrayed him, most notably in the tragic case of Justin Fashanu, who more than two decades earlier had become the first professional footballer to come out and suffered the dreadful consequences. Before long, Smith would be further confounded, not to say rewarded, by a couple more Britons – Steven Davies, then a regular member of England's various cricket squads, and Gareth Thomas, the erstwhile Wales rugby union captain: both had the courage to emerge from the closet while playing, the latter in the winter of his career, the former, even more bravely, in the spring. In 2013, Tom Daley, the teenage 2012 Olympic diving bronze medallist, came out on YouTube and was hailed by the chairman of the Amateur Swimming Association, but there was far less compassion that year for Jason Collins, a veteran for the NBA's Washington Wizards, when he became the first active player in North America's four major team sports to admit his homosexuality; the attitudes that fuelled Smith's sentiments had lost little if any of their destructiveness. Chris Broussard, a habitually provocative ESPN commentator, accused Collins of "living in unrepentant sin" and "walking in open rebellion to God and to Jesus Christ".[97]

On the eve of Wimbledon 2013 the most prominent sporting campaigner for gay rights offered the menfolk her compassion. "In the entertainment world guys have an easier time coming out than women. In the sports world we have had a lot more women coming out than men," said Martina Navratilova at the launch of London Pride. "It is more difficult in team sports as you may not get to play. But that does not explain why there are no gay male tennis players at all. We know they are there, but they are so far in the closet I don't know who they are."[98] Despite Navratilova's prediction that an active player would out himself by 2010, Francisco Rodriguez, who had played for Paraguay in the Davis Cup, remained, in 2013, the first and so far only male player to vacate the closet – and he waited until after his career wound down in 2006, by when his world ranking was a less than lofty 373rd. "If you came out on the tennis tour," he claimed at the time, "you would be an outcast."[99] He also suggested that such a player would be at a competitive disadvantage: the very idea of losing to a gay man would only sharpen his opponents' motivation and edge.

* * *

The word "homosexuality" did not enter a dictionary until the mid-19th century. As open-minded as the French (1791) and Turks (1858) were, not until 1967 was sodomy decriminalised in Britain. Illinois became the first American state to poke its head above the parapet in 1961; it would be another 42 years before homosexuality was legal nationwide. Before Bill Tilden, whose sexual orientation was widely known on the tennis circuit, became the first American to win the All England men's singles title in 1920, there had been the occasional nudge and wink: one newspaper ran a picture of him demonstrating a tennis technique to a young male, captioned "Tilden takes a keen interest in the boy." Even so, noted Mark Hodgkinson in the *Daily Telegraph*, "some commentators have seen a paradox in that, when Tilden's sexuality was still secret from the public, it was said that he had been responsible for shedding tennis's image as a 'sissy' pastime".[100]

It helps, of course, to play a mixed sport, and hence float under the radar. Show-jumpers and ice skaters are probably grateful to be involved in comparatively minor spectator attractions: here, at least, homosexuality is not treated as a disease. "I would say that many gays are involved in the horse world," said Mason Phelps Jr, an American Olympic rider who co-founded the Equestrian AIDS Foundation in 1996. "It is certainly no secret. This is a very accepting community."[101]

Steven Davies believes the same can be said of cricket. "Being a cricketer helps, because it's a decent world, and I haven't had a single jibe." Indeed, he admitted to gaining pleasure from provoking a reaction among teammates "by pretending to take offence on behalf of the gay brethren". He also hoped he'd "opened one or two eyes":

> One colleague "thought all gay guys were as camp as Christmas". He recollected receiving support on Facebook and Twitter: "One guy aged 21 and really into his sport wrote to me saying he was gay and that no one knew about it. He said he felt fake socialising with his friends and that my story helped a lot. Plenty have said that. It makes me feel like I can do some good."[102]

Justin

Fashanu was less fortunate, though it would be naïve to attribute this solely to his having lived in a less tolerant era. In 1980, as a gangly teenage striker, he signed for Nottingham Forest: the first black British footballer to command a £1m transfer fee. Ten years later, having played for England and won the BBC's Goal of the Season award with an unforgettable long-range shot for Norwich City against Manchester United, he came out. The goals, unsurprisingly, dried up. During the long and intense difficulties that followed, he was glad to find a friend in Peter Tatchell. England's most prolific and prominent gay rights campaigner, Tatchell was, and remains, a courageous soul, brave enough to attempt a citizen's arrest of Robert Mugabe (when he stood down as a prospective Green Party candidate for Oxford East in 2009, he explained that it was because he had suffered brain damage caused in part by the response of Mugabe's bodyguards). Tatchell met Fashanu at Heaven, one of

London's first hip gay nightclubs. "During that decade of closeted double-life, he found it immensely difficult to cope with the strain of hiding his gayness in the macho world of football – not to mention the stress of living a secret gay life while constantly in the media spotlight."[103]

Amid such a hostile, stressful atmosphere, Fashanu's troubles were exacerbated by the unsympathetic, at times antagonistic attitude of the Forest manager, Brian Clough, a man who, for all his socialist principles, was in no way resistant to motivating through fear. "The pressure Fashanu was under from Clough made it extra hard to come to terms with his sexuality," recollected Tatchell.

> *When we first became friends, he was only 20 and just starting to realise he was gay. Justin had considerable difficulty in accepting his sexual orientation, but through our talks – often late at night on the phone from his hotel in Nottingham – he began to feel good about his gayness. Although he had not publicly declared his homosexuality in the early 1980s, I was already partly out. Despite the evident risk of his own exposure by association, Fashanu thought nothing of going out with me to night-clubs, parties, family celebrations and high-profile events where he was the guest of honour. He knew journalists and photographers would be there. It was almost as if he wanted to be outed by the press to end the pretence and pressure of leading a secretive double-life.*[104]

Around late 1982, recalled Tatchell, Fashanu wanted to come out. "He was fed up living a lie. We talked through the pros and cons many times. It was I who advised him to wait until he (hopefully) sorted out his problems with Brian Clough and got his football career more firmly established." Seeking refuge in evangelical Christianity was not, perhaps, the wisest move, bringing him face to face with sanctified homophobia. "Desperate attempts at relationships with women failed," remembered Tatchell. "His longing for the love of men never went away. While publicly proclaiming Christian celibacy, he ended up resorting to furtive gay sex. That made it impossible for him to have a stable gay relationship. Caught between God and gayness, he suffered terrible emotional and psychological turmoil."

What persuaded Fashanu to come out – in *The Sun* – was the suicide of a 17-year-old gay friend who had been thrown out of his family home by homophobic parents. "I felt angry at the waste of his life and guilty because I had not been able to help him," he would relate in the book *Stonewall 25*. "I wanted to do something positive to stop such deaths happening again, so I decided to set an example and come out in the papers." At the time, claims Tatchell, he and Fashanu knew a dozen gay or bisexual professional players who lacked such bravery.

While Fashanu's career as a top-flight player, hindered by a chronic knee injury, was over by then, he was still earning a living with his feet. The response to his confession made that increasingly difficult. What hurt the most was the response of the community to whom he had looked for support, affirming the extent to which Clough's perspective was not confined to those who had grown up in a society where homosexuality was illegal. *The Voice* described his coming-out as "an affront to the black community... damaging... pathetic and unforgiveable". Tony Sewell, a columnist with the black London weekly, was especially devoid of compassion: "We heteros are sick and tired of tortured queens playing hide and seek around their closets. Homosexuals are the greatest queer-bashers around. No other group of people are so preoccupied with making their own sexuality look dirty." Even Fashanu's brother, John, a prominent player himself, called him "a gay outcast" (he later apologised but, to his sibling, it was a numbing betrayal). Small wonder Justin told Tatchell he felt "incredibly, almost suicidally, lonely".

Finding a coaching job in the US, he appeared to be putting the worst behind him, but in April 1998 a warrant was issued for his arrest on charges of sexual assault against a 17-year-old. Fashanu hanged himself. His suicide note denied the charges, claiming that he was being blackmailed by his accuser.

If he has been sorely neglected, he has assuredly not been forgotten, least of all by my former University of Brighton colleague, the academic and documentarist Ian McDonald. Two days before the 10th anniversary of Fashanu's death, he helped launch the Justin Campaign against homophobia in football, at the city's Equality Walk, organised, as ever, by Stonewall, the tireless lesbian and gay campaigners. That year, fresh from directing an acclaimed documentary about the local gay team, *Brighton Bandits*, also saw him make another, *A Lonely Vigil*, a five-minute short about a young gay footballer's journey from Brighton to London to commemorate Fashanu, subsequently refashioned as *Shame – Remembering Justin Fashanu*. Two years after that he plunged in again, making the more ambitious *Justin*. In making *Brighton Bandits*, his aim was "to dispel stereotypes that gay men do not play football and as a more humane way of raising questions about homophobia in sport". Why, for instance, "are there not any out gay professionals when there is such a thriving gay football culture? And why are there so few people even talking about this issue?"[105]

Freeing the bonds

The legacy of Fashanu's torment was such that, more than two decades after his tragic end, no English footballer had followed his courageous lead, though a Swede had. That said, Anton Hysén's emergence from the closet in 2011 was largely accidental. Interviewed by *Offside*, a football magazine, his father Glenn, formerly a Liverpool stalwart, casually mentioned the midfielder's sexuality, whereupon the journalist approached Hysén Jr and asked whether he wanted to come out. He grasped the unexpected opportunity. "It's all fucked up," he told his eager inquisitor. "Where the hell are all the others? No one is coming out."[106]

More articulate was Anders Lindegaard, Manchester United's heterosexual Danish goalkeeper, in an impassioned blog the following year. It came in the wake of a report from the House of Commons committee for Culture, Media and Sport claiming that homophobia "may now be a bigger problem in football than other forms of discrimination".[107] Homosexuality was taboo, Lindegaard asserted, because of the intolerance in the stands. "I think first and foremost that a homosexual colleague is afraid of the reception he could get from the fans. My impression is that the players would not have trouble accepting a homosexual. Homosexuality in football is a taboo subject. The atmosphere on the pitch and in the stands is tough. The mechanisms are primitive and it is often expressed through a classic stereotype that a real man should be brave, strong and aggressive. And it is not the image that a football fan associates with a gay person. The problem for me is that a lot of football fans are stuck in a time of intolerance that does not deserve to be compared with modern society's development in the last decades." Homosexuals, he concluded, were "in need of a hero... someone who dares to stand up for their sexuality".[108]

All too typical was another blog, written in February 2013 by Robbie Rogers, the US-born former Leeds United winger who had been capped 18 times by his country of birth. Announcing his retirement at a tender 25, he simultaneously came out, surprising his Leeds manager Neil Warnock (or so he insisted). It was a heart-rending confession:

> *For the past 25 years, I have been afraid... to show who I really was because of fear. Fear that judgement and rejection would hold me back from my dreams and aspirations. Fear that my loved ones would be farthest from me if they knew my secret. Fear that my secret would get in the way of my dreams. I will always be thankful for my career. I will remember Beijing, the MLS Cup, and most of all my teammates. Now is my time to step away. It's 1am in London as I write this and I could not be happier with my decision. My secret is gone, I am a free man. I can move on and live my life as my creator intended.*[109]

Less than six months later, in one of this young century's more welcome and positive U-turns, Rogers unretired, signing for Los Angeles Galaxy. It seemed far from coincidental that, just a few weeks earlier, Jason Collins had declared his true colours. Addressing 500 kids at an LGBT youth forum supplied a further prod. "I seriously felt like a coward," Rogers confessed. "These kids are standing up for themselves and changing the world, and I'm 25, I have a platform and a voice to be a role model. How much of a coward was I to not step up to the plate? I don't know what I was so afraid of. It's been such a positive experience for me. The one thing I've learned from all of this is being gay is not that big of a deal to people… times are just becoming more accepting."[110]

Gordon Taylor, the PFA chief executive, said he was aware of other gay footballers whose stated wish was to continue living a double life. "There is still some way to go, I believe, until that would not be a focus of attention. It's the job of people like me to be brave enough to support those players and for them to be convinced of that."[111]

For Simon Barnes, the criticism of David Beckham that followed his retirement in 2013 emphasised the distance sportingkind still had to travel. "In that revisionism I detect more than a hint of homophobia. Beckham's status as a gay icon continues to upset a certain class of footballing man… and if that's how they treat a heterosexual who happens to have something of an unembarrassed feminine side, it's no wonder that no British footballer has dared come out since Justin Fashanu. The Dark Age continues."[112]

Daley v Carl

Daley Thompson had a wicked sense of humour. He had needed every drop. The London-born son of a Scottish mother and a Nigerian father, he was 12 when the latter, a taxi driver, was shot dead. Daley was all cheeky irreverence; being a cocky sportsman in 1980s England was daring enough; being cocky *and* black was enormously risky. Temperamentally unable to resist a challenge, he won everyone over with a combination of unflagging effort, sheer will and undiluted charisma. In 1980 he won the Olympic decathlon: the planet had no finer all-round athlete. He did it again in LA four years later, convincing no less a judge than Sebastian Coe, himself a double Olympic gold medalist, that he was Britain's greatest Olympian. By way of celebration, he pulled on a t-shirt that gave voice to what most of the watching world had been thinking about the shamelessly partisan manner in which the Games had been broadcast: "Thanks America for a good games and a great time... But what about the television coverage?" On the podium, while the national anthem was playing and the Union Jack was being unfurled, he whistled along. Then, at the press conference, he unzipped his tracksuit to reveal another t-shirt, this one emblazoned with a far more provocative message: "Is the world's second greatest athlete gay?"

Few were left in any doubt that he was referring to the man who had matched Jesse Owens by winning four golds in LA, Carl Lewis, about whose sexuality gossipy tongues had long wagged. Hindsight and enlightenment have rendered Thompson's taunt increasingly unamusing, not to say less savoury. While advocating his credentials to light the Olympic flame in 2012, *The Mirror*'s Mike Walters applauded his "delicious audacity". To the blogger "Fagburn", it was merely evidence of "a homophobic c***".[113]

Given his own struggles to conquer prejudice, it was, at the time, all too easy to forgive Thompson – not least because the term "homophobic" had yet to gain much traction in the global lexicon – but as the years have worn on that jibe has assumed ever greater cause for regret, for his admirers if not himself. Lewis, who would be voted the 20th century's greatest athlete by the IOC, *Sports Illustrated* and the United Nations Education, Scientific and Cultural Organisation (UNESCO), had suffered at the hands of his rivals; presumably inspired in good part by jealousy, it was they who spread the story that he was gay. Lewis's denials were measured but firm, but was it simply coincidence that Coca-Cola withdrew an advertising deal and Nike stopped employing him in the US? "If you're a male athlete," rationalised a Nike executive, "I think the American public wants you to look macho." In fact, as Dwight Stone, the high-jumper, noted, the truth was irrelevant: Madison Avenue *perceived* Lewis as homosexual. "They started looking for ways to get rid of me," Lewis would recall. "Everyone was so scared and cynical, they didn't know what to do."[114] At the time of writing, the world still remained none the wiser.

Strong women, deep closets

The lesbian athlete, with her reputation for masculine style, body type, and desire, represents a refusal to issue this reassurance [of being a "normal" woman]. Her sexual autonomy and her rejection of conventional femininity – as defined through heterosexuality – make her the locus for enduring fears that women in sport transgress gender lines and disrupt the social order.

Susan Cahn[115]

The lingering association of women's sports with lesbianism makes many women in sport defensive about their athleticism and insistent on being perceived as heterosexual. This sensitivity to the negative connotations of the "lesbian label" and the association of women's sports with lesbians create a hostile athletic climate in which many lesbian athletes and coaches hide their identities to protect their access to sports.

Pat Griffin[116]

The second of those quotations comes from the foreword to *Strong Women, Deep Closets*, an insightful analysis of lesbians and homophobia in sport written in the late 1990s by Pat Griffin, a former athlete and coach. Donna Lopiano, then executive director of the US Women's Sports Foundation, denounced five grotesque generalisations commonly applied to large and diverse groups of human beings:

All football players are dumb
All African-Americans have rhythm
All white men can't jump

All Jews are wealthy but frugal
All female athletes are lesbians

Odious as such a comparison might seem, it has been easier being a lesbian athlete than the male equivalent: while gay sportsmen almost invariably stay firmly in the nether reaches of the closet, the default image of women athletes, for many, has been unmistakeable: they are *all* lesbians. Mind you, the following, published in the *Daily Sketch* during the 1931 Wimbledon, does at least hint at a progressive flexibility of thought:

> *The claim of women to equality with men is understandable, but that so many of them should wish to imitate the appearance of the less beauteous sex is not so easy to understand. It began with bobbing, and reached its logical hirsute conclusion in the Eton crop. And, having lost her hair, many a girl is now making strenuous attempts to lose her curves. And concurrently with these changes the conquest of trousers had been steadily proceeding... although mere man may regret the loss of feminine furbelows more than he resents the theft of his trousers, he realises that it is useless to rail against the spirit of the age. Whether we like it or not, girls will be boys.*[117]

Now imagine anyone observing with anything but disgust that, whether we like it or not, in a sporting context, boys will be girls.

Community and intimacy

Led with such vindictive creativity by Senator Joe McCarthy, the communist witch-hunts that robbed so many Americans of their status and jobs are seen as having fuelled and legitimised a wider pursuit of perceived subversives. For homosexuals, who were barred from political office as well as the military, this inevitably generated renewed hostility. By the same token, argued Griffin, "sport provided a place where lesbians and other women who did not fit the feminine and heterosexual ideal could find other women who shared their experience and interests". Many lesbians found "community and intimacy", albeit only so long as they kept the lid on their sexual orientation.

"In this social climate, women athletes were highly visible public representations of the lesbian image: women who defied traditional feminine values and trespassed on male territory. Where suggestions of the association between lesbianism and athletics had been hinted at earlier, the image of the mannish lesbian athlete became a well-known stereotype... As the gulf between perceptions of female athleticism and attractive hetero-sexuality widened, women's sports advocates maintained their apologetic, defensive position. They continued trying to prove women athletes' femininity, heterosexual appeal, and hetero-sexual 'success', despite the general public's scepticism on all three counts."[118]

In those archly conservative 1950s, Babe Didrikson, that matchless "muscle moll" of the 1930s and 1940s, adopted a strategy to elicit mainstream approval and hence increase her marketability: not only did she dare to wear skirts and makeup, she got married. She also denied her earlier Olympic accomplishments, tarred as they were by their reliance on unfeminine power and muscularity. How apt, notes Griffin with a touch of rose-tintedness, that she focused her talents on golf, an "appropriately" middle-class and "feminine" sport. The response to this reinvention was positive, which probably explains why it took the best part of half a century for the publication of Susan Cayleff's biography to reveal to the public at large Didrikson's relationship with Betty Dodd.

While the revolutions and counter-revolutions of the following decade brought progress, those closets remained deep. When Billie Jean King, now 62 and still married, resurfaced in that HBO documentary, Alexandra Stanley saw her as "stout, wrinkled and as plain-spoken as ever", suggesting, almost incredulously, that she "could pass for a retired school-teacher or civil servant". King recalled being a gay role model, albeit an unwilling one. She was driven out of her closet by an ex-girlfriend who in 1981 had sued her, in vain, for palimony.

By 1968, she said, she had come to terms with the realisation that her sexual preferences were not what she had imagined.

As yet, however – understandably, given the savage homophobia of the era – she felt unable to tell her husband, much less her Catholic parents: "The whole world was in tumult, and so was I. I was so ashamed." And it was Larry, she said, who, without consulting her, added her name to the lengthy list of prominent women who in the 1972 debut issue of *Ms.* magazine, proclaimed (as opposed to sheepishly confessed) that they had had abortions.

Not too long afterwards, Billie Jean's pal Elton John, for whom she had once sung background vocals, wrote his No.1 hit *Philadelphia Freedom* to honour her and her World Team Tennis franchise, the aptly anointed Philadelphia Freedoms.

Martina – Part 2

Martina Navratilova had three towering mountains to climb en route to becoming one of the most relentless and successful competitive artists the world has ever seen (to King, her sporting and philosophical role model, she was the finest of all female tennis players). She was a woman, she was born behind the Iron Curtain and, most forbiddingly of all, she was not heterosexual. "My green card was just one of the big changes in my life that took place around my nineteenth birthday. Another changer was discovering that my childhood crushes on some of my female teachers had not been 'just a phase'. Once I started travelling to the States, I realised I felt more comfortable around women than men."

It was all about freedom. "Once I became a regular on the circuit, I saw a lot of women doing what they wanted to do. I saw them making business decisions for themselves, tennis decisions, and smaller decisions about where they wanted to live, how they wanted to eat and dress, what movies they wanted to see. They were professionals, their lives not always defined by men. That sounds like a political statement when I say it, yet it really wasn't a matter of dogma. I just perceived some women doing what they wanted to do, and felt comfortable in their society. Of course, not all the professionals I admired were so-called gay. Nothing so simple. But I came to realise my attractions – social, emotional, professional, intellectual, sexual – were towards women."[119]

Though few were aware of this change, it says much for Navratilova's youthful ingenuousness that she did not foresee how her relative forthrightness might play out in a world where, in 1985, it would take AIDS to persuade Rock Hudson to become the first Hollywood icon to publicly declare his gayness; a world where the singer Cher could be hailed as courageous for accepting a part as a lesbian in the movie *Silkwood*. "I was one of the up-and-coming female tennis players in the world," remembered Navratilova, "and I didn't imagine my sexuality would become a major issue to anybody. It seemed *my* business somehow." Despite her brushes with international intrigue, she had yet to grasp what it meant to be a public figure. Nor was subterfuge her forte. "Right from my first affair in the States, I wanted privacy but I was also uncomfortable about pretending to be something I wasn't. Somebody once said to me, 'Society isn't ready for it.' And I told her, 'Hey, we're society, too.'"[120]

Her sexuality had become an open secret (though she insisted she was bisexual) but that didn't stop her feeling "pretty lonely" when she came out in a *New York Daily News* interview in the summer of 1981. She had been the victim, as she saw it, of "a betrayal of trust", though she also blamed herself. What complicated matters was that while she was prepared to open up, Nancy Liberman, her live-in partner and de facto fitness coach who also happened to be the country's best-known female basketballer, wanted to remain firmly in the closet.

A few weeks earlier, not insignificantly, that palimony lawsuit had been brought against King by Marilyn Barnett, her travelling secretary for many years. At the time, Billie Jean was still married to Larry, though the pair had long lived separate lives. Leading WTA executives, she claimed, had pleaded with her not to come out. "If you decide to come out," went the message, "we won't have a tour." Within a year, Avon, the tour's chief sponsor, had pulled out. Over the next 36 months, by King's conservative reckoning, she lost more than $1.5m in endorsements. Evert, livid, wrote an editorial for *World Tennis* magazine, "In Defence of Billie Jean".[121]

To be absolutely fair, Steve Goldstein, the journalist Navratilova accused of betraying her, did hold the interview back for months, keeping his editors at bay as he waited – rather gallantly – until she had received her US citizenship. She was in Monte Carlo when he rang to say that he was ready to publish. "It was gullible and naïve of me to have shared my strongest feelings with a reporter who had other priorities than my security, my happiness," she would reflect. "But you live and learn. I've always been candid with the press… but after that episode, I cut back on intimate conversations." Protecting Lieberman overrode all.

"Coming out was not considered a wise business decision," Navratilova would recall three decades later at the annual Equality Dinner at London's Dorchester Hotel, a charity event hosted by Stonewall. "I think the phrase I heard was 'career suicide'. I'm told I lost millions in sponsorship, but in my heart I know I gained things of much greater value – the opportunity to live my life with integrity and the knowledge that others might have come out because of my example."[122]

* * *

In 1995, Ben Wright, the CBS golf commentator, told a newspaper reporter not only that the rising visibility of lesbians was a liability for the women's Tour but that they were ruining it by "parading" their sexuality. When the media erupted, Wright accused the reporter of concocting the quotes, persuading CBS and the LPGA players to man the ramparts in his defence. Support ebbed away once he acknowledged the veracity of the quote in private, whereupon the network dropped him.[123]

The Fatal Insult

When, in October 2012, Orlando Cruz, a 31-year-old Puerto Rican featherweight, outed himself as a "proud gay man", the cheers for the first male professional boxer to admit his homo-sexuality rang loud and long. That said, broadly speaking, he had been beaten to it by Charles Jones, the London architect and so-called "White Collar" fighter whose bout with Igor the Pianist at London's Real Fight Club had been the subject of an ITV documentary broadcast in 2005.[124] "I'm not a gay man who happens to box," said Jones. "I'm a boxer who happens to be gay and doesn't give a toss who knows it."[125]

Amid the richly warranted paens to Cruz, references abounded to the most tragic episode in the annals of sport and sexual orientation. Professional boxers and their accomplices will do anything to sell tickets; fighters, moreover, are a law unto themselves when it comes to rousing the forces that enable them to fight for a living. Knowing the ropes inside out could still never have prepared the heart for the ballad of Benny and Emile.

Rewind to 24 March 1962, to the duel for the world welter-weight crown (undisputed version): Benny "Kid" Paret v Emile Griffith at that modern Coliseum, Madison Square Garden. "The Kid was illiterate in two languages," Dan Klores, the playwright, filmmaker and director of *Ring of Fire: The Emile Griffith Story*, recalled on the fight's 50th anniversary. "He had arrived from Cuba a few years before Fidel Castro took over. His family stayed behind, so he was left trusting his older, wiser and charismatic manager, Manuel Alfaro, a successful entrepreneur and nightclub owner. They had a plan. After he beat Griffith, Benny would have a few additional title [defences], then he could own a butcher shop on the Grand Concourse. It would mean success."[126] Griffith grew up "a man-child" at a boys' detention home in the Virgin Islands. "With a body by David, 28-inch waist, 46-inch chest, 146 pounds, he spent his adolescence and early teenage years standing in brutal heat, barefoot on rocks, forced to hold water buckets in each arm, punished for whatever sadistic thoughts entered the minds of authority figures, thirsty for escape. At night, the men or bigger boys came to him. They took."[127]

His mother moved to New York but left her eight children behind. Emile, the oldest, was the first to be summoned north, where he played baseball, swam and "defended the weak on the Harlem streets". A grade-school dropout, with "a high, delightful, innocent singsong voice", he was working in a hat factory in the garment district when his shirtless torso attracted the attention of Gil Clancy, an Irish trainer and Second World War veteran with a master's in education, and Howie Albert, an ex-pug working in the garment industry. "It was the only partnership in history," attested Clancy with the assurance of one who had honed the joke over decades, "where the Irishman and Jew teamed up, and the mick had the brains."

Storming through the Golden Gloves, Griffith made equally short work of his professional foes. "The myths and narratives," noted Klores, "created a clean biography: he was a hat designer, creative, and he loved blonde Scandinavian beauties. Two facts were straight, though. He was a vicious counter-puncher, and after each victory, he honoured Mommy's dream by moving up one of his siblings. Soon, he bought a house in the Hollis section of Queens, for the entire clan."

Griffith soon dethroned Paret, who subsequently reversed the result, setting up the rubber match. "Emile's escape," related Klores, "became the gay bars around Times Square, private places of peace, affection and sex. 'Where does he go?' Clancy said. 'I don't know,' his brother or Albert would reply. 'Has anyone seen my Junior?' Mommy said. One friend was shot, crippled for life. Emile cried and cried. The pain made worse with no one to tell."

Come the day of the fight, Griffith was wary of what Paret might do at the weigh-in. The previous year, prior to their last encounter, the barbed banter on the scales had seen Paret win the mental skirmishing, whispering in his opponent's ear "*maricón, maricón*" – a homophobic Spanish slur. "If he says anything to me before the fight, I'll knock him out," Griffith assured Clancy, then mounted the scales. "Watch out," warned the trainer, but not quickly enough. Paret "had already slipped behind him", related Gary Smith, "wriggling his body, thrusting his pelvis, grabbing Emile's ass. 'Hey, *maricón*,' Paret coos, 'I'm going to get you *and* your husband.' Emile blinks, in his underwear, at a room full of boxing aficionados, reporters and photographers. If he doesn't respond, that means he's afraid, means he's weak… means he may be just what Paret says he is. Clancy steps between them. 'Save it for tonight,' he begs Emile."[128]

It was a time when a clutch of renowned writers – Allen Ginsberg, James Baldwin and Gore Vidal – were just about the only Americans commonly known to be gay; when homosexual actors such as Hudson and Montgomery Clift hid beneath the skirts of their celluloid lovers and press agents and studio bosses; when, fearing the impact on his career, Liberace, a flamboyant and flagrantly camp pianist played convincingly by Michael Douglas in *Behind the Candelabra* – a 2013 biopic based on the memoirs of one of the entertainer's young lovers that makes unremittingly depressing watching – filed lawsuits against those casting aspersions about his sexuality, in Britain as well as the US.

At first, Paret had reason to believe his ruse had worked again, flooring Griffith in round six. He was soon disabused of this, sustaining a brutal pounding for the next six rounds. The final moments, beamed to the nation's hearths, found the referee, Ruby Goldstein, hesitating to intercede as Griffith battered his way toward victory. After his previous such appointment, Goldstein had been berated on the *Ed Sullivan Show*, his squirming witnessed by tens of millions, for halting the fight *too* quickly.

Griffith trapped Paret on the ropes with, as Klores graphically described it, "one arm draped over, the other doing anything to stop the blows: 18, 19, 20, 21, 22, 23, 24, maybe more, all to the head. Benny's arms stopped moving. So did Goldstein's legs. Finally, Manuel jumped into the ring. Emile had reclaimed his title."[129]

Doubtless drawn to boxing as a literary subject by its endless supply of metaphorical inspiration, Norman Mailer likened the force and relentlessness of Griffith's right fist to "a baseball bat demolishing a pumpkin". Paret was taken to an ambulance on a stretcher, unconscious. Griffith tried in vain for several hours to reach his hospital bedside, then dashed through the streets, running a gauntlet of pedestrians spewing insults. Paret's supporters fired off hate mail, convinced he had intended to kill their man. For nine days Benny lingered in a coma; on the 10th he died.

"There's smoke hanging over his death," wrote Smith, referring to half a dozen possible catalysts, including the desire of Paret's manager "to squeeze one more payday from a shot fighter who told his wife the day before the bout that he didn't feel right and didn't want to fight". None of the conjecture, though, would stop Griffith going down in sporting lore as "the man who killed Paret for calling him a faggot".

When Howard Tuckner attempted to explain to *New York Times* readers, with all due delicacy, the meaning of *maricón*, an editor changed "homosexual" to "anti-man". Having televised that grisly tableau, ABC ended its fistic broadcasts, a shift emulated by other US networks; not until the following decade would boxing return to free television. Never again did Goldstein referee a fight.

Hate mail continued to pour in from Cuba. Griffith frequented gay bars, married briefly and continued to pick up world titles for fun. "We certainly raised our eyebrows," wrote the veteran British sportswriter Alan Hubbard, recalling a bout between Griffith and the Welshman Brian Curvis at Wembley two years later. "When we went to his dressing room afterwards he was passionately kissing one of his cornermen."[130] In 1992, Emile came close to death and spent months in hospital after – as he apparently claimed to friends – being badly beaten up outside a gay bar. In 2005, when Smith interviewed him at a nursing home in upstate New York, he said he had no memory of it whatsoever. "I'm *not* gay! It's craziness," he told Smith. Later in the same conversation came a variation: "I will dance with anybody. I've chased men and women. I like men and women both. But I don't like that word: *homosexual, gay* or *faggot*. I don't know what I am."[131]

When Emile met Benny's son in 2005, he wept as they hugged. "I didn't mean to kill him," he assured Matthew Syed in 2007, in an interview *The Times* did not publish until after his death in

July 2013. "I am so sorry it happened. I wake up at night. I have nightmares about it."[132]

Griffith was 75 when he died at a New York care facility, having fallen prey to pugilistic dementia. For his last two years he had been in a vegetative state. Only now did Syed feel able to relate the circumstances of their encounter. Accompanying Griffith had been Ron Ross, his staunch friend and biographer, and Luis Rodrigo, his adopted son, now his companion and carer. "As the interview progressed," recalled Syed, "and I watched the interplay between Rodrigo and Griffith, it slowly dawned on me that the deepest secret of all remained intact. This was not a father-son relationship, as both men publicly claimed. It was a romantic one." Rodrigo confirmed this but requested, in order to protect his lover's image, that it remain a secret; so did Griffith and Ross. "It's OK to write about it now," Ross told Syed in a phone call shortly after the fighter's demise. "It's time."

In his biography, Griffith summed up the perversity of it all: "I kill a man and most people forgive me. However, I love a man and many say this is unforgiveable and this makes me an evil person."[133]

Sincerely, Chris Kluwe

It scarce needs adding that signs of resistance to homophobia have also been mixed at best in the ultra-macho world of the NFL. Asked, shortly before the 2013 Super Bowl, if he would ever accept a gay teammate, Chris Culliver of the San Francisco 49ers, who had already done his image as a redoubtable sexist no harm that week by tweeting demeaning comments about the female menstrual cycle, replied: "No, we don't got no gay people on the team, they gotta get up out of here if they do. Can't be with that sweet stuff. Nah… can't be… in the locker room man. Nah."[134] The ensuing uproar persuaded Culliver to issue what Dave Zirin described as "the finest, most heartfelt apology a 49er public relations intern ever had to write".[135] That Culliver felt obliged to show regret may be progress of sorts, though he was doubtless motivated by the commercial ramifications. Meanwhile, reports emanating later that year from an NFL Combine – a pre-college draft period akin to an extended university open day – claimed that Manti Te'o, a promising Notre Dame linebacker, and Nick Kasa, the Colorado Buffaloes tight end, were asked by suitors whether they were, respectively, homosexual and heterosexual. "There was a couple of questions by coaches," said Kasa, such as, "Do you have a girlfriend?" and "Do you like girls?"[136]

Set against those episodes has been the vocal support for lesbian and gay rights of Brendan Ayanbadejo, a veteran on the Baltimore Ravens' NFL roster, and especially Chris Kluwe, a self-professed libertarian and punter with the Minnesota Vikings. In November 2012, Ayanbadejo endorsed a ballot initiative for Maryland to join those American states recognising same-sex marriage. In a letter to the Ravens' owner, Steve Biscotti, Emmett Burns, a Baltimore County state delegate, could barely contain his wrath and indignation. "I find it inconceivable that one of your players would publicly endorse same-sex marriage, specifically as a Raven Football player," fulminated Burns. "I believe Mr Ayanbadejo should concentrate on football and steer clear of dividing the fan base." Burns also urged the Ravens to "inhibit such expressions from your employees and that he be ordered to cease and desist such injurious actions".[137]

"It's an equality issue," responded Ayanbadejo. "I see the big picture. There was a time when women didn't have rights. Black people didn't have rights. Right now, gay rights is a big issue and it's been for a long time. We're slowly chopping down the barriers to equality."[138] Support came rapidly via a swift and eloquent corrective from Kluwe, who would insist in 2013 that there were "definitely" gay players in the NFL but that he himself was "straight".[139] The following comments, written for the website deadspin, were hailed by Zirin as the "greatest political statement by any athlete ever":

> *I can assure you that gay people getting married will have zero effect on your life. They won't come into your house and steal your children. They won't magically turn you into a lustful c**kmonster. They won't even overthrow the government in an*

orgy of hedonistic debauchery because all of a sudden they have the same legal rights as the other 90 percent of our population – rights like Social Security benefits, child care tax credits, Family and Medical Leave to take care of loved ones, and COBRA healthcare for spouses and children. You know what having these rights will make gays? Full-fledged American citizens just like everyone else, with the freedom to pursue happiness and all that entails. Do the civil-rights struggles of the past 200 years mean absolutely nothing to you? In closing, I would like to say that I hope this letter, in some small way, causes you to reflect upon the magnitude of the colossal foot in mouth clusterf*ck you so brazenly unleashed on a man whose only crime was speaking out for something he believed in. Best of luck in the next election; I'm fairly certain you might need it.

Sincerely, Chris Kluwe[140]

A kiss is just a kiss

In the wake of the slew of anti-LGBT legislation enacted by the Russian hosts of the 2014 Winter Olympics in Sochi, and the defiant podium kiss shared by two female Russian athletes at the 2013 World Athletics Championships in Moscow, the witty, whimsical and always insightful Caitlin Moran made two notably laudable suggestions in *The Times*. First, all competitors should be obliged to kiss: "What more perfect way to show how, ultimately, all love is the same?" Second, that "accepting the logic of Russia's argument – that homosexuality is 'non-traditional… all athletes [should] eschew everything 'non-traditional'". The following captures the essence of the columnist's ethical counter-punch to President Vladimir Putin's endorsement of homophobia:

This would include: non-wooden skis, electrical ski-lifts, artificial fibres, freestyle ski-ing and snowboarding, the participation of every female athlete, and the playing of the national anthems of Canada, Bosnia and Herzegovina, Slovenia, South Africa, Qatar, Tunisia, Zimbabwe, Georgia, Libya, Romania and Australia (all adopted since the Eighties, therefore not "traditional", and therefore, by Russian logic, "gay"). As the world's dullest, most dangerous and uncomfortable Olympics unfolds, everyone has time to have the thought: "Progress. Hmm. Was that a bad thing?"

Of course, there is an argument that, with luck, Sochi 2014's human rights campaign won't need any of these things. After all, at the Berlin 1936 Olympics, during an eerily similar rise in fascism, Jesse Owens elegantly trashed Hitler's poisonous ideology simply by going out there and just... running faster than anyone else. Every gay athlete who holds up a medal at Sochi 2014 will be the living promotion of a very certain thing: human dignity and love always, in the end, out-runs fascism. Because it has to.[141]

Endnotes

Introduction

1   Fleder, Rob (ed), *Damn Yankees: Twenty-Four Major League Writers on the World's Most Loved (and Hated) Team*, HarperCollins, 2012, p. 3

2   Berkoff, Stephen, 'Letters to the Editor', *The Times*, 28 March 2012, p. 25

3   Savage, Michael, '"One final tear-sodden climax"', *The Times*, 11 September 2012, pp. 4-5

4   "Summer of Hope and Glory", *The Times*, 10 September 2012, p. 2

5   McIlvanney, Hugh, "Lightning Bolt's echoes of Ali", *Sunday Times*, 12 August 2012, Sport, p. 24

6   Pickup, Oliver, *Daily Telegraph*, 3 July 2013, http://www.telegraph.co.uk/sport/othersports/athletics/10157145/Usain-Bolt-denies-using-performance-enhancing-drugs-ahead-of-Paris-Diamond-League-meeting.html

7   McIlvanney, Hugh, "Bolt carries burden of faith", *Sunday Times*, 28 July 2013, Sport, p. 11

8   Barnes, Simon, "Clarity hard to find in era of Accidental Doping", *The Times*, 29 July 2013, p. 56

9   Moore, Richard, *The Dirtiest Race In History – Ben Johnson, Carl Lewis and the 1988 Olympic 100m Final*, Bloomsbury, 2012, p. vii

10 Ibid, p. 299

11 Mandela, Nelson, Laureus World Sports Awards, Monaco, 2000

12 Billen, Andrew, '"I had an animal response to fame: Leave me alone. I will go away"', *The Times*, 23 February 2013, Saturday Review, p. 10

13 Letter to *The Guardian*, reprinted in *The Guardian Weekly*, 28 September 2012, p. 23

14 Syed, Matthew, "Overreaction to unforgettable summer in danger of blinding the nation to real challenges", *The Times*, 13 September 2012, p. 76

15 Cash, Pat, "String up new technology and return to nature", *Sunday Times*, 26 May 2013, Sport, p. 12

16 Sky Sports statistics via email from Gemma Nash, Sky Sports News, 8 November 2012

17 Glanville, Brian, Bert Trautmann obituary, *The Guardian*, 19 July 2013, http://www.guardian.co.uk/football/2013/jul/19/bert-trautmann

18 Taylor, Louise, "Bert Trautmann: from Nazi paratrooper to hero of Manchester City", *The Guardian*, 11 April 2010, http://www.guardian.co.uk/football/2010/apr/11/bert-trautmann-nazis-manchester-city

19 Shindler, Colin, "Safe Hans!", *Daily Mail*, 2 November 2004

20 Ibid

21 The Arthur Conan Doyle Collection, http://www.conandoylecollection.co.uk/July2013.html

22 Weide, Robert B. (dir), *Woody Allen: A Documentary*, 2012

23 Hider, James, "Love of sport got me through five years of Hamas captivity, says Israeli soldier", *The Times*, 19 October 2012, p. 42

24 Walton, Darren, "New study shows tennis star Roger Federer is most popular athlete amongst Australian sports fans", Australian Associated Press, 25 October 2012, http://www.foxsports.com.au/other-sports/new-study-shows-tennis-star-roger-federer-is-most-popular-athlete-amongst-australian-sports-fans/story-e6frf56c-1226503307023#.USCV2irKdAM

25 Westerby, John, "Sense of relief fosters new belief for Wales", *The Times*, 11 February 2013, p. 55

26 Zirin, Dave, "Redskins: The Clock is Now Ticking On Changing the Name", *The Nation*, 11 February 2013, http://www.thenation.com/blog/172806/redskins-clock-now-ticking-changing-name#

27 Sangakkara, Kumar, MCC Spirit of Cricket Cowdrey Lecture, Lord's, 4 July 2011 (transcript published in *Daily Telegraph*, 5 July 2011, http://www.telegraph.co.uk/sport/cricket/international/srilanka/8618261/Kumar-Sangakkaras-2011-MCC-Spirit-of-Cricket-Cowdrey-Lecture-in-full.html)

28 Smith, David, "Somalia edges to peace, with football part of the endgame", *The Guardian Weekly*, 26 October 2012, p. 7

29 Ibid

30 McIlvanney, Hugh, "The Best years of our lives", *The Observer*, 18 October 1992, www.kilmarnockacademy.co.uk/famoushmcilvanneybestyears.htm

31 Glanville, Brian, *Champions of Europe – The history, romance and intrigue of the European Cup*, Guinness , 1991, p. 54

32 Steen, Rob, "The Game-Changers: George Best", *The Cambridge Companion to Football*, Cambridge University Press, 2013

33 Davies, Gerald, "Genius of King John in stark contrast to the modern day", *The Times*, 8 March 2013, p. 85

34 Shone, Tom, "Very political, very strategic, very shrewd", *Sunday Times*, 20 January 2013, Culture section, p. 5

35 Weide, *Woody Allen: A Documentary*

Chapter 1 – The Sound (and Fury) Of The Crowd

1 Hider, James, "Referee who stabbed player is beheaded by fans", *The Times*, 8 July 2013, p. 27

2 Zirin, Dave, *Bad Sports: How Owners Are Ruining The Games We Love*, Scribner, 2010, p. 7

3 Zirin, p. 183

4 Engineer, Tariq, "Stadium crowds show the IPL the money", Cricinfo, 15 June 2012, http://www.espncricinfo.com/magazine/content/story/568291.html

5 BBC1, 5 July 2013

6 Ackford, Paul, *The Times*, 1 February 2014, Six Nations section, p. 7

7 Runciman, David, "Home sweet home?", *Observer Sports Monthly*, 3 February 2008, http://www.guardian.co.uk/sport/2008/feb/03/features.sportmonthly16

8   Moskowitz, Tobias and Wertheim, L. John, *Scorecasting: The Hidden Influences Behind How Sports Are Played and Games Are Won*, Random House, 2011, pp. 112-3

9   Seymour, Harold, *Baseball: The Golden Age*, Oxford University Press, 1971, p. 76

10 Sissons, Ric, *The Players: A Social History of the Professional Cricketer*, The Kingswood Press, 1988, p. 129

11 Ibid, p. 130

12 Fifa.com, http://www.fifa.com/worldcup/archive

13 http://www.populstat.info/Americas/uruguayc.htm

14 Vecsey, George, *Baseball: A History of America's Favourite Game*, Modern Library, 2008 (pbk), p. 100

15 Ibid, p. 101

16 Ibid, p. 100

17 Hughes, Matt, "If I can cope with Drogba screaming at me I can cope with anything", *The Times*, 18 April 2012, pp. 60-1

18 Collins, Patrick, *Among The Fans*, Wisden Books, 2011, p. 207

19 Galeano, Eduardo, *Football in Sun and Shadow*, Fourth Estate, 2003, p. 109

20 Barnes, Simon, "Football tolerates everything but change", *The Times*, 5 April 2012, p. 91

21 Paul Davis quoted in Syed, Matthew, "Culture of fandom behind foul chants in theatres of spit", *The Times*, 7 December 2012, http://www.thetimes.co.uk/tto/sport/football/article3623469.ece

22 Syed, Matthew, "There's a fine line between rank and rancour", *The Times*, 6 June 2012, p. 51

23 Holt, Richard, *Sport and the British*, Oxford University Press, 1992 (pbk), p. 145

24 "Record home attendances of English football clubs", Wikipedia, http://en.wikipedia.org/wiki/Record_home_attendances_of_English_football_clubs

25 "Largest Attendance At A Boxing Match", Guinness World Records, http://community.guinnessworldrecords.com/_Largest-attendance-at-a-boxing-match/blog/2935223/7691.html (accessed on 3 April 2012)

26 Gustkey, Earl, *LA Times*, 21 February 1993, http://articles.latimes.com/1993-02-21/sports/sp-960_1_greg-haugen/2

27 Boxrec Boxing Encyclopedia, http://boxrec.com/media/index.php/Tony_Zale_vs._Billy_Pryor

28 Sport Industry Group, 5 August 2011, http://www.sportindustry.biz/news/view/10227/record-crowds-at-uk-sporting-events

29 Email from John Randall, 16 June 2012

30 Deloittes, *Economic Impact of British Racing*, 2006, p. 28, http://www.britishhorseracing.com/inside_horseracing/about/BHB_Economic_Impact_of_British_Racing_Study_(26.05.06).pdf

31 British Horseracing Association press release, 24 January 2012, http://www.britishhorseracing.presscentre.com/Press-Releases/Statement-from-Paul-Bittar-regarding-Racecourse-Attendances-264.aspx

32 Aintree.co.uk, 9 April 2011, http://www.aintree.co.uk/news/bypassing_fences

33 Wood, Greg, "Ascot, rather than racing, deserves credit for Royal meeting success", *The Guardian*, 20 June 2011, http://www.guardian.co.uk/sport/blog/2011/jun/20/ascot-gets-credit-royal-success

34 Sammons, Jeffrey T., *Beyond The Ring – The Role of Boxing in American Society*, University of Illinois Press, 1990, p. 158

35 Mullen, Megan Gwynne, *The Rise of Cable Programming in the United States: Revolution Or Evolution?*, p. 57

36 Steel, Donald, *The Guinness Book of Golfing Facts and Feats*, Guinness Superlatives Ltd, 1982 (2nd edition), p. 64

37 PricewaterhouseCoopers media release, 4 August 2011, http://www.ukmediacentre.pwc.com/News-Releases/Attendances-rise-at-UK-s-biggest-annual-sporting-events-10dc.aspx

38 *The Tour de France 2007: The Grand Depart – Research Summary*, http://www.tfl.gov.uk/assets/downloads/businessandpartners/tour-de-france-research-summary.pdf

39 "Olympic attendance rate at over 90 per cent", Official Website of the Beijing 2008, 12 August 2008 Olympic Games, http://en.beijing2008.cn/venues/n214538308.shtml

40 Nurburgringers.net, http://www.nurburgring-history.co.uk/#/1940-1949/4530032102

41 Langmaid, Aaron, "Critics – attendance figures inflated at Australian GP", *Herald Sun*, 15 March 2012, http://www.heraldsun.com.au/sport/critics-attendance-figuers-inflated-at-australian-gp/story-fn7q3txe-1226300085706

42 Buford, Bill, *Among the Thugs*, Secker & Warburg, 1991, p. 195

43 Sheehan, George with Moore, Kenny, *Running and Being: The Total Experience*, 1978, Second Wind II, p. 193

44 Frosdick, Steve and Marsh, Peter, *Football Hooliganism*, Willan Publishing, 2005

45 Seymour, p. 77

46 Ibid

47 Marsh, Peter, *New Scientist*, 24 September 1981, http://books.google.co.uk/endbooks?id=_0beD5LVNugC&pg=PA804&lpg=PA804&dq=Desmond+Morris+and+The+Soccer+Tribe

48 Morris, Desmond, *The Soccer Tribe*, Jonathan Cape, 1981, p. 268

49 Wade, Stephen, "In Argentina, Hooligans Turn Football Into a Deadly Game", *The Jakarta Globe*, 26 April 2011, http://www.thejakartaglobe.com/archive/in-argentina-hooligans-turn-football-into-a-deadly-game/

50 Kuper, Simon, *Football Against the Enemy*, Orion, 1996 (pbk), p. 191

51 Ibid

52 Davies, Andrew, *Irish Historical Studies*, November 2006, Vol. 35, No. 138, pp. 200-19

53 Gallagher, Tom, *Glasgow: the uneasy peace: religious tension in modern Scotland*, Manchester University Press, 1987, p. 1

54 *Football Focus*, BBC1, 26 March 1988, quoted in Holt, Richard (ed), *Sport and the Working-Class in Modern Britain*, Manchester University Press, 1990, p. 180

55 Armstrong, Gary and Giulianotti, Richard, *Fear and loathing in world football*, Berg, 2001. pp. 25-6

56 Romanos, Joseph, *Great Sporting Rivals*, Exisle Publishing, 2004, p. 93

57 Walker, Graham, "The Ibrox Stadium Disaster of 1971" in Darby, Paul, Johnes, Martin and Mellor, Gavin (eds), *Soccer and Disaster: International Perspectives*, Routledge, 2005, pp. 44-5

58 Ibid, p. 53

59 Davis and Mcintyre quoted in Syed, Matthew, "Culture of fandom behind foul chants in theatres of spit", *The Times*, 7 December 2012, pp. 82-3

60 "Ralph Brand, Rangers legend", *The Scotsman*, April 22, 2011, http://www.scotsman.com/sport/interview-ralph-brand-rangers-legend-1-1595584

61 Murray, Bill, *The Old Firm: Sectarianism, Sport and Society in Scotland*, John Donald Publishing, 2000, quoted in

62 Murray, Ewan, "Why Mo Johnston still stirs emotions across Glasgow", *The Guardian*, 10 July 2009, http://www.guardian.co.uk/football/blog/2009/jul/10/maurice-mo-johnston-rangers-celtic

63 "Old Firm on the ball for economy", BBC News, 29 June 2005, http://news.bbc.co.uk/1/hi/scotland/4635535.stm

64 Richman, Darren, "When Cantona Kicked That Racist – 18 Years On", The Republic of Mancunia, 5 January 2013, http://therepublikofmancunia.com/when-cantona-kicked-that-racist-18-years-later/

65 Williams, Richard, "A martyr to his own myth", *The Independent on Sunday*, 29 January 1995, http://www.independent.co.uk/sport/a-martyr-to-his-own-myth--football-1570233.html

66 Kay, Oliver, "Warped tribalism insults forgotten victims", *The Times*, 15 September 2012, Sport, p. 6

67 Wilson, Paul, "Heysel was the worst thing imaginable, says Phil Neal", *The Guardian*, 28 May 2010, http://www.guardian.co.uk/football/blog/2010/may/28/heysel-disaster-25th-anniversary

68 Kay, "Warped tribalism insults forgotten victims"

69 "A national tragedy: Ibrox disaster, 1902", *The Herald*, 7 April 2008, http://www.heraldscotland.com/a-national-tragedy-ibrox-disaster-1902-1.878072

70 Quoted in "The Guide to Safety at Sports Grounds", http://www.football-safety.com/policy_guide.cfm

71 Evans, Tony, "City's reputation restored but no sense of victory", *The Times*, 13 September 2012, p. 1

72 Greenslade, Roy, 'The Sun's Hillsborough source has never been a secret – it was the police', *The Guardian*, 17 October 2011, http://www.guardian.co.uk/media/greenslade/2011/oct/17/sun-hillsborough-disaster

73 Taylor, The Rt Hon Lord Justice, *The Hillsborough Stadium Disaster*, Final Report, HMSO, January 1990, http://embedit.in/9wT6UMh9jN

74 Cameron, David, "David Cameron's full statement on the Hillsborough panel's report", guardian.co.uk, 12 September 2012, http://www.guardian.co.uk/football/2012/sep/12/david-cameron-hillsborough-report-statement

75 "Hillsborough – How They Buried the Truth", *Panorama*, BBC1, broadcast 20 May 2013

76 Topping, Alexandra, "Galaxy of stars hope Hillsborough single will be Christmas No.1", *The Guardian*, 14 December 2012, http://www.guardian.co.uk/music/2012/dec/14/hillsborough-single-christmas-hollies-remake

77 Barrett, Tony, "FA's attempts to apologise come up woefully short", *The Times*, 14 September 2012, p. 87

78   Anderson, Jon, "Football's own goal", *Sunday Times*, 23 September 2012, Letters, p. 22

79   Kahn, Roger, *The Boys of Summer*, Harper & Row, 1972 (pbk), p. xvi

80   Daley, Arthur, *New York Times*, 14 October 1957, reprinted in Daley, Arthur, *The Arthur Daley Years*, New York Times Publishing Company, 1975, p. 167

81   D'Antonio, Michael, *Forever Blue: The True Story of Walter O'Malley, Baseball's Most Controversial Owner, and the Dodgers of Brooklyn and Los Angeles*, Riverhead Books, 2009, p. 190

82   Caro, Robert, A., *The Power Broker: Robert Moses and the Fall of New York*, Vintage, 1975, p. 59

83   Ibid, p. 142

84   Caro, p. 1018

85   Kahn, pp. 335-6

86   Daley, *New York Times*, 14 October 1957

87   Ibid

88   D'Antonio, p. 1

89   Ibid, p. 3

90   Zirin, Dave, "Do You Know Your Enemy? Why we should all root for the Miami Heat to beat the Oklahoma City Thunder", *The Nation*, 12 June 2012, http://www.thenation.com/blog/168311/do-you-know-your-enemy-why-we-should-all-root-miami-heat-beat-oklahoma-city-thunder

91   Ibid

92   Ibid

93   Brown, Maury, "How Sports Attendance Figures Speak Lies", *Forbes*, 25 May 2011, http://www.forbes.com/sites/sportsmoney/2011/05/25/how-sports-attendance-figures-speak-lies

94   "Goodall expresses concern for stadium attendance in interview", Associated Press, 27 January 2012, http://www.nfl.com/news/story/09000d5d826606fa/article/goodell-expresses-concern-for-stadium-attendance-in-interview

95   Ibid

96   Ibid

97   Williams, John, "Fandom: Consumers, Hooligans and Activists", p. 200, 203

98   Ibid, p. 206

99   Ibid, p. 206

100 Margalit, Avital, "'You'll Never Walk Alone': On Property, Community and Football Fans", *Theoretical Inquiries in Law* 10 (2008), p. 222, quoted in Williams, "Fans: Consumers, Hooligans and Activists", p. 204

101 Williams, "Fans: Consumers, Hooligans and Activists", p. 208

102 Ruddock, Andy, Hutchins, Brett and Rowe, David, 'Contradictions in Media Sport Culture: The Re-Inscription of Football Supporter Traditions through On-Line Media', *European Journal of Cultural Studies*, 13, 3 (2010), p. 328, quoted in Williams, "Fans: Consumers, Hooligans and Activists", p. 205

103 Ibid, p. 209

104 Johnson, K.C., "The invisible fan", *Chicago Times*, 26 September 2011, http://articles.chicagotribune.com/2011-09-26/sports/ct-spt-0927-bartman-chicago--20110927_1_cubs-five-outs-scapegoat-bartman-alex-gibney

105 Ibid

106 McCarthy, Michael, "Catching Hell: Review of Steve Bartman documentary", *USA Today*, 25 April 2011, http://content.usatoday.com/communities/gameon/post/2011/04/the-most-hated-man-in-chicago-espn-tells-steve-bartman-story/1

107 Dorsey, James, "The Turbulent World of Middle East Soccer", 27 January 2013, http://mideastsoccer.blogspot.co.uk/

108 Zirin, Dave, "Soccer and Egypt's Current 'State of Emergency'", *The Nation*, 29 January 2013, http://www.thenation.com/blog/172498/soccer-and-egypts-current-state-emergency#

109 Dorsey, James, "The Turbulent World of Middle East Soccer"

110 Dorsey, James, "Ultras and the Military: Dangerous Games", al-akbar.com, 3 February 2012, http://english.al-akhbar.com/node/3851

111 Dorsey, James, "Egyptian Soccer Violence: A Test of Morsi's Political Savvy", Middle East Online, 27 January 2013, http://www.middle-east-online.com/english/?id=56670

112 Collins, Patrick, *Among The Fans*, p. 146

113 Norman, Matthew, "Let's pack England's phoney Barmy Army off from Ashes series to Helmand", *Daily Telegraph*, 27 December 2010, http://www.telegraph.co.uk/sport/cricket/international/theashes/8225795/Matthew-Norman-lets-pack-Englands-phoney-Barmy-Army-off-from-Ashes-series-in-Australia-to-Helmand.html

114 White, Jim, "The Barmy Army's time has come at last", *Daily Telegraph*, 29 December 2010, http://www.telegraph.co.uk/comment/columnists/jimwhite/8230305/The-Ashes-2010-The-Barmy-Armys-time-has-come-at-last.html

115 Dyson, Jonathan, "Special Report: World will soon be worth more to the Premier League than UK", *Independent on Sunday*, 17 February 2013, http://www.independent.co.uk/sport/football/premier-league/special-report-world-will-soon-be-worth-more-to-premier-league-than-uk-8498204.html

116 Ibid

Chapter 2 – Class Wars

1 Birley, Derek, *Land of sport and glory: Sport and British society 1887-1910*, Manchester University Press, 1995, p. 1

2 Barnes, Simon, "Tradition becoming a poor second to filthy lucre", *The Times*, 13 February 2013, p. 60

3 O'Connor, Ashling, "Squash takes firm step closer to inclusion in 2020", *The Times*, 30 May 2013, p. 55

4 Harris, Tim, *Sport: Almost Everything You Ever Wanted To Know*, Yellow Jersey Press, 2007, p. xiv

5 Allison, Lincoln, lecture at Chelsea School of Sport, University of Brighton, 2012, published in Lincoln Allison and Rusty MacLean, "There's a Deathless Myth on the Close Tonight: Re-assessing Rugby's Place in the History of Sport", *The International Journal of the History of Sport*, 29:13, 1866-1884, http://dx.doi.org/10.1080/09523367.2012.708612

6   Russell, Dave, "The Origins of Association Football" in Steen, Rob, Novick, Jed and Richards, Huw (eds), *The Cambridge Companion to Football*, CUP, 2013, p. 13

7   Bowen, Rowland, *Cricket: A History of its Growth and Development*, Eyre & Spottiswoode, 1970, pp. 29-30

8   Allison and MacLean, "There's a Deathless Myth on the Close Tonight"

9   Block, David, *Baseball before we knew it: a search for the roots of the game*, University of Nebraska Press, 2005, p. 178

10 Vecsey, George, *Baseball: A History of America's Favourite Game*, The Modern Library, 2008 (pbk), p. 19

11 Society for International Hockey Research, http://www.sihrhockey.org/origins_main.cfm

12 Harvie, Robin, *Why We Run: A Story of Obsession*, John Murray, 2011, http://books.google.co.uk/books?id=tS1ieg9gkCsC&pg=PT84&lpg=PT84&d-q=greater+glory+for+any+man+alive+than+ that+which+he+wins+by+his+hands+and+feet

13 Welldon, J. E. C., "The imperial purpose of education", *Proceedings of the Royal Colonial Institute*, XXVI, 1894-5, p. 839

14 Derham, Patrick, "Play up! Play up!", *The Times*, Letters, 8 August 2012, p. 23

15 Perrottet, p. xvii

16 Birley, *Land of Sport and Glory*, p. 3

17 Birley, Derek, *Sport and the making of Britain*, Manchester University Press, 1996 (pbk), p. 130

18 Ibid, p. 144

19 Perkin, Harold, *The Origins of Modern English Society, 1780-1880*, Routledge, 1969, p. 280

20 Collins, Patrick, "Why did we send in the Marines for fourth-form disco?", *Mail on Sunday*, 13 October 2012, http://www.dailymail.co.uk/sport/foot-ball/article-2217364/Why-did-send-Marines-fourth-form-disco.html

21 Coleman, Kathleen, "Gladiators: Heroes of the Roman Amphitheatre", BBC History, 17 February 2011, http://www.bbc.co.uk/history/ancient/romans/gladiators_01.shtml

22 Ibid

23 Reed, Nancy B., "A Chariot Race for Athens' Finest: The *Apobates* Contest Re-Examined", *Journal of Sport History*, 1990, 17:3, p. 306, http://www.la84foundation.org/SportsLibrary/JSH/JSH1990/JSH1703/jsh1703c.pdf

24 Marcellinus, Ammianus, *The Later Roman Empire*, Book 14, 7, http://inter-netbiblecollege.net/Lessons/Large%20Scale%20Backsliding%20in%20the%20Roman%20Empire.pdf

25 "Boxing Equipment and History", Olympic.org, http://www.olympic.org/boxing-equipmentand-history?tab=history

26 Norridge, Julian, *Can We Have Our Balls Back, Please? How the British Invented Sport (And then almost forgot how to play it)*, Penguin (pbk), 2009, p. 7

27 Quoted in Perrottet, p. xix

28 Hurley, Jon, *Tom Cribb – The Life Of The Black Diamond*, The History Press, 2009, p. 3

29 Letter to author, 18 January 2013

30   Wynne-Thomas, Peter, *The History of Cricket – From The Weald to The World*, Norwich: The Stationery Office, 1997, pp. 26-7

31   Norridge, p. 71

32   Williams, Huw, "Get up close and personal with the world's oldest football", BBC News, 19 May 2012, http://www.bbc.co.uk/news/uk-scotland-tayside-central-18119054; "Scottish football more than 500 years old", BBC News, 18 October 2011, http://www.bbc.co.uk/news/uk-scotland-15348386

33   Browning, Robert, *A History of Golf – The Royal and Ancient Game*, A&C Black, 1990 (pbk), p. 1

34   Ibid, p. 2

35   Ibid

36   Ibid, p. 60

37   Ibid, p. 36

38   Ibid, p. 37

39   Ibid, p. 38

40   "History of British Horseracing", British Horseracing Authority website, http://www.britishhorseracing.com/inside_horseracing/racingindustry/history.asp

41   "James I Discovers Newmarket", Newmarketracecourses.co.uk, http://www.newmarketrace courses.co.uk/about-the-home-of-racing/newmarket-history/james-i-discovers-newmarket/)

42   Ibid, http://www.newmarketracecourses.co.uk/about-the-home-of-racing/newmarket-history/newmarket-timeline/

43   Ibid

44   Ice hockey's first world champion was crowned in 1920 but the climax was played out at the Olympics until 1968

45   Shakespeare, William, *Henry V*, Act 1, Scene 2

46   Arlott, John, *The Oxford Companion to Sports and Games*, Paladin, 1977 (pbk), pp. 731-2

47   Harris, p. 27

48   Ibid, pp. 26-7

49   Arlott, p. 732

50   Ibid

51   "Racing certainty", *The Times*, 26 June 2013, p. 4

52   Birley, p. 136

53   Ibid, p. 137

54   Linklater, Magnus, "Even the privileged face the 6am Lord's shuffle", *The Times*, 20 July 2013, Sport, p. 5

55   Warner, Sir Pelham, *Lord's 1787-1945*, first published in 1946, reprinted as part of The Pavilion Library series celebrating MCC's 200th birthday in 1987, p. 28

56   Email from Neil Robinson, 28 June 2012

57   Chadwick, Adam, *A Portrait of Lord's: 200 Years of Cricket History*, Scala Arts & Heritage, 2013, p. 8

58   Ibid, p. 39

59   Malvern, Jack, "First choose a beautiful sitter: rules that can send the value of a painting sky high", *The Times*, 15 June 2013, p. 9

60 Underdown, David, *Start of Play – Cricket and Culture in Eighteenth Century England*, Allen Lane, 2000, pp. 22-3

61 Ibid, p. 23

62 Light, Rob, "Cricket in the eighteenth century", *The Cambridge Companion to Cricket*, Cambridge University Press, 2011, p. 28

63 Mote, Ashley, *The Glory Days of Cricket*, Robson Books, 1999, p. 182 and 188, quoted in *The Cambridge Companion to Cricket*, p. 28

64 Wynne-Thomas, pp. 40-41

65 Ibid, p. 41

66 Ibid

67 Ibid, p. 42

68 Das, Deb K., "Cricket in the USA", Cricinfo, http://static.espncricinfo.com/db/NATIONAL/ICC_MEMBERS/USA/USA_HISTORY.html

69 Wynne-Thomas, p. 42

70 Ramnarayan, V., *Mosquitoes and Other Jolly Rovers: The Story of Tamil Nadu Cricket*, East West Books, 2002, p. 24, quoted in Majumdar, Boria, *Twenty-Two Yards To Freedom: A Social History of Indian Cricket*, Viking, 2004, p. 5

71 Bandopadhyaya, Rakhaldas, "Smriti Tarpan" in Roy, Jagadindranath and Mukhopdhyay, Prabhatkumar (eds), *Manasi o Marmabani*, Kolkata, 1925-6, pp. 618-9, quoted in Majumdar, p. 34

72 Vats, Vaibhav, "Why Does the Rashtriya Swayamsevak Sangh Resent Cricket?", *New York Times*, 2 July 2013, http://india.blogs.nytimes.com/2013/07/02/why-does-the-rashtriya-swayemsewaksangh-resent-cricket/?_r=0

73 Nandy, Ashis, *The Tao of Cricket, On Games of Destiny and the Destiny of Games*, Penguin, 1989

74 Struner, Nancy L., review of Click, Patricia C., *The Spirit of the Times. Amusements in Nineteenth-Century Baltimore, Norfolk, and Richmond*, University Press of Virginia, 1989, published in *Journal of Sport History*, 1990, 17:3, p. 369, http://www.la84foundation.org/SportsLibrary/JSH/JSH1990/JSH1703/jsh1703c.pdf

75 Ibid

76 Norridge, pp. 284-5

77 Hosler, D., Burkett, S. L., and Tarkanian, M. J., "Prehistoric polymers: Rubber processing in Ancient Mesoamerica", *Science*, June 1999, 284 (5422), pp. 1988-1991

78 Tignor, Stephen, *High Strung: Bjorn Borg, John McEnroe and the Untold Story of Tennis's Fiercest Rivalry*, Harper, 2011, p. 19

79 Wynne-Thomas, p. 45

80 Lewis, Peter N., *The Dawn of Professional Golf*, Hobbs and McEwan, 1995, p. 12

81 Russell, p. 20

82 Landow, George, P., "Thomas Hughes's Defence of Fagging at Rugby", The Victorian Web, http://www.victorianweb.org/authors/hughes/fag.html (accessed on 15 June 2013)

83 Hughes, Thomas, *Tom Brown's School Days*, Macmillan, 1857, p. 394

84 Landow

85 Sloan, William Milligan, *Report of the United States Olympic Committee*, 1920, pp. 74-5, quoted in Lucas, p. 59

86 Mandle, W. F., "Wills, Thomas Wentworth (1835–1880)" in Australian Dictionary of Biography, http://adb.anu.edu.au./biography/wills-thomas-wentworth-4863 (accessed on 11 January 2013), quoted in Allison and MacLean

87 Allison and MacLean, "There's a Deathless Myth on the Close Tonight"

88 Marqusee, Mike, *Anyone But England – Cricket and the National Malaise*, Verso, 1994, p. 30

89 "A lower order collapse", *The Economist*, 12 March 2013, http://www.economist.com/blogs/gametheory/2013/03/class-and-cricket

90 Kidd, Patrick, "Public schools dominate England cricket", *The Times*, 2 August 2013, p. 4

91 Priestley, J. B., *The Good Companions*, Penguin, 1976 (pbk)

92 Russell, p. 21

93 Ibid, p. 14

94 Ibid, p.20

95 Ibid

96 Quoted in Stead, Peter, "Brought to Book: Football and Literature" in Steen, Rob, Novick, Jed and Richards, Huw (eds), *The Cambridge Companion to Football*, Cambridge University Press, 2013, p. 249

97 Barzun, Jacques, *God's Country and Mine: A Declaration of Love Spiced with a Few Harsh Words*, New York: Vintage Books, 1959, quoted at http://quote.webcircle.com/cgi-bin/features.cgi?id Feature=2

98 Ward, Geoffrey C., and Burns, Ken, *Baseball: An Illustrated History*, Alfred A. Knopf, 1994, p. 59

99 *New York Gazette Revived*, 6 May 1751, p. 2, quoted in Hise, Beth, "'How is it Umpire?' The 1744 Laws of Cricket and Their Influence on the Development of Baseball in America", *Base Ball – A Journal of the Early Game*, Spring 2011, http://ourgame.mlblogs.com/2011/07/01/1744-laws-ofcricket/

100 Ibid

101 http://www.19cbaseball.com/leagues.html

102 Quoted widely, including in Frommer, Harvey, *Old-Time Baseball: America's Pastime in the Gilded Age*, Rowman & Littlefield, 2006, p. 35

103 Ward and Burns, p. 59

104 Seymour, Harold, *Baseball: The Golden Age*, Oxford University Press, 1971, p. 4

105 Ibid

106 Ibid, p. 3

107 Carroll, Bob, *Baseball Between the Lines*, Perigree Books, 1993, p. 12

108 Ward, John Montgomery, *Baseball: How to Become a Player With the Origin, History and Explanation of the Game*, Philadelphia, 1888, quoted in Ryczek, William, J., *Baseball's First Inning: A History of the National Pastime Through the Civil War*, McFarland & Company, 2009, p. 22

109 Quoted in Block, p. 13

110 Ibid, p. 21

111 Carroll, p. 14

112 Ryczek, p. 23

113 Martinez, David H., *The Book of Baseball Literacy*, Plume, New York, 1996, p. 280

114 Zoss, Joel and Bowman, John, *Diamonds in the Rough: The Untold History of Baseball*, University of Nebraska Press, 2004, p. 39

115 Ibid

116 Broadbent, Rick, "'My crash did hurt. If it was dead safe I wouldn't do it. And I do get off on the pain'", *The Times*, 6 May 2012, p. 49

117 Ibid

118 Ibid

119 "'Bloody Monday' At Harvard", *New York Times*, 5 October 1903

120 Silverman, Jeff and Hardy III, Charles, "Pennsylvania Football", ExplorePAhistory.com, http://explorepahistory.com/story.php?storyId=1-9 -1A&chapter=3 (accessed on 28 June 2013)

121 Braunwart, Bob and Carroll, Bob, *The Journey to Camp: The Origins of American Football to 1889*, Professional Football Researchers Association, http://www.profootballresearchers.org/Articles/Camp_And_Followers. pdf, (accessed on 27 June 2013)

122 Ibid

123 Willis, Chris, *Old Leather: An Oral History of Early Pro Football in Ohio, 1920-1935*, p. xiv

124 Peterson, Robert W., *Cages To Jumpshots: Pro Basketball's Early Years*, Oxford University Press, 1990 (pbk), p. 16

125 Ibid, p. 18

126 Ibid

127 "Newly found documents shed light on basketball's birth", 13 November 2006, http://sports.espn.go.com/nba/news/story?id=2660882

128 Peterson, p. 20

129 Ibid

130 http://www.eliteleague.co.uk/eihl-history-s12540

131 Richards, Huw, "Austria and Hungary: The Danubian School" in Steen, R., Novick, J. and Richards, H. (eds), *The Cambridge Companion to Football*, Cambridge University Press, 2013, p. 50

132 Lanfranchi, Pierre, 'Notes on the Development of Football in Europe' in R. Guilianotti and J. Williams (eds.), *Game without Frontiers: Football, Identities and Modernity*, Arena, 1994, p. 35, quoted in Richards, 'Austria and Hungary: The Danubian School'

133 *Neues Wiener Journal*, 15 November 1924, quoted in R. Horak and W. Maderthaner, "A Culture of Urban Cosmopolitanism: Uridil and Sindelar as Viennese Coffee-House Heroes" in R. Holt, J. A. Mangan and P. Lanfranchi (eds.), *European Heroes, Myth, Identities, Sport*, Frank Cass, 1996, p. 139.

134 Guttmann, Allen, *Games and Empires: Modern Sports and Cultural Imperialism*, Columbia University Press, 1994, p. 2

135 Stone, Oliver, "Oliver Stone's Untold History of the United States", Episode 10, 14 January 2013

136 Gillis, Richard and Miller, Andrew, "The Rich List", *The Cricketer*, August 2012, p. 40-1

Chapter 3 – Odds and Sods

1 Syed, Matthew, "Raising stakes in playing fields of false hope", *The Times*, 23 January 2013, p. 53

2 Ramesh, Randeep, "High-stakes betting machines 'suck money from the poor'", *The Guardian Weekly*, 11 January 2013, p. 17

3 Burgess, Kaya, "Gambling ads 'must be more responsible'", *The Times*, 25 February 2013, p. 15

4 Hines, Nico, "Online gambling is where the money is, Rich List shows", *The Times*, 20 April 2013, p. 16

5 Arlott, p. 732

6 Atherton, Mike, *Gambling*, Hodder, 2007 (pbk), p. 191

7 Perrottet, Tony, *The Naked Olympics*, Random House, 2004, p. 85

8 Armstrong, Jim, "IOC chief says corruption the next big fight", *Associated Press*, 14 July 2011, http://www.toastedrav.com/post/90227_ioc_chief_says_corruption_the_next_big_fight_

9 O'Connor, Ashling, "Turkey escapes heat of fixing row", *The Times*, 8 March 2013, p. 95

10 Lewis, Ron, "Mega-bout in doubt as judges land low blows for Pacquiao", *The Times*, 11 June 2012, p. 57

11 "Jess Willard Knocks Out Jack Johnson in Twenty-sixth Round", *Sioux City Journal*, 6 April 1915, http://www.boxinggyms.com/news/willard_johnson1915/willard1915sioux.htm

12 Atherton, Mike, *Gambling*, Hodder & Stoughton (pbk), 2007, p. 119

13 Quoted in Atherton, *Gambling*, p. 179

14 Ibid, p. 180

15 King's College London, http://www.kcl.ac.uk/depsta/iss/archives/wellington/duel10.htm

16 Wilson, Christopher, "Meet the abominable Queen of the turf", Mail Online, 4 June 2010, http://www.dailymail.co.uk/femail/article-1283831/Meet-abominable-Queen-turf.html

17 Cobb, John, "Why nothing could be easier than nobbling a racehorse", *The Independent*, 28 January 1998

18 Wright, Rob, "Chopra among nine charged with race-fixing", *The Times*, 5 October 2012, p. 77; Lee, Alan, "Chopra among nine warned off", *The Times*, 26 January 2013, Sport, p. 23

19 Quoted in Atherton, *Gambling*, p. 181

20 Birley, Derek, *Sport and the making of Britain*, Manchester University Press, 1996, p. 177

21 Rae, Simon, *W.G. Grace – A Life*, Faber & Faber, 1998, p. 160

22 Ibid, p. 161

23 Ward, Geoffrey C., and Burns, Ken, *Baseball: An Illustrated History*, Alfred A. Knopf, 1994, p. 25

24 Lardner, John, *Strong Cigars and Lovely Women*, Newsweek, 1951, p. 105

25 Ward and Burns, p. 23

26 Ibid, p. 26

27 Ibid, p. 26

28 Seymour, Harold, *Baseball – The Golden Age*, Oxford University Press, 1971, pp. 288-9

29 Lieb, Frederick G., *The Baseball Story*, Putnam, 1950, quoted in Seymour, p. 289

30 Seymour, pp. 288-9

31 Ibid, pp. 290-1

32 *Guardian*, December 2, 2006

33 Jackson, Jamie, "Triumph and despair", *The Observer*, 4 July 2004

34 Hawkins, Ed, "No match too big or too small when billions are staked in insatiable Asian markets", *The Times*, 5 February 2013, p. 66

35 Obituary, *Wisden Cricketers' Almanack 2003*, John Wisden, 2003, pp. 1619-25

36 Steen, Rob, "Hansie: The Making of a martyr", *Wisden Cricketers' Almanack 2005*, John Wisden, 2005, p. 81

37 Sky Sports, 1 June 2012

38 Boswell, Thomas, "Rose case wilting for lack of evidence", *Pittsburgh Post-Gazette*, 27 April 1989, http://news.google.com/newspapers?nid=1129&dat=19890427&id=KbBRAAAAIBAJ&sjid=_W0DAAAAIBAJ&pg=5892,8977188

39 Costa, Brian, "4,256 hits, Millions in Autographs", *The Wall Street Journal*, 30 May 2013, http://bleacherreport.com/tb/dawN2?utm_source=newsletter&utm_medium=newsletter&utm_campaign=mlb

40 Carter, Jimmy, "It's Time to Forgive Pete Rose", *USA Today*, 30 October 1995, quoted at baseballalmanac.com, http://www.baseball-almanac.com/players/p_rosed.shtml

41 Daugherty, Paul, "Rose-colored glasses cloud truth for Roger Clemens", *USA Today*, 12 May 2009, http://usatoday30.usatoday.com/sports/columnist/daugherty/2009-05-12-clemens-rose_N.htm

42 "What others are saying", CBC Sports, http://www.cbc.ca/sports/indepth/peterose/stories/reaction.html (accessed on 4 June 2014)

43 Seymour, Harold, *Baseball: The Golden Age*, p. 295

44 Ibid, p. 296

45 Ibid, p. 301

46 Ibid, p. 337

47 Ibid, p. 338

48 Carney, Gene, *Burying The Black Sox – How Baseball's Cover-Up of the 1919 World Series Fix Almost Succeeded*, Potomac Books, 2006, p. 75

49 Ibid, p. 300-1

Chapter 4 – Ringmasters Inc

1 Barnes, Simon, "Generation game holds key to better world", *The Times*, 25 February 2013, p. 53

2 "Olympic-sized corruption plagues Sochi Winter Games, report claims", NBCNews.com, 30 May 2013, http://worldnews.nbcnews.com/_news/2013/05/30/18631119-olympic-sized-corruption-plagues-sochi-winter-games-report-claims?lite

3 Vasilyeva, Nataliya, "Russian critic: wide corruption at Sochi games", Reuters, 30 May 2013, http://news.yahoo.com/russian-critic-wide-corruption-sochi-games-131742967.html

4 "Sport Power 100", *The Times*, 31 March 2012, Sport section, pp. 14-15

5 Ibid

6   Sangakkara, MCC Spirit of Cricket Lecture

7   Stead, Phil, *Red Dragons: The Story of Welsh Football – Y Lolfa*, Talybont, 2013, p. 168

8   Ibid, pp. 196-7

9   Fernando, Andrew, "SLC to probe Jayawardene's comments to newspaper", Cricinfo, 22 December 2012, http://www.espncricinfo.com/srilanka/content/current/story/598264.html

10   Steen, Rob, "Sheepskins Coats and Nannygoats: The View from the Pressbox", *The Cambridge Companion to Football*, Cambridge University Press, 2013, p. 220

11   Holt, Richard, *Oxford Dictionary of National Biography*, 2004, http://www.oxforddnb.com/view/printable/39536

12   Booth, Keith, *The Father of Modern Sport: The Life and Times of Charles W. Alcock*, The Parrs Wood Press, 2002, p. xi

13   Ibid, pp. 109-111

14   Ibid, p. 110

15   Ferry, Jules, "Speech Before the French Chamber of Deputies, March 28 1884" in Robiquet, Paul (ed), *Discours et Opinions de Jules Ferry*, Armand Colin & Cie., 1897

16   Lucas, John, A., "Baron de Coubertin and Thomas Arnold", *Bulletin du Comité International Olympique*, No.98-99, 15 August 1967, p. 58, http://www.la84foundation.org/OlympicInformation   Center/OlympicReview/1967/BDCE98/BDCE98e.pdf

17   Allison and MacLean, "There's a Deathless Myth on the Close Tonight"

18   De Coubertin, Pierre, "Une Campagne de Vingt et Un Ans, 1887-1908", *Librairie de l'Education physique*, p. 2, quoted in Lucas, p. 58

19   Lucas, p. 59

20   Ibid, p. 60

21   De Coubertin, Baron, *Olympism: Selected Writings*, Comité Internationnal Olympique, 2000, p. 352

22   Ibid, p. 167

23   Ibid, p. 209

24   Müller, Norbert, "Olympic education", http://olympicstudies.uab.es/lec/pdf/muller.pdf

25   Harris, *Sport: Almost Everything You Ever Wanted To Know*, p. 108

26   Arlott, *The Oxford Companion to Sports and Games*, p. 642

27   Richards, Huw, "The Game-Changers: Henri Delaunay" in Steen, Rob, Novick, Jed and Richards, Huw (eds), *The Cambridge Companion to Football*, CUP, 2013, p. 46

28   Hare, Geoff, *Football in France: A Cultural History*, Berg, 2003, p. 34, quoted in Richards

29   Ferriday, Patrick, *Before The Lights Went Out: The 1912 Triangular Tournament*, Von Kramm, 2011, p. 100

30   Ibid, p. 88

31   Haigh, Gideon, "Behind The Scenes At The ICC: Fear and loathing in Dubai", *Wisden Cricketers' Almanack 2012*, John Wisden, 2012, p. 65

32   Seymour, *Baseball: The Golden Age*, p. 9

33   Ibid, p. 183

34 Edelman, Marc, "Moving Past Collusion in Major League Baseball: Healing old wounds, and preventing new ones", *Wayne Law Review*, 2008, Vol 54, No.3, p. 605 (available for download at http://papers.ssrn.com/sol3/papers.cfm?abstract_id=1341333)

35 Ibid, p. 197

36 Ibid, pp. 197-9

37 Ward and Burns, pp. 121-3

38 Ibid

39 Rice, Grantland, *The Tumult And The Shouting*, Cassell & Co, 1956, pp. 19-20

40 Creamer, Robert, W., *Babe: The Legend Comes To Life*, Simon & Schuster, 1974, pp. 233-4

41 Seymour, p. 367

42 Ibid, p. 320

43 Ibid, p. 368

44 Ibid, p. 323

45 Golenbock, Peter, *Dem Bums: An Oral History of the Brooklyn Dodgers*, Dover Publications, 2010 (pbk), p. 110

46 Pietrusza, David, *Judge and Jury: The Life and Times of Judge Kenesaw Mountain Landis*, Diamond Communications, 1998, p. xv

47 Lester, Larry, "Can You Read, Judge Landis?", *Black Ball: A Negro Leagues Journal*, Fall 2008, 1:2, pp. 4-5, http://www.larrylester42.com/uploads/1/9/5/4/19545937/can_u_read_printed_w_cover.pdf

48 Ibid, p. 1

49 Povich, Shirley, *Washington Post*, 7 April 1939, p. 21, quoted in Lester, p. 7

50 Lester, p. 11

51 *New York Times*, April 18, 1945, quoted in Lester, p. 13

52 Harris, Ed, *Philadelphia Tribune*, 7 August 1941, quoted in Lester, p. 10

53 Quoted in Virtue, John, *South of the Color Barrier: How Jorge Pasquel and the Mexcian Leagues Pushed Baseball Toward Racial Integration*, McFarland & Company, 1996, p. 32

54 Quoted in Lester, pp. 13-16

55 Interview with Lester, 31 October 1997, quoted in Lester, p. 12

56 *Los Angeles Times*, 17 July 1942, quoted in Lester, p. 17

57 Ibid

58 Lacey, Sam, *Baltimore Afro-American*, 10 November 1945, quoted in Lester, p. 22

59 Seymour, p. 422

60 Lester, p. 23

61 Phil Woosnam obituary, *The Times*, 24 July 2013, p. 52

62 Ibid

63 Sykes, Tom, "David Beckham is Retiring, But We Still Love Him", *The Daily Beast*, 16 May 2013, http://www.thedailybeast.com/articles/2013/05/16/david-beckham-is-retiring-but-we-still-love-him.html

64 Reuters, "Former NASL commissioner Phil Woosnam dies", 21 July 2013

65 Carlos, John, University of Brighton Annual Sport Journalism Lecture, 17 May 2012

66 Jennings, Andrew, "Journalists? They're media masseurs", *British Journalism Review*, June 2012, Vol. 23, No. 2, 2012, pages 25-31, http://www.bjr.org.uk/data/2012/no2_jennings

67 Interview with author, November 2006

68 Ibid

69 Simson, Vyv and Jennings, Andrew, *The New Lords of the Rings: Power, Money and Drugs in the Modern Olympics*, Simon & Schuster, 1992, p. 25

70 Ibid, p. 24

71 Ibid, pp. 24-5

72 Simson and Jennings, *The New Lords of the Rings: Power, Money and Drugs in the Modern Olympics*, pp. 10-11

73 Powell, Jeff, "Passion, humility and loyalty: Ian Wooldridge transcended sport", *Daily Mail*, 6 March 2007, http://www.dailymail.co.uk/news/article-440333/Passion-humanity-loyalty-Ian-Wooldridge-transcended-sport.html

74 Wooldridge, Ian, *Searching for Heroes – fifty years of sporting encounters*, Hodder & Stoughton, 2007, p. 287

75 Ibid

76 Shepard, Alicia, C., "An Olympian Scandal", *American Journalism Review*, Spring 1999, http://www.ajr.org/Article.asp?id=505

77 Simson and Jennings, p. 173

78 Ibid, p. 182

79 Ibid

80 "Leading European clubs continue rebellion over international fixtures", *Daily Mail*, 24 February 2012, http://www.dailymail.co.uk/sport/football/article-2105886/FIFA-boycott-European-clubs.html

81 Kay, Oliver, *The Times*, 28 April 2012, Sport section, p. 10

82 Pinheiro, Daniela, "The president", *piaui*, Edition 58, July 2011, http://revistapiaui.estadao.com.br/edicao-58/the-faces-of-futebol/the-president

83 Sugden, John and Tomlinson, Alan, *Badfellas*, Mainstream, 2003, p. 63

84 Ibid, p. 68

85 This section draws on "Sheepskin Coats and Nannygoats", my chapter for The *Cambridge Companion to Football*, pp. 217-30

86 McIlvanney, *The Observer*, 6 July 1986, reprinted in "Jewels in a Dung Heap", *McIlvanney on Football*, Mainstream, 1997, p. 267

87 Goldblatt, David, "Kickbacks but no penalties", *The Independent* , 9 June 2006

88 McIlvanney, "Jewels in a dung heap"; Sugden and Tomlinson, *Badfellas*, p. 71

89 Sugden and Tomlinson, p. 69

90 Jennings, *Foul! The Secret World of FIFA: Bribes, Vote-Rigging and Ticket Scandals*, Harper Collins, 2006

91 O'Connor, Ashling, "Court papers show Fifa pair received bribes totalling £80m", *The Times*, 12 July 2012, p. 58

92 O'Connor, Ashling, "Blatter on the defensive over bribe scandal", *The Times*, 13 July 2012, p. 70

93 Jennings, Andrew, "What I Told The FBI About FIFA Crooks", *Transparency in Sport*, 27 March 2013, http://transparencyinsportblog.wordpress.com/2013/03/27/what-i-told-the-fbi-about-the- fifa-crooks/

94 Email to author, 10 May 2013

95 Jennings, "What I Told The FBI About FIFA Crooks"

96 Ibid

[97]   Ugra, Sharda, "A league in need of cleansing", ESPNcricinfo, 28 May 2013, http://www.espncricinfo.com/magazine/content/current/story/638260.html

[98]   "Lessons from cricket", *The Economist*, 25 May 2013, http://www.economist.com/news/leaders/21578396-mismanagement-indian-cricket-reveals-indias-wider-failings-lessons-cricket

[99]   Guha, Ramachandra, "The serpent in the garden", ESPNcricinfo, 1 June 2013, http://www.espncricinfo.com/magazine/content/story/638602.html

[100] Hitchens, Christopher, "Fool's Gold: How the Olympics and other international competitions breed conflict and bring out the worst in human nature", *Newsweek*, 5 February 2010, http://www.newsweek.com/id/233007

[101] "Luge slider dead in Olympics Accident", The Huffington Post, 12 February 2010, http://www.huffingtonpost.com/2010/02/12/nodar-kumaritashvili-cras_n_460474.html

[102] Starkman, Randy, "Canada painted as bad guy in Olympic Oval fuss", *Toronto Star*, 10 March 2009, http://www.thestar.com/sports/olympics/2009/03/10/canada_painted_as_bad_guy_in_olympic_oval_fuss.html (accessed on 23 June 2013)

[103] Broadbent, Rick, "Triumph overcomes tragedy after host nation takes Games to its heart", *The Times*, 1 March 2010

[104] Ibid

[105] Zirin, Dave, "Sportsmanship: The Great Olympic Fraud", *The Progressive*, 15 February 2010, http://www.progressive.org/zirin022510.html

[106] Ibid

[107] Hinds, Richard, "Price of gold soars on the London medal exchange", *Sydney Morning Herald*, 30 October 2009, http://www.smh.com.au/news/sport/price-of-gold-soars-on-the-london-medal-exchange/2009/10/30/1256835151545.html

[108] Will, George F., "Players Are Bought And Sold? Say It Ain't So", *Washington Post*, 24 June 1976, reprinted in Will, George F., *Bunts*, Simon & Schuster, 1999, p. 30

[109] Quoted in Vrooman, John, "The Economic Structure of the NFL" in Quinn, Kevin G., *The Economics of the National Football League*, Springer, 2012, p. 7

[110] ESPN, http://espn.go.com/mlb/attendance

[111] Vrooman, "The Economic Structure of the NFL", Quinn, p. 7

[112] Zirin, Dave, "Rahm Emanuel's Zombie Pigs vs Chicago's Angry Birds", *The Nation*, 22 May 2013, http://www.thenation.com/blog/174478/rahm-emanuels-zombie-pigs-vs-chicagos-angry-birds#

Chapter 5 – The First Taboo
I. From "Gentlemen" to Shamateurs

[1]   Flatman, Barry, "Heaviest footballer eats hecklers for breakfast", *Sunday Times*, 23 December 2012, Sport, p. 7

[2]   Barnes, Simon, "Toff at the top until nurture took its course", *The Times*, 2 August 2013, p. 60

[3]   Arlott, John, *Arlott on Cricket*, Harper Collins Willow, 1984, pp. 22-3

4   Barnes, Simon, "Toff at the top until nurture took its course", *The Times*, 2 August 2013, p. 60

5   Angell, Roger, *Once More Around the Park – A Baseball Reader*, Ballantine Books, 1991, p. 137

6   Ibid

7   Gibson, Bob, with Wheeler, Lonnie, *Stranger to the Game: The Autobiography of Bob Gibson*, Viking, 1994, quoted in Wendel, Tim, *Summer of '68 – The Season That Changed Baseball, and America Forever*, Da Capo, 2012, p. 2

8   Ibid, p. 22

9   Ibid

10   Ibid

11   Syed, Matthew, "Money is not the root of all sport's evils", *The Times*, 5 June 2013, p. 57

12   Ibid

13   Downes, Steven and Mackay, Duncan, *Running Scared: How Athletics Lost Its Innocence*, Mainstream, 1996, p. 220

14   Perrottet, *The Naked Olympics*, p. 52

15   "Dwayne Wade: No pay for Olympics", ESPN, 13 April 2012, http://espn.go.com/nba/story/_/id/7805591/miami-heat-dwyane-wade-backs-compensation-olympics

16   Johnson, Michael, "Don't blame some for lacking Olympic ideal", *The Times*, 30 April 2012, p. 61

17   Perrottet, pp. 53-4

18   Birley, Derek, *A Social History of English Cricket*, Aurum, 2003 (pbk), p. 87

19   Lee, Christopher, *From the Sea End – The Official History of Sussex County Cricket Club*, Partridge Press, 1989, pp. 92-3

20   Birley, p. 85

21   Letter to author, 18 January 2013

22   Birley, p. 86

23   Ibid, p. 87

24   Ibid, p. 83

25   http://www.britishpathe.com/video/cricket-1

26   Sissons, *The Players*, pp. 167-8

27   Streeton, Richard, *P.G.H. Fender – A Biography*, Faber & Faber, 1981, p. 134

28   Ibid, p. 22

29   Ibid, p. 23

30   Cardus, Neville, *English Cricket*, Collins, 1945, pp. 22-3

31   Available on YouTube, http://www.youtube.com/watch?v=7-kMhFe18IA

32   Ranjitsinhji, Prince K. S., *The Jubilee Book of Cricket*, William Blackwood & Sons, 1897, quoted in Cardus, Neville, *English Cricket*, p. 22

33   Booth, *The Father of Modern Sport*, p. 180

34   Quoted in Ball, Peter and Hopps, David, *The Book of Cricket Quotations*, Stanley Paul, 1990, p. 116

35   Rae, Simon, *W.G. Grace – A Life*, Faber & Faber, 1998, pp. xi-xii

36   Ibid, pp. 146-7

37   Ibid, p. 185

38   Ibid, p. xii

39   Knox, Malcolm, *Never a Gentleman's Game: The Scandal-Filled Early Years of Test Cricket*, Hardie Grant, 2012

40 Richards, Huw, *A Game For Hooligans: The History of Rugby Union*, Mainstream, 2006, p. 40

41 Ibid, p. 41

42 Ibid, p. 57

43 Quoted in Richards, p. 57

44 Ibid, p. 59

45 Ibid, pp. 59-60

46 Collins, Tony, *Rugby's Great Split: Class, Culture and the Origins of Rugby League Football*, Routledge, 2006, 2nd edition, p. 48

47 *Yorkshire Post*, 20 September 1886, quoted in Collins, p. 48

48 Budd, Arthur, "The Rugby Union Game" in *Football Annual*, 1886, p. 52, quoted in Collins, p. 49

49 *Yorkshire Post*, 11 October 1886, quoted in Collins, p. 50

50 Collins, p. 51

51 Ibid, p. 58

52 Moorhouse, Geoffrey, *A People's Game: The Official History of Rugby League*, Hodder & Stoughton, 1996, 2nd edition, p. 44

53 *Yorkshire Post*, 30 August 1895, quoted in Moorhouse, p. 44

54 Moorhouse, p. 44

55 Richards, p. 79

56 Collins, p. 197

57 Browning, pp. 75-6

58 Ibid, p. 80

59 Lewis, p. 7

60 Ibid, pp. 14-15

61 Ibid, p. 11

62 Ibid, pp. 15-16

63 Ibid, p. 16

64 Ibid

65 Ibid, p. 8

66 Ibid, p. 18

67 Ibid, p. 49-50

68 Vecsey, *Baseball: A History of America's Favourite Game*, p. 24

69 Booth, p. 173

70 Silverman, Jeff and Hardy III, Charles, "Pennsylvania Football", ExplorePAhistory.com, http://explorepahistory.com/story.php?storyId=1-9-1A&chapter=3 (accessed on 28 June 2013)

71 Weiner, Evan, *America's Passion: How a Coal Miner's Game Became the NFL in the 20th Century*, Smashwords, 2012 (pdf), p. 14

72 "Chronology 1869-1939", Pro Football Hall of Fame, http://www.profootballhof.com/history/general/chronology/1869-1939.aspx (accessed on 27 June 2013)

73 Ibid, p. 16

74 Barker, Matthew, "The Gerry Hitchens Story; William Garbutt", Book review, *When Saturday Comes*, January 2012, http://www.wsc.co.uk/content/view/4743/28/

75 Mason, Tony, *Association Football And English Society 1863-1915*, The Harvester Press, 1980, p. 69

76 *Midland Athlete*, 12 October, 29 December 1881, quoted in Mason, p. 70

77 Booth, p. 178

78 Ibid

79 Ibid, p. 166

80 Ibid, p. 187

81 Mason, p. 71

82 *Athletic News*, 24 October, 14 November 1883, quoted in Mason, p. 72

83 Russell, Dave, "Kicking off: The origins of professional football" in Steen, Rob, Novick, Jed and Richards, Huw (eds), *The Cambridge Companion to Football*, p. 22

84 Ibid

85 Ibid, p. 23

86 Ibid, p. 24

87 *Athletic News*, 23 June 1885, quoted in Mason, p. 36

88 Mason, p. 44

89 Ibid, p. 45

90 Ibid, p. 46

91 Ibid, p. 45

92 Quoted in Rippon, Anton, sportsjournalists.co.uk, "Dirty tackle? Or fair comment? You be the judge", 21 September 2012, http://www.sportsjournalists.co.uk/other-bodies/football-writers/dirty-tackle-or-fair-comment-you-be-the-judge/

93 Ibid

94 Ibid

95 Ibid, p. 47

96 Quoted in Mason, p. 48

97 Quoted in http://www.cmgww.com/sports/thorpe/quotes/quotes.html

98 "Carlisle's Olympic Heroes", *The Red Man*, September 1912, http://home.epix.net/~landis/thorpe.html

99 "Jim Thorpe cruelly treated by authorities", Reuters, 9 August 2004, reprinted in *Sports Illustrated*, http://sportsillustrated.cnn.com/2004/olympics/2004/08/08/bc.olympics.athletics.thorpe/

100 Young, William A., *John Tortes "Chief" Myers: A Baseball Biography*, McFarland & Company, 2012, p. 58

101 Gould, Stephen Jay, *Triumph and Tragedy in Mudville*, Jonathan Cape, 2004, pp. 109-11

102 Rice, p. 146

103 Seymour, *Baseball: The Golden Age*, p. v

104 Mosedale, John, *The Greatest of All*, Doubleday, 1974, quoted in Weinberger, Miro and Riley, Dan, *The Yankees Reader*, Houghton Mifflin, 1991, p.50

105 Ward and Burns, p. 154

106 Ibid, p. 155

107 Creamer, Robert, "Babe, The Legend Comes To Life", *Sports Illustrated*, 18 March 1974, http://bleacherreport.com/tb/d82d2?utm_source=newsletter&utm_medium=newsletter&utm_campaign=mlb

108 Ibid

109 Mosedale, *The Greatest of All*, quoted in Weinberger and Riley, *The Yankees Reader*, p. 50

110 Lieb, Frederick J., *New York Evening Telegram*, 18 April 1923, quoted in Weinberger and Riley, p. 45

111   Ibid, p. 46
112   Montville, Leigh, "Media Babe" in Fleder, Rob (ed), *Damn Yankees: Twenty-Four Major League Writers on the World's Most Loved (and Hated) Team*, HarperCollins, 2012, pp. 109-10
113   Barker, Ralph, *Ten Great Bowlers*, Chatto and Windus, 1967, pp. 124-55
114   *The Times*, 23 October, 1965, p. 10
115   Creamer, pp. 22-3

Chapter 5 – The First Taboo
II. Pride and Prejudice

1   Henderson, Jon, *The Last Champion: The Life of Fred Perry*, Yellow Jersey Press, 2009, p. 4
2   Ibid
3   Ibid
4   Jefferys, Kevin, "Fred Perry: the icon and the outcast", *BBC History Magazine*, http://www.historyextra.com/feature/fred-perry-icon-and-outcast
5   Evans, Richard, *Open Tennis – The First Twenty Years*, Bloomsbury, 1988, p. 4
6   Little, Alan, *Suzanne Lenglen: Tennis Idol of the Twenties*, Wimbledon Lawn Tennis Museum, 2007 edition, p. 110
7   Berry, Eliot, *Topspin: Ups and Downs in Big-Time Tennis*, Henry Holt, 1996, quoted in Talk Tennis, http://tt.tennis-warehouse.com/archive/index.php/t-450723.html
8   Ibid, p. 5
9   Ibid, p. 230
10   Ibid, pp. 260-1
11   Ibid, p. 6
12   Evans, p. 3
13   Ibid, p. 5
14   "Herman David dies", *Catholic Herald*, 1 March 1974, http://archive.catholicherald.co.uk/article/1st-march-1974/10/herman-david-dies
15   Evans, p. 14
16   Ibid
17   Tignor, Stephen, *High Strung: Bjorn Borg, John McEnroe and the Untold Story of Tennis's Fiercest Rivalry*, Harper, 2011, p. 23
18   Ibid
19   Bergman, Justin, "Rod Laver returns to Australian Open 50 years after winning the Grand Slam", Associated Press, 25 January 2012, http://www.thestar.com/sports/tennis/2012/01/25/rod_laver_returns_to_australian_open_in_melbourne_50_years_after_winning_the_grand_slam.html?
20   Stutchbury, Greg, "Rod Laver recalls amateur days as 50th anniversary is celebrated", Reuters, 25 January 2012, http://www.dnaindia.com/sport/report_rod-laver-recalls-amateur-days-as-50th-anniversary-celebrated_1642088
21   Forbes, p. 201
22   Mark McCormack obituary by Milicia, Joe, *Pittsburgh Post-Gazette*, 17 May 2003, http://old.post-gazette.com/obituaries/20030517mccormack0517p4.asp

23 Hopkins, John, *Nick Faldo in perspective*, George Allen & Unwin, 1985, p. 50

24 Ibid, p. 124

25 Haigh, Gideon, "1977 and all that: cricket's revolution as event, history and drama", History Council of Victoria Annual Lecture, 2012

26 Ibid

27 Haigh, Gideon, *The Cricket War – The Inside Story of Kerry Packer's World Series Cricket*, The Text Publishing Company, 1993 (pbk), p. 34

28 Lewis, Tony, "The Establishment needed a shock", *The Cricketer*, February 2013, p. 45

29 Letter to Kerry Packer read out by Tony Greig during his 2012 MCC Spirit of Cricket Lecture at Lord's, reprinted in Nicholas, Mark, "Kerry played guitar", Cricinfo, 28 June 2012, http://www.espncricinfo.com/magazine/content/story/570263.html

30 Haigh, *The Summer Game*, Text Publishing, 1997, p. 274

31 Piesse, Ken, "I left cricket far too early", Cricinfo, 23 January 2013, http://www.espncricinfo.com/magazine/content/story/587966.html

32 Haigh, *The Cricket War*, p. 71

33 Steen, Rob, *Desmond Haynes: Lion of Barbados*, Witherby, 1993, p. 59

34 Ibid, pp. 70-1

35 Ibid, p. 73

36 Ibid

37 Ibid, p. 73

38 Ross, Gordon, "The Packer Circus", *Wisden Cricketers' Almanack 1978*, Sporting Handbooks, 1978, pp. 125-7

39 Brearley, Mike & Doust, Dudley, *The Ashes Retained*, Hodder and Stoughton, 1979, p. 98

40 Haigh, "1977 and all that"

41 Lewis, Tony, "The Establishment needed a shock"

42 Haigh, *The Cricket War*, pp. 225-6

43 Haigh, "1977 and all that"

44 Ibid

45 Downes and Mackay, *Running Scared: How Athletics Lost Its Innocence*, p. 217

46 Ibid

47 Ibid, p. 221

48 Email to author, July 25, 2012

49 Interview with author, October 20, 2006

50 Richards, Huw, *A Game For Hooligans*, p. 196

51 Ibid

52 Ibid

53 Ibid, p. 226

54 Edwards, Gareth, *Gareth: The autobiography of a rugby legend*, Arrow Books, 1979 (pbk), p. 85

55 Ibid, p. 86

56 Ibid, pp. 86-7

57 Ibid, p. 87

58 Quoted in Richards, p. 197

59 Ibid, p. 244

60 Ibid, p. 245

61 Ibid

62 Lynagh, Michael, "Why you have to know your enemy - and referee too", *The Times*, 29 June 2013, Sport, p. 13

63 Marcano, Arturo J and Fidler, David P, "Global baseball: Latin America" in Cassuto, Leonard and Partridge, Stephen (eds), *Cambridge Companion to Baseball*, Cambridge University Press, 2011, p. 172

64 Ibid, p. 170

65 Wendell, Tim, *The New Face of Baseball: The One-Hundred Year Rise and Triumph of Latinos in America's Favourite Sport*, HarperCollins, 2003, p. xii

66 Marcano, Arturo J. and Fidler, David P., "Global baseball: Latin America" in Cassuto, Leonard and Partridge, Stephen (eds), *The Cambridge Companion to Baseball*, Cambridge University Press, 2010, pp. 172-3

67 Zirin, Dave, "Why Major League Baseball Owners Will Cheer the Death of Hugo Chávez", *The Nation*, 6 March 2013, http://www.thenation.com/blog/173233/why-major-league-baseball-owners-will-cheer-death-hugo-chavez#

68 Ibid, p. 175

69 Ibid, p. 175

70 Ibid, p. 176

71 Biertempfel, Rob, "Gayo Leads Bucs in Dominican Republic", *Pittsburgh Tribune-Review*, 10 May 2009, quoted in Marcano and Fidler, p. 176

72 "Yanks fire Latin American scouts amid probe, official says", ESPN.com, 14 January 2010, http://sports.espn.go.com/mlb/news/story?id=3537389

73 Sports Law Blog, 12 November 2012, http://sports-law.blogspot.co.uk/2010/11/3-ks-for-kickbacks-white-sox-are-latest.html

74 Passan, Jeff, "Story of Miguel Sano chronicles ugly, sleazy side of baseball's Dominican Republic pipeline", Yahoo.com, 2 July 2012, http://sports.yahoo.com/news/story-of-miguel-sano-chronicles-ugly--sleazy-side-of-baseball-s-dominican-talent-pipeline.html

75 McCullough, Andy, "Mets GM Sandy Alderson appointed to MLB committee to study amateur draft", *New Jersey Star-Ledger*, 15 December 2011, http://www.nj.com/mets/index.ssf/2011/12/mets_gm_sandy_alderson_appoint.html

76 Marcano and Fidler, p. 182

77 Brown, David, "Sandy Alderson is kidding us, himself about Dominican fraud", Yahoo.com, 29 January 2012, http://sports.yahoo.com/blogs/mlb-big-league-stew/sandy-alderson-kidding-us-himself-domini-can-fraud-101146784.html

78 Gordon, Ian, "Inside Major League Baseball's Dominican Sweatshop System", motherjones.com, March/April 2013, http://www.motherjones.com/politics/2013/03/baseball-dominican-system-yewri-guillen

79 Ibid

80 Thamel, Pete, "Real NCAA Penalty for Penn State, but No Cheers Yet", *New York Times*, 23 July 2012, http://www.nytimes.com/2012/07/24/sports/ncaafootball/in-penn-state-scandal-weighing-penalty-and-role-of-money.html?pagewanted=all

81 Branch, Taylor, "The Shame of College Sports", *The Atlantic*, 7 September 2011, http://www.theatlantic.com/magazine/archive/2011/10/the-shame-of-college-sports/308643/4/

82 Ibid

83 Berkowitz, Steve, "NCAA legal filing reveals fears of college sports officials", *USA Today*, 15 March 2013, http://www.usatoday.com/story/sports/college/2013/03/15/ncaa-lawsuit-filing-ed-obannon-case/1989925/

84 Hruby, Patrick, "The Gold-Plating of College Sports", sportsonearth.com, March 2013, http://www.sportsonearth.com/article/42924176/

85 NCAA.org, http://www.ncaa.org/wps/wcm/connect/public/ncaa/about+the+ncaa/history (last accessed on 8 October 2012)

86 Wolff, Alexander, "Beyond Repair", *Sports Illustrated*, 12 June 1995, pp. 20-26

87 NCAA press release, 1 December 1995, https://web1.ncaa.org/LSDBi/exec/miSearch?mi SearchSubmit=publicReport&key=63&publicTerms=THIS

88 Robinson, Charles, "Renegade Miami football booster spells out illicit payments to players", Yahoo! Sports, 16 August 2011, http://sports.yahoo.com/investigations/news?slug=cr-renegade_miami_booster_details_illicit_benefits_081611

89 Mandel, Stewart, "Credibility of NCAA enforcement will be tested by Miami allegations", *Sports Illustrated*, 16 August 2011, http://sportsillustrated.cnn.com/2011/writers/stewart_mandel/08/16/miami.hurricanes.allegations.reaction/index.html#tyntHFL

90 Wolff, Alexander, "16 Years Later, It's Time To Get Real", *Sports Illustrated*, 29 August 2011, http://sportsillustrated.cnn.com/vault/article/magazine/MAG1189725/2/index.htm

91 Wise, Mike, "Jerry Sandusky sentencing brings an end to sordid tale, but no closure for victims", *Washington Post*, 9 October 2012, http://www.washingtonpost.com/sports/colleges/jerry-sandusky-sentencing-brings-an-end-to-sordid-tale-but-no-closure-for-victims/2012/10/09/45c7516c-1253-11e2-ba83-a7a396e6b2a7_story.html?hpid=z4

92 Scolforo, Mark and Rubinkam, Michael, "Sandusky Headed to Prison But Scandal Persists", Associated Press, 9 October 2012, http://abcnews.go.com/Sports/wireStory/sandusky-30-years-denies-wrongdoing-17436593#.UHVmXyqF_hJ

93 Thamel, Pete, "Real NCAA Penalty for Penn State, but No Cheers Yet"

94 Zirin, Dave, "The Smartest – or Dumbest – Tweet an Athlete Ever Sent", *The Nation*, 8 October 2012, http://www.thenation.com/blog/170414/smartest-or-dumbest-tweet-athlete-ever-sent#

95 Dosh, Kristi, "A Close Look at Ohio State's Football Revenue", Forbes.com, 31 May 2011, http://www.forbes.com/sites/sportsmoney/2011/05/31/a-close-look-at-ohio-states-football-revenue/

96 Ibid

Chapter 6 – Well-Paid Slaves

1 Peter Gabriel interview, *Mojo*, September 2013, p. 43

2 Moran, Caitlin, "Celebrity Watch", *The Times 2*, 8 February 2013, p. 2

3 Snyder, Brad, *A Well-Paid Slave – Curt Flood's Fight for Free Agency in Professional Sports*, Viking, 2006, pp. 103-4

4 Collins, Patrick, "Olympic lessons in pride and prejudice", *Mail on Sunday*, 28 July 2012, http://www.dailymail.co.uk/sport/article-2180378/Patrick-Collins-Olympic-lesson-pride-prejudice.html

5 Kahn, Roger, *A Flame of Pure Fire: Jack Dempsey and the Roaring '20s*, Harcourt Brace, 1999, p. 400

6 Badenhausen, Kurt, "The World's 100 Highest-Paid Athletes", Forbes.com, 18 June 2012, http://www.forbes.com/sites/kurtbadenhausen/2012/06/18/mayweather-tops-list-of-the-worlds-100-highest-paid-athletes/

7 "Arbitration ends with no hearings", Associated Press, 18 February 2013, http://espn.go.com/mlb/spring2013/story/_/id/8958928/mlb-players-pitch-first-arbitration-shutout-39-year-history

8 Dobell, George, "Players could boycott BPL – Tim May", Cricinfo, 30 January 2013

9 Green, Benny, *The Wisden Papers 1888-1946*, Stanley Paul, 1989, p. 73

10 Sissons, Ric, *The Players*, pp. 178-9

11 Ibid, pp. 179-80

12 Bradley, James, "Inventing Australians and Constructing Englishness: Cricket and the Creation of a National Consciousness, 1860-1914", in Cashman, Richard (ed), *Sporting Traditions, The Journal of the Australian Society for Sports*, 1995, p. 45, http://www.la84foundation.org/Sports Library/SportingTraditions/1995/st1102/st1102d.pdf

13 Quoted in Williamson, Martin, "Nottinghamshire's general strike", Cricinfo, 4 June 2005, http://www.espncricinfo.com/ci/content/story/210469.html

14 Vamplew, Wray, review of Sissons, Ric, *George Lohmann: The Beau Ideal*, Pluto Press, 1991, in *Sporting Traditions: The Journal of the Australian Society for Sports*, 1991, p. 229, http://www.la84foundation.org/SportsLibrary/SportingTraditions/1991/st0702/st0702r.pdf

15 Pardon, Sydney, "Some Current Topics", *Wisden Cricketers' Almanack 1897*, quoted in Green, p. 77

16 Ward, Geoffrey C. and Burns, Ken, *Baseball: An Illustrated History*, Alfred A. Knopf, 1994, p. 39

17 Ibid, p. 40

18 Richards, Huw, "The Game-Changers: Billy Meredith" in Steen, Rob, Novick, Jed and Richards, Huw (eds), *The Cambridge Companion to Football*, Cambridge University Press, 2013, p. 31

19 "The Birth Of The Union", Thepfa.com, http://www.thepfa.com/thepfa/history/1900s

20 Carter, Neil, *The Football Manager: A History*, Routledge, 2006, p. 22

21 Richards, p. 30

22 Johnson, Walter, "Baseball Slavery: The Great American Principle of Dog Eat Dog", *Baseball Magazine*, 1911, quoted in Ward and Burns, p. 111

23 Hobson, Richard, "Warne implores Australia to let mongrel off the leash", *The Times*, 6 July 2013, Sport, p. 14

24 Cashman, Richard (Ed), *The Oxford Companion to Australian Cricket*, Oxford University Press, 1996, p. 343

25 Haigh, Gideon, *The Big Ship – Warwick Armstrong and the Making of Modern Cricket*, Aurum, 2002, p. 215

26 Ibid, p. 216

27 Ibid, p. 221

28 Quoted in Haigh, p. 227

29   "Shock For Players – 'New Deal' Slashed", *Daily Mirror*, 14 January 1958, http://www.mirrorfootball.co.uk/incoming/article13898.ece/BINARY/JimmyHill4.pdf

30   Ibid

31   "Smile You Are On TV", Thepfa.com, http://www.thepfa.com/thepfa/history/1950s

32   Greenfield, Steve and Osborn, Guy, *Regulating Football: Commodification, Consumption and the Law*, Pluto Press, 2001, p. 76

33   Guthrie, Jimmy, *Soccer Rebel: The Evolution of the Professional Footballer*, Pentagon Books, 1976, p. 70, quoted in Greenfield and Osborn, p. 76

34   Ibid

35   Ibid

36   King, Anthony, *End of the Terraces: The Transformation of English Football*, Leicester University Press, 2002 (2nd edition), p. 43

37   Hill, Jimmy, *Striking For Soccer*, Davis, 1961, pp. 129-30, quoted in King, p. 44

38   "Ain't No Stopping Us Now", Thepfa.com, http://www.thepfa.com/thepfa/history/1960s

39   Gardiner, Simon (ed), *Sports Law*, Cavendish Publishing, 2006 (3rd edition), p. 211

40   *Eastham v Newcastle United Football Club* [1963] 1 Ch 413, p. 438

41   Kodes, Jan and Kolar, Peter, *Jan Kodes: A Journey to Glory from Behind the Iron Curtain*, New Chapter Press, 2010

42   Evans, p. 77

43   Ibid, p. 79

44   Keating, Frank, "When SW19 turned to the picket line", *The Guardian*, 23 June 2003, http://www.guardian.co.uk/sport/2003/jun/23/tennis.wimbledon200311

45   Ibid, pp. 85-6, p. 91

46   Keating, "When SW19 turned to the picket line"

47   Evans, p. 92

48   Keating, "When SW19 turned to the picket line"

49   Evans, p. 95

50   Eason, Kevin, "Drivers threaten strike over tyre failures", *The Times*, 5 July 2013, p. 60

51   Badenhausen, Kurt, "The World's Highest-Paid Athletes", Forbes.com, 31 May 2011, http://www.forbes.com/sites/kurtbadenhausen/2011/05/31/the-worlds-highest-paid-athletes

52   Stewart, Jackie, *Winning Is Not Enough*, Headline, 2007, p. 154

53   Ibid, pp. 134-5

54   "Grand Prix Hall of Fame – Jackie Stewart", http://www.ddavid.com/formula1/stew_bio.htm

55   Ibid, pp. 155-6

56   Ibid, p. 156

57   Ibid, p. 259

58   Ibid, p. 173

59   Sid Watkins obituary, *The Times*, 14 September 2012, p. 64

60   Rawlings, Nate, "Jim Bunning Remembers Marvin Miller, Baseball's 'Moses'", Time.com, 28 November 2012, http://keepingscore.blogs.time.com/2012/11/28/jim-bunning-remembers-marvin-miller-baseballs-moses/

61   Ibid.
62   Wertheim, Jon, "Marvin Miller on Barry Bonds, drug testing and the NFL labor situation", SI.com, 12 April 2011, http://sportsillustrated.cnn.com/2011/writers/jon_wertheim/04/12/marvin.miller/index.html
63   "Thanks Marvin", http://www.thanksmarvin.com/index-main.html (accessed on 30 November 2012)
64   Zirin, Dave, "The Labor Movement Never Stands Still", 2004 interview with Marvin Miller reprinted in *The Nation*, 27 November 2012, http://www.thenation.com/blog/171466/labor-movement-never-stands-still-interview-marvin-miller-1917-2012#
65   Ward and Burns, *Baseball: An Illustrated History*, p. 354
66   Bryant, Howard, *Juicing the Game: Drugs, Power, and the Fight for the Soul of Major League Baseball*, Viking, 2005, p. 37
67   Ibid, p. 40
68   Ibid, p. 40-1
69   Snyder, p. 347
70   Will, George F., "Dred Scott In Spikes", *Washington Post*, 24 June 1976, reprinted in Will, George F., *Bunts*, Touchstone, 1999 (pbk), p. 279
71   Jaffe, Jay, "Take Me Out of the Hall Game", baseballprospectus.com, 29 May 2008, http://www.baseballprospectus.com/article.php?articleid=7591
72   http://www.baseball-reference.com/bullpen/Collusion
73   Vincent, Fay, *The Last Commissioner*, Simon & Schuster, 2007, pp. 281-6, quoted in Edelman, p. 633
74   Steen, Rob, "Owners pull plug on World Series", *The Independent*, 15 September 1994, http://www.highbeam.com/doc/1P2-4675884.html
75   Bryant, p. 53
76   Wertheim, Jon, "Marvin Miller on Barry Bonds, drug testing and the NFL labor situation"
77   Kastrinakis, Antony, "Bosman is still suffering", The Sun, 28 February 2011, http://www.thesun.co.uk/sol/homepage/sport/football/3436116/Jean-Marc-Bosman-is-skint-and-suffering-as-footballers-earn-millions.html
78   Gillis, Richard, "The business of pleasure", *The Wisden Cricketer*, July 2008, p. 48
79   Liew, Jonathan, "Meet Twenty20 specialist Kieron Pollard – the world's most valuable cricketer", *Daily Telegraph*, 12 July 2011, http://www.telegraph.co.uk/sport/cricket/twenty20/8632819/Meet-Twenty20-specialist-Kieron-Pollard-the-worlds-most-valuable-cricketer.html
80   "West Indies Cricket Impasse Over; Jamaica's Chris Gayle to Return", *Caribbean Journal*, 5 April 2012, http://www.caribjournal.com/2012/04/05/west-indies-cricket-impasse-over-jamaicas-chris-gayle-to-return
81   Wertheim, Jon, "Marvin Miller on Barry Bonds, drug testing and the NFL labor situation"
82   Zirin, Dave, "Taking Sides in the Looming NFL Lockout", *The Nation*, 3 March 2011, http://www.thenation.com/blog/158995/taking-sides-looming-nfl-lockout
83   "NFL owners and players reach deal", BBC Sport, 25 July 2011, http://m.bbc.co.uk/sport/american-football/14284718

84 Brady, Tom and Brees, Drew, "Injured pro athletes deserve workers' comp", *San Francisco Chronicle*, 24 June 2013, http://www.sfchronicle.com/opinion/openforum/article/Injured-pro-athletes-deserve-workers-comp-4617644.php

85 Broadbent, Rick, "Crunch looming nearer for games of risk", *The Times*, 29 November 2013, p. 89

86 Lee, Alan, "Nine trainers escape censure for use of steroids", *The Times*, 8 August 2013, p. 55

87 Lee, Alan, "O'Neill overcomes desperate day to remain National supporter", *The Times*, 4 April 2013, p. 62

88 Stojaspol, Jan, "Horses Gain, Fans Snooze At 'Safe' Pardubicka Race", *The Prague Post*, 12 October 1994, http://www.praguepost.com/archivescontent/17191-horses-gain-fans-snooze-at-safe-pardubicka-race-horses-gain-fans-lose-easy-f.html

89 Barnes, Simon, "National must follow example of going soft", *The Times*, 7 December 2012, p. 74

90 Ibid

91 Stephens, Andy, "Aintree holds its breath as changes scrutinised", *The Times*, 4 April 2013, p. 64

92 Leake, Jonathan, "20 mounts of leading jockey die in 5 years", *Sunday Times*, 27 May 2012, p. 8

93 Ibid

Chapter 7 – The Us Syndrome

1 Bilton, Chris, "The Feel Good Factor", http://www2.warwick.ac.uk/knowledge/culture/feelgoodfactor/

2 Keating, Frank, "The World Cup defeat that lost an election", *The Guardian*, 21 April 2010, http://www.guardian.co.uk/football/blog/2010/apr/21/world-cup-1970-harold-wilson

3 Hobsbawm, Eric, *The Age of Extremes: 1914-1991*, Abacus, 2001 (pbk), p. 198

4 O'Connor, Ashling, "World Cup switch turns up heat", *The Times*, 7 June 2013, p. 70

5 Barnes, Simon, "Why Lions are on list of endangered species", *The Times*, 7 June 2013, p. 69

6 Bishop, Hwyel and Jaworski, Adam, "We Beat 'em': Nationalism and the Hegemony of Homogeneity in the British Press Reportage of Germany versus England during Euro 2000", *Discourse & Society*, Sage 2003, pp. 243-71, http://www.labwales.org.uk/encap/resources/publications/jaworski-adam/papers/bishop%20and%20jaworski%202003.pdf

7 Orwell, George, "The Sporting Spirit", *Tribune*, 1945, http://orwell.ru/library/articles/spirit/english/e_spirit

8 http://www.chancetoshine.org

9 *The Times*, 12 June 2012, p. 1

10 Smith, Rory, "Home hero keeps the dream alive", *The Times*, 13 June 2012, p. 59

11 Thompson, Adam, "Barricaded inside café as fans raged outside", *Bedfordshire on Sunday*, 28 June 2012, http://www.bedfordshire-news.co.uk/News/Barricaded-inside-caf-as-fans-raged-outside-27062012.htm

12   Gill, A.A., "True blue comes in many different shades", *Sunday Times*, 12 August 2012, Culture, p. 15

13   Horlock, Alex, "'The spirit of 1939 Germany pervades through Britain: Angry Morrissey attacks patriotic response to Team GB Olympic success by comparing sport to Nazism", *Daily Mail*, 6 August 2012, http://www.dailymail.co.uk/news/article-2184449/London-2012-Olympics-Morrissey-hits-Games-Royal-Family.html

14   Brown, David, "Spurs manager 'received bungs in bank account named after his dog'", *The Times*, 24 January 2012

15   Ralph, Alex, "Tynes living out his dream with Giants", *The Times*, 24 January 2012

16   Araton, Harvey, "Mixed Doubles Team In a World Gone Mad", *New York Times*, 2 July 2002, http://www.nytimes.com/2002/07/02/sports/sports-of-the-times-mixed-doubles-team-in-a-world-gone-mad.html

17   Parris, Matthew, "The lights are going out across Planet Earth", *The Times*, 4 August 2012, p. 25

18   Hider, James, "Huge crowds protest at Brazil football match", *The Times*, 27 June 2013, p. 37

19   Syed, Matthew, "When tears of joy turn to misery of reality", *The Times*, 26 June 2013, p. 57

20   Harris, Jon, "Cricket in Canada: a historical review", Cricinfo.com, 16 May 2001, http://www.espncricinfo.com/canada/content/story/106282.html

21   Ibid

22   Bowen, Rowland, *Cricket: A History of its Growth and Development*, Eyre & Spottiswoode, 1970, p. 97

23   Tatz, Colin, *Aborigines in Sport*, The Australian Society For Sports History, Studies in Sport No.3, 1987, p. 25-6

24   Ibid

25   Mullaney, D.J., *The Times*, 17 March 1977, quoted in Williams, Marcus (ed), *The Way To Lord's – Cricketing Letters To The Times*, Willow Books, 1983, p. 35-6

26   Clark, Geoff, "Passport to nowhere", *Online Opinion*, 15 February 2002, http://www.onlineopinion.com.au/view.asp?article=1073

27   Connolly, Paul, "The Aboriginal Innings", *The Global Mail*, 14 December 2012, http://www.theglobalmail.org/feature/the-aboriginal-innings/520/

28   Wark, Stuart, "The Aboriginal question", ESPNcricinfo, 26 June 2013, http://www.espncricinfo.com/blogs/content/story/644795.html

29   Steen, Rob and McLellan, Alastair, *500-1: The Miracle of Headingley '81*, BBC Books, 2001, pp. 253-4

30   Ibid, p. 23

31   Birley, *A Social History of English Cricket*, p. 124

32   Hobson, Richard, "Australia prove point to gamblers", *The Times*, 11 July 2013, p. 63

33   Selvey, Mike, "The Real Story Of The Ashes", *The Cricketer*, June 2013, p. 16

34   Frith, David, "Ivo and the Ashes" in Milton, Howard and Barnard, Derek (eds), *The End Of The Beginning Of The Ashes*, The Cricket Society, 2011

35   BBC News report, 23 May 1989, http://www.youtube.com/watch?v=Q3qP5oaSeuE

36   Football Association minutes, 3 October 1872, quoted in James, Brian, *England v Scotland*, The Sportsmans Book Club, 1970, p. 17

37   Ibid, p. 18

38   Ibid, p. 19

39   "England's 800th match", thefa.com, 21 May 2003, http://nav.thefa.com/sitecore/content/TheFA/Home/England/News/2003/49322

40   Quoted in Wilson, Jonathan, *The Anatomy of England: A History in Ten Matches*, Orion, 2010

41   Ibid, p. 20

42   Quoted on Queen of the South FC official website, http://qosfc.com/new_legendsview.aspx?playerid=1039

43   Quoted in James, p. 29

44   Quoted in Alexander, Douglas, "Historic fixture retains its soul", *Sunday Times*, 17 June 2012, Sport, p. 3

45   James, p. 224

46   Quoted in Perryman, Mark, *Ingerland – Travels With A Football Nation*, Simon & Schuster, 2006, pp. 20-1

47   Mallon, Bill, "The 1900 Olympics Games – Results of All Competitors in All Events, with Commentary", McFarland & Company, 1998, http://www.la84foundation.org/6oic/OfficialReports/Mallon/1900.pdf

48   "L'Alliance française y était!", Alliance Française de Londres, http://www.alliancefrancaise.org.uk/m_1908.htm

49   *The Times*, 2 April 2008, quoted in "L'Alliance française y était!"

50   *Report of the American Olympic Committee 1928*, American Olympic Committee, 1929, p. 6., quoted in Brichford, Maynard, "Avery Brundage and American Nationalism at the Olympic Games" in *The Global Nexus Engaged: Past, Present, Future Interdisciplinary Olympic Studies*, Sixth International Symposium for Olympic Research, October 2002, http://www.la84foundation.org/SportsLibrary/ISOR/ISOR2002zc.pdf

51   Brundage, Avery, *The Speeches of President Avery Brundage 1952-1968*, Commite International Olympique, 1969, p. 7; Bushnell, Asa S. (ed), *United States 1952 Olympic Book*, United States Olympic Association, 1953, quoted in Brichford, Maynard, "Avery Brundage and American Nationalism at the Olympic Games"

52   Ibid

53   Bellos, Alex, *Futebol: The Brazilian Way Of Life*, Bloomsbury, 2003 (pbk), p. ix

54   Kuper, Simon, *Football Against the Enemy*, p. 197

55   Richards, Huw, "The culture of football", cambridgeblog.org, 3 August 2013, http://www.cambridgeblog.org/2013/08/huw-richards-on-the-culture-of-football/

56   James, Stuart, "Steve McClaren determined to defy critics at Nottingham Forest", *The Guardian*, 5 August 2011, http://www.theguardian.com/football/2011/aug/05/steve-mcclaren-nottingham-forest

57   Richards, "The culture of football"

58   Palenski, Ron, *Century in Black: 100 Years of All Black Test Rugby*, Hodder, Moa Beckett, 2003, pp. 16-17

59   Marshall, Justin, "All Blacks still aiming for excellence", Stuff.co.nz, 8 October 2012, http://www.stuff.co.nz/sport/rugby/opinion/7781143/Opinion-All-Blacks-still-aiming-for-excellence

60 Belich, Jamie, *Paradise Reforged: A History of New Zealand From The 1880s to The Year 2000*, University of Hawai'i Press, 2001, p. 380

61 Ibid

62 Ibid, p. 388

63 http://www.teara.govt.nz/en/the-new-zealanders/page-4

64 Belich, p. 387

65 Hassan, David, and O'Shea, Philip, "Terrorism and the abnormality of sport in Northern Ireland", *International Review for the Sociology of Sport*, June 2012, Vol. 47 no. 3, pp. 397-413

66 Holt, Richard, and Mason, Tony, *Sport in Britain 1945-2000*, Blackwell, 2000, p. 139

67 Hayes, Cathy, Irishcentral.com, 3 June 2011, http://www.irishcentral.com/news/Irish-boxing-legend-Barry-McGuigan-carried-a-gun-due-to-threat-of-IRA-123091558.html#ixzz1tvpEGNik

68 Lewis, Ron, "Frampton follows McGuigan in bid to unite a divided city", *The Times*, 8 February 2013, pp. 62-3

69 Ibid

70 "Petrol Bombs and Peace", BBC Three, 2 August 2013

71 Ibid

72 Holt and Mason, p. 138

73 Birley, Derek, *Sport and the making of Britain*, Manchester University Press, 1996, pp. 281-2

74 Ibid, p. 282

75 Con Martin obituary, *The Times*, 18 March 2013, p. 46

76 Holt and Mason, pp. 138-9

77 Boswell, Thomas, "Maybe Not Yet, but the WBC is Destined to be a Classic", *Washington Post*, 28 February 2006, http://www.washingtonpost.com/wp-dyn/content/article/2006/02/27/AR2006022701357.html

78 Stark, Jayson, "Busting the WBC injury myth", ESPN.com, 17 January 2013, http://espn.go.com/mlb/blog/_/name/stark_jayson/id/8853591/busting-world-baseball-classic-injury-myth

79 McCarron, Anthony, "Only winning the World Baseball Classic will do for Team USA as Joe Torre's team prepares for Friday's opener against Mexico", *Daily News*, 7 March 2013, http://www.nydailynews.com/sports/baseball/team-usa-heading-wbc-article-1.1282620

80 Kernan, Kevin, "Team USA Humbled by Mexico in World Baseball Classic", *New York Post*, 9 March 2013, http://www.nypost.com/p/sports/team_usa_humbled_by_mexico_in_world_h3EDr0M5VZW31UyC592sSI

81 Ball, Peter and Hopps, David, *The Book of Cricket Quotations*, Stanley Paul, 1990, 2nd edition, p. 75

82 "Too Luxurious", *The Adelaide Advertiser*, 17 November 1930, http://trove.nla.gov.au/ndp/del/article/29848245

83 Steel, Mark, "Behind Bodyline", *The New Ball Volume 1: England v Australia*, 1999, p. 116

84 Page, Michael, *Bradman: The Illustrated Biography*, Macmillan, 1983, pp. 93-4

85 Quoted in Shillinglaw, Tony, *Bradman Revisited: The Legacy of Sir Donald Bradman*, The Parrs Wood Press, 2003, p. 162

86 http://neuroskeptic.blogspot.co.uk/2009/10/whos-greatest-sportsperson.html

87 Jardine, Douglas, *In Quest of The Ashes*, Hutchinson, 1933, and Methuen, 2005 (reprint), p. 41

88 Quoted in Frith, David, *Bodyline Autopsy*, p. 181

89 Ibid

90 Ibid, p. 194

91 Ibid, p. 197

92 Ibid, p. 199

93 Steel, Mark, "Behind Bodyline", p. 122

94 Larwood, pp. 212-3

95 Ibid, p. 19

96 Jardine, Douglas, *In Quest of The Ashes*, Methuen, 2005 (reprint), p. 241

97 Ibid, p. ix

98 Fingleton, Jack, *Cricket Crisis*, Michael Joseph, 1984 (reprint), p. xvii

99 Ryan, Christian, *Wisden Cricketers' Almanack 2013*, p.18

100 Bala, Rajan, *The Covers Are Off*, Rupa, 2004, p. 48

101 Bal, Sambit, "Chennai applauds Pakistan", Cricinfo, 26 July 2009, http://www.espncricinfo.com/magazine/content/story/410452.html

102 Ibid

103 Menon, Suresh, "Crossing The Line In The Sand", *The Cricketer*, March 2013, p. 51

104 Ibid, p. 53

105 Syed, Matthew, 'Ninety-minute patriots ward off faction replays', *The Times*, 25 January 2012

106 Hobsbawm, Eric, *Nations and nationalism since 1870: programme, myth, reality*, Cambridge University Press, 1990, pp. 142-3

107 Darby, Paul, "Africa: Towards Global Football Citizenship?" in Steen, Rob, Novick, Jed and Richards, Huw (eds.), *The Cambridge Companion to Football*, Cambridge University Press, 2012, p.104

108 Ibid

109 Dobell, George, "The team have tended to win when I've done well", Cricinfo, 6 July 2012, http://www.espncricinfo.com/magazine/content/story/571224.html

110 Barnes, Simon, "The importance of being too earnest", *The Times*, 12 April 1990, quoted in Farringdon, Neil, Kilvington, Daniel, Price, John and Saeed, Amir, *Race, Racism And Sports Journalism*, Routledge, 2011, p. 87

111 Henderson, Robert, "Is it in the blood?", *Wisden Cricket Monthly*, June 1995, quoted in Marqusee, Mike, "In search of the equivocal Englishman" in Carrington, Ben and Mcdonald, Ian (eds), *'Race', Sport and British Society*, Routledge, 2001, p. 121

112 Quoted in Steen, Rob, "Whatever happened to the black cricketer?", *The Wisden Cricketer*, August 2004, and in Steen, Rob, "Calypso collapso", *The Observer*, 25 July 2004, http://www.guardian.co.uk/sport/2004/jul/25/cricket.comment3

113 Webb, Dale, *Prize Fighter*, Mainstream, 2000, p. 19

114 Bruno, Frank, and Mitchell, Kevin, *Fighting Back*, Yellow Jersey Press, 2006, p. 161

115 Ibid, pp. 167-9

116 Dabydeen, David and Gilmore, John, *The Oxford Companion to Black British History*, OUP, 2007, p. 468

117 Weintraub, Robert, "No Love for Lennox", slate.com, 25 June 2003, http://www.slate.com/articles/sports/sports_nut/2003/06/no_love_for_lennox.html

118 Ibid

119 Friedman, Steve, "After the Fall", *Runner's World*, October 2009, http://www.runnersworld.com/article/0,7120,s6-243-297--13308-F,00.html

120 Ibid

121 Ibid

122 Kidd, Patrick, "Say it loud, I'm European and I'm proud(ish)", *The Times*, 1 October 2012, times2, p. 6

123 Couch, Greg, "Plenty of blame to share in epic choke", 1 October 2012, http://msn.foxsports.com/golf/story/tiger-woods-united-states-choke-away-ryder-cup-to-europe-on-home-soil-093012

124 Marqusee, Mike, "Nations for Sale" in Steen, Rob (ed), *The New Ball Vol. 4: Imperial Bedrooms*, TwoHeads Publishing, 2001

125 Email to author, 20 October 2012

Chapter 8 – Reluctant Partners

1 Marqusee, Mike, "Politics, our missing link – Contending for the Living", *Red Pepper*, August 2012

2 "David Cameron shows his wicket side", *The Sun*, 19 February 2013, http://www.thesun.co.uk/sol/homepage/news/politics/4801695/David-Cameron-plays-cricket-in-India-with-locals.html

3 Zirin, Dave, *A People's History of Sport in the United States*, New York: The New Press, 2008, p. xii

4 Hyde, Marina, "So, South vs. North Korea at table tennis. 'Yeah, there's a little bit of niggle here…'", *The Observer*, 5 August 2012, p. 9

5 Kyle, Donald G., *Sport and Spectacle in the Ancient World*, Blackwell, 2007, p. 29

6 König, Jason, *Athletics and Literature in the Roman Empire*, Cambridge University Press, 2005, p. 2

7 Quoted in Zirin, pp. 2-3

8 Tomlinson, Alan, and Whannel, Gary, *Five-ring circus: Money, Power and Politics at the Olympic Games*, Pluto Press, 1984, pp. 76-7

9 Ibid, pp. 18-19

10 Harding, Luke, "Tajikistan bans *The Dictator*", *The Guardian*, 18 May 2012, http://www.guardian.co.uk/film/2012/may/18/tajikistan-bans-dictator-baron-cohen

11 Karim, Fariha, "Sorrell's shame over Falklands war memorial stunt", *The Times*, 5 May 2012, p. 13

12 Agnew, Paddy, "Italy: Football as Politics – Mussolini to Berlusconi" in Steen, Novick and Richards, *The Cambridge Companion to Football*, p. 68

13 Martin, *Football and Fascism*, Berg, 2004, p. 3

14 Teja, Angela, "Italian sport and international relations under fascism" in Arnaud, P. and Riordan, J. (eds), *Sport and International Politics*, Routledge, 1998, p. 161

15 Zanetti, Gianfrancesco and Tornabuoni, G., *Il giuoco del calcio*, p. 43, quoted in Simon Martin, *Football and Fascism*, Berg, 2004, and Agnew, p. 75
16 Ibid
17 Quoted in Sammons, Jeffrey T., *Beyond the Ring – The Role of Boxing in American Society*, University of Illinois Press, 1990, p. 101
18 Murray, Bill, *The World's Game: A History of Soccer*, University of Illinois Press, 1996, p. 68
19 Foot, John, *Calcio: A History of Italian Football*, First Estate, 2006, p. 355
20 Sammons, p. 101
21 Ibid
22 Ibid, p. 102
23 Ibid
24 Ibid
25 Beck, Peter, "England v Germany 1938: Football as Propaganda", *History Today*, July 1980, http://www.historytoday.com/peter-beck/england-v-germany-1938-football-propaganda
26 Brohm, Jean-Marie, *Sport, a prison of measured time*, Pluto Press, 1989, p. 180
27 Ibid
28 Ibid
29 Ibid
30 Mustill, Edd, "A workers' Olympics?", Workers' Liberty, 1 August 2012, http://www.workersliberty.org/story/2012/08/01/workers-olympics
31 "The New Great Power: The First Workers' Olympics, 1925", http://www.tate.org.uk/whats-on/tate-modern/film/new-great-power-first-workers-olympics-1925
32 Simson, Vyv and Jennings, Andrew, *The Lords of the Rings: Politics, Money and Drugs in the Modern Olympics*, Simon & Schuster, 1992, p. 3
33 Email to author, 25 January 2013
34 Doherty, Thomas, *Hollywood and Hitler 1933-1939*, Columbia University Press, 2013
35 Guttmann, Allen, "The 'Nazi Olympics' and the American boycott controversy" in Arnaud, Pierre and Riordan, Jim (eds), *Sport and International Politics*, Routledge, 1998, p. 32
36 http://www.ushmm.org/museum/exhibit/online/olympics/videos/?content=exhib_video
37 Marvin, Carolyn, "Avery Brundage and American Participation in the 1936 Olympic Games", Departmental Paper, Annenberg School for Communication, University of Pennsylvania, 1982, http://repository.upenn.edu/cgi/viewcontent.cgi?article=1073
38 IOC Historical Archives, http://www.olympic.org/Assets/OSC%20Section/pdf/LRes_19E.pdf
39 Quoted in Mayer, Paul Yogi, *Jews And The Olympic Games – Sport: A Springboard for Minorities*, Vallentine Mitchell, 2004, p. 95
40 Ibid, p. 96
41 Ibid
42 *The Commonweal*, November 8, 1935, quoted in "The Nazi Olympics", Jewish Virtual Library, http://www.jewishvirtuallibrary.org/jsource/Holocaust/olympics.html

43 Guttmann, Allen, *The Games Must Go On: Avery Brundage and the Olympic Movement*, Columbia University Press, 1984, p. 72

44 Ibid

45 Ibid, p. 67

46 *The Commonweal*, November 8, 1935

47 Schaap, Jeremy, *Triumph*, Houghton Mifflin, 2007, p. 45, quoted in Zirin, Dave, *A People's History of Sports in the United States*, The New Press, 2008, p. 77

48 http://www.jewishvirtuallibrary.org/jsource/Holocaust/olympics.html

49 Povich, Shirley, *All Those Mornings…At the Post*, Public Affairs, 2005, p. 47

50 Mayer, pp. 100-1

51 Ibid, p. 104-5

52 http://www.ushmm.org/museum/exhibit/online/olympics/videos/? content=exhib_video

53 Mayer, p. 103

54 Ibid, p. 115

55 http://www.ushmm.org/museum/exhibit/online/olympics/videos/? content=exhib_video

56 Harrison, Donald H., "Jewish athlete still bitter at ruined chance to win gold medal", *San Diego Jewish Press-Heritage*, 2 July 1999, http://www.jewish-sightseeing.com/germany/berlin/olympic_stadium/19990702-glickman.htm

57 Guttmann, p. 45

58 Povich, p. 43

59 Zirin, p. 78

60 Sammons, pp. 105-6

61 Hitler, Adolf, *Mein Kampf*, Stackpole Sons, 1939, pp. 397-8, quoted in Sammons, p. 106

62 Ibid, p. 115

63 Ibid, p. 107

64 Sammons, p. 108

65 *New Orleans Times-Picayune*, 21 June 1938, section 2, p. 5, quoted in Sammons

66 *Charlotte Observer*, 14 December 1936, section 2, p. 5, quoted in Sammons

67 Sammons, p. 110

68 Quoted in Stradling, Jay, *More Than A Game: When Sport and History Collide*, Pier 9, 2009, p. 49

69 McRae, Donald, *In Black & White: The Untold Story of Joe Louis and Jesse Owens*, Scribner, 2003 (pbk), p. 211

70 Sammons, p. 115

71 Stradling, p. 49

72 Ibid, p. 117

73 Ibid, p. 116

74 Ibid

75 Weisbord, Robert and Hedderich, Norbert, "Max Schmeling: Righteous ring warror?", *History Today*, January 1993, http://www.pages.drexel.edu/~rosenl/sports%20Folder/Max%20Schmeling%20Ring.pdf

76 Ibid

77 Edelman, Robert, *Spartak Moscow: A History of the People's Team in the Workers' State*, Cornell University, 2009, p. 78

78 Ibid, p. 126

79 Miller, Stevie, "Spartak and survival – the story of Nikolai Starostin", BBC Sport, 4 December 2012, http://www.bbc.co.uk/sport/0/football/20518141

80 Dougan, Andy, *Dynamo: Defending the Honour of Kiev*, Fourth Estate, 2001, p. 222

81 Ibid

82 Ibid, pp. 228-9

83 Ibid, pp. 229-30

84 Jung Woo Lee and Bairner, Alan, abstract for "The Difficult Dialogue: Communism, Nationalism, and Political Propaganda in North Korean Sport", *Journal of Sport and Social Issues*, November 2009, vol. 33 no. 4, pp. 390-410

85 Kirby, Rob, "Dictators and Soccer: Kim Jong-Il and North Korea (or Football, Famine, and Giant Rabbits)", 18 January 2013, http://cultfootball.com/2013/01/dictators-and-soccer-kim-jong-il-and-north-korea-or-football-famine-and-giant-rabbits/

86 "Home advantage", *The Economist*, 17 November 2011, http://www.economist.com/blogs/banyan/2011/11/football-north-korea

87 Gibson, *Stranger to the Game*, quoted in Wendel, *Summer of '68*, p. 30

88 This section is a remixed and extended version of my interview with John Carlos on 15 May 2012, published as "A salutary lesson in the power of sport" in the *Independent on Sunday*, 20 May 2012, Sport, pp. 16-17

89 Carlos, John, with Zirin, Dave, *The John Carlos Story*, Haymarket Books, 2011, p. 110

90 Ibid, p. 112

91 Ibid, p. 113

92 Ibid

93 Wilson, Peter, "Will Mankind Ever Grow Up?", *Daily Mirror*, 17 October 1968, p. 30

94 Hitchen, Brian, "Protest Negroes Are Sent Home", *Daily Mirror*, 19 October 1968, p. 32

95 Povich, Shirley, "Olympic Protest", *Washington Post*, 19 October 1968, reprinted in Povich, Shirley, *All Those Mornings… At The Post*, Public Affairs, 2005, p. 242

96 Wilson, Peter, *Daily Mirror*, 18 October 1968

97 Zirin, Dave, "After Forty-four Years, It's About Time Brent Musberger Apologised to John Carlos and Tommie Smith", *The Nation*, 4 June 2012, http://www.thenation.com/blog/168209/after-44-years-its-time-brent-musburger-apologized-john-carlos-and-tommie-smith

98 Sandomir, Richard, "Now on Film: Raised fists And the Yogi love letters", *New York Times*, 6 August 1999, http://www.nytimes.com/1999/08/06/sports/tv-sports-now-on-film-raised-fists-and-the-yogi-love-letters.html

99 Email to author from Andrew Jennings, 9 June 2012

100 Salutethemovie.com, 21 August 2012, http://salutethemovie.com/peter-norman-apology/

101 Krüger, Michael F., Nielsen, Stefan and Becker, Christian, "The Munich Olympics 1972: Its Impact on the Relationship Between State, Sports and

Anti-Doping Policy in West Germany", *Sport in History*, 32:4, 2012, pp. 526-549, http://dx.doi.org/10.1080/17460263.2012.756424

102 Wertheim, Jon, "Munich widow's fight for moment of silence at opener falls on deaf ears", *Sports Illustrated*, 27 July 2012, http://sportsillustrated. cnn.com/2012/olympics/2012/writers/jon_wertheim/07/27/2012-olympics-opening-ceremony-munich/index.html

103 Ibid

104 Bowers, Larry, "Athletic Drug Testing", *Clinics in Sports Medicine*, 1 April 1998

105 Hunt, Thomas M., Dimeo, Paul, Bowers, Matthew T. and Jedlicka, Scott R., "The Diplomatic Context of Doping in the Former German Democratic Republic: A Revisionist Examination", *The International Journal of the History of Sport*, 29:18, December, 2012, pp. 2486–2499

106 "Memorandum For the President's File by the President's Deputy Assistant for National Security Affairs (Haig)", *Foreign Relations of the United States, 1969 to 1976*, Volume XL, 335, 28 December 1971, http://history.state.gov/historicaldocuments/frus1969-76v40/d335

107 Hunt et al, p. 2490

108 Ibid

109 Hunt et al, p. 2491

110 Ibid

111 LaCour, Jean Pierre, *France Soir*, 9 September 1973, quoted in *Swimming World*, October 1973, http://www.swimmingworldmagazine.com/lane9/news/13191.asp

112 Rosen, Daniel M., *Dope: A History of Performance-Enhancement in Sports from the Nineteenth Century to Today*, Praegar, 2008, p. 52

113 Hunt et al, p. 2493

114 Harding, Luke, "Forgotten victims of East German doping take their battle to court", *The Guardian*, 1 November 2005, http://www.guardian.co.uk/sport/2005/nov/01/athletics.gdnsport3

115 Kuhrt, Nicola and Wensierski, Peter, "Deadly Side Effects: New Details Emerge In East German Drug Test Scandal", *Der Spiegel*, 14 May 2013, http://www.spiegel.de/international/germany/western-drugmakers-tested-medicines-on-unwitting-east-germans-a-899594.html

116 Mackay, Duncan, "East Germans compensated for systematic doping", *The Guardian*, 14 December 2006, http://www.guardian.co.uk/sport/2006/dec/14/athletics.gdnsport3

117 Vinton, Nathaniel, "Regimen of Red Bull doctor Bernd Pansold and East Germans still leaves toll on athletes", *New York Daily News*, 24 May 2013, http://www.nydailynews.com/sports/i-team/red-bull-doc-leaves-decades-damage-behind-article-1.1353500

118 Ibid

119 Costello, Mike, "East Germany athletes were 'chemical field tests'", BBC Radio 5 Live, 23 April 2013, http://www.bbc.co.uk/sport/0/athletics/22269445

120 Ibid

121 Cole, Barbara, *The East German Sports System: Image And Reality*, history dissertation, Texas Tech University, pp. 371-2,

122 Ibid, p. 373

123 Vinton, Nathaniel, "Regimen of Red Bull doctor Bernd Pansold and East Germans still leaves toll on athletes", *The Daily Beast*, 24 May 2013, http://www.nydailynews.com/sports/i-team/red-bull-doc-leaves-decades-damage-behind-article-1.1353500

124 Fahey, Ciaran, "West Germany Systematically Doped Athletes, Report Claims", Associated Press, 3 August 2013, http://www.huffingtonpost.com/2013/08/03/report-west-germany-systematical-ly-doped-athletes_n_3701556.html

125 Ibid

126 Ibid

127 Navratilova, Martina with Vecsey, George, *Being Myself*, Grafton, 1986, pp. 17-18

128 Ibid, pp. 154-5

129 Ibid, p. 159

130 Ibid, pp. 171-2

131 Ibid, p. 173

132 "Navratilova Sets the Record Straight", Connie Chung Tonight, CNN, 17 July 2002, http://transcripts.cnn.com/TRANSCRIPTS/0207/17/cct.00.html

133 "Martina Navratilova returns to her Czech roots". *Daily Telegraph*, 12 March 2008,

134 "Cuban boxing champion Teofilo Stevenson dies", BBC News, 12 June 2012, http://www.bbc.co.uk/news/world-latin-america-18405802

135 Cheema, Hassan, "Is Pakistan 'ready' for internationals?", Dawn.com, 16 April 2012, http://dawn.com/2012/04/16/is-pakistan-ready-for-internationals

136 Woolf, Lord, and Pricewaterhouse Coopers, *An independent governance review of the International Cricket Council*, 1 February 2012, http://static.espncricinfo.com/db/DOWNLOAD/0000/0093/woolfe_report.pdf

137 Samiuddin, Osman, "ICC gives boards two years to fall in line", Cricinfo, 30 June 2011, http://www.espncricinfo.com/ci-icc/content/story/521351.html

138 Ibid

139 *Wichaar*, 30 March 2012, http://www.wichaar.com/news/293/ARTICLE/29200/2013-03-04.html

140 Farooq, Umar, "Islamabad High Court suspends Ashraf as PCB chairman", ESPNcricinfo, 28 May 2013, http://www.espncricinfo.com/pakistan/content/story/638164.html

141 Woolf, *An independent governance review of the International Cricket Council*

142 Mohammad Isam, "ICC reviewing stance against government interference", Cricinfo, 17 November 2012, http://www.espncricinfo.com/ci-icc/content/current/story/591750.html

143 "Chequered Flag", *The Times*, 23 April 2012, p. 2

144 Custis, Shaun, "Now the war in Ivory Coast is over, I can build my country a £3m hospital – Chelsea star Didier Drogba", *The Sun*, 16 February 2012, http://www.thesun.co.uk/sol/homepage/features/4132856/Drogba-Now-the-war-in-Ivory-Coast-is-over-I-can-build-my-country-a-3m-hospital.html

145 Gambari, Afolabi, "Nigeria's Super Eagles threatened by extinction", *National Mirror*, 26 January 2012, http://nationalmirroronline.net/mobile/insight/29915.html

146 Vasili, Phil, "Colonialism and football: the first Nigerian tour to Britain", *Race & Class*, 36:4, p. 55

147 "Chequered Flag", *The Times*, 23 April 2012, p. 2

148 Eason, Kevin, "Chicanery of the ruling elite hides dark and brutal road to conflict", *The Times*, 18 April 2013, p 66

149 Weaver, Paul, "Clouded in shame, a race no team wanted", *The Guardian*, 23 April 2012, p. 3

150 Eason, Kevin, "Human rights protesters may make Bahrain a race apart again", *The Times*, 17 December 2012, p. 52

151 "Bahrain protest rally draws thousands ahead of F1 Grand Prix", BBC News, 20 April 2013, http://www.bbc.co.uk/news/world-middle-east-22212896

152 "Bahrain's Parade", *The Times*, 16 April 2012, p. 2

153 Kuper, Simon, *Football Against The Enemy*, Phoenix, 1996 (pbk), pp. 174-5

154 Ibid, p. 179

155 Moores, Ezequiel Fernandez, "Maradona's Folly May Be Argentina's past", *New York Times*, 21 June 2006, http://kickingscreaming.blogs.nytimes.com/2006/06/21/maradonas-folly-may-be-argentinas-past/

156 Pelaez, Vicky, "Operation Condor played out on football pitch", *The Moscow News*, 7 March 2012, http://themoscownews.com/international/20120307/189517599.html

157 Glanville, Brian, *The Story of the World Cup*, Faber & Faber, 2005 (paperback), p. 230

158 Pelaez, "Operation Condor played out on football pitch"

159 "Videla trial opens in Argentina", BBC News, 3 July 2010, http://www.bbc.co.uk/news/10496171

160 Pelaez, "Operation Condor played out on football pitch"

Chapter 9 – No Normal Sport In An Abnormal Society
I. Disunited States

1 Miller, Jackson B., "'Indians', 'Braves' and 'Redskins': A Performative Struggle for the Control of an Image", *Quarterly Journal of Speech*, May 1999, http://www.uky.edu/~addesa01/documents/Indians.pdf

2 Jones, Mike, "Members of Congress urge Snyder to change Redskins name", *Washington Post*, 28 May 2013, http://www.washingtonpost.com/blogs/football-insider/wp/2013/05/28/members-of-congress-urge-snyder-to-change-redskins-name/

3 Hoberman, John, *Darwin's Athletes: How Sport has Damaged Black America and Preserved the Myth of Race*, Houghton Mifflin, 1997, p. 8

4 Sammons, Jeffrey T., "A Proportionate and Measured Response to the Provocation That is *Darwin's Athletes*", *Journal of Sport History*, Fall 1997, 24:3, pp. 378-88, http://library.la84.org/SportsLibrary/JSH/JSH1997/JSH2403/jsh2403g.pdf

5 Sammons, Jeffrey T., "Why Physicians Should Oppose Boxing: An Interdisciplinary History Perspective", *The Journal of the American Medical Association*, 10 March 1989, 26:10, p. 1486.

6 Sammons, "A Proportionate and Measured Response to the Provocation That is *Darwin's Athletes*", pp. 387-8

7   Walsh, David, "Slavery gave me a flying start on the track to glory, says Johnson", *Sunday Times*, 8 July 2012, Sport, p. 13

8   Broadbent, Rick, "'It's not about the colour of your skin but speed,' says Lemaitre", *The Times*, 25 May 2013, Sport, p. 21

9   "Bannister: Black Sprinters Have Anatomical Edge", *LA Times*, 14 September 1995, http://articles.latimes.com/1995-09-14/sports/sp-45793_1_black-athletes

10 Walsh, "Slavery gave me a flying start on the track to glory, says Johnson"

11 Finn, Andharanand, *Running With The Kenyans: Discovering the secrets of the fastest people on earth*, Faber and Faber, 2012, p. 18

12 Ibid, p. 142-3

13 *The Difference*, Channel 4, first broadcast 26 November 2000

14 Arlidge, John, "Black runners have 'speed genes'", *The Observer*, 26 November 2000, http://www.guardian.co.uk/world/2000/nov/26/johnarlidge.theobserver

15 Morgan, Jon, "Sports and Genetics", *Baltimore Sun* , 27 February 2000, http://www.jonentine.com/reviews/baltimore_sun.htm

16 Walsh, David, "Slavery gave me a flying start on the track to glory, says Johnson", *Sunday Times*, 8 July 2012, Sport, p. 13

17 Epstein, David, "Sports Genes", *Sports Illustrated*, 17 May 2010, http://sportsillustrated.cnn.com/vault/article/magazine/MAG1169440/1/index.htm

18 Mosley, Albert, "Racial Differences In Sports: What's Ethics Got To Do With It?", http://www.smith.edu/philosophy/Taboo55.html

19 Du Bois, W.E.Burghardt, *The Sociological Souls of Black Folk – Essays and sketches*, Lexington Books, 2001, p. 133

20 Burns, Ken (director), *An Unforgiveable Blackness – The Rise And Fall of Jack Johnson*, http://www.pbs.org/unforgivableblackness/rebel

21 Du Bois, W.E.B., "The Prize Fighter", *The Crisis*, August 1914, quoted in Zirin, Dave, *A People's History of Sports in the United States*, The New Press, 2008, p. 45

22 Ibid

23 "Jess Willard knocks out Jack Johnson in Twenty-sixth round", *Sioux City Journal*, 6 April 1915, http://www.boxinggyms.com/news/willard_johnson1915/willard1915sioux.htm

24 Burns, *An Unforgivable Blackness*, http://www.pbs.org/unforgivableblackness/knockout/women.html

25 Oates, Joyce Carol, "The Cruelest Sport", *New York Review of Books*, 13 February 1992, http://www.nybooks.com/articles/archives/1992/feb/13/the-cruelest-sport

26 Ibid, quoted in Gems, Gerald R., and Pfister, Gertrud, *Understanding American Sports*, Routledge, 2009, p. 235

27 Gems and Pfister, pp. 232-3

28 Ashe, Arthur, *A Hard Road to Glory: A History of the African American Athlete, 1619-1918*, John Wiley, 1992, p. 102, quoted in Zirin, p. 41

29 http://fritzpollard.org

30 Sammons, *Beyond the Ring – The Role of Boxing in American Society*, p. 73

31 Edmonds, Anthony, O., *Joe Louis*, Eerdmans, 1973, p. 35, quoted in Sammons

32 Schwartz, Larry, "Brown Bomber was a hero to all", ESPN.com, http://espn.go.com/sports century/features/00016109.html
33 Ashe, Arthur and Rampersad, Arnold, *Days of Grace – A Memoir*, Ballantine Books, 1994 (pbk), p. 193
34 Ibid, p. 194
35 McRae, *In Black & White: The Untold Story of Joe Louis and Jesse Owens*, p. 4
36 Wiggins, David K. and Miller, Patrick B., *The Unlevel Playing Field*, University of Illinois Press, 2003, p. 165, quoted in Zirin, pp. 75-6
37 Rice, *The Tumult and the Shouting*, p. 160
38 McRae, p. 153
39 Rice, p. 159
40 Rice, p. 160
41 McRae, p. 167
42 Owens, Jesse and Neimark, Paul, G., *Blackthink: My Life As Black Man and White Man*, Morrow, 1970, p. 190
43 McRae, p. 167
44 *Afro American*, 9 August 1936
45 Weber, Mark, *The Journal of Historical Review*, Spring 1984, 5:1, pp. 123-5, http://www.ihr.org/jhr/v5n1p123.html
46 Cassavell, A. J., "Wearing No. 42 with pride, MLB honors Jackie", *Bleacher Report*, 16 April 2013, http://mlb.mlb.com/news/article.jsp?ymd=20130413&content_id=44707692
47 Goodbody, John, "In one giant leap..." DuBois, p. 89
48 Broadbent, Rick, "Dramatic saga of trailblazing icon retains relevance in the modern world", *The Times*, 29 April 2013, p. 51
49 Falkner, David, *Great Time Coming – The Life of Jackie Robinson, from Baseball to Birmingham*, Simon & Schuster, 1995, p. 78
50 Ibid, p. 79
51 Mann, Arthur, *The Jackie Robinson Story*, New York: Grosset & Dunlap, 1951, cited in Falkner, pp. 104-5
52 Falkner, p. 105
53 Eig, Jonathan, *Opening Day: The Story of Jackie Robinson's First Season*, Simon & Schuster, 2007, p. 74
54 Eig, p. 109
55 Quoted in Berkow, Ira, "Two Men Who Did the Right Thing", *New York Times*, 2 November 2005
56 Ibid
57 Eig, p. 156
58 Ibid, pp. 157-7
59 Ibid, p. 350
60 Ibid, p. 349
61 Peterson, *Cages To Jump Shots: Pro Basketball's Early Years*, University of Nebraska Press, 1990, p. 170
62 Ibid, pp. 170-1
63 Peterson, p. 105
64 Green, Ben, *Spinning the World: The Rise, Fall, and Return to Greatness of the Harlem Globetrotters*, HarperCollins, 2009, p. 156
65 Ibid
66 http://www.library.fordham.edu/cubanbaseball/e_bellan.html

67 "NJ Lawmaker Wants Major League Baseball to Honor Roberto Clemente", *New Jersey Today*, 15 May 2012, http://njtoday.net/2012/05/15/nj-lawmaker-wants-major-league-baseball-to-honor-roberto-clemente/

68 Cited in Zirin, Dave, *A People's History of the United States*, The New Press, 2008, p. 196

69 Lapchick, Richard, et al, "The 2012 Racial and Gender Report Card", 25 April 2012, The Institute for Diversity and Ethics in Sport, http://www.tidesport.org/RGRC/2012/2012%20MLB%20RGRC.pdf

70 Ceasar, Stephen, "Hispanic population tops 50m in US", *Los Angeles Times*, 24 March 2011, http://articles.latimes.com/2011/mar/24/nation/la-na-census-hispanic-20110325

71 Voight, David Quentin, *American Baseball Volume III: From Postwar Expansion to the Electronic Age*, The Pennsylvania State University Press, 1983, p. 244

72 Ibid

73 Maraniss, David, *Clemente – The Passion and Grace of Baseball's Last Hero*, Simon & Schuster, 2006, p. 70

74 Ibid, p. 71

75 Ibid, p. 148

76 Ibid, p. 174

77 Angell, Roger, *The Summer Game*, Simon & Schuster, 1987 (reprint), p. 275

78 Maraniss, pp. 264-5

79 Ibid, p. 354

80 Ibid, p. 1

81 Weinbaum, William, "The Legacy of Al Campanis", espn.go.com, 30 March 2012, http://espn.go.com/espn/otl/story/_/id/7751398/how-al-campanis-controversial-racial-remarks-cost-career-highlighted-mlb-hiring-practices

82 Johnson, Eric, " 'Nightline' Classic: Al Campanis", abcnews.go.com, 12 April 2007, http://abcnews.go.com/Nightline/ESPNSports/story?id=3034914#.T3cBmq5lhRY

83 Zirin, Dave, "The NFL: Where Dr King's Dream Goes to Die", *The Nation*, 21 January 2013, http://www.thenation.com/blog/172336/nfl-where-dr-kings-dream-goes-die#

84 Zirin, Dave, "25 Years Since Al Campanis Shocked Baseball: What's Changed and What Hasn't", *The Nation*, 16 April 2012, http://www.thenation.com/blog/167400/25-years-al-campanis-shocked-baseball-whats-changed-and-whats-stayed-same

85 Early, Gerald, "Where Have We Gone, Mr Robinson?", *Time*, 12 April 2007, http://www.time.com/time/magazine/article/0,9171,1609796,00.html

86 Valerie Plame, a former undercover FBI spy, was at the centre of a scandal after initiating a lawsuit charging that senior officials in President George W. Bush's administration had orchestrated a campaign to leak her name to reporters and thus compromise her covert status. This was done, she alleged, as retribution for a 2003 *New York Times* column by her husband about Iraq's nuclear ambitions, which did not quite match the version peddled by Tony Blair and his subordinates. The case went all the way to the Supreme Court, thwarted at every turn.

87 Zirin, Dave, "The Great American Witch-hunt: How Barry Bonds Became a Convicted Felon", *The Nation*, 13 April 2011

88 Ortiz, Jorge, L., "Barry Bonds found guilty of obstruction of justice", *USA Today*, 13 April 2011, http://content.usatoday.com/communities/dailyp-itch/post/2011/04/barry-bonds-found-guilty-of-obstruction-of-justice/1#.US5K2CrKde0

89 "Barry Bonds appeals obstruction conviction", UPI, 13 February 2013, http://www.upi.com/Sports_News/2013/02/13/Barry-Bonds-appeals-obstruction-conviction/UPI-34161360801146/

90 Quoted by several sources, including Nightengale, Bob, "Reason for Bonds' bad image split between steroids and racism", *USA Today*, 6 April 2006, http://usatoday30.usatoday.com/sports/baseball/nl/giants/2006-03-29-bonds-cover_x.htm

91 Zirin, Dave, "The Great American Witch-hunt: How Barry Bonds Became a Convicted Felon"

Chapter 9 – No Normal Sport In An Abnormal Society
II. For the Common Wealth

1   Clifford, Angela, "Serfdom or Ethnic Cleansing? – A British Discussion on Palestine – Churchill's Evidence to the Peel Commission" (1937), Athol Books, Belfast and London, 2003, p. 34, quoted at http://lists.econ.utah.edu/pipermail/rad-green/2011-June/044631.html

2   "The Churchill you didn't know", *The Guardian*, 28 November 2002

3   Majumdar, Boria, *Lost Histories of Indian Cricket*, Routledge, 2006, p. 1

4   Guha, Ramachandra, *A Corner of a Foreign Field: The Indian History of a British Sport*, Picador, 2002 (pbk), p. 20

5   Quoted in Wilde, Simon, *Ranji – The Strange Genius of Ranjitsinhji*, Aurum Press, 2005 (pbk), p. 39

6   Sen, Satadru, "Chameleon Games: Ranjitsinhji's Politics of Race and Gender" in *Journal of Colonialism and Colonial History*, 2001, quoted in Majumdar, p. 8

7   Wilde, Simon, *Ranji – The Strange Genius of Ranjitsinhji*, Aurum Press, 2005 (pbk), p. 71

8   Quoted in Majumdar, *Lost Histories of Indian Cricket*, p. 15

9   Bowen, p. 97

10 Beckles, Hilary McD., *The First West Indies Cricket Tour – Canada and the United States in 1886*, University of the West Indies Press, 2007, p. xi

11 Ibid

12 Beckles, *The Development of West Indies Cricket: Vol. 1 The Age of Nationalism*, The University of the West Indies Press, 1998, p. 35

13 Ibid, p. 46

14 James, C.L.R., *Beyond a Boundary*, Stanley Paul, 1990 (fifth reprint; pbk), p. 107

15 Ibid, p. 110

16 Ibid, p. 111

17 Quoted in James, pp. 112-3

18 Ibid, p. 110

19 Stollmeyer, Jeffrey, *Everything Under The Sun: My Life in West Indies Cricket*, Stanley Paul, 1983, p. 36

20 James, p. 113

21 Ibid, p. 51

22 Ibid, p. 146

23 This section draws on the author's essay for *The Nightwatchman*, aka the *Wisden Quarterly*, in 2013.

24 James, p. 195

25 Eytle, Ernest, *Frank Worrell*, The Sportsmans Book Club, 1965, p. 8

26 James, *Beyond a Boundary*, pp. 232-3

27 Figueroa, John in Brown, Stewart and McDonald, Ian (eds), *The Bowling Was Superfine: West Indian Writing And West Indian Cricket*, Peepal Tree, 2012, quoted in Ugra, Sharda, "Large-hearted, red-blooded, Caribbean", Cricinfo, 24 February 2013, http://www.espncricinfo.com/magazine/content/story/605650.html

28 James, p. 225

29 James, C. L. R, *The Nation*, 15 May 1959, quoted in Grimshaw, Anna (ed), *A Majestic Innings: Writings on Cricket*, 2006, p. 89

30 Ibid, p. 90

31 Eytle, p. 10

32 James, p. 252

33 Email to author, 12 August 2012

34 Barnes, Simon, "The man who took the game to apartheid", *The Times*, 9 December 2013, p. 57

35 Beckles, *The Age of Nationalism*, p. 44

36 Reddy, Enuga S., "Sports and the liberation struggle: a tribute to Sam Ramsamy and others who fought apartheid sport", http://scnc.ukzn.ac.za/doc/SPORT/SPORTRAM.htm

37 Ibid, pp. 112-3

38 Ibid, p. 114

39 Ibid, p. 115

40 Ibid, p. 116

41 Ibid, pp. 117-8

42 Ibid, pp. 119-20

43 "The 1981 Springbok Rugby Tour", New Zealand History online, http://www.nzhistory.net.nz/culture/1981-springbok-tour

44 Ibid

45 Richards, p. 207

46 "The 1981 Springbok Rugby Tour", New Zealand History online, http://www.nzhistory.net.nz/culture/1981-springbok-tour

47 Richards, p. 207

48 Hewitt, Duncan, Interview with John Taylor, 4 April 2012

49 Turnbull, Simon, "John Taylor: Rebel with a cause", *The Independent*, 30 May 2009, http://www.independent.co.uk/sport/rugby/rugby-union/international/john-taylor-rebel-with-a-cause-1693205.html

50 Ibid

51 Williamson, Martin, "Cricket's forgotten skeleton", Cricinfo, 5 December 2009, http://www.espncricinfo.com/magazine/content/story/438099.html

52 Stollmeyer, p. 219

53 Manley, Michael, *A History of West Indies Cricket*, 1988, p. 305

54 Quoted in May, Peter, *The Rebel Tours – Cricket's Crisis of Conscience*, Cheltenham: SportsBooks Limited, 2009, p.140

55 Lister, Simon, *Supercat – The authorised biography of Clive Lloyd*, Bath: Fairfield Books, 2007, p. 140

56 Lister, Simon, *Supercat*

57 Quoted in Roehler, Gordon, "Calypso, Literature and West Indian Cricket: Era of Dominance" in *Anthurium: A Caribbean Studies Journal*, 6:1, http://scholarlyrepository.miami.edu/anthurium/vol6/iss1/4

58 Schofield, Daniel, "'If being a mercenary is fighting for someone's cause, then I was'", *The Times*, 21 March 2013, p. 74

59 Quoted in Liew, Jonathan, "Nineteen Eighty-Three", *The Cricketer*, April 2013, p. 40

60 Liew, "Nineteen Eighty-Three"

61 Schofield, "'If being a mercenary is fighting for someone's cause, then I was'"

62 Brown, Kevin, "End race-based affirmative action? No", *New York Daily News*, 2 June 2013, http://www.nydailynews.com/opinion/race-based-affirmative-action-article-1.1360153

63 Thomen, Carl, *Is it Cricket? An Ethical Evaluation of Race Quotas in Sport*, University of Cape Town, 2008, p. 94

64 Ibid, p. 3

65 Cricket South Africa website, http://www.cricket.co.za/proteas.aspx

66 "South African cricket still seeing arguments in black and white", *The Guardian*, 7 January 2002, http://www.guardian.co.uk/sport/2002/jan/07/comment.southafricacricketteam

67 Quoted in Thomen, *Is it cricket? An ethical evaluation of race quotas in sport*, p. 16

68 Email to author, 24 May 2013

69 Email from John Young, 25 May 2013

70 "Olonga: 'why I wore that black armband'", newzimbabwe.com, 11 December 2009, http://www.newzimbabwe.com/pages/olonga3.11959.html

71 Hussain, Nasser with Newman, Paul, *Playing With Fire*, Michael Joseph, 2004, p. 5

72 Sheringham, Sam, "Andy Flower & Henry Olonga: the 'death of democracy' remembered", BBC Sport, 7 February 2013, http://www.bbc.co.uk/sport/0/cricket/21359274; Moonda, Firdoose, "Andy Flower recalls armband protest", Cricinfo, 7 February 2013, http://www.espncricinfo.com/zimbabwe/content/current/story/603792.html

Chapter 10 – The Grass Ceiling

1 Cohen, Nick, "Hate porn, sure, but be wary of banning it", *The Observer*, 30 June 2013, p. 33

2 Westerby, John, "Sister act makes sweeping statement at storied ground", *The Times*, 4 April 2012, http://www.thetimes.co.uk/tto/sport/cricket/article3374672.ece

3   Smith, Joan, *The Public Woman*, The Westbourne Press, 2013, quoted in *Sunday Times* review, 26 May 2013, Culture, p. 38

4   Goodwin, Christopher, *Sunday Times*, 14 July 2013, Culture, p. 6

5   Burke, Monte, "The Ten Richest Sporting Events in the World", *Forbes*, 24 May 2012, http://www.forbes.com/sites/monteburke/2012/05/24/the-ten-richest-sporting-events-in-the-world/

6   Mills, Brett D., *Women of Ancient Greece: Participating in Sport?*, Education Resources Information Centre, 1994, http://www.eric.ed.gov/ERICWebPortal/search/detailmini.jsp?_nfpb= true&_&ERICExtSearch_SearchValue_0=ED370951&ERICExtSearch_SearchType_0=no&accno=ED370951

7   Dillon, Matthew, *Girls And Women In Classical Greek Religion*, Routledge, 2002, p. 131

8   Williams, Jean, "Football and Feminism" in Steen, Rob, Novick, Jed and Richards, Huw, *The Cambridge Companion to Football*, Cambridge University Press, 2013, p. 184

9   BBC Sport, 27 June 2013, http://www.bbc.co.uk/sport/0/tennis/23067434

10   Davis, Toby, "Serena up for battle of the sexes against Murray", Reuters, 27 June 2013, http://uk.reuters.com/article/2013/06/27/tennis-wimbledon-williams-idUKL5N0F33I220130627

11   Rosin, Hanna, *The End of Men – And The Rise Of Women*, Riverhead, 2012, based on her article in *Atlantic Monthly*, 8 June 2010, http://www.theatlantic.com/magazine/archive/2010/07/the-end-of-men/308135

12   Brohm, Jean-Marie, "Twenty Theses on Sport", *Quel Corps?*, April-May 1975, quoted in *Sport – A Prison of Measured Time: Essays by Jean-Marie Brohm*, translated by Fraser, Ian, Ink Links, 1978, p. 182

13   *Clare Balding's Secrets of a Suffragette*, Channel 4, 26 May 2013

14   Tanner, Michael, *The Suffragette Derby*, Robson Press, 2013

15   *The Devon And Exeter Gazette*, 5 June 1913, p. 6, courtesy of British Museum

16   *Derby Daily Telegraph*, 12 June 1913, courtesy of British Museum

17   "A Memorable Derby", *The Times*, 5 June 1913, p. 9, http://www.heretical.com/suffrage/1913tms1.html

18   Pankhurst, Emmeline, *My Own Story*, New York: Hearst International Library, 1914, www.teachnet-uk.org.uk/.../History.../Emily%20Davison%20sources2.doc

19   Ibid

20   McGowan, Harriet, "More friendly sports needed PE teachers told", teachingpersonnel.com, 2 May 2012, http://www.teachingpersonnel.com/news/2012/5/2/more-female-friendly-sports-needed,-pe-teachers-told/

21   *New York Times*, 22 March 2007

22   Owen, Oliver, "Wolff determined to defeat the sceptics and the sexists", *The Times*, 20 October 2012, Sport, p. 17

23   Eason, Kevin, "Pioneer Patrick takes the lonely road to Hollywood-style stardom", *The Times*, 23 February 2013, Sport, p. 18

24   Schneider, Frank, *Bild*, 19 February 2013, http://www.bild.de/sport/motorsport/formel-1/kein-angebot-fuer-nascar-superfrau-danica-patrick-29189588.bild.html

25   O'Connor, Ashling, "Women lack mental strength for Formula One, says Stirling Moss", *The Times*, 16 April 2013, p. 19

26 Ibid

27 Hughes, Mark, "Hot in Daytona", *Sunday Times*, 24 February 2013, Sport, p. 14

28 Sylvester, Rachel, "Yes, they're the most democratic Games", *The Times*, 31 July 2012, p. 19

29 Quoted in Pope, Stacey, "'The Love of My Life': The meaning and importance of sport for Female Fans", *Journal of Sport and Social Issues*, May 2013

30 Giulianotti, Richard, "Supporters, followers, fans, and flâneurs", *Journal of Sport and Social Issues*, 2002, 26(1), 25-46

31 Pope, "'The Love of My Life': The meaning and importance of sport for Female Fans"

32 Ibid

33 Ibid

34 Anon, 'Women's "International" Dick, Kerr's, the women's "soccer" side, defeated the French women's team 5-1 (Exclusive)', *Daily Mirror*, 18 May 1921, p. 8. I am grateful to Neil Carter for all references to the *Daily Mirror*

35 Williams, Jean, "Football and Feminism", p. 186

36 Williams, Jean, *A Game for Rough Girls: A History of Women's Football in England*, Routledge , 2003, p. 20

37 Ibid, p. 187

38 Little, Alan, *Suzanne Lenglen – Tennis Idol of the Twenties*, Wimbledon Lawn Tennis Museum, 2007, p. 17

39 Holt, Richard, *Sport and Society in Modern France*, Macmillan, 1981, pp. 178-9, quoted in Wagg, Stephen, "'Her Dainty Strength': Suzanne Lenglen, Wimbledon and the Coming of Female Sport Celebrity" in Wagg, Stephen (ed), *Myths and Milestones in the History of Sport*, Palgrave Macmillan, 2011, p. 123

40 Hargreaves, Jennifer, *Sporting Females: Critical issues in the history and sociology of women's sports*, Routledge, 1994, p. 117

41 Ibid, p. 88-9

42 Wagg, p. 124

43 Kidd, Bruce, "The Women's Olympic Games: Important Breakthrough Obscured by Time", *Canadian Association for the Advancement of Women and Sport and Physical Activity Action Bulletin*, Spring 1994, http://www.caaws.ca/e/milestones/women_history/olympic_games.cfm

44 Macaulay, Lt. Col. A.D.C., *Behind the Scenes at Wimbledon*, Collins, 1965, p. 33, quoted in Wagg, p. 137

45 Daley, Arthur, "A Remarkable Woman", *New York Times*, 30 September 1956, quoted in Tuite, James (ed), *The Arthur Daley Years*, The New York Times, 1975, p. 148

46 Ibid

47 Ibid, p. 149

48 Babe Didrikson entry at sportsreference.com, http://www.sports-reference.com/olympics/athletes/di/babe-didrikson-1.html

49 Bijkerk, Anthony, "Fanny Blankers-Koen – A Biography", *Journal of Olympic History*, 12:2, pp. 56-60, http://www.aafla.org/SportsLibrary/JOH/JOHv12n2/johv12n2r.pdf; Fimrite, Ron, "Grace under pressure – four times over", *Sports Illustrated*, 1 August 1996, http://sportsillustrated.cnn.com/events/1996/olympics/daily/aug1/flashback.html

50 Cahn, Susan, K., *Coming On Strong – Gender and Sexuality in Twentieth-Century Women's Sport*, Harvard University Press, 1994, p. 132

51 Ibid

52 Ibid

53 Ibid, pp. 132-3

54 "About Title IX", http://bailiwick.lib.uiowa.edu/ge/aboutRE.html

55 "Last Hurrah for US Women", BBC Sport website, 3 September 2004, http:bbc.co.uk/sport/hi/football/world_football/3622770.stm (accessed on 15 January 2012).

56 Zirin, Dave, "Serena Williams and Getting 'Emotional' for Title IX", thenation.com, 9 July 2012, http://www.thenation.com/blog/168793/serena-williams-and-getting-emotional-title-ix

57 Quoted in Zirin, Dave, "Nine-Year-Old Girl Plays Football, Kicks Ass and Maybe Changes the World", *The Nation*, 11 November 2012, http://www.thenation.com/blog/171186/nine-year-old-girl-plays-football-kicks-ass-and-maybe-changes-world#

58 Wilks, Hannah, "The women's game is not equal to the men's game. It's actually far superior", *The Times*, 7 July 2012, Sport, p. 2

59 McIlvanney, Hugh, "In sport, equality isn't always fair", *Sunday Times*, 1 July 2012, Sport, p. 14

60 Mewshaw, Michael, *Ladies of the Court: Grace And Disgrace On The Women's Tennis Tour*, Little, Brown, 1993, p. 325

61 Navratilova, Martina with Vecsey, George, *Being Myself*, Grafton, 1986, pp. 190-1

62 Stanley, Alessandra, "The Legacy of Billie Jean King: an Athlete Who Demanded Equal Pay", *New York Times*, 26 April 2006, http://www.nytimes.com/2006/04/26/arts/television/26stan.html

63 Forbes, Gordon, *A Handful of Summers*, Sportspages, 1994 (pbk), p. 198

64 Ibid, p. 198

65 Overend, Jonathan, "WTA Anniversary: The Day Sport Changed Forever", bbc.co.uk, 11 June 2013, http://www.bbc.co.uk/sport/0/tennis/22833297

66 Harman, Neil, "King can be well pleased with health of the WTA", *The Times*, 20 June 2013, p. 68

67 Erskine, James (dir), *The Battle of the Sexes*, UK, 2013

68 Quoted by several sources, including Syed, Matthew, "How sex returned to the circuit", *The Times*, 27 June 2013, times2, p. 5

69 Harman, "King can be well pleased with health of the WTA"

70 *Billie-Jean: Portrait of a Pioneer*, broadcast on HBO, 26 April 2006, quoted in Buzinski, Jim, "King a true pioneer", outsports.com, http://www.outsports.com/tennis/2006/bjkhboreview.htm

71 "Bobby Riggs on 60 Minutes", YouTube, first broadcast on ABC TV, 1973, http://www.youtube.com/watch?v=dxHrO8pwSww (accessed on 4 June 2012)

72 Harman, "King can be well pleased with health of the WTA"

73 "Wimbledon pays equal prize money", BBC Sport, 22 February 2007, http://news.bbc.co.uk/sport1/hi/tennis/6385295.stm

74 Ibid

75 Navratilova, Martina with Vecsey, George, *Being Myself*, p. 285

76 "ANC condemns Semenya gender row", *Mail and Guardian Online*, 20 August 2009, http://www.mg.co.za/article/2009-08-20-anc-condemns-semenya-gender-row

77 Farrington, Neil, Kilvington, Daniel, Price, John and Saeed, Amir, "Athletics: The fastest 'race'?", *Race, Racism And Sports Journalism*, Routledge, 2012, pp. 50-1

78 Ibid, p. 57

79 Ibid

80 Salt, Don and Brain, Zoe, "Intersex: The space between the genders", *Cosmos*, 15 June 2007, http://www.cosmosmagazine.com/node/1462

81 Caudwell, Jayne, "Sex watch: surveying men's and women's sexed bodies at the Olympics" in Sugden, John and Tomlinson, Alan (eds), *Watching the Olympics: power, politics and representation*, Routledge, 2011, p. 161

82 Nyong'o, Tavia, "The unforgiveable transgression of being Caster Semenya", *Women and Performance: A Journal of Feminist Theory* 20 (1), 95-100, quoted in Caudwell, p. 161

83 Kessel, Anna, "Rivals 'laughed and stared' at Caster Semenya, says Jenny Meadows", *The Guardian*, 21 July 2010, http://www.guardian.co.uk/sport/2010/jul/21/caster-semenya-jenny-meadows

84 Arbuthnott, George and Barnes, David, "Four female Olympic stars were genetically male", *Sunday Times*, 23 June 2013, p. 15

85 Parks Pieper, Lindsey, "Gender Regulation: Renee Richards Revisited", *International Journal for the History of Sport*, 2012, 29:5, pp. 675-690

86 Pitt, Nick, "Lee Puts House In Order", *Sunday Times*, 26 May 2013, Sport, p. 15

87 Quotes from Glenda Jackson, Vivien Saunders and Peter Dawson from "R&A defends all-male policy", Golftoday.co.uk, March 2003, http://www.golftoday.co.uk/news/yeartodate/news03/randa2.html

88 Bort, Julie, "IBM CEO Ginny Rometty Faces Off Against Golf's Most Sexist Club", *Business Insider*, 30 March 2012, http://www.businessinsider.com/ibm-ceo-ginny-rometty-faces-off-against-golfs-most-sexist-club-2012-3

89 McIlvanney, Hugh, "Augusta retains pride in its prejudices", *Sunday Times*, Sport section, p. 16

90 Pavia, Will, "Obama joins civil rights battle for the Rosa Parks of women's golf", *The Times*, 7 April 2012, p. 4

91 Davies, Patricia, "No woman? No cry. Augusta National will grow up eventually and see sense", *The Times*, 7 April 2012, Sport section, p. 2

92 Brennan, Christine, "Finally! Augusta does right thing and admits women", *USA Today*, 20 August 2012, http://www.usatoday.com/sports/golf/masters/story/2012-08-20/Masters-women-Condoleeza-Rice-Darla-Moore-Christine-Brennan/57160258/1

93 Zirin, Dave, "Condi Rice's Membership at August National Is Nothing to Celebrate", *The Nation*, 20 August 2012, http://www.thenation.com/blog/169475/condi-rices-membership-augusta-national-nothing-celebrate

94 Harris, Cathy, "Top golfer attacks decision to stage Open at club that excludes women", *The Times*, 15 July 2013, p. 7

95 "Open and Shut Case", *The Times*, 15 July 2013, p. 24

96 Smith, Gary, "The Shadow Boxer", *Sports Illustrated*, 18 April 2005, http://sportsillustrated.cnn.com/2005/magazine/04/12/griffith0418/index.html

[97] Broussard, Chris, "Outside the Lines", ESPN, 29 April 2013

[98] Harding, Eleanor, "Martina: Gay male players hide in closet", *Daily Mail*, 24 June 2013, p. 3

[99] Thorpe, David, "Love Story", Out.com, 7 June 2008, http://www.out.com/entertainment/ 2008/07/06/love-story

[100] Hodgkinson, Mark, "Fame and Shame of a tennis pioneer", *The Age*, 16 January 2007, http://www.theage.com.au/news/tennis/fame-and-shame-of-a-tennis-pioneer/2007/01/15/1168709679591.html originally published as "The Sad End of Bill Tilden", *Daily Telegraph*, 16 January 2007

[101] Glbtq.com, http://www.glbtq.com/arts/olympic_equestrians.html

[102] Davies, *Wisden 2013*, p. 89

[103] Tatchell, Peter, "Justin Fashanu – Homophobia Destroyed Him", http://www.petertatchell.net/sport/justin_fashanu.htm

[104] Ibid

[105] Tucker, James Marcus, "Kick It Out", *One + One: The Brighton Filmmakers Journal*, July 2007, p. 14, http://oneplusonejournal.co.uk/wp-content/uploads/2012/07/FMJ_Issue1.pdf

[106] Richards, Giles and Christenson, Marcus, "Anton Hysen states case for coming out and for his father's speech", *The Guardian*, 13 March 2011, http://www.guardian.co.uk/football/2011/mar/13/anton-glenn-hysen-gay-pride?INTCMP=SRCH

[107] "Racism in Football: Culture, Media and Sport Committee", 19 September 2012, http://www.publications.parliament.uk/pa/cm201213/cmselect/cmcumeds/89/8904.htm

[108] Ducker, James, "Homosexual players need a gay hero, says Lindegaard", *The Times*, 28 November 2012, p. 83

[109] Walder, Seth, "US national team player Robbie Rogers reveals he's gay, stepping away from soccer", *New York Daily News*, 15 February 2013, http://www.nydailynews.com/sports/more-sports/u-s-national-team-soccer-player-reveals-gay-article-1.1265595

[110] Foss, Mike and Brady, Erik, "Rogers coming back as first openly gay player in MLS", *USA Today*, 24 May 2013, http://www.usatoday.com/story/sports/mls/2013/05/24/robbie-rogers-mls-galaxy-openly-gay/2160105/

[111] Rumsby, Ben, "Former Leeds winger relieved to say he is gay", *Daily Telegraph*, 16 February 2013, Sport, p. 6

[112] Barnes, Simon, "Small-minded have gloried at Beckham's exit", *The Times*, 20 May 2013, p. 54

[113] Fagburn, "Daley Thompson: Why Sportsmen Don't Come Out", 15 October 2011, http://www.fagburn.com/2011/10/daley-thompson-why-sportsmen-dont-come.html

[114] Anthony, Andrew, "Speed: the sequel", *The Observer*, 30 September 2007, http://www.guardian.co.uk/sport/2007/sep/30/athletics.features

[115] Cahn S., "Coming on strong: Gender and sexuality in twentieth-century women's sport", quoted in Tredway, Kristi, "Judith Butler redux – the heterosexual matrix and the out lesbian athlete: Amélie Mauresmo, gender performance, and women's professional tennis", Journal of the Philosophy of Sport, 16 April 2013

[116] Griffin, Pat, *Strong Women, Deep Closets: Lesbians and Homophobia in Sport*, Human Kinetics, 1998, p. ix

117 Quoted in "'Bare-leg' Tennis, and the Bitter Rivalry between Helen Wills and Helen Jacobs", 29 June 2012, http://www.nickelinthemachine.com/tag/lesbianism/

118 Griffin, Pat, *Strong Women, Deep Closets: Lesbians and Homophobia in Sport*, pp. 38-9

119 Navratilova, Martina with Vecsey, George, *Being Myself*, p. 177

120 Ibid, pp. 179-80

121 Howard, Johnette, *The Rivals: Chris Evert vs. Martina Navratilova – Their Epic Duels and Extraordinary Friendship*, Broadway Books, 2005 (pbk),pp. 176-7

122 "Martina Navratilova and Gareth Thomas speak at Stonewall's Equality Dinner", April 2010, https://www.stonewall.org.uk/media/current_releases/3891.asp

123 Zipay, S, "CBS drops Wright as golf analyst", *Newsday*, 10 January 1996, A52, quoted in Griffin, *Strong Women, Deep Closets: Lesbians and Homophobia in Sport*, p. 47

124 *Fight Night: White Collar Boxing*, ITV, broadcast in 2005

125 Hubbard, Alan, "Emile and the Pink Pounder drag fight game out of the closet", *The Independent on Sunday*, 27 December 2009, http://www.independent.co.uk/sport/general/others/boxing-emile-and-the-pink-pounder-drag-fight-game-out-of-closet-1850993.html

126 Klores, Dan, "Junior, the Kid, the Fight", *New York Times*, 31 March 2012, http://www.nytimes.com/2012/04/01/sports/emile-griffith-benny-paret-and-the-fatal-fight.html?pagewanted=all

127 Ibid

128 Ibid

129 Ibid

130 Hubbard, Alan, "The phrase 'come out fighting' has been given a completely new meaning", insidethegames.biz, 8 October 2012, http://www.insidethegames.biz/blogs/1011210

131 Smith, "The Shadow Boxer"

132 Syed, Matthew, "Now fight is over, boxer's last secret comes out", *The Times*, 27 July 2013, p. 12

133 Quoted in Hubbard

134 Rogers, Martin, "Niners CB says openly gay players would not be welcomed on the team", Yahoo! Sports, 30 January 2013, http://sports.yahoo.com/news/nfl--report--niners-cb-says-openly-gay-players-would-not-be-welcomed-on-the-team-190346715.html

135 Zirin, Dave, "Is it Getting Better? Homophobia Rocks Super Bowl", *The Nation*, 1 February 2013, http://www.thenation.com/blog/172590/it-getting-better-homophobia-rocks-super-bowl

136 ESPN Radio, Denver, quoted in Busbee, Jay, "Colorado's Nick Kasa says he was asked at combine, 'Do you like girls?'", Yahoo! Sports, 27 February 2013, http://sports.yahoo.com/blogs/nfl-shutdown-corner/colorado-nick-kasa-says-asked-combine-girls-151539932--nfl.html

137 "Maryland politician's letter denouncing Brendon Ayanbadejo's support of gay marriage", yahoo.com, 6 September 2012, http://sports.yahoo.com/news/nfl--maryland-politician's-letter-denouncing-brendon-ayanbade-jo's-support-of-gay-marriage.html

138 Klemko, Robert, "Brendon Ayanbadejo responds to delegate on gay marriage", *USA Today*, 7 September 2012, http://www.usatoday.com/sports/football/nfl/ravens/story/2012-09-07/brendan-ayanbadejo-gay-marriage/57680822/1

139 Huffington Post, 26 June 2013, http://www.huffingtonpost.com/2013/06/26/chris-kluwe-gay-nfl-player_n_3505296.html

140 Kluwe, Chris, "They Won't Magically Turn You Into A Lustful Cockmonster: Chris Kluwe Explains Gay Marriage to the Politician Who Is Offended By An NFL Player Supporting It", deadspin.com, 7 September 2012, http://deadspin.com/5941348/they-wont-magically-turn-you-into-a-lustful-cockmonster-chris-kluwe-explains-gay-marriage-to-the-politician-who-is-offended-by-an-nfl-player-supporting-it. Quoted in Zirin, Dave, "Chris Kluwe and the Greatest Political Statement By Any Athlete Ever", *The Nation*, 8 September 2012, http://www.thenation.com/blog/169818/chris-kluwe-and-greatest-political-statement-any-athlete-ever

141 Moran, Caitlin, *The Times Magazine*, 28 September 2013, p. 5

Index

affirmative action (positive
    discrimination) 652–4, 687
Africa(n) Cup of Nations 475–6, 562,
    567
Alcock, Charles William 201–4, 287–8,
    360, 435
Ali, Muhammad 52, 295, 495, 510, 538,
    562, 578, 580, 589
American football 52–3, 153–6, 160,
    357–8, 422, 457
  administration 249–50
  amateur v. professional status
    284–6, 338, 345–54
  Bloody Mondays 153
  floodlights 42
  and homosexuality 723
  nationalism 422
  players' rights 404–6
  racial issues 615
  student-athletes 345–6
Ancient Olympics 78, 110, 115–16,
    260, 263
animal welfare issues 407–10
Anti-Nazi League 518, 525
antisocial behaviour 48–9: see also
    hooliganism
apartheid 186, 319, 446, 477, 489–91,
    545, 575, 603, 630, 632–44
archery 128
Argentina 60–1, 100, 139, 234, 439,
    445, 459, 504–5, 570–4
Ashe, Arthur 311, 378, 592–3, 637–8
Association of Football Players' and
    Trainers' Union (AFPU) 365,
    369, 370
Association of Tennis Professionals
    (ATP) 45, 311, 375–8
athletics 288, 296, 329–30, 455
  genetics and 583–4

nationalism 445–6
and politics 539–45
and professionalism 254, 259–60,
    297–9
racial issues 580–5
transgender politics 693–8
women's participation in 671, 681–2
attendance figures 49–57
Augusta National Golf Club 699–702
Australian Cricket Board (ACB) 200,
    318–19, 327–8
Australian Football League (AFL) 52,
    142, 430
Ayanbadejo, Brendon 723

badminton 122, 456
Baer, Max 524–5
Bahrain 489, 568
Bahrain F1 Grand Prix 567–9
Bailey, Abe 211–12
Bailey, Donovan 330, 580
Bangladesh Cricket Board (BCB) 359,
    566
Bangladesh Premier League 359, 404
Barmy Army 41, 97–100
barras bravas 60–1
baseball 146–51, 160, 338–45, 686
  administration 213–24, 248–9,
    340–1, 358
  amateur v. professional status
    255–7, 282–4, 300–5
  American exceptionalism 455,
    457–62
  attendance figures 50, 52
  and community, loss of 80–7
  doping 189, 397–8, 618–20
  floodlights 42–3
  gambling 178, 180, 187–93
  history/myths of 108, 138–9

home advantage 39–40
hooliganism 58–9, 68
match fixing 177–81, 187–93
owners' collusion 395
players' rights 362–3, 387–95
players' strike 391, 396–7
racial issues 220–24, 591, 597–604, 608–20
reserve clause 215–17, 283, 362–3, 389, 392–3, 395
Royal Rooters 59
ticket sales 88–90
timing of games 43–4
basketball 15, 156–61, 359, 455–7, 459
globalisation 338
home advantage 39
Israeli Women's Premier League 359
match-fixing 349
racial issues 604–8
strikes 359
Belgian Football Union (BFU) 70
Bergmann, Gretel 521–2
Best, George 31
Bharat Army 41
Black Sox scandal 168, 190–3
Blankers-Koen, Fanny 682–4
Board of Control for Cricket in India (BCCI) 240–2, 244, 401, 564
Boat Race 51, 134, 670
Bolt, Usain 4, 17
Bonds, Barry 22, 618–20
Bosman ruling 399–400
bowls 456
boxing 13, 357–8, 407
    attendance figures 50–2
    history/myths of 115–16, 139
    and homosexuality 717–25
    match fixing 169, 170–1
    nationalism 423, 449–51, 484–8
    Northern Ireland/Eire 449–51
    and politics 509–10, 524–8, 561–2, 587
    racial issues 578–80, 585–90
Braddock, James J. 526–7
Bradman, Donald 52, 464–7, 470, 623
British American Football League 160
British Athletics Federation (BAF) 330
British Basketball League 161

British Empire 111–12, 132–3, 140, 205–6
British Football Association 290
British Open 14, 53, 138, 280–1, 699
Brundage, Avery 121–2, 296–7, 329, 440–2, 516–20, 522–4, 538–9, 541–4, 546, 594, 684
Bruno, Frank 486–8, 585
Budd, Zola 489–91

canoeing 456
capitalism 154, 244, 249, 502
Carlos, John 227, 539–42, 545
Chase, Hal 179–81
Chatrier, Philippe 311, 376–8
Clay, Cassius, *see* Ali, Muhammad
Clemente, Roberto 608–10, 612–15
collective identity 90–3
college sports 345–54
Committee in Defence of West Indies Cricket 324
Commonwealth Games 455, 480, 641–2
Communism 502, 516–17, 529–31, 552
Confederation of African Football (CAF) 567
Constantine, Learie 626–30, 632
corruption 60–1, 194, 197, 207, 228, 231–3, 235: *see also* match fixing
Cotswold Olympicks 117
Coubertin, Baron de, *see* de Coubertin, Pierre de Frédy, Baron
cricket 15, 25, 29–30, 32, 39–41, 163, 165, 359–62, 445, 456
    administration 197, 200–1, 211–13, 240–5
    admission charges 127
    affirmative action 653–4
    amateur v. professional status 264–73, 287–8, 316–28
    Americans and 305–6
    The Ashes 52, 367–8, 414, 416, 431–4, 462–72, 478
    attendance figures 52–5
    bodyline (leg theory) controversy 462–72
    Chance To Shine programme 143
    corruption in 243–4
    gambling 168, 171–2, 175–7, 184–5

Gentlemen v Players 136, 267
history/myths of 105–6, 118–19,
    125, 127–33, 136, 138–43
and homosexuality 703, 705
India 133, 472–5
indigenous Australian players
    427–31
match fixing 175–7, 184–5
nationalism 414, 416, 423, 425–34,
    462–75, 477–8, 480–4, 494–6
New Zealand 562–3
Pakistan 472–5, 565–6
players' rights 361–2, 367–9, 400–1
players' strikes 361
and politics 497–8, 562–6
and private schools 143
quotas and 652–7
racial issues 425–30, 480–4, 622–34,
    647–60
Tebbit test 482–3
Twenty20 format: 9, 199, 242, 245,
    359, 269, 401–4, 495, 563
Varsity cricket match 134
West Indies 185, 212, 322–4, 401–3,
    480, 562, 623–34, 647–51
women in 674
croquet 134, 220, 665
Curtis Cup 418–19
cycling 54, 198–9, 418, 590, 666

Dassler, Adolph (Adi) and Horst
    229–30, 263
David, Herman 311–13
Davison, Emily Wilding 668–70
de Coubertin, Pierre de Frédy,
    Baron 111–12, 204–8, 259–60,
    503
Delaunay, Henri 209–11
Dempsey, Jack 50, 357, 590
Didrikson, Mildred "Babe" 662,
    681–2, 714
D'Oliveira, Basil 477–8, 632–3
doping 5–7, 169, 671
    baseball 189, 397–8, 618–20
    cycling 198–9
    East Germany 500, 548–58
    horse racing 173–4, 407–8
    Olympic Games 548–58
    West Germany 500, 557–8

Drogba, Didier 566–7
Du Bois, William Edward Burghardt
    585, 588, 597
duelling 172–3

Eastham, George 374–5
Edwards, Gareth 333–5, 446
Elite Ice Hockey League 159–60
Emanuel, Rahm 251–2
Empire Games 455
Epsom 51, 121, 125–6, 174–5, 668–70
equestrianism 456, 665, 672, 704–5
Erhardt Conference 160
European Club Association (ECA)
    233–4
Evangelisti, Giovanni 232–3
exceptionalism, American 2, 153–4,
    156, 159, 163, 362, 455–62

FA Cup 19, 54–5, 66–7, 138, 202–3
    286–8
Fascism 502, 505–9
Fashanu, Justin 705–8
Federal League 216–17, 219, 366
Federation of International Amateur
    Athletics Associations 329
Federation of International Cricketers
    Associations (FICA) 359
fencing 208, 456, 665
FIFA 195, 200, 209–10, 231, 233–40,
    424, 476, 499, 640, 678–9
FIFA World Cup 41, 54, 131, 164, 455,
    504, 507–9, 535, 566, 571
    1966: England 13, 88, 122
    1978: Argentina 61, 570–4
    2022: Qatar 27, 235, 415
FIGC (Federazione Italiana Giuoco
    Calcio) 507
Flood, Curt 356, 362, 392–3, 400
floodlights 42–4
Flower, Andy 658–60
football 143–5, 161–3, 358, 399–400,
    455
    administration 198, 200–3, 209–11,
        233–40
    amateur v. professional status
        286–95
    attendance figures 50, 54–5
    Brazil 54, 442–3, 445

debt to public schools 144–5
Egypt 95–7
European 443–4
floodlights 27–8
gambling 170, 181–4
Germany 511–12
history/myths of 105, 119, 137–9
home advantage 39, 42
and homosexuality 703, 705–10
hooliganism 57–71, 91–2
Ibrox disasters 63, 71–2
and indigenous players 430
Italy 505–9
match fixing 181–4
Mogadishu national stadium 30
nationalism 412–14, 416–22, 434–8,
    443–4, 452–3, 475–7
Nigeria 567
North Korea 535–8
Old Firm 59–65
players' rights 371, 399–400
players' strikes 365
and politics 498–9, 505–9, 511–12,
    531–5, 566–7, 570–4
racial issues 577–8, 590
retain-and-transfer system 364–5,
    373–5
safety issues 63, 65, 67–9, 97
ultras 96–8
women's participation in 666,
    677–9
see also FIFA; FIFA World Cup
Formula 1 (F1) 164, 380–7, 456
Fraternity of Professional Base Ball
    Players of America 366
free agency system 248, 341–2, 391–2,
    399

Gaelic Athletic Association (GAA)
    452–3
gambling 166–8, 170–8, 180–8
Gardiner Conference 160
Gayle, Chris 402–3
Geipel, Ines 553–5
Gibson, Bob 255–7, 539
gladiators 114–16
Glickman, Marty 516, 522–3
Goebbels, Joseph 502, 515, 522, 525–7,
    529, 533

golf 358, 454–5
    amateur v. professional status
        279–82, 315–16
    attendance figures 53
    Canada Cup 454
    history/myths of 119–20, 138–9
    nationalism 418–19, 491–4
    Open Championship Charter 280
    women in 674, 682, 698–702
Grace, W. G. 177, 203, 269–72, 360,
    362, 478
Grand Prix Drivers Association
    (GPDA) 379, 382, 384, 386–7
Grange, Harold Edward 'Red' 285
Greig, Tony 319–21, 324–6, 481
Griffith, Emile 718–22
Guillén, Yewri 344–5
Guthrie, Jimmy 370–2
gymnastics 139, 208, 510, 576

hammer throw 151
Havelange, João 229, 235–9, 519
Haynes, Desmond 323–4
Headley, George 623, 628–9
Heineken Cup 53
hero worship 40
Heysel Stadium disaster 69–71
Hill, Jimmy 369, 371–4
Hillsborough disaster 73–80
Hitler, Adolf 502, 506, 510–12, 515,
    519–23, 525–6, 589, 596
hockey 108–9, 456, 665
home advantage 38–42, 245–6
homosexuality 703–12, 717–25
hooliganism 57–71, 91–2
horse racing
    animal welfare issues 407–10
    attendance figures 51
    The Derby 125–6, 174–5, 668–9
    doping 173–4, 407–8
    and gambling 171, 173–5
    Grand National 137, 408–9
    history/myths of 121, 125–6, 130–1,
        138
    The Oaks 25
    racial issues 590
    St Leger 25, 125
    women in 672
    women' rights protest 668–9

Hussain, Nasser 482–4, 659–60

Ibrox disasters 63, 71–2
ice hockey 108–10, 122, 139, 159, 396, 455–7, 477, 500
Indian Premier League (IPL) 38, 55, 240–5, 400–1, 495
Intercollegiate Football Association 156
International Association of Athletics Federations (IAAF) 55, 229, 232, 489, 683, 694–7
International Cricket Council (ICC) 29, 164, 168, 169, 200–1, 211–13, 241, 243–4, 251, 284, 321, 563–6
International Football Association Board 137, 139
International Ice Hockey Federation 159
International (Lawn) Tennis Federation (ITF/ILTF) 310, 311, 313, 376–9, 454
International Management Group (IMG) 313, 315
International Olympic Committee (IOC) 200, 207, 227–33, 261–2, 424
International Rugby Board (IRB) 335, 449
International Tennis Players' Association (ITPA) 375–6
Irish Amateur Boxing Association 449
Isle of Man Tourist Trophy (TT) 152–3, 380

Jahncke, Ernest Lee 519
James, C. L. R. 626–34
Jardine, Douglas 464, 466–8, 471
Jayawardene, Mahela 199–200
Jewish Labour Committee 518
Jockey Club 121, 125–6
John, Barry 31–2
Johnson, Ben 6–7
Johnson, Jack 357, 585–9
Johnson, Michael 261–2, 583
Jordan, Michael 295, 306, 313, 459, 617

Kay, Tony 181
Kenya/Kenyan athletes 445–6, 581–4

King, Billie Jean 499, 688–92, 714–15, 716–17
King, John Barton 305–6
Kramer, Jack 308, 310–11, 376–8, 691–2
Krieger, Andreas/Heidi 554–5

lacrosse 15, 139, 456
Landis, Kenesaw Mountain 192, 217, 219–24, 598–9
Larwood, Harold 464, 466–8, 470–1
Laver, Rod 32, 313–14
lawn tennis 134–6
Le Mans 24-Hour race 56, 385, 455
Lemaitre, Christophe 580–1
Lenglen, Suzanne 309, 679–81
lesbianism 672, 712–17
Lewis, Carl 32, 711–12
Lewis, Lennox 485–8
Lloyd, Clive 322–3, 624, 648–50
Lohmann, George 359–62
London Marathon 51, 141
Long, Lutz 595–6
Lord, Thomas 128
Louis, Joe (Joe Louis Barrow) 509–10, 525–9, 539, 575, 591–4, 598
luge 245–6

McAlister, Peter 367–8
McCormack, Mark 313, 315–16
McGuigan, Barry 450–1
Major League Baseball Players Association (MLBPA) 387, 393, 396
Major League Soccer 226–7, 338
Mandela, Nelson 7, 186, 336, 484, 567, 632–5
Maradona, Diego 32, 233, 571–2
Marylebone Cricket Club (MCC) 127–9, 135–6, 176–7, 197, 200, 265–6, 271, 275, 287, 319, 361, 428, 469, 471, 629
Massasoit Convention 154, 156
match fixing 168–70, 176–93, 349
Mayer, Paul Yogi 520–3
Mays, Carl 217–18
media 74–6, 88–90, 369–70
micro-fixing, *see* spot-fixing
Miller, Marvin 387–95, 397–9, 404

Mills Commission Report 149
motorsports 55–7, 152–3, 358, 379–87, 419, 455, 567–70, 672–4
Muldoon, Robert 641–2
multinationalism 422
Murray, Andy 38, 44–5, 666–7, 687
Musberger, Brent 541, 543
Mussolini, Benito 502, 505–9
Myers-Briggs Type Indicator (MBTI) 26

Naismith, James 156–9
NASCAR (National Association for Stock Car Racing) 380–1, 673
National Association for the Advancement of Coloured People (NAACP) 87, 525
National Collegiate Athletic Association (NCAA) 346–52
National Tennis League (NTL) 313
nationalism/national identity 412–22, 434–8
    American exceptionalism 2, 153–4, 156, 159, 163, 362, 455–62
    American football 422
    athletics 445–6
    boxing 423, 449–51, 484–8
    Brazil 424, 442–3
    cricket 414, 416, 423, 425–34, 462–72, 478, 480–4, 494–5
    England v. Australia 414, 416, 427–34, 462–72
    England v. Scotland 434–8
    England v. West Germany 412–13
    football 412–14, 416–22, 434–8, 442–4, 452–3, 475–7
    golf 418, 491–4
    India v. Pakistan 472–5
    and internationalism 477–84
    Ireland 448–53
    motor racing 419
    New Zealand 445–8
    Olympics 418, 420–1, 439–42, 488–91
    rugby union 418–19, 444–8
    tennis 423, 454, 477–9
Navratilova, Martina 477–8, 558–61, 688, 693, 703–4, 715–17
Nazism 500, 502

netball 159
North American Soccer League (NASL) 225

Old Firm 59–65
Olonga, Henry 658–60
Olympic Games
    1896 Athens 204, 208, 664–5
    1900 Paris 439
    1904 St Louis 439
    1908 London 439
    1912 Stockholm 296, 503, 517
    1932 Los Angeles 681–2
    1936 Berlin 500, 515–24, 533, 593–6
    1948 London 682–3
    1956 Melbourne 54, 538, 548
    1968 Mexico City 445–6, 538–45
    1972 Munich 545–8, 550
    1976 Montreal 328, 538, 548, 550, 558
    1980 Moscow 538, 551
    1984 Los Angeles 329, 489–90, 538
    1988 Seoul 446, 551
    1996 Atlanta 54
    2000 Sydney 12, 247
    2008 Beijing 4, 54, 247, 503–4, 538
    2012 London 3–4, 54, 128, 489, 500, 547
    2016 Rio de Janeiro 424
    administration 196, 200, 207–8, 227–33
    amateurism v. professionalism 254, 260–3, 328–31
    attendance figures 54
    corruption 194, 231–3
    doping 548–58
    history/myths of 110–12, 115–17
    nationalism 418, 420–1, 439–42, 488–91
    and politics 500–1, 512–24, 530–1, 538–48
    sports, inclusion of 103–4
    women in 664–6, 675, 680, 682–5
Olympic Project for Human Rights (OPHR) 538–9
Olympism 207, 247–8
O'Malley, Walter 80–6, 250
Operation Last Bet, Italy 182–3
Owens, Jesse 32, 515, 522–3, 541–2, 593–7

Pacific Coast League (PCL) 215
Packer, Kerry 317–28, 335–6
Pacquiao, Manny 170, 357
Pakistan Cricket Board (PCB) 565
Panesar, Monty (Mudhsuden Singh)
    480–1
Paralympics 8, 11–12, 54, 420
Paret, Benny "Kid" 718–22
Pelé 32, 226, 299, 465, 498–9, 571
People's Olympiad, Barcelona (1936)
    513–14
Perry, Fred 307–10
Pilic, Nikki 375–7
polo 134, 622
popular culture, and feel-good factor
    411–8
positive discrimination (affirmative
    action) 652–4, 687
Professional Footballers' Association
    (PFA) 369, 371, 373

Qatar 27, 235, 415, 489, 675

racial issues 12, 700
    indigenous players 427–31, 577–8
    segregation 220–24, 598
Ramsey, Alf 131, 412–3
Ranjitsinhji Vibhaji (Kumar Shri
    Ranjitsinhji, Ranji) 270, 305, 622–3
Raskin, Richard (Renée Richards)
    693, 698
real tennis 122–5
Red Sport International (RSI,
    Sportintern) 513
Richards, Vivian (Viv) 403, 623–4, 648
Rickey, Branch 224, 599–600, 602
Riggs, Bobby 690–2
Robinson, Jackie 81, 86, 224, 392, 499,
    597–8
Robinson, Sugar Ray 52, 598–604,
    615–16
Rogers, Robbie 709–10
Rogge, Jacques 169, 196, 246, 547–8
Rose, Pete 187–9
Rous, Stanley 236, 511
rowing 456
rugby 144
    All Blacks 27, 336, 444–7, 446–7,
        641–3
    amateur v. professional status
        273–9, 331–8
    history/myths of 106–8, 136, 138–9
    and homosexuality 703
    and indigenous players 430
    nationalism 418–9, 444–8
    New Zealand 446–8
    Northern Ireland/Eire 449
    and professionalism 259, 331–8
    racial issues 641–6
    rugby union 15, 27, 38–9, 53, 163,
        449, 456
    Springboks 641–2, 654
    Wales 446
Rugby Football Union 273, 277–8
rugby league 333, 336–8
    Rugby League Challenge Cup 278,
        279
Rugby League World Cup 279
Rugby School 106–7, 112, 141–2, 205–6
Runciman, David 39, 42
Ruth, Babe (George Herman Ruth) 26,
    32, 300–6, 357
Ryder Cup 454–5, 491–4

sailing 138
Samaranch y Torelló, Don Juan
    Antonio 230–1, 237, 514, 544
Saperstein, Abe 605–8
Schmeling, Max 524–9, 594
Semenya, Caster 693–7
show jumping 456, 672, 704–5
Six Nations Championship 27, 53, 278
Smith, Tommie 539–44
snooker 49, 455
Snow, John 324–5
Sobers, Garry 4, 32, 185, 428, 623, 632,
    634
social media 97, 101–2
Socialist Workers' Sport International
    (SASI) 512–13
Solheim Cup 455
Somali Football Federation (SFF) 30
Spalding, Albert 147–50, 160, 363, 686
speed skating 246, 576
speedway 456
sphairistikè 134–5
Spitzer, Ankie 546, 547–8
Sport Power 100 (*The Times*) 195–6

spot-fixing 168, 187, 243–4
squash 103–4, 122, 445
Sri Lanka Cricket (SLC) 199
Sri Lankan civil war 562
Stalin, Josef 80, 251, 502, 530–33
Starostin, Nikolai 531–3
Stevenson, Teofilo 561–2
Stewart, Jackie 379, 380, 383–6
Stoller, Sam 522–3
Sullivan, John L. 139, 586
swimming 208, 262, 576, 664–5

table tennis 29, 122, 247–8, 455,
    500–1
Tartan Army 438
Tatum, Reece "Goose" 606–7
Taylor, John 644–6
Taylor Report 76–7
tennis 32, 44–5, 49, 53–4, 163, 358
    affirmative action 687
    amateur v. professional status
        307–14
    Davis Cup 139, 163, 307, 376–7,
        415–16, 454, 640
    history/myths of 106, 121–5, 134–6,
        139
    and homosexuality 703–4
    lawn tennis 134–6
    nationalism 413, 423, 454, 477–9
    in Olympic Games 665
    players' rights 375–9
    and politics 510, 525, 558–61
    racial issues 638–41
    transgender politics 493
    women in 358, 679–81, 686–93
The Times 2–3, 195–6, 409–10
Thompson, Daley 486, 710–11
Thorpe, Jim 285, 296–9, 517
transgender politics 693–8
Trautmann, Bert (Bernhard Carl)
    17–19

UEFA 69–70, 91, 170, 210–11, 233, 399
ultras 96–8
US Lawn Tennis Association (USLTA)
    376

Videla, General Jorge 570, 573–4
video analysis 26

violence, see hooliganism
volleyball 231, 456

Walker Cup 454
Walsh, Stella (Stanisława
    Walasiewicz) 695–6
Warne, Shane 366
water-skiing 456
Watkins, Dr Sid 381, 386–7
Wheatley Report 72
Wightman Cup 454–5
Winter Olympics 194, 231–2, 489,
    520–1
women
    in athletics 671, 681–2
    in cricket 674
    earnings 358, 663, 672, 690–2
    and fandom 675–7
    in football 666, 455–6
    in golf 674, 682, 698–702
    in horse racing 672
    in motor racing 672–4
    in Olympic Games 664–6, 675,
        681–5
    in show jumping 672
    in tennis 358, 679–81, 686–93
    Title IX: 685–6
    women's rights demonstrations
        668–71
Women's Olympic Games 681
Women's Tennis Association 690
Women's World Games 665, 678
Woolf Report 564, 566
Woosnam, Phil 225–7
Workers' Olympiad 512–13
World Baseball Classic (WBC) 459–62
World Championship Tennis (WCT)
    311, 314, 376
World Rugby Corporation (WRC) 335
World Series Cricket (WSC) 317–18,
    321–8
World Table-Tennis Championships
    29
Worrell, Frank 630–2, 633–4
wrestling 103–4, 169, 208, 664–5

xenophobia 12, 483

Zimbabwe 212, 242, 657–60